READINGS IN AMERICAN GOVERNMENT

Frank Bryan

Department of Political Science
University of Vermont

West Publishing Company

Saint Paul   New York   Los Angeles   San Francisco

Credits

Chapter I (1.) From *Inventing America* by Garry Wills (New York: Doubleday & Co., 1978). Reprinted by permission of the author, Garry Wills. (2.) From *The Declaration of Independence* by Carl Becker (New York: Harcourt Brace, 1922). (3.) From *Democracy in America* by Alexis De Tocqueville (New York: J. & H. G. Langley, 1841). (4.) Excerpts from *The Liberal Tradition in America*, copyright © 1955 and renewed 1983 by Louis Hartz, reprinted by permission of Harcourt Brace Jovanovich, Inc. (5.) Excerpts from *Outside, Looking In* by Dorothy Buckton James. Copyright © 1972 by Dorothy Buckton James. Reprinted by permission of HarperCollins Publishers. (6.) Reprinted from *The End of Liberalism, Ideology, Policy, and the Crisis of Public Authority*, by Theodore J. Lowi, by permission of W. W. Norton & Company, Inc. Copyright © 1969 by W. W. Norton & Company, Inc. (7.) From "Don't Count Out Conservatism," by Irving Kristol, *New York Times Magazine*, June 14, 1987. Copyright © 1987 by The New York Times Company. Reprinted by permission. (8.) From "Hurrah for the L-Word," by Arthur Schlesinger, Jr. *Wall Street Journal*, October 21, 1988. Reprinted with permission of The Wall Street Journal © 1988 Dow Jones & Company, Inc. All rights reserved.

Credits continued on page A1.

Cover photo: David W. Hamilton/The Image Bank.

ISBN 0–314–85391–X

CONTENTS

Chapter II   THE CONSTITUTION: FROM VALUES TO RULES

Changing the Constitution

Chapter III   **CIVIL RIGHTS AND LIBERTIES: PLAYING BY THE RULES**

Civil Rights for Blacks

Freedom of Speech, Press, and Choice

When Rights and Liberties Collide

PART B
THE ARCHITECTURE OF GOVERNANCE 123

Chapter IV   DIVIDING POWER: FEDERALISM AND THE REPUBLIC

Creating and Adjusting the Framework

The View from the States

Federalism's Missing Pieces

The Federalism You Don't See

PART C
THE POLITICAL PROCESS

PART D
THE INSTITUTIONS OF GOVERNANCE 335

Chapter X   CONGRESS

The Original Design

Home Is Where the Heart Is, or Is It?

Saving Your Incumbency

How Decisions Get Made

Chapter XI   THE PRESIDENCY

The Original Design

The Presidency in Operation

Judging Presidents

Chapter XII   THE BUREAUCRACY

Overview

Two Views of Bureaucracy

A Different Version

Chapter XIII   THE COURTS

Creating and Adjusting the Framework

Contents

Choosing Judges

Inside the Court

PREFACE

All of us who make our living teaching American Government and Politics in front of undergraduates must have said it at least once a semester, "If only I had time to put together my own book of readings." There are two things wrong with this sentence: First, readers are not books. The problem with a reader is that you can't drop nonchalant lines in conversations with colleagues like: "In the (yawn) BOOK I just published with . . ." Second, "put" is definitely the wrong verb. "Scratch," "rake," "claw," even "scrape" seem more appropriate. Doing (it's *tough* to think of a proper verb for this) a reader has taught me a couple of things. Writing, although painful, is much easier than editing. I should have appreciated my old readers more.

Once when I said I'd like to do (how's that?) a reader of my own, Clark Baxter of West Publishing overheard me. The result is now I have one of my own. The irony is that I'm trying to convince you to use it. Let's be honest. In a reader the preface is not written for the reader. Believe me, our students are not concerned with the conceptual soundness of the book's epistemological paradigms. Prefaces to readers are in-house memos written for the ones who *assign* them. In the preface, we get a chance to convince our colleagues that our reader is new, fresh, and innovative.

Such is my admiration for my competitors that I will follow their lead and list the reasons why my reader is newer, fresher, and more innovative than theirs.

Actually, my serious judgment is that most of us are doing about the same thing. There is nothing in this book unique to all readers (unless it is the inclusion of a piece from *Mother Jones*). With that in mind, however, I do claim there are emphases here which, in combination, do make it different.

Also. Twenty-three years of teaching at two state universities (Vermont and Montana), a small Catholic College (St. Michael's) and several semesters at Middlebury College and Johnson State College give me the confidence to stake a claim on the turf of experience. By my quick estimate this includes over 60 sections of the basic course using five different textbooks and four different readers. Whatever else this book is, it's my best shot at what experience tells me undergraduates should, can, and *will* read to supplement textbook-based courses in American Politics and Government.

* *Choice.* This is the key. It is presumptuous to believe that any of us can pick three or four supplementary readings per chapter and in that small cluster there will be enough variety to fit your needs. There are ninety-one readings in this book. Your choices here are almost double those of the standard model. This is the book's most distinguishing characteristic. Without it, many of the additional options in the book would be impossible.

* *Basics.* Here this book is like most others. It includes the basics from *Federalist* No. 10 to David Truman and Robert Dahl. But because of the number of readings included, we were able to include a wider range of fundamental sources.

* *Relevance.* Students should be assigned current material—books and/or authors whose names are familiar, *The Power Game*, Arthur Schlesinger, Jr., *The Brethren*, Judge Souter, David Broder, Irving Kristol. They should also be assigned books and scholars referenced in their textbooks—Lowi, Parenti, Ladd, James MacGregor Burns, Sabato, Mansbridge, Mayhew, Fenno, Fiorina, Barber, Rosenbloom, and so on.

* *Issues.* Care was taken to spice each section with illustrative examples from the give and take of contemporary politics. In this I did not hesitate to use journalists and political scientists that write for more popular journals. The future of liberalism, abortion, the drinking age, Democrats v. Republicans, flag burning, AIDS, the language of hate on campus, PACs and campaign finance, bias in the news are examples.

* *Original Sources.* In each chapter (where relevant), I included a selection from *The Federalist Papers* and a Court case. Thus *Federalist* No. 39, and *McCulloch v. Maryland* (for federalism), *Federalist* No. 51 and *U.S. v. Nixon* (for checks and balances), *Federalist* No. 78 and *Marbury v. Madison* (for the Courts). In other cases a secondary source was featured that dealt with historical and structural issues: Barry D. Karl on American bureaucracy is an example.

* *Theory.* Few readers have a chapter on what I call "the roots of our values." This one does. It contains selections both historical and current. Garry Wills, Carl Becker, Alexis De Tocqueville, Louis Hartz, Dorothy Buckton James, Theodore Lowi, Arthur Schlesinger, and Irving Kristol provide both depth and range.

In terms of the book's organization, it's standard. Additionally, it includes *Thinking It Over* questions at the end of each reading that are designed to do more than ask questions. Some suggest paper topics. Some direct students to comparative reading. Some seek to prompt a debate. Some suggest a survey research project or a case study. I have *not* included chapter summaries. My view is these are not read by students. I have, however, included *Setting the Scene* introductions to each reading, in effect breaking up chapter summaries into more digestible portions.

I certainly do owe thanks to a lot of people. First to the dozen or so anonymous readers to which West sent the original list of selections for their comments and suggestions: whoever you are, I suspect you'll see some of your ideas in this book and thank you for them. At the University of Vermont I'd especially like to thank Eileen Burgin, John Burke, Ken Holland, Steve Nelson, and Tom Rice for their comments and suggestions. A special thank you to Bob Pepperman Taylor who not only made many useful suggestions but also suffers the misfortune of having his office next door. Finally, thank you to Lee. She knew when I said, "Piece of cake. Just a book of readings. It'll be fun!" that I remained somewhat of an ass. But (so far) she's hung around anyway. The real work was hers.

PART

A

FOUNDATIONS

Chapter I

THE ROOTS OF OUR VALUES

1.
INVENTING AMERICA
by Garry Wills

Setting the Scene: Here one of America's leading essayists takes a look at the Declaration of Independence as seen through the eyes of Abraham Lincoln. As Americans we think we are different, says Wills. We even think we are God-like and our country was inspired by a higher order. Much of this comes from the kind of misreading of the Declaration of which Lincoln is guilty. America was not founded on a "creed." The creed we invented as we went along. America was *founded* on the aspirations of practical persons for whom "the highest test of a thing was its immediate practicality to the living generation."

. . . In 1975, the lieutenant governor of Pennsylvania wrote around to scholars for a list of appropriate modern leaders who might re-enact the signing of the Declaration on July 4, 1976. . . . the man was asking for the impossible, for a resurrection of the dead. Most of those brought in for such a ceremony would not know what on earth they were admitting to. And those who might know, and still wanted to sign, would have to justify their act in ways so devious as to defeat speculation on their motives.

It is not surprising that we should misunderstand the Declaration. It is written in the lost language of the Enlightenment. It is dark with unexamined lights. Besides, we have a very powerful document from the nineteenth century to help us along in our error. What the State of Pennsylvania was contemplating in 1975, the President of the United States had already accomplished in 1863—the recontracting of our society on the basis of the Declaration as our fundamental charter. This was accomplished by the principal political stylist of his day—indeed, of our entire history. Abraham Lincoln was a great and conscious verbal craftsman. The man who writes, "The world will little note, nor long remember, what we do here," has done his best—by mere ripple and interplay of liquids—to make sure the world will remember; as it has. . . .

He obviously gave some thought to the first six words of his most famous exordium: "Four score and seven years ago . . ." . . . "Four score and seven" is a very stilted way of saying eighty-seven. Lincoln himself, speaking at Springfield in 1857, talked of the Declaration's passage "some eighty years ago." . . . And later in the speech Lincoln cited the exact figure: "eighty-one years ago." . . .

Admittedly, "Four score and seven" rolls—it has less the accountant's style than the prophet's. You hear it and don't immediately start subtracting eighty-seven from 1863. ("Let's see, that gives us 1776.") And Lincoln had good reason to prefer that you hold off, for a while, on the computation till he made his case for it. It was not a necessary, or even obvious, number to choose for our date of national origin.

It is customary to settle for a vague justification of Lincoln's language as achieving dignity by periphrasis. But what, precisely, makes "four score" so dignified? One thing. The English Bible. That does the trick. Only in "three-score and ten" for the allotted life of man was "score" commonly used for twice-ten in the Victorian era. Lincoln is stirring biblical echoes in his opening phrase, and he keeps on stirring as he goes.

"Four score and seven years ago our fathers brought forth . . ." Fathers is another religious term. Faith of our Fathers. The language of the hymnal. Pilgrim Fathers. Washington as Father of his Country. "Fathers" of the Constitution. But Lincoln is not talking about the founders, in the sense of the framers, the men of 1787; if he were, he would have been forced to say "Three score and sixteen years ago" or "Four score minus four years ago," which is better history but inferior music.

"Our fathers *brought forth* . . ." Just what does that mean? Not simply that they introduced something onto this continent. If so, where was it before they brought it in? And how could it be called a *new* nation if merely transferred? No, "bring forth" cannot mean anything like "introduce from abroad." Lincoln is talking about generation on the spot. The nation . . . is not only new, but newborn. The suggested image is, throughout, of . . . a marriage of male heaven ("our fathers") and female earth ("this continent"). And it is a miraculous conception, a virgin birth. The nation is conceived by a mental act, in the spirit of liberty, and *dedicated* (as Jesus was in the temple) to a proposition. The proposition to which it is dedicated forms the bridge back from Lincoln to Jefferson, from the Address to the Declaration—"the proposition that all men are created equal." . . .

The mere idea of a sudden "birth" for America is very misleading. In the first place, the continent was not all that "virgin." It has not only Indians to be pitchforked toward the interior, but long-standing colonial governments which had reached a high degree of self-rule. Benjamin Harrison V arrived at the Continental Congress of 1774 as a member of the Virginia Assembly, in which Benjamin Harrison I had sat—and Benjamin Harrison II, *and* Benjamin Harrison III, *and* Benjamin Harrison IV. These were men with a century of governing behind them. America was already old before she got a chance to be "born" from an idea, as the myth of virgin birth demands.

The Declaration lends itself to that myth in ways the Articles or the Constitution could never do. They are messier enterprises, with the stamp of compromise upon them. To this the Articles add a note of failure and the Constitution adds a note of illegality. The convention that drew up our Constitution went far beyond its mandate; in effect, smuggled a new nation in upon the continent rather than bringing it forth by intellectual impregnation. The founding legend begins to look more like a case of Sabine rape than virginal conception.

Of course, to Lincoln—and to those progressive historians who fleshed out his insight—the compromises of the Constitution were a natural struggling of the flesh, unable to live up to the pure spirit of the nation's Idea. The Church may at times not live up to the demands of Faith, but Faith was given us entire at the outset. We move, here, from nineteenth-century Fundamentalism to liberal Protestantism, to the idea of a development in the Church's living of doctrinal truth. At Springfield, Lincoln put it this way:

> They [the Declaration's signers] meant simply to declare the right, so that enforcement of it might follow as fast as circumstances should permit. They meant to set up a standard maxim for free society, which would be familiar to all, and revered by all; constantly looked to, constantly labored for, and even though never perfectly attained, constantly approximated, and thereby constantly spreading and deepening its influence and augmenting the happiness and value of life to all people of all colors everywhere. The assertion that "all men are created equal" was of no practical use in effecting our separation from Great Britain; and it was placed in the Declaration not for that, but for future use. Its authors meant it to be—as, thank God, it is now proving itself—a stumbling block [like St. Paul's preaching at Galatians 5:11] to all those who in after times might seek to turn a free people back into the hateful paths of despotism.

The *new* nation was not conceived in blood and conquest, like other nations, nor by mere accident or legal convenience. There was a necessity in its conception. But does this extraordinary birth of itself make the nation too etherial to survive in our real world? "Now we are engaged in a great civil war testing whether that nation, or any nation so conceived and so dedicated, can long endure." We move from St. Luke to St. John, to the hour and the power of darkness. Lincoln hints here, as he did elsewhere, at the Civil War as the nation's crucifixion. The country set apart by miraculous birth undergoes its supreme test and achieves—resurrection: "that this nation under God shall have a *new birth* of freedom." The nation must be twice-born, according to the gospel pattern, to become a sign for the nations, a pledge that "government of the people, by the people, and for the people shall not perish from the earth."

Well, now, that is a very nice myth. It flatters us with our special status, our central importance to all men's aspirations. If we tried to live up to its implications, we might all be better human beings. So what's the matter with keeping the myth?

. . . A belief in our extraordinary birth, outside the processes of time, has led us to think of ourselves as a nation apart, with a special destiny, the hope of all those outside America's shores. This feeling, of course, antedated Lincoln. It was part of the Puritan ideal, of the city set on a hilltop. It turned George Washington into a Moses during the revolutionary period. It arose from Protestant America's strong feeling of kinship with the chosen people of its Old Testament. It returned in visions of manifest destiny at the beginning of this century. But Lincoln's was the most profound statement of this belief in a special American fate. . . .

After his election in 1860, Lincoln said on his way to Washington: "It [the Revolution] was not the mere matter of separation of the colonies from the motherland, but [of] that sentiment in the Declaration of Independence, which gave liberty not alone to the people of this country, but hope to all the world, for all future time. It was that which gave promise that in due time the weights would be lifted from the shoulders of all men, and that all should have an equal chance. This is the sentiment embodied in the Declaration of Independence."

One way we felt we should save the world was to stay pure of it. If we were set apart, we should stay apart, to influence others precisely because we would not join them in the ruck of things. On the other hand, *when* we intervened in the affairs of the world, it would have to be for the highest and most total reasons—to save and transform the world, to give it a new life patterned after ours; to make the world safe for democracy, to free the captives, to bring self-determination to others. In 1960, John F. Kennedy adapted a phrase from Lincoln—who was, in turn, adapting the Bible—to say that the world cannot exist half-slave and half-free. The possession parable of the house divided against itself was used by Lincoln to show that the North must prevail over the South's demoniac "possession" by slavery. Kennedy expanded that to make us willing to throw Communist devils out of Russia, China, Cuba, or Vietnam.

Since we had a special mission, we could assume special powers. President Woodrow Wilson, invading Mexico because its electoral arrangements displeased him, said that our bayonets would teach the country to elect good men—men, say, like Woodrow Wilson. The virtue of our aims sanctified the means—so we could indulge in a righteous Hiroshima or two, in napalm and saturation bombing, in a Diem coup, or a Chile *putsch.* Lincoln spoke of shed American blood as expiatory and cleansing, as a washing in the blood of the Lamb; and if we shed even our own blood, might we not shed that of others for their salvation?

This touches only one manifestation of our messianic sense, our willingness to redeem men in blood. The heart of that urge comes from our dedication to a *proposition.* In 1921, when Gilbert Chesterton applied for entry to America as a visiting lecturer, he was amused by the questions he had to answer. Was he an anarchist? A polygamist? Did he advocate the overthrow of America by force? "I have stood on the other side of Jordan, in the land ruled by a rude Arab chief, where the police looked so like brigands that one wondered what the brigands looked like. But they did not ask me whether I had come to subvert the power of the Shereef; and they did not exhibit the faintest curiosity about my personal views on the ethical basis of civil authority." Only America, the land of the free, asked him what he thought about the kind of freedom it was peddling—and asked him not as a settler or possible immigrant, but merely as a visitor. He especially loved the idea that subverters of the nation would serenely declare, on a question form, their intention to subvert.

Chesterton, being as generous as he could to this odd inquisition, granted that America, with its ambition of combining the most disparate ingredients in one republic, had to have a mold of some kind: "The experiment of a democracy of diverse races has been compared to a melting pot. But even that metaphor implies that the pot itself is of a certain shape and a certain substance; a pretty solid substance. The melting pot must not melt." Chesterton rightly called the mold religious, and looked for the source of our religion in the Declaration of Independence (as that was understood by Lincoln): "America is the only nation in the world that is founded on a creed. That creed is set forth with dogmatic and even theological lucidity in the Declaration of Independence, perhaps the only piece of practical politics that is also theoretical politics and also great literature."

Certainly Lincoln felt that the Declaration's importance was doctrinal, a test of virtue and citizenship: "All honor to Jefferson—to the man who, in the concrete pressure of a struggle for national independence by a single people, had the coolness, forecast, and capacity to introduce into a merely revolutionary document, an abstract truth, and so to embalm it there, that today and in all coming days, it shall be a rebuke and a stumbling block to the very harbingers of reappearing tyranny and oppression" (Letter to H. L. Pierce, 1859). America is the American *idea* for Lincoln, and that idea is contained in the Declaration: "I have insisted that, in legislating for new countries where it [slavery] does not exist, there is no just rule other than of moral and abstract right. With reference to those new countries, those maxims as to the right of people to 'life, liberty, and the pursuit of happiness' were the just rules to be constantly referred to: (1858). . . .

This whole way of thinking would, on many grounds, have been alien to Thomas Jefferson. . . . With Locke, he had rejected innate ideas. He considered Plato's self-existent Ideas the great delusion of Western history. He did not believe one could "embalm" an idea in a text, lay it away in some heaven of the mind, for later generations to be constantly aspiring after. He denied that a spiritual ideal could be posed over-against some fleshly struggle toward it. He did not think material circumstances an obstacle to Reality. They, and they alone, *were* reality for him. He would not have accepted Lincoln's mystique of national union as a transcendentally "given" imperative.

He would never encourage people to yearn back toward some ideal of perfection delivered to their forebears. He opposed "entailing" opinions on a later generation; he wanted constitutions revised often, since accumulated knowledge must make later generations wiser than that which drew up *any* old document . . .

To the extent that Chesterton read the Declaration as "dogmatic and even theological," he was misreading it. Jefferson would take such terms as an insult if applied to his draft. He thought most theology an enemy to man's freedom, and he opposed any religious tests for holding office or citizenship.

The dry intellectual formulae of the eighteenth century were traced in fine acids of doubt, leaving them difficult to decipher across the intervals of time and fashion. When the Declaration is read in Lincoln's romantic glass, darkly, its content becomes entirely a victim of guess and bias. Proof of this is easily obtained: Lincoln congratulates Jefferson for not being "merely" practical, for laying up a timeless truth, usable in future ages, though his own contemporaries could not recognize it. That praise includes almost everything Jefferson opposed. For him, the highest test of a thing was its immediate practicality to the living generation.

I have concentrated, here, on misreadings that derive from Lincoln, or are strengthened by his views, not because I think all our errors traceable to Gettysburg. Far from it. My point is that this is only one of *many* intervening filters that distort the text. The Declaration is not only part of our history; we are part of its history. We have cited it, over the years, for many purposes, including the purpose of deceiving ourselves; and it has become a misshapen thing in our minds.

Thinking It Over

1. If the Declaration of Independence has been misread, does it really matter? If so, why?

2. Isn't Wills being a little hard on Lincoln whose interest in delivering the Gettysburg Address was not (as is Wills') to be insightful about history and literature? Or does the very offhandedness of the Address (Lincoln wrote it on the train to Gettysburg in a few minutes' time) underscore the point Wills is making?

2.
THE DECLARATION OF INDEPENDENCE
by Carl Becker

Setting the Scene: It is generally agreed that the following is one of the clearest statements on the Declaration of Independence we have. You will enjoy Becker's style, fresh and to the point, as he takes you through the text. It is hard to read Becker's essay and not want to pause to pay Thomas Jefferson a moment of tribute for a job well done. At one and the same time Becker convinces us that what the Declaration does is "no big thing" and yet is a profound, almost immaculate revolutionary document.

The purpose of the Declaration is set forth in the first paragraph—a striking sentence, in which simplicity of statement is somehow combined with an urbane solemnity of manner in such a way as to give that felicitous, haunting cadence which is the peculiar quality of Jefferson's best writing.

When in the course of human events, it becomes necessary for one people to dissolve the political bands, which have connected them with another, and to assume, among the powers of the earth, the separate and equal station, to which the laws of nature and of nature's God entitle them a decent respect to the Opinions of mankind requires that they should declare the causes which impel them to the separation. . . .

The ostensible purpose of the Declaration was, therefore, to lay before the world the causes which impelled the colonies to separate from Great Britain. We do in fact find, in the Declaration, a list or catalogue of acts, attributed to the king of Great Britain, and alleged to have been done by him with the deliberate purpose of establishing over the colonies "an absolute tyranny." These "causes" which the Declaration sets forth are not quite the same as those which a careful student of history, seeking the antecedents of the Revolution, would set forth. The reason is that the framers of the Declaration were not writing history, but making it. They were seeking to convince the world that they were justified in doing what they had done; and so their statement of "causes" is not the bare record of what the king had done, but rather a presentation of his acts in general terms, and in the form of an indictment intended to clear the colonists of all responsibility and to throw all the blame on the king. From whatever causes, the colonists were in rebellion against established and long recognized political authority. The Declaration was not primarily concerned with the causes of this rebellion; its primary purpose was to present those causes in such a way as to furnish a moral and legal justification for that rebellion. The Declaration was essentially an attempt to prove that rebellion was not the proper word for what they were doing.

Rebellion against established authority is always a serious matter. In that day kings were commonly claiming to rule by divine right, and according to this notion there could be no 'right' of rebellion. The framers of the Declaration knew very well that however long their list of grievances against the king of Great Britain might be, and however oppressive they might make out his acts to have been, something more would be required to prove to the world that in separating from Great Britain they were not really engaged in rebellion against a rightful authority. What they needed, in addition to many specific grievances against their particular king, was a fundamental presupposition against kings in general. What they needed was a theory of government that provided a place for rebellion, that made it respectable, and even meritorious under certain circumstances.

Before enumerating the specific grievance against the king of Great Britain, Jefferson therefore proceeded to formulate a general political philosophy—a philosophy upon which the case of the colonies could solidly rest. This philosophy, which affirms the right of a people to establish and to overturn its own government, is formulated in the first part of the second paragraph of the Declaration.

> We hold these truths to be self-evident, That all men are created equal, that they are endowed by their creator with certain unalienable rights; that among these are life, liberty & the pursuit of happiness; that to secure these rights governments are instituted among men, deriving their just powers from the consent of the governed; that whenever any form of government becomes destructive of these ends, it is the right of the people to alter or to abolish it, and to institute new government, laying its foundation on such principles and organizing its powers in such form, as to them shall seem most likely to effect their safety and happiness.

This is a frank assertion of the right of revolution, whenever "the people" are convinced that the existing government has become destructive of the ends for which all government is instituted among men. Many difficulties lie concealed in the words "the people"; but it is sufficient to note in passing that a large part of the people in the colonies, not being convinced that the British government had as yet become destructive of their liberties, or for some other reason, were either indifferently or strongly opposed to separation. Yet the leaders of the Revolution, being now committed to independence, found it politically expedient to act on the assumption that the opposition was negligible. Very naturally, therefore, Jefferson endeavored to make it appear that the people of the colonies were thoroughly united in wishing to 'institute new government' in place of the government of the king.

Accordingly, having affirmed the right of revolution under certain conditions, the Declaration goes on to state that as a matter of fact these conditions prevail in the colonies, and that 'the people' have submitted to them as long as it is humanly possible to do.

> Prudence, indeed, will dictate, that government long established should not be changed for light and transient causes; and accordingly all experience hath shewn that mankind are more disposed to suffer, while evils are sufferable than to right themselves by abolishing the forms, to which they are accustomed. But when a long train of abuses & usurpations pursuing invariably the same object evinces a design

Summation I: Four Counts against the Ideology

(1) Interest-group liberalism as public philosophy corrupts democratic government because it deranges and confuses expectations about democratic institutions. Liberalism promotes popular decision-making but derogates from the decisions so made by misapplying the notion to the implementation as well as the formulation of policy. It derogates from the processes by treating all values in the process as equivalent interests. It derogates from democratic rights by allowing their exercise in foreign policy, and by assuming they are being exercised when access is provided. Liberal practices reveal a basic disrespect for democracy. Liberal leaders do not wield the authority of democratic government with the resoluteness of men certain of the legitimacy of their positions, the integrity of their institutions, or the justness of the programs they serve.

(2) Interest-group liberalism renders government impotent. Liberal governments cannot plan. Liberals are copious in plans but irresolute in planning. Nineteenth-century liberalism was standards without plans. This was an anachronism in the modern state. But twentieth-century liberalism turned out to be plans without standards. As an anachronism it, too, ought to pass. But doctrines are not organisms. They die only in combat over the minds of men, and no doctrine yet exists capable of doing the job. All the popular alternatives are so very irrelevant, helping to explain the longevity of interest-group liberalism. . . .

The Departments of Agriculture, Commerce, and Labor provide illustrations, but hardly exhaust illustrations, of such impotence. Here clearly one sees how liberalism has become a doctrine whose means are its ends, whose combatants are its clientele, whose standards are not even those of the mob but worse, are those the bargainers can fashion to fit the bargain. Delegation of power has become alienation of public domain—the gift of sovereignty to private satrapies. The political barriers to withdrawal of delegation are high enough. But liberalism reinforces these through the rhetoric of justification and often even permanent legal reinforcement: Public corporations—justified, oddly, as efficient planning instruments—permanently alienate rights of central coordination to the directors and to those who own the corporation bonds. Or, as Walter Adams finds, the "most pervasive method . . . for alienating public domain is the certificate of convenience and necessity, or some variation thereof in the form of an exclusive franchise, license or permit . . . . [G]overnment has become increasingly careless and subservient in issuing them. The net result is a general legalization of private monopoly . . . ."[1] While the best examples still are probably . . . self-governing systems of agriculture policy, these are obviously only a small proportion of all the barriers the interest-group liberal ideology has erected to democratic use of government.

(3) Interest-group liberalism demoralizes government, because liberal governments cannot achieve justice. The question of justice has engaged the best minds for almost as long as there have been notions of state and politics, certainly ever since Plato defined the ideal as one in which republic and justice were synonymous. And since that time philosophers have been unable to agree on what justice is. But outside the ideal, in the realms of actual

---

[1]Adams and Gray, *op. cit.,* pp. 47-48.

government and citizenship, the problem is much simpler. We do not have to define justice at all in order to weight and assess justice in government, because in the case of liberal policies we are prevented by what the law would call a "jurisdictional fact." In the famous jurisdictional case of *Marbury v. Madison* Chief Justice Marshall held that even if all the Justices hated President Jefferson for refusing to accept Marbury and the other "midnight judges" appointed by Adams, there was nothing they could do. They had no authority to judge President Jefferson's action one way or another because the Supreme Court did not possess such jurisdiction over the President. In much the same way, there is something about liberalism that prevents us from raising the question of justice at all, no matter what definition of justice is used.

Liberal governments cannot achieve justice because their policies lack the *sine qua non* of justice—that quality without which a consideration of justice cannot even be initiated. Considerations of the justice in or achieved by an action cannot be made unless a deliberate and conscious attempt was made by the actor to derive his action from a general rule or moral principle governing such a class of acts. One can speak personally of good rules and bad rules, but a homily or a sentiment, like liberal legislation, is not a rule at all. The best rule is one which is relevant to the decision or action in question and is general in the sense that those involved with it have no direct control over its operation. A general rule is, hence, *a priori*. Any governing regime that makes a virtue of avoiding such rules puts itself totally outside the context of justice.

Take the homely example of the bull and the china shop. Suppose it was an op art shop and that we consider op worthy only of the junk pile. That being the case, the bull did us a great service, the more so because it was something we always dreamed of doing but were prevented by law from entering and breaking. But however much we may be pleased, we cannot judge the act. We can only like or dislike the consequences. The consequences are haphazard; the bull cannot have intended them. The act was a thoughtless, animal act which bears absolutely no relation to any aesthetic principle. We don't judge the bull. We only celebrate our good fortune. Without the general rule, the bull can reenact his scenes of creative destruction daily and still not be capable of achieving, in this case, aesthetic justice. The whole idea of justice is absurd.

The general rule ought to be a legislative rule because the United States espouses the ideal of representative democracy. However, that is merely an extrinsic feature of the rule. . . . All that counts is the character of the rule itself. Without the rule we can only like or dislike the consequences of the governmental action. In the question of whether justice is achieved, a government without good rules, and without acts carefully derived therefrom, is merely a big bull in an immense china shop.

(4) Finally, interest-group liberalism corrupts democratic government in the degree to which it weakens the capacity of governments to live by democratic formalisms. . . . Liberalism weakens democratic institutions by opposing formal procedure with informal bargaining. Liberalism derogates from democracy by derogating from all formality in favor of informality. Formalism is constraining; playing it "by the book" is a role often unpopular in American war films and sports films precisely because it can dramatize personal rigidity and the plight of the individual in collective situations. Because of the impersonality of

formal procedures, there is inevitably a separation in the real world between the forms and the realities, and this kind of separation gives rise to cynicism, for informality means that some will escape their collective fate better than others. There has as a consequence always been a certain amount of cynicism toward public objects in the United States, and this may be to the good, since a little cynicism is the father of healthy sophistication. However, when the informal is elevated to a positive virtue, and hard-won access becomes a share of official authority, cynicism becomes distrust. It ends in reluctance to submit one's fate to the governmental process under any condition, as is the case in the United States in the mid-1960's.

Public officials more and more frequently find their fates paradoxical and their treatment at the hands of the public fickle and unjust when in fact they are only reaping the results of their own behavior, including their direct and informal treatment of the public and the institutions through which they serve the public. The more government operates by the spreading of access, the more public order seems to suffer. The more public men pursue their constituencies, the more they seem to find their constituencies alienated. Liberalism has promoted concentration of democratic authority but deconcentration of democratic power. Liberalism has opposed privilege in policy formulation only to foster it, quite systematically, in the implementation of policy. Liberalism has consistently failed to recognize, in short, that in a democracy forms are important. In a medieval monarchy all formalisms were at court. Democracy proves, for better or worse, that the masses like that sort of thing too.

Another homely parable may help. In the good old days, everyone in the big city knew that traffic tickets could be fixed. Not everyone could get his ticket fixed, but nonetheless a man who honestly paid his ticket suffered in some degree a dual loss: his money, and his self-esteem for having so little access. Cynicism was widespread, violations were many, but perhaps it did not matter, for there were so few automobiles. Suppose, however, that as the automobile population increased a certain city faced a traffic crisis and the system of ticket fixing came into ill repute. Suppose a mayor, victorious on the Traffic Ticket, decided that, rather than eliminate fixing by universalizing enforcement, he would instead reform the system by universalizing the privileges of ticket fixing. One can imagine how the system would work. One can imagine that some sense of equality would prevail, because everyone could be made almost equally free to bargain with the ticket administrators. But one would find it difficult to imagine how this would make the total city government more legitimate. Meanwhile, the purpose of the ticket would soon have been destroyed.

Traffic regulation, fortunately, was not so reformed. But many other government activities were. The operative principles of interest-group liberalism possess the mentality of a world of universalized ticket fixing: Destroy privilege by universalizing it. Reduce conflict by yielding to it. Redistribute power by the maxim of each according to his claim. Reserve an official place for every major structure of power. Achieve order by worshiping the processes (as distinguished from the forms and the procedures) by which order is presumed to be established.

If these operative principles will achieve equilibrium—and such is far from proven[2]—that is all they will achieve. Democracy will have disappeared, because all of these maxims are founded upon profound lack of confidence in democracy. Democracy fails when it lacks confidence in its own authority.

Democratic forms were supposed to precede and accompany the formulation of policies so that policies could be implemented authoritatively and firmly. Democracy is indeed a form of absolutism, but ours was fairly well contrived to be an absolutist government under the strong control of consent-building prior to taking authoritative action in law. Interest-group liberalism fights the absolutism of democracy but succeeds only in taking away its authoritativeness.

Thinking It Over

1. Summarize Lowi's four charges against interest group liberalism and then match them against the reality of any one episode of policy-making in America with which you are familiar. Does the indictment hold?

2. One way to think productively about interest group liberalism is to extend the sports analogy. Here are a series of terms. Match them.

For Politics:
(1) Congress
(2) Interest groups
(3) Congresspersons
(4) Lobbyists

For Sports:
(A) Umpires or referees
(B) Madison Square Garden
(C) "Magic" Johnson and Patrick Ewing
(D) The Los Angeles Lakers and the the New York Knicks

---

[2]*Cf.* David Easton, *The Political System* (New York: Alfred A. Knopf, 1953), Chapter 11; *cf.* also Easton, *A Systems Analysis of Political Life* (New York: John Wiley, 1965), Chapter 2.

7.
DON'T COUNT OUT CONSERVATISM
by Irving Kristol

Setting the Scene: Writing as the Reagan era draws to a close, a leading spokesperson for the "new right" (see James' reading above), Irving Kristol argues that reports of the demise of conservatism in America are speculations tied to the moment (Reagan's "lame duck" status) and not to enduring trends. After a defense of social and economic policy under Reagan which focuses on the fallacies of the liberal attack and the inadequacies of liberal solutions, Kristol sets about making a more positive case for conservatism. That is where we join him.

All of this testifies to the impasse that American liberalism now finds itself in, and to the fact that a political climate inhospitable to the liberal mode of thinking is still with us. But it constitutes negative evidence. Are there not some independent reasons for believing that "the Force" is with American conservatism?

Well, yes. To begin with, there is the interesting socioeconomic fact that the industrial working class, together with its trade unions, is a shrinking factor in American life. The potential political significance of this fact is weighty.

Today, only about 16 percent of the American labor force is made up of blue-collar, industrial workers—and that percentage is declining. It is not the case, as some think, that our industrial base is temporarily distressed. The shrinkage has been going on for more than a decade now, even though our industrial production (as distinct from industrial employment) is no lower today than it was 10 years ago. We just don't need all of those industrial workers, and will apparently need fewer every year.

So far, attention has been focused on the pains caused by this transition—pains that are real enough, even if they can only be alleviated, not "cured." But there are larger meanings implicit here. White-collar workers or service workers generally tend either not to be unionized at all, or not to be involved in the kind of ideological trade unionism—with its overall social-democratic agenda—that has traditionally characterized much of the industrial working class. Whatever their income levels, men and women in the service sectors are more inclined to think of themselves as middle class rather than working class. This does not necessarily prevent them from voting for liberal candidates, but it makes it a lot easier for them to identify with conservative politics.

One should not leap to the assumption that the American industrial working class is in the process of vanishing from the political scene. Like farmers (now less than 3 percent of the population) they will remain a very influential "interest group," their attention and energy directed to their most pressing economic concerns. But, along with their trade unions, they will no longer be a major component of a liberal coalition committed to "social change." And this is bound to have a consequential effect on the ideological climate in which American politics lives and breathes.

At the opposite pole from such socioeconomic considerations is the "war of ideas," where conservative writers and thinkers have been consistently, if slowly, gaining ground. There is no doubt that conservative and neo-conservative along with some neo-liberal writers are today the more interesting of the breed. (Neo-liberals are included because for the most part they are bashful, equivocating neo-conservatives.) The most original writings on social policy in these past years have come from Charles Murray, on economic policy from George Gilder and a nucleus of "supply-siders," on education from Allan Bloom. These writings are "controversial," which means they help define the intellectual agenda.

Talent attracts talent, in social thought as in physics or mathematics, and the increasing number of talented young conservative writers on public affairs is straining the resources of the magazines that publish them, the institutions that house them and the foundations that support them. This is frustrating and exasperating for the individuals and institutions involved, but it is a sign of conservative health, not of conservative decline.

In the area of foreign policy, the spectrum of discourse has shifted so decisively to the right that whole portions of the liberal vocabulary have, to all intents and purposes, been forgotten. Who today looks on the United Nations and other such international organizations as reliable instruments of American foreign policy? Who seriously declaims on the virtues of "international law" among a "world community of nations" as a relevant solution to American foreign policy problems? The entire outlook once designated as "liberal internationalism" is a shambles, with even NATO coming under critical scrutiny. Our State Department is still committed to this outlook, but everyone else now talks about our "national interest." It is the conception of our "national interest" that sets the terms for all our debates on foreign policy.

Specifically, the debate centers on the issue of whether it is in our national interest to attempt actively to shape the future world order by the use of American power; or, instead, to create an America that provides an example to humanity so splendid as to move other nations toward an emulation of our model. This last approach has been an integral part of traditional American isolationism, and it is fair to say that it is becoming the dominant theme of liberal thinking on foreign policy. But there are some crucial differences between the older isolationism, which still has adherents in middle America, and the current liberal version.

To begin with, the traditional isolationist is highly nationalistic, thinking the United States to be too good a nation to get involved in a corrupt, un-American world. Liberal-isolationism today disapproves of "excessive" nationalist fervor, and believes the United States is too radically imperfect to play a constructive role in world affairs. Similarly, traditional isolationism has always approved of a strong defense establishment—it is inconceivable, for instance, that traditional isolationists would find any reason to be hostile to the Strategic *Defense* Initiative. In contrast, current liberal isolationism prefers social spending to defense spending, and detest the S.D.I.

Perhaps most important, traditional American isolationism was never totally isolationist. It regarded the Western Hemisphere as a predestined "sphere of influence" for the United States, accepted without cavil the import of the Monroe Doctrine, and saw no problem in projecting American power in the Caribbean and Latin America. Essentially, that isolationism was opposed to "entanglements" with the power politics of European nations. Even with regard to the Pacific, it was never entirely averse to a modest extension of American hegemony.

So, despite the confusion that now prevails in public attitudes toward American foreign policy, it seems probable that liberal isolationism is so profoundly against the American grain as to have little real purchase on the future. It is President Reagan's activism that has appropriated the spirit of American nationalism—an activism that makes us "stand tall," as the saying goes. It is this kind of activism that is gradually supplanting both traditional isolationism and traditional internationalism. The American people approved the invasion of Grenada, while liberals deplored it. They approved the bombing of Libya, while liberals mocked it. In general, they seem approving of unilateral, decisive military intervention when our national interest might be served by it. They certainly do agree that there ought to be "no more Vietnams." But it is as easy to draw activist-nationalist inferences from that proposition as liberal-isolationist ones. And one does sense that the American people are inclined to do the former rather than the latter.

What the Reagan Administration has *not* been able to do is articulate any kind of comprehensive conservative viewpoint. This is an Administration that from the beginning has been a transitional affair, but has lacked the self-consciousness to know it. That was bound to be the case because it is a Republican administration. The Republican Party even today is primarily wedded to the fiscal conservatism of the business community and shares its aversion to any kind of governmental activism—or, indeed, to any kind of ideological conservative enthusiasm. It is predominantly a party that is happy to benefit opportunistically from the rising tide of evangelical Christianity, but is a lot more comfortable in the board room than in church. it is a party that approves, for commercial as well as nationalist reasons, of a large military establishment, but cannot be bothered to engage in any hard thinking about how to use it. And it is a party that, when in office, always finds itself floundering in one squalid financial scandal after another—it does, after all, take money (as distinct from sex) seriously.

But the times-they-are-a-changing, and Ronald Reagan has been the political catalyst for that change. There is now in Congress, and infiltrating the party on the local level in state after state, a new breed of conservative activists who will claim to be heirs to the Reagan legacy but in truth are much more than that. They have set their sights on a reformation of the Republican Party and of American conservatism—which is why they are regarded by traditional Republicans with such suspicion and apprehension. They are still an amorphous, if powerful, tendency rather than a clearly defined faction with a coherent program. But no one who observes closely what is happening to the Republican Party and American conservatism today can doubt that the Force is with them. And while that Force is the authentic Reagan legacy, it will have to be defined and implemented by a future conservative administration.

Thinking It Over

1. If one were to compare President Bush's policy in the Persian Gulf with Kristol's analysis, would one conclude that Bush was acting as a conservative?

2. As you view the world of American politics now, is there evidence to suggest that Kristol's "the-times-they-are-a-changing" optimism (in the direction of a more coherent conservative viewpoint) of 1987 is justified?

8.
HURRAH FOR THE L-WORD
by Arthur Schlesinger, Jr.

Setting the Scene: This is a different kind of article from Irving Kristol's defense of conservatism (see above). On the eve of the 1988 Presidential election Arthur Schlesinger, Jr., one of America's great defenders of liberalism, reviews its traditions and calls its supporters back to the fold. At a time when "the L-word" is on a list of words you can't say in public, Schlesinger argues that its principles are as sound in 1988 as ever before and that if abandoned the "republic will pay a fearful price." What follows is an example of political advocacy at its best.

I write as an unrepentant, unreconstructed, unregenerate and unabashed liberal who wonders why so many of his fellow citizens have allowed themselves to be gulled by the Republicans into regarding what Ronald Reagan archly calls "the L-word" as the greatest menace to the republic since the fluoridation of water. These same fellow citizens, when asked to name the 20th-century presidents they most admire, generally come up with Franklin Roosevelt, Harry Truman and John Kennedy. What in the world do they think Roosevelt, Truman and Kennedy were? Conservatives?

Some Republicans *do* astonishingly insist that they were conservatives. In a genial debate we had the other day in Bakersfield, Calif., Pierre (alias Pete) du Pont IV claimed that FDR was the hero of the "conservative majority" of his day. He then went on to denounce me as a socialist. One could not help recalling that Pierre du Pont III joined with other members of the family half a century ago to finance the American Liberty League, an organization of rich reactionaries dedicated not to the celebration of Franklin Roosevelt but to denouncing him—as a socialist. ("The American Liberty League," Jim Farley said at the time, "ought to be called the American Cellophane League. . . . First, it's a du Pont product and second, you can see right through it."

The New Deal

Let the record read: Franklin Roosevelt was a liberal, and proud of it, and his New Deal created modern America. When FDR came to Washington in 1933, unrestrained capitalism, the unregulated market and the unchecked rule of the rich had brought our capitalist democracy to the brink of disaster. There was no old-age insurance, no unemployment compensation, no guarantee of bank deposits, no farm price supports, no federal regulations of the securities exchanges. The conservative leaders of the country had been too busy taking care of the rich to think of the rest of the American people.

In fact, they were fulfilling the old prediction of Karl Marx that capitalism would be destroyed by its own contradictions. Their laissez-faire policies were plunging the republic into depression and class war. Nor has capitalism triumphed over Karl Marx in the years since by fidelity to laissez faire and devil-take-the-hindmost. It has triumphed because of the long campaign mounted by liberals in the teeth of envenomed conservative resistance to reduce the suffering, and thereby the revolutionary passions, of those to whom accidents of birth or fortune deny an equal chance in life.

Karl Marx failed to foresee the ability of democratic governments to show a sense of social responsibility. Those who would not have government abandon social responsibility in the name of unbridled individualism are doing Marx's work for him.

What Franklin Roosevelt did was to rescue capitalism from the capitalists. By humanizing the economic order and giving the poor a stake and a chance in the American system, he renewed and revitalized democracy.

It was liberal leadership that gave the American people Social Security—over the intense opposition of the Republicans. Liberal leadership gave workers the right to organize in unions of their own choosing. Fifty years ago, liberal leadership established a minimum wage (of 25 cents and hour)—and the Republicans fought just as hard against it then as they fought (alas, successfully) this month against a bill to raise the minimum wage beyond a paltry $3.35 an hour.

Those terrible liberals, who the president and vice president tell us have ruined America, equipped the economy with built-in economic stabilizers and social safety nets that have saved us from a major depression for half a century. Before the New Deal the U.S. went through a severe depression roughly every 20 years: 1819, 1837, 1857, 1873, 1893, 1907, 1929. We have had no serious economic collapse since the Great Depression—and that is because every tendency toward depression has been contained by the world the New Deal made.

This is what American liberalism is all about: economic opportunity, social justice, civil freedom. The liberal remaking of America was rooted in the understanding, firmly grounded in our history, that the rich always rule in their own interest. "They act," as Orestes Brownson wrote a century ago, "on the beautiful maxim, 'Let the government take care of the rich, and the rich will take care of the poor,' instead of the far safer maxim, 'Let government take care of the weak, the strong can take care of themselves.'"

What FDR began, Harry Truman and John Kennedy and Lyndon Johnson carried forward. "We have rejected the discredited theory that the fortunes of the nation should be in the hands of a privileged few," said Harry Truman. "Instead, we believe that our economic system should rest on a democratic foundation and that wealth should be created for the benefit of all. . . . Every segment of our population and every individual has a right to expect from his government a fair deal."

Now Ronald Reagan has revived the theory that Harry Truman supposed had long since been discredited. The country-club ticket of 1988 is running on that discredited theory today. To keep power in the hands of a privileged few, the well-paid Republican propaganda apparatus has distracted the electorate by putting across a caricature of liberalism and blaming liberals for everything that happened to the republic from 1961 till Ronald Reagan rode his white horse into Washington in 1981.

In fact, there has not been a liberal administration in Washington since the Great Society vanished into the Vietnam quagmire in 1966. Richard Nixon a liberal? Gerald Ford a liberal? Jimmy Carter, the most conservative Democratic president since Grover Cleveland and almost as assiduous a critic of affirmative government as Mr. Reagan himself, a liberal? Someone must be kidding. We have not had a liberal administration for more than 20 years.

For better or for worse, conservative government and conservative policies are responsible for the present state of the union—for the harsh fact that the gap between rich and poor is greater today than it has been at any time since the Census Bureau started collecting data on the subject; that the number of poor people has increased by eight million since 1978 and that one-fifth of the children of the republic are today living in poverty; that the national debt has nearly trebled since 1981; that what was once the world's leading creditor nation has been transformed into the world's leading debtor nation and that our real estate, banks, industrial base and national economic policy are increasingly in hock to foreigners; that corruption is rampant in both public and private sectors; that our schools and cities and environment and housing and health care and highways and dams and bridges and tunnels are in decay; that a reckless and duplicitous foreign policy has gravely reduced international confidence in the U.S.

This is where government by the rich for the rich has landed us. The Republicans this time around are trying, with some apparent success, to divert the country from serious issues by demanding a compulsory Pledge of Allegiance to the flag (written in fact by a socialist) and reviling the American Civil Liberties Union (an organization dedicated to the Bill of Rights of the Constitution) and lamenting the Massachusetts furlough system (instituted not by Michael Dukakis but by his Republican Predecessor).

But the Republican caricature of liberalism has nothing to do with what Roosevelt and Truman, Kennedy and Johnson were all about—and what Michael Dukakis is all about today. What liberalism is all about is to recall a generous-spirited people to its better self—to remind us that we are all members one of another and that the conservative philosophy of cosseting the rich and devil-take-the-hindmost is not only ignoble but, as past generations have bitterly learned, self-destructive, breeding economic depression, class conflict and moral squalor.

Pioneers on New Frontiers

The presidents we admire and celebrate most—Jefferson and Jackson and Lincoln and Theodore Roosevelt and Wilson and FDR and Harry Truman and JFK—were all, in the context of their times, vigorous and unashamed liberals. They were all pioneers on new frontiers, seeking out the ways of the future, meeting new problems with new remedies, carrying the message of constructive change in a world that never stops changing. From the start of the republic liberalism has always blazed the trail into the future—and conservatism has always deployed all the weapons of caricature and calumny and irrelevance to conceal the historic conservative objective of unchecked rule by those who already have far more than their fair share of the nation's treasure.

The conservatives have got away with this kind of campaign before, and they may well get away with it in 1988. The republic will very likely pay a fearful price for succumbing once again to conservative cynicism and conservative guff.

Thinking It Over

1. Read Christopher Lasch's article on the need for *less* objectivity in the media (included in Chapter VIII below). Is Schlesinger's approach what he had in mind?

2. If one defines conservatism as a faith in the values and traditions of the past, is there a case to be made that on this dimension at least Schlesinger is a conservative?

Chapter II

THE CONSTITUTION: FROM VALUES TO RULES

9.
THE CONSTITUTION
AS AN ELITIST DOCUMENT
by Michael Parenti

Setting the Scene: Michael Parenti is a leading American political scientist of the left. His book *Democracy for the Few* has had a wide audience and its title symbolizes Parenti's view of the American political System. What follows (from another source) is vintage Parenti—a very persuasive interpretation of the Constitution that seeks to underscore the notion that those who fashioned our fundamental law in 1887 had an ax to grind and they ground it very well indeed. What they were about was the preservation of their own special status.

The Constitution was framed by financially successful planters, merchants, lawyers, and creditors, many linked by kinship and marriage and by years of service in Congress, the military, or diplomatic service. They congregated in Philadelphia in 1787 for the professed purpose of revising the Articles of Confederation and strengthening the powers of the central government. They were impelled by a desire to do something about the increasingly insurgent spirit evidenced among poorer people. Fearful of losing control of their state governments, the framers looked to a national government as a means of protecting their interests. Even in a state like South Carolina, where the propertied class was distinguished by the intensity of its desire to avoid any strong federation, the rich and the well-born, once faced with the possibility of rule by the common people "and realizing that a political alliance with conservatives from other states would be a safeguard if the radicals should capture the state government . . . gave up 'state rights' for 'nationalism' without hesitation."[1] It swiftly became their view that a central government would be less accessible to the populace and would be better able to provide the protections and services that their class so needed.

The landed, manufacturing, and merchant interests needed a central government that would provide a stable currency; impose uniform standards for trade; tax directly; regulate commerce; improve roads, canals, and harbors; provide protection against foreign imports and against the discrimination suffered by American shipping; and provide a national force to subjugate the Indians and secure the value of western lands. They needed a government that would honor at face value the huge sums of public securities they held and would protect them from paper-money schemes and from the large debtor class, the land-hungry agrarians, and the growing numbers of urban poor.

The nationalist conviction that arose so swiftly among men of property during the 1780s was not the product of a strange transcendent inspiration; it was not a "dream of nation-building" that suddenly possessed them as might a collective religious experience. (If so, they were remarkably successful in keeping it a secret in their public and private communications.) Rather, their newly acquired nationalism was a practical and urgent response to material conditions affecting them in a most immediate way. Gorham of Massachusetts, Hamilton of New York, Morris of Pennsylvania, Washington of Virginia, and Pinckney of South Carolina had a greater identity of interest with each other than with debt-burdened neighbors in their home counties. Their like-minded commitment to a central government was born of a common class interest stronger than state boundaries.

The rebellious populace of that day has been portrayed as irresponsible and parochial spendthrifts who never paid their debts and who believed in nothing more than timid state governments and inflated paper money. Little is said by most scholars of the period . . . about the actual plight of the common people, the great bulk of whom lived at a subsistence level. Farm tenants were burdened by heavy rents and hard labor. Small farmers were hurt by the low prices merchants offered for their crops and by the high costs for merchandised goods. They often bought land at inflated prices, only to see its value collapse and to find themselves unable to meet their mortgage obligations. Their labor and their crops usually were theirs in name only. To survive, they frequently had to borrow money at high interest rates. To meet their debts, they mortgaged their future crops and went still deeper into debt. Large numbers were caught in that cycle of rural indebtedness which is the common fate of agrarian peoples in many countries to this day. The artisans, small tradesmen, and workers (or "mechanics," as they were called) in the towns were not much better off, being "dependent on the wealthy merchants who ruled them economically and socially."[2]

During the 1780s, the jails were crowded with debtors. Among the people, there grew the feeling that the revolution against England had been fought for naught. Angry, armed crowds in several states began blocking foreclosures and sales of seized property, and opening up jails. They gathered at county towns to prevent the courts from presiding over

---

[1]Merrill Jensen, *The Articles of Confederation* (Madison: University of Wisconsin Press, 1948), p. 30.
[2]Ibid., pp. 9-10. . . .

debtor cases. In the winter of 1787, farmers in western Massachusetts led by Daniel Shays took up arms. But their rebellion was forcibly put down by the state militia after some ragged skirmishes. . . .

Containing the Spread of Democracy

The specter of Shays' Rebellion hovered over the delegates who gathered in Philadelphia three months later, confirming their worst fears about the populace. They were determined that persons of birth and fortune should control the affairs of the nation and check the "leveling impulses" of that propertyless multitude which composed "the majority faction." "To secure the public good and private rights against the danger of such a faction," wrote James Madison in *Federalist* No. 10, "and at the same time preserve the spirit and form of popular government is then the great object to which our inquiries are directed." Here Madison touched the heart of the matter: how to keep the *spirit* and *form* of popular government with only a minimum of the *substance*, how to provide the appearance of republicanism without suffering its leveling effects, how to construct a government that would win mass acquiescence but would not tamper with the existing class structure, a government strong enough both to service the growing needs of an entrepreneurial class while withstanding the egalitarian demands of the poor and propertyless.

The framers of the Constitution could agree with Madison when he wrote in the same *Federalist* No. 10 that "the most common and durable source of factions has been the various and unequal distribution of property. Those who hold and those who are without property have ever formed distinct interests in society." They were of the opinion that democracy was "the worst of all political evils," as Elbridge Gerry put it. Both he and Madison warned of "the danger of the leveling spirit." "The people," said Roger Sherman, "should have as little to do as may be about the Government." And according to Alexander Hamilton, "All communities divide themselves into the few and the many. The first are the rich and the well-born, the other the mass of the people. . . . The people are turbulent and changing; they seldom judge or determine right."[3]

The delegates spent many weeks debating their interests, but these were the differences of merchants, slave owners, and manufacturers, a debate of haves versus haves in which each group sought safeguards within the new Constitution for its particular concerns. Added to this were the inevitable disagreements that arise over the best means of achieving agreed-upon ends. Questions of structure and authority occupied a good deal of the delegates' time: How much representation should the large and small states have? How might the legislature be organized? How should the executive be selected? What length of tenure should exist for the different officeholders? *Yet, questions of enormous significance, relating to the new government's ability to protect the interests of property, were agreed upon with surprisingly little debate.* For on these issues, there were no dirt farmers or poor artisans attending the

---

[3]The quotations by Gerry, Madison, Sherman, and Hamilton are taken from Max Farrand, ed., *Records of the Federal Convention* (New Haven: Yale University Press, 1927), vol. 1, passim. . . .

convention to proffer an opposing viewpoint. The debate between haves and have-nots never occurred.

The portions of the Constitution giving the federal government the power to support commerce and protect property were decided upon after amiable deliberation and with remarkable dispatch considering their importance. Thus all of Article I, Section 8 was adopted within a few days.[4] This section gave to Congress the powers needed by the propertied class for the expansion of its commerce, trade, and industry, specifically the authority to (1) regulate commerce among the states and with foreign nations and Indian tribes, (2) lay and collect taxes and impose duties and tariffs on imports but not on commercial exports, (3) establish a national currency and regulate its value, (4) "borrow Money on the credit of the United States"— measure of special interest to credits, (5) fix the standard of weights and measures necessary for trade, (6) protect the value of securities and currency against counterfeiting, (7) establish "uniform Laws on the subject of Bankruptcies throughout the United States," and (8) "pay the Debts and provide for the common Defense and general Welfare of the United States."

Some of the delegates were land speculators who expressed a concern about western holdings; accordingly, Congress was given the "Power to dispose of and make all needful Rules and Regulations respecting the Territory or other Property belong to the United States. . . ." Some delegates speculated in highly inflated and nearly worthless Confederation securities. Under Article VI, all debts incurred by the confederation were valid against the new government, a provision that allowed speculators to make generous profits when their securities were honored at face value.

In the interest of merchants and creditors, the states were prohibited from issuing paper money or imposing duties on imports and exports or interfering with the payment of debts by passing any "Law impairing the Obligation of Contracts." The Constitution guaranteed "Full Faith and Credit" in each state "to the Acts, Records, and judicial Proceedings" of other states, thus allowing creditors to pursue their debtors more effectively.

The property interests of slave owners were looked after. To give the slave-owning states a greater influence, three-fifths of the slave population were to be counted when calculating the representation deserved by each state in the lower house. The importation of slaves was allowed until 1808. Under Article IV, slaves who escaped from one state to another had to be delivered to the original owner upon claim, a provision unanimously adopted at the convention.

The framers believed the states acted with insufficient force against popular uprisings, so Congress was given the task of "organizing, arming, and disciplining the Militia" and calling it forth, among other reasons, to "suppress Insurrections." The federal government was empowered to protect the states "against domestic Violence." Provision was made for "the Erection of Forts, Magazines, Arsenals, dock-Yards and other needful Buildings" and for the maintenance of an army federal presence within the potentially insurrectionary

---

[4]John Bach McMaster, "Framing the Constitution," in his *The Political Depravity of the Founding Fathers* (New York: Farrar, Straus, 1964, originally published in 1896), p. 137. . . .

states—a provision that was to prove a godsend a century later when the army was used repeatedly to break strikes by miners, railroad employees, and factory workers.

In keeping with their desire to contain the majority, the founders inserted "auxiliary precautions" *designed to fragment power without democratizing it.* By separating the executive, legislative, and judiciary functions and then providing a system of checks and balances among the various branches, including staggered elections, executive veto, Senate confirmation of appointments and ratification of treaties, and a bicameral legislature, they hoped to dilute the impact of popular sentiments. They also contrived an elaborate and difficult process for amending the Constitution. *To the extent that it existed at all, the majoritarian principle was tightly locked into a system of minority vetoes, making sweeping popular actions nearly impossible.*

The propertyless majority, as Madison pointed out in *Federalist* No. 10, must not be allowed to concert in common cause against the established economic order. First, it was necessary to prevent unity of public sentiment by enlarging the polity and then compartmentalizing it into geographically insulated political communities. The larger the nation, the greater the "variety of parties and interests" and the more difficult it would be for a majority to find itself and act in unison. As Madison argued, "A rage for paper money, for an abolition of debts, for an equal division of property, or for any other wicked project will be less apt to pervade the whole body of the union than a particular member of it. . . ." An uprising of impoverished farmers could threaten Massachusetts at one time and Rhode Island at another, but a national government would be large and varied enough to contain each of these and insulate the rest of the nation from the contamination of rebellion.

Thinking It Over

1. Assume Parenti is correct in his interpretation. Do the elitist characteristics of the Constitution of 1887 prevail today or has the document changed to reflect a general democratization of society and politics?

2. Parenti emphasizes that the Constitution "fragments power without democratizing it." Square this observation with the characteristics of an "elitist" society. In short, the pluralist might argue that fragmentation precludes elitism. Where would Madison fit in this argument?

10.
THE FOUNDING FATHERS:
A REFORM CAUCUS IN ACTION
by John P. Roche

Setting the Scene: When you read Roche's article, you will be reading one of the most often assigned articles in political science classes in the United States. Roche has carefully examined *all the records* that came out of the Philadelphia convention that produced the Constitution. What happened there, he argues, was a meeting of very practical politicians who viewed their mission in terms of producing a form of government that would save the Republic from disintegration. Roche treats us to a refreshing and unique look at the founders of our country, persons who were perfectly willing to sacrifice theory to practical politics when the chips were down.

Indeed, in my view, there is one fundamental truth about the Founding Fathers . . . they were first and foremost superb democratic politicians . . . They were, with their colleagues, *political men*—not metaphysicians, disembodied conservatives or Agents of History—and as recent research into the nature of American politics in the 1780s confirms, . . .they were committed (perhaps willy-nilly) to working within the democratic framework, with a universe of public approval. . . . [T]he Philadelphia Convention was not a College of Cardinals or a council of Platonic guardians working within a manipulative, pre-democratic framework; it was a *nationalist* reform caucus which had to operate with great delicacy and skill in a political cosmos full of enemies to achieve the one definitive goal—popular approbation . . .

In this context, let us examine the problems they confronted and the solutions they evolved. The Convention has been described picturesquely as a counter-revolutionary junta and the Constitution as a *coup d' etat*, . . . but this has been accomplished by withdrawing the whole history of the movement for constitutional reform from its true context. No doubt the goals of the constitutional elite were "subversive" to the existing political order, but it is overlooked that their subversion could only have succeeded if the people of the United States endorsed it by regularized procedures. Indubitably they were "plotting" to establish a much stronger central government than existed under the Articles, but only in the sense in which one could argue equally well that John F. Kennedy was, from 1956 to 1960, "plotting" to become President. In short, on the fundamental *procedural* level, the Constitutionalists had to work according to the prevailing rules of the game. . . .

When the Constitutionalists went forth to subvert the Confederation, they utilized the mechanisms of political legitimacy. And the roadblocks which confronted them were formidable. At the same time, they were endowed with certain potent political assets. The history of the United States from 1786 to 1790 was largely one of a masterful employment of political expertise by the Constitutionalists as against bumbling, erratic behavior by the opponents of reform. Effectively the Constitutionalists had to induce the states, by democratic techniques of coercion, to emasculate themselves. . . .

The group which undertook this struggle was an interesting amalgam of a few dedicated nationalists with the self-interested spokesmen of various parochial bailiwicks. The Georgians, for example, wanted a strong central authority to provide military protection for their huge, underpopulated state against the Creek Confederacy; Jerseymen and Connecticuters wanted to escape from economic bondage to New York; the Virginians hoped to establish a system which would give that great state its rightful place in the councils of the republic. . . . There was, of course, a large element of personality in the affair: there is reason to suspect that Patrick Henry's opposition to the Convention and the Constitution was founded on his conviction that Jefferson was behind both, and a close study of local politics elsewhere would surely reveal that others supported the Constitution for the simple (and politically quite sufficient) reason that the "wrong" people were against it.

To say this is not to suggest that the Constitution rested on a foundation of impure or base motives. It is rather to argue that in politics there are no immaculate conceptions, and that in the drive for a stronger general government, motives of all sorts played a part . . .

As Stanley Elkins and Eric McKitrick have suggested in a perceptive essay,[1] what distinguished the leaders of the Constitutionalist caucus from their enemies was a "Continental" approach to political, economic and military issues. To the extent that they shared an institutional base of operations, it was the Continental Congress (thirty-nine of the delegates to the Federal Convention had served in Congress . . .), and this was hardly a locale which inspired respect for the state governments. . . . [O]ne can surmise that membership in the Congress under the Articles of Confederation worked to establish a continental frame of reference, that a Congressman from Pennsylvania and one from South Carolina would share a universe of discourse which provided them with a conceptual common denominator *vis à vis* their respective state legislatures. This was particularly true with respect to external affairs: the average state legislator was probably about as concerned with foreign policy then as he is today, but Congressmen were constantly forced to take the broad view of American prestige, were compelled to listen to the reports of secretary John Jay and to the dispatches and pleas from their frustrated envoys in Britain, France and Spain. . . . From considerations such as these, a "Continental" ideology developed which seems to have demanded a revision of our domestic institutions primarily on the ground that only by invigorating our general government could we assume our rightful place in the international arena. . . .

. . . [T]he great achievement of the Constitutionalists was their ultimate success in convincing the elected representatives of a majority of the white male population that change was imperative. A small group of political leaders with a Continental vision and essentially a consciousness of the United States' *international* impotence, provided the matrix of the movement. To their standard other leaders rallied with their own parallel ambitions. Their

---

[1]Stanley Elkins and Eric McKitrick, "The Founding Fathers: Young Men of the Revolution," *Political Science Quarterly*, Vol. 76, p. 181 (1961).

great assets were (1) the presence in their caucus of the one authentic American "father figure," George Washington, whose prestige was enormous; . . . (2) the energy and talent of their leadership (in which one must include the towering intellectuals of the time, John Adams and Thomas Jefferson, despite their absence abroad), and their communications "network," which was far superior to anything on the opposition side; . . . (3) the preemptive skill which made "their" issue The Issue and kept the locally oriented opposition permanently on the defensive; and (4) the subjective consideration that these men were spokesmen of a new and compelling credo: *American* nationalism, that ill-defined but nonetheless potent sense of collective purpose that emerged from the American Revolution . . .

The Constitutionalists got the jump on the "opposition" (a collective noun: opposition*s* would be more correct) at the outset with the demand for a Convention. Their opponents were caught in an old political trap: they were not being asked to approve any specific program of reform, but only to endorse a meeting to discuss and recommend needed reforms. If they took a hard line at the first stage, they were put in the position of glorifying the *status quo* and of denying the need for *any* changes. Moreover, the Constitutionalists could go to the people with a persuasive argument for "fair play"—"How can you condemn reform before you know precisely what is involved?" Since the state legislatures obviously would have the final say on any proposals that might emerge from the Convention, the Constitutionalists were merely reasonable men asking for a chance. Besides, since they did not make any concrete proposals at that stage, they were in a position to capitalize on every sort of generalized discontent with the Confederation.

Perhaps because of their poor intelligence system, perhaps because of over-confidence generated by the failure of all previous efforts to alter the Articles, . . . the opposition awoke too late to the dangers that confronted them in 1787. . . . Even George Clinton, who seems to have been the first opposition leader to awake to the possibility of trouble, could not prevent the New York legislature from appointing Alexander Hamilton—though he did have the foresight to send two of his henchmen to dominate the delegation. . . .

With delegations safely named, the focus shifted to Philadelphia. While waiting for a quorum to assemble, James Madison got busy and drafted the so-called Randolph or Virginia Plan with the aid of the Virginia delegation. This was a political master-stroke. Its consequence was that once business got underway, the framework of discussion was established on Madison's terms. There was no interminable argument over agenda; instead the delegates took the Virginia Resolutions—"just for purposes of discussion"—as their point of departure. . . .

Standard treatments of the Convention divide the delegates into "nationalists" and "states'-righters" with various improvised shadings ("moderate nationalists," etc.), but . . . [w]hat is striking to one who analyzes the Convention as a case-study in democratic politics is the lack of clear-cut ideological divisions in the Convention. Indeed, I submit that the evidence—Madison's *Notes*, the correspondence of the delegates, and debates on ratification—indicates that this was a remarkably homogeneous body on the ideological level. Yates and Lansing, Clinton's two chaperones for Hamilton, left in disgust on July 10. . . . Luther Martin, Maryland's bibulous narcissist, left on September 4 in a huff when he discovered that others did not share his self-esteem; others went home for personal reasons. But the hard core of delegates accepted a grinding regimen throughout the attrition of a Philadelphia summer precisely because they shared the Constitutionalist goal.

Basic differences of opinion emerged, of course, but these were not ideological; they were *structural*. If the so-called "states'-rights" group had not accepted the fundamental purposes of the Convention, they could simply have pulled out and by doing so have aborted the whole enterprise.   Instead of bolting, they returned day after day to argue and to compromise.   An interesting symbol of this basic homogeneity was the initial agreement on secrecy: these professional politicians did not want to become prisoners of publicity; they wanted to retain that freedom of maneuver which is only possible when men are not forced to take public stands in the preliminary stages of negotiation. . . .

Commentators on the Constitution who have read *The Federalist* in lieu of reading the actual debates have credited the Fathers with the invention of a sublime concept called "Federalism." . . . Unfortunately *The Federalist* is probative evidence for only one proposition: that Hamilton and Madison were inspired propagandists with a genius for retrospective symmetry. Federalism, as the theory is generally defined, was an improvisation which was later promoted into a political theory. . . .   In any event, the final balance in the Constitution between the states and the nation must have come as a great disappointment to Madison, while Hamilton's unitary views are too well known to need elucidation.

It is indeed astonishing how those who have glibly designated James Madison the "father" of Federalism have overlooked the solid body of fact which indicates that he shared Hamilton's quest for a unitary central government.   To be specific, they have avoided examining the clear import of the Madison-Virginia Plan, . . . and have disregarded Madison's dogged inch-by-inch retreat from the bastions of centralization. The Virginia Plan envisioned a unitary national government effectively freed from and dominant over the states. The lower house of the national legislature was to be elected directly by the people of the states with membership proportional to population. The upper house was to be selected by the lower and the two chambers would elect the executive and choose the judges. The national government would be thus cut completely loose from the states. . . .

The structure of the general government was freed from state control in a truly radical fashion, but the scope of the authority of the national sovereign as Madison initially formulated it was breathtaking—it was a formulation worthy of the Sage of Malmesbury himself.   The national legislature was to be empowered to disallow the acts of state legislatures, . . . and the central government was vested, in addition to the powers of the nation under the Articles of Confederation, with plenary authority wherever ". . . the separate States are incompetent or in which the harmony of the United States may be interrupted by the exercise of individual legislation."[2] Finally, just to lock the door against state intrusion, the national Congress was to be given the power to use military force on recalcitrant states.[3]

---

[2]Resolution 6.
[3]*Ibid.*

This was Madison's "model" of an ideal national government, though it later received little publicity in *The Federalist*.

The interesting thing was the reaction of the Convention to this militant program for a strong autonomous central government. Some delegates were startled, some obviously leery of so comprehensive a project of reform, . . . but nobody walked out. Moreover, in the two weeks that followed, the Virginia Plan received substantial endorsement *en principe;* the initial temper of the gathering can be deduced from the approval "without debate or dissent," on May 31, of the Sixth Resolution which granted Congress the authority to disallow state legislation ". . . . contravening *in its opinion* the Articles of Union." Indeed, an amendment was included to bar states from contravening national treaties.[4]

The Virginia Plan may therefore be considered, in ideological terms, as the delegates' Utopia, but as the discussions continued and became more specific, many of those present began to have second thoughts. After all, they were not residents of Utopia or guardians in Plato's Republic who could simply impose a philosophical ideal on subordinate strata of the population. They were practical politicians in a democratic society, and no matter what their private dreams might be, they had to take home an acceptable package and defend it—and their own political futures—against predictable attack. On June 14 the breaking point between dream and reality took place. Apparently realizing that under the Virginia Plan, Massachusetts, Virginia and Pennsylvania could virtually dominate the national government—and probably appreciating that to sell this program to "the folks back home" would be impossible—the delegates from the small states dug in their heels and demanded time for a consideration of alternatives. One gets a graphic sense of the inner politics from John Dickinson's reproach to Madison: "You see the consequences of pushing things too far. Some of the members from the small States wish for two branches in the General Legislature and are friends to a good National Government; but we would sooner submit to a foreign power than . . . be deprived of an equality of suffrage in both branches of the Legislature, and thereby be thrown under the domination of the large States."[5] . . .

According to the standard script, at this point the "states'-rights" group intervened in force behind the New Jersey Plan, which has been characteristically portrayed as a reversion to the *status quo* under the Articles of Confederation with but minor modifications. A careful examination of the evidence indicates that only in a marginal sense is this an accurate description. It is true that the New Jersey Plan put the states back into the institutional picture, but one could argue that to do so was a recognition of political reality rather than an affirmation of states'-rights. A serious case can be made that the advocates of the New Jersey Plan, far from being ideological addicts of states'-rights, intended to substitute for the Virginia Plan a system which would both retain strong national power and have a chance of adoption in the states. The leading spokesman for the project asserted quite clearly that his views were based more on counsels of expediency than on principle; said Paterson on June

---

[4]*Farrand*, I, 54 (Italics added.)

[5]*Ibid.,* p. 242. Delaware's delegates had been instructed by their general assembly to maintain in any new system the voting equality of the states. *Farrand*, III, 574.

16: "I came here not to speak my own sentiments, but the sentiments of those who sent me. Our object is not such a Governmt. as may be best in itself, but such a one as our Constituents have authorized us to prepare, and as they will approve."[6] This is Madison's version; in Yates' transcription, there is a crucial sentence following the remarks above: "I believe that a little practical virtue is to be preferred to the finest theoretical principles, which cannot be carried into effect."[7] In his preliminary speech on June 9, Paterson had stated ". . . to the public mind we must accommodate ourselves,"[8] . . .

This was a defense of political acumen, not of states'-rights. In fact, Paterson's notes of his speech can easily be construed as an argument for attaining the substantive objectives of the Virginia Plan by a sound political route, *i.e.,* pouring the new wine in the old bottles. With a shrewd eye, Paterson queried:

> Will the Operation and Force of the [central] Govt. depend upon the mode of Represents.—No—it will depend upon the Quantum of Power lodged in the leg. ex. and judy. Departments—Give [the existing] Congress the same Powers that you intend to give the two Branches, [under the Virginia Plan] and I apprehend they will act with as much Propriety and more Energy. . . .[9]

In other words, the advocates of the New Jersey Plan concentrated their fire on what they held to be the *political liabilities* of the Virginia Plan—which were matters of institutional structure—rather than on the proposed scope of national authority. Indeed, the Supremacy Clause of the Constitution first saw the light of day in Paterson's Sixth Resolution; the New Jersey Plan contemplated the use of military force to secure compliance with national law; and finally Paterson made clear his view that under either the Virginia or the New Jersey systems, the general government would ". . . act on individuals and not on states."[10] From the states'-rights viewpoint, this was heresy: the fundament of that doctrine was the proposition that any central government had as its constituents the states, not the people, and could only reach the people through the agency of the state government.

On Tuesday morning, June 19 . . . James Madison led off with a long, carefully reasoned speech analyzing the New Jersey Plan which, while intellectually vigorous in its criticisms, was quite conciliatory in mood. "The great difficulty," he observed, "lies in the affair of Representation; and if this could be adjusted, all others would be surmountable."[11] (As events were to demonstrate, this diagnosis was correct.) When he finished, a vote was taken on whether to continue with the Virginia Plan as the nucleus for a new constitution: seven states voted "Yes"; New York, New Jersey, and Delaware voted "No"; and Maryland, whose

---

[6]*Ibid.,* p. 250.
[7]*Ibid.,* p. 258.
[8]*Ibid.,* p. 178.
[9]*Ibid.,* pp. 275-76.
[10]. . . *ibid.* at p. 276.
[11]*Farrand,* I, 321.

position often depended on which delegates happened to be on the floor, divided. . . . Paterson, it seems lost decisively; yet in a fundamental sense he and his allies had achieved their purpose: from that day onward, it could never be forgotten that the state governments loomed ominously in the background and that no verbal incantations could exorcise their power. Moreover, nobody bolted the convention: Paterson and his colleagues took their defeat in stride and set to work to modify the Virginia Plan, particularly with respect to its provisions on representation in the national legislature. . . .

For the next two weeks, the delegates circled around the problem of legislative representation. The Connecticut delegation appears to have evolved a possible compromise quite early in the debates, but the Virginians and particularly Madison (unaware that he would later be acclaimed as the prophet of "federalism") fought obdurately against providing for equal representation of states in the second chamber. . . . On July 2, the ice began to break . . . . The Convention had reached the stage where it was "ripe" for a solution (presumably all the therapeutic speeches had been made), and the South Carolinians proposed a committee. Madison and James Wilson wanted none of it, but with only Pennsylvania dissenting, the body voted to establish a working party on the problem of representation.

The members of this committee, one from each state, were elected by the delegates—and a very interesting committee it was. Despite the fact that the Virginia Plan had held majority support up to that date, neither Madison nor Randolph was selected . . . . From the composition, it was clear that this was not to be a "fighting" committee: the emphasis in membership was on what might be described as "second-level political entrepreneurs." On the basis of the discussions up that time, only Luther Martin of Maryland could be described as a "bitter-ender." Admittedly, some divination enters into this sort of analysis, but one does get a sense of the mood of the delegates from these choices—including the interesting selection of Benjamin Franklin, despite his age and intellectual wobbliness, over the brilliant and incisive Wilson or the sharp, polemical Gouverneur Morris, to represent Pennsylvania. His passion for conciliation was more valuable at this juncture than Wilson's logical genius, or Morris' acerbic wit.

It would be tedious to continue a blow-by-blow analysis of the work of the delegates; the critical fight was over representation of the states and once the Connecticut Compromise was adopted on July 17, the Convention was over the hump. Madison, James Wilson, and Gouverneur Morris of New York (who was there representing Pennsylvania!) fought the compromise all the way in a last-ditch effort to get a unitary state with parliamentary supremacy. But their allies deserted them and they demonstrated after their defeat the essentially opportunist character of their objections—using "opportunist" here in a non-pejorative sense, to indicate a willingness to swallow their objections and get on with the business. Moreover, once the compromise had carried (by five states to four, with one state divided), its advocates threw themselves vigorously into the job of strengthening the general governments's substantive powers—as might have been predicted, indeed, from Paterson's early statements. It nourishes an increased respect for Madison's devotion to the art of politics, to realize that this dogged fighter could sit down six months later and prepare essays for *The Federalist* in contradiction to his basic convictions about the true course the

Convention should have taken . . .

Drawing on their vast collective political experience, utilizing every weapon in the politician's arsenal, looking constantly over their shoulders at their constituents, the delegates put together a Constitution. It was a make-shift affair; some sticky issues (for example, the qualification of voters) they ducked entirely; others they mastered with that ancient instrument of political sagacity, studied ambiguity (for example, citizenship), and some they just overlooked. . . .

The Framers were busy and distinguished men, anxious to get back to their families, their positions, and their constituents, not members of the French Academy devoting a lifetime to a dictionary. They were trying to do an important job, and do it in such a fashion that their handiwork would be acceptable to very diverse constituencies. No one was rhapsodic about the final document, but it was a beginning, a move in the right direction, and one they had reason to believe the people would endorse. . . .

Probably our greatest difficulty is that we know so much more about what the Framers *should have meant* than they themselves did. We are intimately acquainted with the problems that their Constitution should have been designed to master; in short, we have read the mystery story backwards. If we are to get the right "feel" for their time and their circumstances, we must in Maitland's phrase, ". . . think ourselves back into a twilight." Obviously, no one can pretend completely to escape from the solipsistic web of his own environment, but if the effort is made, it is possible to appreciate the past roughly on its own terms. The first step in this process is to abandon the academic premise that because we can ask a question, there must be an answer.

Thus we can ask what the Framers meant when they gave Congress the power to regulate interstate and foreign commerce, and we emerge, reluctantly perhaps, with the reply that (Professor Crosskey to the contrary notwithstanding) . . . they may not have known what they meant, that there may not have been any semantic consensus. The Convention was not a seminar in analytic philosophy or linguistic analysis. Commerce was *commerce*—and if different interpretations of the word arose, later generations could worry about the problem of definition. The delegates were in a hurry to get a new government established; when definitional arguments arose, they characteristically took refuge in ambiguity. If different men voted for the same proposition for varying reasons, that was politics (and still is); if later generations were unsettled by this lack of precision, that would be their problem. . . .

The Constitution, then, was not an apotheosis of "constitutionalism," a triumph of architectonic genius; it was a patch-work sewn together under the pressure of both time and events by a group of extremely talented democratic politicians. They refused to attempt the establishment of a strong, centralized sovereignty on the principle of legislative supremacy for the excellent reason that the people would not accept it. They risked their political fortunes by opposing the established doctrines of state sovereignty because they were convinced that the existing system was leading to national impotence and probably foreign domination. For two years, they worked to get a convention established. For over three months, in what must have seemed to the faithful participants an endless process of give-and-take, they reasoned, cajoled, threatened, and bargained amongst themselves. The result was a Constitution which the people, in fact, by democratic processes, did accept, and a new and far better national government was established.

To conclude, the Constitution was neither a victory for abstract theory nor a great practical success. Well over half a million men had to die on the battlefields of the Civil War before certain constitutional principles could be defined—a baleful consideration which is somehow overlooked in our customary tributes to the farsighted genius of the Framers and to the supposed American talent for "constitutionalism." The Constitution was, however, a vivid demonstration of effective democratic political action, and of the forging of a national elite which literally persuaded its countrymen to hoist themselves by their own boot straps. American pro-consuls would be wise not to translate the Constitution into Japanese, or Swahili, or treat it as a work of semi-Divine origin; but when students of comparative politics examine the process of nation-building in countries newly freed from colonial rule, they may find the American experience instructive as a classic example of the potentialities of a democratic elite.

Thinking It Over

1. Is it not possible to make the case that both Parenti and Roche are correct? See if you can manage that in a short essay.

2. What are the pros and cons of the Virginia and New Jersey plans? What is Roche's view on the *seriousness* of either of them as models for the final document?

11.
THE AMERICAN CONSTITUTION AS IDEOLOGY
by Everett Carll Ladd

Setting the Scene: Why, asks Everett Ladd has the Constitution lasted so long and performed so well? His answer, delivered in the prose that has made him one of the most readable political scientists in America, is based on the "Toys R-Us" model which holds that we are what we think and the Constitution is both. It is the *linkage* between the Constitution and the nation that is key. While parrying the thrusts of the Constitution's critics with ease and dispatch, Ladd spins a convincing case for a fundamental optimism as we judge the future of the Constitution.

The United States is celebrating the 200th anniversary of its most notable political accomplishment—the framing of the Constitution. The 55 delegates to the Constitutional Convention in Philadelphia began their work in May 1787 and completed it four months later, on Sept. 17. By mid-1788 the Constitution had been ratified, replacing the Articles of Confederation as the law of the land. A new president and Congress took office under the Constitution in the spring of 1789.

Longevity.

For two centuries, then, in unbroken succession, the US has been governed under a single basic law. In the same span France has been governed by 10 separate and distinct constitutional orders: five republics, two empires, one monarchy, one plebiscitary dictatorship, and the puppet dictatorship installed at Vichy during World War II. The US Constitution has no peer in longevity.

In many regards, the US has been transformed over the past 200 years: A seaboard farming nation of 4 million people, mostly of British background, has become a continent-spanning country of 240 million, its economy built upon advanced technology, its citizenry of great ethnic and religious diversity. Government does a whole lot more now than it did then—compare today's $1 trillion budget with that enacted by the first Congress, of $4 million. But the *way* the US government operates in the age of President Reagan, Treasury Secretary James Baker III, and House Speaker James Wright, is remarkably like the way it functioned under President George Washington, Treasury Secretary Alexander Hamilton, and Speaker James Madison. In its animating spirit, not just its formal language, the Constitution of 1987 is the Constitution of 1787.

Were the founders somehow confronted with American life of 1987, they would surely experience culture shock: Penthouse magazine; fast-food Chinese restaurants dispensing carry-out Moo Sho pork; nine-year-olds "debugging software" on their PCs; television programs showing animal life in the high desert of the Canadian arctic; and live 12-meter yacht competition "down under." But in the sphere of government they would be right at home. More than anything else, they would feel variously exasperated and reassured by the most extraordinary of their governmental progeny—separation of powers. It is indeed alive and well: President and Congress are still paired in that unique political dance, as separate institutions performing shared functions, each possessed of an arsenal of checks on the other. These determinedly independent institutions are required to work together in complex power sharing before anything can be done in any policy area.

Why the Striking Persistence?

For the Constitution to stand largely unchanging while so much of the world around it is transformed is extraordinary by any standard, and now at the beginning of this bicentennial year it is worth asking how and why it came about. If pressed most Americans would probably respond: "The Constitution has lasted because it protects our liberties and lets us govern ourselves reasonably well. It has never really been broken, so why should we have fixed or replaced it?"

Some thoughtful students of our constitutional system, don't at all agree with this answer, of course. For the last hundred years, friendly critics have argued that the Constitution is a splendid effort—that needs basic repair. They have concentrated their criticism on the separation of powers, which, they argue, hamstrings the executive, blurs responsibility and accountability, and makes it impossible for the country to frame coherent, integrated policy to meet increasingly complex problems. The young Woodrow Wilson argued in "Congressional Government" that we can best show our reverence for what the founders accomplished by being open-eyed and courageous about the pressing need for change in the face of new challenges. Groups like the Committee on the Constitutional System make the same case today.

My own view is that the Constitution is a brilliant piece of governmental engineering, based on generally sound first premises. For example, separation of powers isn't simply a prudent defense against the danger of tyrannical government; it is a sensible precaution against insufficiently competent and knowledgeable governmental officials. Barriers to precipitate action and the requirement of interbranch compromise are sound responses to the fact that politicians often really don't know what to do. This said, I would not argue that the Constitution has lasted simply because it works well. It has remained constant as our basic law because the values and picture of the world on which it is based square with our own.

The Nation is the Ideology is the Regime.

The historian Ralph Barton Perry once observed of the US that "history affords few parallel instances of a state thus abruptly created, and consciously dedicated to a body of ideas whose acceptance constitutes its underlying bond of agreement." Unlike most countries where the sense of being a nation is derived from common ethnic identity and memories, the

US is a nation founded upon an ideology. A young American socialist, Leon Samson, wrote in the 1930s that "when we examine the meaning of Americanism, we discover that Americanism is to the American not a tradition or a territory, not what France is to a Frenchman or England to an Englishman, but a doctrine—what socialism is to a socialist." Samson understood how essential it is to American unity that people of diverse ethnic backgrounds could become securely American by espousing a set of political ideas and values.

Derived from European liberalism of the 17th and 18th centuries and enlarged by American experience, the American ideology is given force and coherence by a far-reaching commitment to the individual. According to the ideology, society in general and government in particular exist, or should exist, to fulfill the rights of each to "Life, Liberty, and the Pursuit of Happiness." To realize their rights fully, individuals must have freedom, the opportunity to make their own choices with a minimum of restraint. The worth of each individual should be seen as equal. Private property is a primary means through which individuals define themselves, protect themselves, and locate their own niche in society. For individuals to be strong and their rights protected, government must be limited and popular.

Out of an expanding and more self-conscious commitment to the ideology, a sense of being not English but American emerged in the colonies before 1776. John Adams described this development as "the real American revolution." And after independence, the solidifying ideological consensus was articulated in the Constitution. Initial disagreements between Federalists and anti-Federalists pale before the rapidity and extent of the Constitution's triumph as a pure reflection of the American ideology—the political idea given governmental form.

The US Constitution embodies the ideology's view of man and of government in its relationship to man. People have both rights and interests: Government must respect the former, and it should permit the individualistic pursuit of the latter so long as basic rights are not infringed or national unity impaired. The polity would be failing if striving individuals were unable to advance their interests within it—or if they were able to be too successful, since *every* special interest is inherently "activated by some common impulse or passion . . . adverse to the rights of other citizens, or to the permanent and aggregate interests of the community" (as James Madison put it in Federalist Paper No. 10). The answer must be found in an elaborate social-political pluralism, where no group or interest can get too strong. Underlying the entire constitutional arrangement, then as now, is the classical liberal distrust of power as a threat to the sovereign individual. The answer to this problem of power: Disperse it and limit it.

Political historian Louis Hartz wrote with mixed admiration and frustration of America's "cult of constitution worship." Not many people can recite the provisions of Article 1, Section 8, or explain the 14th Amendment, but in its largest sense, as a statement of political philosophy and ideals, the US Constitution is exceedingly well understood and strongly supported. It is seen, correctly, as an embodiment of the country's most fundamental political values. And since those values define today, as in 1787, what it means to be American, the Constitution is virtually untouchable. Liberals and conservatives disagree over what certain constitutional provisions require, but together they see being "unconstitutional" as the equivalent of being un-American." The only fundamental constitutional debate the US ever had culminated in an attempt at dissolving the American union—and a civil war in which 618,000 people perished.

I have no quarrel generally with the argument that constitutions should be seen as attempts at governmental engineering. It follows that, if an existing system can be better designed to meet current conditions, it is prudent to do so. This perspective doesn't help us much, however, in assessing the US Constitution on its 200th anniversary. Far more than a piece of governmental engineering, the Constitution is the expression of a nation-defining consensus on political values. In the Constitution's 200th anniversary, we celebrate the persistence of that consensus and the founders' near "perfect pitch" in expressing it.

Thinking It Over

1. What does Ladd mean by the sentence: "The nation is the ideology is the regime"?

2. The "current wisdom" is that the constitution has survived because it is "flexible." Would Ladd agree? Do you?

12.
THE FEDERALIST PAPERS, NO. 10
by James Madison

Setting the Scene: **Ask what the most important source on the American Constitution is and you will be told** *The Federalist Papers.* **Ask what the single most important** *Federalist Paper* **is and you will be told** *Federalist* No. 10 by James Madison. Enough said.

Among the numerous advantages promised by a well-constructed Union, none deserves to be more accurately developed than its tendency to break and control the violence of faction. The friend of popular government never finds himself so much alarmed for their character and fate as when he contemplates their propensity to this dangerous vice. He will not fail, therefore, to set a due value on any plan which, without violating the principles to which he is attached, provides a proper cure for it. . . .

By a faction I understand a number of citizens, whether amounting to a majority or minority of the whole, who are united and actuated by some common impulse of passion, or of interest, adverse to the rights of other citizens, or to the permanent and aggregate interests of the community.

There are two methods of curing the mischiefs of faction: the one, by removing its causes; the other, by controlling its effects.

There are again two methods of removing the causes of faction: the one, by destroying the liberty which is essential to its existence; the other, by giving to every citizen the same opinion, the same passions, and the same interests.

It could never be more truly said than of the first remedy that it was worse than the disease. Liberty is to faction what air is to fire, an aliment without which it instantly expires. But it could not be a less folly to abolish liberty, which is essential to political life, because it nourishes faction than it would be to wish the annihilation of air, which is essential to animal life, because it imparts to fire its destructive agency.

The second expedient is as impracticable as the first would be unwise. As long as the reason of man continues fallible, and he is at liberty to exercise it, different opinions will be formed. As long as the connection subsists between his reason and his self-love, his opinions and his passions will have a reciprocal influence on each other; and the former will be objects to which the latter will attach themselves. The diversity in the faculties of men, from which the rights of property originate, is not less an insuperable obstacle to a uniformity of interests. The protection of these faculties is the first object of government. From the protection of different and unequal faculties of acquiring property, the possession of different degrees and kinds of property immediately results; and from the influence of these on the sentiments and views of the respective proprietors ensues a division of the society into different interests and parties.

The latent causes of faction are thus sown in the nature of man; and we see them everywhere brought into different degrees of activity, according to the different circumstances of civil society. A zeal for different opinions concerning religion, concerning government, and many other points, as well of speculation as of practice; an attachment to different leaders ambitiously contending for pre-eminence and power; or to persons of other descriptions whose fortunes have been interesting to the human passions, have, in turn, divided mankind into parties, inflamed them with mutual animosity, and rendered them much more disposed to vex and oppress each other than to co-operate for their common good. So strong is this propensity of mankind to fall into mutual animosities that where no substantial occasion presents itself the most frivolous and fanciful distinctions have been sufficient to kindle their unfriendly passions and excite their most violent conflict. But the most common and durable source of factions has been the various and unequal distribution of property. Those who hold and those who are without property have ever formed distinct interests in society. Those who are creditors, and those who are debtors, fall under a like discrimination. A landed interest, a manufacturing interest, a mercantile interest, a moneyed interest, with many lesser interests, grow up of necessity in civilized nations, and divide them into different classes, actuated by different sentiments and views. The regulation of these various and interfering interests forms the principal task of modern legislation and involves the spirit of party and faction in the necessary and ordinary operations of government. . . .

It is vain to say that enlightened statesmen will be able to adjust these clashing interests and render them all subservient to the public good. Enlightened statesmen will not always be at the helm. Nor, in many cases, can such an adjustment be made at all without taking into view indirect and remote considerations, which will rarely prevail over the immediate interest which one party may find in disregarding the rights of another or the good of the whole.

The inference to which we are brought is that the *causes* of faction cannot be removed and that relief is only to be sought in the means of controlling its *effects*.

If a faction consists of less than a majority, relief is supplied by the republican principle, which enables the majority to defeat its sinister views by regular vote. It may clog the administration, it may convulse the society; but it will be unable to execute and mask its violence under the forms of the Constitution. When a majority is included in a faction, the form of popular government, on the other hand, enables it to sacrifice to its ruling passion or interest both the public good and the rights of other citizens. To secure the public good and private rights against the danger of such a faction, and at the same time to preserve the spirit and the form of popular government, is then the great object to which our inquiries are directed. . . .

By what means is this object attainable? Evidently by one of two only. Either the existence of the same passion or interest in a majority at the same time must be prevented, or the majority, having such coexistent passion or interest, must be rendered, by their number and local situation, unable to concert and carry into effect schemes of oppression. If the impulse and the opportunity be suffered to coincide, we well know that neither moral nor religious motives can be relied on as an adequate control. They are not found to be such on the injustice and violence of individuals, and lose their efficacy in proportion to the number combined together, that is, in proportion as their efficacy becomes needful.

From this view of the subject it may be concluded that a pure democracy, by which I mean a society consisting of a small number of citizens, who assemble and administer the government in person, can admit of no cure for the mischiefs of faction. A common passion or interest will, in almost every case, be felt by a majority of the whole; a communication and concert results from the form of government itself; and there is nothing to check the inducements to sacrifice the weaker party or an obnoxious individual. Hence it is that such democracies have ever been spectacles of turbulence and contention; have ever been found incompatible with personal security or the rights of property; and have in general been as short in their lives as they have been violent in their deaths. Theoretic politicians, who have patronized this species of government, have erroneously supposed that by reducing mankind to a perfect equality in their political rights, they would at the same time be perfectly equalized and assimilated in their possessions, their opinions, and their passions.

A republic, by which I mean a government in which the scheme of representation takes place, opens a different prospect and promises the cure for which we are seeking. Let us examine the points in which it varies from pure democracy, and we shall comprehend both the nature of the cure and the efficacy which it must derive from the Union.

The two great points of difference between a democracy and a republic are: first, the delegation of the government, in the latter, to a small number of citizens elected by the rest; secondly, the greater number of citizens and greater sphere of country over which the latter may be extended.

The effect of the first difference is, on the one hand, to refine and enlarge the public views by passing them through the medium of a chosen body of citizens, whose wisdom may best discern the true interest of their country and whose patriotism and love of justice will be least likely to sacrifice it to temporary or partial considerations. Under such a regulation it may well happen that the public voice, pronounced by the representatives of the people, will be more consonant to the public good than if pronounced by the people themselves, convened for the purpose. On the other hand, the effect may be inverted. Men of factious tempers, of local prejudices, or of sinister designs, may, by intrigue, by corruption, or by other means, first obtain the suffrages, and then betray the interests of the people. The question resulting is, whether small or extensive republics are more favorable to the election of proper guardians of the public weal; and it is clearly decided in favor of the latter by two obvious considerations.

In the first place it is to be remarked that however small the republic may be the representatives must be raised to a certain number in order to guard against the cabals of a few; and that however large it may be they must be limited to a certain number in order to guard against the confusion of a multitude. Hence, the number of representatives in the two cases not being in proportion to that of the constituents, and being proportionally greatest in the small republic, it follows that if the proportion of fit characters be not less in the large than in the small republic; the former will present a greater option, and consequently a greater probability of a fit choice.

In the next place, as each representative will be chosen by a greater number of citizens in the large than in the small republic, it will be more difficult for unworthy candidates to practice with success the vicious arts by which elections are too often carried; and the suffrages of the people being more free, will be more likely to center on men who possess the most attractive merit and the most diffusive and established characters. . . .

The other point of difference is the greater number of citizens and extent of territory which may be brought within the compass of republican than of democratic government; and it is this circumstance principally which renders factious combinations less to be dreaded in the former than in the latter. The smaller the society, the fewer probably will be the distinct parties and interests composing it; the fewer the distinct parties and interests, the more frequently will a majority be found of the same party; and the smaller the number of individuals composing a majority, and the smaller the compass within which they are laced, the more easily will they concert and execute their plans of oppression. Extend the sphere and you take in a greater variety of parties and interests; you make it less probable that a majority of the whole will have a common motive to invade the rights of other citizens; or if such a common motive exists, it will be more difficult for all who feel it to discover their own strength and to act in unison with each other. Besides other impediments, it may be remarked that, where there is a consciousness of unjust or dishonorable purposes, communication is always checked by distrust in proportion to the number whose concurrence is necessary.

Hence, it clearly appears that the same advantage which a republic has over a democracy in controlling the effects of faction is enjoyed by a large over a small republic—is enjoyed by the Union over the States composing it. Does this advantage consist in the substitution of representatives whose enlightened views and virtuous sentiments render them superior to local prejudices and to schemes of injustice? It will not be denied that the representation of the Union will be most likely to possess these requisite endowments. Does it consist in the greater security afforded by a greater variety of parties, against the event of any one party being able to outnumber and oppress the rest? In an equal degree does the increased variety of parties comprised within the Union increase this security. Does it, in fine, consist in the greater obstacles opposed to the concert and accomplishment of the secret wishes of an unjust and interested majority? Here again the extent of the Union gives it the most palpable advantage.

Thinking It Over

1. Madison is fundamentally concerned with controlling "the violence of faction." What kind of violence? What kind of faction?

2. A lot has changed since Madison wrote *Federalist* No. 10. Would you say the worries he expressed then are more or less relevant today?

13.
A MAN FOR 1987: JAMES MADISON UNSUNG HERO OF THE CONSTITUTION
by Fred Barbash

Setting the Scene: James Madison, more than any other single person shaped the Constitution. Here we see the incredible obstacles he overcame and the momentous deeds he performed. Here we see Madison not from the perspective of the document, but from the perspective of the person. Fred Barbash makes a convincing case that Madison deserved to be carved into the stone of Mount Rushmore "every bit as much" as the other Presidents who reside there today.

He was a small man, "no bigger than a snowflake," as someone wrote of him. As a youth, he thought himself too sickly to achieve much in this world, and when the Revolutionary War came, he thought himself too frail to fight. He was timid and self-conscious as a public speaker, sitting in utter silence through sessions of the Virginia Assembly, preferring the detail of committee work to speech-making on the floor. Some thought him anti-social, humorless, bookish—altogether "little and ordinary," as one acquaintance put it.

A modern public relations man's nightmare, James Madison could probably never ascend to political leadership today, as America observes the bicentennial of his great achievement, the Constitution. But, tomorrow is the 236th anniversary of his birth, and, speaking of national heroes, it is time we gave him his due.

Madison's example is especially useful now, at a time when the republic is going through one of its periodic crises. For lurking behind the iran-contra affair is the same fundamental problem Madison addressed 200 years ago—the tension between our democratic values and the need for a strong central government, or, as he put it, how best to "enable the government to control the governed, and in the next place, oblige it to control itself."

He resolved it with a system of checks and balances, which in many quarters is now regarded as a nuisance. It was no nuisance to Madison and his colleagues. Checks and balances, especially the checks, were the very essence of our government, no exceptions made for foreign policy, secret wars or anything else. "All men having power ought to be distrusted to a certain degree," he said in the convention.

Consider what he accomplished in 1787, and while doing that remember how long it often takes in *our* time to address a single pressing social problem—a decade, if at all; half a decade at best.

- In 1787, James Madison, in a few months time, dreamed up and saw through to completion the creation of an entirely new political system, a new political culture.

• He did it even though the odds, virtually all our traditions and many of the era's most powerful politicians, were against him. He did it at the age of 36. And he did it outside "established channels." Some even thought the whole enterprise of the convention illegal. He was clever enough and determined enough to browbeat the nation's most popular man, George Washington, into attending, as a powerful and badly needed symbol of legitimacy.

• Finally, he proceeded without any aides scurrying about, telling him what to say and think; without feasibility studies, without consultants, pollsters or public relations experts. Madison was an intellectual. He shut out the world when he thought. His dreams and schemes were often laid in solitude.

His vehicle was the Constitutional Convention, held in the statehouse in Philadelphia from May 25 through Sept. 17, 1787. Madison himself never fully claimed the credit for it, because he and most of the other delegates at the convention strictly observed the vow of secrecy they had taken. The world did not become completely aware of his profound influence until he died, and his widow, Dolley, sold his notes of the debates in the convention.

Studying Madison's achievement 200 years later can be a distressing experience. The gap between the quality of political leadership he offered and the discount brand we now suffer through is enormous. It wasn't simply his powerful intellect. It was the political savvy, the guile, the sense of timing, the single-mindedness and the audacity he combined with that intellect that was so stunning. He was an intellectual who got things done, who transformed theory into reality as effectively as any political leader in modern world history.

To be sure, Madison was exceptional even then. So are many of the propositions he stood for, as demonstrated by Watergate, the Iran-contra affair and other scandals as well as the permissive attitude shown by many Americans and the courts to the exercise of governmental authority. But if he was exceptional, his beliefs were not. Madison believed that a government could exercise only that authority granted to it by the Constitution. The burden was on government to justify its acts. Now, the burden has shifted. Now, governmental authority is assumed, and it is up to an outraged litigant, or an outraged citizenry, to prove its abuse.

Was life simpler? Not really. The country was smaller, about 3 million people. But the years between the American revolution and the convention were among the most turbulent in our history. Putting it as succinctly as possible: The national treasury was empty; everyone, rich and poor, was in debt; detachments of the army mutinied; inflation was rampant; the currencies were nearly worthless, and the trade deficit was horrendous. Barbary Pirates preyed on our shipping; the 13 states feuded bitterly, and last but not least, a violent insurrection of farmers, Shays Rebellion, broke out.

We had a Congress—a one house affair established under the Articles of Confederation. But it lacked any real power, including the power to tax, to regulate trade, to enact laws binding on individuals. Often, this Congress could not even muster a quorum to do business. (There was no national executive or national judiciary, because there were no real laws to execute or to interpret.)

The states were king then. For the first (and last) time in our history, they were completely sovereign, with no higher federal authority or crown to overrule their laws. The Congress was kept "imbecilic," as they put it then, by the state governments, which chose and controlled the delegates to the Congress. Any augmentation of Congress' power required the unanimous consent of the states—which never gave it.

Enter James Madison. At the age of 29, in the year 1780, the Commonwealth of Virginia dispatched him to Philadelphia as one of its delegates to the Congress. Reading his correspondence, one almost immediately feels the disillusionment he felt with this once-illustrious body whose direct forebear, the Continental Congress, had brought America the Declaration of Independence and steered her through the war. Madison soon joined a small band of nationalists—among them Alexander Hamilton of New York and James Wilson of Pennsylvania—in several efforts to increase the authority of the national government. All of them failed.

It is difficult to determine exactly when Madison decided the time had come for a total transformation. It might have been on a stifling 90-degree plus day in June 1783, when a rag-tag band of former Revolutionary War troops, muskets at the ready, marched to the statehouse in Philadelphia, where Congress was meeting, surrounded it and threatened to keep everyone hostage until they were paid the months of back wages owed them. Congress asked Pennsylvania for a detachment of militia—and Pennsylvania declined. Shortly thereafter, Madison and the rest of the Congress fled to Princeton, N.J. From that day forward, Congress wandered from city to city like some nomadic tribe, a laughing-stock.

One of the remarkable traits Madison possessed was the ability to see opportunity in a crisis, rather than letting crisis weigh him down and paralyze him. "This picture of our affairs is not a flattering one," he wrote Thomas Jefferson with sublime understatement after the humiliation of 1783. "But we have been witnesses of so many cases in which evils and errors have been the parents of their own remedy, that we cannot but view it with consolations of hope."

Soon he returned to Virginia and began a solitary intellectual odyssey that would change the world. In the winter of 1785, he retreated to his family home in Orange, at the foot of the Blue Ridge, surrounded himself with history books, and began an intensive study of failed confederacies—"ancient and modern."

This immersion in history was, at least in part, in preparation for a gathering of delegates from the states scheduled for Annapolis in September, 1786, to come up with a solution to the country's worsening trade crisis. However, there are many indications that even then, Madison had something much grander in mind.

The study turned out to be merely the first step in his development over the following year of a theory of politics and government for America, and of a plan to bring the theory to life. In brief: The proximate cause of America's troubles lay in the unrestrained power of the states, which declined to cede sufficient authority to a central government to allow America to function as a nation. At the same time, the states trespassed on national prerogatives (he noted that the United States could not even live up to treaty obligations because of state intransigence), abused their neighbors and even oppressed their own citizens by enacting laws breaching property rights and favoring one religion over another. If nothing was done, America would remain a collection of feuding, fussing and thoroughly inconsequential little nations, vulnerable forever to the designs of aggressive foreign powers.

The dynamic that drove the states to these depths, he believed, could be traced to the unique combination of government by majority rule, and factionalism—the inevitable tendency of interest groups, be they creditors, debtors, Anglicans or Baptists, to pursue their own selfish ends.

The solution was not to abandon republicanism, or to stamp out the liberty people enjoyed to pursue their own interests. Republicanism was not the trouble. The trouble was republicanism operating in small spheres, where it was too easy for factions to gang up. The remedy was "an enlargement of the sphere," the creation of a much larger political arena, with a new power center, in which there would be so many competing groups that none would dominate and none would be dominated. The factions, their influence dispersed through the branches of the government, would neutralize one another.

He acknowledged that the prevailing American ideology favored small government close to the people and deeply distrusted big, centralized government as a threat to liberty. The threat, he said, comes not from big government, but from big government improperly constituted. The tripartite system of separated powers and checks and balances, in his view, would keep the government under control.

Thus was born his idea of "the extended republic." Madison's new Congress would not only have the authority to tax, to regulate trade, to make laws binding on individuals. It would be empowered to veto any and all state laws contrary to the Constitution. This was national supremacy with a vengeance.

Since this was to be a government over individuals, rather than over states, individuals, not the state governments, would elect members of the Congress. The states, as states, were to have no representation whatsoever. They would be stripped of authority, bypassed. Finally, and for the same reasons, Madison's scheme would put an end to the principle by which each state had an equal vote: Representation in the Congress—in both houses—would be according to the size of each district.

A new power center would indeed be created, the sphere enlarged, the republic extended.

Why Madison thought the states would ever go along with this defanging is baffling, considering that they had never unanimously approved even a minor augmentation of Congress' power. That he was acutely aware of the explosiveness of his plan was demonstrated by the secrecy with which he treated it as he set about the task of organizing a convention. He told only his closest allies what he was thinking. He would spring it on the others when the convention began.

The idea of a convention itself was highly suspect. For one thing, conventions were considered extra-legal, bypassing established channels of change. The Articles of Confederation expressly required that Congress propose any amendments. For another, conventions had been used by radicals in New England to attack established institutions. They were thus considered by the propertied classes more suitable for tearing down than for building up. Finally, even those who desired change doubted the convention's success. They might hold a convention and nobody would come. Indeed, the little meeting in Annapolis the prior year had attracted only 12 delegates from five states, before issuing (with the connivance of Madison and Alexander Hamilton) its famous and purposely vague sounding call for a second convention, to be held in May, 1787 in Philadelphia.

The convention had an image problem. To solve it, Madison took three slightly devious steps.

First, he and his allies went to the Confederation Congress in search of an endorsement for the convention, but without telling it just what they had in mind. After months of inaction, the endorsement was approved, but with severe restrictions on the convention's mandate (which were ultimately ignored by Madison.)

Second, aware that he was by now tainted as an extreme nationalist, Madison went in search of some more moderate, more respectable figure to front for him. He found his man in Edmund Randolph—the extremely respectable, and extremely moderate governor of Virginia. Randolph threw himself into the task, using his office as governor to correspond with all the other governors and legislatures, urging them to send delegates. Madison ultimately also convinced Randolph to introduce the plan on the floor of the convention, where it became know as "Mr. Randolph's Plan" or "The Virginia Plan," even though most of it was Madison's plan.

Third, at the top of the list of delegates from Virginia, Madison and Randolph put the name of George Washington—the most adored figure in the land. If he couldn't be a drawing card, no one could. They did this without consulting Washington, and then trumpeted the news throughout the land: the great man will attend. Washington was not pleased. At that time (late winter, 1787) he had no intention of abandoning his retirement at Mount Vernon, no desire, as he put it, to "embark again on a sea of troubles." Though Washington sympathized with Madison's cause, he too had grave doubts that a convention would succeed.

Eventually, if reluctantly, Washington agreed to attend.

Although the convention altered many of Madison's most cherished ideas (the congressional veto power over state laws became the supremacy clause; state representation and a remnant of state equality was preserved in the Senate), his plan served as the cornerstone.

Madison, of course, did not do it alone. But it is fair to say that the Constitution would not have come about without him—not then. True, Madison was not the sort to be carved into Mount Rushmore—he would look ridiculous there. But in terms of making a significant and lasting contribution to our welfare, he deserves to be there every bit as much as the other four presidents.

Thinking It Over

1. Is it accurate to charge that the American political system now precludes persons like James Madison from aspiring to the Presidency?

2. Here is an idea for an essay. Ask the question "In today's world, would we *want* a person like Madison in the oval office? You might want to do a little extra reading to answer the question: Was he as good a President as he was activist and intellectual?

14.
PLURALIST DEMOCRACY IN THE UNITED STATES: CONFLICT AND CONSENT
by Robert A. Dahl

Setting the Scene: **Below** one of America's leading political scientists writes about Madison, factions and his solution for the problems of controlling them. In this reading you will review with Dahl the key dilemma that marks governance in a mass, complex society. This is followed by a brief explanation of the concept of *pluralism*. There is no better **single** way to understand (and appreciate) the importance of Madison's thinking and its impact on modern politics than to read the works of persons like Lowi (earlier) and now Robert Dahl.

The Dangers of Faction

Nothing weighed more heavily on the minds of the Founders than the dangers of faction. In an impressive and justly famous analysis (that foreshadowed the remarks quoted above from *The Federalist*), James Madison expressed during the second week of the Constitutional Convention a concern that must have been widely shared among the other delegates:

> All civilized Societies would be divided into different Sects, Factions & interests as they happened to consist of rich & poor, debtors & creditors, the landed, the manufacturing, the commercial interests, the inhabitants of this district or that district, the followers of this political leader or that political leader, the disciples of this religious Sect or that religious Sect.

Madison took it for granted, then, that cleavages could occur in many ways; economic relationships, geographical location, religious feelings, even loyalties to particular leaders, all could lead to conflict. And what would restrain one faction in its struggles with another? Honesty? Reputation? Conscience? Religion? In Madison's view, all limits to faction that depend, like these, on the willingness of an individual or a group to exercise self-restraint are bound to be inadequate.

Like most of the other delegates, Madison was more inclined to stress the dangers that could arise from a willful or tempestuous majority than from a minority; for he assumed that in a republic a majority could more easily have its own way. But he was not unmindful of the possibility that minority factions might also threaten a republic.

> . . . According to the Republican theory indeed, Right & power both being vested in the majority, are held to be synonymous. According to fact & experience, a minority may in an appeal to force be an over-match for the majority. 1. If the minority

happen to include all such as possess the skill & habits of military life, with such as possess the great pecuniary resources, one third may conquer the remaining two thirds. 2. one third of those who participate in the choice of rulers may be rendered a majority by the accession of those whose poverty disqualifies them from a suffrage, & who for obvious reasons may be more ready to join the standard of sedition than that of the established Government. 3. where slavery exists, the Republican Theory becomes still more fallacious.

Precisely what are the dangers of faction that preoccupied the Founders? Curiously enough, none of the men at the Convention ever seems to have stated exactly what he had in mind. On this question even the clearest minds, like those of Madison and Wilson, gave forth cloudy answers. When the delegates descended from vague generalities to concrete cases, the examples they chose generally involved attempts to change the distribution of property. In fact, a careful reading of the record of debates suggests the cynical answer that when the delegates at the Constitutional Convention spoke of the dangers of faction they were usually thinking of attacks on property—their own. Here, for example, is what Madison said at one point:

> . . . No agrarian attempts have yet been made in this Country, but symptoms, of a leveling spirit, as we have understood, have sufficiently appeared in certain quarters to give notice of the future danger. How is this danger to be guarded agst. on republican principles? How is the danger in all cases of interested coalitions to oppress the minority to be guarded agst?

With the aid of the experience that has accumulated since 1787, perhaps men today can see the problem of faction more clearly than the delegates to the Convention were able to do. We have learned some hard lessons. When someone says he opposes factions and parties, what he usually means, it seems, is that he opposes every faction, every party, every interest—except his own. If one believes that policies proposed by others will deprive him of something he values, or if he so strongly believes his own policies are right that he would impose them on other people no matter what they prefer, he finds it easy to define what the others wish to do as tyranny and what he himself wishes to do as obvious justice.

Many of the concrete concerns of the Founders were, I believe, of this kind. To some extent, they elevated their own privileges into universal matters of abstract and universal right; groups who might interfere with their privileges were, in their eyes, dangerous factions. In this respect they carried partisan attitudes into the Convention, yet were usually unaware that they did so. They were not necessarily cynical, but merely human. (Does one have a right to expect more from men simply because they make a constitution?)

Yet it is too facile to jump to the conclusion that the fear of faction expressed by the Founders represented nothing more than sordid self-interest. Whatever their motives and biases may have been, whatever the extent to which they were influenced by their own socio-economic positions and ideological perspectives, the problem they confronted was genuine, important, timely, persistent and worthy of the concern they gave it. For the problem of faction is simply the mirror image of the problem of gaining consent—of governing with the consent of the governed. And governing with the consent of the governed . . . has values both ideal and practical. Goals of personal freedom, human dignity, enlightened self-interest, and political stability all justify a serious concern for gaining consent, and hence for keeping conflict within bounds, so that in the best of circumstances all citizens will feel that what they hold most dear is respected and protected by the government—while even in the worst of circumstances they will feel that the laws are at least tolerable, and do not encourage disloyalty, violence, or civil wars.

As practical men, the Founders were concerned lest conflicts get out of hand. Faction has been the bane of previous republics; faction was a worrisome fact of recent experience; and faction would be a standing danger to the new republic.

> . . . In Greece & Rome the rich & poor, the creditors & debtors, as well as the patricians & plebians alternately oppressed each other with equal unmercifulness. What a source of oppression was the relation between the parent cities of Rome, Athens & Carthage, & their respective provinces: the former possessing the power, & the latter being sufficiently distinguished to be separate objects of it? Why was America so justly apprehensive of Parliamentary injustice? Because G. Britain had a separate interest real or supposed, & if her authority had been admitted, could have pursued that interest at our expense. We have seen the mere distinction of colour made in the most enlightened period of time, a ground of the most oppressive dominion ever exercised by man over man. What has been the source of those unjust laws complained of among ourselves? Has it not been the real or supposed interest of the major number? Debtors have defrauded their creditors. The landed interest has borne hard on the mercantile interest. The Holders of one species of property have thrown a disproportion of taxes on the holders of another species.

Yet, being realists, they also knew that conflict is inevitable. Conflict, as Madison said, is sown in the nature of man. An autocratic government might suppress the symptoms of conflict, as modern dictators have succeeded in doing; but even an autocracy cannot eliminate the causes. By establishing a republic in which citizens would enjoy a large measure of personal freedom, the Founders were found to make it easy for conflict to erupt. How, then, was conflict to be managed? How could it be moderated so that it would not wreck the new Republic? How could government be carried on with something like the general consent of the people? . . .

Even if people cannot always agree on specific policies . . . a solution is to gain their consent for a process. It is perfectly reasonable of me to say that I approve of the process by which certain kinds of decisions are made, even if I do not always like the specific results. Thus the consent of the governed may be interpreted to mean their approval of the processes by which decisions are arrived at and their willingness to abide by these decisions even when these seem wrong.

But what kind of a process shall I require? If I hold that no one can, as a general matter, know my goals and values better than I myself, then no doubt I will insist that the process of making decisions must provide me with a full opportunity to make my views known; and even if I am willing to leave details to experts, I do not want anyone else to have more power over the decision, in the last say, that I do. A solution along these lines might well appeal to me as the best attainable, given the inescapable conditions mentioned earlier: that my need for human fellowship impels me to live in a society, that I cannot live with others without sometimes disagreeing with them, and that I must therefore find some way to adjust our conflicts that will appeal to all of us as fair . . .

But how is this solution to be applied? What kind of process will insure that I shall have a full opportunity to make my views known, and that no one else will have more power over decisions, in the last say, than I do?

There are a number of different answers to these questions, and it is with two of these that we are concerned. Purely as a matter of abstract theory, the one is admirably clear and explicit; this is decision-making by the sovereign majority. Yet no country seems to have adopted this method in entirely. The other is in greater or lesser degree the pattern that seems to have evolved in the countries we usually call 'democratic.' Yet the pattern is so blurred and chaotic—and there are so many variations from country to country—that it is difficult to describe. . . .

In the vision of democracy as decision-making by the sovereign majority, the citizens of a given country all approve of the principle of majority rule, according to which all conflicts over the policies of government are settled, sooner or later, by a majority of citizens or voters—either directly in a public assembly or in a referendum, or indirectly through elected representatives. . . .

It seems reasonable to conjecture that the more diverse the beliefs held among a body of people, the less likely it is that they will approve of the idea of making decisions by majority rule. To the extent that this conjecture is valid, it is a severe restriction on the principle of rule by a sovereign majority, particularly in modern heterogeneous societies. For it seems entirely reasonable to hold that diversity of beliefs is likely to be greater the larger the number of citizens, the bigger the territory over which they are spread, and the greater the distinctions of race, ethnic group, regional culture, occupation, social class, income, property, and so on. Some advocates of rule by the sovereign majority have therefore argued, as Rousseau did, that majority decisions would be acceptable only among very small and highly homogeneous bodies of people, groups no larger perhaps than a town or a very small city. According to this view, nations even as small as Norway, and certainly as large as the United States, are unsuitable for democracy. . . .

The practical solutions that democratic countries have evolved are a good deal less clear than a straightforward application of the principle of majority rule. . . .

. . . [T]he United States has limited the sovereignty of the majority . . . so far . . . that it is sometimes called a pluralistic system, a term I propose to use here.

The fundamental axiom in the theory and practise of American pluralism is, I believe, this: Instead of a single center of sovereign power there must be multiple centers of power, none of which is or can be wholly sovereign. Although the only legitimate sovereign is the people in the perspective of American pluralism even the people ought never to be an absolute sovereign; consequently no part of the people, such as a majority, ought to be absolutely sovereign.

Why this axiom? The theory and practise of American pluralism tend to assume, as I see it, that the existence of multiple centers of power, none of which is wholly sovereign, will help (may indeed be necessary) to tame power, to secure the consent of all, and to settle conflicts peacefully:

¶ Because one center of power is set against another, power itself will be tamed, civilized, controlled, and limited to decent human purposes, while coercion, the most evil form of power, will be reduced to a minimum.

¶ Because even minorities are provided with opportunities to veto solutions they strongly object to, the consent of all will be won in the long run.

¶ Because constant negotiations among different centers of power are necessary in order to make decisions, citizens and leaders will perfect the precious art of dealing peacefully with their conflicts, and not merely to the benefit of one partisan but to the mutual benefit of all the parties to a conflict.

These are, I think, the basic postulates and even the unconscious ways of thought that are central to the American attempt to cope with the inescapable problems of power, conflict, and consent.

Thinking It Over

1.   What is Robert Dahl's solution for the problem of faction?

2.   Many people ask this question in reference to Dahl's model for American politics: Is that the best we can expect from our political system? Is that a fair question? If not, why? If so, answer it.

15.
WHY WE LOST THE ERA
by Jane J. Mansbridge

Setting the Scene: It is not easy to amend the Constitution. Huge majorities are needed in both Houses of Congress and most of the states must approve. In the following reading Professor Mansbridge takes a clear-eyed look at the campaign to ratify the Equal Rights Amendment. It was a campaign that failed. Not everything Jane Mansbridge says about it will please those who fought so hard to secure Constitutional protection for women's rights. But her conclusions ring true and they go a long way in explaining how the great proportion of changes in the way we govern ourselves in America take place outside the Constitution.

1. Equality of rights under the law shall not be denied or abridged by the United States or by any State on account of sex.
2. The Congress shall have the power to enforce, by appropriate legislation, the provisions of this article.
3. This amendment shall take effect two years after the date of ratification.

— *Complete text of the Equal Rights Amendment*

In March 1972 the Equal Rights Amendment to the United States Constitution—the ERA—passed the Senate of the United States with a vote of 84 to 8, fifteen votes more than the two-thirds required for constitutional amendments. In the ensuing ten years—from 1972 to 1982—a majority of Americans consistently told interviewers that they favored this amendment to the Constitution. Yet on June 30, 1982, the deadline for ratifying the amendment passed with only thirty-five of the required thirty-eight states having ratified.

How did this happen?

. . . [I]f the ERA had been ratified, the Supreme Court would have been unlikely to use it to bring about major changes in the relations between American men and women, at least in the foreseeable future. Nor did the American public want any significant change in gender roles, whether at work, at home, or in society at large. The groups that fought for the ERA and the groups that fought against it, however, had a stake in believing that the ERA *would* produce these kinds of changes. With both the proponents and the opponents exaggerating the likely effects of the ERA, legislators in wavering states became convinced that the ERA might, in fact, produce important substantive changes—and the necessary votes were lost. Considering the large number of legislative votes required to amend the Constitution, the puzzle is not why the ERA died but why it came so close to passing.

Contrary to widespread belief, public support for the ERA did not increase in the course of the ten-year struggle. In key wavering states where the ERA was most debated, public support actually declined. Much of the support for the Amendment was superficial, because it was based on a support for abstract rights, not for real changes. Many nominal supporters took strong antifeminist positions on other issues, and their support evaporated when the ERA became linked in their minds to feminist positions they rejected.

The irony in all this is that ERA would have had much less substantive effect than either proponents or opponents claimed. Because the ERA applied only to the government and not to private businesses and corporations, it would have had no noticeable effect, at least in the short run, on the gap between men's and women's wages. Furthermore, during the 1970s, the Supreme Court began to use the Fourteenth Amendment to the Constitution to declare unconstitutional almost all the laws and practices that Congress had intended to make unconstitutional when it passed the ERA in 1972. The exceptions were laws and practices that most Americans approved. Thus, by the late 1970s it was hard to show that the ERA would have made any of the substantive changes that most Americans favored.

While the ERA would have had few immediate, tangible effects, I nonetheless believe that its defeat was a major setback for equality between men and women. Its direct effects would have been slight, but its indirect effects on both judges and legislators would probably have led in the long run to interpretations of existing laws and enactment of new laws that would have benefited women. The lack of immediate benefits did, however, deeply influence the course of the public debate. Because ERA activists had little of an immediate, practical nature to lose if the ERA was defeated, they had little reason to describe it in a way that would make it acceptable to middle-of-the-road legislators. As a consequence, the most influential leaders in the pro-ERA organizations and many of the activists in those organizations chose to interpret the ERA as delivering radical results.

Most proponents contended, for example, that the ERA would require the military to send women draftees into combat on the same basis as men. ERA proponents adopted this position even though it reduced their chances of achieving the short-run goal of passing the ERA and despite the fact that the Court was not likely to interpret the ERA as having this effect. They did so in part because their ideology called for full equality with men, not for equality with exceptions. In a somewhat similar manner, certain feminist lawyers argued in state courts that state ERAs required states to fund medically necessary abortions if they were funding all medically necessary services for men. Such arguments also reduced the chances that legislators in the key unratified states would vote for the federal ERA.

The struggle reveals how impossible it is, even in the most favorable circumstances, to dispense with "ideology" in favor of practical political reasoning when the actors in the drama give their energies voluntarily, without pay or other material incentives. Volunteers always have mixed motives, but most are trying to do good and promote justice. As a result, most would rather lose fighting for a cause they believe in than win fighting for a cause they feel is morally compromised.

Because the ERA offered its supporters no tangible benefits, activists worked hard for it only if they believed strongly in equality for women. They had no reason to "betray" that principle by compromise for compromise offered no concrete benefits, either to them personally or to women generally. ERA opponents took relatively extreme positions for similar reasons. But their "radicalism" cost them less, because they had only to disrupt an emerging consensus, not to produce one.

Refusing to compromise is, of course, often better than winning. It is not the focus on principle rather than practice that should give the reader of this story pause. It is the difficulty both sides had assimilating information about the struggle in which they were engaged. This institutionalized deafness meant that neither the activists nor the general public could make even an informed guess about what passage of the ERA would accomplish. As a result, there was no serious national debate about whether the Amendment was the best way of accomplishing what the proponents sought or whether it really threatened the values that opponents sought to defend. Nor did the proponents, who ran the gamut from feminist lawyers to grass-roots activists, ever engage one another in a wide-ranging discussion of strategy.

The only possible way to have persuaded three more state legislature to ratify the ERA would have been to insist—correctly—that it would do relatively little in the short run, and to insist equally strongly—and correctly—on the importance of placing the principle in the Constitution to guide the Supreme Court in its long-run evolution of constitutional law. In addition, the pro-ERA movement would have had to develop an ongoing, district-based political network capable of turning generalized public sympathy for reforms that benefit women into political pressure on specific legislators in the marginal unratified states. But even this strategy might not have worked. Comparatively few state legislators were open to persuasion on this issue, and the troops for district-based organizing were often hard to mobilize—or keep mobilized.

The movement away from principle and the increasing focus on substantive effects was probably an inevitable result of the ten-year struggle for the ERA. Inevitable or not, the shift did occur. In the near future, therefore, the only way to convince legislators that the ERA would not have undesirable substantive effects would be to add explicit amendments limiting its application to the military, abortion, and so on. No principled feminist, including myself, favors an ERA that includes such "crippling" amendments. In the present political climate, therefore, the future of the ERA looks even dimmer than its past.

The death of the ERA was, of course, also related to broader changes in American political attitudes. Two of these changes were especially relevant: growing legislative skepticism about the consequences of giving the U.S. Supreme Court authority to review legislation, and the growing organizational power of the new Right.

Suspicion of the Supreme Court, and of the role of lawyers and judges generally, certainly played a significant role in the ERA's demise. For its advocates, the ERA was a device for allowing the Supreme Court to impose the principle of equality between the sexes on recalcitrant state legislators. For legislators, that was precisely the problem. They did not want their actions reviewed, much less reversed, by federal judges whom they did not even appoint. There was a larger problem as well. The ERA embodied a principle, which was supposed to apply, without exception, to specific pieces of legislation.   But most people—including most legislators—do not derive their preferences from principles. Instead, they derive their principles from their preferences, endorsing principles they associate with outcomes they like. Because the justices of the Supreme Court of the United States put somewhat more weight than ordinary citizens do on the principles they have evolved from the Constitution, they often find themselves taking controversial or even unpopular stands. As a result, much of the public has come to view the Court as "out of control." Although the Court's unpopular decisions have not yet reduced its power, they took their toll on the ERA. If the primary cause of the ERA's defeat was the fear that it would lead to major changes in the roles of men and women, a major subsidiary cause was legislative backlash against "progressive" Court decisions, starting with the 1954 school desegregation decision. Many state legislators were unwilling to give the Court "new words to play with," rightly fearing that this could eventually have all sorts of unforeseeable consequences they might not like and would not be able to reverse.

The same sense of impotence in the face of national changes that fueled the reaction against the Court also fed the conservative backlash against feminism and the growth of the "new" Right. For many conservative Americans, the personal became political for the first time when questions of family, children, sexual behavior, and women's roles became subjects of political debate. Leaders of the "old" Radical Right, who had traditionally focused on national defense and the Communist menace, became aware of the organizing potential of these "women's" issues only slowly. Once assimilated, however, the "new" issues turned out to have two great organizational virtues. First, they provided a link with fundamentalist churches. The evangelizing culture and the stable geographic base of the fundamentalist churches made them powerful actors in state legislatures once they ventured into the political process. Second, "women's issues" not only gave a focus to the reaction against the changes in child rearing, sexual behavior, divorce, and the use of drugs that had taken place in the 1960s and 1970s, they also mobilized a group, traditional homemakers, that had lost status over the two previous decades and was feeling the psychological effects of the loss. The new women's issues, combined with improvements in computer technology that reduced the cost of processing large numbers of names, made it feasible for the first time to contact by direct mail and thus bring into concerted political activities many who had previously been concerned only with a single issue or not been involved in politics at all.

State legislators were predisposed to oppose a constitutional amendment that gave the federal government power in one of the few areas that was still primarily in the province of the states, namely, family law. The entry of new conservative activists into the political process enhanced this "natural" resistance. As fundamentalist women became more prominent in the opposition, the ERA came to be seen as an issue that pitted women against women and, moreover, women of the Right against women of the Left. Once the ERA lost its aura of benefiting all women and became a partisan issue, it lost its chance of gaining the supermajority required for a constitutional amendment.

There are two lessons to be learned from the story told here. The first is a lesson about the politics of promoting "the common good." We have known for a long time of the extraordinary inequities built into the way different groups can influence legislators in a pluralist democratic system. We have also known that because it is harder to organize for the general interest than for particular interests, the general interest will—all other things being equal—count less in the political process than most people want it to. The story of the ERA struggle reveals a third, less widely recognized, obstacle to promoting the common good. Organizing on behalf of the general interest usually requires volunteers, and mobilizing volunteers often requires an exaggerated, black or white vision of events to justify spending time and money on the cause. Ironically, the greatest cost in organizing for the public interest may be the distortion, in the course of organizing, of that interest itself.

A second, practical lesson follows from the first. While organizations that depend on volunteers to promote the common good seem to have an inherent tendency toward ideological purity and polarized perceptions, they can develop institutions that help correct these tendencies, ranging from small-group techniques through formal systems of representation. Although ongoing organizations are susceptible to the temptations of speaking only to themselves, they are also our main repositories of past experience and our main mechanism for avoiding the endless repetition of past errors. Effectively promoting the common good thus requires that we keep such organizations strong and consistently funded, while at the same time trying to ensure internal dialogue on substantive issues.

Thinking It Over

1. How could a professor resist. . . . Why *was* the ERA defeated? In fifty words or less, please.

2. How does Professor Mansbridge, in light of her fundamental argument, defend the notion that the defeat of the ERA was "a major setback for equality between men and women"?

Chapter III

CIVIL RIGHTS & LIBERTIES: PLAYING BY THE RULES

16.
BROWN V. BOARD OF EDUCATION

Setting the Scene: The Supreme Court has never handed down a case with such sweeping significance for social policy as the one you are about to read. While the abortion decisions have been more fiercely contested in the streets of Washington, *Brown* set in motion a revolution. One thing the present generation must bear in mind was that segregation was *real*. A simpler term for it is *racism*. The implications of that fact are hard to grasp if one has never seen it in person. The picture of a black woman with two kids lowering her head and walking to the back of a bus to where a "Coloreds" sign swayed in the gloom, for instance, will be etched in my mind forever even though I was only twelve the year mom took us south from Vermont for a year to find work. The world was a *very* different place in 1952 when a unanimous Court decreed that separation of the races was unconstitutional. I want you to understand this case intellectually. But more than that, try to find a way to *sense* its significance, to *feel* the injustice to which it speaks, and to *understand* the passion that rightly fills the souls of those who have experienced racism.

Chief Justice Warren delivered the opinion of the Court:

These cases come to us from the States of Kansas, South Carolina, Virginia and Delaware. They are premised on different facts and different local conditions, but a common legal question justified their consideration together in this consolidated opinion.

In each of the cases, minors of the Negro race, through their legal representatives, seek the aid of the courts in obtaining admission to the public schools of their community on a nonsegregated basis. In each instance they had been denied admission to schools attended by white children under laws requiring or permitting segregation according to race. This segregation was alleged to deprive the plaintiffs of the equal protection of the laws under the Fourteenth Amendment. In each of the cases other than the Delaware case, a three-judge federal district court denied relief to the plaintiffs on the so-called "separate but equal" doctrine announced by this Court in *Plessy v. Ferguson* . . . Under that doctrine, equality of treatment is accorded when the races are provided substantially equal facilities, even though these facilities be separate. In the Delaware case, the Supreme Court of Delaware adhered to that doctrine, but ordered that the plaintiffs be admitted to the white schools because of their superiority to the Negro schools.

The plaintiffs contend that segregated public schools are not "equal" and cannot be made "equal," and that hence they are deprived of the equal protection of the laws. Because of the obvious importance of the question presented, the Court took jurisdiction. Argument was heard in the 1952 Term, and reargument was heard this Term on certain questions propounded by the Court.

Reargument was largely devoted to the circumstances surrounding the adoption of the Fourteenth Amendment in 1868. It covered exhaustively consideration of the Amendment in Congress, ratification by the states, then existing practices in racial segregation, and the views of proponents and opponents of the Amendment. This discussion and our own investigation convince us that, although these sources cast some light, it is not enough to resolve the problem with which we are faced. At best, they are inconclusive. The most avid proponents of the post-War Amendments undoubtedly intended them to remove all legal distinctions among "all persons born or naturalized in the United States." Their opponents, just as certainly, were antagonistic to both the letter and the spirit of the Amendments and wished them to have the most limited effect. What others in Congress and the state legislatures had in mind cannot be determined with any degree of certainty.

An additional reason for the inconclusive nature of the Amendment's history, with respect to segregated schools, is the status of public education at that time. In the South, the movement toward free common schools, supported by general taxation, had not yet taken hold. Education of white children was largely in the hands of private groups. Education of Negroes was almost nonexistent, and practically all of the race were illiterate. In fact, any education of Negroes was forbidden by law in some states. Today, in contrast, many Negroes have achieved outstanding success in the arts and sciences as well as in the business and professional world. It is true that public school education at the time of the Amendment had advanced further in the North, but the effect of the Amendment on Northern States was generally ignored in the congressional debates. Even in the North, the conditions of public education did not approximate those existing today. The curriculum was usually rudimentary; ungraded schools were common in rural areas; the school term was but three months a year in many states; and compulsory school attendance was virtually unknown. As a consequence, it is not surprising that there should be so little in the history of the Fourteenth Amendment relating to its intended effect on public education.

In the first cases in this Court construing the Fourteenth Amendment, decided shortly after its adoption, the Court interpreted it as proscribing all state-imposed discriminations against the Negro race. The doctrine of "separate but equal" did not make its appearance in this Court until 1896 in the case of *Plessy v. Ferguson, supra,* involving not education but transportation. American courts have since labored with the doctrine for over half a century. In this Court, there have been six cases involving the "separate but equal" doctrine in the field of public education. In *Cumming v. County Board of Education* . . . and *Gong Lum v. Rice* . . . the validity of the doctrine itself was not challenged. In more recent cases, all on the graduate school level, inequality was found in that specific benefits enjoyed by white students were denied to Negro students of the same educational qualifications (*Missouri ex rel. Gaines v. Canada* . . . *Sipuel v. Oklahoma* . . . *Sweatt v. Painter* . . . *McLaurin v. Oklahoma State Regents* . . .) In none of these cases was it necessary to re-examine the doctrine to grant relief to the Negro plaintiff. And in *Sweatt v. Painter, supra*, the Court expressly reserved decision on the question whether *Plessy v. Ferguson* should be held inapplicable to public education.

In the instant cases, that question is directly presented. Here, unlike *Sweatt v. Painter*, there are findings below that the Negro and white schools involved have been equalized, or are being equalized, with respect to buildings, curricula, qualifications and salaries of teachers, and other "tangible" factors. Our decision, therefore, cannot turn on merely a comparison of these tangible factors in the Negro and white schools involved in each of the cases. We must look instead to the effect of segregation itself on public education.

In approaching this problem, we cannot turn the clock back to 1868 when the Amendment was adopted, or even to 1896 when *Plessy v. Ferguson* was written. We must consider public education in the light of its full development and its present place in American life throughout the Nation. Only in this way can it be determined if segregation in public schools deprives these plaintiffs of the equal protection of the laws.

Today, education is perhaps the most important function of state and local governments. Compulsory school attendance laws and the great expenditures for education both demonstrate our recognition of the importance of education to our democratic society. It is required in the performance of our most basic public responsibilities, even service in the armed forces. It is the very foundation of good citizenship. Today it is a principal instrument in awakening the child to cultural values, in preparing him for later professional training, and in helping him to adjust normally to his environment. In these days, it is doubtful that any child may reasonably be expected to succeed in life if he is denied the opportunity of an education. Such an opportunity, where the state has undertaken to provide it, is a right which must be made available to all one equal terms.

We come then to the question presented: Does segregation of children in public schools solely on the basis of race, even though the physical facilities and other "tangible" factors may be equal, deprive the children of the minority group of equal educational opportunities? We believe that it does.

In *Sweatt v. Painter, supra*, in finding that a segregated law school for Negroes could not provide them equal educational opportunities, this Court relied in large part on "those qualities which are incapable of objective measurement but which make for greatness in a law school." In *McLaurin v. Oklahoma State Regents, supra*, the Court, in requiring that a negro admitted to a white graduate school be treated like all other students, again resorted to intangible considerations: ". . . his ability to study, to engage in discussions and exchange views with other students, and, in general, to learn his profession." Such considerations apply with added force to children in grade and high schools. To separate them from others of similar age and qualifications solely because of their race generates a feeling of inferiority as to their status in the community that may affect their hearts and minds in a way unlikely ever to be undone. The effect of this separation on their educational opportunities was well stated by a finding in the Kansas case by a court which nevertheless felt compelled to rule against the Negro plaintiffs:

> Segregation of white and colored children in public schools has a detrimental effect upon the colored children. The impact is greater when it has the sanction of the law; for the policy of separating the races is usually interpreted as denoting the inferiority of the negro group. A sense of inferiority affects the motivation of a child to learn. Segregation with the sanction of law, therefore, has a tendency to [retard] the educational and mental development of negro children and to deprive them of some of the benefits they would receive in a racial[ly] integrated school system.

Whatever may have been the extent of psychological knowledge at the time of *Plessy v. Ferguson*, this finding is amply supported by modern authority. Any language in *Plessy v. Ferguson* contrary to this finding is rejected.

We conclude that in the field of public education the doctrine of "separate but equal" has no place. Separate educational facilities are inherently unequal. Therefore, we hold that the plaintiffs and others similarly situated for whom the actions have been brought are, by reason of the segregation complained of, deprived of the equal protection of the laws guaranteed by the Fourteenth Amendment. This disposition makes unnecessary any discussion whether such segregation also violates the Due Process Clause of the Fourteenth Amendment.

Because these are class actions, because of the wide applicability of this decision, and because of the great variety of local conditions, the formulation of decrees in these cases presents problems of considerable complexity. On reargument, the consideration of appropriate relief was necessarily subordinated to the primary question—the constitutionality of segregation in public education. We have now announced that such segregation is a denial of the equal protection of the laws. In order that we may have the full assistance of the parties in formulating decrees, the cases will be restored to the docket, and the parties are requested to present further argument on Questions 4 and 5 previously propounded by the Court for the reargument this Term. The Attorney General of the united States is again invited to participate. The Attorneys General of the states requiring or permitting segregation in public education will also be permitted to appear as *amici curiae* upon request to do so by September 15, 1954, and submission of briefs by October 1, 1954.

It is so ordered

Thinking It Over

1. It is generally agreed that the majority of Americans would not have voted for the Brown decision had it been put to a vote in 1954. What does that say about American democracy?

2. Face the tough question. Isn't the Brown case clear evidence that the Court makes policy? The Constitution that allowed racism the day before they decided, disapproved of it twenty-four hours later. What's all the fuss about? What's the big deal? Of *course* the Court makes policy. Comment.

17.
THE DECLINING SIGNIFICANCE OF RACE
by William J. Wilson

Setting the Scene: In the piece that follows, you will be introduced to a fundamental debate that still rages in America. Do we remain a racist society? William J. Wilson would certainly agree there are racists in America, but the overall pattern of black repression, he argues, is related to "fundamental changes in the economy." Blacks are imprisoned by their socio-economic status, not the color of their skin. We join his argument after he has made the case that a "history of discrimination and oppression created a huge black underclass" in the first place.

The Polity and American Race Relations

If the patterned ways in which racial groups have interacted historically have been shaped in major measure by different systems of production, they have also been undeniably influenced by the changing policies and laws of the state. For analytical purposes, it would be a mistake to treat the influences of the polity and the economy as if they were separate and unrelated. The legal and political systems in the antebellum South were effectively used as instruments of the slaveholding elite to strengthen and legitimate the institution of slavery. But as industrialization altered the economic class structure in the postbellum South, the organizing power and political consciousness of the white lower class increased and its members were able to gain enough control of the political and juridical systems to legalize a new system of racial domination, (Jim Crow segregation) that clearly reflected their class interests.

In effect, throughout the preindustrial period of race relations and the greater portion of the industrial period the role of the polity was to legitimate, reinforce, and regulate patterns of racial inequality. However, it would be unwarranted to assume that the relationship between the economic and political aspects of race necessarily implies that the latter is simply a derivative phenomenon based on the more fundamental processes of the former. The increasing intervention, since the mid-twentieth century, of state and federal government agencies in resolving or mediating racial conflicts has convincingly demonstrated the political system's autonomy in handling contemporary racial problems. Instead of merely formalizing existing racial alignments as in previous periods, the political system has, since the initial state and municipal legislation of the 1940s, increasingly created changes leading to the erosion of traditional racial alignments; in other words, instead of reinforcing racial barriers created during the preindustrial and industrial periods, the political system in recent years has tended to promote racial equality.

Thus, in the previous periods the polity was quite clearly an instrument of the white population in suppressing blacks. The government's racial practices varied, as I indicated above, depending on which segment of the white population was able to assert its class interests. However, in the past two decades the interests of the black population have been significantly reflected in the racial policies of the government, and this change is one of the clearest indications that the racial balance of power had been significantly altered. Since the early 1940s the black population has steadily gained political resources and, with the help of sympathetic white allies, has shown an increasing tendency to utilize these resources in promoting or protecting its group interests.

By the mid-twentieth century the black vote had proved to be a major vehicle for political pressure. The black vote not only influenced the outcome of national elections but many congressional, state, and municipal elections as well. Fear of the Negro vote produced enactment of public accommodation and fair employment practices laws in northern and western municipalities and states prior to the passage of federal civil rights legislation in 1964. This political resurgence for black Americans increased their sense of power, raised their expectations, and provided the foundations for the proliferation of demands which shaped the black revolt during the 1960s. But there were other factors that helped to buttress Negro demands and contributed to the developing sense of power and rising expectations, namely, a growing, politically active black middle class following World War II and the emergence of the newly independent African states.

The growth of the black middle class was concurrent with the growth of the black urban population. It was in the urban areas, with their expanding occupational opportunities, that a small but significant number of blacks were able to upgrade their occupations, increase their income, and improve their standard of living. The middle-class segment of an oppressed minority is most likely to participate in a drive for social justice that is disciplined and sustained. In the early phases of the civil rights movement, the black middle class channeled its energies through organizations such as the National Association for the Advancement of Colored People, which emphasized developing political resources and successful litigation through the courts. These developments were paralleled by the attack against traditional racial alignments in other parts of the world. The emerging newly independent African states led the assault. In America, the so-called "leader of the free world," the manifestation of racial tension and violence has been a constant source of embarrassment to national government officials. This sensitivity to world opinion made the national government more vulnerable to pressures of black protest at the very time when blacks had the greatest propensity to protest.

The development of black political resources that made the government more sensitive to Negro demands, the motivation and morale of the growing black middle class that resulted in the political drive for racial equality, and the emergence of the newly independent African states that increased the federal government's vulnerability to civil rights pressures all combined to create a new sense of power among black Americans and to raise their expectations as they prepared to enter the explosive decade of the 1960s. The national government was also aware of this developing sense of power and responded to the pressures of black protest in the 1960s with an unprecedented series of legislative enactments to protect black civil rights.

The problem for blacks today, in terms of government practices, is no longer one of legalized racial inequality. Rather the problem for blacks, especially the black underclass, is that the government is not organized to deal with the new barriers imposed by structural changes in the economy. With the passage of equal employment legislation and the authorization of affirmative action programs the government has helped clear the path for more privileged blacks, who have the requisite education and training, to enter the mainstream of American occupations. However, such government programs do not confront the impersonal economic barriers confronting members of the black underclass, who have been effectively screened out of the corporate and government industries. And the very attempts of the government to eliminate traditional racial barriers through such programs as affirmative action have had the unintentional effect of contributing to the growing economic class divisions within the black community.

Class Stratification and Changing Black Experiences

The problems of black Americans have always been compounded because of their low position in both the economic order (the average economic class position of blacks as a group) and the social order (the social prestige or honor accorded individual blacks because of their ascribed racial status). It is of course true that the low economic position of blacks has helped to shape the categorical social definitions attached to blacks as a racial groups, but it is also true that the more blacks become segmented in terms of economic class position, the more their concerns about the social significance of race will vary.

In the preindustrial period of American race relations there was of course very little variation in the economic class position of blacks. The system of racial caste oppression relegated virtually all blacks to the bottom of the economic class hierarchy. Moreover, the social definitions of racial differences were heavily influenced by the ideology of racism and the doctrine of paternalism, both of which clearly assigned a subordinate status for blacks vis-à-vis whites. Occasionally, a few individual free blacks would emerge and accumulate some wealth or property, but they were the overwhelming exception. Thus the uniformly low economic class position of blacks reinforced and, in the eyes of most whites, substantiated the social definitions that asserted Negroes were culturally and biogenetically inferior to whites. The uniformly low economic class position of blacks also removed the basis for any meaningful distinction between race issues and class issues within the black community.

The development of a black middle class accompanied the change from a preindustrial to an industrial system of production. Still, despite the fact that some blacks were able to upgrade their occupation and increase their education and income, there were severe limits on the areas in which blacks could in fact advance. Throughout most of the industrial period of race relations, the growth of the black middle class occurred because of the expansion of institutions created to serve the needs of a growing urbanized black population. The black doctor, lawyer, teacher, minister, businessman, mortician, excluded from the white community, was able to create a niche in the segregated black community. Although the income levels and life-styles of the black professionals were noticeably and sometimes conspicuously different from those of the black masses, the two groups had one basic thing in common, a racial status contemptuously regarded by most whites in society. If E. Franklin

Frazier's analysis of the black bourgeoise is correct, the black professionals throughout the industrial period of American race relations tended to react to their low position in the social order by an ostentatious display of material possessions and a conspicuous effort to disassociate themselves from the black masses.[1]

Still, as long as the members of the black middle class were stigmatized by their racial status; as long as they were denied the social recognition accorded their white counterparts; more concretely, as long as they remained restricted in where they could live, work, socialize, and be educated, race would continue to be a far more salient and important issue in shaping their sense of group position than their economic class position. Indeed, it was the black middle class that provided the leadership and generated the momentum for the civil rights movement during the mid-twentieth century. The influence and interests of this class were clearly reflected in the way the race issues were defined and articulated. Thus, the concept of "freedom" quite clearly implied, in the early stages of the movement, the right to swim in certain swimming pools, to eat in certain restaurants, to attend certain movie theaters, and to have the same voting privileges as whites. These basic concerns were reflected in the 1964 Civil Rights Bill which helped to create the illusion that, when the needs of the black middle class were met, so were the needs of the entire black community.

However, although the civil rights movement initially failed to address the basic needs of the members of the black lower class, it did increase their awareness of racial oppression, heighten their expectations about improving race relations, and increase their impatience with existing racial arrangements. These feelings were dramatically manifested in a series of violent ghetto outbursts that rocked the nation throughout the late 1960s. These outbreaks constituted the most massive and sustained expression of lower-class black dissatisfaction in the nation's history. They also forced the political system to recognize the problems of human survival and de facto segregation in the nation's ghettoes—problems pertaining to unemployment and underemployment, inferior ghetto schools, and deteriorated housing.

However, in the period of modern industrial race relations, it would be difficult indeed to comprehend the plight of inner-city blacks by exclusively focusing on racial discrimination. For in a very real sense, the current problems of lower-class blacks are substantially related to fundamental structural changes in the economy. A history of discrimination and oppression created a huge black underclass, and the technological and economic revolutions have combined to insure it a permanent status.

As the black middle class rides on the wave of political and social changes, benefiting from the growth of employment opportunities in the growing corporate and government sectors of the economy, the black underclass falls behind the larger society in every conceivable respect. The economic and political systems in the United States have demonstrated remarkable flexibility in allowing talented blacks to fill positions of prestige and influence at the same time that these systems have shown persistent rigidity in handling the problems of lower-class blacks. As a result, for the first time in American history class

---

[1]E. Franklin Frazier, *Black Bourgeoisie* (New York: The Free Press, 1957). See also Nathan Hare, *Black Anglo-Saxons* (New York: Collier, 1965).

issues can meaningfully compete with race issues in the way blacks develop or maintain a sense of group position. . . .

Conclusion

. . . I have tried to show that race relations in American society have been historically characterized by three major stages and that each stage is represented by a unique form of racial interaction which is shaped by the particular arrangement of the economy and the polity. My central argument is that different systems of production and/or different policies of the state have imposed different constraints on the way in which racial groups interact—constraints that have structured the relations between racial groups and produced dissimilar contexts not only for the manifestation of racial antagonisms but also for racial-group access to rewards and privileges. I emphasized in this connection that in the preindustrial and industrial periods of American race relations the systems of production primarily shaped the patterns of racial stratification and the role of the polity was to legitimate, reinforce, or regulate these patterns. In the modern industrial period, however, both the system of production and the polity assume major importance in creating new patterns of race relations and in altering the context of racial strife. Whereas the preindustrial and industrial stages were principally related to group struggles over economic resources as different segments of the white population overtly sought to create and solidify economic racial domination (ranging from the exploitation of black labor in the preindustrial period to the elimination of black competition for jobs in the industrial period) through various forms of political, juridical, and social discrimination; in the modern industrial period fundamental economic and political changes have made economic class position more important than race in determining black chances for occupational mobility. Finally, I have outlined the importance of racial norms or belief systems, especially as they relate to the general problem of race and class conflict in the preindustrial and industrial periods.

My argument that race relations in America have moved from economic racial oppression to a form of class subordination for the less privileged blacks is not meant to suggest that racial conflicts have disappeared or have even been substantially reduced. On the contrary, the basis of such conflicts have shifted from the economic sector to the sociopolitical order and therefore do not play as great a role in determining the life chances of individual black Americans as in the previous periods of overt economic racial oppression.

Thinking It Over

1. What credit does Wilson give the political system in the field of race relations? Has government worked to exacerbate the problems of status-induced abuses or to alleviate them?

2. If Wilson is correct, does his position weaken or strengthen the case for mandatory bussing of school children to promote equality?

18.
THE MYTH OF BLACK PROGRESS
by Alphonso Pinkney

Setting The Scene: It is obvious that Pinkney's reading should be considered in comparison with Wilson's. In fact Pinkney criticizes Wilson directly in his book. The major points of contention are two: While Wilson says blacks have made considerable progress in recent years, Pinkney holds black progress is largely a myth. Pinkney also claims that it is race itself and not socio-economic status that continues to imprison blacks in the status to which a racist America assigned them in the first place. Overall, Pinkney is concerned with the difference between "equality in principle and equality in practice."

Reports of the ongoing oppression of Afro-Americans are commonplace: In 1983 a five-year-old black child was murdered in California by a white police officer who claimed that the child had a handgun; four blacks were indiscriminately killed by New Orleans police following the murder of a white police officer; a black transit worker was killed by a white mob in Brooklyn as he stopped with co-workers in a delicatessen for food; white voters refused to support well-qualified black candidates; the black candidate for mayor of Chicago, along with a Democratic candidate for president, was refused permission to speak by a crowd of white racists at a Roman Catholic church on Palm Sunday; spokespersons for the administration continued to take positions opposed to the aspirations of blacks; twice as many black adults were unemployed as whites and among teenagers it was three blacks for every white; Little Rock resegregated its schools because of white boycotts.

At the same time we are bombarded with books and articles, by blacks and whites, claiming that in this country race is no longer a salient variable in relations between blacks and whites. These writers have given support to the conservative trend in the United States. Some of them hold important positions in the administration and others are courted by government policy makers. These people continue to hold fast to their ahistorical positions in the face of the continuing oppression of black people. While their motives are difficult to fathom their positions no doubt fuel the antiblack feelings of conservatives, in and out of government. And, equally crucial, in many instances their pronouncements directly contradict the data gathered by government agencies. . . .

It is ironic that at a time when there appeared to be some minor progress in improving the citizenship status of black people in the United States, and some official commitment to racial equality, the national mood shifted rather abruptly to one of continued subjugation and racial oppression. Beginning with the *Brown v. Board of Education* decision of the Supreme Court in 1954 and continuing through most of the decade of the 1960s, there was reason for America's black citizens to suspect that their liberation from oppression was underway and that those citizens opposed to equality for blacks were in a small minority. And it appeared that government agencies supported their aspirations. But as is so characteristic of American society, the national mood shifted radically, and through a variety of actions at all levels, blacks found themselves with fewer allies in their quest for equality. Public support for black progress virtually disappeared, and blacks were once again being blamed for their plight in a society where racism has historically been an integral part of all of its institutions and has served to maintain and protect white privilege. How is it possible that after a few years of apparent commitment to full equality for black people, the mood of the American people could shift so drastically?

Clearly there are many answers to this question, but of special relevance to the present work is the confusion between equality in principle and equality in practice. Social scientists, government officials, and the general public have tended to assume, however naively, that the legislative and judicial acts on behalf of America's black colony between 1954 and 1968, which served to elevate the citizenship status of black people to that of white people, thereby accomplishing equality in principle, would lead to immediate equality in practice. Such was not the case.

It is undeniable that some progress toward eliminating discriminatory barriers against blacks was achieved in the last half of the 1950s and the decade of the 1960s, but these actions failed largely because racial discrimination is deeply rooted in the structure of American institutions. In many cases, those in power in these institutions profit from the maintenance of racial discrimination, for it is to their economic advantage. When a law is enacted, for example, those entrusted with its enforcement usually have available to them a variety of means for evading it with impunity. And it is frequently the responsibility of the victims to prove the case against wealthy corporations with unlimited funds for legal expenses. Consequently, the long-standing problems of poverty, unemployment, job discrimination, inadequate housing, and barriers to education continue to reinforce the subordinate position of Afro-Americans. Deeply ingrained white racism serves to justify the oppression of blacks. . . .

Social Scientists and the Myth of Black Progress

Several works have appeared in recent years by sociologists and other social scientists alleging that race is no longer an important variable in American society. Others have maintained that black Americans of comparable educational achievement have reached income parity with white Americans. There are even those who maintain that black people in the United States now enjoy some advantages over white people, particularly in education and employment, and that more than half of all black families have achieved middle-class status. Some claim that affirmative action programs have served to close the income gap between black and white Americans, and that legislative acts and court decisions of the 1960s and 1970s have transformed American society into an egalitarian one in practice as well as in principle.

It is the contention here that these works put forth major myths regarding race relations in the United States. They present an erroneous picture of the status of black people, and all too often influence public policy ostensibly aimed at alleviating problems and powerlessness among Afro-Americans and other people of color. When not making exaggerated claims on the question of black progress, these social scientists tend to blame Afro-Americans (the victims) for their lack of progress rather than the forces in the society that serve to maintain their oppression (the perpetrators).

. . .

Problems of Race

In interviews with twenty middle-class blacks in Philadelphia a reporter for the *Wall Street Journal* found that racism was a persistent problem in that city and its suburbs.[1] As a psychologist put it, "Middle class or not, I get watched when I walk into a department store, and I still have to cash my check at a bank that knows me." A school teacher: "My physician is white, and you should see the stares I get when I'm in his waiting room. The whites act like they think I'm going to clean the place when they leave. They think all blacks go to clinics." On the matter of housing discrimination, these middle-class blacks reported that, no matter how much they earn, they are steered by real estate brokers to five or six areas when they shop for an apartment or a house. One informant said he was warned about the possibility of being "burned out" when he asked to be shown a home in one section of the city.

The Census Bureau reports that between 1970 and 1977 the number of blacks living in the suburbs increased by 34 percent.[2] But a move to the suburbs can bring terror for black people as fire bombings and shootings continue. Since federal fair housing laws were enacted in 1968, middle-class blacks have moved to the suburbs in larger numbers than ever before, but the enforcement of these laws has been lax. Consequently, many black families who have purchased houses have been prevented from moving in because of racist terror or threats. In recent years, a black college teacher's home in Chicago was fire bombed and vandalized; crosses were burned at black suburban homes around the country; rocks were thrown through windows and arson was attempted at a black home in Cleveland Heights; a vacant home was burned in New Jersey when rumors were spread that a black family had bought it; in Rockaway, New York, a duplex was set afire nine times in a single year.[3] Such practices are likely to continue as long as American society remains stratified along ethnic lines. And though there is some amelioration in this regard, it is reasonable to assume that racism will remain a factor in American life for the indefinite future.

The United States Commission on Civil Rights concluded that *"discriminatory mortgage lending practices have restricted the home ownership opportunities of middle-income minorities and women, thereby subjecting them more often to higher housing costs and inferior housing and denying them a principal means of saving and accumulating wealth."*[4]

---

[1]Alsop, "Middle-Class Blacks Worry." [Ronald Alsop, "Middle-Class Blacks Worry About Slipping, Still Face Racial Bias," *Wall Street Journal*, November 3, 1980, p. 1.]

[2]*New York Times*, December 3, 1978, p. 82.

[3]Dorothy Newman et al., *Protest, Politics and Prosperity: Black Americans and White Institutions, 1940-1975* (New York: Pantheon Books, 1978), p. 139.

[4]*Twenty Years After Brown: Equal Opportunity in Housing* (Washington, D.C.: U.S. Commission on Civil Rights, 1975), p. 173. Emphasis in original.

Members of the black middle class may possess the same degree of education, the same income, and the same occupational status as whites, but they are still considered black first and middle class second. Therefore, many associate with one another out of choice, but many also are prohibited from joining the social clubs of whites. There exist, throughout the country, many private clubs that discriminate against minorities and women. It is in these clubs that many political and corporate decisions are made. There are even cities in the country with black mayors who are not permitted to join or attend these private clubs. The black middle class, consequently, continues to rely on friendship cliques, social service clubs, fraternities and sororities to a greater extent than do their white counterparts. . . .

Racial discrimination in housing is not limited to members of the black middle class. It affects wealthy blacks as well. This is the area of American society about which white persons are most intransigent, and it is one of the areas where social class plays only a minor role.

The following incident, involving one of the greatest basketball players of all time, illustrates the difficulty even rich blacks have moving into neighborhoods that are totally white. Oscar Robertson, voted one of the five best basketball players of all time, lives in Cincinnati, Ohio. He was considering purchasing a house on the city's most prestigious street, but its residents would not tolerate a black neighbor, not even one who was internationally known (he was co-captain of the American Olympic basketball team that won a Gold Medal) and wealthy. "In the end, the problem resolved itself when Robertson decided against the property and bought a house in another part of town."[5]

If one visits blacks in the wealthy suburbs of many American cities there is almost certain to be discussion of some form of harassment from their white neighbors. They fear that neighbors and white vigilante groups will fire bomb their homes or otherwise cause personal or property damage. This suspicion is not paranoia, but is based on the large number of such incidents that one reads about almost daily. Given the conservatism sweeping the country, with its heavy dose of racism, there is every indication that such shootings and fire bombings will continue, for they are fueled by individuals at the highest levels of government and some of the so-called religious leaders. In other words, these individuals have created a climate in which expressions of racist sentiment thrive.

Middle-class black travelers, while facing fewer problems than in the past, are still subjected to discrimination and insults. A black journalist and her husband were visiting in New York from Chicago. When a white maid entered the hotel room she was overheard to say, "I guess they let anybody in here these days."[6] And black people are frequently given undesirable rooms like those near elevators or in dark corners.

The occupational positions held by most members of the black middle class since the second half of the 1960s place these people in precarious situations. Often they were employed to comply with affirmative action guidelines, and their positions are without power. They are reluctant to employ too many blacks for fear of criticism. A black superintendent

---

[5]Birmingham, *Certain People,* pp. 24-5. [Stephen Birmingham, *Certain People: America's Black Elite* (Boston: Little, Brown, 1977).]

[6]*New York Times,* April 15, 1979, sec. 10, p. 1.

of prisons in a large city, who was probably appointed to the post because of the high percentage of black prisoners, explains his dilemma: "If I hire two people, one better be black and one better be white. If I hire two blacks, people will say, 'Aha, I know what he's up to,' and if I hire two whites, I'll be called an Uncle Tom."[7]

A black physician in Mississippi was refused permission to practice in a hospital. "In the fall of 1977, I began private practice in Canton [Mississippi] and applied for medical staff privileges at Madison General. Even though I am the only private physician here who has been certified by the American Board of Family Practice, and even though my references are laudatory, the hospital denied my application without even an interview."[8]

In some respects middle-class blacks are more likely to encounter racism than their poor fellow blacks in the slums, for the poor blacks are likely to be shielded from white people. Hence, they are spared the subtle discrimination encountered by members of the middle class in employment and public accommodations. One might not know if one is passed over for promotion because of race or some other factor, but given the nature of American society, it is not unreasonable to first assume that race was the deciding factor.

Thinking It Over

1. The obvious question is: Who is more correct in your view, Wilson or Pinkney? Surely there is ample material in this comparison for a powerful essay or term paper.

2. Pinkney quotes a middle class black from Philadelphia as follows: "Middle class or not, I get watched when I walk into a department store, and I still have to cash my check at a bank that knows me." There is a lot of gut validity to that statement. Put yourself in Wilson's shoes for a moment and see if you can deal with it.

---

[7]Alsop, "Middle-Class Blacks Worry," p. 28.
[8]Frazier, *Black Bourgeoisie*, p. 235. [E. Franklin Frazier, *Black Bourgeoisie* (New York: Free Press, 1957).]

19.
TEXAS V. JOHNSON

Setting the Scene: When Gregory Lee Johnson burned an American flag in front of the Dallas City Hall while a crowd chanted "America, the red, white and blue, we spit on you," he was arrested, sentenced to one year in jail and fined $2,000. In the case that follows, the court held that an American's right to freedom of speech as expressed in the Constitution protected Johnson from the Texas law. Go free, said the Court. Many, many Americans would have liked to have told Mr. Johnson where to go and it was not, we may safely conclude, "free." The storm of anger at the Court's decision caused an amendment to the Constitution to be proposed and sent to Congress which would expressly forbid burning the flag. It also precipitated much huffing and puffing as politicians postured for political purposes. President Bush supported the amendment. (No surprise there.) But it was killed in Congress. Listen to the Court as it calmly seeks out the reasoning that will defend our right to express ourselves through other than traditional means.

Chief Justice Brennan delivered the opinion of the Court:

After publicly burning an American flag as a means of political protest, Gregory Lee Johnson was convicted of desecrating a flag in violation of Texas law. This case presents the question whether his conviction is consistent with the First Amendment. We hold that it is not.

While the Republican National Convention was taking place in Dallas in 1984, respondent Johnson participated in a political demonstration dubbed the "Republican War Chest Tour." As explained in literature distributed by the demonstrators and in speeches made by them, the purpose of this event was to protest the policies of the Reagan administration and of certain Dallas-based corporations. The demonstrators marched through the Dallas streets, chanting political slogans and stopping at several corporate locations to stage "die-ins' intended to dramatize the consequences of nuclear war. On several occasions they spray-painted the walls of buildings and overturned potted plants, but Johnson himself took no part in such activities. He did, however, accept an American flag handed to him by a fellow protestor who had taken it from a flag pole outside one of the targeted buildings.

The demonstration ended in front of Dallas City Hall, where Johnson unfurled the American flag, doused it with kerosene, and set it on fire. While the flag burned, the protestors chanted, "America, the red, white, and blue, we spit on you." After the demonstrators dispersed, a witness to the flag-burning collected the flag's remains and buried them in his backyard. No one was physically injured or threatened with injury, though several witnesses testified that they had been seriously offended by the flag-burning.

Of the approximately 100 demonstrators, Johnson alone was charged with a crime. The only criminal offense with which he was charged was the desecration of a venerated object in violation of Tex Penal Code . . . (1989).[1]   After a trial, he was convicted, sentenced to one year in prison, and fined $2,000. . . .

The First Amendment literally forbids the abridgement only of "speech," but we have long recognized that its protection does not end at the spoken or written word. While we have rejected "the view that an apparently limitless variety of conduct can be labeled 'speech' whenever the person engaging in the conduct intends thereby to express an idea," (*United States v O'Brien*) . . . we have acknowledged that conduct may be "sufficiently imbued with elements of communication to fall within the scope of the First and Fourteenth Amendments." . . .

In deciding whether particular conduct possesses sufficient communicative elements to bring the First Amendment into play, we have asked whether "[a]n intent to convey a particularized message was present, and [whether] the likelihood was great that the message would be understood by those who viewed it." . . . Hence, we have recognized the expressive nature of students' wearing of black armbands to protest American military involvement in Vietnam . . . of a sit-in by blacks in a "whites only" area to protest segregation . . . of the wearing of American military uniforms in a dramatic presentation criticizing American involvement in Vietnam . . . and of picketing about a wide variety of causes . . .

Especially pertinent to this case are our decision recognizing the communicative nature of conduct relating to flags. Attaching a peace sign to the flag . . . and displaying a red flag . . . we have held, all may find shelter under the First Amendment. See also *Smith v Goguen* . . . (treating flag "contemptuously" by wearing pants with small flag sewn into their seat is expressive conduct). That we have had little difficulty identifying an expressive element in conduct relating to flags should not be surprising. The very purpose of a national flag is to serve as a symbol of our country . . . Pregnant with expressive content, the flag as readily signifies this Nation as does the combination of letters found in "America" . . .

The State of Texas conceded for purposes of its oral argument in this case that Johnson's conduct was expressive conduct . . . and this concession seems to us as prudent as was Washington's in Spence. Johnson burned an American flag as part—indeed, as the culmination—of a political demonstration that coincided with the convening of the Republican Party and its renomination of Ronald Reagan for President. The expressive, overtly political nature of this conduct was both intentional and overwhelmingly apparent. At his trial, Johnson explained his reasons for burning the flag as follows: "The American Flag was burned as Ronald Reagan was being renominated as President.   And a more powerful statement of symbolic speech, whether you agree with it or not, couldn't have been

---

[1]Tex Penal Code Ann § 42.09 (1989) provides in full:

"§ 42.09. Desecration of Venerated Object

"(a) A person commits an offense if he intentionally or knowingly desecrates:

"(1) a public monument;

"(2) a place of worship or burial; or

"(3) a state or national flag.

"(b) For purposes of this section, 'desecrate' means deface, damage, or otherwise physically mistreat in a way that the actor knows will seriously offend one or more persons likely to observe or discover his action.

"(c) An offense under this section is a Class A misdemeanor."

made at that time. It's quite a just position [juxtaposition]. We had new patriotism and no patriotism." . . .

The State offers two separate interests to justify this conviction: preventing breaches of the peace, and preserving the flag as a symbol of nationhood and national unity. We hold that the first interest is not implicated on this record and that the second is related to the suppression of expression. [Editor's note: After justifying its holding on the "breach of peace" question, the Court turns to the question of "suppression of free expression."] . . .

It remains to consider whether the State's interest in preserving the flag as a symbol of nationhood and national unity justifies Johnson's conviction.

. . . The State's argument is not that it has an interest simply in maintaining the flag as a symbol of *something*, no matter what it symbolizes; indeed, if that were the State's position, it would be difficult to see how that interest is endangered by highly symbolic conduct such as Johnson's. Rather, the States's claim is that it has an interest in preserving the flag as a symbol of *nationhood* and *national unity*, a symbol with a determinate range of meanings. Brief for Petitioner 20-24. According to Texas, if one physically treats the flag in a way that would tend to cast doubt on either the idea that nationhood and national unity are the flag's referents or that national unity actually exists, the message conveyed thereby is a harmful one and therefore may be prohibited. . . .

If there is a bedrock principle underlying the First Amendment, it is that the Government may not prohibit the expression of an idea simply because society finds the idea itself offensive or disagreeable. . . .

We have not recognized an exception to this principle even where our flag has been involved. In *Street v New York* . . . we held that a State may not criminally punish a person for uttering words critical of the flag. Rejecting the argument that the conviction could be sustained on the ground that Street had "failed to show the respect for our national symbol which may properly be demanded of every citizen," we concluded that "the constitutionally guaranteed 'freedom to be intellectually . . . diverse or even contrary,' and the 'right to differ as to things that touch the heart of the existing order,' encompass the freedom to express publicly one's opinions about our flag, including those opinions which are defiant or contemptuous" . . . Nor may the Government, we have held, compel conduct that would evince respect for the flag. "To sustain the compulsory flag salute we are required to say that a Bill of Rights which guards the individual's right to speak his own mind, left it open to public authorities to compel him to utter what is not in his mind." . . .

In holding in Barnette that the Constitution did not leave this course open to the Government, Justice Jackson described one of our society's defining principles in words deserving of their frequent repetition: "If there is any fixed star in our constitutional constellation, it is that no official, high or petty, can prescribe what shall be orthodox in politics, nationalism, religion, or other matters of opinion or force citizens to confess by word or act their faith therein." . . . In Spence, we held that the same interest asserted by Texas here was insufficient to support a criminal conviction under a flag-misuse statute for the taping of a peace sign to an American flag. "Given the protected character of [Spence's] expression and in light of the fact that no interest the State may have in preserving the physical integrity of a privately owned flag was significantly impaired on these facts," we held, "the conviction must be invalidated" . . . (White, J., concurring in judgment) (to convict person who had sewn a flag onto the seat of his pants for "contemptuous" treatment of the flag would be "[t]o convict not to protect the physical integrity or to protect against acts interfering with the proper use of the flag, but to punish for communicating ideas unacceptable to the controlling majority in the legislature").

In short, nothing in our precedents suggest that a State may foster its own view of the flag by prohibiting expressive conduct relating to it. . . . To bring its argument outside our precedents, Texas attempts to convince us that even if its interest in preserving the flag's symbolic role does not allow it to prohibit words or some expressive conduct critical of the flag, it does permit it to forbid the outright destruction of the flag . . .

Texas' focus on the precise nature of Johnson's expression, moreover, misses the point of our prior decisions: their enduring lesson, that the Government may not prohibit expression simply because it disagrees with its message, is not dependent on the particular mode in which one chooses to express an idea. . . . If we were to hold that a State may forbid flag-burning wherever it is likely to endanger the flag's symbolic role, but allow it wherever burning a flag promotes that role—as where, for example, a person ceremoniously burns a dirty flag—we would be saying that when it comes to impairing the flag's physical integrity, the flag itself may be used as a symbol—as a substitute for the written or spoken word or a "short cut from mind to mind"—only in one direction. We would be permitting a State to "prescribe what shall be orthodox" by saying that one may burn the flag to convey one's attitude toward it and its referents only if one does not endanger the flag's representation of nationhood and national unity.

We never before have held that the Government may ensure that a symbol be used to express only one view of that symbol or its referents. Indeed, in *Schacht v United States*, we invalidated a federal statute permitting an actor portraying a member of one of our armed forces to "'wear the uniform of that armed force if the portrayal does not tend to discredit that armed force.'" . . . This proviso, we held, "which leaves Americans free to praise the war in Vietnam but can send persons like Schacht to prison for opposing it, cannot survive in a country which has the First Amendment." . . .

We perceive no basis on which to hold that the principle underlying our decision in Schacht does not apply to this case. To conclude that the Government may permit designated symbols to be used to communicate only a limited set of messages would be to enter territory having no discernible or defensible boundaries. Could the Government, on this theory, prohibit the burning of state flags? Of copies of the Presidential seal? Of the Constitution? In evaluating these choices under the First Amendment, how would we decide which symbols were sufficiently special to warrant this unique status? To do so, we would be forced to consult our own political preferences, and impose them on the citizenry, in the very way that the First Amendment forbids us to do. . . .

There is, moreover, no indication—either in the text of the Constitution or in our cases interpreting it—that a separate juridical category exists for the American flag alone. Indeed, we would not be surprised to learn that the persons who framed our Constitution and wrote the Amendment that we now construe were not known for their reverence for the Union Jack. The First Amendment does not guarantee that other concepts virtually sacred to our Nation as a whole—such as the principle that discrimination on the basis of race is odious and destructive—will go unquestioned in the marketplace of ideas. See *Brandenburg v Ohio* . . . We decline, therefore, to create for the flag an exception to the joust of principles protected by the First Amendment.

It is not the State's ends, but its means, to which we object. It cannot be gainsaid that there is a special place reserved for the flag in this Nation, and thus we do not doubt that the Government has a legitimate interest in making efforts to "preserv[e] the national flag as an unalloyed symbol of our country." . . . We reject the suggestion, urged at oral argument by counsel for Johnson, that the government lacks "any state interest whatsoever" in regulating the manner in which the flag may be displayed. . . . Congress has, for example, enacted precatory regulations describing the proper treatment of the flag, and we cast no doubt on the legitimacy of its interest in making such recommendations. To say that the Government has an interest in encouraging proper treatment of the flag, however, is not to say that it may criminally punish a person for burning a flag as a means of political protest. "National unity as an end which officials may foster by persuasion and example is not in question. The problem is whether under our Constitution compulsion as here employed is a permissible means for its achievement." . . .

We are fortified in today's conclusion by our conviction that forbidding criminal punishment for conduct such as Johnson's will not endanger the special role played by our flag or the feelings it inspires. To paraphrase Justice Holmes, we submit that nobody can suppose that this one gesture of an unknown man will change our Nation's attitude towards its flag. . . . Indeed, Texas' argument that the burning of an American flag "'is an act having a high likelihood to cause a breach of the peace,'" . . . and its statute's implicit assumption that physical mistreatment of the flag will lead to "serious offense," tend to confirm that the flag's special role is not in danger; if it were, no one would riot or take offense because a flag had been burned.

We are tempted to say, in fact, that the flag's deservedly cherished place in our community will be strengthened, not weakened, by our holding today. Our decision is a reaffirmation of the principles of freedom and inclusiveness that the flag best reflects, and of the conviction that our toleration of criticism such as Johnson's is a sign and source of our strength. Indeed, one of the proudest images of our flag, the one immortalized in our own national anthem, is of the bombardment it survived at Fort McHenry. It is the Nation's resilience, not its rigidity, that Texas sees reflected in the flag—and it is that resilience that we reassert today.

The way to preserve the flag's special role is not to punish those who feel differently about these matters. It is to persuade them that they are wrong. "To courageous, self-reliant men, with confidence in the power of free and fearless reasoning applied through the processes of popular government, no danger flowing from speech can be deemed clear and present, unless the incidence of the evil apprehended is so imminent that it may befall before there is opportunity for full discussion. If there be time to expose through discussion the falsehood and fallacies, to avert the evil by the processes of education, the remedy to be applied is more speech, not enforced silence" . . . And, precisely because it is our flag that is involved, one's response to the flag-burner may exploit the uniquely persuasive power of the flag itself. We can imagine no more appropriate response to burning a flag than waving one's own, no better way to counter a flag-burner's message than by saluting the flag that burns, no surer means of preserving the dignity even of the flag that burned than by—as one witness here did—according its remains a respectful burial. We do not consecrate the flag by punishing its desecration, for in doing so we dilute the freedom that this cherished emblem represents.

Johnson was convicted for engaging in expressive conduct. The State's interest in preventing breaches of the peace does not support his conviction because Johnson's conduct did not threaten to disturb the peace. Nor does the State's interest in preserving the flag as a symbol of nationhood and national unity justify his criminal conviction for engaging in political expression. The judgment of the Texas Court of Criminal Appeals is therefore affirmed.

Thinking It Over

1. See if you can defend President Bush's position: there is no reason why we could not expressly and carefully exclude burning the flag from the right to express yourself in non traditional ways without giving up the *principle* that freedom of *speech* can take many forms. We could, in other words, make it the "exception that proves the rule."

2. Consider the following: An American soldier just back from overseas duty and still in uniform is approached on a busy street by a young man wearing an American flag around his shoulders. He takes off the flag, throws it to the ground in front of the soldier, spits on it, and sets it on fire, yelling "Here's what I think of the flag you defend!" Would this young man be protected in his actions by the Court as Gregory Lee Johnson was?

20.
HUSTLER MAGAZINE V. FALWELL

Setting the Scene: When Larry Flint published a particularly disgusting parody of Jerry Falwell a "nationally-known minister" in *Hustler* magazine, Falwell did him the great favor of publicizing it and the magazine by taking him to Court, thereby, one assumes, increasing the sales substantially. Flint also won the case. The reasoning used by public figures to prevent attacks on themselves in print is extensive and varied. This case reviews much of this reasoning for you, shows why it does not apply to *Hustler* and also why even this most vile story about a minister and his mom is also protected by the Constitution. Once again the First Amendment emerged unscathed.

Chief Justice Rehnquist delivered the opinion of the Court:

Petitioner Hustler Magazine, Inc., is a magazine of nationwide circulation. Respondent Jerry Falwell, a nationally known minister who has been active as a commentator on politics and public affairs, sued petitioner and its publisher, petitioner Larry Flynt, to recover damages for invasion of privacy, libel, and intentional infliction of emotional distress. The District Court directed a verdict against respondent on the privacy claim, and submitted the other two claims to a jury. The jury found for petitioners on the defamation claim, but found for respondent on the claim for intentional infliction of emotional distress and awarded damages. We now consider whether this award is consistent with the First and Fourteenth Amendments of the United States Constitution.

The inside front cover of the November 1983 issue of Hustler Magazine featured a "parody" of an advertisement for Campari Liqueur that contained the name and picture of respondent and was entitled "Jerry Falwell talks about his first time." This parody was modeled after actual Campari ads that included interviews with various celebrities about their "first times." Although it was apparent by the end of each interview that this meant the first time they sampled Campari, the ads clearly played on the sexual double entendre of the general subject of "first times." Copying the form and layout of these Campari ads, Huster's editors chose respondent as the featured celebrity and drafted an alleged "interview" with him in which he states that his "first time" was during a drunken incestuous rendezvous with his mother in an outhouse. The Hustler parody portrays respondent and his mother as drunk and immoral, and suggests that respondent is a hypocrite who preaches only when he is drunk. In small print at the bottom of the page, the ad contains the disclaimer, "ad parody—not to be taken seriously." The magazine's table of contents also lists the ad as "Fiction; Ad and Personality Parody." . . .

This case presents us with a novel question involving First Amendment limitations upon a State's authority to protect its citizens from the intentional infliction of emotional distress. We must decide whether a public figure may recover damages for emotional harm caused by the publication of an ad parody offensive to him, and doubtless gross and repugnant in the eyes of most. Respondent would have us find that State's interest in protecting public figures from emotional distress is sufficient to deny First Amendment protection to speech that is patently offensive and is intended to inflict emotional injury, even when that speech could not reasonably have been interpreted as stating actual facts about the public figure involved. This we decline to do.

At the heart of the First Amendment is the recognition of the fundamental importance of the free flow of ideas and opinions on matters of public interest and concern. "[T]he freedom to speak one's mind is not only an aspect of individual liberty—and thus a good unto itself—but also is essential to the common quest for truth and the vitality of society as whole." *Bose Corp. v. Consumers Union of United States.* . . . We have therefore been particularly vigilant to ensure that individual expressions of ideas remain free from governmentally imposed sanctions. The First Amendment recognizes no such thing as a "false" idea. *Gertz v. Robert Welch, Inc.* . . . As Justice Holmes wrote, "when men have realized that time has upset many fighting faiths, they may come to believe even more than they believe the very foundations of their own conduct that the ultimate good desired is better reached by free trade in ideas—that the best test of truth is the power of the thought to get itself accepted in the competition of the market. . . ." *Abrams v. United States* . . . (dissenting opinion).

The sort of robust political debate encouraged by the First Amendment is bound to produce speech that is critical of those who hold public office or those public figures who are "intimately involved in the resolution of important public questions or, by reason of their fame, shape events in areas of concern to society at large." *Associated Press v. Walker* . . . Justice Frankfurter put it succinctly in *Baumgartner v. United States* . . . when he said that "[o]ne of the prerogatives of American citizenship is the right to criticize public men and measures." Such criticism, inevitably, will not always be reasoned or moderate; public figures as well as public officials will be subject to "vehement, caustic, and sometimes unpleasantly sharp attacks" . . . "[T]he candidate who vaunts his spotless record and sterling integrity cannot convincingly cry 'Foul!' when an opponent or an industrious reporter attempts to demonstrate the contrary." *Monitor Patriot Co. v. Roy* . . .

Of course, this does not mean that *any* speech about a public figure is immune from sanction in the form of damages. Since *New York Times Co. v. Sullivan, supra,* we have consistently ruled that a public figure may hold a speaker liable for the damage to reputation caused by publication of a defamatory falsehood, but only if the statement was made "with knowledge that it was false or with reckless disregard of whether it was false or not." . . . False statements of fact are particularly valueless; they interfere with the truth-seeking function of the marketplace of ideas, and they cause damage to an individual's reputation that cannot easily be repaired by counterspeech, however persuasive or effective. . . . But even though falsehoods have little value in and of themselves, they are "nevertheless inevitable in free debate" . . . and a rule that would impose strict liability on a publisher for false factual assertions would have an undoubted "chilling" effect on speech relating to public figures that does have constitutional value. "Freedoms of expression require "'breathing space.'" *Philadelphia Newspapers, Inc. v. Hepps* . . . This breathing space is provided by a constitutional rule that allows public figures to recover for libel or defamation only when they can prove *both* that the statement was false and that the statement was made with the requisite level of culpability.

Respondent argues, however, that a different standard should apply in this case because here the State seeks to prevent not reputational damage, but the severe emotional distress suffered by the person who is the subject of an offensive publication. . . . In respondent's view, and in the view of the Court of Appeals, so long as the utterance was intended to inflict emotional distress, was outrageous, and did in fact inflict serious emotional distress, it is of no constitutional import whether the statement was a fact or an opinion, or whether it was true or false. It is the intent to cause injury that is the gravamen of the tort, and the State's interest in preventing emotional harm simply outweighs whatever interest a speaker may have in speech of this type.

Generally speaking the law does not regard the intent to inflict emotional distress as one which should receive much solicitude, and it is quite understandable that most if not all jurisdictions have chosen to make it civilly culpable where the conduct in question is sufficiently "outrageous." But in the world of debate about public affairs, many things done with motives that are less than admirable are protected by the First Amendment. In *Garrison v. Louisiana* . . . we held that even when a speaker or writer is motivated by hatred or ill-will his expression was protected by the First Amendment:

> "Debate on public issues will not be uninhibited if the speaker must run the risk that it will be proved in court that he spoke out of hatred; even if he did speak out of hatred, utterances honestly believed contribute to the free interchange of ideas and the ascertainment of truth." . . .

Thus while such a bad motive may be deemed controlling for purposes of tort liability in other areas of the law, we think the First Amendment prohibits such a result in the area of public debate about public figures.

Were we to hold otherwise, there can be little doubt that political cartoonists and satirists would be subjected to damages awards without any showing that their work falsely defamed its subject. Webster's defines a caricature as "the deliberately distorted picturing or imitating of a person, literary style, etc. by exaggerating features or mannerisms for satirical effect." Webster's New Unabridged Twentieth Century Dictionary of the English Language 275 (2d ed. 1979). The appeal of the political cartoon or caricature is often based on exploitation of unfortunate physical traits or politically embarrassing events—an exploitation often calculated to injure the feelings of the subject of the portrayal. The art of the cartoonist is often not reasoned or evenhanded, but slashing and one-sided. One cartoonist expressed the nature of the art in these words:

> "The political cartoon is a weapon of attack, of scorn and ridicule and satire; it is least effective when it tries to pat some politician on the back. It is usually as welcome as a bee sting and is always controversial in some quarters." Long, The Political Cartoon: Journalism's Strongest Weapon, The Quill, 56, 57 (Nov. 1962).

Several famous examples of this type of intentionally injurious speech were drawn by Thomas Nast, probably the greatest American cartoonist to date, who was associated for many years during the post-Civil War era with Harper's Weekly. In the pages of that publication Nast conducted a graphic vendetta against William M. "Boss" Tweed and his corrupt associates in New York City's "Tweed Ring." It has been described by one historian of the subject as "a sustained attack which in its passion and effectiveness stands alone in the history of American graphic art." M. Keller, The Art and Politics of Thomas Nast 177 (1968). Another writer explains that the success of the Nast cartoon was achieved "because of the emotional impact of its presentation. It continuously goes beyond the bounds of good taste and conventional manners." C. Press, The Political Cartoon 251 (1981).

Despite their sometimes caustic nature, from the early cartoon portraying George Washington as an ass down to the present day, graphic depictions and satirical cartoons have played a prominent role in public and political debate. Nast's castigation of the Tweed Ring, Walt McDougall's characterization of Presidential candidate James G. Blaine's banquet with the millionaires at Delmonico's as "The Royal Feast of Belshazzar," and numerous other efforts have undoubtedly had an effect on the course and outcome of contemporaneous debate. Lincoln's tall, gangling posture, Teddy Roosevelt's glasses and teeth, and Franklin D. Roosevelt's jutting jaw and cigarette holder have been memorialized by political cartoons with an effect that could not have been obtained by the photographer or the portrait artist. From the viewpoint of history it is clear that our political discourse would have been considerably poorer without them.

Respondent contends, however, that the caricature in question here was so "outrageous" as to distinguish it from more traditional political cartoons. There is no doubt that the caricature of respondent and his mother published in Hustler is at best a distant cousin of the political cartoons described above, and a rather poor relation at that. If it were possible by laying down a principled standard to separate the one from the other, public discourse would probably suffer little or no harm. But we doubt that there is any such standard, and we are quite sure that the pejorative description "outrageous" does not supply one. "Outrageousness" in the area of political and social discourse has an inherent subjectiveness about it which would allow a jury to impose liability on the basis of the jurors' tastes or views, or perhaps on the basis of their dislike of a particular expression. An "outrageousness" standard thus runs afoul of our longstanding refusal to allow damages to be awarded because the speech in question may have an adverse emotional impact on the audience. See *NAACP v. Claiborne Hardware Co.* . . . . ("Speech does not lose its protected character . . . simply because it may embarrass others or coerce them into action"). And, as we stated in *FCC v. Pacifica Foundation* . . .

"[T]he fact that society may find speech offensive is not a sufficient reason for suppressing it. Indeed, if it is the speaker's opinion that gives offense, that consequence is a reason for according it constitutional protection. For it is a central tenet of the First Amendment that the government must remain neutral in the marketplace of ideas." . . .

See also *Street v. New York* . . . ("It is firmly settled that . . . the public expression of ideas may not be prohibited merely because the ideas are themselves offensive to some of their hearers").

Admittedly, these oft-repeated First Amendment principles, like other principles, are subject to limitations. We recognized in *Pacifica Foundation*, that speech that is "'vulgar,' 'offensive,' and 'shocking'" is "not entitled to absolute constitutional protection under all circumstances." In *Chaplinsky v. New Hampshire* . . . we held that a State could lawfully punish an individual for the use of insulting "'fighting' words—those which by their very utterance inflict injury or tend to incite an immediate breach of the peace." . . . These limitations are but recognition of the observation in *Dun & Bradstreet, Inc. v. Greenmoss Builders, Inc.* . . . that this court has "long recognized that not all speech is of equal First Amendment importance." But the sort of expression involved in this case does not seem to us to be governed by any exception to the general First Amendment principles stated above.

We conclude that public figures and public officials may not recover for the tort of intentional infliction of emotional distress by reason of publications such as the one here at issue without showing in addition that the publication contains a false statement of fact which was made with "actual malice," *i.e.,* with knowledge that the statement was false or with reckless disregard as to whether or not it was true. This . . . reflects our considered judgment that such a standard is necessary to give adequate "breathing space" to the freedoms protected by the First Amendment . . .

. . . The judgment of the Court of Appeals is accordingly

Reversed.

Thinking It Over

1. Deal with this argument: "Let's get serious. What appeared in *Hustler* was far enough removed from a cartoon that the Court had better come up with a standard. Maybe they should use the reasoning one of their own judges once employed in defining pornography—'I can't define it, but I know it when I see it.'"

2. Did the framers of the First Amendment intend to protect people like Larry Flynt or is this another example of the "living Constitution"? Irrespective of what was intended, is it a good or bad thing?

21.
ROE V. WADE

Setting the Scene: I'm going to ask you to do something difficult—something the great portion of Americans have refused to do. I want you to think objectively about *Roe v. Wade.* In fact I *dare* you to. The case is vastly misunderstood, which is not surprising given the public passion associated with its implications. But like it or not, there is no escaping *Roe.* Somewhere along the line between conception and eighteen years (when people can vote) the growth of the human embryo must be given legal status—that is, declared a human life for purposes of citizenship. (I'm being a tad facetious here to cover those among you who support infanticide). This *is* a question for the state. It *is* a political question. Whether you like *Roe* or not (and neither extreme on the abortion decision should), it does reflect serious thinking about one of the critical issues of our time. Give yourself a chance to elevate your own thinking on the subject.

Chief Justice Blackmun delivered the opinion of the Court:

The Texas statutes that concern us here are Arts. 1191-1194 and 1196 of the State's Penal Code. . . . These make it a crime to "procure an abortion," as therein defined, or to attempt one, except with respect to "an abortion procured or attempted by medical advice for the purpose of saving the life of the mother." Similar statutes are in existence in a majority of the States. . . .

Jane Roe,[1] a single woman who was residing in Dallas County, Texas, instituted this federal action in March 1970 against the District Attorney of the county. She sought a declaratory judgment that the Texas criminal abortion statutes were unconstitutional on their face, and an injunction restraining the defendant from enforcing the statutes.

Roe alleged that she was unmarried and pregnant; that she wished to terminate her pregnancy by an abortion "performed by a competent, licensed physician, under safe, clinical conditions"; that she was unable to get a "legal" abortion in Texas because her life did not appear to be threatened by the continuation of her pregnancy; and that she could not afford to travel to another jurisdiction in order to secure a legal abortion under safe conditions. She claimed that the Texas statutes were unconstitutionally vague and that they abridged her right of personal privacy, protected by the First, Fourth, Fifth, Ninth, and Fourteenth Amendments. By an amendment to her complaint Roe purported to sue "on behalf of herself and all other women" similarly situated. . . .

The principal thrust of appellant's attack on the Texas statutes is that they improperly invade a right, said to be possessed by the pregnant woman, to choose to terminate her pregnancy. Appellant would discover this right in the concept of personal "liberty" embodied

---

[1]The name is a pseudonym.

in the Fourteenth Amendment's Due Process Clause; or in personal, marital, familial, and sexual privacy said to be protected by the Bill of Rights or its penumbras, see *Griswold v. Griswold v. Connecticut* . . .(1965); *Eisenstadt v. Baird* . . . (1972) . . . (White, J., concurring in result); or among those rights reserved to the people by the Ninth Amendment, *Griswold v. Connecticut* . . . (Goldberg, J. concurring). . . .

Three reasons have been advanced to explain historically the enactment of criminal abortion laws in the 19th century and to justify their continued existence.

It has been argued occasionally that these laws were the product of a Victorian social concern to discourage illicit sexual conduct.   Texas, however, does not advance this justification in the present case, and it appears that no court or commentator has taken the argument seriously. . . . The appellants and *amici* contend, moreover, that this is not a proper state purpose at all and suggest that, if it were, the Texas statutes are overboard in protecting it since the law fails to distinguish between married and unwed mothers.

A second reason is concerned with abortion as a medical procedure. When most criminal abortion laws were first enacted, the procedure was a hazardous one for the woman. . . . This was particularly true prior to the development of antisepsis. Antiseptic techniques, of course, were based on discoveries by Lister, Pasteur, and others first announced in 1867, but were not generally accepted and employed until about the turn of the century. Abortion mortality was high. Even after 1900, and perhaps until as late as the development of antibiotics in the 1940's, standard modern techniques such as dilation and curettage were not nearly so safe as they are today. Thus, it has been argued that a State's real concern in enacting a criminal abortion law was to protect the pregnant woman, that is, to restrain her from submitting to a procedure that placed her life in serious jeopardy.

Modern medical techniques have altered this situation. Appellants and various *amici* refer to medical data indicating that abortion in early pregnancy, that is, prior to the end of the first trimester, although not without its risk, is now relatively safe. Mortality rates for women undergoing early abortions, where the procedure is legal, appear to be as low as or lower than the rates for normal childbirth. . . . Consequently, any interest of the State in protecting the woman from an inherently hazardous procedure, except when it would be equally dangerous for her to forgo it, has largely disappeared. Of course, important state interests in the areas of health and medical standards to remain. The State has a legitimate interest in seeing to it that abortion, like any other medical procedure, is performed under circumstances that insure maximum safety for the patient. This interest obviously extends at least to the performing physician and his staff, to the facilities involved, to the availability of after-care, and to adequate provision for any complication or emergency that might arise. The prevalence of high morality rates at illegal "abortion mills" strengthens, rather than weakens, the State's interest in regulating the conditions under which abortions are performed. Moreover, the risk to the woman increases as her pregnancy continues. Thus, the State retains a definite interest in protecting the woman's own health and safety when an abortion is proposed at a late stage of pregnancy.

The third reason is the State's interest—some phrase it in terms of duty—in protecting prenatal life. Some of the argument for this justification rests on the theory that a new human life is present from the moment of conception. . . . The State's interest and general obligation to protect life then extends, it is argued, to prenatal life. Only when the life of the pregnant mother herself is at stake, balanced against the life she carries within her, should the interest of the embryo or fetus not prevail. Logically, of course, a legitimate state interest in this area need not stand or fall on acceptance of the belief that life begins at conception or at some other point prior to live birth. In assessing the State's interest, recognition may be given to the less rigid claim that as long as at least *potential* life is involved, the State may assert interests beyond the protection of the pregnant woman alone.

Parties challenging state abortion laws have sharply disputed in some courts the contention that a purpose of these laws, when enacted, was to protect prenatal life. . . . Pointing to the absence of legislative history to support the contention, they claim that most state laws were designed solely to protect the woman. Because medical advances have lessened this concern, at least with respect to abortion in early pregnancy, they argue that with respect to such abortions the laws can no longer be justified by any state interest. There is some scholarly support for this view of original purpose. . . . The few state courts called upon to interpret their laws in the late 19th and early 20th centuries did focus on the State's interest in protecting the woman's health rather than in preserving the embryo and fetus. . . . Proponents of this view point out that in many States, including Texas, . . . by statute or judicial interpretation, the pregnant woman herself could not be prosecuted for self-abortion or for cooperating in an abortion performed upon her by another. . . . They claim that adoption of the "quickening" distinction through received common law and state statutes tacitly recognizes the greater health hazards inherent in late abortion and impliedly repudiates the theory that life begins at conception.

It is with these interests, and the weight to be attached to them, that this case is concerned.

The Constitution does not explicitly mention any right of privacy. In a line of decisions, however, going back perhaps as far as *Union Pacific R. Co. v. Botsford* . . . the Court has recognized that a right of personal privacy, or a guarantee of certain areas or zones of privacy, does exist under the Constitution. In varying contexts, the Court or individual Justices have, indeed, found at least the roots of that right in the First Amendment, *Stanley v. Georgia* . . . (1969); in the Fourth and Fifth Amendments, *Terry v. Ohio* . . . (1968), *Katz v. United States* . . . (1967); *Boyd v. United States* . . . (1886) . . . in the penumbras of the Bill of Rights, *Griswold v. Connecticut* . . . in the Ninth Amendment . . . or in the concept of liberty guaranteed by the first section of the Fourteenth Amendment, see *Meyer v. Nebraska* . . . (1923). These decisions make it clear that only personal rights that can be deemed "fundamental" or "implicit in the concept of ordered liberty," *Palko v. Connecticut* . . . (1937), are included in this guarantee of personal privacy. They also make it clear that the right has some extension to activities relating to marriage, *Loving v. Virginia* . . . (1967); procreation, *Skinner v. Oklahoma* . . . (1942); contraception, *Eisenstadt v. Baird* . . . family relationships, *Prince v. Massachusetts* . . . (1944); and child rearing and education, *Pierce v. Society of Sisters* . . . (1925) . . . .

This right of privacy, whether it be founded in the Fourteenth Amendment's concept of personal liberty and restrictions upon state action, as we feel it is, or, as the District Court determined, in the Ninth Amendment's reservation of rights to the people, is broad enough to encompass a woman's decision whether or not to terminate her pregnancy. The detriment that the State would impose upon the pregnant woman by denying this choice altogether is apparent. Specific and direct harm medically diagnosable even in early pregnancy may be involved. Maternity, or additional offspring, may force upon the woman a distressful life and future. Psychological harm may be imminent. Mental and physical health may be taxed by child care. There is also the distress, for all concerned, associated with the unwanted child, and there is the problem of bringing a child into a family already unable, psychologically and otherwise, to care for it. In other cases, as in this one, the additional difficulties and continuing stigma of unwed motherhood may be involved. All these are factors the woman and her responsible physician necessarily will consider in consultation.

On the basis of elements such as these, appellant and some *amici* argue that the woman's right is absolute and that she is entitled to terminate her pregnancy at whatever time, in whatever way, and for whatever reason she alone chooses. With this we do not agree. Appellant's arguments that Texas either has no valid interest at all in regulating the abortion decision, or no interest strong enough to support any limitation upon the woman's sole determination, are unpersuasive. The Court's decisions recognizing a right of privacy also acknowledge that some state regulation in areas protected by that right is appropriate. As noted above, a State may properly assert important interests in safe-guarding health, in maintaining medical standards, and in protecting potential life. At some point in pregnancy, these respective interests become sufficiently compelling to sustain regulation of the factors that govern the abortion decision. The privacy right involved, therefore, cannot be said to be absolute. In fact, it is not clear to us that the claim asserted by some *amici* that one has an unlimited right to do with one's body as one pleases bears a close relationship to the right of privacy previously articulated in the Court's decision. The Court has refused to recognize an unlimited right of this kind in the past. *Jacobson v. Massachusetts* . . . (1905) (vaccination); *Buck v. Bell* . . . (1927) (sterilization).

We, therefore, conclude that the right of personal privacy includes the abortion decision, but that this right is not unqualified and must be considered against important state interests in regulation.

We note that those federal and state courts that have recently considered abortion law challenges have reached the same conclusion. . . .

Although the results are divided, most of these courts have agreed that the right of privacy, however based, is broad enough to cover the abortion decision; that the right, nonetheless, is not absolute and is subject to some limitations; and that at some point the state interests as to protection of health, medical standards, and prenatal life, become dominant. We agree with this approach.

Where certain "fundamental rights" are involved, the Court has held that regulation limiting these rights may be justified only by a "compelling state interest," . . . and that legislative enactments must be narrowly drawn to express only the legitimate state interests at stake. . . .

In the recent abortion cases, cited above, courts have recognized these principles. Those striking down state laws have generally scrutinized the State's interests in protecting health and potential life, and have concluded that neither interest justified broad limitations on the reasons for which a physician and his pregnant patient might decide that she should have an abortion in the early stages of pregnancy. Courts sustaining state laws have held that the State's determinations to protect health or prenatal life are dominant and constitutionally justifiable.

The District Court held that the appellee failed to meet his burden of demonstrating that the Texas statute's infringement upon Roe's rights was necessary to support a compelling state interest, and that, although the appellee presented "several compelling justifications for state presence in the area of abortions," the statutes outstripped these justifications and swept "far beyond any areas of compelling state interest." 314 F. Supp., at 1222-1223. Appellant and appellee both contest that holding. Appellant, as has been indicated, claims an absolute right that bars any state imposition of criminal penalties in the area. Appellee argues that the State's determination to recognize and protect prenatal life from and after conception constitutes a compelling state interest. As noted above, we do not agree fully with either formulation.

A. The appellee and certain *amici* argue that the fetus is a "person" within the language and meaning of the Fourteenth Amendment. In support of this, they outline at length and in detail the well-known facts of fetal development. If this suggestion of personhood is established, the appellant's case, of course, collapses, for the fetus' right to life would then be guaranteed specifically by the Amendment. The appellant conceded as much on reargument. . . . On the other hand, the appellee conceded on reargument . . . that no case could be cited that holds that a fetus is a person within the meaning of the Fourteenth Amendment.

The Constitution does not define "person" in so many words. Section 1 of the Fourteenth Amendment contains three references to "person." The first, in defining "citizens," speaks of "persons born or naturalized in the United States." The word also appears both in the Due Process Clause and in the Equal Protection Clause. "Person" is used in other places in the Constitution . . . . But in nearly all these instances, the use of the word is such that it has application only postnatally. None indicates, with any assurance, that it has any possible prenatal application. . . .

All this, together with our observation, *supra*, that throughout the major portion of the 19th century prevailing legal abortion practices were far freer than they are today, persuades us that the word "person," as used in the Fourteenth Amendment, does not include the unborn.[2] . . .

B. The pregnant woman cannot be isolated in her privacy. She carries an embryo and, later, a fetus, if one accepts the medical definitions of the developing young in the human

---

[2] Cf. the Wisconsin abortion statute, defining "unborn child" to mean "a human being from the time of conception until it is born alive," Wis. Stat. § 940.04 (6) (1969), and the new Connecticut statute, Pub. Act No. 1 (May 1972 special session), declaring it to be the public policy of the State and the legislative intent "to protect and preserve human life from the moment of conception."

uterus. . . . The situation therefore is inherently different from marital intimacy, or bedroom possession of obscene material, or marriage, or procreation, or education, with which *Eisenstadt* and *Griswold, Stanley, Loving, Skinner,* and *Pierce* and *Meyer* were respectively concerned. As we have intimated above, it is reasonable and appropriate for a State to decide that at some point in time another interest, that of health of the mother or that of potential human life, becomes significantly involved. The woman's privacy is no longer sole and any right of privacy she possesses must be measured accordingly.

Texas urges that, apart from the Fourteenth Amendment, life begins at conception and is present throughout pregnancy, and that, therefore, the State has a compelling interest in protecting that life from and after conception. We need not resolve the difficult question of when life begins. When those trained in the respective disciplines of medicine, philosophy, and theology are unable to arrive at any consensus, the judiciary, at this point in the development of man's knowledge, is not in a position to speculate as to the answer. . . .

In view of all this, we do not agree that, by adopting one theory of life, Texas may override the rights of the pregnant woman that are at stake. We repeat, however, that the State does have an important and legitimate interest in preserving and protecting the health of the pregnant woman, whether she be a resident of the State or a nonresident who seeks medical consultation and treatment there, and that it has still *another* important and legitimate interest in protecting the potentiality of human life. These interests are separate and distinct. Each grows in substantiality as the woman approaches term and, at a point during pregnancy, each becomes "compelling."

With respect to the State's important and legitimate interest in the health of the mother, the "compelling" point, in the light of present medical knowledge, is at approximately the end of the first trimester. This is so because of the now-established medical fact . . . that until the end of the first trimester mortality in abortion may be less than mortality in normal childbirth. It follows that, from and after this point, a State may regulate the abortion procedure to the extent that the regulation reasonably relates to the preservation and protection of maternal health. Examples of permissible state regulation in this area are requirements as to the qualifications of the person who is to perform the abortion; as to the licensure of that person; as to the facility in which the procedure is to be performed, that is, whether it must be a hospital or may be a clinic or some other place of less-than-hospital status; as to the licensing of the facility; and the like.

This means, on the other hand, that, for the period of pregnancy prior to this "compelling" point, the attending physician, in consultation with his patient, is free to determine, without regulation by the State, that, in his medical judgment, the patient's pregnancy should be terminated. If that decision is reached, the judgment may be effectuated by an abortion free of interference by the State.

With respect to the State's important and legitimate interest in potential life, the "compelling" point is at viability. This is so because the fetus then presumably has the capability of meaningful life outside the mother's womb. State regulation protective of fetal life after viability thus has both logical and biological justifications. If the State is interested in protecting fetal life after viability, it may go so far as to proscribe abortion during that period, except when it is necessary to preserve the life or health of the mother.

Measured against these standards, Art. 1196 of the Texas Penal Code, in restricting legal abortions to those "procured or attempted by medical advice for the purpose of saving the life of the mother," sweeps too broadly. The statute makes no distinction between abortions performed early in pregnancy and those performed later, and it limits to a single reason, "saving" the mother's life, the legal justification for the procedure. The statute, therefore, cannot survive the constitutional attack made upon it here. . .

To summarize and to repeat:

1. A state criminal abortion statute of the current Texas type, that excepts from criminality only a *lifesaving* procedure on behalf of the mother, without regard to pregnancy stage and without recognition of the other interests involved, is violative of the Due Process Clause of the Fourteenth Amendment.

(a) For the stage prior to approximately the end of the first trimester, the abortion decision and its effectuation must be left to the medical judgment of the pregnant woman's attending physician.

(b) For the stage subsequent to approximately the end of the first trimester, the State, in promoting its interest in the health of the mother, may, if it chooses, regulate the abortion procedure in ways that are reasonably related to maternal health.

(c) For the stage subsequent to viability, the State in promoting its interest in the potentiality of human life may, if it chooses, regulate, and even proscribe, abortion except where it is necessary, in appropriate medical judgment, for the preservation of the life or health of the mother.

2. The State may define the term "physician," as it has been employed in the preceding paragraphs of this Part XI of this opinion, to mean only a physician currently licensed by the State, and may proscribe any abortion by a person who is not a physician as so defined. . . .

This holding, we feel, is consistent with the relative weights of the respective interests involved, with the lessons and examples of medical and legal history, with the lenity of the common law, and with the demands of the profound problems of the present day. The decision leaves the State free to lace increasing restrictions on abortion as the period of pregnancy lengthens, so long as those restrictions are tailored to the recognized state interests. The decision vindicates the right of the physician to administer medical treatment according to his professional judgment up to the points where important state interests provide compelling justifications for intervention. Up to those points, the abortion decision in all its aspects is inherently, and primarily, a medical decision, and basic responsibility for it must rest with the physician. If an individual practitioner abuses the privilege of exercising proper medical judgment, the usual remedies, judicial and intra-professional, are available. . . .

Mr. Justice Rehnquist, dissenting. . . .

. . . I have difficulty in concluding, as the Court does, that the right of "privacy" is involved in this case. Texas, by the statute here challenged, bars the performance of a medical abortion by a licensed physician on a plaintiff such as Roe. A transaction resulting in an operation such as this is not "private" in the ordinary usage of that word. Nor is the "privacy" that the Court finds here even a distant relative of the freedom from searches and seizures protected by the Fourth Amendment to the Constitution, which the Court has referred to as embodying a right to privacy. *Katz v. United States* . . . (1967).

If the Court means by the term "privacy" no more than that the claim of a person to be free from unwanted state regulation of consensual transactions may be a form of "liberty" protected by the Fourteenth Amendment, there is no doubt that similar claims have been upheld in our earlier decisions on the basis of that liberty. I agree with the statement of Mr. Justice Stewart in his concurring opinion that the "liberty," against deprivation of which without due process the Fourteenth Amendment protects, embraces more than the rights found in the Bill of Rights. But that liberty is not guaranteed absolutely against deprivation, only against deprivation without due process of law. The test traditionally applied in the area of social and economic legislation is whether or not a law such as that challenged has a rational relation to a valid state objective. *Williamson v. Lee Optical Co.* . . . (1955). The Due Process Clause of the Fourteenth Amendment undoubtedly does place a limit, albeit a broad one, on legislative power to enact laws such as this. If the Texas statute were to prohibit an abortion even where the mother's life is in jeopardy, I have little doubt that such a statute would lack a rational relation to a valid state objective under the test stated in *Williamson, supra*. But the Court's sweeping invalidation of any restrictions on abortion during the first trimester is impossible to justify under that standard, and the conscious weighing of competing factors that the Courts' opinion apparently substitutes for the established test is far more appropriate to a legislative judgment than to a judicial one.

The Court eschews the history of the Fourteenth Amendment in its reliance on the "compelling state interest" test. . . . But the Court adds a new wrinkle to this test by transposing it from the legal considerations associated with the Equal Protection Clause of the Fourteenth Amendment to this case arising under the Due Process Clause of the Fourteenth Amendment. Unless I misapprehend the consequences of this transplanting of the "compelling state interest test," the Court's opinion will accomplish the seemingly impossible feat of leaving this area of the law more confused than it found it.

While the Court's opinion quotes from the dissent of Mr. Justice Holmes in *Lochner v. New York* . . . (1905), the result it reaches is more closely attuned to the majority opinion of Mr. Justice Peckham in that case. As in *Lochner* and similar cases applying substantive due process standards to economic and social welfare legislation, the adoption of the compelling state interest standard will inevitably require this Court to examine the legislative policies and pass on the wisdom of these policies in the very process of deciding whether a particular state interest put forward may or may not be "compelling." The decision here to break pregnancy into three distinct terms and to outline the permissible restrictions the State may impose in each one, for example, partakes more of judicial legislation than it does of a determination of the intent of the drafters of the Fourteenth Amendment. . . .

There apparently was no question concerning the validity of this provision or of any of the other state statutes when the Fourteenth Amendment was adopted. The only conclusion possible from this history is that the drafters did not intend to have the Fourteenth Amendment withdraw from the States the power to legislate with respect to this matter. . . .

For all of the foregoing reasons, I respectfully dissent.

Thinking It Over

1. Sandra Day O'Connor, the first and only woman ever to serve on the Supreme Court, said the *Roe* decision was a case "on a collision course with itself." What did she mean by that?

2. What is the Constitutional principle on which *Roe* is based? Where is it found? Are you convinced by Rehnquist's attack on the Court's application of this principle?

22.
HATE GOES TO COLLEGE
by Steve France

Setting the Scene: One of the most difficult dilemmas for the political system occurs when two rights collide. Here we consider the clash between equality and free speech. Campuses all over the country have been reacting to outbursts of racial bigotry and expressions of hate based on lifestyle and other forms of diversity. In all matters where opinions are deeply felt it is hard to screw up your courage (and it *does* take courage) and think objectively. Remember this. If you are correct in your views, articles like the one that follows—if you give them a chance—can only help you. If you are wrong, there is no better time than right now to begin to do something about it.

The incidents are familiar: At the University of Michigan the student-run radio station broadcasts a racial joke. At the University of Wisconsin a fraternity holds a mock slave auction. At Stanford a picture of Beethoven is given fuller lips and dark frizzy hair, and then posted in a black-studies dormitory. Swastikas, epithets and Ku Klux Klan imagery poison the environment of many a campus.

Coast to coast, it seems racial tensions on American university campuses have been rising for several years. Increasingly rough words are being spoken, lines defiantly drawn. And the schools themselves are in an exquisite dilemma, forced to defend by turns the principle of free speech that, more than anything else, defines the spirit of truth-seeking for which universities are said to stand, and the right of their students—especially those who are members of racial and other minorities—to seek the truth in surroundings free of hatred and intimidation.

In response to a growing number of incidents, many universities have enacted "conduct codes" prohibiting certain types of racist and other anti-minority speech. That tactic has sparked great concern among some civil libertarians, who believe it violates the First Amendment. Many of them express bewilderment that civil-rights activists who have turned so often to the Bill of Rights are now advocating limits on the right of free speech.

To understand the debate it is necessary to understand the philosophical distance travelled by civil-rights activists since the Civil Rights Act was passed in 1964. The experience of those 26 years has raised doubts among many activists about the adequacy of traditional American notions of equality and minority rights.

It used to be that the goal of the civil-rights movement was integration, the "melting pot." But over the years that idea has fallen out of favor, dismissed as white, male, Eurocentric. Why, reformers ask, should our goal be to homogenize diverse cultures in our society to conform to the standards of the dominant culture? Shouldn't we encourage diversity and pluralism instead, and work affirmatively to ensure that minorities enjoy equal power and prestige?

In this view, physical integration of minorities into the mainstream is inadequate. Integration must be joined with commitment to diversity. Thus Kathleen Mahoney, a Canadian law professor, argues that her country has rightly rejected the melting pot in favor of "a mosaic approach to cultural diversity."

But pursuit of this egalitarian ideal in the United States will require painful changes in traditional First Amendment doctrines that protect speech attacking racial minorities, gays and women, say Mahoney and many American professors, students and activists.

So far the changes have indeed been painful. The University of Michigan, for example, adopted a conduct code to suppress speech offensive to minorities, but a federal judge declared it to be unconstitutionally overboard. (*Doe v. University of Michigan* . . .[1989]) But many other codes remain in force, or are being developed, at other schools.

Last summer the University of Wisconsin instituted one of the toughest codes. It subjects students to discipline for "discriminatory comments or expressive behavior directed at an individual that intentionally demean the race, sex, religion, color, creed, disability, sexual orientation, national origin, ancestry or age of the individual, and create a demeaning environment for education."

Some argue that because the Wisconsin rule is restricted to statements directed at an individual, it fails to reach general expressions of racism, sexism and homophobia. The intent requirement has been criticized as creating too many difficult problems of proof for those who would invoke the protections of the code. At least two constitutional-law professors, Mari Matsuda of the University of Hawaii and Charles R. Lawrence III of Stanford, argue that such codes should protect only members of "historical victim groups" and not members of dominant social groups.

Most civil libertarians, on the other hand, complain that the conduct codes are unwise and unworkable as social policy, and unconstitutional as a matter of First Amendment law. Led by the American Civil Liberties Union (which represented the plaintiff in the Michigan case), they have opposed the codes around the country. In March the ACLU sued to have the Wisconsin code declared unconstitutional.

But even veteran ACLU attorneys admit that they find it painful to be fighting against civil-rights activists, many of whom are old allies or themselves members of the ACLU. Inured to charges that they are "the criminals' lobby," that they sympathize with subversives and condone various outrages, they squirm at implications that they are insensitive to minorities. At last year's convention, for example, as a gesture of sensitivity to minority concerns, the union formally considered a resolution in favor of campus codes.

"I found it amazing that 10 years after the Skokie case [upholding the right of neo-Nazis to march through a heavily Jewish suburb of Chicago] we were thinking about endorsing censorship," says Nadine Strossen, the ACLU's general counsel.

Nonetheless, in arguing against a proposed Stanford rule to punish abusive speech, Strossen is careful to establish her civil-rights credentials, emphasizing the ACLU's "deep commitment to eradicating racism throughout society."

Nor does she easily accept the notion that her disagreement with campus-code advocates involves a profound difference in basic political philosophy. Rather, Strossen and other optimists on both sides of the debate believe that their differences can be reconciled, with an eventual net gain in mutual understanding.

To a degree, this hope seems based on the belief that campus-code advocates don't really mean what they say. While remaining respectful of their motivations, the optimists see the chorus of calls for speech restrictions as a reaction to a rising tide of racist campus incidents and to society's indifference to minority concerns. Therefore, they reason, genuine compromise is possible, once the First Amendment is understood and the good faith of its defenders established. . . .

The reason a true compromise may not be easy to reach is that both sides believe they have unequivocal commitments to the twin goals of equality *and* free speech.

Strossen denies that the price of protecting free speech is a diminution of the commitment to equality: "This false dichotomy," she says, "simply drives artificial wedges between would-be allies in what should be a common struggle to promote civil rights and civil liberties."

But First Amendment revisionists also deny that their proposals require a balancing approach to the Constitution. They really mean it when they argue that sanctions on discriminatory speech *promote* free speech.

"Freedom of expression as defined by women and minority groups looks different than freedom of speech defined by others," comments Mahoney.

"Speech is meaningless to people who do not have equality. I mean substantive as well as procedural equality," Mari Matsuda says in arguing for content- and viewpoint-based limits on speech—an idea she frankly admits is "heresy in First Amendment doctrine."

"Equality is a necessary precondition to free speech," Charles Lawrence states in an article suggesting that "content regulation of racist speech is not just permissible but, in certain circumstances, may be required by the Constitution."

In arguing for a broad rule at Stanford, several minority-student groups put the matter squarely. Rather than reduce free speech, they said, such a rule would increase free speech and "vigorous debate."

Aside from the severe emotional distress caused by racist speech, and its tendency to spread the infection of racism, the most insistent claim made by advocates of regulation is that racist speech "silences" its victims. It "warn[s] them that they will suffer some kind of harm," according to a group of Stanford minority students, if they speak up for their rights in society.

To maintain our traditional First Amendment tolerance of hate speech is, Matsuda says, to impose "a psychic tax on those least able to pay." At best, First Amendment "romantics" show insensitivity to the hurtful, silencing impact of discriminatory speech. At worst, the traditional view acts as a self-serving cover for the continued domination of majority elites. . . .

Despite the radical implications of such arguments, Strossen urges the revisionists to recognize "how narrow are the actual differences between us regarding the extent to which racist speech should be prohibited." She even concedes that banning certain forms of racist expression would make a symbolic contribution to "our all-important struggle to eradicate the cancer of racism itself."

Consistent with this rosy view of the philosophical distance between the two sides,

Strossen and others have emphasized the pragmatic reasons against trying to regulate discriminatory speech. After easily demonstrating that such regulation is unconstitutional, they point out reasons why it is also unworkable and unproductive.

Alan Borovoy, general counsel of the Canadian Civil Liberties Association, argues that it is difficult for "a blunt instrument like the criminal law to distinguish destructive hatred from constructive tension" in the complex matter of intergroup relations. Prosecutors are placed on a slippery slope from which they are likely to fall into punishing useful speech just because some find it offensive.

In addition, even when the indicted speech is truly vicious, prosecution can play into the hands of the speaker by giving him a resounding public forum in which to expound his hateful opinions. Borovoy notes that Adolf Hitler used anti-hate speech laws in Weimar Germany to publicize his cause and play the martyr.

Strossen points out that unless such laws punish only racist speech against minorities they are likely to be used against intemperate members of minority groups, who are the intended beneficiaries of the laws. After all, the laws, as political instruments, are ultimately controlled by the majority. She cites the fact that the University of Michigan applied its rule to several minority students before it was struck down.

Civil libertarians also contend that racist speech serves as a warning system by revealing anti-social pathologies. Once warned, healthy individuals and institutions can be mobilized against the threat and can better develop immunities. Viewed in this light, tolerance of hateful speech is not a matter of indulgence or sympathy with the views expressed, but a vital way for society to develop stronger resistance mechanisms.

Gerald Gunther says that he feels almost grateful on the rare occasions when a student in his constitutional-law class expresses unpopular, retrograde views against affirmative action or other well-established liberal doctrines. Without the spark of live conflict the classroom discussion tends to languish.

Although these pragmatic arguments are forcefully presented and despite revisionists' protestations against the "ringing rhetoric" of First Amendment romantics, civil libertarians tend to speak in muted tones when opposing hate-speech rules. They do not loudly invoke the fundamental political principles of free-speech doctrine.

Have liberal civil libertarians in fact subtly silenced themselves? Some have done more than that.

The ACLU's southern and northern California affiliates have approved a hate-speech policy similar to the Grey compromise at Stanford. There are signs this softness is based on ACLU leaders' sympathy for the revisionist view that equality should be defined as a group right, not merely as the individual's right, to be free from discrimination.

According to Strossen, who says her position on the issue is hardening as she continues to reflect on it, the concept of a cultural mosaic as a substitute for the melting-pot ideal is based on giving group rights priority over individual rights. As long as rights belong just to individuals and are not limited by group rights, in this view, historical patterns of inequality will be perpetuated.

The ACLU's national legal director, John Powell, opposes campus speech codes but says "our concept of equality under the 14th Amendment is anemic and underdeveloped. I'm not sure just where its contours are, but is not just a matter of not discriminating against individuals."

If he saw equality as just a matter of individual rights, he says, he might find it logically hard to reconcile himself to affirmative-action policies (though he is quick to characterize those policies as "a strategy, not a principle").

The revisionist view of free speech does seem akin to affirmative action in certain ways, Strossen admits. In any case, those who are opposed to affirmative action are ferocious in their condemnation of the hate-speech rules.

Thus Alan Keyes, a former official in the Reagan administration and the Republican candidate for a Maryland Senate seat in 1988 (he lost to Paul Sarbanes), denounces them as patronizing, paternalistic forms of a well-intentioned racism that cripples blacks. He says he would feel cheated by an education that insulated him from contact with white racist views. "I wouldn't want to graduate and the first time I get into a debate with a real gutter fighter on any issue of importance, they look at me and call me 'nigger,' and I lose my mind," he says.

Even without official punishment of conservative views, students feel social pressure to conform to "the new secular orthodoxy on social issues," says Wayne State Law School Professor Robert Sedler, who argued the case against Michigan's hate-speech rule. "The '60s New Left radicals have taken over lots of university establishments. They can be just as fascistic as anyone."

Shelby Steele, a professor of English at San Jose State University and a frequent writer on the subject of race, believes the reigning orthodoxy of race relations tends to exacerbate tensions. In his view, the cult of diversity and pluralism destroys students' ability to understand their own racial anxieties (white guilt, black fear of inferiority) and their hope of seeing each other's essential human likeness.

Subjected to "a machinery of separatism that, in the name of sacred difference, redraws the ugly lines of segregation," students are forced into ever more extreme conflicts, Steele says. Gutless school officials cave in to whatever demands minorities put on the table, "rather than work with them to assess their real needs."

Steele longs to hear again the message he heard from Martin Luther King in 1964, the summer before he entered college: "When you are behind in a foot race, the only way to get ahead is to run faster than the man in front of you. So when your white roommate says he's tired and goes to sleep, you stay up and burn the midnight oil."

For Steele, this statement was a recognition that success in an integrated society would be difficult, but that the difficulty should be viewed as a challenge to be assumed, rather than a reason to abandon the idea of integration.

First Amendment revisionists seem to be on solid ground when they argue that free-speech values do not exist in a political vacuum. However, that fact may in the end work to their disadvantage—casting doubt on the wisdom of their fundamental social ideal.

Liberals who wish to defend traditional values of free speech may find themselves defending far more of our political value system than they would like. That system gives primacy to individual rights and the building of a common national identity—principles in harmony with the old ideals of integration and the melting pot.

Given a choice between abandoning the First Amendment or upholding those principles, liberals may be forced to reject much of their current minority agenda.

In the end, the debate over free speech on campus is really about what kind of social equality we believe is possible and just. The last several years of struggling with that question have not given much comfort to those who believe in the melting pot and the wisdom of the country's founders.

Thinking It Over

1. There seems to be in law a protection against insult based on the "fighting words" principle. Why is the "fighting words" principle not enough if one seeks to protect minorities from the language of hate?

2. How would you have come down on Stanford University's rule against discriminatory speech as it originally read? Defend your position.

PART

B

THE ARCHITECTURE

OF GOVERNANCE

Chapter IV

DIVIDING POWER: FEDERALISM & THE REPUBLIC

23.
THE FEDERALIST PAPERS, NO. 39
by James Madison

Setting the Scene: Federalist No. 39 describes a perfect example of political engineering. That is to say, the framers *had* a pair of concepts, republicanism and federalism and they sought to build, to *engineer*, a structure based on those theories. Your task is to keep this in mind as you read. You'll need to pay attention to the definition of both terms and stay alert to the causal relationships between them and the framework proposed to give them life.

The last paper having concluded the observations which were meant to introduce a candid survey of the plan of government reported by the convention, we now proceed to the execution of that part of our undertaking.

The first question that offers itself is, whether the general form and aspect of the government be strictly republican? It is evident that no other form would be reconcilable with the genius of the people of America; with the fundamental principles of the Revolution; or with that honorable determination which animates every votary of freedom, to rest all our political experiments on the capacity of mankind for self-government. If the plan of the convention, therefore, be found to depart from the republican character, its advocates must abandon it as no longer defensible.

What, then, are the distinctive characters of the republican form? . . .

If we resort for a criterion to the different principles on which different forms of government are established, we may define a republic to be, or at least may bestow that name on, a government which derives all its powers directly or indirectly from the great body of the people, and is administered by person holding their offices during pleasure, for a limited period, or during good behavior. It is *essential* to such a government that it be derived from the great body of the society, not from an inconsiderable proportion, or a favored class of it; otherwise a handful of tyrannical nobles, exercising their oppressions by a delegation of their powers, might aspire to the rank of republicans, and claim for their government the honorable title of republic. It is *sufficient* for such a government that the persons administering it be appointed, either directly or indirectly, by the people; and that they hold their appointments by either of the tenures just specified; otherwise every government in the United States, as well as every other popular government that has been or can be well organized or well executed, would be degraded from the republican character. . . .

On comparing the Constitution planned by the convention with the standard here fixed, we perceive at once that it is, in the most rigid sense, conformable to it. The House of Representatives, like that of one branch at least of all the State legislatures, is elected immediately by the great body of the people. The Senate, like the present Congress, and the Senate of Maryland, derives its appointment indirectly from the people. The President is indirectly derived from the choice of the people, according to the example in most of the States. Even the judges with all other officers of the Union, will, as in the several States, be the choice, though a remote choice, of the people themselves. The duration of the appointments is equally conformable to the republican standard, and to the model of State constitutions. The House of Representatives is periodically elective, as in all the States; and for the period of two years, as in the State of South Carolina. The Senate is elective, for the period of six years; which is but one year more than the period of the Senate of Maryland, and but two more than that of the Senates of New York and Virginia. The President is to continue in office for the period of four years; as in New York and Delaware the chief magistrate is elected for three years, and in South Carolina for two years. In the other States the election is annual. In several of the States, however, no constitutional provision is made for the impeachment of the chief magistrate. And in Delaware and Virginia he is not impeachable till out of office. The President of the United States is impeachable at any time during his continuance in office. The tenure by which the judges are to hold their places, is, as it unquestionably ought to be, that of good behavior. The tenure of the ministerial offices generally, will be a subject of legal regulation, conformably to the reason of the case and the example of the State constitutions.

Could any further proof be required of the republican complexion of this system, the most decisive one might be found in its absolute prohibition of titles of nobility, both under the federal and the State governments; and in its express guaranty of the republican form to each of the latter.

"But it was not sufficient," say the adversaries of the proposed Constitution, "for the convention to adhere to the republican form. They ought, with equal care, to have preserved the *federal* form, which regards the Union as a *Confederacy* of sovereign states; instead of which, they have framed a *national* government, which regards the Union as a *consolidation* of the States." And it is asked by what authority this bold and radical innovation was undertaken? The handle which has been made of this objection requires that it should be examined with some precision.

Without inquiring into the accuracy of the distinction on which the objection is founded, it will be necessary to a just estimate of its force, first, to ascertain the real character of the government in question; secondly, to inquire how far the convention were authorized to propose such a government; and thirdly, how far the duty they owed to their country could supply any defect of regular authority.

First.—In order to ascertain the real character of the government, it may be considered in relation to the foundation on which it is to be established; to the sources from which its ordinary powers are to be drawn; to the operation of those powers; to the extent of them; and to the authority by which future changes in the government are to be introduced.

On examining the first relation, it appears, on one hand, that the Constitution is to be founded on the assent and ratification of the people of America, given by deputies elected for the special purpose; but, on the other, that this assent and ratification is to be given by the people, not as individuals composing one entire nation, but as composing the distinct and independent States to which they respectively belong. It is to be the assent and ratification of the several States, derived from the supreme authority in each State,—the authority of the people themselves. The act, therefore, establishing the Constitution, will not be a *national*, but a *federal* act.

That it will be a federal and not a national act, as these terms are understood by the objectors; the act of the people, as forming so many independent States, not as forming one aggregate nation, is obvious from this single consideration, that it is to result neither from the decision of a *majority* of the people of the Union, nor from that of a *majority* of the States. It must result from the *unanimous* assent of the several States that are parties to it, differing no otherwise from their ordinary assent than in its being expressed, not by the legislative authority, but by that of the people themselves. Were the people regarded in this transaction as forming one nation, the will of the majority of the whole people of the United States would bind the minority, in the same manner as the majority in each State must bind the minority; and the will of the majority must be determined either by a comparison of the individual votes, or by considering the will of the majority of the States as evidence of the will of a majority of the people of the United States. Neither of these rules has been adopted. Each State, in ratifying the Constitution, is considered as a sovereign body, independent of all others, and only to be bound by its own voluntary act. In this relation, then, the new Constitution will, if established, be a *federal*, and not a *national* constitution.

The next relation is, to the sources from which the ordinary powers of government are to be derived. The House of Representatives will derive its powers from the people of America; and the people will be represented in the same proportion, and on the same principle, as they are in the legislature of a particular State. So far the government is *national*, not *federal*. The Senate, on the other hand, will derive its powers from the States, as political and coequal societies; and these will be represented on the principle of equality in the Senate, as they now are in the existing Congress. So far the government is *federal*, not *national*. The executive power will be derived from a very compound source. The immediate election of the President is to be made by the States in their political characters.

The votes allotted to them are in a compound ratio, which considers them partly as distinct and coequal societies, partly as unequal members of the same society. The eventual election, again, is to be made by that branch of the legislature which consists of the national representatives; but in this particular act they are to be thrown into the form of individual delegations, from so many distinct and coequal bodies politic. From this aspect of the government, it appears to be of a mixed character, presenting at least as many *federal* as *national* features.

The difference between a federal and national government, as it relates to the *operation of the government*, is supposed to consist in this, that in the former the powers operate on the political bodies composing the Confederacy, in their political capacities; in the latter, on the individual citizens composing the nation, in their individual capacities. On trying the Constitution by this criterion, it falls under the *national*, not the *federal* character. . . .

But if the government be national with regard to the *operation* of its powers, it changes its aspect again when we contemplate it in relation to the extent of its powers. The idea of a national government involves in it, not only an authority over the individual citizens, but an indefinite supremacy over all persons and things, so far as they are objects of lawful government. Among a people consolidated into one nation, this supremacy is completely vested in the national legislature. Among communities united for particular purposes, it is vested partly in the general and partly in the municipal legislatures. In the former case, all local authorities are subordinate to the supreme; and may be controlled, directed, or abolished by it as pleasure. In the latter, the local or municipal authorities form distinct and independent portions of the supremacy, no more subject, within their respective spheres, to the general authority, than the general authority is subject to them, within its own sphere. In this relation, then, the proposed government cannot be deemed a *national* one; since its jurisdiction extends to certain enumerated objects only, leaves to the several States a residuary and inviolable sovereignty over all other objects. It is true that in controversies relating to the boundary between the two jurisdictions, the tribunal which is ultimately to decide, is to be established under the general government. But this does not change the principle of the case. The decision is to be impartially made, according to the rules of the Constitution; and all the usual and most effectual precautions are taken to secure this impartiality. Some such tribunal is clearly essential to prevent an appeal to the sword and a dissolution of the compact; and that it ought to be established under the general rather than under the local governments, or, to speak more properly, that it could be safely established under the first alone, is a position not likely to be combated.

If we try the Constitution by its last relation to the authority by which amendments are to be made, we find it neither wholly *national* nor wholly *federal*. Were it wholly national, the supreme and ultimate authority would reside in the *majority* of the people of the Union; and this authority would be competent at all times, like that of a majority of every national society, to alter or abolish its established government. Were it wholly federal, on the other hand, the concurrence of each State in the Union would be essential to every alteration that would be binding on all. The mode provided by the plan of the convention is not founded on either of these principles. In requiring more than a majority, and particularly in computing the proportion by *States*, not by *citizens*, it departs from the *national* and advances toward the *federal* character; in rendering the concurrence of less than the whole number of States sufficient, it loses again the *federal* and partakes of the *national* character.

The proposed Constitution, therefore, is in strictness, neither a national nor a federal Constitution, but a composition of both. In its foundation it is federal, not national; in the sources from which the ordinary powers of the government are drawn, it is partly federal and partly national; in the operation of these powers, it is national, not federal; in the extent of them, again, it is federal, not national; and, finally in the authoritative mode of introducing amendments, it is neither wholly federal nor wholly national.

Thinking It Over

1. Is there an inherent contradiction between republicanism and federalism as defined by Madison?

2. The features Madison describes to insure that republican principles survive have been changed considerably to further democratization of the political process. If Madison were alive today, would he see the government in Washington as still being fundamentally republican in character?

24.
MCCULLOCH V. MARYLAND

Setting the Scene: Perhaps no other Supreme Court decision is as ripe with questions of governance as *McCulloch v. Maryland.* Two critical decisions are made here, both in the direction of empowering the national, at the expense of the state governments. It is in this case that we find the famous axiom "the power to tax is the power to destroy" and it is from this case that the national government gained massive new flexibility to act based on Chief Justice John Marshall's interpretation of the "necessary and proper" clause. This case will give you a first-hand appreciation for Marshall's ability to state an argument well.

Chief Justice Marshall delivered the opinion of the Court:

In the case now to be determined, the defendant, a sovereign state, denies the obligation of a law enacted by the legislature of the Union, and the plaintiff, on his part, contests the validity of an act which has been passed by the legislature of that State. The constitution of our country, in its most interesting and vital parts, is to be considered; the conflicting powers of the government of the Union and of its members, as marked in that constitution, are to be discussed; and an opinion given which may essentially influence the great operations of the government. No tribunal can approach such a question without a deep sense of its importance, and the awful responsibility involved in its decision. But it must be decided peacefully, or remain a source of hostile legislation, perhaps of hostility of a still more serious nature; and if it is to be so decided, by this tribunal alone can the decision be made. On the Supreme Court of the United States has the constitution of our country devolved this important duty.

The first question made in the cause is, has Congress power to incorporate a bank? . . .

In discussing this question, the counsel for the State of Maryland have deemed it of some importance, in the construction of the constitution, to consider that instrument not as emanating from the people, but as the act of sovereign and independent States. The powers of the general government, it has been said, are delegated by the States, who alone are truly sovereign; and must be exercised in subordination to the States, who alone possess supreme dominion.

It would be difficult to sustain this proposition. The convention which framed the constitution was indeed elected by the state legislatures. But the instrument, when it came from their hands, was a mere proposal, without obligation, or pretensions to it. It was reported to the then existing congress of the United States, with a request that it might "be submitted to a convention of delegates, chosen in each State by the people thereof, under the recommendation of its legislature, for their assent and ratification." This mode of proceeding was adopted; and by the convention, by congress, and by the State legislatures, the instrument was submitted to the people. They acted upon it in the only manner in which they can act safely, effectively, and wisely, on such a subject, by assembling in convention. It is true, they assembled in their several States; and where else should they have assembled? No political dreamer was ever wild enough to think of breaking down the lines which separate the States, and of compounding the American people into one common mass. Of consequence, when they act, they act in their States. But the measures they adopt do not, on that account, cease to be the measures of the people themselves, or become the measures of the State governments.

From these conventions the constitution derives its whole authority. The government proceeds directly from the people; is "ordained and established" in the name of the people; and is declared to be ordained, "in order to form a more perfect union, establish justice, insure domestic tranquility, and secure the blessings of liberty to themselves and to their posterity." The assent of the States, in their sovereign capacity, is implied in calling a convention, and thus submitting that instrument to the people. But the people were at perfect liberty to accept or reject it; and their act was final. It required not the affirmance, and could not be negatived, by the State governments. The constitution, when thus adopted, was of complete obligation, and bound the State sovereignties. . . .

This government is acknowledged by all to be one of enumerated powers. The principle, that it can exercise only the powers granted to it, would seem too apparent to have required to be enforced by all those arguments which its enlightened friends, while it was depending before the people, found it necessary to urge. That principle is now universally admitted. But the question respecting the extent of the powers actually granted, is perpetually arising, and will probably continue to arise, as long as our system shall exist. . . .

If any one proposition could command the universal assent of mankind, we might expect it would be this: that the government of the Union, though limited in its powers, is supreme within its sphere of action. This would seem to result necessarily from its nature. It is the government of all; its powers are delegated by all; it represents all, and acts for all. Though any one State may be willing to control its operations, no State is willing to allow others to control them. The nation, on those subjects on which it can act, must necessarily bind its component parts. But this question is not left to mere reason: the people have, in express terms, decided it by saying, "this constitution, and the laws of the United States, which shall be made in pursuance thereof," "shall be the supreme law of the land," and by requiring that the members of the State legislatures, and the officers of the executive and judicial departments of the States shall take the oath of fidelity to it.

The government of the United States, then, though limited in its powers, is supreme; and its laws, when made in pursuance of the constitution, form the supreme law of the land, "anything in the constitution or laws of any State to the contrary notwithstanding."

Among the enumerated powers, we do not find that of establishing a bank or creating a corporation. But there is no phrase in the instrument which, like the articles of confederation, excludes incidental or implied powers; and which requires that everything granted shall be expressly and minutely described. Even the 10th amendment, which was framed for the purpose of quieting the excessive jealousies which had been excited, omits the word "expressly," and declares only that the powers "not delegated to the United States, nor prohibited to the States, are reserved to the States or to the people"; thus leaving the question whether the particular power which may become the subject of contest has been delegated to the one government, or prohibited to the other, to depend on a fair construction of the whole instrument. The men who drew and adopted this amendment had experienced the embarrassments resulting from the insertion of this word in the articles of confederation, and probably omitted it to avoid those embarrassments. A constitution, to contain an accurate detail of all the subdivisions of which its great powers will admit, and of all the means by which they may be carried into execution, would partake of the prolixity of a legal code, and could scarcely be embraced by the human mind. It would probably never be understood by the public. Its nature, therefore, requires, that only its great outlines should be marked, its important objects designated, and the minor ingredients which compose those objects be deduced from the nature of the objects themselves. . . .

Although, among the enumerated powers of government, we do not find the word "bank" or "incorporation," we find the great powers to lay and collect taxes; to borrow money; to regulate commerce; to declare and conduct a war; and to raise and support armies and navies. The sword and the purse, all the external relations, and no inconsiderable portion of the industry of the nation, are entrusted to its government. It can never be pretended that these vast powers draw after them others of inferior importance, merely because they are inferior. Such an idea can never be advanced. But it may with great reason be contended, that a government, entrusted with such ample powers, on the due execution of which the happiness and prosperity of the nation so vitally depends, must also be entrusted with ample means for their execution. . . .

But the constitution of the United States has not left the right of congress to employ the necessary means for the execution of the powers conferred on the government to general reasoning. To its enumeration of powers is added that of making "all laws which shall be necessary and proper, for carrying into execution the foregoing powers, and all other powers vested by this constitution, in the government of the United States, or in any department thereof." . . .

But the argument on which most reliance is placed, is drawn from the peculiar language of this clause. Congress is not empowered by it to make all laws, which may have relation to the powers conferred on the government, but such only as may be "necessary and proper" for carrying them into execution. The word "necessary" is considered as controlling the whole sentence, and as limiting the right to pass laws for the execution of the granted powers, to such as are indispensable, and without which the power would be nugatory. That it excludes the choice of means, and leaves to congress, in each case, that only which is most direct and simple.

Is it true that this is the sense in which the word "necessary" is always used? Does it always import an absolute physical necessity, so strong that one thing, to which another may be termed necessary, cannot exist without that other? We think it does not. If reference be had to its use, in the common affairs of the world, or in approved authors, we find that it frequently imports no more than that one thing is convenient, or useful, or essential to another. To employ the means necessary to an end, is generally understood as employing any means calculated to produce the end, and not as being confined to those single means, without which the end would be entirely unattainable. . . .

We admit, as all must admit, that the powers of the government are limited, and that its limits are not to be transcended. But we think the sound construction of the constitution must allow to the national legislature that discretion, with respect to the means by which the powers it confers are to be carried into execution, which will enable that body to perform the high duties assigned to it, in the manner most beneficial to the people. Let the end be legitimate, let it be within the scope of the constitution, and all means which are appropriate, which are plainly adapted to that end, which are not prohibited, but consist with the letter and spirit of the constitution, are constitutional. . . .

After the most deliberate consideration, it is the unanimous and decided opinion of this court that the act to incorporate the Bank of the United States is a law made in pursuance of the constitution, and is a part of the supreme law of the land. The branches, proceeding from the same stock, and being conducive to the complete accomplishment of the object, are equally constitutional. . . .

It being the opinion of the court that the act incorporating the bank is constitutional, and that the power of establishing a branch in the State of Maryland might be properly exercised by the bank itself, we proceed to inquire:—

Whether the State of Maryland may, without violating the constitution, tax that branch? . . .

That the power to tax involves the power to destroy; that the power to destroy may defeat and render useless the power to create; that there is a plain repugnance, in conferring on one government a power to control the constitutional measures of another, which other, with respect to those very measures, is declared to be supreme over that which exerts the control, are propositions not to be denied. . . .

If the States may tax one Instrument, employed by the government in the execution of its powers, they may tax any and every other Instrument. They may tax the mail; they may tax the mint; they may tax patent-rights; they may tax the papers of the custom-house; they may tax judicial process; they may tax all the means employed by the government, to an excess which would defeat all the ends of government. This was not intended by the American people. They did not design to make their government dependent on the States . . .

If the controlling power of the States be established; if their supremacy as to taxation be acknowledged; what is to restrain their exercising this control in any shape they may please to give it? Their sovereignty is not confined to taxation. That is not the only mode in which it might be displayed. The question is, in truth, a question of supremacy; and if the right of the States to tax the means employed by the general government be conceded, the declaration that the constitution, and the laws made in pursuance thereof, shall be the supreme law of the land, is empty and unmeaning declamation. . . .

The court has bestowed on this subject its most deliberate consideration. The result is a conviction that the States have no power, by taxation or otherwise, to retard, impede, burden, or in any manner control the operations of the constitutional laws enacted by congress to carry into execution the powers vested in the general government. This is, we think, the unavoidable consequence of that supremacy which the constitution has declared.

We are unanimously of opinion that the law passed by the legislature of Maryland, imposing a tax on the Bank of the United States, is unconstitutional. . . .

Thinking It Over

1. One of the most fascinating questions to contemplate after reading *McCulloch v. Maryland* is: How far can the elastic clause be stretched? If the national government has the power to "regulate interstate commerce" and it can do anything "necessary and proper" on behalf of that function, would it not be possible for it to perform almost any function at all?

2. The Supreme Court is, after all, a national court, one of three branches of the *federal* government. Reading *McCulloch* carefully, is it not possible to detect in Marshall a bias toward the center—toward the government that pays his wages?

25.
THE MALIGNED STATES
by Ira Sharkansky

Setting the Scene: There has been in your lifetime a renewed interest in assigning more governmental responsibility to the states. The reading below is from an important contribution to the cause for revitalizing the states, which appeared in the early 1970s. To fully understand its importance, one must recognize that for most of this century, it *was* the case that many of the states were simply too lax on issues of civil rights to be trusted with broad new social programs. The cry for more authority at the state level was defined, then, as "states' rights." Rights or not, it is being recognized more and more that the national government simply can't do everything. It is also believed that it is safer now from the perspective of civil rights to give the states the chance to play a larger role. The following was written as these twin conclusions were dawning on a federal system having difficulty governing from the center.

The states are powerful. Considering domestic public services only—and leaving out national defense and international relations—the states are growing in importance more than any other level of government. Since World War II the states have grown more than the national and local governments in their contributions to public services. After a heady 10 years of domestic innovations, international experiments with the Alliance for Progress, the war in Southeast Asia, and the excessive centralization of the national government's power in the White House, the Washington of the Ford administration became preoccupied with a tidy administration domestically and a strong, if not extended, position militarily. At the local level, city halls around the country scream poverty and look over their shoulders to the near bankruptcy of New York City. Meanwhile, the states have become more and more the workhorses rather than the weak sisters of the Federal system.

One of the ironies in American politics is that states reap so much negative publicity. Most public comments about the states say they are weak. That, indeed, is putting it mildly. They are said to be habitats of corrupt, evil, or simply ineffective politicians and bureaucrats. The states lack the image of innovation on the frontier of social and economic activity. The main political action seems to be in the cities and Washington. "States' Rights" conjures up the anachronisms of Klan members and backward programs in education, health, and welfare. . . .

The inferior prestige of state governments is not a recent development. In 1933 a specialist in public administration wrote, "The American State is finished. I do not predict that the States will go, but affirm that they have gone."[1] Professor Martin Landau traces what he considers to be the decline of the states:

---

[1] Sanford, p. 21. [Terry Sanford, *Storm over the States* (New York: McGraw-Hill, 1967).]

We have Woodrow Wilson's description, in 1885, of the "altered and declining status of the states." The pragmatic Frank Goodnow concludes in 1916 that industrialization has caused "the old distinction" between interstate and intrastate commerce "almost to disappear." And there is [Harold] Laski's tale of obsolescence and Max Lerner speaking of the ghost of federalism which "haunts a nation in which every force drives toward centralization." . . . Leonard White states "that competent observers at home and abroad have declared that American federalism is approaching its end." Roscoe Drummond put it more directly: "our federal system no longer exists."[2]

. . .

What underpinnings of the state governments have kept them alive for so long? They receive support from a combination of constitutional provisions, laws, extralegal political institutions, custom, and attachment to the differences that have marked our regions since colonial times. The Constitution guarantees the states equal representation in the United States Senate, a state basis for selecting members of the United States House of Representatives, and state roles in the electoral college and the process of constitutional amendment. Some constitutional provisions make a direct grant of authority to the state governments, while others protect the states by assuring their citizens a role in making important decisions for the national government. The use of states as the electoral units for the House, Senate, and Presidency allow leading politicians in each state to exact promises from national candidates in exchange for their own campaign support. Insofar as the officials of leading cities have some influence over their state's political party (Chicago's late Mayor Richard Daley is the best example in recent years), this consultative role of state leaders in national politics also serves the interests of the cities.

Formal constitutional provisions merely set the stage for the protection of state and local interests within the Federal structure. A series of laws, customs, and political institutions provides the detailed bulwarks for state interests. The national government supported the activities of state and local governments with financial assistance totaling $53 billion in 1975. These programs are not simply imposed on the states. They are offered under terms that Congress defines as a result of consultations with the officials of state and local governments, and they are administered by procedures that are tolerable to most state officials and their friends in Congress.

Prominent, but extralegal, bulwarks of state governments are the political parties and "civil societies" that use state institutions to pursue or protect their goals. The American party system has state roots.[3] The 50 state parties are the key elements in national party structures. Members of the House and Senate and Presidential candidates owe political obligations to the leaders of state party organizations. Candidates' financial support comes from state party organizations. Presidential candidates gain their party nominations in state

---

[2]Martin Landau, "Baker v. Carr and the Ghost of Federalism," in Charles Cnudde and Deane E. Neubauer, eds., *Empirical Democratic Theory* (Chicago: Markham, 1969), p. 135.

[3]Morton Grodzins, "American Political Parties and the American System," *Western Political Quarterly*, 13 (December 1960), pp. 974-998; and Daniel J. Elazar, *American Federalism: A View from the States* (New York: Thomas Y. Crowell).

primaries and national conventions that are governed by the leaders of state parties. The national party offers few tangible incentives for state cooperation and holds no formal sanction over state recalcitrants. Some governors campaign openly in opposition to national party leaders, and some members of Congress compile voting records sharply at odds with their party's President. National Democrats have a problem with Southern conservatives who vote and campaign against their social, labor, and economic policies. In the fall of 1964 Barry Goldwater had to campaign against prominent state Republicans in New York, Illinois, and Michigan.

State populations show their loyalty to localities and regions in the face of outside pressure. This is most pronounced in the South, where state officials and private citizens responded in concert against Federal statutes and administrative "guidelines" that require racial integration. State officers and citizen groups in all regions seek Federal contracts for industries, Federal expenditures on military installations or public works, and national recognition of state historical celebrations and scenic attractions. These efforts involve chambers of commerce, elected officials of state and local governments, members of Congress, and individual business executives.

A feature that heightens the importance of the states in the Federal structure is the mixture of government responsibilities. There is no important domestic activity that is handled or financed solely by the Federal, state, or local governments. The fields that consume most domestic expenditures—education, highways, welfare, health, natural resources, public safety—are funded with a combination of Federal grants or loans and state and local taxes or service charges, and they are staffed partly by the personnel of national, state, and local governments. This means that national and local authorities must take account of state preferences in virtually all major policy decisions.

. . .

The states are not alone. They all draw sizable funds from the United States Treasury, and almost all state agencies receive some directives from the national government. Extensive Federal aid to state and local governments came with the Depression. It grew from $232 million in 1932 to $945 million in 1940, and it has continued growing to $60.5 billion in 1977.

Even for a partisan of the states, it is necessary to concede that the national government helps a great deal. Yet portions of the Federal help are arbitrary in their design and misallocated in their administration; in some programs, Federal agencies generate major problems for state officials and citizens. It is easy to exaggerate the role of the national government. One of the great ironies in Federal-state relations is that both ultraliberal critics of the state governments and ultraconservative advocates of states rights argue that Washington has more control over the states than is actually the case. For the liberal, the national government is responsible for much of what is good about the states. For the conservative, the national government chokes any state efforts at individuality or creativity. Both partisans are wrong. There is much slippage in Washington's control over the grants-in-aid programs. State officials have important influence over the programs' design and implementation. Even in the programs with reputations for rigid central control, the states have shown creative efforts in their own policies.

Virtually all major Federal grants-in-aid borrowed heavily from the experiments of state governments. Numerous state universities antedate Federal acts for the support of land-grant colleges; there was an extensive system of limited access highways before the Interstate and Defense Highway Act; the Office of Economic Opportunity took important cues from projects funded by the Ford Foundation in conjunction with New York and North Carolina; 10 states provided old-age pensions by 1930—5 years before Old Age Assistance came with the United States Social Security Act.[4]

One critic of Federal programs writes that they emphasize glamorous additions to basic programs funded with state money, and that the Federal contributions are puffed up in their importance by public relations.

> Some . . . have had the impression that highways are built mostly with Federal dollars. This impression may be, in part, the result of effective public relations. Most states take it for granted that the taxpayers, seeing grading and paving machines and new roads, assume the state gasoline tax is at work. But the Federal government doesn't risk such assumptions. For every road built or improved, the state or the contractor must erect a sign proclaiming "Your Highway Taxes at Work" in eight-inch block letters, with the amounts of the funds from each government, and other information as required by Act of Congress . . . and spelled out by almost ten pages of guidelines. It is a small matter, but worth noting, that the signs applauding the work must be 6 feet by 13 feet when the Federal funds are 90 percent . . . but only 4 feet by 8 feet when the Federal funds are 50 percent of the costs . . . All state schools must comply with the sign requirements, and even a little church college has to put the congregations in the back pews and post a red, white, and blue sign if it received Federal money under the Higher Education Facilities Act . . . It is proper to remember, however, for all the advantages brought by the extras, the train was put on the track in the first place by the states, and continues to be moved by state fuel and engineers.[5]

Some states play their own public relations game with the Federally required signs. When the University of Georgia put the necessary red, white, and blue signs outside the projects being supported with Federal money, it attached a small sign: "This sign imposed on the State of Georgia by requirements of the U.S. Department of Health, Education, and Welfare."

The Federal programs are charged with more serious deficiencies than upstaging the states in public relations. A whole set of problems results from the variety of different programs with overlapping target groups. Without any effective means of coordination, state officials face certain frustration in their efforts to develop programs that cut across the boundaries of different Federal activities. Related programs are supported by different agencies of the same Cabinet Department or by agencies in different Cabinet Departments.

---

[4]James T. Patterson, *The New Deal and the States: Federalism in Transition* (Princeton, N.J.: Princeton University Press, 1969), chap. 1.

[5]Terry Sanford, *Storm over the States* (New York: McGraw-Hill, 1967), pp. 62-63.

The President's budget for 1977 lists education funds amounting to $18.2 billion divided among the activities of all 11 Cabinet Departments, the Library of Congress, 2 units in the Executive Office of the President, and 11 independent offices. The Federal government sponsors coordinating mechanisms at the levels of state governments and metropolitan areas, and it has established coordinating committees for the Federal departments and agencies in Washington and regional offices. Yet there remain serious problems of Federal units that seem bent on avoiding any compromise of their own missions for the sake of coordination and surplus of coordinating mechanisms that beg for coordination among themselves. The coordinators need a coordinator.

> If the community-level coordinating structures . . . are left to the sponsorship of individual Federal agencies, it is doubtful that any of them will prove effective in knitting together in the communities the programs of many Federal agencies . . .
>
> The facts of bureaucratic life are that no Cabinet department has ever been able to act effectively, for long, as a central coordinator of other departments of equal rank that are its competitors for authority and funds. Nor does coordination spring readily from the mutual adjustment of Cabinet-level equals within the Federal hierarchy.[6]

Federal programs also impose arbitrary procedures on state recipients and evade the stickiest issues in the activities they help to finance. Public assistance programs are notorious for the inequities between state welfare programs that they encourage, and the highway programs leave the states to absorb the inevitable tensions produced by route selection and the uprooting of business and population . . .

Any inquiry into the accomplishments, problems, and opportunities of state governments must recognize that they are not solely responsible for each failure or success. They are enmeshed in numerous and complex relationships with the national government on one side and with their local governments on the other side. Federal relationships offer money and technical assistance to state governments and impose program requirements and obligations that narrow the range in which state officials can design their own activities. There are hardly any state programs of importance that are free from the resources or the demands of other government authorities. Some of what is wrong or right with state programs should properly be blamed or credited to other governments.

---

[6]James L. Sundquist, *Making Federalism Work* (Washington: Brookings, 1969), p. 244.

Thinking It Over

1. Be honest now, isn't it the case that you know a lot more about the Congress than you do your state legislature? If that be so, wouldn't it be better for you if the Congress held onto its policy-making authority?

2. What is meant by the observation that the states are the "laboratories" of the federal system?

26.
21 OR ELSE MANDATE ANGERS STATES
by Elaine S. Knapp

Setting the Scene: Most of you reading this cannot buy a beer in a bar even though you are adult, voting-age citizens. Elaine Knapp will explain to you why that is so. It is a story of blackmail—federal blackmail. But it also explains a lot about the kind of federalism that falls through the cracks. This brand of federalism has almost nothing to do with the Constitution and almost everything to do with political power.

State officials are angry with the congressional ultimatum to raise the drinking age to 21 or lose highway funds. Even supporters of a higher drinking age resent the federal "blackmail." There is talk of opposing the federal mandate and predictions that the heavy federal hand will make it difficult to raise the age in some states.

Still, it is felt that the loss of federal funds will be too great for many states not to act.

The 27 states with lower drinking ages could lose 5 percent of their federal highway funds in fiscal 1986 and 10 percent in fiscal 1987. Withheld funds would be released once a state raised its drinking age, however.

The measure slid quickly through Congress despite protests from state officials over the federal pre-emption of state power. The federal proposal was termed a "drastic pre-emption of state authority" by the chairman of The Council of State Governments (CSG), acting on behalf of CSG's Executive Committee. North Dakota Rep. Roy Hausauer, in a letter to the chief sponsor of the bill in the Senate, wrote that state officials strongly opposed the bill "as a misuse of federal spending power through the grant-in-aid system. In an era in which we expected to see more authority returned to the states, and in which more states are imposing tougher sanctions for drunk driving, federal preemption in this area is especially inappropriate."

New York Sen. John J. Marchi, a CSG Executive Committee member, wrote U.S. Senate Majority Leader Howard Baker that although the objective of reducing highway deaths was laudable, the use of "legislative blackmail" was not.

The U.S. Senate, preferring the stick to the carrot, rejected a substitute measure to provide incentives for states that set the drinking age at 21. The majority disregarded the plea of U.S. Sen. Gordon J. Humphrey, R-N.H., who asked, "Where do we stop enlarging the power of the federal government and protect the sovereignty of the states?" . . .

Laws in 23 states provide for a 21-year-old drinking age for all alcoholic beverages. Another eight states and the District of Columbia have combination drinking ages, generally 21 for distilled spirits and 18 to 19 for beer and wine. The drinking age is 20 in four states, 19 in 12 states and 18 in three others.

Many states lowered the drinking age in the 1970s, influenced by a constitutional amendment giving 18-year-olds the right to vote and by the Vietnam War in which 18-year-olds fought and died.

The trend in recent years, spurred by the movement against drunk driving, has been to raise the drinking age. From 1976 to 1983, 21 states raised their drinking ages (to 19, 20 or 21). Four states—Arizona, Nebraska, Rhode Island and Tennessee—passed minimum 21-year-old drinking ages in 1984 sessions. Rhode Island's and Tennessee's laws took effect this year; the rest take effect in 1985. The drinking age was raised to 21 by 1983 sessions in Alaska, Delaware, New Jersey and Oklahoma. A 1982 Maryland law will gradually raise the drinking age until it reaches 21 on July 1, 1985. . . .

The quick passage of the federal bill caught even supporters off guard. The measure moved swiftly through Congress after being attached to a $5 billion highway bill (H.R. 5504) by U.S. Rep. James J. Howard, D-N.J. Rep. Howard, chairman of the House Public Works and Transportation Committee, a decade ago played a key role in legislation that likewise penalized states unless they passed a 55 mph speed limit.

After the amendment sailed through the House on a voice vote June 7, President Reagan reversed his position and supported the bill. Previously, the administration has argued that the law would be more effectively enforced if states acted voluntarily. However, June 13, Secretary of Transportation Elizabeth Hanford Dole announced administration support for the legislation. She said that state "momentum appears to have stalled," noting that efforts to raise the drinking age to 21 failed in many states this year. According to the U.S. DOT, bills were introduced but failed to pass in 17 states to set a minimum age of 21. Bills are still pending in Louisiana and Massachusetts.

Rather than approve the House-passed highway bill, the Senate passed the drinking age provision as an amendment to a child restraint bill (H.R. 4616). The measure, sponsored by Sen. Frank R. Lautenberg, D-N.J., passed 81 to 16 on June 26. The Senate added provisions to increase highway safety funds by up to 5 percent for states that enact specified mandatory sentences for drunk drivers. States will be eligible if they mandate a 90-day license suspension and two days in jail or 100 hours of community service on a first offense: a one-year license suspension and 10 days in jail on a second offense; a three-year license suspension and 120 days in jail on third offense, and a 30-day jail sentence for conviction of driving on a suspended, revoked or restricted license. The House gave final congressional approval to the bill June 28 . . .

So-called "blood borders" which teenagers cross to legally buy liquor are a primary target of the federal legislation. Sen. Lautenberg said New Jersey had a problem "known as border-slaughter, because our neighboring state of New York as a lower legal minimum." The presidential commission concluded only a uniform drinking age would solve the problem of teenagers crossing state lines to drink. U.S. Sen. Richard G. Lugar, R-Ind., cited the recent defeat of a "21 bill" by the New York Legislature as evidence "that not all states will act on their own." He declared, "Surely the national interest in protecting the lives of our young people outweighs the states' interest in setting a drinking age lower than 21 years."

The Coalition of Northeast Governors (CONEG) had resolved in December to work for a regional uniform minimum drinking age. The minimum age is 21 in New Jersey, Pennsylvania and Rhode Island, but is 20 in Connecticut, Massachusetts, and New Hampshire, and 19 in New York. A major lobbying effort by New York Gov. Mario Cuomo failed to push through a higher age limit this session, however. A poll of CONEG states in mid-June showed concern with "pre-emption and the withholding of federal monies" under the federal measure. . . .

Both congressional sponsors denied the federal legislation was a mandate to states. Sen. Lautenberg and Rep. Howard called their measures a means "to encourage" states to raise their minimum drinking age to 21. Rep. Howard said his amendment "allows each state to make its own determination on whether to raise the drinking age," and then face the loss of federal funds if it did not. Sen. Lautenberg said it was "the same approach taken to enforce the 55 mph speed limit." Acknowledging the bill was "strong medicine" and that he was reluctant to deny federal aid to states, Sen. Lautenberg concluded it was necessary to save lives. The parallel with the 55 mph national speed limit was also cited by U.S. Rep. Glenn Anderson, D-Calif., who said the approach was effective because sanctions have not been used yet.

Loss of federal funds in one program for inaction in another area is called a "crossover" sanction. This method was also used to force states to adopt billboard controls as required by the 1965 Highway Beautification Act. However, the DOT did not threaten states with loss of aid until several years after the 1968 deadline for compliance. Only South Dakota lost federal highway funds over the billboard issue. . . .

Crossover sanctions are viewed as severe remedies and, further, make states angry. Implementation of them can run into political trouble for federal agencies. For instance, Congress took away the power of the National Highway Traffic Safety Administration to withhold aid from states without motorcycle helmet laws.

The possibility of further federal intrusion into state responsibilities was raised by U.S. DOT Secretary Dole July 11. She said that the choice might be between mandatory state seat belt legislation and a federal requirement for air bags in motor vehicles . . .

The federal drinking age measure is viewed by state officials as another pre-emption of state authority. However, state officials have mixed feelings. Many agree with the concept of a 21-year-old drinking age or with at least a uniform drinking age. The disagreement is with the federal method to achieve it. The use of federal sanctions is seen as a big federal stick by states. For many, the issue is not the merit of a higher drinking age, but roughshod misuse of federal power. . . .

Iowa has turned down a 21-year-old drinking age five times since 1972, noted Speaker Don Avenson. However, the vote was close this past session in the House. The 1984 session did pass a tough drunk driving law, including a provision to revoke the license of drivers under age 19 who drink and drive. The pressure to raise the drinking age has been building, Speaker Avenson said, fueled by statistics of alcohol-related deaths among young drivers. However, the feeling was the persons with the responsibility of adulthood at age 18 ought also to have the privileges of adulthood.

As far as the federal law is concerned, Speaker Avenson said that most legislators were relieved that the political decision was taken out of their hands, but were angry at the federal pre-emption of state powers. "Personally, I am very upset," Speaker Avenson said. "I am tired of federal mandates in areas I believe the constitution reserves to the states." Iowa most likely will pass the 21-year-old drinking age within the next two years, he predicted.

Likewise, mandatory seat belts will eventually be required by the state, but similar federal pressure would not help passage, he said. "These pre-emptions can only go on so long before there's a backlash," the speaker concluded. . . .

The mood now in Wyoming is not to raise the minimum age, said Rep. Patrick H. Meenan. Saying he was "appalled" by the federal mandate, Rep. Meenan declared that raising the drinking age was not the issue, but the "federal government sticking its nose in state" affairs was. "I was surprised; it seems contrary to everything Reagan said he would do, as far as states' rights," Rep. Meenan said of the federal sanctions.

Wyoming legislators have defeated bills to raise the drinking age from 19 which is also the age of majority there. Other arguments were that a higher drinking age would deny jobs to youth in restaurants and lounges and that it is better to have youth drink in licensed places "than out on the prairie." Neither did Wyoming legislators feel a higher age would reduce highway deaths, because 21- to 24-year-old drivers are more of a problem. Rep. Meenan noted that there was quite a bit of sentiment to raise the drinking age, due to concern over drunk driving. However, the state did further tighten its drunk driving laws. He noted that the U.S. DOT lobbied hard for a higher age in Wyoming and other states, and speculates that the DOT focused its efforts in Congress after states refused to go along with it.

"Everyone talks bravely" now about not going along, but that could change as the loss of federal funds nears, Rep. Meenan acknowledged. Still, he wonders "what would happen if all states told them to jump in the lake."

Georgia House Speaker Thomas B. Murphy called the federal measure a "form of blackmail." He sees the recent action by DOT Secretary Dole as another move to "blackmail the states into passing mandatory seat belts." Speaker Murphy said, "If Congress cannot accomplish something, it blackmails the states into doing it." Speaker Murphy predicted that most states, including Georgia, would raise the drinking age rather than lose millions in highway funds. A bill to raise the drinking age from 19 to 21 in Georgia failed to get out of committee in the 1984 session. "I was opposed to it," the speaker declared. He noted that 18-year-olds were old enough to fight for their country, inherit and buy property, but "can't spend 75 cents on a beer."

In Virginia, where a measure to raise the legal age for beer from 19 failed this session, Gov. Charles S. Robb, a proponent of the higher age, called the federal action coercive. "There are states' rights issues involved," Gov. Robb said. An opponent of the higher age, Virginia Sen. Peter K. Babalas, said the state would not "have much choice if we want federal highway funds."

Thinking It Over

1. The Supreme Court has upheld the right of the federal government to use "cross-over" sanctions. Try to construct in your own mind the kind of argument it used.

2. Is there any way the reserved powers clause which is a part of the Constitution can be squared with the use of cross-over sanctions which are not found in the Constitution?

27.
NEW FEDERALISM: INTERGOVERNMENTAL REFORM FROM NIXON TO REAGAN
by Timothy J. Conlan

Setting the Scene: Two of the last four Presidents we have elected have had a kind of "new federalism" in the core of their domestic agenda. This is no small potatoes. Both Richard Nixon and Ronald Reagan were deeply committed to adjusting the balance of power in favor of the states and doing so in fundamental measure. They were in office for 14 of the 20 years between 1968 and 1988 and both were overwhelmingly reelected after their first four years. If there is no new federalism in the 1990s, it isn't as though it hasn't been tried.

It has been argued since Aristotle that genuine democracy can flourish only in small political entities. . . . Thus Montesquieu argued in the mid-eighteenth century that "it is natural for a republic to have only a small territory." His arguments were well known to leading American colonists at the time of the Revolution, and antifederalist opponents of the federal Constitution used them to justify their own passionate views. Men like Patrick Henry, Luther Martin, and Richard Henry Lee were against the creation of a stronger national government because they thought that it would be a threat to individual liberty and to the survival of the states.

These arguments were ultimately rejected by those attending the Constitutional Convention and by the states that ratified the Constitution. Yet the practical and philosophical merits of small versus large governments and the proper balance of power and authority between the federal government and the states have remained concerns throughout American history. . . .

With their New Federalism initiatives, both Nixon and Reagan revived these old questions. . . .

There are, in short, at least three answers to the question, "Why New Federalism?" A coherent program of decentralization was a plausible policy response to real and contemporary problems of governmental management and performance. It also provided a solution that reinforced natural partisan predispositions and was grounded in a long philosophical tradition.

Yet . . . the New Federalism programs of Nixon and Reagan, and the political reactions to them, were as different as they were alike. Those differences reveal much about the nature of contemporary American politics—both about the framework of ideas that organize the political agenda and give rise to specific policies and about the structure of political interests and institutions that constitute the policymaking system.

At the philosophical level, although Nixon and Reagan shared a belief that the federal government had grown too large and influential and that local decisionmaking is generally preferable to national, they differed fundamentally in their beliefs about the desirable ends of decentralization and the role of the public sector. Although actions do not always follow rhetoric and every administration's policies are diverse and evolving, the policies of their administrations proved consistent, on the whole, with their philosophies.

Nixon was deeply suspicious of the federal bureaucracy and the national policymaking system, which he thought was dominated by "iron triangles" of congressional committees, federal agencies, and interest groups. His New Federalism policies were designed in part to disrupt this system. Overall, however, Nixon viewed his federalism strategy as a means of improving and strengthening government, especially at the state and local levels. It was not a path toward dismantling it. Time and again he argued that the American people were "fed up with government that doesn't deliver" and that New Federalism reforms were needed to "close the gap between promise and performance."[1] Improved governmental efficiency and management were part of his solution, to "make government run better at less cost."[2] Since the main problem in the system was thought to be an overextended federal government, he also prescribed decentralization. Yet if the goal of improved performance required nationalizing certain shared or local functions—such as welfare or environmental regulation—in order to rationalize the financing and delivery of public services, Nixon accepted that conclusion.

Nixon's New Federalism reforms were therefore presented as a program for strengthening government and making it more active and creative. . . . Programs like revenue sharing and block grants were designed to reward and promote governmental activism and problem solving at state and local levels, and to give such governments "a new sense of responsibility." As President Nixon put it, "If we put more power in more places, we can make government more creative in more places."[3] . . .

Reagan, in contrast, has viewed New Federalism as part of a broader strategy to reduce the role of government in society at every level. The major focus of his retrenchment program, of course, has been the federal government, and his rhetoric on this score has often been extreme. "We need relief from the oppression of big government," he told an assembly of state legislators in 1981, and went on to lay out his proposal for restoring balance to the federal system. Unlike Nixon, he made no mention of rationalizing roles and responsibilities and encouraging the renaissance of state and local creativity and activism. Instead, balance was to be achieved by purely negative means—by enhancing state and local governments in relative terms, by pruning their resources less drastically than at the federal level. "We're strengthening federalism by cutting back on the activities of the Federal government," he told the legislators.[4] He argued, in short, that a reduced role for the federal government would

---

[1] Statement on signing the State and Local Fiscal Assistance Act, October 20, 1972. Quoted in "Nixon Goal: A Leaner but Stronger Government," *National Journal*, December 16, 1972, p. 1911.

[2] Interview with the *Evening Star* and *Washington Daily News*, November 9, 1972, in ibid.

[3] Quoted in "New Federalism II: Philosophy—Great Society Failures, conservative Approach to Government Underlie New Federalism Drive," *National Journal*, December 16, 1972, p. 1916.

[4] Reagan, "National Conference of State Legislature," pp. 834-35.

by itself mean an enhanced role for state and local governments.

Far from encouraging states and localities to step in to fill the void left by federal tax and budget cuts, the Reagan administration focused many of its most severe budget cuts on programs that subsidized activism at the state and local levels. In one of the most pointed and ironic contrasts with his Republican predecessor, Reagan even urged that general revenue sharing—which had been the programmatic heart of Nixon's New Federalism—be eliminated. Reagan subsequently denounced state efforts to raise the taxes needed to replace these budget cuts and to assume new responsibilities—despite earlier assurances that his revenue policies were designed to create "tax room" for states.[5] . . .

Reagan's positive vision, though heavily localistic, lacks a strong role for government of any kind. His quest for community entails "an end to giantism, for a return to the human scale." This is not the scale of local government, but "the scale of the local fraternal lodge, the church organization, the block club, the farm bureau"—in short, the scale of the private association.[6] It is this vision of private communal action that spurred the administration to emphasize "voluntarism, the mobilization of private groupings to deal with our social ills." Ronald Reagan's strategy was precisely what he detailed in his first economic message to Congress: "we leave to private initiative all the functions that individuals can perform privately," and only reluctantly turn to states and localities to address public needs, with federal action as a last resort.

. . .

Paradoxical Politics

The political responses to the reform initiatives of Nixon and Reagan and the political coalitions both administrations constructed to achieve their goals differed as much as their objectives. Paradoxically, the activist and nationally oriented Nixon was overwhelmed by the centrifugal parochialism and fragmentation of the 1970s. In contrast, Reagan, the antigovernment crusader, won crucial victories through his mastery of national politics.

Nixon proposed a coherent and internally consistent program of federalism reform. Nonetheless, Congress addressed the proposal in a segmented and individualized fashion, as can be seen in the treatment of Nixon's block grants. The political responses to these proposals were based principally on the attitudes and interests within each policy subsystem. The pattern of idiosyncratic politics was repeated across the entire range of Nixon's reform agenda. General revenue sharing, for example, failed to arouse the kind of congressional unanimity that greeted most of the president's block grant proposals within each policy area. Rather, GRS caused sharp divisions within Congress that cut across party lines. . . . The politics of the family assistance plan were different again, although cross-party cleavages were present here too. In the House, FAP attracted broad bipartisan support, largely in deference to the president and the influential chairman and ranking member of the Ways and Means Committee. In the Senate, however, FAP twice collapsed when conservatives and

---

[5]See Ronald Reagan, fund-raising letter on behalf of the Republican Governors Association/Republican National Committee, n.d., p. 3.

[6]Quoted in Schambra, "Progressive Liberalism," p. 47.

liberals joined forces to fight its provisions for precisely the opposite reasons.

The politics of Reagan's New Federalism evolved in two distinct phases, each characterized by a far higher degree of policy interdependence than was evident in the 1970s. The first phase was marked by the president's budget and tax victories of 1981. In that single year, the fragmented subsystem politics that colored Nixon's reform efforts gave way to a highly visible, majoritarian style of presidential policy leadership as Reagan successfully constructed a partisan-conservative phalanx that pushed much of his fiscal policy through Congress more or less intact. The highly polarized and unified partisan coalitions in Congress proved critical in key votes on the president's program, and the overall levels of party voting in Congress remained high throughout the 1980s. This greater degree of political interdependence was reinforced by new budgetary procedures that served to integrate diverse spending and authorization issues on the president's terms. . . .

This pattern did not continue past 1981, for several reasons. With the control of congress divided between the Democrats in the House and Republicans in the Senate, Reagan lacked the political resources needed to build majority coalitions on a strictly partisan basis, and the situation merely grew worse after the 1982 elections. Moreover, Congress had arguably made the "easiest" fiscal decisions in 1981, so that the president found it far more difficult to hold his coalition together when the highly controversial proposals of subsequent years came up for debate.

In addition, that coalition itself was unstable. Although the party-building activities of the Republicans in the late 1970s contributed to the president's victory, their new-found strength was short-lived, even in the Senate. To complicate matters, the president's first-year success in the House was due in part to the very atomization that characterized Congress in the late 1970s. As Steven Smith has argued, the policymaking implications of Congress's fragmentation into semiautonomous committees and subcommittees are quite different from those of extreme individualization, even though legislative decentralization is being promoted in both cases.[7] Depending on the degree of subcommittee proliferation and autonomy, the politics within this committee framework retains elements of the functional insulation and stability that characterized the earlier, oligarchical Congress. . . .

Although Reagan's majoritarian style of leadership lost effectiveness after 1981, intergovernmental policymaking did not return to the fragmented patterns of the 1970s. Rather, by institutionalizing a "new politics of deficits,"[8] the fiscal policies adopted in 1981 ushered in a new phase of rationalizing politics, as the domestic policy agenda became preoccupied with the fiscal, institutional, and policy consequences of the 1981 initiatives. Opportunities and incentives for new entrepreneurial initiatives were reduced and redirected as zero-sum budgeting created new patterns of policy interdependence. The numbers of new laws introduced and passed declined, and those proposed and adopted have been restructured by the new policymaking environment.

---

[7]Steven S. Smith, "New Patterns of Decisionmaking in Congress," in John E. Chubb and Paul E. Peterson, eds., *The New Direction in American Politics* (Brookings, 1985), pp. 203-34.

[8]Paul E. Peterson, "The Politics of Deficits," in Chubb and Peterson, eds., *New Direction in American Politics*, pp. 365-97.

The Ironies of Reform

The New Federalism initiatives of Nixon and Reagan both left ironic legacies that changed the direction not only of the federal system but also of American politics and policy in general. Richard Nixon sought to simplify and streamline intergovernmental relations and to produce a more decentralized and rationalized federal system than the one he inherited. Yet he left behind a system of massive intergovernmental interdependence and institutionalized new and higher levels of federal fiscal and regulatory dominance. Ronald Reagan enjoyed more success in his efforts to refocus the policy agenda and accomplish desired changes in policy direction. Yet he, too, will leave behind a legacy of support for governmental activism nationwide.

In his efforts to reduce the size and activity of the welfare state, Reagan has accomplished more than most analysts thought likely when he entered office. Federal spending priorities, popular expectations, and the federal policymaking environment have all been substantially altered during the Reagan presidency. Since 1980 nondefense discretionary spending has declined by 29 percent as a proportion of GNP, and general federal revenues are down 13 percent. Entitlement growth as a percentage of GNP has been limited to just 5 percent during this period, and federal aid to state and local governments has been reduced by one-fourth. As a result, federal grants as a percentage of total federal outlays and as a percent of state and local outlays have declined in importance . . . .

In some respects, however, the welfare state is stronger today as a result. Just as the New Deal helped save capitalism from its own worst excesses, so Reagan's agenda has trimmed questionable programs and answered concerns about governability and uncontrolled governmental growth. As a result, the underpinnings of popular support for the welfare state are in some ways stronger today than when Ronald Reagan took office. Americans have always been ambivalent toward governmental activism. At one level, they hold the views of "ideological conservatives" who are suspicious of governmental authority in the abstract, while at another level they are "operational liberals" who pragmatically support a broad range of government programs to address social problems.[9] According to opinion polls, the first set of conservative attitudes gained ascendancy in the early 1980s, thereby generating the plausible if simplistic belief that Reagan had received a popular mandate for his domestic policies. By 1986, however, American public opinion had reverted to older patterns of broad support for governmental spending, and polls indicated that Americans no longer supported substantial budget cuts in virtually any area of domestic policy. Indeed, recent research on Americans' confidence in public and private institutions indicates that, thanks in large part to Ronald Reagan, confidence in the federal government has rebounded more strongly than for any other major institution in society.[10]

Thus, depending on uncertainties surrounding the economy and a viable deficit reduction

---

[9]Lloyd Free and Hadley Cantril, *The Political Beliefs of Americans: A Study of Public Opinion* (New Brunswick, N.J.: Rutgers University Press, 1967), p. 180.

[10]Seymour Martin Lipset and William Schneider, "The Confidence Gap during the Reagan Years, 1981-1987," *Political Science Quarterly,* vol. 102 (Spring 1987), p. 21.

process, Reagan has apparently squeezed much of what is likely to be extracted from the American welfare state, producing at best a stable and somewhat lower public sector share of the economy. Much of what remains is now firmly institutionalized.[11] Given politicians' relentless search for new and creative program initiatives to deal with contemporary problems, however, even this achievement may ultimately prove to be only a temporary interregnum in the long-term growth of American government.

Thinking It Over

1. What is the fundamental difference between the new federalism of Richard Nixon and Ronald Reagan?

2. After reading Conlan's article, is it fair to ask if the states really *want* more extensive responsibility in the federal system?

---

[11]See John E. Chubb, "Federalism and the Bias for Centralization," in Chubb and Peterson, eds., *New Direction in American Politics,* pp. 273-306.

28.
CRAZY-QUILT FEDERALISM
by W. John Moore

Setting the Scene: Local governments are creatures of the states. Yet the public services we receive from government are very often delivered at the local level. In this article, W. John Moore deals with the inherent problems that arise when local governments are *in competition* with the state governments for federal money and when state governments can simply mandate functions to the localities without providing the funds to pay for them. The localities have no protection whatever in the federal Constitution yet they are critical to our democracy. Most textbooks in American government discuss federalism in terms of "picket fences" and "layer cakes." Reading this piece you'll understand why Moore believes the proper term is "crazy quilt."

Across the street from the capitol in Sacramento, about 300 country supervisors, local judges and sheriffs congregated on a warm night last summer in the old Crest theater. There they devised what they termed an "August assault" for getting more aid from the state. Trios of officials fanned out from the theater, badgering their state legislators about money for local courts.

Under legislation approved in 1987, California had agreed to an overhaul of the state's legal system that could save counties from paying $350 million annually for state trial courts. County officials had hoped to divert some of that money to county-provided services ranging from welfare to medical care. But controversial language in the law forces the 58 counties to share at least some of that money with California cities.

The rally was meant to highlight more than just another monetary dispute, according to Larry E. Naake, executive director of the County Supervisors Association of California. For years, Naake said, the state has justified a quick fix of the counties' financial needs rather than adopting a comprehensive reform package to sort out which chores shall be done by various levels of government. "This is not just a fiscal crisis, but a crisis in governance," Naake argued. "The tail end of federalism never reached down to the local level." . . .

Abandoned by Washington, many local officials have turned to the states. The local officials have an ambitious agenda. They want more money, fewer restrictions on taxes and spending and less-intrusive state regulatory requirements.

During an era in which state governments have enjoyed a dramatic renaissance as power has shifted away from Washington, city-state relations remain in flux. "We are on the brink of a period of significant change in the way state and local governments interact," the task force on state-local relations of the National Conference of State Legislatures (NCSL) concluded in a 1987 report. . . .

Although federal aid to both states and localities declined by 37 per cent in real terms from 1980-87, the biggest cuts came in local programs. The $6.9 billion general revenue sharing program of 1980 was shelved in 1986. Urban development action grants fell from $675 million in 1980 to $215 million in 1988, and that program's demise is expected soon. Federal community development block grants fell from about $4 billion to $2.9 billion over the same eight years.

The states did not have the financial wherewithal to replace all the federal money. Nor did many state officials feel that a specific cutback in a program such as general revenue sharing should coerce the states into filling the void. "Our philosophy is that we are not here to bail out the federal government," said Michigan Treasurer Robert A. Bowman. "We have our own budget to balance."

But some states are contributing. Census Bureau figures show that total state spending jumped 7.4 per cent from fiscal 1986-87, to $456 billion. (The rate of growth in state spending was down slightly from the 8.5 per cent average increase during the 1980s, however.)

"State aid to local government is growing every year," said Gerald H. Miller, executive director of the National Association of State Budget Officers in Washington. "There is no question about that." The association's latest survey showed that 15 states adopted spending or tax proposals to help local governments in fiscal 1988. California agreed to spend $15.3 million to stabilize counties' growing health and welfare costs. New Jersey provided $18 million to pay for county court costs. Utah will take over financing of local district courts. Vermont established a municipal and regional planning fund, financed by an increase in the state's property transfer tax. . . .

Through its legislative power, the state not only determines local government revenues, it also can require cities and towns to comply with a host of administrative, environmental and personnel regulations that cost local governments millions of dollars annually. Only rarely do the states reimburse local governments for complying with these mandates. As a result, the mandate question, mirroring a federal-state dispute on the same issue, has emerged as one of the bitterest state-local disputes. In Texas, for example, the state, raising the banner of economic development, has knocked down local impact fees and tough permit requirements. And some states also determine the number of hours and the amount of vacation time for some local employees, including fire fighters and police officers. . . .

More than 100 years ago, a crusty chief judge of the Iowa Supreme Court named John F. Dillon curtly dismissed the importance of cities and counties. Local governments, he held in an 1868 decision, are "mere tenants at the will of the legislature." He later enunciated his famous rule on intergovernmental relations in his *Commentaries on the Law of Municipal Corporations* (Little, Brown & Co., 1911, fifth edition). Any powers not explicitly given to cities and towns are retained by state government, he wrote.

Not every state government follows Dillon's strict precepts. The growth of state advisory commissions on intergovernmental relations in the past several years suggests that both state and local officials understand that their relationship has changed because of Reagan Administration policies giving the states more power. But many states have their local governments on a short leash. A decade ago, New York had 11 statutes in 40 volumes containing 6,000 pages of requirements and directives for local governments. Forty-eight states restrict local governments' ability to raise revenues. Virtually every state government exercises control over local governments through costly and sometimes burdensome regulations. . . .

On the expenditure side of the equation, local governments are troubled by an increasing array of burdensome state mandates that have forced cities and towns to spend millions on everything from garbage disposal to workers' compensation. Many of these state mandates undoubtedly promote public health and safety, city officials acknowledged, but the unexpected costs can ruin local budgets. When New Jersey blocked communities in Essex County from dumping garbage in a landfill near the Meadowlands sports complex, local governments responded by shipping the garbage out of state. Pamela E. Goldstein, a spokesman for Newark Mayor Sharpe James, said disposal costs skyrocketed from $26 to $106 per ton, upping Newark's annual garbage costs from $6 million to $30 million in fiscal 1988.

In their fulminations against state mandates, mayors and county supervisors echoed the usual complaints voiced by state leaders about expensive directives from Washington. In recent years, for example, the Illinois legislature has reduced local property tax rates by increasing the homestead exemption, increased local employee pension requirements and demanded that cities and counties engage in collective bargaining with their employees.

"The problem is that when the legislature runs out of money to do good things, they tend to do good things with laws," said Donald A. Slater, executive director of the League of Minnesota Cities. "Local government must then execute those good things without being compensated for them." For example, Slater noted, Minnesota's 1983 comparable worth statue requires that men and women employees be paid the same salaries for similar jobs. State officials, he said, estimated that the law, whose penalty provisions took effect this year, will cost local governments 2-3 per cent of annual payroll costs. Slater estimated that compliance costs will more likely be in the 5 per cent range. With payroll costs accounting for up to 70 per cent of a municipality's budget and the penalty for noncompliance being a reduction in state aid, the comparable worth statute "is not a toothless tiger," Slater added.

Local officials have long hoped that state laws requiring cities and counties to be reimbursed by the state for implementing new mandates would help local government finances. But most of the states have simply ducked the requirements. And state courts in such key states as California have been reluctant to give mandate reimbursement provisions much legal punch.

Congress's General Accounting Office (GAO), in a September study, noted that 14 states have enacted such laws but that only California has appropriated significant sums ($144 million in fiscal 1987) to cover the costs of state mandates. In Florida, where mandate reimbursement has been law since 1978, the number of unfinanced mandates has increased, the GAO reported. "No state agency is in charge of enforcing the statute, no reimbursement policies or procedures have been established and no provisions are made for a local appeals process," the study said. And in Illinois, the General Assembly passed a mandate reimbursement law in 1979 but has enacted 57 mandates since then that have cost local governments $148 million, according to the GAO.

Despite the niggardly amounts of state aid to reimburse local governments, specialists in intergovernmental affairs, said that the state laws have probably deterred states from dumping costly new requirements on local governments. The real significance of these provisions, the Urban Institute's Shannon said, is not the amount of money that flows from the state to local governments but the fact that these laws "tend to slow down the proliferation of state mandates."

But Pumas County (Calif.) Supervisor Bill Coates scoffs at the notion that Sacramento has learned any important lessons from California's mandate reimbursement law. The battle over the trial court money has left a bitter taste in his mouth. Because of various state laws and regulations, the Northern California county can put only 7 per cent of its budget into discretionary spending, including police protection and libraries. The rest goes to pay for state-ordered programs. "It's like we've given them our checkbook," he complained. "Local citizens see their money spent on things they don't want, while the programs that are most critical to them are dying off."

Coates, who joined other local officials in the march on the capitol, said that more-drastic tactics are needed to convince California state legislators that the problem is serious. He supports a possible 1989 initiative that would bring county governments an extra half-cent of the state sales tax. And he wants to tighten the language in California's mandate reimbursement law.

To accomplish these feats, Coates and other officials are willing to make a Faustian pact with their longtime opponent, Paul Gann, a driving force behind Proposition 13. Coates said that their willingness to work with Gann demonstrates the intensity of the county officials' concerns. "We're getting tougher," he said, "and we intend to start a hell of a fight."

Thinking It Over

1. If you had it in your power, would you reverse "Dillon's Rule"? Why?

2. If you were rewriting the Constitution today, would you ignore local governments (in effect continuing their status as "creatures of the states") or would you give them standing in the federal Constitution? Explain.

29.
KENNEDY JUSTICE
by Victor S. Navasky

Setting the Scene: There is much in federalism that doesn't meet the eye. James Meredith's enrollment of the University of Mississippi will make all past and any future lines you stand in before a registration window seem like a piece of cake. This story takes place during the fall of 1962, seven years after the Supreme Court ordered the integration of public schools. The first black student at "Old Miss" is being registered. The officers in charge? Bobby Kennedy, the President's brother and the Attorney General of the United States, and the Governor of Mississippi, Ross Barnett. What follows are recorded phone conversations between the two. Bear in mind the problem is complex and depends on one's point of view. Bobby Kennedy is trying to get Mississippi to comply with a Supreme Court decision. He wants to make federalism work. Barnett's problem is to save face. He's got to *seem* like he's going down fighting. James Meredith would like to be able to attend class without getting shot. We pick up the conversation on Monday, September 17, as Kennedy and Barnett haggle over the *city* in which Meredith should register (Oxford, where the University is—or Jackson, the state capital) and the *day* (Thursday when everyone else registers) or Monday (when there aren't as many people around). You'll note Ross Barnett refers to Bobby Kennedy as "General" from time to time. That is the nickname Kennedy liked when he was "Attorney General."

[*Monday, September 17th.*]

AG: *If he comes to Jackson will he be registered?*

Gov.:   *It is up to the Trustees whether or not they will permit him to register. We have a constitutional Board of Trustees. They have the right to control and direct all of the activities of the university. It may be the majority will not permit him to register. I couldn't promise they will register him. He will have the same opportunities in Jackson as up there. His whole transcript of grades are here.*

AG: *On the time, should we work that out?*

Gov.:   *Yes, send another telegram saying that he may present himself at 3 o'clock tomorrow—2:30 or 3. The Board, you see, has the authority to decide those things. That is the matter conclusively. It is bound on the discretion of the Board of Trustees. That's my judgment about it.*
They are going to make a mistake if they go to Oxford. The Board of Trustees has decided they want him to present himself in Jackson. If he doesn't do what the Board says, it won't be our fault.

AG: *If he goes to Oxford, you won't take responsibility for his safety?*

Gov.:   *It will be in violation of the orders of the Board. These people are very peaceful. This thing is serious to the people in the South and all over the world. This thing—it has the whole nation upset. We have telegrams from California to Maine.*

> *You would be surprised at the sentiment on this thing.*
> *He's been notified where to come.*

AG: *How many students have they told to come to Jackson? Have telegrams been sent to other students?*

Gov.:   *I couldn't answer that. I know of one.*

The Kennedy response to James Meredith's lonely fight to integrate Ole Miss was typical of its general civil rights posture in a number of respects. First, there was never any doubt that the Kennedy Administration would be on the side of Meredith, on the side of integration. Second, it should be noted that what Kennedy Justice did was react, respond to a situation somebody else had created, and the response was delayed at that. Third, there was the long-drawn-out attempt to achieve through negotiation and mediation what the courts had already made mandatory by their orders. Fourth, policies were articulated in terms of . . . [a] theory of federalism which highlighted court orders. Fifth, despite the rhetorical adhesion to orderly legal process, if preserving the peace required informal pseudo-legal arrangements, there was no hesitation to make them. And finally, there was the introduction of troops, of force, only as a last resort.

The theory of federalism—which posited an elaborate system of deferences to state and local authority—was attractive to Attorney General Robert Kennedy not because it accorded with his understanding of history or the Constitution (although he undoubtedly came to believe that it did), but because it neatly reconciled the three codes of conduct by which the Department of Justice was governed in the kennedy era:

The code of the FBI, as we have already seen, posited the unavailability of the FBI and/or total self-determination over its deployment (and thereby limited the Justice Department's potential for flexible and creative response).

The code of the Kenndys . . . had principal relevance in the matter of priorities. Despite the lofty campaign promises, early Kennedy priorities put civil rights somewhere around the middle of the list—after organized crime, after Jimmy Hoffa, after anti-trust (although this soon fell to the back of the pack), after juvenile delinquency, but ahead of internal security, ahead of crime in the streets, ahead of such unglamorous fields as civil, lands and natural resources litigation.

And the code of the Ivy League Gentleman, which assumed that reasonable men can work everything out in due course.

"We came to see," Nicholas Katzenbach recalls, "that you could not on any level give the Southern Governors an excuse for not enforcing the law of the United States. It was our theory that if you take over the law enforcement from them, you won't be able to maintain it and they will abdicate. From this came the attempt to preserve the federal system until we could get through the idea that local officials have an obligation to enforce the law."

In other words, let George do it. George Wallace, that is, who vowed after an early electoral defeat to a segregationist opponent, "I'll never be outniggered again." Or Ross Barnett . . .

Tuesday, September 18, 1962. *The Attorney General agrees to ask Meredith to wait until the following Monday instead of registering on Thursday like everyone else.*

The Attorney General and Governor Ross Barnett, 12:30 p.m.

RFK: *Governor, how are you?*

Barnett: *Fine, General, how are you?*

RFK: *Governor, I had a representative of the Department talk to this boy's lawyer and he in turn talked to Meredith and he feels strongly that he would like to register at Oxford and it's our judgment that it is the best judgment.*

Barnett: *General, I think you're making a mistake there.*

RFK: *Well, I think it's up to the boy—*

Barnett: *It's up to him, I know.*

RFK: *The vast majority of the students are registering in Oxford and he doesn't feel he should do anything unusual. But I think you can provide for his safety, can you not?*

Barnett: *Of course, we will have to do that. We'll do that all right. What day now does he want to register?*

RFK: *Thursday.*

Barnett: *He wouldn't want to wait until Monday?*

RFK: *Next Monday? He would rather do it Thursday.*

Barnett: *They're going to have a lot of folks registering there Thursday. I'm trying to figure this thing out. From a psychological standpoint the atmosphere will be better, that's what I'm thinking about. They'll register all through next Monday.*

RFK: *Do you want me to take this up again? I will be glad to do that. If you want him to register Monday, I'll be glad—*

Barnett: *We insist that he come then. It would just save us a lot of trouble and it would be easier. I don't understand why he won't come here.*

RFK: *The students are registering at Oxford and he wants to register at Oxford.*

Barnett: *See if he will do this. See if—in other words, there are going to be a lot of them registering Thursday and most of them will go home Friday morning. Even if you try to have it that it could be Monday or even Saturday.*

RFK: *I'm going up to Massachusetts to vote, so I can give you a ring tomorrow morning. You would rather have him register Saturday or Monday? Let me go to work on that. I will try to do that later today.*

Barnett: *Friday would be better than Thursday.*

RFK: *Any day but Thursday?*

Barnett: *They're going to have such a gang up there at Ole Miss and a lot of them might resent it. General, some men here insist that he come to the Jackson State Office Building on the tenth floor where the Trustees meet. The registrar is here and he'll miss the whole crowd and it would be so much better for everybody. Frankly I think if you don't agree with me there is nothing—he'll just have to come up there.*

RFK: *I think he has considered it. Let me go over this again. First, we approached his lawyer and his lawyer said, "We want to go to Oxford." Then I told our attorney*

this is not a decision for the lawyer, this should be taken up with the boy. I didn't
talk to him myself.

Barnett: *You'll call me tomorrow morning?*

RFK: *I will talk to you tomorrow morning and see if we can move it to another day.*
Thank you, Governor.

Barnett: *Thank you, General. . . .*

[Ten days pass during which Meredith has been physically restrained by the Governor from registering at "Old Miss" as Barnett attempts one stalling tactic after another. There have been several showdowns on campus, the legislature has passed a law refusing Meredith's admission, and most importantly, a *federal* Court has cited Barnett with an injunction and issued a citation of contempt. Barnett is now caught betwen a rock (the federal Court) and a hard place (the poeple of Mississippi). Kennedy is suggesting it will go easier on him if Meredith is already registered when he goes to Court.]

Robert Kennedy and Governor Ross Barnett, September 27, 1962, 3:50 p.m.

Barnett: *General, I felt like I ought to call you back. What we talked about, General, it is*
something that I think this thing ought to wait until you send him back here. Why
can't you wait until Saturday morning? Here's the thing about it. We want the
people to subside a little bit.

RFK: *I think the problem for you, Governor, you will have that court case tomorrow and*
that's why your lawyers wanted it done today.

Barnett: *Can't you pass that case for a while?*

RFK: *They won't do that. You can't do that now.*

Barnett: *I think this case ought to be put off. I am honest with you.*

RFK: *I will call them back and we won't do it.* [Won't take Meredith to be registered.]

Barnett: *We better postpone this thing and some of the others will be in touch with you*
about this thing. Let's not have any misunderstanding. We can't afford to have
that. At five o'clock it's getting pretty dark down here.

RFK: *I think you are making a mistake on it. I think the problem on Saturday is going*
to be much more difficult. I think it is going to be much more difficult and your
situation before the courts will be more difficult. I think it is a great advantage
to do it today as your lawyers—

Barnett: *The people probably will find it out.* [That Barnett backed down because of the
Court]

RFK: *There's not going to be any mention of it from here.*

Barnett: *Certainly not here. Our conversations weren't taken down here.*

RFK: *You never had anything that's come out of this office and I never said I talked to*
you and I have never made one statement about you or anything to do with
Mississippi, so I think—

Barnett: *One man said, "You will all compromise in this thing?"*

onto the plan for radically different motives. This had the façade of compromise. Reagan, like Gramm, wanted the automatic slicer to chop Democratic-style domestic programs. Most Senate Republicans wanted not only to cut domestic programs but to pressure Reagan to raise taxes and trim back on defense; twenty-seven Democrats felt the same way. On October 9, the Senate passed the plan by a 75-24 vote—as part of a bill raising the debt ceiling above $2 trillion.

Escaping Blame: Reverse Houdini

When Congress gets tangled in the partisan warfare of divided government, it often ties itself in knots. All sides resort to one-upmanship. That is what happened on Gramm-Rudman. The House Democratic leadership, initially stunned by the Senate vote, eventually put a reverse squeeze on Republicans. It was a case study in the legislative power game.

Old-line Democratic committee chairmen wanted to fight. The group that Tip O'Neill nicknamed the "old oaks" (Claude Pepper of Florida, Jack Brooks of Texas, Jamie Whitten of Mississippi, Peter Rodino of New Jersey, and John Dingell of Michigan) urged the speaker to kill Gramm-Rudman—to pass the debt-ceiling bill without it. They saw it as an outrageous, unconstitutional giveaway of congressional power to the president, because his budget director would get authority to decide when and how to carry out the automatic budget cuts.

But O'Neill knew the Democrats had no chance unless they were unified, and revolt was rippling through the rank and file. Democratic conservatives liked the budget-balancing purpose of Gramm-Rudman. Moderate Democrats feared looking passive on the deficit while the Republicans were billboarding a new panacea. Whip Tom Foley told the committee chairmen they were outgunned.

"You're the toughest unit in the U.S. Army," Foley kidded them. "You're willing to take on machine-gun emplacements with your hands, kick the treads off Tiger tanks with G.I. boots." But he warned them that it would take winning all the Democrats—"and you can't get that kind of vote!"[3]

Within forty-eight hours, O'Neill had adopted a Democratic damage-control strategy: Matching the Republican squeeze play. With two moderates in charge, Foley and Gephardt, the Democratic tactic was to endorse Gramm-Rudman's goals and then revise its specifics. There followed two months of tense maneuvering. House Democrats eventually got agreement from Senate Republicans to suspend Gramm-Rudman during a recession. They also inserted provisions to protect Congress. Their plan provided that the Congressional Budget Office share with the budget director the power of deciding when to activate automatic budget cuts—and empowered the comptroller general (an agent of Congress) to specify the actual cuts. Those provisions got bipartisan support.

But House Democrats also played blame-game politics: a game of political chicken.

---

[3]Thomas Foley, interview with the author, February 6, 1986. His version was confirmed by two of Speaker O'Neill's aides.

They decided to expose the Republicans by tightening the Gramm-Rudman scheme to make the public howl at the cuts it imposed. "Let's really make it hurt," was the Democratic war cry.

"There's no doubt there was a strain of partisan political vengeance," Foley told me. "The feeling was, 'Let's get revenge on those bastards. They want deficit reduction—let's give it to 'em early in the year so they're gonna have to explain to their constituents why all these programs are cut out six months before the election.'"[4]

Gramm's original bill had been a clever blame-game ploy. It gave Senate Republicans a partisan advantage—publicity for fighting the deficit in 1985 and 1986, but delaying actual cuts until after the 1986 elections. Democrats ridiculed it as a tactic to save Republican Senate seats in 1986. The Democratic countersqueeze was to make Gramm-Rudman bite into programs in early 1986, so that voters would feel the pinch before the 1986 elections and punish Republican candidates. To compound the political pain, Democrats also pushed for deeper cuts in 1986.

Foley, Gephardt, and company also made sure the axe would fall fully on Pentagon spending and fought to exempt their pet social programs from automatic cuts. In the end, the Democrats spared a string of programs from Gramm's guillotine: Social Security, veterans pensions, and such programs for the poor as food stamps, Medicaid, child nutrition, supplemental income for the elderly, and welfare for families with dependent children. Cuts on Medicare and four other health programs were limited.

Finally, the Gramm-Rudman law passed by large majorities, creating optimism in financial markets that the government was serious about licking the deficit. But the lopsided majorities were misleading. At the White House, officials admitted privately that they were counting on the law's being ruled unconstitutional. Members of Congress filed suit.

Indeed, the Supreme Court ruled the automatic cutting mechanism unconstitutional, as the canniest White House and congressional strategists had expected. The Court saved the politicians from themselves, as some had intended. . . .

The Gramm-Rudman law had a fallback procedure: The automatic budget-cutting could take effect, provided that Congress and the president agreed. But that never happened; the blame-game rivals kept on arguing. Even if the Court had upheld Gramm-Rudman, the conflicting motives of Reagan, Senate Republicans, and House Democrats suggest there would have been endless maneuvers to avoid its full and fair implementation—because a genuine budget compromise had not been reached.

In short, the 1985 Gramm-Rudman act turned out to be not a model of political responsibility but an exercise in the politics of evasion. Not that everyone's intentions were cynical. Many in Congress wanted to curb the deficit, and some worked hard to that end. But after President Reagan blocked the consensus approach, all sides vied to look good fighting the deficit, while using the fine print to protect their pet programs—thus perpetuating big deficits. Instead of the deficit declining, it shot up. The 1986 Gramm-Rudman target was $144 billion, but the deficit hit a record level of $220.6 billion.

---

[4]*Ibid.*

Unintentionally, Gramm-Rudman became a metaphor for divided government. Because no one wanted to deliver any bad news to voters, the politicians invented a Rube Goldberg contraption that made the dirty work of cutting programs and raising taxes seem impersonal. Congress literally tied itself in knots. Barney Frank of Massachusetts called Gramm-Rudman a "reverse Houdini." Houdini was known for miraculous escapes from impossible predicaments; Frank felt Congress was great at the opposite—locking itself into unbreakable deadlocks, so voters cannot fault anyone in particular. That is what Gramm-Rudman did. It offered everyone from President Reagan to the most junior Democrat in Congress what politicians love—political cover: a way to look well intentioned but avoid blame for unpleasant action.

Thinking It Over

1. Define: the "blame game."

2. Our fascination with watching the blame game played out through the eyes of Hedrick Smith may cause us to lose sight of the forest because we are so caught up in the trees. In this case the "forest" is a concept—divided government. But is that really the *cause* of all that's going on? Is there a way to preserve the benefits of the separation of powers and at the same time prevent the power game from being played?

33.
THE TRIUMPH OF POLITICS
by David A. Stockman

Setting the Scene: David Stockman came to the Reagan administration as the quintessential "fair haired boy." Bright, articulate, ambitious, hard working. As it turned out he was the man primarily responsible for attempting to convince Ronald Reagan that the budget deficits could not be blamed on Congress alone, that his "supply side" theories had not been applied correctly, and that he *must* raise taxes or face massive deficits down the line. This reading is ripe with insights for political scientists. Its purpose here is to demonstrate that there is no such thing as "the executive branch." There is the bureaucracy (referred to below by references to the cabinet), there is a huge and complex Presidential staff (represented by Stockman, Meese, Darman, and others) and there is the President (Ronald Reagan). We join Stockman as he desperately searches for away to convince Ronald Reagan that raising taxes and not simply cutting spending is the only approach consistent with reality.

It was January 1983, and Jim Baker and I were in the third-floor residence of the White House, briefing the President.

"You're telling me this trigger tax is actually going to happen, aren't you?" The President sounded crushed.

"Yes," I answered, "I don't see how it can be avoided."

"Oh darn, oh darn. It just can't be. I never thought it would come to this." Slowly he took out his pen and scratched "RR" on the paper I had brought to him. His 1984 budget was thus approved, calling for a tax increase of $50 billion per year, on top of the large tax increase he had approved just a few months earlier. I had never seen him look so utterly dejected.

Ordinarily, Ronald Reagan was an incorrigible optimist. One of his favorite stories was the one about the two boys getting their Christmas presents. The first boy was a pessimist, the second an optimist. The pessimist gets a roomful of toys. He's miserable, because he's sure there's some catch involved. The optimist gets a roomful of horse manure. He's delighted. He digs around in the room for hours on end. With all that horse manure, he figured there just *had* to be a pony in there somewhere!

Well, I had just unloaded several tons of horse manure into the Cabinet Room, and it appeared that Ronald Reagan had finally given up looking for the pony. God knows he had tried. But now even he understood that major tax increases were needed to restore the Treasury's depleted coffers. Over the previous two months I had given him evidence upon evidence that if we didn't impose this trigger tax, the already frightening deficit would soar to $277 billion by 1986. As it stood now, we would accumulate *$1.4 trillion* in red ink over five years.

Yet up to now he had stoutly resisted any further tax increase, no matter what the evidence. In his mind, the three-year $100 billion tax increase (TEFRA) that Bob Dole and the College of Cardinals had insisted upon the summer before would be the absolute limit of his retreat. He had accepted that only with great reluctance, as a quid pro quo for additional congressional spending cuts. In fact, he had managed to convince himself that it wasn't really a tax increase at all.

"This bill only collects taxes we are owed already," he told the group of dubious House Republicans in the Cabinet Room. "It won't raise taxes on the legitimate taxpayer at all."

That was true only if you considered people who bought cigarettes and owned a telephone "illegitimate" taxpayers; they and millions of others were the ones who would now be paying more taxes. In order to get him to go along with it, we had gussied up Bob Dole's tax increase bill so that it seemed like some bench warrant issued at midnight to permit a raid on America's criminal underground.

But even that had not been enough. Over 1982, as the economy plunged deeper into recession and inflation continued to collapse, Rosy Scenario looked less and less rosy. The structural deficit turned out not to be $150 billion, as we had thought during the November 1981 debate, but nearly double that. By the end of 1982, the fiscal situation was an utter, mind-numbing catastrophe.

To convince the President it really was as bad as I was saying, I invented a multiple-choice budget quiz. The regular budget briefings weren't doing the job. I thought this might be the way.

The quiz divided the entire budget up into about fifty spending components and gave him three spending-cut choices on each, ranging from a nick to a heavy whack. Next to each choice was a description of what the impact of the cut would be (how many people would be thrown out into the snow), and of its political prospects (e.g., "previously defeated 27-2 in committee").

One typical example of a heavy whack showed that he could save $1.3 billion by eliminating the tourism bureau, dropping 2.5 million households from the heating assistance aid program, cutting child welfare grants by 35 percent, and eliminating the senior employment program and the minority business program entirely. By contrast, if he merely nicked this set of programs, he would save only $47 million.

The President took the quiz in November 1982. During several long sessions in the Cabinet Room we had gone through all fifty budget components. The quiz allowed him systematically to look at the whole $900 billion budget, to see it brick-by-brick. It also allowed him to get his hands dirty, maybe even bloody, with the practical chore of nitty-gritty cutting. Once the President went through it, he would understand that the budget was not a matter of too many bureaucrats and filing cabinets, but a politically explosive, vast, complex network of subsidies, grants, and entitlements. He would see that to cut COLAs by $14 billion meant taking $1,263 dollars a year out of the pockets of 36 million Social Security recipients and several million more military and civilian retirees.

The President enjoyed the quiz immensely. He sat there day after day with his pencil. He listened to his senior staff and the economic team discuss the relevant policy and political ramifications, then announced his choice and marked the appropriate box.

And rarely chose to make a whack. They were mostly nicks. "Yes," he would say, "we can't go that far." Or, "No, we better go for the moderate option or there will be a drumbeat from the opposition."

The last session was on a Friday afternoon. I could tell the President was delighted about having endured the ordeal. It had occasioned a number of anecdotes about the federal monster and he had happily dispensed them to the group assembled at the cabinet table.

When we told him what his grade was early the next week, he was not so pleased. He had flunked the exam. After making all his cuts, the five-year deficit remained at a staggering $800 billion.

I went into the meeting in which I would present the President with his grade, thinking, "Well, the moment of truth has finally come." But not yet. I still did not understand how determined the President was to find his pony.

I made sure that his report card highlighted all the positive aspects of the cuts he had made, but it also showed the negative ones, too. Such as the fact that the remaining deficits meant the government would need to borrow *over half* of the nation's net private savings over the next four years. Such as the fact that under his budget, the total national debt would reach *two trillion dollars* by 1988.

When the discussion turned to taxes, his fist came down squarely on the table.

"I don't want to hear any more talk about taxes," he insisted. "The problem is *deficit spending!*"

It is difficult politely to correct the President of the United States when he has blatantly contradicted himself. The $800 billion worth of deficits were the result of the spending he didn't want to cut.

But now came two new ideas. "It's time we got something out to the people," said the President, "and that is to show them we didn't cause deficits. Now, what would they have been under the policies before we got here?

"And we should also show them where the deficits would be if Congress had given us all the cuts we asked for."

I cautioned that neither approach would make the huge deficit numbers in front of us go away. Moreover, that what the President was suggesting might not prove as exculpatory as he thought.

But now Meese began chanting the California mantra. "That's just the point," he echoed. "We *inherited* this mess. Bad as it is, we need to get out how much worse it would be under the old tax-and-spend approach of Carter."

Soon a Saturday radio speech was being cooked up along the lines of, If "we" flunked the test, "they" would have flunked it worse. I was instructed to make the numbers prove all this.

Well, you couldn't. No known method of accounting could. The numbers simply would not prove either point. A few days later I sent the President a memo saying, "I would recommend you not pursue these points in the Saturday speech."

My memo pointed out that by 1968 the deficit would still be $150 billion, even if Congress had enacted *every* cut in our original budget. It would have actually been $200 billion save for the magic asterisk. And, in truth, we had never "actually proposed this due to the deadlock over Social Security."

As for the mess we'd inherited from Jimmy Carter, well, oops! Under his policies, the deficit by 1986 would only have been $80 billion. "A weak argument for our case," I noted.

I succeeded in aborting the radio speech pinning the blame on the donkey. Now it was time to take another look at the problem. But what could be done?

One day Dick Darman and I were sitting on his office couch wringing our hands, when he suddenly got up and darted for a pad of paper lying on his desk.

"Don't get offended now," he began, "but you might as well know it. When you sit there going over the deficit projections, the man's eyes glaze over. He tunes out completely because he doesn't fully appreciate that the pony is already built into the numbers."

Darman meant that the President did not think in terms of more than one year at a time. He looked only at the current year's deficit numbers and wrote them off as attributable to the recession. He just didn't believe in the over $250 billion figure for the out-years, because he thought the coming economic recovery would drastically shrink the deficit numbers by 1987 or 1988. Never mind that the briefing book already showed that these numbers were based on a booming recovery beginning in 1983 and lasting through the end of the decade.

"The economic assumptions are all right there," I protested to Darman.

"But they're on a *different page* than the budget numbers," said Darman. "He doesn't make the connection." He sketched furiously on his pad. When he finished, I saw what he was up to, and was chagrined I hadn't thought of it myself.

His sketch showed a chart done in the exaggerated manner of the political cartoonist. At the center were big red bars showing the deficits rising year after year. Off to the side were black bars showing unemployment declining year after year. The President would see his pony (economic recovery and optimism) *and* the deficits on the same page. It would be impossible to miss the point.

Back to the OMB graphics department. Soon I had the finished chart. It was a thing of beauty.

"I've got the pony galloping one way on the same page with the deficit soaring the other," I bubbled over, showing it to Darman. "This has got to do the trick!"

By any kind of reasoning I can think of, it should have worked. Right there on one page you saw the economy getting better and the triple-digit deficit getting worse. . . .

I took the chart in to the next meeting in the Cabinet Room. The President just stared at the first page and turned it. But the next page showed the same point: The spending bar was at 24.5 percent of GNP and the revenue bar with existing taxes was at 18.9 percent of GNP. He turned the page again, and saw the same point again. The deficit bar for 1986 absorbed 72 percent of net private savings, "crowding out investment and economic growth."

And when he turned the page again, there it was again: a bar for the CETA boondoggle under Carter at $9 billion; but the bar for the 1983 enacted budget was only $3.7 billion, meaning we didn't have much left to cut. By contrast, a few pages further the bar for Social Security and retirement programs was $212 billion, or *fifty times* as high; and basically we had no hope for savings except for the minor trimmings that Jim Baker's bipartisan Social Security Commission was still heatedly debating.

After going through all the pages, the President sat at the cabinet table, staring at the paper, looking concussed. No one in the room seemed to have the nerve to bring up the tax increase issue yet again, and I was weary of being the only person who would. I'd been sure Darman's graphs would finally cause the President to say, "Yes, we do need more revenue." But now there was an awkward silence.

Meese finally spoke up with the usual solution. "We'll have to go back to the drawing board over Thanksgiving," he said, "and then we'll see where we are in December after the cabinet comes in with their ideas for new budget savings."

Back to the drawing board! We had all—the President included—just spent a full week chained to the drawing board and we still had come out $800 billion in the red.

New cuts from the Cabinet! The cabinet had not volunteered so much as a single cut on its own since Inauguration Day.

But that's the way it was to be.

Thinking It Over

1. When Madison wrote, the executive branch consisted of the President and a handful of others. Would he be as worried about the problems of concentrated power today as he was in 1787?

2. Can you think of a better way of communicating with the President than the way Stockman chose?

34.
THE DEADLOCK OF DEMOCRACY
by James MacGregor Burns

Setting the Scene: James MacGregor Burns' book does many things.   But fundamentally it treats the deadlock into which our national government has stumbled.   Without political parties there is nothing to provide a "web of influence" and hold the disparate branches of government together.   What the part of the book reprinted here does, however, is to provide a critical summary of Madisonianism.   In fact I know of no other short piece that so well ties Madison and the checks and balances thesis to problems of governance in the modern period.   This is the kind of essay that falls into the category "if you only had time to read one . . ."

In his first paper, Number 10, he [Madison] came to grips with the crucial problem of breaking and controlling the violence of faction, which he defined as a "number of citizens, whether amounting to a majority or minority of the whole, who are united and actuated by some common impulse of passion, or of interest, adverse to the rights of other citizens, or to the permanent and aggregate interests of the community."   The origins of such factions were in the nature of man, in his passions and interests, economic, religious, and otherwise. The cause of faction, Madison wrote, could not and should not be removed, for that cause was liberty, which must never be suppressed.   But the effects of faction could be controlled by enlarging the society to be governed, since the larger the society, the greater the "variety of parties and interests" and the less likely that any one faction will have a majority.   The greater variety could be found in a broader Republic, with its national Congress representing many sections and groups and hence able to break and control the violence of faction, whether of a popular majority or minority.

Like a careful cook, Madison wanted to dissolve indigestible lumps and fiery spices in the blander waters of a large pot.   His crucial assumption here was that the broader republic would overcome faction.   Why?   If, say, inflationists in one state could get control of the state legislature, why could not inflationists in all states join hands and gain control of the new Congress?   Here Madison marshaled his arguments convincingly.   For one thing, he said, in a large republic the people would have to delegate decisions to representatives of bigger constituencies, and hence factional feelings would be refined and tempered by carefully chosen leaders whose views were more refined and broad minded than factional leaders.   To be sure, factional and even sinister representatives might get elected and betray the people, but this would be less likely where representatives had to appeal to a "greater number of citizens in the large than in the small republic."   The new Constitution, providing for two layers of government, would be a fine balance, a "happy combination" of local and general representation.   But even more important, under a greater variety of parties and interests, "you make it less probable that a majority of the whole will have a common motive to invade the rights of the citizens; or if such a common motive exists, it will be more difficult for all who feel it to discover their own strength, and to act in unison with one another." Thus inflationists in different states could not easily join together because in the broader sphere other differences would keep them apart—for example, Madison had noted prophetically, the basic conflict between North and South.

But Madison still was not satisfied. There was still the possibility that even in the new Union a majority of the people might gang up on the minority. To be sure, Montesquieu's old safeguard might work: divide up national power among different officials, legislative, executive, and judicial, "for the accumulation of powers . . . in the same hands . . . may justly be pronounced the very definition of tyranny." But even this might not be enough, for what if the different officials—Congressmen, President, and federal judges—got together and pooled their power for the interests of some oppressive majority?

The answer to this question became the archpin of the whole constitutional framework. That answer was the system of checks and balances. "The great security against a gradual concentration of the several powers in the same department, consists in giving to those who administer each department the necessary constitutional means and personal motives to resist encroachments of the others," Madison wrote in the fifty-first paper, which rivals the tenth in intellectual sweep and power. ". . . Ambition must be made to counteract ambition. The interest of the man must be connected with the constitutional rights of the place." Was it a reflection on human nature that such devices should be necessary to control the abuses of government? Yes, Madison admitted, and reverting to his first premise as to the nature of man, he asked: "But what is government itself, but the greatest of all reflections on human nature? If men were angels, no government would be necessary."

"Ambition must be made to counteract ambition"—in these seven words Madison drove straight to the heart of the whole problem; here he showed his genius as a political scientist. For he was not content with a flimsy separation of power that lunging politicians could smash through like paper. He was calling for barricade after barricade against the thrust of a popular majority—and the ultimate and impassable barricade was a system of checks and balances that would use man's essential human nature—his interests, his passions, his ambitions—to control itself. For Madison's ultimate checks and balances were political; they built into the engine of government automatic stabilizing devices that were sure to counterbalance one another because they were powered by separate sources of political energy. The ambitions of Presidents and Senators and Representatives and judges were bound to collide because each was responsible to separate constituencies in the "greater variety of parties and interests of the new federal republic." And each official, of course, had some kind of constitutional weapon—the President's veto, for example, or the Senators' power over treaties—that could be used against other officials and the sectional or economic or ideological interests they represented.

It was a stunning solution to the Framers' problem of checking the tyranny of the majority. Yet the solution contained a major flaw, or at least inconsistency, in the thinking behind it—a flaw so relevant to our later analysis that we must note it even in the same breath that we pay tribute to this profound scholar and politician.

The trouble was this: if, as Madison said, the first great protection against naked majority rule was the broader diversity of interests in a larger republic and hence the greater difficulty of concerting their "plans of oppression," why was not this enough in itself? Why would not any popular majority representing such a variety of interests perforce become so broad and moderate in its goals as never to threaten any major or even minor or individual interest? Why was it necessary to have what Madison called "auxiliary precautions" of checks and balances built right into the frame of government? Because, he said, experience had taught men the necessity of them. What experience? Madison must have meant the experience of societies so deeply divided between rich and poor, between master and slave, between sections, between religions, that victory for one side meant coercion or annihilation of the other. But the America he knew was not such a society. No ideological conflict racked the nation; as Louis Hartz has shown, Americans were united—to the extent they thought about such things—over the liberal creed of John Locke. No sharp class or religious conflict had torn the country into two warring halves. The same diversity that Madison used as an argument for broader union would have required any majority to appeal to so many interests, to straddle so many issues, that it must act in a moderate, broadly representative fashion.

The key to Madison's thinking is his central aim to stop people from turning easily to government for help. Today, when many people want protection by or through government, and not just protection from government, the power of a minority to stop the majority from acting through government may be as arbitrary as majority rule seemed to Madison. The fact is that Madison believed in a government of sharply limited powers. His efforts at Philadelphia to shift powers from the states to the new national government were intended more to thwart popular majorities in the states from passing laws for their own ends than to empower national majorities to pass laws for *their* ends. For the new national government was supposed to tame and temper popular majorities—which some states had been unable to do. This meant weaker government—but it was Madison, after all, who said that the necessity of any government was a misfortune and a reflection on human nature. Government, in short, was a necessary evil that must be curbed, not an instrument for the realization of men's higher ideals or a nation's broader interests. Hence he could sponsor what Richard Hofstadter has called a harmonious system of mutual frustration. . . .

Certainly the implications of Madison's insight are clear today. Around every position established under the new Constitution—around "the interest of the man," whether President, legislator, or even judge or bureaucrat—a circle of sub-leaders and followers would also grow, the size of the circle depending on the importance of the office and the appeal and skills of the leader. Other factions would grow around politicians outside government, trying to get in. And of course the Constitution left intact a proliferation of offices in the states, counties, and localities, which in turn were the centers of thousands of other little circles of political action and influence.

These officeholders, their rivals, and the circles of sub-leaders and personal followers around them comprise a web of influence stretching across the formal governmental system. This is not to deny the importance of political parties and interest groups, of opinion-shaping agencies such as the press, of the thick crust of traditional habits and attitudes, of ideological and social forces, and of other factors. It is to say that, given the stability and durability of our constitutional system, these offices establish the main structure of political combat and government power.

. . .

I have advanced the thesis that under the Madisonian system personal factions would grow up around each officeholder and office seeker, from President to fence viewer, and would buttress the constitutional and legal checks and balances with political or human forces. Governmental offices would give some structure and stability to the flux of political energy, for as Madison said, "The interest of the man must be connected with the constitutional rights of the place." Hence my thesis implies that if the structure of power-wielding offices remains substantially the same over time, the pattern of politics—of political factions, leader-follower relations, area groupings, for example—would also persist over time. The pattern would not always be very clear, of course. Fierce storms such as civil war, or long-gathering tides such as urbanization, or sudden squalls such as those personified by a Hearst or a Huey Long or a McCarthy, might wash over the familiar channels, but the old political patterns would reappear once the storm was gone.

This is precisely what has happened in America. We have recently celebrated the 175th anniversary of the Constitutional Convention with the proliferation of offices in that charter essentially as the Framers gave it to us. In a more tranquil age Gladstone described the American Constitution as the finest instrument struck off from the brow of man. While few political scientists would say this today, we can pay tribute to the marvelous resilience and durability of the charter, its capacity to accommodate itself to the wrench of civil war, to depressions, to westward expansion, massive increase and spread of population, several world wars, urbanization, vast immigration and internal migration, cold war, and the demands of leadership in the free world. It has co-existed with the expansion of the suffrage, the democratization of major sectors of government, and the Jeffersonian impulse of strong Presidents. Above all it has survived—no mean feat in a world littered with the scraps of paper once destined to serve nations for the ages.

And with it has survived the Madisonian model of a variety of different offices with mingled powers and separated constituencies. We still have a President, a Congress with two equally powerful chambers, a Supreme Court with its own source of authority, and separate system of state and local government. The men in the White House and on Capitol Hill still confront one another in much the same posture of competition as they did a century and a half ago. Rivalry between governors and legislatures, between national and state politicians, between city mayors and state legislatures continues unabated, as does the struggle of individuals and institutions within each unit of government. Our economy and our national life have become integrated in many respects, while our politics has remained fragmented.

Thinking It Over

1. What is the "arch pin" of our "constitutional framework" according to Burns? What is the "major flaw" in the thinking behind it?

2. If Burns is right, is there any way to use Madisonianism productively to govern a post modern society?

35.
THE DECLINE OF THE AMERICAN NATIONAL GOVERNMENT
by Robert J. Pranger

Setting the Scene: Traditionally, those who have advocated a larger role for state and local governments in America have been motivated by a desire to bring government closer to the people. In the reading that follows, however, we have a scholar who fears for the health of the *national* government; not because it is too strong, but because it is too weak. But the implications of Pranger's thinking do not necessarily lead to a bigger central government. Instead Pranger argues that in the modern period our national system has become "localism writ large" and the national government, as an arena seeking to attend to all interests, has left unattended those things fundamental to the nation. This is the very negative and dangerous legacy of checks and balances.

Much has been made of the ascendancy of the national government over the states and of the alleged decline of liberty as a result. Indeed, some have tried to trace liberty's history in the United States to the failing prosperity of the states—under the rubric of "states' rights." But less has been said of the decline of the national government with regard to its special function in the American federal system, that of promoting the public good. While some have argued that the states and local governments, being closer to the grassroots, will sustain community while the national government will nurture power of vast magnitude, a very different view was taken by the founders of the American republic: national power would diffuse ambition, mitigate despotism, lend itself to cosmopolitan toleration and considerations of public good, whereas local power would bring into sharp focus narrow interest, factious ambition and power politics. The federal system would act as a firebreak. Out of fear that the struggle for factional power might leap over local boundaries and spread nationally to build a majority with formidable, tyrannical impulses, the continuities from local to state to national politics would be broken just enough to provide insurmountable obstacles for the spread of such a wild fire. If the evils of faction might spring from local competition, then the union would promote wider loyalties to a common citizenship and a correspondingly richer view of liberty that would embrace a politics of wide variety as well as a politics of self-interested competition.

A decline of the national government has taken place in terms of public perceptions to its civic purpose, from one of zealous umpire responsible to the community as a whole to one of ultimate preemptor where ambition may repair from local conflict to large scale warfare. At the turn of the century, Arthur F. Bentley announced general conceptions of the nation dead, in his *The Process of Government* (1908). He would leave abstractions such as the public good to metaphysicians; there was no politics save that of interest at all levels of government. Although Madison may have said substantially the same thing, he sought, in federalism, *remedies* to excessive factionalism and *provisions* for the public good.

In the course of this decline of truly national functions, the redemptive nature of broad national politics has been replaced by localism writ large or, better stated, by the nationalization of local politics so that there is no longer an American community at all. Cosmopolitan tolerance has given way to universal, provincial selfishness. In a word, the contemporary eclipse of community in America may not stem as some might think, from the deterioration of closely knit localities under the corrosive influences of mass society, but from the disintegration of a national center capable of providing a base for a broad general will. Without central focus, the concept of public good quickly becomes little more than a national sum of private ambitions. The founding fathers clearly saw a difference between such ambitions and public welfare, albeit they were, given their individualistic assumptions about *all* politics (note Madison on interest), somewhat unspecific about the difference. Such decline of community as there is comes from national as well as local difficulties.

The purpose of the federal system of national unity in the United States has been to couple liberty with safety. This means that free movement and speech would be couched in constitutional and procedural terms, within the established institutional forms of republican or representative government. Inside such a constitutional shell—but only inside—could two types of liberty safely coexist without either doing damage to the other or to the common union. And, after all, the zeal for liberty of the founders of the American republic was equalled only by their desire for union.

First, there was the important liberty for self-fulfillment, the freedom to follow one's ambitions. Such liberty has behind it, however, the impulse of preemption over others, because, by definition, ambition includes the desire—praiseworthy or inordinate—for "rank, fame or power" (Webster). This form of liberty was well-established in 18th-century economics, with hardy roots in the 17th-century liberalism of Harrington, Hobbes, Locke and the Levellers. Such ambition could take the more mundane forms of everyday competition, or it might lead to more unusual efforts at individual creativity.

At the same time, however, there is a second form of liberty, also well defined by the 18th century, that of toleration or the liberty to deviate unimpeded by peremptory claims of others. This too had 17th-century progenitors. The federalist genius was to protect liberty in both forms, but protection that was to take the role of constitutionalizing them so that they might coexist, prosper and yet not injure the union. From the federal perspective, the core of this doctrine of safe liberty is found in Federalist Paper Number 10.

While interconnected, the two forms of liberty ("passion" or preemption and "opinion" or deviation, according to Madison), represented distinct political forms with characteristic virtues, styles of political action, dangers and public policies. Behind the liberty to preempt and the liberty to deviate stood, respectively, the politics of ambition and the politics of variation. The curious title of this essay refers to the decline in the national government's most unusual contribution to the federal union, a strong politics of variation, and the rise of the national government as ultimate preemptor under the politics of ambition. This shift in political emphasis at the national level has had important consequences for the federal system as conceived by the founders of the republic, the chief one being that a national center of union, with its common citizenship, is now in eclipse. . . .

To review the argument up to this point, the founding fathers established a government whose purpose was to gain the full blessings of liberty for all citizens. This purpose was to be attained, however, not by manifestos of principle but by a system of government founded solely on individual liberty, a system whose "public good" would be the maximization of this liberty within a republican or representative form of government. In a way, this would be anarchy secured against its own excesses, a safe liberty, a form of political economy somewhat like laissez-faire. Instead of defining the nation, it was believed that the nation would define itself spatially and temporally as it explored the full potentials of its main purpose. The "fullness" of liberty would be twofold, the liberty to preempt others or to compete with others, and the liberty to deviate through the practices of toleration for others. For preemptive liberty, there were two virtues, the one emphasizing self-interested competition or ambition, the other encouraging assertive creativity. In the case of the liberty to deviate, the main virtue was diversity or toleration. Political styles varied according to the types of politics and their virtues: demanding and asserting constituted the two main ways that preemptive liberty could manifest itself in action, while listening would be the modus operandi for toleration. Under the politics of preemption political issues would encompass those of "Who *gets* what, when and how?" and "Who *creates* what, when and how?", whereas the politics of deviation asks the question, "Who *expresses* what, when and How?" How would federalism, one of the main principles of the American constitution, operate to maximize both liberties? In the case of preemptive liberty, it encourages competition and creation at all levels of government, but builds barriers at the national level against reaching the point of majority tyranny. The liberty to deviate works to build a center or forum for toleration at the national level, under the idea of a limited government, and within this forum—side by side with competitive politics—to explore the full ramifications of the American sovereign principle, full liberty.

The two liberties and their politics are generically related to the main species of politics, power and participation. In establishing on the basis of full liberty an American commonwealth, the founding fathers blended power and participation, hierarchy and community, in the federal system. Surprisingly enough for those who associate genuine community with physical intimacy, the American national government would be designed to play as large—or larger—a role in community formation as it would in building the pyramidal structures of American government.

Preemption belongs to the politics of power. In the case of both competition and creation the central symbolism is one of domination of some over others in the context of scarcity. That America has been a nation of abundance did not affect the politics of competition, because this abundance was more an effect of full liberty than it was the cause of that liberty. Americans found abundance in the course of their history, a history they made themselves. In any event, preemptive action builds pyramidal hierarchy, no matter how shifting this hierarchy might be. And in the United States, "the circulation of elites," as Pareto called the process by which neophytes moved from powerlessness to power, was very rapid indeed. The political system most typical of hierarchy is more like the Versailles of Louis XIV, however, than like a New England town meeting. It was not simply the practicality of the town meeting that disappeared in American history, it was the idea of an established forum tolerant of all divergent opinions that gave way before the intense political combativeness of self-interested competition. Yet more important than the downfall of the New England town meeting, was the decline of the national government as a forum for the widest diversity of viewpoints, a forum insulated from majority-seeking factions who would invade the national center to preempt others.

Political toleration or the politics of variation belongs to the broad generic activity of participation. The last activity works to provide a common ground for all citizens to contribute to defining and exploring the most important issues confronting the whole polity. Here a politics is created constantly by citizens seeking common ground with their fellows, first by expressing their wants and then by listening to others. If the pyramidal hierarchy of Versailles typifies the politics of power, the congregational community of certain early American colonies characterizes the politics of participation.

On the one hand is power, the politics of some preempting others; on the other is participation, the politics of some sharing common involvements with others. Both are essential to the common, public life of politics, yet balance between them is vital so that authority may rest on genuine feelings of civic obligation, and so that obligation may be finding on fellow citizens: commonality and unity, order and diversity, leadership and citizenship, sanction and justice. Such balance is rare indeed.

For the founding fathers, federalism played an odd role in this balanced liberty between power and participation, hierarchy and community. An American today, so used to the awesome power of the national government with its towering organizational structures and imposing leaders, would find it hard to transport himself back to the early days of the republic when a much less hierarchical conception of the nation was envisaged. Contemporary experience is with the vast political distance that seems to separate national leaders from ordinary citizens, in spite of revolutions in communications and transportation. for the founding fathers, on the other hand, the national center was to operate as a community of citizens rather than as the most powerful hierarchy. In fact, it is hard to find a conception of "levels" of government among the federalists (except Hamilton, perhaps), where the national government was considered higher or more powerful than the states, because the issue of separated power was one of providing full liberty and not full power. The national government was not conceived in hierarchical terms, because its distinguishing characteristic was its forum for national community rather than national preemptive organization. So political distance between citizen and nation could not be great, not because Washington was easier to reach from Baltimore in the 19th than in the 20th century, but because civic perceptions envisaged Washington as the center for a national will that transcended petty factionalism and local involvement.

Until recently a profound nationalistic enthusiasm was widespread in the United States. Today there is a much more reserved attitude toward the nation, especially among educated people. Why? Some have blamed the Vietnam War or a more general technocratic organization that has produced citizen alienation and powerlessness. Another explanation might be that the national center can no longer generate nationalistic enthusiasm because it no longer operates as a center for the nation as a whole. When coalition enrichment rather than an open forum for all dominates a government, one can expect citizens to see little hope that any individual expression will count for much. This hopelessness seems widespread today. Domestication of the national government has made it a government like all others—public and private—in the United States, a political system dominated by factious competition. Why should the nation make any special claims to allegiance or any unique contributions to personal liberty under these trends toward homogenization?

In the wake of this domestication process of all areas of American government there has been no adequate symbolic substitute found for the task of pulling Americans together in common undertakings. All forums for variation and expression seem to change into arenas of competitive struggle between citizens. Community seems everywhere in decline, led by the degeneration of the American national community. Indeed, without a central unifying impulse of any kind amidst a sea of fragmented demands, the very idea of a common citizenship begins to lose its meaning. Participation of the citizenry in the polity's common business undergoes eclipse, while power becomes the name of the political game. Then these demands are aggregated by powerful organizations, with citizenship now a matter of organizational membership. Not the nation but the organization becomes parent for us all.

When the open forum at the national level disappears, so does tolerance for diversity. Diverse demands are still made at the national center, but the bureaucratic organization invented to meet these demands has time only for classes of demands and broad categories of persons. Individuals begin to count for less and less, except those extraordinary personages who dominate the Versailles-like world of the national government. In any organization there are boundaries allowing that organization to operate efficiently by narrowing its purposes. A forum, on the other hand, has no interest in efficiency or narrow aids, but almost by definition seeks to broaden the range of permissible issues in an indeterminate fashion. The founding fathers did not fear such broadening, but today's leadership seems more timid. When organized power comes to dominate the national center, the idea of the nation being the broadest forum for its citizenry is replaced by a belief that what organization cannot handle is not a national issue at all. Openness and breadth are superseded by excessive structure and narrowness. Again and again, the citizenry is then confronted with the mirror for itself, an organizational view of good citizenship wherein a national organization will define central political issues in terms of its perception of the demands of a national coalition. If you would know your tasks as a citizen and the permissible limits of your behavior, just as you would know your very political values, "observe" the rules of those organizations established to serve the public!

Such mirrors for good citizenship have nothing to do with effective civic participation. They have just as little to do with the intentions of the founding fathers for the national government's unique role in the federal system, which was to create a common sense of the public good through the politics of variation and the forum and not through the politics of preemption and organization. Wherever the activities of citizenship are predestined by what national officials and their bureaucratic organizations do, citizenship is in eclipse. "Citizenship" becomes "membership." "Civic virtue," as a question for every citizen, is domesticated into pure self-interest. And pure self-interest is only one side of liberty.

Thinking It Over

1.   What does Pranger mean by preemptive liberty?

2.   Late in his term President Jimmy Carter delivered a famous address in which he said America was suffering from a deep national malaise. If Pranger were to have defined malaise and given the speech, what would his central thesis have been?

PART
C

THE POLITICAL PROCESS

Chapter VI

POLITICAL SOCIALIZATION AND PUBLIC OPINION

36.
THE POLITICAL LIFE OF CHILDREN
by Robert Coles

Setting the Scene: The nature of a political system is shaped by the values held by its people. Every system's survival depends on its capacity to insure that the people who matter in the system understand the rules of the game. Remember in grade school when the teacher had you *vote* on whether or not the class would play kickball or basketball at recess? What was going on there was political socialization. In many countries of the world school children never vote. They are *told.* That is socialization too. Although there is disagreement as to exactly when, most studies show that people acquire their dominant value structures very early in life. If we are to understand how the political process works, we must start our investigation with children. In the reading below Robert Coles shares with us a series of interviews in which he sought to discover patterns of political beliefs among the very young. They are often poignant. They are always revealing.

. . . Presumably at some time a child begins to develop assumptions about his or her situation as an individual: The country beckons, or it doesn't; the political order is just or fearful and harmful or crooked to the core; the people who hold office, near and far, can be counted upon, or are, quite definitely, enemies, or indifferent, if not contemptuous. Race awareness, we know, takes root among preschool children; by three or four, they not only spot others who are black or white, or Indian or Chicano, but are quick to come up with pejorative or congratulatory remarks, tied to the person recognized as "other." . . . Professor Connell's studies show that some young Australian children are canny indeed about the

197

motives and purposes of their own and other government. Those same children, incidentally, are quick to distinguish themselves, racially, from the Vietnamese or the Japanese, whom they saw on television. Why do we so often assume that it takes ten or twenty years for children to begin to understand exactly what it is that works for or against them in the world?

In the South, for years, I heard black children speak of sheriffs and policemen as "devils," without picking up the hint they were giving me of attitudes long held. . . . In 1965, In McComb, Mississippi, I asked a six-year-old child who was President. She said she didn't know, "but they killed President Kennedy and they killed Medgar Evers." I asked who "they" were. She said, "the people who don't like us." There is a limit beyond which a guest begins to feel ever ruder and more arrogantly intrusive than he already may have good cause to feel. I may then have felt myself to have gone too far, because I shut up, and did not pursue the obvious chain of psychiatric interrogation: *Which* people don't like you, and *why* don't they, and so on. I realize now that I had made a psychological judgment, maybe a discovery: This child knows a great deal about what social scientists call the subject of "race relations," and I would be foolish, as well as insulting to her, if I persisted in making her spell out not only the obvious, but the exceedingly painful. And too, I probably felt (more than realized) that she would begin to wonder whether there was any point in talking about such matters with a white doctor. She was fully capable of a firm political assessment: The relatively well-off people don't *themselves* want to be reminded too pointedly how things work in their favor. It is a discomforting accusation.

Eventually, as soon of the civil rights workers in rural Alabama and Mississippi turned their attention to the education of children, after dealing with issues like lunch-counter desegregation or voting rights, one began to hear astonishing exchanges between schoolchildren and activists in the Student Nonviolent Coordinating Committee (SNCC) and the Congress of Racial Equality (CORE), or, up in the hollows of Kentucky and West Virginia, the Appalachian Volunteers. A young man or woman would enter a home to urge upon parents a course of action with respect to school desegregation, or a county official's attitude toward the school budget, and suddenly a child would speak up: "I don't like the teachers; they say bad things to us. They're always calling us names; they make you feel no good. We saw the man on the television, the governor, and he wasn't any good either." It is all too easy to take for granted such remarks, spoken by a ten-year-old boy whose father is a tenant farmer near Belzoni in the Mississippi Delta: Black children, badly treated by white *or* black schoolteachers (the latter can sometimes be especially mean to poor children of their own race) will inevitably pick up the rejection and scorn that others feel toward them. Yet, when a child of ten links the governor of his state with the schoolteachers who look down upon him in a rural, still all-black elementary school, he is making a significant judgment.

From that Belzoni boy, much more was to be heard, not then but at a later time. Many rural blacks in the South knew all along that those who came to fight on their behalf would soon enough leave; the apathy and lethargy they displayed to the political activists who asked for a signature, a declaration of support, a willingness to march, to picket were, in fact, also expressions of a political judgment. When asked whether he would one day want to vote, as blacks were then in small numbers beginning to do, the boy had this to say: "Maybe; I don't know. My daddy says what's the use, because even if every one of us voted, the whites would still run Mississippi and still own everything, the whole country. The teacher told us the President is a good man, and he's from the South, and he's trying to do good by the white, and by the colored. To tell the truth, I don't believe her. My sister, she laughed when I told her what the teacher said. My sister said that if I believe everything I hear teachers say, and the governor, and the President—then I'm still a baby, and have a lot of growing up to do. Well, I told her I try on something I hear, to see if it fits, but I know when it doesn't, and I throw it away real fast, because I'll tell you, if you're colored, you'd better learn the difference between a piece of real meat and streak o'lean. My mother cooks them their steaks, up at the boss man's house, and she knows the difference; and she's taught us. And I'll bet it's mostly streak o'lean that they hand out to you, a sheriff or a governor or a President. If they'd be handing out good meat, it would be better. But like my daddy says, there's nothing you can expect to get for the asking from the white people, so it's good the civil rights people are getting the government mad and worrying the President, even if the teachers say we should obey the law and salute the flag and America isn't second to any country. If you're not white, you're second, and a lot of whites, they're second, too; and my sister says that's the scene, and if you don't know what scene you're watching, you're dumb, dumb, dumb."

He was not especially precocious, for all his implicit sociological and political shrewdness. He never went to high school—and now, decades after he spoke like that, he works compliantly on a large Delta plantation. When I asked him, a grown man, the father of two children, what he thinks of the President, or the governor, or Watergate, or any of the important issues that have faced America and the world, he shrugged his shoulders and presented a blank look, or else smiled in a way that can only mystify: Does he, deep down, have some views, or is he utterly without them? After a drink or two he will speak his mind fully: "It's no good for the black man here, no matter who's up there in Washington as President or down in Jackson as governor. That's all I know. Watergate? They caught a few crooks and liars, I guess. Where are all the rest of them? Still in charge of us, still up to no good."

No one wiretaps his phone; he has none. But if he so much as speaks out of turn, the consequences are obvious. The black children I have known in our South, or in our northern ghettos sound—at six, eight, nine, or ten—like some articulate, politically conscious middle-class white college students. As these children grow older, they tend to become much less candid, though they do not change their opinions. While a number of American youths are becoming more critical politically (even disenchanted with the objects of childhood idealizations), many black youths in the South and mountain youths of Appalachia become less outspoken about what they have, it seems, known for a long time—that their situation in life, the conditions they must continue to face, day in, day out, are consequentially connected to the nation's political leadership. The black man whom I quoted as a child, and whom I have seen every year at least twice since I left Mississippi two decades ago, puts his feelings in perspective all too tersely: "I knew what's going on for us a long time, and I haven't seen a good reason yet to change my mind."

As a boy he watched not "the spectacle of gladiatorial games," but this kind of spectacle, no less persuasive: "You remember, when I was a kid I told you about the whippings they gave my daddy for saying he wanted to register to vote. Well, the sheriff did it; and that's the law for you. Now I can go vote, but the same sheriff is there, and even if the bigger politicians watch their language a little better these days, it's no different here. The other day my boy was called 'a little nigger' by the sheriff, just because he didn't say 'yes, sir' when told to stay on the sidewalk until the policeman said it's all right to cross the street. Later he asked me why the governor keeps talking about 'the good people' of the state and the 'bloc vote.' Actually, he's heard me say to my wife that the whites are 'the good people' and we're 'the bloc vote'—bloc instead of black is the way they do it these days!"

A cussing sheriff will do as well as a gladiator or two. The poor, or those who belong to the so-called working class, always live closer to the law, closer to the whims and fancies of political authority. A nine-year-old boy from Marion County, West Virginia, described the relationship between poor people, and those who get elected to office: "You make the wrong move, and they'll be on you, telling you off and ready to lock you up, if need be." What had he seen? What "trained" (Mlle. Weil's word) in him a specific attitude toward West Virginia's, America's government? The spectacle of a father's funeral; the man was one of seventy-eight miners killed in an "accident" whose causes, immediate and more distant, his children knew quite well. The boy sat in the church, with many other children; he heard various "principalities and powers" being exposed for their negligence, and worse. He saw on television the Secretary of Labor and the Secretary of the Interior and the governor and the mayor and a host of county officials and the president of the coal company utter their lamentations, apologies, and excuses: the litany of self-justifying explanations that miners' wives have a way of hearing as if a sounding brass or a tinkling cymbal. In the words of the child, again: "My mother says they can do what they want, the company people; and the sheriff, he listens to them, and that's it, they get their way. Last year there was going to be a strike, and daddy took us and we saw the company people and the sheriff and his people, and they were talking buddy-buddy." Another "spectacle" that does not go unnoticed by children whose parents live or die, depending upon how sensitive they are to the implications of such a "spectacle."

Many upper-middle-class suburban children have quite a contrasting view of their nation and its leaders. A black child of eight, from southern Alabama, just above Mobile, told me in 1968 that she knew one thing for sure about who was going to be President: he'd be a white man; and as for his policies, "no matter what he said to be polite, he'd never really stand up for us." Already she knew herself to be a member of "us," as against "them." A few miles away, a white child of nine, the son a lawyer and plantation owner, had a rather different perspective on the presidency: "The man who's elected will be a good man; even if he's not too good before he goes to Washington, he'll probably turn out good. This is the best nation there is, so the leader has to be the best, too." A child with keen ears who picks up exactly his father's mixture of patriotism and not easily acknowledged skepticism? Yes, but also a child who himself—by the tone of his voice and his earnestness—has come to believe in his nation's destiny, and in the office of the presidency. How about the governor? "He's better known than most governors," the boy boasts. Then he offers his source: "My daddy says that we have a better governor than they do in Louisiana or in Georgia." (The child has cousins in both states.) "And he says that our governor makes everyone stop and listen to him, so he's real good. He knows how to win; he won't let us be beaten by the Yankees."

More sectional bombast, absorbed rather too well by a boy who, now a teenager, hasn't had the slightest inclination to develop the "cynicism" a number of students of "political socialization" have repeatedly emphasized? Or the response of a child who knows what his parents really consider important, really believe in—and fear? "I took my boy over to my daddy's house," the child's father recalls, "and we watched Governor Wallace standing up to those people in Washington; he told the President of the United States that he was wrong." The boy was then four, and no doubt he would not at nine, never mind at fifteen, recall the specific event his father and grandfather both remember so clearly. But time and again he has heard members of his family stress how precarious they feel, in relation to Yankee (federal) power, and therefore how loyal they are to a governor who gives the illusion of successfully defending cherished social and political prerogatives.

Up North, in a suburb outside Boston, it is quite another story. At nine a girl speaks of America and its leaders like this: "I haven't been to Europe yet, but my parents came back last year and they were happy to be home." Then, after indicating how happy she was to have them home, she comments on the rest of the world, as opposed to her country: "It's better to be born here. Maybe you can live good in other places, but this is the best country. We have a good government. Everyone is good in it—if he's the President, he's ahead of everyone else, and if he's a governor, that means he's also one of the people who decide what the country is going to do. There might be a war, and somebody has to send the troops by plane across the ocean. If there is a lot of trouble someplace, then the government takes care of it. I'm going to Washington next year to see all the buildings. My brother went two years ago. He really liked the trip. He came back and said he wouldn't mind being in the government; it would be cool to go on that underground railroad the senators have. He said he visited someone's office, and he was given a pencil and a postcard, and he wrote a letter to say thank you, and he got a letter back. His whole class went, and they were taken all over. They went to see some battlefield, too."

She doesn't know which battlefields, however; nor does she know which war was fought on those fields. She is one of those whom southern children of her age have already learned to identify as "Yankees," even to fear of envy. There are no equivalents for her, however—no name she is wont to hurl at Southerners, or for that matter, anyone else. True, she learned long ago, at about four or five, that black children, whom she sees on television but has never gone to school with, are "funny" and the one Japanese child she had as a classmate in kindergarten was "strange, because of her eyes"; but such children never come up spontaneously in her remarks, and when they are brought up in conversation with a visitor, she is quick to change the subject or go firmly silent. Nor is there any great amount of prejudice in her, at least of a kind that she has directly on her mind. Her drawings reveal her to care about flowers, which she likes to help her mother arrange, about horses, which she loves to ride, and about stars, which she is proud to know rather a lot about.

The last interest prompts from her a bit of apologetic explanation: "My brother started being interested in the stars; my daddy gave him a telescope and a book. Then he lost interest. Then I started using the telescope, and my daddy said I shouldn't, because maybe my brother would mind, but he doesn't." And, in fact, her parents do have rather firm ideas about what boys ought to be interested in, what girls ought to find appealing. Men run for political office, she knows, and sometimes women do, but rarely; anyway, she won't be one of them. In 1971 she thought the President was "a very good man; he has to be—otherwise he wouldn't be President." The same held for the governor and the town officials who make sure that all goes well in her neighborhood. When the Watergate incident began to capture more and more of her parents' attention, she listened and wondered and tried to accommodate her lasting faith with her new knowledge: "The President made a mistake. It's too bad. You shouldn't do wrong; if you're President, it's bad for everyone when you go against the law. But the country is good. The President must feel real bad, for the mistake he made." After which she talks about *her* mistakes: she broke a valuable piece of china; she isn't doing as well in school as either her parents or her teachers feel she ought be doing; and not least, she forgets to make her bed a lot of the time, and her mother or the maid has to remind her of that responsibility. Then she briefly returns to the President, this time with a comment not unlike those "intuitive" ones made by Australian children (in New South Wales) to Professor Connell: "A friend of mine said she didn't believe a word the President says, because he himself doesn't believe what he says, so why should we." What did the girl herself believe? "Well, I believe my parents, but I believe my friend, too. Do you think the President's wife believes him? If he doesn't believe himself, what about her?" So much for the ambiguities of childhood, not to mention such legal and psychiatric matters as guilt, knowing deception, self-serving illusions, and political guile.

Unlike black children, or Appalachian children, or even the children of well-to-do southern white families, the girl I have just quoted has no vivid, politically tinged memories of her own, nor any conveyed by her parents—no governor's defiance; no sit-ins or demonstrations; no sheriff's car or sheriff's voice; no mass funeral after a mine disaster; no experience with a welfare worker; no strike, with the police there to "mediate"; no sudden layoff, followed by accusations and recriminations and drastically curbed family spending. Such unforgettable events in the lives of children very definitely help shape their attitudes toward their nation and its political authority. The black children I have come to know in different parts of this country, even those from relatively well-off homes, say critical things about America and its leaders at an earlier age than white children do—and connect their general observations to specific experiences. A black child of eight, in rural Mississippi or in a northern ghetto, an Indian or Chicano or Appalachian child, can sound like a disillusioned old radical.

The pledge of allegiance to the flag can be an occasion for boredom, at the very least, among some elementary schoolchildren; the phrase "with liberty and justice for all" simply rings hollow, or is perceived as an ironic boast. Here is what a *white* schoolteachers in Barbour County, Alabama, has observed over the years: "I'm no great fan of the colored; I don't have anything against them, either. I do my work, teaching the colored, and I like the children I teach, because they don't put on airs with you, the way some of our own children do—if their daddy is big and important. The uppity niggers—well, they leave this state. We won't put up with them. The good colored people, they're fine. I grew up with them. I know their children, and I try to teach them as best I can. I understand how they feel; I believe I do. I have a very bright boy, James; he told me that he didn't want to draw a picture of the American flag. I asked him why not. He said that he just wasn't interested. It's hard for them—they don't feel completely part of this country. I had a girl once, she was quite fresh; she told me that she didn't believe a word of that salute to the flag, and she didn't believe a word of what I read to them about our history. I sent her to the principal. I was ready to have her expelled, for good. The principal said she was going to be a civil rights type one day, but by then I'd simmered down. 'To tell the truth,' I said, 'I don't believe most of the colored children think any different than her.' A lot of times I skip the salute to the flag; the children start laughing, and they forget the words, and they become restless. It's not a good way to start the day. I'd have to threaten them, If I wanted them to behave while saluting. So, we go right into our arithmetic lessons."

In contrast, among middle-class white children of our northern suburbs, who have no Confederate flag to divide their loyalties, the morning salute can be an occasion for real emotional expression. It is all too easy for some of us to be amused at, or to scorn, the roots of smug nationalism. But for thousands of such children, as for their parents, the flag has a great deal of meaning, and the political authority of the federal, state, and local governments is not to be impugned in any way. Among many working-class families policemen, firemen, clerks in the post office or city hall are likely to be friends, relatives, neighbors. Among upper-middle-class families, one can observe a strong sense of loyalty to a system that clearly, to them, has been friendly indeed. And the children learn to express what their parents feel and often enough say, loud and clear.

"My uncle is a sergeant in the army," the nine-year-old son of a Boston factory worker told me. He went on to remind me that another uncle belongs to the Boston Police Department. The child has watched parades, been taken to an army base, visited an old warship, climbed the steps of a historic shrine. He has seen the flag in school and in church. He has heard his country prayed for, extolled, defended against all sorts of critics. He said when he was eight, and in the third grade, that he would one day be a policeman. Other friends of his, without relatives on the force, echo the ambition. Now nearer to ten, he speaks of motorcycles and baseball and hockey; and when he goes to a game he sings the national anthem in a strong and sure voice. Our government? It is "the best you can have." Our President" He's "good."

One pushes a little: Is the President in any trouble now? (It is 1973, and the President is Nixon.) Yes, he is, and he might have made some mistakes. Beyond that the child will not easily go. His parents had for the first time voted Republican in 1972, and now they are disappointed with, disgusted by, the president's Watergate-related behavior. But they have been reluctant to be too critical of the President in front of their children: "I don't want to make the kids feel that there's anything wrong with the *country*," the father says. There's *plenty* wrong with the President, he admits, and with the way the country is being run—and, he adds, with big business, so greedy all the time, as well as with the universities and those who go to them or teach at them; but America, he believes, is the greatest nation that ever has been—something, one has to remember, every President's speech-writers, Democratic or Republican, liberal or conservative, manage to work into just about every televised address.

Only indirectly, in drawings or comic exaggeration or metaphorical flights of fancy does the boy dare show what he has been making of Watergate, news of which has, of course, come to him primarily through television. Asked to draw a picture of the President, the boy laughs, says he doesn't know how (he had had no such trouble a year earlier), and finally manages to sketch an exceedingly small man, literally half the size of the earlier portrait. then, as he prepares to hand over the completed project, he has second thoughts. He adds a blue sky. Then he blackens the sky. He puts earth under the man, but not, as is his usual custom, grass. Then he proceeds to make two big round black circles, with what seem to be pieces of string attached to them. What are they? He is not sure: "Well, either they could be bombs, and someone could light the fuse, and they could explode and he'd get hurt, and people would be sad; or they could be balls and chains—you know, if you're going to jail" . . .

Way across the tracks, out in part of "rich suburbia," as I hear factory workers sometimes refer to certain towns well to the north and west of Boston, adults have a slightly different kind of love of country—less outspoken, perhaps, less defensive, but not casual and certainly appreciative. In those towns, too, children respond quite directly and sensitively to the various messages they have learned from their parents—and to a number of low-key "spectacles": flags out on July Fourth; the deference paid to civil employees; pictures of father in uniform during one or another war; and perhaps most of all, conversations heard at the table. "My father hears bad news on television, and he says 'thank God we're Americans,'" says a girl of eleven. She goes on to register her mother's gentle, thoughtful qualification: "It's lucky we live where we do." Her mother's sister, older and attracted to the cultural activity that only a city can offer, has to live a more nervous life: "My aunt has huge locks on her doors. My mother leaves the keys right in the car." Nevertheless, the United States of America, for the girl's aunt as well as her parents, is nowhere near collapse: "Everything is going to be all right with the country. This is the best place to live in the whole world. That's what my aunt says." The girl pauses. Now is the time to ask her what *she* has to say. But she needs no prodding; immediately she goes on: "No place is perfect. We're in trouble now. The President and his friends, they've been caught doing bad things. It's too bad. My older brother argues with daddy; he told daddy that it's wrong to let the President get away with all he'd done, while everyone else has to go to jail; and he told daddy there's a lot of trouble in the country, and no one is doing anything to stop the trouble. The President, I think he's running as fast as he can from the police. I guess I would if I knew I'd done wrong. But I'd never be able to get to Egypt or Russia, so he's lucky, that President." (Nixon has just gone to both countries.)

It is simply not altogether true, as concluded in some studies of "political socialization," that she and other children like her *only* tend to "idealize" the President, or give a totally "romanticized" kind of loyalty to the country, on the basis of what they hear, or choose to hear, from their parents or teachers. Many parents do select carefully what they say in front of their children; and children are indeed encouraged by their teachers, and the books they read, to see presidents and governors and Supreme Court justices and senators as figures much larger than life. Yet, in no time—at least these days—children can lay such influences aside, much to the astonishment even of parents who *don't* try to shield their children from "bad news" or "the evils of this world," two ways of putting it that one hears again and again. Black children laugh at books given them to read in school, snicker while the teacher recites historical pieties that exclude mention of many things, and often challenge their own parents when they understandably try to temper the actuality of black people in America. White children, too, as James Agee noticed in the 1930s, pick up the hypocrisies and banalities about them and connect what they see or hear to a larger vision—a notion of those who have a lot and those who have very little at all.

"The President checks in with the people who own the coal company," a miner's shy son, aged eleven, remarked in Harlan, Kentucky, where the Duke Power Company was fighting hard to prevent the United Mine Workers from becoming a spokesman of the workers. The child may well be incorrect; but one suspects that log of the calls made by the President would show him in contact with people very much like those who are on the board of the Duke Power Company, as opposed to people like the boy's parents. By the same token, when a child whose father happens to be on the board of a utility company, or a lawyer who represents such clients, appears to overlook whatever remarks his or her parents have made about the United States and instead emphasizes without exception the nation's virtues, including those of its leaders, by no means is psychological distortion necessarily at work. The child may well have taken the measure of what has been heard (and overheard) and come to a conclusion: this is what his parents really believe. The reason they believe it is to support a whole way of life—the one we are all living. And so, it is best for the child to keep certain thoughts (in older people, called "views") to himself.

Too complicated and subtle an analysis for a child under ten, or even under fifteen? We who in this century have learned to give children credit for the most astonishing refinements of perception or feeling about the nuances of family life or the ups and downs of neighborhood play, for some reason we are less inclined to picture those same children as canny social observers or political analysts. No one teaches children sociology or psychology; yet, children are constantly noticing who gets along with whom, and why. If in school, or even when approached by a visitor with a questionnaire (or more casually, with an all-too-interested face and manner), those same children tighten up and say little or nothing, or come up with platitudinous remarks, they may well have applied another of their sophisticated psychological judgments—reserving the expression of any controversial political asides for another, a more private occasion.

Thinking It Over

1. Recollect your own upbringing. How close do you fit Coles' models? Has he left you out?

2. Coles seems to tie a considerable amount of his explanation of why attitudes among children differ to economic status. Do you agree? Do you have any qualifiers?

37.
CHILDREN IN THE POLITICAL SYSTEM
by David Easton and Jack Dennis

Setting the Scene: This reading is a very small portion of a very large study of political socialization among children. Although it covered children with a wide range of socio-economic backgrounds from places all across America, its major focus is on children of the middle class, broadly defined. It is a fascinating study, not only for its findings but also for its methodology. I think you will find the *way* Easton and Dennis went about determining the "child's view of politics" both unique and useful.

Symbolic Associations of the Government Concept

As it appears that the child is rather likely to develop some working conception of government in these early years, we can move on to ask: What is the specific content of this concept? We might well expect that because of the inherent ambiguity and generality of the term, even for adults, considerable differences and disjunctiveness would characterize it for aggregates of children. Our findings to, in part, support this expectation. Yet there are clearly some dominant patterns in these collective conceptions, and these patterns vary to a large degree with the age and grade level of the children.

To get fairly directly at the dominant patterns in this period and at the way in which they change, we devised a pictorial representation of government. It took the form of the ten symbols . . . [Policeman, Washington, Uncle Sam, Voting, Supreme Court, Capitol, Congress, Flag, Statue of Liberty, President]. These symbols emerged distinctively in our pretest data when children were asked either to define government or to free associate with a list of words, one of which was government.

The pattern of response to these ten symbols is shown in Table 6-2. Several interesting facts are suggested. If we take 20 percent as a rough guide to what we might expect purely by chance as a maximum level of response to each of the ten symbol options (for two-answer format), we see that only four of these pictures were chosen with a frequency greater than chance. These four were George Washington, Voting, Congress, and President Kennedy. These are selected with considerably greater frequency than any of the others, although this dominance varies with grade level. For the youngest children, the two most popular options are the two Presidents, Washington and Kennedy. But these choices drop in the later grades. . . .

It would appear that, in terms of these symbols, the youngest child's perception of government is quite likely to be framed by the few personal figures of high governmental authority that cross his cognitive horizon, probably both in the school (where the portraits of presidents are often prominently displayed) and outside. The young child focuses most directly upon personal or perhaps charismatic aspects of the political authorities for his interpretation of what government is. But as he moves into the middle years (grades 4 to 6),

Table 6-2 Development of a Cognitive Image of Government: Symbolic Associations* (percent of children and teachers responding)†

Grade	Police-man	George Wash-ington	Uncle Sam	Voting	Supreme Court	Capitol	Congress	Flag	Statue of Liberty	President Kennedy	I Don't Know	N § Re-sponding	N Not Responding
Grade 2	8%	39	16	4	5	14	6	16	12	46	16%	1619	36
Grade 3	4	27	19	8	6	16	13	16	14	47	13	1662	16
Grade 4	6	14	18	11	10	17	29	13	13	37	13	1726	23
Grade 5	3	7	19	19	17	12	49	12	11	39	5	1789	14
Grade 6	2	5	17	28	17	10	50	11	17	31	5	1740	9
Grade 7	3	3	18	39	14	9	44	13	19	28	3	1714	9
Grade 8	2	2	16	47	16	7	49	12	20	23	2	1689	6
Teachers‡	1%	1	5	72	13	5	71	6	8	15	0%	390	1

*CA-9, page 4, item 24: "Here are some pictures that show what our government is. Pick the *two* pictures that show best what our government is."

†Percentages should add to 200 in the two-answer format, but do not, because of the failure of some children to make two choices; this is especially the case for those answering "I don't know."

‡We have added the responses of the teachers of these children for the sake of comparison; the teachers were given a similar questionnaire at the time of administration of the children's questionnaire.

§N = the number of cases making some response. This number was used as the base for the percentages.

there is a greater likelihood that his attention will turn to rather different prominent aspects of the authorities. Thus he revises his notions to include the Congress and drops George Washington—who suffers a precipitous decline after his initial showing.

Undoubtedly, the growing response to Congress reflects an awareness of several things. (These conclusions are supported by various other data as well.) First, the older children become more aware of the group character of government and do not simply identify it with single persons. Second, the more frequent choice of Congress probably also reflects a greater awareness of governmental institutions—particularly the ongoing organizations engaged in lawmaking (as suggested undoubtedly in the beginning social studies, history, or civics texts). Children move from a very personalized conception of governmental authority to one that emphasizes the "legal-rational," institutionalized aspects, to continue the Weberian parallel. We may characterize this more generally as a shift from a personalized to an impersonal image of government. Third, children appear to reflect a greater awareness of the representative character of these institutions. Impersonalization of authority is coincident with some growth in the recognition of regime norms, in this case of the rules of behavior that contribute to representation. This conclusion is borne out to some degree by the marked age shift which occurs as represented by the older child's greater tendency to pick Voting as the best picture of our government. By grade 8 nearly half the children chose Voting. This suggests some beginning awareness of the regime rules associated with popular democracy and the expected role of ordinary people in it.

The child's conception of government is, therefore, brought in stages from far to near, from one small set of persons to many people, from a personalized to an impersonalized form of authority, and toward an awareness of the institutionalization in our system of such regime norms as are embodied in the idea of a representative, popular democracy. Not that all the children are going through these stages of cognitive development. . . . But the patterns which emerge seem very striking and are supported in various ways by our other data.

Generally, therefore, in these data about the cognitive development of this rather abstract category of the individual's political thought, we detect more than a mere glimmering of a concept. Furthermore, the emergent conception in this instance reflects some fairly wide and regularly changing comprehension for aggregates of children.

This suggests that society is probably expending considerable energy in an effort to transmit a concept deemed appropriate in the American political system. If we compare children with their teachers, for example (Table 6-2), we find that the latter most roundly endorse the two options dominant for the eighth-grade children. The proportions are even higher for the teachers—who may be important agents contributing to the child's political and general conceptual development—so that in terms of the statistical norms, they stand perhaps closer to the end state suggested by the direction of movement of the children. One could hypothesize, therefore, that a part of society's efforts to inform the child is reflected in the responses of the teachers.

The Concept of Government and the Lawmaking Function

A supporting piece of evidence which is connected to the general pattern of development just described, but which supplements it from the standpoint of governmental functions (rather than from the structural aspects of the concept alone), has to do with the child's changing awareness of the chief lawmakers in our system of government. One thing we found was that, of the various kinds of political or other functions that the child most readily associates with government, the making of laws is very prominent. When the child is asked "What does the government do?" he is quite likely to answer that he, it, or they make the laws. In one instance, Andrew, aged eight, son of a truck driver and loader and in third grade at a Chicago-area school, was asked in a personal interview "What is government?" He replied: "It's like governor. It keeps all the laws." In the same vein, but at a little older age, Patrick, ten, son of a commercial photographer and in fifth grade in the Chicago area, replied: "That's where they make the law, pass it on, and give it to the Supreme Court, then to the President, and then it is passed on to us and it—well, we are supposed to abide by it."

We could use this transparent awareness of the lawmaking activity to probe further into the child's image of government. A questionnaire item that we presented in this connection read: "Who makes the laws? Put an X next to the one who does the most to make the laws." The options were: (1) Congress, (2) President, (3) Supreme Court, (4) I Don't Know. The same pictures as before were used. In Table 6-3 we see the patterns of change over the grade span for this aspect of the child's understanding.

Table 6-3 Development of an Awareness of the Chief Lawmaker* (percent of children and teachers responding)

Grade	Congress	President	Supreme Court	I Don't Know	Total	N Responding	N Not Responding
Grade 2	5%	76	11	9	100%	1627	28
Grade 3	11	66	17	6	100	1648	30
Grade 4	28	44	21	7	100	1723	26
Grade 5	57	19	20	3	99	1793	10
Grade 6	65	13	18	3	99	1743	6
Grade 7	72	9	16	3	100	1712	11
Grade 8	85	5	8	1	99	1690	5
Teachers	96%	1	3	0	100%	339	5

*CA-9, page 7, item 33. "Whom makes the laws? Put an X next to the one who does the most to make the laws." A smaller set of the same pictures as in item 24 was used.

Here the president's early dominance is apparent, but Congress gradually supplants him by grade 5. Thus, by the middle grades the child is increasingly prone to identify Congress as both the chief source of lawmaking and a more representative symbol of our government than the President.

If this trend should continue into adulthood, we would expect considerable support for Congress as the primary institution of government vis-à-vis the President. We would expect that, of the opposing observations of Max Lerner and Robert Lane, for example, those of Lane would be given greater credence. Lerner observed (as cited by Lane) that "When the American thinks of his government, he thinks first of the President as its symbol."[1] If "first" means while he is a second or third grader, then Lerner is correct. But this does not appear to be the sense in which he is using the word.

In light of the developmental trends we see in our data, our respondents seem to resemble more closely the "common men" in Lane's Eastport study. Lane found that his respondents were more likely to perceive government in terms of its legislative functions than of its administrative or judicial ones.[2] Government is thought of in terms of its products, the laws it makes.[3] As far as the common men in Eastport were concerned, Congress was the most important focus of their concept of government. They considered government and Congress as benign, helpful, and responsive—an organization "working for the people, not merely restraining them."[4]

All these findings converge with our data as far as the developmental trends are concerned. The oldest children in our test group are those who most resemble the common men of Eastport. Our data are an indication that this image of government is not confined to the period of Lane's study but has more general application. Over the grades our respondents increasingly tend to see government with Congress as its center, law as its most visible product, and, as we shall later note, benign, helpful, protective, and responsive qualities in its manner of operation.

Thinking It Over

1. You must know children in the second grade, about seven years old. What symbols would *they* associate with government and politics? Would these symbols change in the poor neighborhoods of our largest cities?

2. This study was done over twenty years ago. Would it hold true today? Here is an opportunity for an interesting and useful paper. See if you can get the teachers of a local school to cooperate. Then repeat the study yourself. To make it simple, compare only second and eighth graders. Because you would be using an empirical base to test a predictive model, the elements of a complete (if very limited) scientific inquiry are present.

---

[1]Max Lerner, *America as a Civilization* (New York: Simon and Schuster, 1957), p. 377.
[2]R. Lane, *Political Ideology* (New York: Free Press, 1962), p. 146.
[3]Ibid., pp. 147-148.
[4]Ibid., pp. 145-149.

38.
THE PHANTOM PUBLIC
by Walter Lippmann

Setting the Scene: Writing in the 1920s Walter Lippmann was a dominant influence in the development of journalism in this century. He was a prolific writer and respected scholar whose work still helps set the agenda for scholastic interest in public opinion and the media. The following excerpt is from his classic interpretation of the role of public opinion in American democracy. From its first paragraph, I suspect you will find much that seems not to have changed.

The private citizen today has come to feel rather like a deaf spectator in the back row, who ought to keep his mind on the mystery off there, but cannot quite manage to keep awake. He knows he is somehow affected by what is going on. Rules and regulations continually, taxes annually and wars occasionally remind him that he is being swept along by great drifts of circumstance.

Yet these public affairs are in no convincing way his affairs. They are for the most part invisible. They are managed, if they are managed at all, at distant centers, from behind the scenes, by unnamed powers. As a private person he does not know for certain what is going on, or who is doing it, or where he is being carried. No newspaper reports his environment so that he can grasp it; no school has taught him how to imagine it; his ideals, often, do not fit with it; listening to speeches, uttering opinions and voting do not, he finds, enable him to govern it. He lives in a world which he cannot see, does not understand and is unable to direct.

There is then nothing particularly new in the disenchantment which the private citizen expresses by not voting at all, by voting only for the head of the ticket, by staying away from the primaries, by not reading speeches and documents, by the whole list of sins of omission for which he is denounced. I shall not denounce him further. My sympathies are with him, for I believe that he has been saddled with an impossible task and that he is asked to practice an unattainable ideal. I find it so myself for, although public business is my main interest and I give most of my time to watching it, I cannot find time to do what is expected of me in the theory of democracy; that is, to know what is going on and to have an opinion worth expressing on every question which confronts a self-governing community. And I have not happened to meet anybody, from a President of the United States to a professor of political science, who came anywhere near to embodying the accepted ideal of the sovereign and omnicompetent citizen. . . .

. . . [V]arious remedies [to the problem of political apathy], eugenic, educational, ethical, populist and socialist, all assume that either the voters are inherently competent to direct the course of affairs or that they are making progress toward such an ideal. I think it is a false ideal. I do not mean an undesirable ideal. I mean an unattainable ideal, bad only in the sense that it is bad for a fat man to try to be a ballet dancer. An ideal should express the true possibilities of its subject. When it does not it perverts the true possibilities. The ideal of the omnicompetent, sovereign citizen is, in my opinion, such a false ideal. It is unattainable. The pursuit of it is misleading. The failure to achieve it has produced the current disenchantment. . . .

If all men had to conceive the whole process of government all the time the world's work would obviously never be carried on. Men make no attempt to consider society as a whole. The farmer decides whether to plant wheat or corn, the mechanic whether to take the job offered at the Pennsylvania or the Erie shops, whether to buy a Ford or a piano, and, if a Ford, whether to buy it from the garage on Elm Street or from the dealer who sent him a circular. These decisions are among fairly narrow choices offered to him; he can no more choose among all the jobs in the world than he can consider marrying any woman in the world. These choices in detail are in their cumulative mass the government of society. They may rest on ignorant or enlightened opinions, but, whether he comes to them by accident or scientific instruction, they are specific and particular among at best a few concrete alternatives and they lead to a definite, visible result.

But men are supposed to hold public opinions about the general conduct of society. The mechanic is supposed not only to choose between working for the Pennsylvania or the Erie but to decide how in the interests of the nation all the railroads of the country shall be regulated. . . .

Since the general opinions of large numbers of persons are almost certain to be a vague and confusing medley, action cannot be taken until these opinions have been factored down, canalized, compressed and made uniform. The making of one general will out of a multitude of general wishes is not an Hegelian mystery, as so many social philosophers have imagined, but an art well known to leaders, politicians and steering committees.[1] It consists essentially in the use of symbols which assemble emotions after they have been detached from their ideas. Because feelings are much less specific than ideas, and yet more poignant, the leader is able to make a homogeneous will out of a heterogeneous mass of desires. The process, therefore, by which general opinions are brought to cooperation consists of an intensification of feeling and a degradation of significance. . . .

For great masses of people, though each of them may have more or less distinct views, must when they act converge to an identical result. And the more complex the collection of men the more ambiguous must be the unity and the simpler the common ideas. . . .

I do not wish to labor the argument any further than may be necessary to establish the theory that what the public does is not to express its opinions but to align itself for or against a proposal. If that theory is accepted, we must abandon the notion that democratic government can be the direct expression of the will of the people. We must abandon the notion that the people govern. Instead we must adapt the theory that, by their occasional mobilization as a majority, people support or oppose the individuals who actually govern. We must say that the popular will does not direct continuously but that it intervenes occasionally. . . .

---

[1] *Cf.* my *Public Opinion*, Chapters XIII and XIV.

We must assume that the members of a public will not anticipate a problem much before its crisis has become obvious, nor stay with the problem long after its crisis is past. They will not know the antecedent events, will not have seen the issue as it developed, will not have thought out or willed a program, and will not be able to predict the consequences of acting on that program. We must assume as a theoretically fixed premise of popular government that normally men as members of a public will not be well informed, continuously interested, nonpartisan, creative or executive. We must assume that a public is inexpert in its curiosity, intermittent, that it discerns only gross distinctions, is slow to be aroused and quickly diverted; that, since it acts by aligning itself, it personalizes whatever it considers, and is interested only when events have been melodramatized as a conflict.

The public will arrive in the middle of the third act and will leave before the last curtain, having stayed just long enough perhaps to decide who is the hero and who the villain of the piece. Yet usually that judgment will necessarily be made apart from the intrinsic merits, on the basis of a sample of behavior, an aspect of a situation, by very rough external evidence. . . .

Thus we strip public opinion of any implied duty to deal with the substance of a problem, to make technical decisions, to attempt justice or impose a moral precept. And instead we say that the ideal of public opinion is to align men during the crisis of a problem in such a way as to favor the action of those individuals who may be able to compose the crisis. . . .

That, I think, is the utmost that public opinion can effectively do. With the substance of the problem it can do nothing usually but meddle ignorantly or tyrannically. It has no need to meddle with it. Men in their active relation to affairs have to deal with the substance, but in that indirect relationship when they can act only through uttering praise or blame, making black crosses on white paper, they have done enough, they have done all they can do if they help to make is possible for the reason of other men to assert itself.

For when public opinion attempts to govern directly it is either a failure or a tyranny. It is not able to master the problem intellectually, nor to deal with it except by wholesale impact. The theory of democracy has not recognized this truth because it has identified the functioning of government with the will of the people. This is a fiction. The intricate business of framing laws and of administering them through several hundred thousand public officials is in no sense the act of the voters nor a translation of their will.

But although the acts of government are not a translation of public opinion, the principal function of government is to do specifically, in greater detail, and more continually what public opinion does crudely, by wholesale, and spasmodically. It enforces some of the working rule of society. It interprets them. It detects and punishes certain kind of aggression. It presides over the framing of new rules. It has organized force which is used to counteract irregular force. . . .

Therefore, instead of describing government as an expression of the people's will, it would seem better to say that government consists of a body of officials, some elected, some appointed, who handle professionally, and in the first instance, problems which come to public opinion spasmodically and on appeal. Where the parties directly responsible do not work out an adjustment, public officials intervene. When the officials fail, public opinion is brought to bear on the issue.

Thinking It Over

1. Over half a century of massive change in communications technology has occurred since Lippmann published *The Phantom Public*. Is it your view that these changes have weakened or strengthened his case?

2. Write an essay entitled "Dan Rather and Walter Lippmann Debate the Role of Television in Presidential Elections."

3. On another matter. Walter Lippmann was a progressive in his day. Yet his entire essay was written in what today would be unacceptable sexist language. How can one not be struck by this and better understand and appreciate those who urge us to be aware of our own shortcomings on this score?

39.
TEFLON POLITICS
by Michael Jay Robinson and Maura Clancey

Setting the Scene: How much do Americans know about the events that shape the public sector? Very little, say the authors of this study. In reading it you may not recognize a good number of the news events to which the authors refer. But at least *you* have an excuse. You were probably too young at the time to pay much attention. The news stories mentioned, however, were *major* stories. They are surely analogous to the major news stories that have appeared in the year you are reading this. "Mass amnesia" is the way the authors describe the condition of the American public when it comes to remembering what's going on in the world.

Ron Nessen likes to say that if it didn't happen on the evening news, then it didn't happen. He should know: Nessen is the only person ever to work from both sides—as a network correspondent and as a presidential press secretary. But what Nessen neglects to say is that even if it *did* happen on the evening news, it still might not have "happened," at least as far as the public is concerned.

We have just completed a national, scientific phone survey of 366 adult Americans (April 14-16), and we are convinced that news coverage—even time on network television—doesn't translate directly into celebrity status or into public awareness. In our poll, whether the question involved Ed Meese's cronies or Gary Hart's original surname, the public enthusiastically exhibited its right *not* to know.

To the Best of Their Recollection

The first item on our questionnaire tapped the public memory about the year's top stories. "Over the last twelve months," we asked, "which news event would you say you remember the most?" We offered no hints.

Questions like this scare people, and about half the respondents who hung up on us during the survey did so after hearing this one. Even those respondents brave enough to continue remembered little about current events, nor did they equate news with political news.

A large proportion of our subjects balked at the idea of remembering a major event—and if they did, we asked them the same question again, giving them as much time as they needed to come up with something—anything. Even so, about one-fourth (23 percent) of our sample could recall nothing in the news from the last twelve months. In fact, the single most memorable news event for the last year turned out to be "can't remember" (see table 1).

Many of those who could recall something came up with events that had taken place two or more years ago—the war in the Falklands, the Tylenol scare, and Brezhnev's death, to name a few. Another fifth of the sample offered nonpolitical events—the sorts of things no self-respecting journalist would consider "real" news: volcano eruptions, weather reports, accidents, and sports news. All told, over 40 percent of our sample mentioned "nothing" or nonpolitical events as what they remembered most in 1983-1984.

To be fair, six of the ten most memorable stories were political (table 1). Nonetheless, our figures suggest the public remembers hard news the way Ronald Reagan remembers hard facts—fitfully, at best. They also suggest that news audiences have at least as great an interest in the mundane as the political. Criminal acts were precisely as memorable as *everything* going on in Central America. Soviet leader Yuri Andropov's death barely surpassed the death of rock/gospel singer Marvin Gaye as the year's most memorable obituary (Andropov having suffered the twin misfortunes of dying outside a major media center and of natural causes, not murder).

Murders and murderers totally outdistanced foreign wars or foreign anything. For example, homicidal maniacs, as a class, proved seven time as memorable as the brutal war between Iran and Iraq.

Table 1

Top Ten Most memorable News Events
In the Last 12 Months

Can't remember	23%
Beirut bombing	14
Campaign/Elections, general	12
Grenada invasion	7
Space shuttle	6
Marine pullout	4
KAL Flight 007	3
Weather	3
Lebanese war	2
Christopher Wilder	2
Hart campaign	2

But it isn't just homespun violence that outdoes politics or foreign affairs—news recollections are about as pedestrian as they are prurient or provincial. In what might be the most memorable finding about less-than-memorable news, the Soviet attack on Flight 007 proved no more newsworthy in the public's collective memory than the year's weather. In fact, the Korean jet massacre—so big in the media—proved only half as salient to the public as news about the U.S. space shuttle program.

These numbers reflect a public far less political than politicians or journalists usually assume, and a public possessing an astoundingly short memory. People recall the politics of yesterday, not the day before. Only four months after Jesse Jackson's stunning success in bringing Lt. Robert Goodman back from his Syrian captivity, for example, a miniscule 1 percent of the public was able to list that series of events among the most memorable. Christopher Wilder, race-car driver turned killer, does "better" than Jackson's rescue mission in refreshing memories because, in part, Wilder made news in April, not in January.

We found public memory about news and world affairs short enough to qualify as mass amnesia. In fact, the thesis that Americans are, more than most, willing to forgive and forget may have less to do with the former than with their astounding capacity for the latter.

Ed Meese and Charles "The Killer" Wick

A week before we conducted our survey, Louis Harris presented America with national polling data that showed the public had decided Attorney General-designate Ed Meese had to go. Our survey indicates that the same public barely knows that Ed Meese was ever here.

We asked our respondents, "Have you heard the name Ed Meese?" One-quarter of the sample said "No." We then asked those who had heard Meese's name why he had been in the news lately. One-quarter of them had to admit they couldn't remember anything at all about Meese, or they told ut things that weren't true. ("His recent tragic death" was a shocking example of misinformation.)

Another 10 percent could recall only that Meese had recently been designated as attorney general. Two percent of our respondents said Meese was about to be made secretary of state, which, we concluded, was either misinformation or a hot tip. And murder being much on the minds of our sample, one woman claimed that Ed Meese was a vicious killer—something not even Senator Howard Metzenbaum has intimated.

About a third (36 percent) of the entire sample did link Ed Meese to financial problems, his indiscretion concerning loans, cuff-links, cronyism, or his insensitivity toward hunger in America.

So how did Louis Harris get these people to volunteer an opinion about someone they didn't recognize? Quite simply, he never asked them whether they knew Meese or not. And, by describing his version of what Meese had done before asking for opinions, Harris could be fairly certain that people would have something to say.

Harris's respondents were faced with the following *lead* item—one that was quintessentially Harris in style: "Agree or disagree: Since federal law says that high officials must report all loans they receive, it looks as though Meese violated the law by not reporting a $15,000 loan from a couple who were close friends, both of whom later got federal jobs paying a combined total of close to $100,000 a year." (77 percent agreed, 15 percent disagreed, 8 percent were not sure.)

Looking at the question, we're not surprised at the results. But the real issue isn't so much Harris's methodology as it is the level of knowledge the public possesses about Attorney General-designate Edwin Meese. After all, it makes little sense to argue that Americans want dismissed from office a man about whom they know nothing.

Perhaps Harris felt safe in assuming people knew Ed Meese. After all, he had dominated a fair share of the news for several weeks. We checked abstracts of the evening news programs for the month of March—the month in which Meese's problems really began.

Meese made the network news forty-three times in just thirty-one days, and he was the lead story on eight separate occasions—total news time: 5,100 seconds. But despite Meese's ongoing status as a lead story on network news during the month before our survey, the Meese mess, no matter how generously defined, failed to penetrate the cognitive map of even four Americans out of ten.

Nonetheless, when compared to Charles Z. Wick, problem-plagued director of the USIA, Ed Meese is a celebrity. Wick's case magnifies everything said so far about levels of public information, extensiveness of news coverage, and the tenuousness of the relationship between the two.

Let's be fair. Since the beginning of the year Charles Wick has received only a fraction of the news coverage that Ed Meese has attracted. Still, back in January when Wick was a hot news story, network evening news featured him no fewer than ten times—five times as often as the networks featured Gary Hart during the same four-week period. Ten bad news reports in a month—half of them presented before the first commercial—puts the Wick affair somewhere between a major media story and an inside-the-Beltway press flap.

The facts in the Wick case were anything but trivial. Having lied to the *New York Times*, having slurred Margaret Thatcher and her sex, having secretly taped phone calls with Jimmy Carter and dozens of other private citizens—all in a year's time—Wick might well have become a household word in a world populated with the politically interested. Yet, in our survey three-quarters of the public had never heard his name! A microscopic *2 percent* of our sample could tell us anything at all accurate about Wick—good, bad, or indifferent. In fact, because Wick was, at the time of our poll, unlucky enough to own the same initials as Christopher Wilder, he was about as likely to be identified as a mass murderer as he was to be linked directly to his secret taping enterprise.

Thinking It Over

1. Here's an easy one. If you haven't already, read Walter Lippmann's remarks in the previous reading. Do Robinson and Clancey's findings confirm Lippmann's thesis?

2. This is another opportunity for a little empirical research. Do a quick and dirty survey (take every fifth person walking *into* a local supermarket [no bags of groceries going in]) and see how they score on a survey like the authors'. *Briefly* interview 25 people. It won't be scientific but you should learn a lot in the process and at the same time provide yourself with some empirical data for a short essay.

40.
ANATOMY OF THE NUCLEAR PROTEST
by Fox Butterfield

Setting the Scene: I can remember in the mid 1950s going to a "ground observer" station built by our community civil defense corps. My task was to watch out for Russian bombers carrying atomic bombs. I did two hours every Tuesday night. Some of you may remember when the threat of nuclear war seemed to be on everyone's mind in the early 1980s. At about that time a protest movement grew up in America dedicated to the proposition that the United States (and certainly the Soviet Union, too—if they would) should freeze the production of nuclear bombs. Both sides had enough blast power already to destroy the other a couple thousand times. Wasn't that enough? The movement got a remarkably positive press. In the following piece, Fox butterfield examines the character and the dynamics of the "freeze movement." Here was a group of people committed to a campaign to *create* popular opinion—to mobilize enough Americans of similar views to sway the politics of the nation.

Randall Forsberg was born in Alabama with "a few Georgia plantations ravaged by Sherman's troops floating around in my past." She graduated from Barnard College in the mid-1960's and became an English teacher at the proper Baldwin School in Bryn Mawr, Pa. There was little in her background to suggest that one day she would produce the idea that has turned the esoteric art of nuclear-arms control into an explosive popular issue.

Alan F. Kay graduated from the Massachusetts Institute of Technology, served in Army intelligence during World War II and got a Ph.D. in math at Harvard. He founded and eventually sold two highly profitable electronics companies, one of which worked for the Pentagon, before retiring to his home in Weston, a green-carpeted expanse of multiacre houses that is Boston's wealthiest suburb. There was little in his biography to suggest that he would provide the first key infusion of cash that enabled Miss Forsberg to translate her potent idea into action.

It was in 1980 that the retired businessman heard the former schoolteacher, now a student of the arms race, make her proposal. She was calling for a freeze—a mutual and verifiable freeze by the United States and the Soviet Union—on the testing, production and deployment of all nuclear weapons. It was a very simple idea—too simple, some critics contended, since it did not allow for the staggering complexities of the arms race. But Mr. Kay recognized that its simplicity could also be a strength: It sidestepped the old hard-to-understand arguments about MIRV's, megatonnage, throw weight and inspection that had long baffled the public. So Mr. Kay contributed the money that set the freeze campaign in motion—$5,000 to help organize the first national conference of peace groups in Washington in March 1981, where it was decided to concentrate on promoting the freeze as a common strategy. He would eventually add a quarter of a million dollars, spread among several antinuclear-war groups.

In the year since that first meeting, the freeze idea has reached what some activists like to call critical mass, borrowing from the lexicon of atomic physics. A poll last spring by The New York Times and CBS News found that 72 percent of Americans favor a nuclear freeze. It has been endorsed by hundreds of town meetings, dozens of city councils and nine state legislatures. Last month, it was approved by the House Foreign Affairs Committee in a nonbinding resolution.

The freeze idea has provided a spark, but it is only part of a larger story, an extraordinary grass-roots, nationwide movement to stop the nuclear arms race. The movement has even influenced President Reagan, leading him to soften his longtime opposition to arms-control talks and inspiring him to offer several sweeping proposals to negotiate sharp reductions in nuclear arsenals with the Soviet Union.

The movement's scope was dramatically illustrated by last month's disarmament rally in New York City, in which an estimated 700,000 people participated, making it the largest political demonstration in the history of the United States. And there are a growing number of politicians in Washington who believe the antinuclear arms issue may play an important role in this November's Congressional elections and the 1984 Presidential contest. Two weeks after the New York rally, the Democratic Party, at its midterm convention in Philadelphia, endorsed a carefully worded freeze resolution that had been drafted by aides to the party's leading Presidential contenders.

The profile of this latest of protests is a far cry from that of the powerful antiwar demonstrations of the late 1960's. The leaders are not bearded radicals but middle-aged and middle-class men and women, many accustomed to positions of responsibility and prestige. They include doctors, lawyers, nurses, scientists, teachers and priests. Their chief battles have been fought, not in street confrontations, but at sermons and lectures, in books and pamphlets . . .

One of the key new activists in the Physicians for Social Responsibility was Dr. Helen M. Caldicott, an outspoken Australian-born pediatrician. She had been passionately involved in the antinuclear movement since she read the novel "On the Beach" as a teen-ager in Melbourne. The book, set in Australia, describes the end of the world in a nuclear war. She became president of the group in 1979 and resigned her practice and a teaching job at the Harvard Medical School.

Since then, Dr. Caldicott, who is 43 years old, has toured the country showing the film "The Last Epidemic," which describes in chilling detail exactly what would happen to San Francisco in a nuclear attack. She sees her work as a logical extension of the practice of medicine: "It is the ultimate form of preventive medicine. If you have a disease and there is no cure for it, you work on prevention."

The Physicians for Social Responsibility has increased its membership from 3,000 a year ago to 16,000 today. Thomas A. Halsted, the groups' director, who once worked for the Arms Control and Disarmament Agency under the Carter Administration, says that it is now gaining more than 300 new adherents a week. The doctors' main organizational tactic until recently has been their careful field work, conducting day-long educational symposiums for groups of 1,500 to 3,000 doctors in a dozen cities around the country. But P.S.R., as it is called, has also begun adopting direct-mail appeals.

This year, the physicians' group will only send out about one million letters, Mr. Halsted said (as many as a million at a time are sent out by some of the more sophisticated political action committees in Washington). The organization has been getting back about $4 for every $1 it spends on its new mailings, he added. And its own budget has increased from $400,000 last year to about $1.6 million this year. Its staff of 24 full-time employees has just moved to new quarters above a Woolworth's store in Cambridge and has opened another small office in Washington. To aid its work, the group has acquired its own computer and also rents time on a bigger computer system at Harvard.

The success of the scientists and doctors groups has been shared by dozens of other such organizations, including High Technology Professionals for Peace, Communicators for Nuclear Disarmament, Educators for Social Responsibility and Musicians Against Nuclear Arms. Alan Sherr, who is president of the Lawyers Alliance for Nuclear Arms Control, believes that organizing by guild has been essential to the movement's success.

Mr. Sherr quit his job as general counsel to the Massachusetts Office of Human Services last January to open a full-time office for the lawyers' group; his new office looks out over Boston's Granary Burial Ground where Paul Revere and Sam Adams are among those interred. The guild approach, he said, "avoids the divisiveness of the Vietnam War protests"—a key factor in convincing older, conservative professionals to join the movement. During the 1960's, such men and women had no desire to be associated with the hippies and the flag-burning that were so prominent in the peace movement of that day. Their feelings are different toward telephone calls or letters from their peers.

Another important factor in convincing middle-class and middle-aged citizens to join the movement have been American churches—particularly the Roman Catholic Church, which has experienced a critical transformation.

According to Bishop Thomas J. Gumbleton, Roman Catholic auxiliary Bishop of Detroit, the change began during the Vietnam War, "though not many bishops publicly identified with it at the time." In 1968, he recalled, the National Conference of Catholic Bishops had written a pastoral letter outlining the possibility "of a conflict between a person's conscience and what the Government asks you to do." This, Bishop Gumbleton said, "highlighted a problem that had been there for many Catholics. We had a heritage as an immigrant church. We tended to overcompensate for this by our patriotism. As Francis Cardinal Spellman used to say, 'My country, right or wrong.'"

But as the Vietnam War continued, the bishops began to re-examine the old arguments concerning a just war. And, as Bishop Gumbleton pointed out, the church's reevaluation of the relationship between the individual and the state intensified with the Supreme Court decision allowing abortion in 1973.

In November 1980, with the collapse of the SALT II treaty and Mr. Reagan's campaign rhetoric about the need to increase America's nuclear arsenal, the Catholic bishops conference began work on a pastoral letter on the arms race. It is due to be issued this fall. Bishop Gumbleton, who is head of the American branch of Pax Christi, a Roman Catholic peace group, would not comment on its contents. But he referred to a statement made last year by Archbishop John R. Roach, president of the bishops conference, in which he proclaimed that "the most dangerous moral issue in the public order confronting us is the arms race." The nuclear freeze has been endorsed by 133 of the nation's 280 active Roman Catholic bishops . . .

Where is the movement headed? Democratic and Republican politicians agree that the antinuclear campaign is becoming far more partisan and political. They disagree about how significant a role it will play this fall and in the 1984 elections.

Patrick H. Caddell, the Carter Administration's pollster, said the mamoth rally in New York tended to confirm his conviction that "the antinuclear-arms movement is the most significant movement since the environmental movement in the late 1960's." In Mr. Caddell's view, the disarmament issue may not come to a head until after November, but he sees it as a long-term movement that is bound to have a strong political impact.

On the other hand, Lance Tarrance Jr., a pollster in Houston who works mainly for Republicans, discounts the surveys, which indicate that three-quarters of the American people favor a freeze. When his interviewers go on to ask people if they want a freeze that would leave the United States militarily behind the Soviet Union, "many people fall off the bandwagon," he said. "Support for the freeze is not firm; it won't hold up under stress."

But the movement has clearly had an impact on President Reagan, affecting his policy if not his personal thinking. The first significant change took place back in November, not long after the widespread teach-in on Veterans Day, when he proposed to the Soviet leader Leonid I. Brezhnev that Washington would forgo placing its new Pershing 2 and cruise missiles on European soil if Moscow would scrap its SS-20 missiles, already targeted on Western Europe.

Mr. Reagan appeared to be trying to outflank the burgeoning antinuclear-arms movement by being conciliatory instead of combative. Then last month he signaled a major switch away from his hard-line policy of linking arms control talks with Soviet aggression around the world. In a commencement speech at Eureka College in Illinois, he proposed a two-step plan in which the United States and the Soviet Union would initially reduce by one-third their inventories of nuclear warheads on land- and sea-based ballistic missiles.

Yet many peace activists remain skeptical about Mr. Reagan's sincerity in wanting nuclear-arms control. At the same time he was making his latest offer to Moscow, the Pentagon, under Secretary of Defense Caspar W. Weinberger, was drafting a five-year plan for fighting nuclear was against the Soviet Union "over a prolonged period." It has also not gone unnoticed that Mr. Reagan's choice to head the United States delegation to the new talks on reducing strategic arms, which began in Geneva on June 29, is a conservative, retired Army lieutenant general, Edward L. Rowny. General Rowny, who resigned from the American SALT II negotiating team to protest what he felt were too great concessions by the Carter Administration to the Soviet Union, has charged that a freeze would lock the United States into an inferior position.

Despite the rapid spread of the antinuclear-arms movement, there is still far from a consensus about how the United States should proceed or whether the freeze proposal itself is a good plan. More than 25 different resolutions to end the arms race have been introduced in Congress, and a freeze resolution was rejected by the Republican-controlled Senate Foreign Relations Committee.

Even some of the most active members of the movement worry that the freeze is too simplistic and impractical. Roger C. Molander, the founder of Ground Zero and a former National Security Council staff member, asks: "Freeze what? Does it mean freezing every last vehicle that is rigged up to deliver nuclear weapons, like the A-6's on aircraft carriers?"

"The freeze campaign is a good way for people to express their concern about the dangers of nuclear war," he continues, "but the lesson we can learn from the last 20 years is that focusing exclusively on arms-control agreements or the development of new weapons is not enough. The hard thing to face up to is that you can't get real arms control without improving relations with the Soviet Union."

Mr. Molander is concerned that Americans are deceiving themselves by concentrating only on affecting United States Government policy. "There is a little too much of the feeling that the whole problem is in this country and that if we can just get our act together, the Russians will go along."

But many of the activists are heartened by their sudden success, particularly as seen in the huge New York rally. Joan Baez, the folk singer and a leader of civil-rights and anti-Vietnam War protests of the 1960's, remarked in New York: "I have been on peace marches since I was probably 14 years old. But never in all those years did I feel the kind of encouragement I do now." Dr. James Muller, secretary of the International Physicians for the Prevention of Nuclear War and an assistant professor of cardiology at the Harvard Medical School, was euphoric after the big rally. "It was far more people than we expected," he said.

Representative Edward J. Markey, Democrat of Massachusetts, one of the original sponsors of the freeze resolution in the House, is also optimistic. A tall, lanky, youthful-looking man of 36, with modishly long brown hair and clear blue eyes, Mr. Markey believes that "freeze workers are going to be the replacements this fall for the Moral Majority in the 1980 election. They may provide the margin in close contests and make them flip-flop, perhaps 20 to 30 seats."

"My belief," Mr. Markey added, "is that Reagan was not put on earth by God to bring us supply-side economics. His role is to sit down with Brezhnev and end the arms race, to do for nuclear arms what Nixon did for China. My role is to create the atmospherics, the public and Congressional support, that will make Reagan the greatest man who ever lived." Mr. Markey paused, then went on with a smile. "He can reject if, of course, but we will have tried."

Thinking It Over

1. To what extent was this a popular movement and to what extent was it an elitist vanguard of well-heeled technocrats on a mission of their own?

2. Comment on the following: The nuclear freeze movement is just the kind of public opinion we need; a thoughtful mobilization of people with brains and education. Even Walter Lippmann would approve. (See Lippmann's remarks in an earlier reading.)

41.
THE POLITICAL IMPACT OF PRIME-TIME TELEVISION: "THE DAY AFTER"
by Stanley Feldman and Lee Sigelman

Setting the Scene: Everyone has an opinion about the effect of television on our lives. But in fact we actually know very little. Take, for instance, the effect of TV on public opinion concerning a critical public issue of the day. What follows is from a scientific study of "The Day After," an ABC movie watched by the second largest TV audience in the history of the United States. What the movie did was to try to scare the hell out of us. It might fairly and usefully be asked, did it? What was the impact of this movie on politics in a democracy? The authors of the following study sought to make that determination. Many of the details have been omitted so that we may concentrate on the results and how they relate to public policy.

The attitudinal effects of the television docudrama "The Day After," which depicted the aftermath of a Soviet nuclear attack on the Kansas City area, are analyzed through data from a panel conducted immediately before and after the program was shown. The effects of the program's byproducts (associated coverage and discussion) outweighed the effects of the program itself. The program seems to have had its greatest direct impact on the salience of and information about nuclear war rather than on attitudes as such.

Analyses of television's political impact (e.g., Robinson, 1976; Iyengar et al., 1982) have long focused on news and documentary programs, largely ignoring prime-time entertainment shows. However, beneath the surface of network entertainment programs rest some fairly elaborate, though often unarticulated, political-ideological foundations (see, e.g., Goldman, 1982), and some of these programs deal directly with important social and political issues. In this study we probe the effects of one such program. "The Day After," an ABC Theatre program, was shown on Sunday, 20 November 1983, to an audience estimated at more than 100 million, making it the second most-watched program in American television history (McFadden, 1983). The makers of "The Day After" set out, in the words of Brandon Stoddard, president of ABC Motion Pictures, to show "ordinary Americans and what their lives would be like after a nuclear war" (quoted by Farber, 1983). This they accomplished in unprecedentedly graphic terms:

We see virtually an entire populace reduced to vaporized silhouettes. We see blistered and blinded human gargoyles suffer slow death from radiation sickness. We see the crumbling of a society's restraints: the most law-abiding citizens emerge from the rubble of ground zero to loot, rape and pillage. As firing squads add to the mass graves, a few valiant survivors . . . struggle to reconnect the severed communal bonds that distinguish life from mere existence.   But their efforts erode as relentlessly as the deathly white ash that wafts down upon the blackened fields. (Waters, 1983)

What effects did watching "The Day After" have?   By providing an answer to this question we hope to shed new light on the political impact of prime-time television. However, before we begin our own account, we need to read some existing evidence into the record. According to a poll conducted by the Warner-Amex Qube cable television network, only 13 percent of 5,500 viewers surveyed following the movie believed there was no hope of avoiding nuclear war. Nor did the movie lead to a major increase in support for a nuclear freeze: 49 percent said they "still support" nuclear arms control, while 29 percent said they "still support" "strength through nuclear arms buildup"; 12 percent said they "now support" arms control, but 6 percent said they "now support" an arms buildup; the remaining 4 percent were "confused" or "don't care" (McFadden, 1983).   In a survey conducted by the *Washington Post* on the day after "The Day After," 850 members of a 1500-person national sample originally interviewed during the first week of November were reinterviewed. Their responses indicated little or no change in support for President Reagan's handling of his job, his nuclear weapons policy, or a nuclear freeze, and no increase in the perception that nuclear war was imminent (Sussman, 1983).   Similarly, an overnight nationwide telephone poll conducted at George Washington University uncovered no change in viewers' estimates of the likelihood of nuclear war, appraisals of President Reagan's job performance, feelings of political powerlessness, or support for unilateral nuclear disarmament, a bilateral nuclear freeze, or decreased defense spending. This evidence led William Adams, the director of the poll, to conclude that those who predicted the movie would produce at least a short-term bonanza in additional antinuclear sentiment among the general public were completely wrong. . . . 'The Day After' failed to change existing views on the horror of nuclear war, the need for mutual arms control, and the strategy of deterrence" (Adams, 1983).

In assessing this evidence, we must recognize, first, that the designs of these surveys were not as rigorous as one might have wished; they employed independently drawn pre- and post-"The Day After" samples or post-only samples, either of which makes it difficult to draw any firm conclusions about changes in people's attitudes, cognitions, and issue salience. In addition, notwithstanding the arguments of both its warmest admirers and its most vociferous opponents, "The Day After" focused on a relatively narrow issue of the *aftermath* of a nuclear strike, not only what led to the attack (a question the moviemakers deliberately avoided), what could be done to avoid such an attack, or the chances that an attack will actually occur. In this light we would argue that assessing the impact of "The Day After" as having little or no effect on attitudes toward issues the movie did not directly address constitutes a very hard test of its effects. . . . Thus, even though existing evidence indicates that a graphic depiction of the aftermath of a nuclear attack did not lead to any wholesale repositioning of the public on policy issues or to any large-scale rethinking of basic political orientations, this does not necessarily mean that "The Day After" had no important effects. . . .

The Impact of "The Day After"

Now that we have examined the impact of the byproducts of "The Day After," it is time to consider the effects of the movie itself. The first thing to note in this regard is that, contrary to expectations, judgments of the movie's realism had virtually no bearing on its effects. The only statistically significant effect associated with Realism is on Defense Spending, with those who considered the movie realistic becoming more likely to call for cutting the defense budget. The only other coefficient for Realism which even approaches any substantial magnitude is in the Relations with Russia equation, but the standard error of this coefficient is so large that any substantive interpretation would be tenuous at best. So, with only a single exception out of fourteen trials, we can say that the impact of "The Day After" was unaffected by judgments about it realism.

. . . [W]atching "The Day After" had a significant impact on the reported salience of nuclear war with viewers giving higher estimates of the amount of time they spent thinking about nuclear war in the second wave of the survey than they had in the first wave . . . this effect was most pronounced among viewers with only six or eight years of schooling and declined perceptibly at higher levels of education; in fact, the increase in salience was almost twice as large for those with a sixth-grade education as it was for college graduates. On the other hand, "The Day After" seems to have had no effect on self-rated knowledge concerning nuclear war, and this noneffect was equally true for all levels of education.

The results for the three emotional impact variables are rather uneven. There is no indication whatsoever that watching the movie led to any more pronounced feelings of anger or to any diminished sense of hopefulness about the nation's defense against nuclear war. Viewers did not, on this evidence, react to "The Day After" in a strongly emotional fashion; the movie did not infuriate them, nor, notwithstanding some of the more extreme predictions that were made about its potentially traumatizing impact, did it drop them into an abyss of despair. It did, however, cause them to become somewhat more worried about America's nuclear defenses that they had been before watching. Combining this effect with the one reported above for Thinking about Nuclear War, we can say the "The Day After" led to increased public concern about the issue of nuclear war. Moreover, just as was true of Thinking about Nuclear War, the movie's effect on the Worry dimension was registered primarily among the least educated viewers and diminished to near zero among those with more years of education. This disproportionate impact on less educated, and presumably less knowledgeable, viewers is consistent with the *tabula rasa* interpretation introduced earlier.

In addition to these clear salience effects, "The Day After" may have generated changes in cognitions concerning the consequences of nuclear war. Since the story line of "The Day After" focused on the aftermath of a nuclear attack, we argued earlier that if the movie had any impact at all on its viewers, that impact should show up most clearly in images of life after the bomb has fallen . . . this was in fact the case. Those who watched the movie became more likely to believe that basic services such as food, shelter, and medical care would not be available after a nuclear attack and that the prospects for their own and the country's survival would be dim. For those with a high school education, the effects are roughly equivalent for Services and Survivability, and both are fairly sizable. . . .

As for more general orientations toward foreign and defense policy issues, "The Day After" seems to have had no effect on the salience of defense policy or on support for nuclear arms limitation. Thus, despite pre-movie pronouncements by both friends and foes of the movie, our data reinforce indications from the Warner Amex-Qube, *Washington Post*, and George Washington University surveys that "The Day After" produced no groundswell for arms limitation—although we should bear in mind that support for arms limitation was very widespread before the movie was shown. Similarly, the movie's effects on attitudes toward U.S. Soviet relations were generally trivial, though an interesting education-based pattern emerges in table 3. For those with very little education, the small impact of the movie was in the direction of a tougher stance toward the Soviet Union, but the opposite was true for college graduates. In fact, those with post-graduate educations moved a significant degree toward a more conciliatory posture.

Interestingly, the very same basic pattern shows up, albeit much more strongly, in attitudes toward defense spending. Having watched the movie, those with little education became more supportive of higher defense spending, but those with high levels of education became more likely to endorse defense spending cutbacks. The tipping point in this regard was twelve years of education. For those with just a high school education, the impact of the movie on attitudes toward defense spending was nil, but closer to the educational extremes the movie had fairly pronounced and directly opposite effects.

Finally, did "The Day After" have any effect on attitudes toward the Reagan administration? Among the most educated people, watching the movie led to a slight increase in the belief that the policies of the Reagan administration were increasing the chances of nuclear war. This effect was, however, very limited. The movie's impact is far more evident in evaluations of President Reagan's handling of foreign policy. Again, this impact varies significantly according to education. For those with less than a college degree, "The Day After" had virtually no effect one way or the other. For those who had completed college, however, watching the movie appears to have led to a substantial decline in evaluations of the president's performance in the foreign policy arena. This education-based effect on policy-related evaluations is entirely consistent with the reactions to "The Day After" among more educated people in the areas of defense spending and relations with Soviet Union.

Conclusion

The foregoing analysis suggests several conclusions about the impact of prime-time television. First of all, we have seen how dangerous it can be to try to estimate the impact of a television docudrama without controlling for associated media coverage of the issue on which the docudrama is focused. The televised panel discussion that followed "The Day After," interpersonal discussions sparked by the program, and especially stories about nuclear war on television and in the newspapers had substantial effects on political attitudes and cognitions. In fact, these effects, taken together, were larger than the impact of "The Day After" itself. Most important, newspaper and television stories about nuclear war significantly affected support for arms limitation and relations with the Soviet Union, whereas

"The Day After" itself had no such effect. Thus, much of the *total* impact of the program apparently resulted from the attention it received in the media rather than from direct viewership. Ironically, then, those who feared that "The Day After" would work to the benefit of the antinuclear movement may have helped bring out that very result by drawing attention to the program. More generally, our analysis suggests that the impact of the media on political attitudes and cognitions can be substantial when a great deal of media attention is focused on a particular subject.

Consistent with our earlier discussion of attitudes, cognitions, and salience, we found that "The Day After" had its greatest impact on salience and information. Less educated people in particular thought and worried more about nuclear war after watching "The Day After." Moreover, viewers became less likely to believe that basic public services would be sufficient following a nuclear attack and that the country would survive. Thus, consistent with a number of previous finds on the effects of movies and television programs, the most pronounced effects of "The Day After" pertained directly to the program's major substantive focus.

The most significant *attitudinal* effects of "The Day After"—on evaluations of defense spending and of President Reagan's handling of American foreign policy—were clearly mediated by education. Less educated viewers came to favor *greater* defense spending and gave Reagan higher marks for his handling of foreign policy. More educated people, on the other hand, grew more disapproving of Reagan and called for more cuts in defense spending. Further analysis not reported here shows that this is not simply a social class effect, for substituting income in place of education or combining the two did not produce the same result, nor is it a simple knowledgeability effect, for replacing education with self-professed knowledge concerning nuclear war failed to generate a similar interaction. Similar tests for interaction effects of perceived realism of "The Day After" produced no substantial effects, however.

On at least some issues, our analysis shows that different types of viewers reacted very differently to the information communicated by "The Day After." Failure to examine interaction effects would thus erroneously have led us to conclude that attitudes toward President Reagan and defense spending were not influenced at all by watching "The Day After." As we have shown, there were instances in which "The Day After" led its viewers not in a single direction but in two, depending upon what they themselves brought to the movie. In the aggregate, then, there seems to have been little overall change in political attitudes as a consequence of "The Day After," though that lack of overall movement masks, to some extent, movement in offsetting directions in different segments of the public.

In explaining the political role of network television news programs, Michael Robinson (1976, pp. 426-32) refers, among other factors, to the sheer size of the audience (which means that mass audiences are exposed to ideas and information they would never deliberately seek out), the high credibility of the news programs (which predisposes viewers to accept what they see and hear), and the thematic nature of television news coverage (which makes news stories readily interpretable for the mass audience). Too often overlooked is the fact that the very same attributes are no less characteristic of some *nonnews* programs as well, including docudramas like "The Day After." The effects we have uncovered, then,

to numbers of candidates, in a manner beyond the reach of individual citizens.

This power to pool political money makes the PACs peculiarly enticing to politicians in frantic search of shortcuts. The PACs, proffering gifts of $5,000 (and even $10,000, to candidates who have both a primary and a general-election contest), offer tempting paths of least resistance.

The PACs' allure is the prime cause of a disturbing trend: congressmen and senators are becoming more and more indebted to outside special-interest PACs. Thus, those lawmakers obligate themselves, morally at least, to accord favored treatment to those PACs' lobbyists, even though those lobbyists are not permitted to vote in their elections. In 1986, for 185 representatives—nearly half the U.S. House—more than 50 percent of their campaign funds came from outside political action committees rather than from their own constituents. Many congressmen got 60 or 80 percent—and in two cases, more than 90 percent—of their money from outside PACs.

The U.S. Constitution calls them "representatives." But when congressmen are obligated to outsiders for 60 percent or 80 percent of their campaign funds, whom do they *really* represent? When, over an eight-year period, a congressman like Banking Committee Chairman Fernand St. Germain, the Rhode Island Democrat, takes nearly a third of a million dollars from banks and other financial institutions, is he the representative of his Rhode Island congressional district? Or is he the representative of the banking industry?

. . .

The crisis in the way we now finance our congressional election campaigns can be summarized in two concise facts:

First: Campaigns have become so expensive that, to wage a winning campaign, the average United States senator must raise nearly $10,000 a week *every week during his or her entire six-year Senate term.*

Second: Under the current system, even the most idealistic senator has no alternative for achieving that task other than to rely on special-interest groups.

The result is this: In the first six months of 1987, thirteen U.S. senators raised over $3 million in campaign funds. More than half of that money came from outside special-interest PACs—far above the normal proportion for senators. Well over half of that came from PACs who were now switching horses and contributing to senators they had previously tried to defeat.

These thirteen are not a random sampling of senators. *All of them had just been elected in November of 1986.*

Their next election is not until 1992.

Thinking It Over

1. All right, you don't like what PACs are doing. But what are you going to do about it? How might one construct an essay entitled "Clipping the Wings of the PACs: A Modest Proposal"?

2. Stern says "Neither factions nor special-interest money is new to American politics. In *Federalist Papers* No. 10, James Madison warned of the dangers of factionalism." If Stern is saying Madison warned us about the dangers associated with multiple interests and therefore supports his (Stern's) thesis, has he read Madison correctly? Comment.

46.
SHOOTING BACK
by Kirk Victor

Setting the Scene: Here is the situation. The Defense Department does not build its own weapons. It contracts with private corporations to build them. It says, in effect, we need 1,000 new jet fighters. If your company would like to build them for us, give us a bid for the contract and we'll consider it along with the bids of other companies. Thus the market place is supposed to keep prices down and protect the taxpayers—Congress becomes a "shopper" in a competitive market. That's the theory. This article is about what happens when Congress (which has its suspicions about the competitiveness of the market) tries to tighten up the nature of the contracts being awarded. The answer is the companies shoot back.

Rep. Charles E. Bennett, D-Fla., recalls that a top executive of a major defense contractor once sat in his office and told him that if Congress didn't want the government to pay for boarding company executives' dogs, it ought to enact appropriate legislation.

"He was not being sarcastic," Bennett said in an interview. "He explained to me that the corporate structure was not designed in a way to weigh things other than for the good of the corporation." In other words, the executive's duty was to the company and its shareholders. It was not his job to protect the public interest: That was Congress's responsibility.

"With that kind of a challenge, knowing full well that they were not going to correct [the problem], we set out to do it," Bennett said. He joined other legislators to amend the 1985 defense authorization bill with an "allowable costs" section that spells out legitimate expenses. . . .

A Common Cause study last year profiled the 10 companies receiving the largest Pentagon procurement and research and development contracts and concluded that the companies' success was the result of a combination of factors, including campaign contributions, home-state jobs, honoraria for members of Congress and large Washington offices that monitor Pentagon spending and maintain close ties with government leaders.

But portraying the defense industry as a monolith is wrong, according to a wide range of industry officials, analysts and congressional sources. On the contrary, defense contractors say, they are fiercely competitive, as an industry official put it, they would "eat each other for breakfast" when vying for a contract.

Even though the companies fight to secure particular contracts—from the B-1 bomber to the F-16 fighter—they have paid little attention to generic issues that affect them all—such as procurement rules that prescribe how government dollars are doled out. "On the general industrywide problems, I don't think they have been an effective lobby," Sen. Jeff Bingaman, D-N.M., chairman of the Armed Services Subcommittee on Defense Industry and Technology, said in an interview. . . .

A cacophony of voices emanating from companies pursuing individual interests makes for an industry that is vulnerable when its practices are suddenly called into question. That is what occurred in the mid-1980s, when headlines told of defense firms selling items to the government at wildly inflated prices—such as $600 toilet seats and $7,000 coffeemakers—and defense contractors became symbols of "waste, fraud and abuse." "Guys who wrote about that knew that the horror stories were aberrations," said Weyman B. (Sandy) Jones, vice president for public affairs at Grumman Corp. "They say it as a metaphor for a larger truth about horrible waste in military contracting—they believed the whole system was wasteful . . . .   The process begins there and the end of it is punitive legislation and regulation that I think demonstrably does not serve the national interest."

Industry officials argue that national security is inextricably linked to industry's good fortunes. With that argument as their rallying cry, the companies have launched a lobbying campaign—they call it "educational"—aimed at gaining a re-examination of recent procurement changes. And the companies already appear to be winning points with some lawmakers on Capitol Hill. . . .

Company Complaints

The focus of the debate is the legislation and regulation that took effect during the past five years under the rubric of "procurement reform." Those changes, industry officials argue, will sharply reduce profits, undermine technological innovation and discourage companies from bidding on programs, thereby creating a long-term threat to U.S. interests.

The distasteful changes cited by industry officials include technical modifications in the way the government pays defense contractors.   Among the changes are "cost-sharing" provisions that require a company to pay for research development on a weapons project even though there is no guarantee that the company will be chose to produce it or that the weapon will even be developed: a reduction, from 90 per cent to 75 per cent, in "progress payments" that provide interest-free financing for work under way, and a lowering of profit margins to about 10 per cent. . . .   New tax law changes have also been attacked by the contractors because they eliminate the right to defer tax payments on profits from uncompleted contracts.

Company officials and industry advocates say these changes will undercut industry's ability to meet U.S. defense needs. "I think that unless the environment is improved for the defense industry, the industrial base is in jeopardy—the ability of this country's defense industrial base to provide an adequate level of protection for our national security," said Jean A. Caffiaux, senior vice president of the electronic Industries Association (EIA).   Also framing the issue in those stark terms is the rejuvenated Aerospace Industries Association of America Inc. (AIA), led by former Rep. Don Fuqua, D-Fla.

By underwriting expensive studies and becoming more accessible to reporters, the associations and industry executives are getting their message out. Defense contractors are also waging aggressive advertising campaigns—for example, on television shows seen by "upscale people in our line of activity," said John H. Bickers, director of advertising for McDonnell Douglas Corp.   On a recent airing of ABC News's *This Week with David Brinkley*, a McDonnell Douglas advertisement ("We're giving America its money's worth") was followed by a Raytheon Co. spot ("Quality starts with fundamentals").

The companies' efforts to cultivate better relations with reporters may already be having an effect. News accounts about the defense industry now stress the difficult times that lie ahead because of procurement reforms and flat defense budgets. A recent *Washington Post* article, for example, highlighted projections of "a bruising industry shakeout that will inevitably force many players into new lines of work in order to survive." That is a far cry from stories of a profit-bloated industry hell-bent on gouging government.

The change in news media coverage troubles Dina Rasor, director of the watchdog Project on Military Procurement in Washington, who despaired that "scandals aren't news anymore." She also denigrated industry's efforts to change the terms of the debate. "They are seeing that it's a good time to reclaim their territory," she said. "I don't see the health of these companies going down—it's like taking a fifth hot fudge sundae from a fat man, and he complains that you're starving him."

And House Armed Services Committee staff member Joseph Cirincione expressed incredulity at the notion that the firms' fortunes had sunk. "All you have to do is to take a look at the executive salaries, bonuses, benefits and life-style of defense contractors to know that those companies are not hurting," he said.

Despite the skeptics, the industry's arguments appear to be gaining an increasingly sympathetic audience on Capitol Hill. "the majority in Congress, at least in my view, are anxious that we maintain a strong industrial base," Bingaman said. "We have to . . . find out exactly what that means and what that requires, but no one wants to see us in the position of having to meet our defense needs by buying abroad."

Assessing Damage

Bingaman's subcommittee last August established an ad hoc panel of 13 senior defense industry officials. Its mandate was to identify "those aspects of the acquisition process that stifle innovation, drain good talent away from defense industries and threaten the technological lead that is the foundation of our nation's security," the Senator said in a statement.

The subcommittee's decision to turn to defense industry executives for advice is a clear signal that the industry's credibility is improving. Nevertheless, a congressional staffer who works on defense issues said that the panel members were "setting the stage" for an appeal to "economic nationalism" but that their agenda really is aimed at rolling back reforms.

In February, the ad hoc group released a report and, in a cover letter to Bingaman and Phil Gramm, R-Texas, the subcommittee's ranking minority member, said that Congress, the Defense Department, and industry must "reestablish a more open and collaborative (rather than adversarial) climate." The 65-page report, accompanied by an "illustrative bill" to implement its recommendations, bluntly criticized the procurement system. "Contractors have little incentive to take on projects that involve technological risk and innovation," it said. "[The Pentagon] and Congress must realize that profit and investment policies are the foundation of industry's ability to serve the nation's needs. National security is not well served by policies which make defense business a poor investment."

John D. Rittenhouse, senior vice president of General Electric Co.'s Aerospace Group and chairman of the ad hoc committee, testified in April hearings of Bingaman's subcommittee that "well-intentioned legislation can actually have profoundly negative impacts on our acquisition system."

"I don't think anyone perceived how bad the hostile environment was going to get," Rittenhouse said in an interview. That environment includes more regulation, more auditing and more contract requirements, he said. He added: "I'm not trying to duck responsibility, but I'm trying to deal with doing what's best for the defense of the country, as corny as that sounds. If we keep adding on to the price of these systems with additional layers of regulations and if we [industry and government] continue to [be] . . . so hostile with each other that we can't work together on these very complex systems, then we're not going to be able to build these complex weapons systems. It's that simple."

Bingaman has introduced a bill that addresses at least some of the industry panel's concerns. One provision puts limits on fixed-price development contracts that force contractors to take on "an inordinate share of the risk," Bingaman said in a statement. Those contracts mean that firms may have to project what a new product will cost before it has been designed.

The industry's arguments gained further momentum with the release in March of a study by the MAC Group, a management consulting firm in Cambridge, Mass. The report was commissioned at a cost of $400,000 by three Washington associations: the AIA, the EIA, and the National Security Industrial Association. The authors stated that they had "complete independence with regard to the methodology, findings and conclusions."

The MAC study's conclusions track those of the industry panel. The study examined how nine profitable defense programs of nine major—but unidentified—contractors would have been affected if recent procurement reforms had been in effect when the programs were begun. The reforms include changes in progress payments, lower profit allowances, elimination of tax deferral benefits, cost sharing on new programs and a requirement that a company pay for at least half of the special tools on projects that may never go forward. Using confidential financial data provided by the firms, the MAC Group found that the reforms would have cut profits by an average of 23 per cent, that companies would have been forced to reduce research and development investment and that they would have had to decline to bid on some programs.

The study said that changes in procurement policy had been fueled by diverse factors—from spare parts scandals to free-market ideology to budgetary constraints. Although the cumulative effect of these changes would not be reflected in industry's financial statements for three or more years, the study grimly predicted a weakened industry vulnerable to foreign competition. In short, it concluded, the policies "are not consistent with the maintenance of a strong defense industrial base."

Industry executives were clearly heartened by the widespread—and rather uncritical—news media coverage of the study. "The press surprisingly wrote it up with a minimum of editorialization," the EIA's Caffiaux said. "It was fair and balanced reporting . . . . If the report had come out four or five years ago, the press would have regarded it as self-serving and ginned up by fat cats."

Defense Secretary Frank C. Carlucci III and other Defense Department officials received a briefing on the study and "understood" the problems, said the AIA's Fuqua.

Eleanor R. Spector, deputy assistant Defense secretary for procurement, said that the government has special obligations in light of its status as the defense contractors' dominant customer. "We don't have the right to push contractors and force them to lose money on our contracts through no inefficiency on their part," she said. On the other hand, she said, "We try to do the right thing by contractors and by the American taxpayers, without being unduly influenced by [industry] studies."

Members of the House Armed Services Committee also made time to hear about the study, and the reception was "quite understanding—not the least bit hostile," said Donald H. White, president and chief operating officer of Hughes Aircraft Co., a unit of General Motors Corp.

Not everyone was sold on the study. Committee aide Cirincione agreed with its conclusion that there has been "a crazy patchwork of reform," but he attributed that in large measure to the contractors "for repeatedly lobbying for changes in procurement law that would favor their particular industry or company."

Other criticisms of industry's thesis are also being voiced. Earlier this month, the GAO noted in a letter to Bennett that the MAC study was based on data from nine firms but made "no attempt to establish the level of over-all industry profitability data, it is not possible to determine the full impact of existing policies."

Peter T. Bower, a co-author of the study, responded that "short of a sample of 100 per cent, GAO can always come back and say it's only a sample."

Well-known whistle-blower A. Ernest Fitzgerald of the Air Force's financial management office, called the study a "self-serving document" because the consultants used the companies' numbers "without any knowledge whether they were true . . . . If I were to put out a report based on things people gave me, nobody would pay attention to it."

But Robert N. Anthony, professor emeritus at Harvard University Graduate School of Business Administration, who also worked on the study, said: "It's the impact [of the reforms] that makes the difference, and that was very carefully controlled. Any bias in the initial figures was unimportant—we had to have a starting point."

Backing Off Bids

As the debate over the study continues, industry critics—and some government officials—are unhappy that it is being used so effectively as a lobbying tool.

A Pentagon official said: "What is unusual about [the study] is that the [industry executives] have united to embrace it to their breast and preach it as if it is the gospel to political leaders as well as [Pentagon] officials. I don't think about half of them understand the assumptions behind the study." He said it presented "a worst case scenario" and that its scare tactics would undermine industry's credibility.'But if it was a worst-case scenario, company executives were not only echoing its themes, but also publicly pointing to examples of how procurement reforms had affected their companies' fortunes.

White said that Hughes Aircraft had decided to make a bid that "was far too high" to win a contract for radar on the Air Force Advanced Tactical Fighter (ATF). The decision "shocked people [because] we are the leading airborne fighter radar company in the world," White said. "It was very difficult not to bid—we worked on this for a long time," he added. The decision was made "not out of pique or principle—we tried to make what we thought was a well-thought-out business judgment." He called the ATF a case of "forced cost-sharing" that "makes contractors less viable, which is not in the long-term interests of the country." And John O'Brien, Grumman's president and chief executive officer, told shareholders that Grumman had decided not to make a low bid on a new aircraft because it "did not make business sense."

Amid such complaints by defense executives, the House in May passed a measure that would require contractors with more than $100 million in negotiated defense contracts to report their profitability, to help determine the validity of industry's arguments. Bennett, who offered the proposal, said in a statement that while contractors complain about lower profits, the GAO and the Navy had conducted studies showing that defense contractors' profits were twice as high as comparable commercial profits. "Anyone who wants to play the game of saying that GAO was wrong must ante up better information," he said. "Otherwise, everyone argues from his own studies."

As the debate over procurement policies intensified, at least one executive offers a dismal forecast. "Only with some emotional, dramatic event will people pay attention—some big contractor will have to go belly-up or some big program will have to be proposed to which there are no bids because companies don't have cash," said John J. Stirk, staff vice president for congressional relations at General Dynamics Corp. "Only with some dramatic event like that will there really be the impetus to correct these problems."

Thinking It Over

1. Fundamentally, what is the defense industry's case? Summarize it in your mind in such a way that you could defend the industry in a heated debate.

2. The government purchases much more than guns: medical care, highways, and spaceships are a few of the other items on its shopping list. If the market place does not work to protect the taxpayer when the government buys weapons, does it work in these other areas? If not, is there a better way to do things?

47.
OLD MONEY, NEW POWER
by John Tierney

Setting the Scene: Just about the time most of you reading this reach your prime earning years, the number of old folks (like I'll be then) will be astronomical. Guess who will be asked to foot the bill for much of the care and services we'll need? You. But the number of you in relation to the number of us is declining. Fewer and fewer earners are being asked to care for more and more retirees. Ask your parents how much comes out of their paychecks *now* for social security (before we baby boomers have retired) and you'll get some idea of the problem. Even now retired Americans are learning how to get what they want from the political process. By the time I retire we should have perfected the art of making sure you youngsters take care of us in a style to which we are accustomed. After all. It's the democratic way.

Ed Bradley, the "60 Minutes" correspondent, was on the podium. He was speaking on an afternoon last May at the national convention of the American Association of Retired Persons, the subject of a famous expose by "60 Minutes" that accused the group of being little more than a front for an insurance company. But that was long ago—back in 1978, when the A.A.R.P. had only 10 million members or so. Since then, it has reorganized and nearly tripled in size, to more than 28 million.

Bradley was talking about the evils of politics. Money from special-interest groups was corrupting Congress, he said, and the public was being ignored. "Who represents Mr. and Mrs. Average?" he asked rhetorically, and the white-haired listeners in Detroit's Cobo Center nodded and applauded. They cheered again when Bradley, after pointing to the lobbies for doctors and health insurers and hospitals, asked in thundering tones, "Where is the lobby for the patients in the hospital?"

It did not seem to occur to Bradley, nor to his equally indignant listeners, that an answer to the question might be right in front of him. An hour earlier, this same audience had watched Michael Dukakis and George Bush on the giant screens in the auditorium, answering questions from the A.A.R.P. and promising to address just what the organization demanded for patients: new curbs on hospital and doctor fees, new Government subsidies for the ill.

Lobbyists for hospitals and doctors have never had such an opportunity to extract promises from the candidates, yet Bradley's listeners could still somehow consider themselves beleaguered. Theirs is a constituency with a $300-billion-a-year political agenda—the combined cost of Medicare and Social Security—and as much power as any lobby in the country. Yet they wouldn't think to include themselves on a list of powerful special-interest groups.

Nor would most other Americans, and you could see why, looking at the conventioneers in Detroit, a huge throng, but such a *nice* throng. They exuded the kindly glow of grandparents. They waited patiently to take their turns bowling at the lane set up in the exhibit hall. They listened politely to speakers ranging from Ralph Nader to Dr. Ruth Westheimer. They signed up for volunteer work at "Hometown USA," a mock village displaying the charitable works of 400,000 members of the A.A.R.P.'s local chapters.

Other exhibits were stocked with brochures and products to help the elderly take care of themselves: special faucets and handles for the arthritic, appliances for the sight-impaired, advice on buying medication and insurance and writing a will.

"A.A.R.P. promotes dignity for the elderly; it cares about our problems," said Julia Barrett, a retired schoolteacher from Farmington, Mich., who was eating lunch in the exhibit hall with two friends. When the subject of government benefits came up, she explained that she was generally opposed to welfare: "Make them work—they should not get paid for sitting around, these welfare people." When it was suggested that the Social Security program might be considered a form of welfare, too, because some recipients today are getting back five times the amount they contributed to the fund, Barrett and her companions turned indignant. They talked of their financial fears, the extravagance of today's young people, the need to respect the aged. "The statistics may show that we're getting extra benefits, but I think we're due them," Barrett said. "We've produced all of our lives. I know I think I'm due them."

Combine this sense of entitlement with the A.A.R.P.'s size, and you get an unprecedented force in American politics. The A.A.R.P. is twice the size of the A.F.L.-C.I.O.—representing more than one fifth of the country's voters. The organization's headquarters is an 8-story building in Washington; the group has 10 regional offices, a staff of 1,200 and a $235 million budget.

The low annual dues, $5 a member—the same for a married couple—provide only a third of the group's revenues. The rest comes mainly from selling products: A.A.R.P. Group Health Insurance Program ($82 million in annual revenues); home and automobile insurance ($17 million); A.A.R.P. Pharmacy Service, and advertising space in Modern Maturity, the group's magazine, which is sent bimonthly to 17.9 million households.

Forty-eight percent of Americans over 50 are A.A.R.P. members. (A person must be 50 or older to join.) They are recruited mainly through direct-mail campaigns and by word of mouth, but the A.A.R.P. also advertises on television.

The A.A.R.P.'s special interests have become Washington's special interests. There may be a budget deficit, but virtually no politician will even discuss cutting two programs that consumer a quarter of all Federal spending: Social Security and Medicare. That kind of talk earns the label "granny-basher."

Medicare, according to some experts, may run out of money before the baby boomers retire, but Congress is expected to give today's elderly another expensive benefit, a long-term care program that the A.A.R.P. is championing.

"A.A.R.P. is becoming the most dangerous lobby in America," says Charles Peters, 61 years old, editor in chief of the *Washington Monthly*, a magazine on politics and government. "The image is that of the nicest kind of old fellows and old ladies, and, in fact, they are perpetuating a myth that the elderly are all needy. That's their fundamental lobbying technique, and our society has to face the fact that it's not true." . . .

The enormous growth in the number of old people in America and their increasing demands for pensions may lead us to expect a new sort of class war—between our younger and older citizens." The economist Frank G. Dickinson wrote those words in 1951, seven years before the A.A.R.P.'s founding, when the first baby boomers were 5 years old. Dickinson predicted that the elderly's demands for "free medical care, free housing, free food—anything you want to name" could lead to "heavy pension taxes that may eventually absorb more than one-fourth of the income of both workers and employers."

The taxes haven't reached quite that level yet, although today's workers are paying for so many different pensions that no one knows exactly what the total burden is. Pensions take up 6.2 percent of the Pentagon's budget, for instance, and 12.5 percent of Amtrak's. And, as Dickinson predicted, Social Security taxes have continued to rise. In 1951, this payroll tax, shared by employer and employee, was 3 percent of a worker's salary; today it's 15 percent, and it will go up slightly in 1990. For more than half of American workers, it's now a bigger burden than the Federal income tax, and some of the gloomier forecasters think the tax would have to reach 25 percent in the next century for the baby boomers to collect their benefits, even taking into account the interest that would have accumulated.

Dickinson also warned that "we will see workers and employers, in spite of their natural respect for age, standing shoulder to shoulder against the hard-driven politicians who promise our senior citizens impossible pensions and encourage the older worker to exploit the younger worker."

In that prediction, Dickinson was utterly wrong. Even though the baby boomers tell pollsters they don't expect to get their fair share back from the Social Security system, and even though they out-number the elderly, they have not stood shoulder to shoulder. There is no group acting as a counterweight to the A.A.R.P.

The closest thing to a voice for the baby boomers is a group—currently with 700 members—called Americans for Generational Equity, and its leaders cringe when they hear it described as an opponent of the A.A.R.P. Its chairman, 54-year-old Senator Dave Durenberger, a Republican of Minnesota, prefers to use Thomas Jefferson as a reference point: "Jefferson said that each generation must feel a moral imperative to leave the next generation better off, and I'm concerned that my generation is going to be the first one not to do that. We have to start scaling back our expectations." Durenberger's role in the Americans for Generational Equity has drawn flak in his re-election campaign this year, and he stresses that he doesn't want to take benefits from today's elderly.

"In the beginning, some people at A.A.R.P. came to the conclusion that this organization was a bunch of granny-bashers, but they realize now that's not the case," Durenberger says.

"We decided that we wouldn't try to compete with A.A.R.P.," says Phillip Longman, a former staff member for the equity group. "Rather than get young people to burn their Social Security cards on the steps of the Capitol, we remained strictly a public education group." Today, the equity organization publishes a journal and holds conferences, but doesn't lobby.

This year, Longman got a personal look at the power of the senior lobby. Having left the Americans for Generational Equity organization, he was working as an aide to Representative Kenneth (Buddy) MacKay, a Florida Democrat, when he spoke his mind on a "West 57th" television segment about the A.A.R.P. Although he wasn't identified on the program as a member of MacKay's staff, the Congressman's office got a couple of calls, and

Longman was dismissed about two weeks later.

Longman suspects the phone calls were an orchestrated effort to do him in. MacKay's administrative aide, Greg Farmer, disputes that and says Longman was going to be discharged anyway, because of his long-standing bias on issues affecting the elderly. Either way, Longman says he doesn't blame MacKay for getting rid of him.

"In his district, you do not fool around with offending voters over 65," Longman says. "The reality in Congress is that nobody can take on the elderly. When A.A.R.P.'s lobbyist shows up, it's like Darth Vader at the door—he tells people how to vote." . . .

The A.A.R.P.'s most important weapon is probably the flood of paper that goes out: the articles in its publication, the grass-roots alerts to get members to write their legislators about certain bills, the studies and position papers that go to Congress and think tanks and journalists. The A.A.R.P.'s legislative staff has doubled since 1984, to 125 positions, including 18 registered lobbyists who visited virtually every member of Congress during the last session.

But do the A.A.R.P.'s positions on the issues correspond to its members' opinions? Do the members even want the group to spend $10 million a year on a legislative division?

The A.A.R.P. regularly polls members and has local-chapter delegates vote on policies at the biannual convention, but a small, closed group appoints the A.A.R.P.'s leadership. Nominations to the board of directors come from a committee set up by the board. Board members are then voted in by delegates—chosen by their local chapters—at the biannual A.A.R.P. convention.

The group's former executive director, Jack W. Carlson, 54, thinks the organization is hardly democratic. Carlson, who was dismissed earlier this year, contends the A.A.R.P. has long been dominated by its New York law firm, Miller, Singer, Raives & Brandes.

Carlson had succeeded Cyril F. Brickfield, a lawyer and a former official of the Veterans Administration. Brickfield was popular with the staff and got along well with the board of directors. Upon retiring last year, he received what was rumored to be a generous bonus—in seven figures, according to one staff member who claims to have seen the contract. (The A.A.R.P. has refused members' requests for disclosure of the salaries of top officials: Carlson says his salary was $200,000 a year.)

As Brickfield's successor, Carlson, a former economist at the Office of Management and Budget under President Richard M. Nixon and an executive at the Chamber of Commerce of the United States, lasted just 15 weeks on the job. Staff members reportedly complained that his political philosophy was too conservative and his management style too autocratic. He resigned in January and was replaced by a veteran A.A.R.P. official, Deets, who had been Brickfield's principal assistant.

"It bothers me that A.A.R.P. is spending so much money to get across the political views of its staff," Carlson says now. "A.A.R.P. started out as basically a commercial venture, and it still largely is, but now it's started to hold itself out as representative of its members. But A.A.R.P. doesn't have any democratic process to determine members' views. There are surveys of members—some biased, some not—but that does not replace democracy. There's no bottom-up process for members to become candidates or set policies. They can't even find out what their officers are being paid."

Last year, Carlson disagreed with the A.A.R.P.'s lobbying staff over its handling of the Pepper bill to provide long-term care at home for the elderly. A.A.R.P. lobbyists committed the group to supporting the bill without consulting the A.A.R.P.'s legislative and executive committees, Carlson complains. Nor did the A.A.R.P. stance necessarily reflect the views of its members. Carlson says: "It was typical. The staff, being relatively young and from Washington—most of them have served in the Federal Government—tend to think of a Federal solution to any problem. But I think many of our members would prefer to see a private or a state solution."

Pepper's bill raises the same basic issue as the battles over Social Security and Medicare: can the Federal Government afford to subsidize not only the needy, but the middle and upper classes? The bill would pay for in-home services, such as cooking, cleaning and nursing care, for any person, regardless of income, who is deemed chronically ill and unable to perform certain tasks. Critics complain that the costs could escalate even faster than Medicare's.

"In practice, the restrictions are so weak that the law would provide a free cook and a free maid to anyone over 65 who wants to ask for one," says Peter Ferrara, 35 a professor at George Mason University Law School and a Heritage Foundation fellow. "I think the elderly realize that most people don't need this kind of help. But the A.A.R.P.'s leaders want to increase their own political muscle in Washington, so they're trying to take a constituency that believes mainly in self-sufficiency and persuade it to be dependent on the Government."

Ferrara's criticism is reminiscent of the words of the A.A.R.P.'s founder, Ethel Percy Andrus, who wrote that "most older persons are able to live in independence" and that the "A.A.R.P. does not welcome the welfare state as the way of life for all older persons." She argued that aid should be focused on the minority that needs it.

Today, more than 30 percent of Federal spending is on the elderly, most of it in universal programs benefiting the middle class. According to the Census Bureau, the over-50 age group has a higher after-tax per capita income than the under-50 age group. But 3.5 million of the elderly still live below the poverty line, according to the A.A.R.P. ($5,255 a year or less for a single person, $6,630 for a couple). Shouldn't the money be restricted to those who need it?

The standard counterargument, sometimes called the "bribe-the-middle-class theory," is that the only practical way to help the aged poor is to help all the aged. Rother, the A.A.R.P.'s legislative director, says: "If you start limiting these programs to those with low incomes, you stigmatize them as welfare programs, and look at how little support there is in this country for welfare programs. And if the benefits are only there for the poor, you're discouraging people from saving for their retirement. You're giving them the wrong message: Spend it all, because then the taxpayers will take care of you."

Public-opinion polls seem to bear out Rother's point: Social Security and Medicare are probably the most popular of all Government programs, and the young are just as opposed as the old to any tampering with benefits.

"The public doesn't support welfare for young people because the average person doesn't expect to go on welfare himself," counters Longman. "But none of us knows whether through bad luck or bad planning or bad health we're going to be in trouble in old age, or whether our parents will be in trouble. That's why I think there's a tremendous constituency for giving benefits just to the poor elderly."

During the last session of Congress there was, in fact, a modest attempt made to reduce the Social Security checks of the middle class by canceling cost-of-living adjustments. The A.A.R.P. refused to go along with the idea; it died in closed-door discussions.

"That tax had a good chance of passing if A.A.R.P. hadn't opposed it," says Charles Peters of the *Washington Monthly*. "I don't think there's any legitimate argument for not taxing those benefits. It's the kind of thing we have to do to reduce the deficit, and that's the only way we'll be able to give more help to those elderly who are truly needy. We should give more to that lonely old lady who is solely dependent on Social Security and lives a threadbare existence. But it is shocking for my Aunt Alice to be able to use her Social Security to go to Europe, which she does."

If Aunt Alice had been a the A.A.R.P.'s convention in Detroit, she could have done some travel planning at booths like the ones for the Norwegian Cruise Line or the Korea Travel Bureau. Some conventioneers acknowledged that there was a certain incongruity in gathering the tour brochures and then going off to cheer politicians assuring them they needed more money from the Government. And some conventioneers, when told about the arguments of A.A.R.P. critics, seemed both surprised and concerned.

"Don't get the wrong idea about us," said Lawrence Heeb, 75, a retired college professor from Lawrence, Kan. "We don't just care about ourselves. We worry about our children and our grandchildren. If there really is a problem, and if it has been demonstrated that those of us retired today are getting over and above what we put into Social Security, then it shouldn't be difficult to come up with a formula for a cutoff above a certain income.

"I know I don't need that extra 4 percent cost-of-living increase, and I would be willing to do without it, I think a lot of our members would feel the same way." But did he think that the A.A.R.P. would officially support an idea like that?

"Oh, no," he said. "There's just no way that A.A.R.P. would. That's not the way an organization like this works."

Thinking It Over

1. See if you can develop a fair way of seeing to it that Aunt Alice doesn't use her social security checks to go to Europe *if* she is getting back *more* than she put in and if she has, let's say, an average income from other sources. Have I phrased this task incorrectly or with a bias? If so, why?

2. Is there any way, consistent with democratic principles to preclude the soaking of the young by the old? Is it fair to retired people to ask that question?

48.
GAY CLOUT
by Carol Matlack

Setting the Scene: Carol Matlack deals with another kind of interest group—one that has recently come out of the closet. Here analysis is of a new group that has had to use the fear of AIDS to wedge its way into the consciousness of the political process. As an interest group its characteristics are the opposite of those groups like the American Association of Retired Persons (see above). In one case the membership is small and issue specific. In the other it is huge and issue diffuse. What follows is an excellent case study of a new player on the block of special interests politics. It is about gays whose current "special" interest is in reality a critical public interest.

On a chilly morning in early December, about 80 AIDS protesters marched from Lafayette Park into the middle of Pennsylvania Avenue, sat down and began shouting taunts at the White House. Within an hour, rubber-gloved police had handcuffed them and loaded them into waiting buses. Except for a few curious passersby and the grizzled residents of the park peering from their makeshift shelters, hardly anyone saw the demonstration. President Bush was at a summit meeting in Malta.

No matter. Gay activists have found other ways of making themselves heard in Washington. In the past few years, they have:
- helped secure increasingly large federal appropriations for AIDS research, which now approach $750 million annually;
- prodded the Food and Drug Administration (FDA) to speed the release of experimental AIDS treatment drugs;
- established one of the country's wealthiest political action committees (PACs), the Human Rights Campaign Fund;
- helped secure overwhelming congressional support for a disability rights bill that included protections for people infected with the AIDS virus.

These achievements are all the more striking because gay activists, until a few years ago, were more apt to regard government as an enemy than as a benefactor.

"They were very libertarian. They didn't want anything except to be left alone," said Rep. Henry A. Waxman, D-Calif., an early supporter of gay civil rights legislation who has worked with gay groups on AIDS and other issues.

"It's what every other group has learned before us," said Jeffrey Levi, the former executive director of the National Gay and Lesbian Task Force who is now a consultant to the New York City-based Gay Men's Health Crisis Inc. "The government can play an active role in helping to build our institutions."

But gay activists have had trouble parlaying their AIDS victories and their fund-raising prowess into success on other fronts. A gay civil rights bill introduced in the early 1970s has picked up scant congressional support, and few Members, even those who benefit from gay PAC donations, are outspoken proponents of gay rights. Even civil rights groups, seemingly natural allies, keep gay-rights activists at arm's length. And gay groups face outright hostility from some lawmakers, notably Rep. William E. Dannemeyer, R-Calif., who has tried to stir public outrage by inserting statements in the *Congressional Record* graphically describing gay sex acts.

The gay-rights movement itself is divided on what it should do next. Some groups will continue to focus almost exclusively on AIDS, while others are trying to revive the gay civil rights bill and other efforts that fell by the wayside when the AIDS epidemic began.

The gay task force and some local activists are gearing up to tackle what could be the toughest fight of all: the repeal of sodomy laws that outlaw homosexual activity in 25 states and the District of Columbia. But other gay leaders warn that the repeal effort plays into the hands of anti-gay politicians and could jeopardize what modest gains the movement has achieved. Most gay leaders agree that they are entering a period of retrenchment, in which gay groups will pay more attention to local organizing and to building public support for their cause. The task force and the Human Rights Campaign Fund are beefing up their field organizing operations, and traditionally litigation-oriented groups such as the New York City-based Lambda Legal Defense and Education Fund are putting more emphasis on education.

Without a reservoir of public goodwill toward gays, elected officials "can choose to ignore us," said Urvashi Vaid, the task force executive director. Many cities have "sizable and well-organized gay and lesbian communities that can make a difference in local elections," she said, "But we still have a long way to go before we are a force that cannot be ignored."

Common Ground On AIDS

As recently as the early 1980s, the gay lobby was all but invisible in Washington. The proposed gay civil rights bill was moribund, and gay activists, shaken by the strength of the religious Right in the 1980 elections, were generally lying low.

Then came AIDS. "It was the AIDS crisis that totally transformed the kind of politics that the gay community needed to do in Washington and the expectations that our constituency had of us as political players," Levi said.

AIDS not only galvanized the gay community, it provided entree for gay leaders with Members of Congress and other officials concerned about the epidemic's spread. "They needed us as much as we needed them," Levi said. "There was common ground and more comfortable ground for them to begin meeting with the gay community."

Working on AIDS legislation also helped gay lobbyists hone their legislative skills. "It's one thing to be lobbying on a bill that is not going to pass for 10 years," Levi said. "It is quite another to be following the appropriations process." Those skills have come in handy; last year, when Sen. Jesse A. Helms, R-N.C., won enough votes to attach an anti-gay amendment to an appropriations bill containing funds for the National Endowment for the Arts, gay lobbyists helped a coalition of arts groups conceive a strategy of securing a House vote instructing House conferees not to accept the Helms proposal.

With the emergence of promising new AIDS treatment drugs such as AZT, the focus of

AIDS lobbying shifted to the FDA—and Washington was introduced to a new group that didn't play by the usual rules. The AIDS Coalition to Unleash Power (ACT UP) was formed in 1987 by activists who were angry at what they perceived as the government's slowness in responding to the epidemic. ACT UP is a seemingly anarchic collection of local groups best known for their street-fighting tactics. Its members have picketed FDA meetings, disrupted Catholic Masses to protest church policies on AIDS and chained themselves to radiators at the Research Triangle Park (N.C.) headquarters of Burroughs Wellcome Co., manufacturer of AZT, to protest high drug prices. But they have also become self-taught experts on drug regulation.

. . . At the urging of ACT UP and other groups, the FDA approved AZT in record time. And it is considering a proposal to provide experimental drugs to AIDS patients before the drugs have been fully tested in clinical trials. (Traditionally, patients could get such drugs only by participating in the trials in which some participants are given placebos.)

In its push to speed up the drug-approval process, ACT UP found a willing audience among deregulation advocates in the Reagan Administration and among pharmaceutical firms who had been fighting the same battle for years, though for different reasons. Last year, the Competitive Enterprise Institute, a conservative economic policy group in Washington, joined forces with AIDS activists to petition the FDA to speed the release of experimental drugs to AIDS patients. And the conservative Heritage Foundation has quoted ACT UP members in some of its pro-deregulation literature.

That has sometimes put ACT UP at odds with consumer advocates, who warn that the release of inadequately tested drugs could not only raise false hopes among AIDS victims, but could also jeopardize clinical trials that could lead to the development of effective new drugs. "It pits the people with AIDS now against those who may have it in the future," said William B. Schultz, an attorney for the Ralph Nader-founded Public Citizen Litigation Group who specializes in FDA matters. Nevertheless, Schultz and other consumer advocates praise ACT UP for making the FDA more responsive to the public.

Champagne Fund?

If ACT UP is the gay-rights movement's guerrilla force, the Human Rights Campaign Fund is its black-tie battalion. Started in 1980 with a $5,000 donation to then-Rep. James Weaver, D-Ore., the Washington-based campaign fund is now the country's 20th-largest PAC, having raised nearly $2.3 million and having given $405,000 to federal candidates and political committees during the 1987-88 election cycle.

No shoestring operation, the campaign fund courts major donors at $250-a-plate dinners featuring Hollywood stars. "Some people call us the Human Rights Champagne Fund," said Eric Rosenthal, the group's political director. But, he said, "we started being paid attention to when we were able to give a quarter of a million dollars."

Although the PAC is bipartisan, its spending tilts heavily toward Democratic incumbents, and in the 1988 elections, it made large contributions to the Democratic Congressional Campaign Committee and the Democratic Senatorial Campaign Committee. It also spent $66,288 on advertisements in North Carolina criticizing Helms, one of its archenemies.

In the past, the campaign fund also served as a conduit for "bundled" contributions collected from individual gay donors and passed along to candidates. The arrangement, which is legal, enabled candidates to avoid public disclosure of their links to the campaign fund. But executive director Tim McFeeley stopped the practice when he joined the campaign fund last summer. "It used to be difficult for politicians, even liberal politicians, to take money from us," he said. "Now, I really want to stress the positive side of being with the gay community."

Privately, some gay activists question whether the campaign fund is getting its money's worth. Some Members, after pocketing hefty checks from the PAC, have voted for anti-gay measures such as a recent amendment to the District of Columbia appropriations bill that, after being watered down, provided a partial exemption from enforcement of the District's gay-rights law for certain religious educational institutions.

"No one's perfect," McFeeley said with a shrug. Even if lawmakers sometimes ignore its wishes, the campaign fund's PAC contributions give it access to Members who might otherwise ignore it, he said.

The gay task force, by contrast, tried to turn up the heat on Members with constituent pressure. Operating out of a cramped Washington storefront, the task force boasts the most established lobbying operation in the gay-rights movement. Chief congressional lobbyist Peri Jude Radecic tracks a wide range of issues, from AIDS to immigration laws to discrimination against gays in the military. She issues "report cards" on Members' voting records and has set up dozens of lobbying visits by gay constituents with their Members.

Increasingly, Radecic said, gay activists are learning to strengthen their hand by working in coalitions. The task force, for example, is working closely with People for the American Way and other groups on a bill that would require the government to collect statistics on hate crimes: These groups want to include attacks on gays in the crimes covered by the legislation. It has been passed by the House, but so far, Helms has managed to block it in the Senate.

The campaign fund, meanwhile, is going high-tech to strengthen its constituent lobbying. It has established a national Mailgram program that delivered more than 40,000 Mailgrams to members of Congress last year. More recently, it has pioneered the use of videotapes featuring lobbying messages from constituents to their Members.

And gay groups are tapping into the momentum of the abortion-rights position. The task force and the campaign fund both strongly oppose anti-abortion legislation.

Gay activists "have been able to build coalitions with other groups over broader issues than the gay agenda per se," Waxman said. "They've been able to mainstream some of the issues they've been [working] on."

Few Friends in Congress

But despite those efforts, gay organizations do not have a large base of support on Capitol Hill. "They have only a few friends in Congress, and they go to those friends over and over again," said a congressional aide who has followed gay-rights issues since the 1970s. "It is not, by any stretch, a powerful lobby."

The offices of Reps. Barney Frank, D-Mass., and Gerry E. Studds, D-Mass., the only openly gay Members, often serve as focal points for gay lobbying. Studds, for example, has taken the lead on pressing for acceptance of gays in the military, although he doesn't serve on the Armed Services Committee.

Frank has been preoccupied recently with a Standards of Official Conduct (Ethics) Committee investigation of his relationship with a male prostitute, but gay activists say that they don't think the incident has seriously damaged his standing in the House. "The fact that Barney had so much respect [from his colleagues] helped him and helped the gay community survive the terrible press," Vaid said. (Studds, in the early 1980s, survived an ethics investigation in which he was stripped of his subcommittee chairmanship for having had a sexual relationship with a House page.)

In the Senate, gay activists lost one of their staunchest allies in 1988 with the defeat of Sen. Lowell P. Weicker Jr., R-Conn.

And though civil rights groups have readily accepted the help of gay lobbyists on the disability rights bill (which was passed overwhelmingly by the Senate in 1989 and has strong support in the House), they have not repaid the favor by endorsing the long-pending gay civil rights bill. Civil rights activists say privately that most of their members would support the bill, but that some religious leaders in the movement strongly believe homosexuality is immoral.

"Outside of AIDS, where we get good support from the disabilities community and the civil rights community and the public health community.," McFeeley said, "on the straightforward gay civil rights kind of issues, we don't have the kind of support that I would like to see."

. . . Still, no one predicts that the gay lobby will soon fade from the scene. "I've been working on Capitol Hill for seven years," McGuire of the AIDS Action Council said, "and I can tell you that the gay community is represented in conversations now that it was simply never a part of before, from health care to civil rights."

Thinking It Over

1. Suppose there were no AIDS crisis. Would the gay community be visible in the political process then? Think about this in terms of democracy's capacity to respect minority rights on a continuing basis not only in theory but also in practice.

2. An earlier article in this chapter decried the power of PACs in the political process. But gays have a PAC too, the Human Rights Campaign Fund. Does this change your view of PACs?

49.
GIANT KILLERS
by Michael Pertschuk

Setting the Scene: If you were to read Michael Pertschuk's book, *Giant Killers*, in its entirety, you might want to run right out and become a lobbyist. The very word "lobbyist" (like "bureaucrat") seems to have pejorative connotations. In this reading, which is from the introduction, Pertschuk reflects on two lobbyists who, over two different lunches, inspired him to write *Giant Killers*. The author is a lobbyist who does not apologize. In his words "this book owes much to these two lunches: to lunch with George, for awakening the sense of play and story which are the mostly untold legacy of an uncelebrated craft; to lunch with David, for the reminder that beyond craft and story lies democratic promise."

All Lobbyists Must Eat

Some of my best friends are lobbyists. And some of the best lobbyists are my friends. Not all represent benign causes, though many among them represent what they believe are public interest causes: nuclear arms control; civil rights; environmental and consumer interests; tax equity; public health; the welfare of Indian tribes, blacks, women, ethnic minorities, and poor children. . . .

But others among them represent cigarette companies; defense contractors; life insurance companies; retailers; big oil and small (but not very) oil; real estate; railroads and airlines; truckers; merchant marine interests; advertising agencies, cable television operators; and, like George W. Koch, big grocery manufacturers—Procter and Gamble, General Foods and Nestle.

George W. Koch is the President of GMA (the Grocery Manufacturers of America). Before that he was chief lobbyist for Sears. George is my friend; he has also been my adversary for nearly twenty years.

In the mid-sixties, I was a staff member of the Senate Commerce Committee, assigned to consumer protection legislation. I saw myself, then, as a latter-day Scarlet Pimpernel—to outward appearances, a mild-mannered clerk; below the surface, a guerilla fighter for truth and light, or, at the moment, truth in packaging and labeling. George led the powers of darkness.

In the late sixties and early seventies, our band of consumer guerillas, emboldened by Ralph Nader's vision, fought for the creation of a Consumer Advocacy Agency. George led the benighted resistance; we were beginning to get used to each other.

By the late seventies, I was at the Federal Trade Commission, determined to rid the country of the blight of television advertising directed to very young children. George led the opposition.

He also refused to let the Grocery Manufacturers of America join in a lawsuit filed by the advertising, broadcasting, and toy industry groups which sought to remove me from the proceeding as biased beyond tolerance. George said he was confident I would be fair and objective in applying the law. I was surprised and moved; I wasn't so sure about myself.

In the first years of the Reagan administration, defrocked as chairman but with three years left in my term as one of the FTC's five commissioners, I lobbied within the commission and in Congress for mandatory salt labeling; preservation of the "Delaney" clause, which bars from food products any trace of substances causing cancer in laboratory animals; and for U.S. support for United Nation's action condemning infant formula promotion in third world countries. George masterminded the opposition to all three.

In many ways, George W. Koch is a remarkable—and good—man. A stubborn rectitude led him to a rare and unsettling challenge to a pillar of the Washington establishment: the Congressional Country Club, of which he was and is a member. At a personal cost of tens of thousands of dollars, George first questioned politely, then confronted, then legally challenged the club's economic exploitation of its mostly black and Hispanic low-income workers. In recounting his lone struggle, the Washington Afro-American said, "If you didn't know that George Koch (pronounced Cook) was a white, middle-class conservative Republican lobbyist for the grocery manufacturing industry, you might think he was Martin Luther King, Jr. Certainly their stories are similar and Koch's courage appears to be as great."

On January 21, 1981, I was still chairman of the Federal Trade Commission, but not for long. This was Ronald Reagan's first day as president. And as a Carter appointee and a demon regulator, I was fated for swift removal as chairman. On my calendar for that day was lunch with George Koch. I hadn't remembered setting the date, and when I arrived at the elegant Four Seasons to join George at his customary table overlooking the garden, he told me that he had set the date with Darlene, my secretary, a month before. He'd figured that the day after the Reagan inaugural, facing my imminent fall from grace and power, feeling displaced and forgotten, I'd need a dose of good cheer—a dash of reassurance and a good meal. George, of course, had been an early and enthusiastic Reagan supporter—but he didn't gloat.

Like ancient veterans of opposing armies, we share an arcane interest in old battle tactics and maneuvers, and we soon lapsed into old war stories and confessions.

"Did you ever wonder," George suddenly asked, "how the Democratic platform in 1972 happened to include an endorsement of the 'amicus amendment'?"

My mind was blank for a moment. "Amicus amendment"? What had that been all about? Then I remembered: the consumer movement was then riding like a juggernaut through Congress. Throughout the late sixties we had gained enactment of a series of major consumer protection measures. By 1972 we were on the threshold of the creation, by Congress, of a powerful new Consumer Advocacy Agency, with broad license to intervene in the proceedings of regulatory agencies which were slow, timid or indifferent to the aggressive pursuit of the consumer interest.

The teeth-gnashing business lobbies had been able only to slow the agency's momentum. Its passage in the next Congress appeared imminent.

As a last line of defense, George and his allies has pressed to limit the consumer advocate to the advisory role of a "friend of court" or "amicus curiae"—a mere kibitzer.

I remembered. I also remembered how stunned I had been when, in the midst of this heated conflict, the Democratic platform emerged from that most liberal of conventions—the McGovern convention—with a ringing endorsement of the "amicus amendment" to the Consumer Agency bill.

"Yes George, I wondered how that happened."

"Mike, you probably don't remember, but as soon as the platform appeared, you called me and asked how it happened, and I didn't tell you. Now I will tell you.

"We had a man on the platform committee. A very distinguished North Carolina lawyer—very proper, very sober, very conservative. You may remember what that convention was like. All sorts of people were delegates—hippies, yippies, old radicals and student radicals, and for the first time, openly, gays.

"The convention was even more of a mad house than usual. The platform committee was the focal point for demands by all that ragtaggle of dissident groups; meetings of the platform committee dragged throughout the day and deep into the night. Our man was sitting next to the representative of the gay caucus on the platform committee. It was well after midnight when the question of the endorsement of the Consumer Advocacy Agency was placed before the committee. Our man had arranged for the amicus language to be proposed to modify the convention's endorsement of the Consumer Agency. His gay neighbor had dozed off and awoke with a start to hear a strange and unfamiliar discussion of the 'amicus amendment.' He turned to our man and asked, 'what is this amicus amendment all about?' And our fellow leaned over, put his hand on his colleague's knee, looked him soulfully in the eye, and said, 'amicus . . . means 'friend'.' Whereupon the gay delegate spoke briefly but passionately in support of the amicus amendment, then lapsed back into a deep sleep. The amendment carried."

What a rotten trick, George: cynical, manipulative, and exploitive!

Like Henry Higgins contemplating the dreary future fate of the ungrateful Eliza Doolittle who has just walked out on him, I thought: "How frightful!" . . . and, then, "How delightful!"

I was seized with an inspiration, "George, that's a great—though shameful—story. With all your wicked ways, you must have dozens like it and must have heard dozens more from your black hat colleagues. I have a few favorites from our side. Why don't we write a book together: *Great Moments in Lobbying History?*"

George was intrigued, but he noted, wisely, that the best stories could not safely be told until the participants were dead (or out of power). We agreed that it was a great potential joint venture for our mutual retirements—or semi-retirements—still many years away, of course.

I was so delighted by George and the lunch that I relaxed my customary fastidiousness and let George pick up the check for that conspiratorial hiatus in the public interest/private interest war.

Yes, lobbying is a game. It can be petty, tedious, boring, and demeaning. But sometimes it's played out on a great stage full of bold strategies, fatal missteps, shrewd tactical feints, and intricate maneuvers. The fate of the world—or at least a share of its fate—may rest not on grand policy debates or the massive realignment of political forces, but upon the play of greed, ambition, quirky alliances and coalitions, deep loyalties and deeper enmities, corroding envy, and yes, affection, even love.

Nobody tells the good tales of lobbying for the sake of the stories—and the craft. We could do that.

Three years later, in the fall of 1984, I had lunch with another old friend, David Cohen.

Early in 1984 David had agreed to serve as the strategist and chief lobbyist for a new coalition of professional groups drawn together in alliance against the nuclear arms buildup: the Union of Concerned Scientists; the Physicians for Social Responsibility; and the Lawyers' Alliance Against Nuclear Arms. At the same time, Kathleen Sheekey, whom we both admired and respected enormously, had become chief lobbyist for Common Cause. David and Kathleen had both been at the center of the fight to stop production of the MX-missile. In the sharing of tasks among the peace groups, Common Cause had taken primary responsibility for coordinating the national effort to half production of the MX, an effort which had fallen short the previous year.

In 1984 Reagan had sought authorization for the production of forty MX missiles. As the anti-MX campaign gained momentum, support for the MX eroded. Soon even military sycophants in Congress were willing to fight for only twenty-one missiles. Four weeks before we met, a desperate White House had compromised further, down to fifteen. Yet the House approved even fifteen by only six votes. Then, two weeks later, the House reversed its action. By two votes it denied all funding for the MX—unless Congress affirmatively approved MX construction the next year.

Against the Pentagon, against the ingrained tradition of deference to the president on military affairs, against the client relationship of armed service committees to defense contractors, they had nonetheless triumphed beyond rational expectations. It had to be a glorious tale, and it was.

It was a tale of how congressmen—cool, calculating, venal and cringing; fiercely independent, fearful, partisan, intimidated, or furious; eager to do the right thing, but uncertain; unconvinced; chronically conditioned to seek the safe middle-wiggled, waffled, walked, ran, turned again, held firm, buckled; then at one moment came together and held firm for the critical twenty minutes of a recorded vote.

It was a tale alive with tensions, stress and high drama (and low comedy), grand strategy, artful maneuver—the bridging of mature lobbying skills to a broad and deeply committed citizen movement.

I went back to my office in high glee. I had captured a treasure. David and Kathleen were as artful a team as had ever practiced the lobbying art. Here was the centerpiece of any book on great moments in lobbying history.

But I also knew that what I had learned was more than a good lobbying story.

It was not just a Washington inside story, nor was it a cynical story. It was a story of democratic possibility, of the hitching of a citizen movement to the skills needed to translate the moral force and energy of that movement into effective action. That's the essence of public interest lobbying at its best, and it is why there really is a difference between the role of the private interest lobbyist and the public interest lobbyist.

This book owes much to these two lunches: to lunch with George, for awakening the sense of play and story which are the mostly untold legacy of an uncelebrated craft; to lunch with David, for the reminder that beyond craft and story lies democratic promise.

Thinking It Over

1. All very well and good. But would a book about George W. Koch's successes as a lobbyist also be about the promise of democracy? Or what about a book on the NRA's success in defeating gun control legislation? Why is it when environmental lobbyists win, it is called a victory for the democratic *process*? When the NRA does, it is not?

2. Michael Pertschuk has made the career of lobbyist seem exciting, even romantic. Call a lobbyist who works in your state. It's easy; you can find them registered at the capital or working as the "public relations officer" of a firm or organization. If that doesn't work, simply call the office of one of the many organizations that obviously have lobbyists in your state—the NRA, the AMA, etc. Arrange for an interview and you've got yourself the foundation of a paper for any number of classes from Political Science to English to Business.

Chapter VIII

THE MEDIA

50.
INVENTING REALITY:
THE POLITICS OF THE MASS MEDIA
by Michael Parenti

Setting the Scene: Most of the critiques of the media in America seem to come from the right—that is, from conservatives who think it's too liberal, from Republicans who think it favors Democrats. Michael Parenti's approach is unique because it comes from the left. Remember, Parenti's perspective is that the corporate structure in America *contains* both conservatives and liberals, and Republicans and Democrats. The real struggle is against an elitist and self-serving status quo of which major institutions of the media are an important component. Look for bias in the media in the treatment of those who seek fundamental change in the corporate capitalist system.

How to Discredit Protesters

On those infrequent occasions when the media took the trouble to report on protests during the seventies and eighties, the coverage was reminiscent of the disparaging treatment accorded demonstrations during the sixties. The *Washington Post*'s story of the May 3, 1981, "March on the Pentagon" can serve as a typical example of how the press treats protests on the left.[1] Buried in Section C along with local news, obituaries, and classified ads, the story,

---

[1] *Washington Post*, May 4, 1981.

written by Mike Sager, begins by describing the demonstrators as a "loose coalition of groups whose causes range from gay rights to Palestinian autonomy." At the outset one might wonder why the *Post* singled out these two groups—in a march protesting U.S. intervention in El Salvador and Reagan's cuts in social programs—unless it was to typify the event as a potpourri of marginal, off-beat characters or in other ways to play upon the negative prejudices of certain sectors of its readership.

The story seems more concerned with describing the protesters than with telling us anything about the content of their protests, about why they were out there in the first place. So we read that the "youthful crowd formed a colorful river of jean-and-tee-shirt-clad humanity" and that "they marched carrying banners for their causes while licking ice-cream bars and taking pictures of each other with complicated camera gear." Furthermore, "Yesterday's minions carried a few placards and repeated a few chants, but some also took time to eat picnic lunches, smoke marijuana, drink beer and work on their tans." These images suggest a frivolous, festive atmosphere that denies the protesters the seriousness of their concerns. It might be noted that a "minion," according to Webster's Unabridged Dictionary is "a term of contempt" describing "one who is a servile follower."

Two fairly large photographs of the event, accompanying the story, show no one consuming picnic lunches, pot, beer, or ice cream, nor is anyone sunbathing. And the photos reveal not "a few placards" but what must be hundreds of placards and banners. To be sure, some of the participants may well have paused to refresh themselves—in a demonstration that continued for some seven hours under the hot Washington sun. What might be questioned is why the *Post* writer treated these minor activities as central to the event.

Judging from the photographs accompanying the story and observations by persons like myself who witnessed the day-long event, the atmosphere was a serious political one and not that of a carnival. But the *Post* had its own scenario to spin: "Many of those interviewed yesterday—from long-haired hippie hold-outs with painted faces to L. L. Bean-clad outdoorsmen to health-conscious joggers who had stopped by to witness the spectacle—said they had come not so much to protest U.S. intervention in El Salvador as to voice their disapproval of the state of the nation under Reagan and the state of the world in general." (No danger of encountering any earnest and knowledgeable political intentions in this crowd.) "In all," continued the *Post*, "the demonstration took on a flea market atmosphere—something for everyone." It was a "hodge-podge collection." Even the headline noted: "25,000 PROTESTERS MARCH FOR MIXED CAUSES."

One could just as readily, and more accurately, see the diversity of issues as a sign of unity and maturity among progressive-minded people joined in struggle against a common enemy. The *Post* story assumed there was an incongruous mix of issues, when in fact the demonstration sought to link a range of domestic and foreign policies. Such issue linkage is somewhat alien to a press that treats political issues as unrelated events and dismisses large popular coalitions as hodge-podge collections.

The crowd was described as "youthful" and the event little more than a rerun of "the Vietnam antiwar rallies of a decade ago." (For years the press repeatedly described, or rather dismissed, demonstrations as tiresome repeats of the Vietnam era.) The emphasis on the supposedly "youthful" quality of the demonstrators plays on the stereotype of youth as not very responsible or rational, making it easier to treat the protest as a product of their immature spirits than as a justifiable response to political reality. But a few columns later we read that participants included trade unionists, retired elderly, lawyers, Hispanic migrant farm workers, feminists, and government employees—certainly a crowd of more than just youthful protesters.

The *Post* reporter accepted the police estimate of the crowd at 25,000, making no mention of the 100,000 claimed by the march organizers. A counterdemonstration, counted by me at 100 to 110 people, was reported in the *Post* story as 300 "clean-cut protesters" from "Re. Moon's Unification Church which is calling for U.S. intervention in El Salvador to rid it of Russian and Cuban communist influence . . ." (Here the *Post* is accepting as established fact the Moonie charge that the Salvadoran revolutionaries are puppets of Moscow and Havana; a less biased statement might have read: "to rid it of *what the counterdemonstrators claim* is Russian and Cuban communist influence.") While the Moonies were only a minute fraction of the people present, they and their concerns were accorded about one-fifth of the story.

Speakers from a wide range of political groups made statements about U.S. policies at home and abroad, yet nothing about these speeches appeared in this rather lengthy article except for a few mocking lines describing one speaker's plea for funds to pay the demonstration costs. In sum, in most of its tone and content the *Post* article was belittling. Readers who had no direct experience with the demonstration might easily have come away thinking they had exercised good sense in choosing not to participate in what must have been a rather inane, circuslike affair.

The *Washington Post* outdid itself a few months later when it reported—or failed to report—the huge Labor Day parade that took place in New York City in September 1981. The parade organizers estimated the marchers at 200,000; the police said 100,000. In either case, the turnout was quite impressive in size and militancy. The *Post*'s story, choosing instead to concentrate on President Reagan's visit to Mayor Edward Koch of New York, allowed only passing reference to the parade, buried toward the end of the article, describing it as a "disappointingly small crowd of less than 100,000 union workers."[2] Actually the parade organizers were jubilant at the enormous size of the turn-out.

The next month a series of civil disobedience actions at the Diablo Canyon nuclear site in California resulted in over 2,000 arrests. For years the protesters had argued that the plant was not sufficiently earthquake-proof, that human error made no nuclear plant safe, that there was no sufficient technology to deal with nuclear waste, radiation leakages, and a serious accident. Television news coverage of the Diablo Canyon protests, ignoring the arguments and evidence offered by the demonstrators, concentrated on the personal appearance of the marchers, their chants and songs, and the confrontation with the police—with much footage devoted to the arrests. Again, the *reason* why people were taking this extraordinary action was lost in a superficial recording of the action itself.

A *Washington Post* editorial did its part in making the Diablo Canyon protesters the issue

---

[2]*Washington Post*, September 8, 1981.

rather than the thing they were protesting, referring to them as "the mindless school of nuclear protest" and the "quintessentially California happening of underworked TV actors and overgrown flower children complete with folk songs and 'affinity groups' . . ." (not Americans who were willing to put their bodies on the line to oppose a human and environmental menace).[3]

The media make a regular practice of undercounting the size of demonstrations. The Solidarity Day march of organized labor on September 19, 1981, in Washington, D.C., was reported at 240,000 by the *New York Times* and 260,000 by the *Washington Post*, both far below the police estimate of 400,000. (And police estimates are usually notorious for undercounting).

On July 2, 1983 the People's Anti-War Mobilization, a broad-based coalition of several hundred peace groups around the country held a demonstration in Washington, D.C., to protest the U.S. intervention in Central America. Parade organizers claimed 20,000 participants. (I and two assistants counted about 14,000 as the demonstrators marched to Lafayette Park; this did not include the substantial numbers who had departed during the previous two hours of speeches to escape the stifling 95-degree heat.)[4] The police estimate of 7,500 was the only one reported in the *Washington Post*.[5] A local evening television news report referred to "several thousand," and showed a brief 30-second clip of the march.

A right-wing counterdemonstration of Moonies, Vietnamese exiles, and a Christian group held on the same day numbered about 200 people by my count. The *Post* reported the police estimate of 500, then added that "unofficial estimates" were much higher. The article did not identify who made the unofficial estimates. This reporting of the counterdemonstration stands in marked contrast to the way the *Post* ignored the "unofficial estimates" of the larger major event and printed without question the low count of the police. Similarly, the story gave almost as much coverage to the tiny pro-war, pro-Reagan group as to the antiwar rally and more photo space. The networks gave *equal* time to both the 14,000 who marched against U.S. intervention in Central America and the 200 or so who gathered in support of it. The *New York Times* carried no story at all but ran a picture of a portion of the congregated crowd on page 12, captioned, "Rally Opposes U.S. Role in Caribbean." The *Times* made no estimate of the crowd size, but noted in the caption that the rally "prompted criticism from Government supporters, who held a rally nearby. No violence was reported."[6] The reference to the absence of violence carried the implication that violence might have been expected—thus continuing the media association of protest with violence. The absence of any reference to crowd size allowed the *Times* to describe the mass rally and the very minor one in equal terms.

Not all protests are slighted or ignored by the U.S. news media. The 1981 crisis in Poland won the rapt attention of the U.S. business-owned press for days on end in a way that

---

[3]Editorial, *Washington Post*, October 6, 1981.

[4]The method we used was to make a count of five hundred marchers, estimating the portion of the street block they occupied, the using that measurement to count out additional blocks of five hundred as subsequent marchers passed by.

[5]*Washington Post*, July 3, 1983.

[6]*New York Times*, July 3, 1983.

no strikes or demonstrations in the United States have ever done. Western sympathizers designated January 30, 1982, as "Solidarity Day" and planned demonstrations in support of Polish Solidarity in various cities. Unlike most demonstrations these were well publicized beforehand in the media. Also widely publicized was the International Communication Agency-produced television show "Let Poland Be Poland" featuring songs and appearances by Hollywood celebrities and statements by political leaders of various countries, offered for prime-time viewing on "Solidarity Day" to some 50 broadcast services around the world. Few political events had ever received such massive and favorable prepublicity, but the turnout on "Solidarity Day" itself did not live up to the media hype preceding it. The *Washington Post* story, bravely headlined: "THOUSANDS HERE AND ABROAD TURN OUT FOR 'SOLIDARITY DAY,'" reported rallies held in cities in the United States and a few foreign capitals, the largest being in Chicago, the city with the biggest ethnic Polish population outside Warsaw, where Secretary of State Haig spoke to a crowd reportedly of 8,000 (no source was given for that figure). In Boston, the three biggest names in the state, Governor Edward King, Senator Edward Kennedy, and Humberto Cardinal Medeiros attracted a crowd reported at 300. In Washington, the *Post* reported "more than 1,000" marched to Lafayette Park (although I counted about 570). The story gives no figures for the rallies in other cities. While the press usually does not cover the speeches made at protest rallies, the *Post* devoted substantial space to the statements made by the speakers at the Chicago, Boston, and Washington gatherings.[7] The evening news programs of all three commercial networks covered the story, offering clips of speakers making statements in support of freedom in Poland, with no mention of the disappointing size of the crowds. (Left demonstrations of such small numbers seldom, if ever, make the evening news of national television.)

In May 1983 the *Post* gave front page play to the "tens of thousands of protesters" in Poland who "boycotted official May Day ceremonies and staged counter-demonstrations."[8] The story noted that the Warsaw government estimated the number of protesters at 40,000 and the number of participants in the pro-government demonstrations at 6.5 million. The *Post* however claimed that "estimates by western correspondents placed the number of demonstrators in Warsaw and Gdansk combined at more than 40,000"—but does not say how much more. Nor does the story refute or comment on the massive 6.5 million turnout in support of the Polish government! This latter, somewhat astonishing figure would seem to have been the real story, but it received only one bare mention buried in a story headlined: "POLES PROTEST IN 20 CITIES ON MAY DAY." In a country where the mass of the populace was reported as in a state of rebellion against the government, how was it that 6.5 million ignored the Solidarity marches and participated in the government-sponsored demonstration? The *Post* leaves us to our own conjectures.

---

[7]*Washington Post*, January 31, 1982.
[8]*Washington Post*, May 2, 1983.

Thinking It Over

1. Do you have any trouble squaring Parenti's account with events in your part of America? From where I sit, all kinds of tiny demonstrations (left or right) seem to get coverage—and the more radical they are, the more coverage they get. Would Parenti argue that (A) I've missed his point, (B) what could one expect if one lived (as I do) in northern Vermont, (C) both explanations are operative?

2. Isn't Parenti's fundamental point correct? Dan Rather works for a large corporation. Why should the bottom line of that capitalist structure be any different from any other? Put another way, are Dan Rather's ratings important to CBS because CBS is concerned about a democratic society getting useful information or is CBS concerned with being able to sell advertising slots to pay Dan's salary and make a profit? Put still another way. Why is there exactly 30 minutes (minus advertising) worth of news every day in America?

51.
ALL THE PRESIDENT'S PATSIES
by Adam Hochschild

Setting the Scene: One of the great dilemmas in the news business (and business *is* the correct term) is this: In order for you as a reporter to excel in getting access to the news, it is important to build relationships with the people who can give you important news stories—hopefully before the competition gets them. But how do you build these relationships without sacrificing your objectivity? Another angle on the dilemma is the argument that many news people covering, say, Presidential candidates for long periods of time during a campaign come to sympathize with the candidate. The following reading in which Adam Hochschild discusses these problems is unique in that it is itself a review of Mark Hertsgaard's book *On Bended Knee: The Press and the Reagan Presidency.* I found this review an excellent way to get at the essence of the book.

Most cub reporters covering a trial or a legislative hearing for the first time learn to do two things: they watch what's going on, and they watch what the *other* reporters are taking notes on—because that, of course, defines what's news. Any serious student of the press therefore must study the subject not as a psychologist looks at the behavior of individuals, but as a zoologist looks at the behavior of herds.

Mark Hertsgaard understands this well. In his excellent new book on Reagan and the media he scrutinizes not only the principal members of the herd—network producers, newspaper editors, White House correspondents—but also the shepherds, Reagan's brilliant staff of public relations men, who kept the herd going obediently in the proper direction. The result is a bit like the work of a military historian who has been able to interview key officers on both sides. Except this war isn't history; it's still going on. And until Contragate and the astrology capers forced the media to admit that the emperor might be missing a few items of clothing, relations between Reagan and the press were not warlike at all, but the opposite.

As we learn in this account, Reagan's principal PR handlers—David Gergen, Larry Speakes, and, above all, Michael Deaver (a man who, to quote ABC's Sam Donaldson, "could have saved the Edsel")—used a variety of ways to keep the herd on track. In early morning staff meetings they set a "line of the day," a theme that the statements and appearances by the president and top officials were to stress that day. Conference phone calls and computer messages carried the word to cabinet members and their public relations staffs.

In times of crisis, this daily drumfire turned into a blitz. When the administration became alarmed by popular enthusiasm for the nuclear freeze in mid-1982, Robert McFarlane told Hertsgaard, he called a meeting of 30 top officials, targeted 14 major media markets, and said he wanted everyone present to spend 4 days in one of those areas in the next 60 days, doing a minimum of one meeting with a newspaper editorial board, one prime-time talk show, one meeting with a civic club, and one campus speech. By year's end, the 30 conscripts had made more than 600 public appearances to denounce the freeze and push the Reagan line on arms control.

Reagan, of course, puts his foot in his mouth whenever he says anything without a script. So in 1982, Deaver ruled that reporters would not be allowed to ask questions at the staged "photo opportunities" at which Reagan shook hands with visiting heads of state and celebrities. White House TV correspondents said that if they couldn't come to such events, then neither would their cameras. Understanding herd behavior, Deaver hung tough; he knew that once one network caved in, they all would. NBC soon gave up and resumed sending its camera crews; within two days, ABC and CBS did too.

Deaver never forgot the lesson, and eventually Reagan almost dispensed with press conferences altogether. In 1984, while campaigning for re-election, he held not a single one between July 25 and Election Day. But because he was president, the press had to report what he said, and because he wouldn't answer questions, they had to report his prepared statements. Reagan's people learned early what Israeli and South African authorities have demonstrated recently: if you allow TV to film only what you want it to film, that's what will go on the air. As Deaver acknowledges to Hertsgaard with remarkable frankness, "They had to take what we were giving them."

That's precisely how it worked. When U.S. planes shot down two Libyan jets, Reagan was triumphantly helicoptered to the deck of an aircraft carrier; little did it matter that it was off the coast of southern California, not Libya. When Reagan called for repealing the corporate income tax, Deaver dampened the outcry by arranging to have his client filmed having a beer with the boys in an Irish bar in Boston. When more than 200 U.S. Marines were killed in a Beirut bombing, Deaver staged a televised reunion at the White House to show the Reagans greeting soldiers and medical students newly "rescued" after the U.S. invasion of Grenada.

What the White House giveth, the White House taketh away. TV cameras were able to film Reagan opening the International Games for the Disabled, but reporters were not allowed close enough to ask him why he had asked Congress to cut funds for the handicapped. When correspondents at another carefully staged appearance at a wildlife refuge started shouting questions, White House officials literally pulled the plug on the TV lights.

One revelation in *On Bended Knee* is that White House media czar David Gergen used to telephone all three networks every day to find out what stories were going to be on the evening news. Then, after the news, he would call again to praise or criticize or suggest changes for later editions to be broadcast in the midwest and West Coast time zones.

Why would any self-respecting journalist *take* such calls? And, apparently, often make changes in response? Imagine the uproar if a network were caught editing its newscasts in accordance with daily phone calls from, say, Jesse Jackson. The main reason the Reagan administration's apparent media wizardry worked so well is that the press allowed it to. "There is," as Hertsgaard observes, "no great challenge in seducing someone who yearns to submit."

Ronald Reagan had the good luck to take office at a time when the press was still on the rebound from Watergate. The episode had led to an exceedingly rare breakdown of the team spirit that usually binds the major media and the national government. Never happy too far from official favor to begin with, the Washington press corps was, in 1980, more than ever in a mood to revive that spirit. And Reagan's personal popularity—although Hertsgaard argues that the media overstated this—and the outpouring of public sympathy for him after the 1981 assassination attempt made journalists still more inclined to treat him gently.

The result, in Hertsgaard's phrase, was "jellybean journalism"—an eagerness to take those calls, to transmit the president's messages, to let Reagan's astounding misstatements about recallable submarine-launched missiles or the ending of segregation in South Africa go by with barely a murmur. The loaded terms used by the White House were repeated by the media. ABC News—soon followed by the other two networks—talked about an economic "recovery" when, in 1983, unemployment dropped from 10.8 percent to 10.4 percent.

In most times and places in history, the mainstream media serve as a transmitter for the ideas of those in power, or very near power. The range of permissible criticism is wider in the *Washington Post* than in *Izvestia*, but both have strict, unwritten limits. Today the manipulative magic of television by its very nature narrows that range still further and places in the hands of a skillful administration an ominous degree of power.

During the 1984 campaign, CBS correspondent Lesley Stahl aired what she thought was a tough piece of reporting about Reagan. The screen showed a string of appearances carefully orchestrated for TV: the president visiting an old folks home, greeting an Olympic athlete, tossing a football, lifting weights, mingling with black and white children. Stahl's voice-over comments explained how the White House effectively used such stage-managing to block out awareness that Reagan was elderly, had cut federal social programs, was weak on civil rights, and so forth. To her amazement, according to Hedrick Smith in his new book, *The Power Game* (Random House), as soon as the evening news was over, Stahl's phone rang and a senior White House official said, "Great piece!"

Stahl asked: "Did you listens to what I said?"

The official said: "Lesley, when you're showing four and a half minutes of great pictures of Ronald Reagan, no one listen to what you say. . . . The Public sees those pictures and they block your message. They didn't even hear what you said. So in our minds, it was a four and a half minute free ad for the Ronald Reagan campaign for re-election."

It's no coincidence that the first president to understand the power of good visuals was Teddy Roosevelt: when he led his Rough Riders up San Juan Hill, he brought along two newsreel cameramen. The charge up the hill was of dubious military value, and the war in which it took place even more dubious, but it propelled TR into the White House. The inherent power of the visual image, brought to the height of its influence by modern TV, will always favor the pleasing message over the painful, the simple solution over the complicated. Who needs Big Brother and the Ministry of Truth when a skillful PR staff, a timid and obedient press, and the overwhelming influence of TV will just as efficiently disconnect image from reality?

Thinking It Over

1. Read *On Bended Knee: The Press and the Reagan Presidency.* Does Hochschild do it justice? Does he omit themes that conflict with his thesis?

2. Write a short essay in which you demonstrate how to solve the newsperson's problem of getting too cozy with the source.

52.
JUST HOW LIBERAL IS THE NEWS?
by Michael Jay Robinson

Setting the Scene: In the article that follows, the author tests what is perhaps the major hypothesis concerning news coverage in America: it is too "liberal." There has been clear evidence over several decades that "media elites" *are* more liberal—considerably more liberal—than the general public. They are also more apt to vote for Democratic candidates. But what matters is their treatment of the news. Is it biased? We join Michael Jay Robinson near the beginning of his article as he discusses the findings of an earlier study by Robert Lichter and Stanley Rothman.

The surveys conducted by Lichter and Rothman do prove beyond all reasonable doubt that the media elite—the Eastern press establishment—*think* more liberally than the nation's economic elite. Their surveys also prove that the national media are, in their personal opinions, decidedly more liberal than their national audience. Over half of the media elite were willing to label themselves liberal, twice the proportion of the public at large. Eighty-five percent of the sample of press people think that homosexuals should be allowed to teach in public school. The national figure is 57 percent. And over 80 percent of the press elite admitted to having voted for George McGovern in 1972, a statistic that, by historic contrast, makes even the voters of Massachusetts look reactionary. . . .

But press behavior—not opinion—is the key. Bias that counts must be in the copy, not just in the minds of those who write it. And our own research shows that, at least in the politics of 1980, the same Eastern press that thinks "New Class" and votes Democratic reports political news in a reasonably nonpolitical way. . . .

Throughout 1980 the Media Analysis Project at George Washington University conducted a presswatch, focusing for the most part on network and wire coverage of the yearlong national political campaign. We concentrated on CBS "Evening News" and the UPI day wire, but we analyzed political reporting from six other news sources as well—NBC, ABC, AP, the *Boston Globe*, the *Columbus Dispatch*, the *Seattle Times*. . . .

During the first eight months of Campaign '80 (January-August), we concentrated on coverage of candidates, not coverage of policy. So, during the ten weeks of the general campaign (Labor Day to Election Day), we took special pains to uncover pro-liberal reporting on what we classified as "the issues"—campaign news about public policy. We went through CBS and UPI copy line by line, checking for any telltale signs of partisanship. Specifically, we were looking for any *normative* statements by reporters that said or even suggested that public policy ought to be this, or ought to be that. The results do not support theories of liberal bias. If the absence of normative statements is the test of unbiased reporting, CBS and UPI passed with honors.

As expected, the wire reporters made no normative statements whatever during the general campaign, at least not about policy or issues. But CBS's evenhandedness came as a surprise. We know (thanks to specific data provided by Lichter and Rothman) that people at CBS news have since 1964 voted for the liberal candidate for president in ratios of *at least* four to one. Notwithstanding this record, CBS "Evening News" people were almost as unwilling as UPI to speak normatively about issues. During the entire general campaign, CBS reporters and anchormen made only two clearly normative remarks about anything, and neither one had much to do with "the issues," let alone with liberalism.[1]

Our study predates the coronation of Dan Rather as "Evening News" anchorman, and the full-time employment of Bill Moyers as "DC" (designated commentator). Our data from 1980 do show that Rather and Moyers are more "analytical" than the news people they replaced, although they are not necessarily more liberal. But in Campaign '80, before they were promoted, even Rather and Moyers avoided normative statements about issues and, like the rest of the reportorial staff, aimed their more subjective assessments at the candidates. That *zero* percent of all the general campaign news coming from CBS (or over UPI) was normative—and that zero percent made value judgments about issues—implies that the Eastern media are generally mute about policy, not that they are premeditatedly liberal. . . .

The Lichter and Rothman surveys indicate that the national media are more pro-Democratic than pro-liberal. Although eight of ten media elites voted for Jimmy Carter in 1976, only about one in ten believes, for instance, that big business should be publicly owned. But news content reveals the national media in 1980 did not favor the Democrats.

One of the oldest tricks in the bag of press biases involves access—getting time or space in the news. The Chandler family, which for a century has owned the *Los Angeles Times*, grew infamous by denying access to opponents while granting it to political friends. Back in the old days, *Los Angeles Times* national correspondent Kyle Palmer described the notion that major party nominees deserved equal space as nothing more than "New York crap." Equal access has been and is an issue in press bias. So, crude as they may be as measures, time and space are important indicators of press fairness.

How did the liberal press do at handicapping the opposition (Republicans) in 1980? The answer is—miserably. As if they were doling it out with a spoon, CBS and UPI gave almost perfectly equal access to the two major party nominees and to the entire field of Democrats and Republicans.

Between Labor Day and Election Day, Jimmy Carter and Ronald Reagan received equal time on "Evening News" an equal space on UPI. On CBS, Reagan had 50.6 percent of the two-party news seconds; Carter got the rest. On UPI Reagan secured 48.1 percent of the two-party news space; Carter had the remainder.

The month by month figures for the first four months of the campaign—the period coming before the asymmetrical convention period—indicate that the news media were dividing access equally, not indulging their political convictions.

---

[1] In October, Walter Cronkite apologized at length for drawing a white X over the candidate's face in a feature story about Ronald Reagan: the white X had been used to show how Reagan had contradicted himself on five issues. And on a second occasion in October, CBS reporter Lem Tucker made a facetious remark about Leon Jaworski. Tucker concluded that Jaworski should change the name of his new "Democrats for Reagan Committee" to "Democrat for Reagan," since Jaworski was its sole member.

If anything, these numbers indicate that it was the competitiveness of the race, not the politics of the news sources, that explains any discrepancy in party access. In January the Democrats had the "real" horse race; in March it was the Republicans. But, early and late, time was pretty much equally divided—and never divided along the ideological frontier. . . .

Time is one thing. But, as social workers tell us, quality time is another. So our study did more than count news seconds; it also judged every story for its *tone*. We divided stories into four types—good press, bad press, ambiguous press, and neutral press. The rules for scoring were complicated, but stated simply, a story was good press if the positive references to the candidate (horse race assessments excluded) outnumbered negative references three to one.[2] A bad press story had a ratio going in the opposite direction—three to one negative. Ambiguous stories fell somewhere in between. Neutral stories had not directional news whatever.

Ignoring horse race assessments, about four-fifths of the CBS news stories were neutral or ambiguous in tone. The remaining fifth were more negative toward the Democrats collectively than toward the Republicans. On "Evening News," (excluding Anderson) bad press represented 14 percent of all the news time for Republican candidates, and 19 percent for the Democrats taken as a field. The Democrats also lost out to the Republicans on UPI—9 percent bad press for the Democrats, 7 percent bad press for the GOP. . . .

It goes beyond our limits here to decide which candidate deserved how much access. But looking at the time given *each* of the candidates on CBS there doesn't seem to be much aggregate evidence over the year to suggest partisan bias, with three possible exceptions—Ed Clarke, Barry Commoner, and John Anderson. Clarke wound up with more votes on file than time on air. And, as a Libertarian, he might well be considered the victim of ideological bias. On CBS, Clarke received a total of 170 seconds of news time, less than 3/10ths of one percent of the total. But Clarke got 170 seconds more than Barry Commoner, the Citizen's Party candidate, who was completely shut out of "Evening News." The media apparently discriminate shamelessly against third parties, not just Libertarians.[3]

All this discussion of neutrality, however, masks one very important "liberal" funding. Early on, one candidate got more time than he deserved by almost any measure. On CBS, John Anderson not only managed to come in second in news time among all Republicans over the entire campaign, he also came in second among Republicans during the original three months of the campaign, *before* he declared his independence and *without* the benefit of any primary victory or any major support in the polls.

. . . The Anderson advantage in access, it turns out, was unique to CBS, or at least unique to the elite media. Anderson, compared with the rest of the Republicans, had poor access on UPI in January, February, and March. It was on CBS that he staged a press coup. This may be a CBS news bias, a network news bias, or an "elite media" bias. But no matter

---

[2] We excluded positive and negative statements made by the candidates or those who had previously endorsed candidates. We also excluded comments by communists, terrorists, criminals, and the Ayatollah. The good press/bad press measure reflects what the reporters or the "man on the street" were saying about the candidate's credentials or behavior.

[3] Barry Commoner's experience demonstrates that new class values don't always play well on network news. During the fall, Commoner had only one story—a negative piece on ABC reporting on his radio ad using the term "bullshit."

which level of press one cites, the Anderson access in the early campaign smacks of liberalism. In fact, extra news time for Anderson in the early campaign probably is the best and the *only* real evidence we uncovered linking the liberal press to liberal press content.

Bruce Morton at CBS explained to us the Anderson press advantage in part by acknowledging that Anderson was saying "interesting things," a remark that is about as close to a concession of philosophical bias as one might expect to hear from a prominent and practicing newsman speaking about his beat.

But the Anderson case was the exception, not the rule. And his exceptionalism was very short-lived. . . .

. . . Can anyone other than a Democrat conclude that political reporting is unbiased against Republicans and conservatives? Perhaps not. Nor will these data persuade many true believers that over the long haul the national press is biased against everybody, but in near equal proportions.

But, for those who might need help in discounting these findings, let me suggest some missing links in my own research. First, and most obvious, is the problem of other sources. CBS and UPI alone are *not* the media—only representatives thereof. Second, this analysis ignores the softer side of the national news, programs like "60 Minutes" which are to objectivity what Lyn Nofziger is to fashion.

The third and perhaps most serious omission is that these data deal only with news about the presidency and about the political campaigns. And, even though these two news categories represent a full third of the national newshole, by subtraction two-thirds of the newshole remains unaccounted for. And, very probably, that two-thirds *is* more partisan, more subjective than the rest.

Had our study gone beyond politics and the presidency per se—had it included *all* the network and wire coverage of the civil wars in Nicaragua and El Salvador, had it included *all* the coverage of the last oil crisis, had it included earlier reports about Three Mile Island or nuclear energy—the results would have been somewhat different from what they were in Campaign '80. But, quite ironically, in 1980 the two long-term news stories we followed that stood outside our formal analysis—the hostage crisis and the Soviet invasion of Afghanistan—if anything implied a conservative press bias, slight as it was.

Anyone who still remains convinced that the national media report the news liberally can also take comfort in one last truth—one last problem with my 1980 statistics. There is no discussion here of news agenda. If the press covered all business scandals objectively, but *only* covered business scandals, that agenda alone would support a theory of partisan bias. If the media always covered cost-overruns at the Pentagon but failed to cover any cheating in AFDC programs, that too would be political bias, regardless of how fair the reports themselves may seem. . . .

Let's not hear a round of applause for the nation's press. One cannot sort through 6,000 news stories coming over wire and television without developing a deep appreciation for all that our news media fail to do. Sensational at times, petty on occasion, superficial almost always, the news media fail almost as often and badly as the citizenry they try to serve.

But these are mostly failures of commercialism, not of partisanship. Why did CBS and UPI in 1980 present seven times as many stories about Billy Carter as about SALT?

Whatever else is true, the reason cannot be that the press was being partisan or liberal. Liberalism seeps into the national news, but never seeps in at rates as great as that which put Billygate on page one time after time and SALT II back near the classifieds. And if liberalism does seep into the news on occasion, as it did for a while with the Anderson campaign, it also seems clear that campaigns cannot float for long on press seepage alone. Nor is a ship of state likely to sink from seepage as modest as that which the liberal press produces. There are places where the press's ideology oozes—even pours—on occasion . . . right wing dictators . . . usually get worse press than most left wing dictators . . . But on issues close to home—*especially voting issues*—most topics get fair, if frivolous, coverage. And in campaign news reporting—the one form of journalism which ties directly to voting—partisan bias counts for next to nothing.

The next generation of media elites may make things much worse—may report the news both commercially *and* politically. At Columbia Journalism School, *the elite* journalism school, Rothman and Lichter find students ranking the *New York Review of Books* as the nation's third most credible news source, a finding that should please nobody but those who publish the *Review* or who contribute generously to the American Civil Liberties Union. But that new news elite at Columbia won't come on watch until the nineties, if ever. As for this generation, when the issue is news reporting—hard news reporting—the problem is not nearly so much new class values as old-time sensationalism and competitiveness. Ratings and circulation are the issue here, not radical chic. So when it comes to news content, liberal bias is a story, but, at best, it's a side-bar story for page three.

Thinking It Over

1. Consider this statement: "As the 1984 election returns came in to CBS news headquarters during the evening of Ronald Reagan's smashing victory, I swear the atmosphere turned more and more dour. The people at CBS tried to be cheerie but it was (to me) obvious they were not. Two years later in the 1986 off-year election, the atmosphere was considerably more up beat, almost bubbly. Reagan's Republicans were taking a beating. I'd bet the house and the car that if you ran those two shows consecutively to someone uninitiated to their content and without the sound, anyone watching would *see* the difference in attitude—would even be *struck* by it." If Michael Jay Robinson read this, what would he say, "That's interesting," or "So what"? Comment.

2. Let's say you are a liberal democrat and Michael Jay Robinson tried to convince you that, well, media elites may be conservatives and disagree strongly with liberal views and almost always vote for Republicans but—not to worry—the news itself is unbiased. How would you feel? Comment.

53.
SCOOP OR SNOOP?
by Dom Bonafede

Setting the Scene: In recent years we have seen a rush of headlines involving the personal lives of candidates for public office. Here we confront an important question in the relationship between the press and politics: how far should reporters go when they seek out information about a candidate's private life? We all agree we have a "right to know." But how much do we have a right to know? When a newspaper claims it operates under the principle "all the news that's fit to print," we may well ask, what does "fit" mean? Just as importantly, who makes that decision? A Presidential candidate has a boyfriend on the side. Who needs to know? Dom Bonafede does an excellent job in posing these kinds of questions to a series of people whose views are important. In doing so, he helps us think about this problem in new and interesting ways.

> The right to be left alone is the most comprehensive of rights and the right most valued in civilized man.
> —Justice Louis D. Brandeis

In Justice Brandeis, the 1988 presidential and vice presidential candidates—the winners as well as all the losers—appears to have a friend. At some time or another, most of the candidates have complained about the news media's intrusions into their private lives, thereby elevating an issue involving press ethics and responsibility that will very likely linger long after this campaign season is over.

Scandalmongers have always rummaged beneath the covers. Saintly George Washington was rumored to have coveted a neighbor's wife; Andrew Jackson was pilloried for marrying his beloved Rachel before her first marriage was legally terminated; Martin Van Buren was rumored to be the illegitimate son of Aaron Burr.

But perhaps never before has scandal, buttressed by gossip and rumors, been as much a part of the currency of politics as it has been in this campaign. The litany of personal transgressions—the trivial and unfounded as well as cardinal lapses in moral conduct, equally trumpeted by the news media—reads like chapter headings in an almanac of the 1988 campaign.

Gary Hart's philandering; the "miraculous" birth of Marion G. (Pat) Robertson's first child; Delaware Sen. Joseph R. Biden Jr.'s plagiarism; rumors of Michael S. Dukakis's "depression" after his gubernatorial defeat; the "youthful indiscretions" of Sen. Dan Quayle (notably the purported use of family influence to get into the Indiana National Guard to avoid combat in Vietnam).

After the Hart episode, reporters inquired of other candidates: "Have you ever committed adultery?" Private lives transacted with public lives in the theater of politics. Blunt, personal questions also have been asked to elicit answers on public policy: Cable News Network anchor Bernard Shaw, during the second debate between the presidential candidates, asked Dukakis if he would still oppose capital punishment even if his wife were raped and murdered.

And recently, an old rumor was fanned into flames by *LA Weekly*, an alternative newspaper in Los Angeles, that George Bush several years ago had a mistress. That rumor spawned another—that *The Washington Post* was about to publish a story on Bush's private life—that contributed to a 43-point drop in the Dow Jones industrial average. *Post* editors promptly denied that the paper planned such a story, but TV networks and major newspapers gingerly reported the story of the rumor, thus disseminating it. And, in an offshoot of that incident, a Dukakis campaign staff aide was forced to resign after telling reporters that "George owes it to the American people to 'fess up."

The news media's role in pursuing and printing such stories has raised as many questions about America's Fourth Estate as it has about the candidates. The performance of the nation's political press is being judged even as it, in effect, sits in judgment on the candidates. . . .

Inherent in this controversy are two questions:

Do presidential candidates surrender their right of privacy when they compete for the nation's highest elective office?

Have the news media exceeded their traditional responsibilities and overstepped the bounds of professional propriety in dogging the intimate lives of the candidates in search of "character"?

Responses are divided among political activists, campaign observers and members of the news media, reflecting the dilemma that arises over an issue touching on the press's independence, institutional accountability, private rights and the public's right to know.

In a sense, the debate has been provoked by the blend of the New Journalism with the New Politics, the first of which relies on subjective assessments and full disclosure, and the second, on imagery and illusions.

Political philosopher Michael Novak of the American Enterprise Institute for Public Policy Research (AEI) observed: "It's curious how a permissive generation of journalists can become so puritanical in probing the lives of public officials. It's hard to tell whether the journalists prey on a love of fallacious gossip, or whether they are responding to a so-called constituency of conscience.

"Since at least the late '60s, we've experienced a politics of conscience in which various candidates play 'purer than thou.' Hence, the candidates themselves have contributed to the legitimization of the politics of scandal. Destroying public lives has become a way of eliminating political opponents." According to Novak: "The amount of evil behavior hasn't changed; it's just been rearranged. Everybody is demanding righteous behavior and flogging themselves. It's a funny, paradoxical generation we live in."

George Reedy, who was President Johnson's press secretary and is now a Marquette University journalism professor, similarly placed some of the blame on the candidates. "When they feature their families in order to get votes, they are inviting the press into their private lives," he said. Reedy maintained that the public is entitled to know anything about a candidate's character that is important enough to change votes. "That's the acid test," he said. "The little slips aren't important; they don't shed any light on character. In a presidential campaign, people are concerned about the character of the candidates, and they have every right to be . . . and the only way to tell character is through their private lives."

How Much Privacy?

One who know firsthand how press revelations can destroy political ambitions is former Sen. Thomas F. Eagleton, D-Mo. Now practicing law in St. Louis, Eagleton abruptly withdrew as George McGovern's vice presidential running mate in 1972 just before newspaper reports that he had a history of mental illness and had been hospitalized at least three times because of it.

"The rules are much different from a half-century ago, during the time of Franklin D. Roosevelt," Eagleton said in a telephone interview. "Then, the press operated under a gentleman's agreement; no pictures were published of FDR in a wheelchair or struggling on crutches. I suspect that more than half of the country didn't know he was a victim of polio.

"Today, it is very doubtful that Roosevelt could be elected President of the United States. There would be pictures on the front page and on TV showing him being carried or trying to get into a car with his legs in braces. People would feel that we need a more vigorous President."

Eagleton is convinced that the news media sometimes go too far. "Those who espouse unlimited freedom of the press say that's wonderful. I say, I wonder. Can freedom of the press be carried to extremes? I suspect it can. . . . The criteria in a presidential campaign should be, is it relevant to the candidate's qualifications to be President?" . . .

Shelley Ross, author of *Fall from Grace: Sex, Scandal and Corruption in American Politics* (Ballantine Books, 1988), writes: "Even in the best of times, scandals are difficult for politicians to overcome. But when they hit in the middle of a presidential campaign, they are especially brutal. While the candidate is hard at work trying to create—and control—a certain image, the media uncovers a scandal and destroys it."

Ross further notes a historical parallel to this year's campaign: "Much like the 1884 presidential campaign, there is no one overriding issue, such as war or depression," she writes. "And just as with Grover Cleveland and James G. Blaine, journalists in the 1988 campaign began covering everything from mistresses and bastard scandals to how a candidate grew rich in office. Needless to say, in 1988 the media has flexed its muscle, showing off a capacity to break a candidate just as easily as it makes one."

Although the right to privacy appeals to Americans' sense of fairness and is implicit in a tradition of individual liberty, it is not explicitly spelled out in the Constitution. Various legal decisions have upheld "the right to be left alone" even as others ruled to the contrary, including a 6-2 Supreme Court decision last May *(California v. Greenwood)* that no right of privacy prevents the police from searching through a person's garbage.

This lack of juridical precision muddles the issue of the right of the press versus the candidates' right to privacy. Consequently, the press becomes the arbiter of whether there are any boundaries on probing candidates' lives.

On this, as on many issues involving journalistic practices and standards, the news media are split. On one side are the absolutists, who believe that a person forfeits the right to privacy after declaring as a presidential candidate. On the other side are the moderates, who argue that there should be limits to how far the media dig, determined by criteria such as whether information is relevant to a candidate's qualifications to hold office.

Conflicting Views

There is almost universal agreement that it is in the public interest that candidates' health and finances be treated as fair game. But conflicts arise over investigations into personal moral histories.

Among the absolutists is Howard Simons, former *Washington Post* managing editor and current curator of the Nieman Fellowship Program at Harvard University, who said: "Yes, they surrender all rights of privacy if they step into that major arena. Everything and anything is important to some segment of society. If they have anything to hide, the public has the right to know down to their socks and psyche. . . . If you want to be in the public limelight, you have to stand in the glare of public scrutiny."

Expressing approval of the media's inquiries about Quayle, Simons said: "We ought to know about his academic record; it tells us something of his formative years, his intellect and intelligence. All is fair game. The public is not dumb, it can sort out what is trivial. It does a pretty good job given the choices it gets."

Taking an opposing view, Ben J. Wattenberg, an AEI senior fellow and syndicated columnist, maintained that candidates should not be compelled to forgo their privacy and that the press should disclose only information that is pertinent to a candidate's ability to hold office. "The press ought to be responsible," he said. "If it finds corruption, yes, release it. It should stay away from sex and psychiatry, unless it curtails a candidate's effectiveness . . . when candidates are put through that kind of wringer—Had they an operation? Did they have a girlfriend in their past? Did they ever have emotional problems?—many will refuse to run. . . . I just think that puttering into everybody's bed covers is overdone" . . .

The Brookings Institution's Stephen Hess, a specialist in the relationship between press and government, contended that presidential candidates "do and should surrender their privacy rights." Presidential candidates, like movie stars, voluntarily give up that right, as evidenced by their retention of public relations consultants and pursuit of publicity, and "once given up, it is very difficult to reclaim," he said. "Geraldine Ferraro [the 1984 Democratic vice presidential nominee] is now a private citizen and tells the press to 'stop bothering me,' but she is still vulnerable. This applies to some degree to their families as well." The trial and conviction of Ferraro's son on a drug charge, for example, was a running news item.

Hess suggested that the news media's clamorous interest in the private lives of public figures is partly caused by sharp competition in the news business. It's not a neat, clean business," he said. "It's a highly competitive business, played by highly competitive people." . . .

The press is no longer simply a silent observer or instant chronicler of events, but rather an integral part of the electoral process. As the role of the two major political parties in selecting a presidential candidate has withered, the news media have assumed the parties' traditional function of assessing candidates and selecting issues. Moreover, the media have, by forfeit, become in some ways the common arbiter of moral principles.

In assessing candidates, helping to set the political agenda and weighing questions of morality, the press operates without formal guidelines, relying on ad hoc, self-defined, self-imposed and self-regulated standards.

Political journalists maintain that character is part of the calculus of leadership and that one of the news media's functions is to help articulate that quality to their audience. . . .

Media Backlash?

A side effect of the media-as-moralist syndrome is that the spotlight has been turned back on the press. The deluge of publicity about the private lives of Hart, Quayle and others made the public unusually sensitive to the pervasive presence of the news media in the campaign.

Surveys universally indicated that the majority of the public thought that the majority of the public thought that the press had engaged in "overkill" and generally agreed with Bush that in Quayle's case, it had indulged in a "feeding frenzy." A survey by the Center for Media and Public Affairs, headed by S. Robert Lichter, showed that the Quayle story "took up more than one-quarter of all evening news broadcasts for nearly two weeks after his nomination."

An internal memo by *Washington Post* ombudsman Richard Harwood took the paper to task for succumbing to "mob psychology" in its extensive coverage of the Quayle episode. The memo, published by the *Post*'s competitor, *The Washington Times*, noted that the *Post*, in a long profile of Quayle the day after his selection, referred to his National Guard service but did not question his motivation. Harwood wrote that the media blitz against Quayle started after Democratic political consultant Robert D. Squier suggested to reporters that they check into Quayle's military and academic background. On one day alone, Harwood said, the paper assigned 15 reporters to the story and, in addition to three A-section stories, published two columns, two "Style" features and two op-ed commentaries on Quayle. "Our handling of this story inspired the largest number of public criticisms I've encountered this year," he wrote. "Many of them were partisan, but some had validity." . . .

In any case, after the GOP convention and the Quayle tempest, Bush's standing in the polls began to climb.

Eagleton said: "This campaign will go down as the most asinine in history because of the media's concern with irrelevancies as, for example, whether Dukakis had ever seen a psychiatrist or whether Mrs. Dukakis once had burned an American flag.

"I think there is a growing sense of revulsion in the never-ending arrogance of the media telling people what they should think and what is important. There is a feeling that these arrogant people in New York determine what our thought patterns are. People sitting in their living rooms resent being dictated to but are likely to believe media types who, after all, provide what amounts to windows on the world."

Some observers sense that the public's reaction has caused the press to reassess its behavior. "Generally, the press is an educable institution; it does something and then reevaluates it," Hess said. "After discussing Robertson's first child, it pulled back." And [CBS news consultant John] Buckley noted, "When [former lobbyist and *Playboy* model] Paula Parkinson claimed Quayle put moves on her, many reporters said, 'Wait a minute,' and took a step backward." . . .

While agreeing that the media's excesses tend to be corrected, Buckley said: "There is still a sense that the media don't know what the rules are. But it's pretty clear that candidates can't spend a weekend with a 25-year-old model and get away with it."

Thinking It Over

1. Would *you* have reported Gary Hart's indiscretion? Dan Quayle's grades in college? Thomas Eagleton's "mental illness"? Mrs. Dukakis' alleged flag burning (if it were true)? Defend your decision. Is it possible to develop a hierarchy of personal news items that range from "report definitely" to "leave alone"? What is the criterion you would use to establish such a listing?

2. Extract from this article the single most insightful comment and explain why you chose it.

54.
DID THE PRESS UNCOVER WATERGATE?
by Edward Jay Epstein

Setting the Scene: If you like claims that take on established views, you'll love Epstein's article. He takes on public opinion, Hollywood, the media, and a whole slew of political pundits. The press, he says, did not uncover Watergate; the government did. It was not Carl Bernstein and Bob Woodward (alias Dustin Hoffman and Robert Redford) and their colleagues. It was the day-to-day operations of rather mundane institutional processes that did the trick. Characters like "Deep throat" may have been good for the movie, but they are irrelevant in explaining Watergate. I know of no article that combines the story of Watergate with the role of the media as well as this one.

A sustaining myth of journalism holds that every great government scandal is revealed through the work of enterprising reporters who by one means or another pierce the official veil of secrecy. The role that government institutions themselves play in exposing official misconduct and corruption therefore tends to be seriously neglected, if not wholly ignored, in the press. This view of journalistic revelation is propagated by the press even in cases where journalists have had palpably little to do with the discovery of corruption. . . .

The natural tendency of journalists to magnify the role of the press in great scandals is perhaps best illustrated by Carl Bernstein and Bob Woodward's autobiographical account of how they "revealed" the Watergate scandals.[1] The dust jacket and national advertisements, very much in the bravado spirit of the book itself, declare: "All America knows about Watergate. Here, for the first time, is the story of how we know. . . . In what must be the most devastating political detective story of the century, the two young Washington *Post* reporters whose brilliant investigative journalism smashed the Watergate scandal wide open tell the whole behind-the-scenes drama the way it happened." In keeping with the mythic view of journalism, however, the book never describes the "behind-the-scenes" investigations which actually "smashed the Watergate scandal wide open"—namely the investigations conducted by the FBI, the federal prosecutors, the grand jury, and the Congressional committees. The work of almost all those institutions, which unearthed and developed all the actual evidence and disclosures of Watergate, is systematically ignored or minimized by Bernstein and Woodward. Instead, they simply focus on those parts of the prosecutors' case, the grand-jury investigation, and the FBI reports that were leaked to them. . . .

After five burglars, including James McCord, who was an employee of the Committee for the Re-election of the President (CRP), were arrested in the headquarters of the Democratic National Committee in the Watergate complex on June 17, 1972, the FBI

---

[1] *All the President's Men*, Simon & Schuster, 349 pp., $8.95.

immediately located three important chains of evidence. First, within a week of the break-in, hundred-dollar bills found on the burglars were easily traced by their serial numbers through the Federal Reserve Bank at Atlanta to the Miami bank account of Bernard Barker, one of the burglars arrested in the Watergate. By June 22, the prosecutors had subpoenaed Barker's bank transactions, and had established that the hundred-dollar bills found in the burglary had originally come from contributions to the Committee for the Re-election of the President and specifically from checks deposited by Kenneth Dahlberg, a CRP regional finance chairman, and others. (Copies of these checks were leaked to Woodward and Bernstein by an investigator for the Florida state's attorney one month later, well after the grand jury was presented with this information—and they "revealed" it in the Washington *Post* on August 1.) And in early June, the treasurer of the Republican National Committee, Hugh W. Sloan, Jr., confirmed to the prosecutors that campaign contributions were given to G. Gordon Liddy, who by then was suspected of being the ringleader of the conspiracy.

Secondly, the FBI, in searching the premises of the burglars, found, within twenty-four hours after their arrest, receipts, address-books, and checks that linked E. Howard Hunt, White House consultant, to the conspiracy. (This information was leaked a few days later by the Washington police to Eugene Bachinski, a Washington *Post* reporter, and subsequently published in that newspaper.) The investigation into Hunt led the prosecutors to his secretary, Kathleen Chenow, who was flown back from England, and, in early July, confirmed that Hunt and Liddy were working on clandestine projects together, and had had telephone calls from Bernard Barker just before Barker was arrested in Watergate. (Months later, in September, defense attorneys who had been given the list of prosecution witnesses leaked Miss Chenow's name to Woodward and Bernstein, who then—after calling her—"revealed" this information to the public.) Thus, in early July, the prosecutors had presented evidence to the grand jury tying Hunt and Liddy to the burglars (as well as Liddy to the money).

The most important chain of evidence involved an eyewitness to the entire conspiracy. The day of the burglary, the FBI discovered a listening post at the Howard Johnson Motor Hotel, across the street from the Watergate, from which conspirators sent radio signals to the burglars inside Watergate (and received transmissions from electronic eavesdropping devices). By checking through the records of phone calls made from this listening post, the FBI easily located Alfred Baldwin, a former FBI agent, who had kept logs of wiretaps for the conspirators and acted as a look-out. By June 25, after the prosecutors offered Baldwin's attorney a deal by which Baldwin could escape prison, Baldwin agreed to cooperate with the government.

The main instrument for extracting information from reluctant witnesses like Baldwin was the prosecutors' skill in threatening, badgering, and negotiating. By July 5, less than three weeks after the burglars were apprehended, Baldwin sketched out the outlines of the conspiracy. He identified Hunt and Liddy as being at the scene and directing the burglary; he described prior break-in attempts, the installation of eavesdropping devices, the monitoring of logs of the eavesdropping, and the delivery of the fruits of the conspiracy to CRP. All this evidence was of course presented to the grand jury in mid-July. (Liddy's name was only mentioned in passing in the press on July 22, when he resigned from CRP, and it was not until the following October that Jack Nelson of the Los Angeles *Times* located and published an interview with Baldwin. To "top" the L.A. *Times*'s interview, Woodward and Bernstein erroneously reported that Baldwin had delivered the logs to three executives at CRP, Robert C. Odle, Jr., Glenn J. Sedam, Jr., and William E. Timmons. In fact, Baldwin delivered the logs to Liddy. In any case, the press was three months behind the prosecutors in disclosing Baldwin's vital account.) The prosecutors needed, however, a witness to corroborate Baldwin, since they realized that any single witness could be discredited by fierce cross-examination. The locating of Thomas J. Gregory, a student working as a minor spy for CRP, was critical for the prosecutors' case since he was able to corroborate important elements in Baldwin's account. (Gregory's existence was never mentioned by the press until the trial.)

The prosecutors and the grand jury thus developed an airtight case against Liddy, Hunt, and the five burglars well in advance of, and without any assistance from, Woodward, Bernstein, or any other reporters. The case was presented to the grand jury and would certainly have been made public in the trial. At best, reporters, including Woodward and Bernstein, only leaked elements of the prosecutors' case to the public in advance of the trial.

By leaking fragments of the prosecutors' case, Woodward and Bernstein, as well as other journalists, did of course add fuel to the fire. But even here, they were not the only ones publicizing the case. Immediately after the arrest of the Watergate burglars and throughout the campaign, Senator George McGovern denounced Watergate in most of his speeches and suggested in no uncertain terms that the White House was behind the burglary. Indeed, his campaign staff hired Walter Sheridan, a former FBI agent on Robert Kennedy's staff, to help "get out" the story. On June 20, three days after the burglary, the Democratic National Committee commenced a civil suit against the Committee for the Re-election of the President that compelled the responsible officials in CRP to give statements under oath (Edward Bennett Williams represented both the Democratic National Committee and the Washington *Post*). The General Accounting Office, an arm of Congress, and Common Cause, a quasi-public foundation, meanwhile forced Republican officials to disclose information about campaign contributions which indirectly added to the publicity about Watergate. Preliminary legal actions taken by the prosecutors (as well as the Florida state's attorney) also divulged important elements of the case. For example, in motions opposing bail for the defendants, the prosecutors disclosed in a brief filed June 23, 1972 that Mexican checks were deposited in Barker's account (although the press, until a month later, when the checks were literally handed to reporters, failed to pursue the "money tree" exposed in the bail motions). In short, even in publicizing Watergate, the press was only one among a number of institutions at work.

But what about Hunt and Liddy's superiors—Jeb Stuart Magruder and John Mitchell? The prosecutors were unable to develop a case against them, since as part of a cover-up, coordinated by the White House counsel John Dean, Magruder swore that he had given Liddy the contributions for a different purpose—to set up a system of informants—and this perjury was corroborated by Mitchell, by Herbert L. Porter, Magruder's assistant, and by Sally Harmony, one of Liddy's secretaries. But neither did Woodward and Bernstein nor any other reporters reveal the existence of the cover-up. The offers of executive clemency, the participation of Dean in the cover-up, the hush money, and the perjury did not emerge in the press in any serious form until after the trial of the Watergate burglars.

In the end, it was not because of the reporting of Woodward and Bernstein, but because of the pressures put on the conspirators by Judge John Sirica, the grand jury, and Congressional committees that the cover-up was unraveled. After the Watergate conspirators were convicted, Judge Sirica made it abundantly clear that they could expect long prison sentences unless they cooperated with the investigation of the Senate Select Committee on Presidential Campaign Activities (the Ervin committee). One of the convicted burglars, James McCord, clearly not content with accepting such a prison sentence, wrote Sirica that perjury had been committed at the trial and the defendants had been induced by "higher-ups" to remain silent. Subsequently, McCord suggested that Magruder, Mitchell, and Dean all were involved in the planning of the burglary and cover-up.

While McCord's assertion turned out to be only hearsay evidence, obtained from Liddy, the grand jury was reconvened, the prosecutors subpoenaed Dean, and the Ervin committee began focusing on the roles of Dean and Magruder. To intensify the pressure on Dean, the prosecutors held long secret sessions with Liddy, and though Liddy steadfastly refused to discuss the case in these well-publicized sessions, the prosecutors intentionally promoted the story that Liddy was talking and implicating Dean and Magruder.

As President Nixon's transcripts confirm, the ruse succeeded: Dean believed that Liddy, who had attended meetings with him and Mitchell which eventually led to Watergate, was plea-bargaining with the prosecutors. Moreover, Dean believed that Magruder, who could also implicate him in both the planning of the burglary and the cover-up, was about to bargain with the prosecutors. And FBI Director L. Patrick Gray, in confirmation hearings before the Senate Judiciary Committee, was publicly suggesting that Dean had interfered in the investigation and lied to the FBI.

Dean realized that he could not testify before the Ervin committee or the grand jury without fatally perjuring himself. Since President Nixon was not able to offer him any safe way out of his predicament, and he feared that the President's assistants would eventually sacrifice him, Dean began negotiating with the prosecutors on March 31 for immunity, and bit by bit, they forced him to disclose the entire cover-up—including the payments of hush money, blackmail threats, offers of executive clemency, the suborning of perjury, etc. In April the prosecutors finally elicited evidence from Dean of the burglary of Daniel Ellsberg's psychiatrist's office and the other "horror stories." Four days after he heard Dean was bargaining with the prosecutors, Magruder also decided to plea-bargain, and corroborated Dean's story.

A final coherent picture of the planning and execution of Watergate, of the cover-up, and of the other "horror stories" was developed by the Ervin committee on television. The American public thus found out about Watergate in hundreds of hours of testimony elicited in plea-bargaining and negotiations for immunity by the prosecutors and then presented and tested in cross-examination by members of the Ervin committee.

What was the role of the press in all this? At best, during the unraveling of the cover-up, the press was able to leak the scheduled testimony a few days in advance of its appearance on television.

If Bernstein and Woodward did not in fact expose the Watergate conspiracy or the cover-up, what did they expose? The answer is that in late September they were diverted to the trail of Donald H. Segretti, a young lawyer who had been playing "dirty tricks" on various Democrats in the primaries. The quest for Segretti dominates both the largest section of their book (almost one-third) and most of their "exclusive" reports in the *Post* until the cover-up collapsed later that March. Unidentified sources within the government gave Bernstein and Woodward FBI "302" reports (which contain "raw"—i.e., unevaluated—interviews), phone-call records, and credit-card records, all of which elaborated Segretti's trail. Through the FBI reports and phone records, they located a number of persons whom Segretti had tried to recruit for his "dirty-tricks" campaign. The reporters assumed that this was all an integral part of Watergate, and wrote that "the Watergate bugging incident stemmed from a massive campaign of political spying and sabotage. . . . The activities, according to information in FBI and Department of Justice files, were aimed at all the major Democratic Presidential contenders." They further postulated that there were fifty other Segretti-type agents, all receiving information from Watergate-type bugging operations.

As it turned out, this was a detour, if not a false trail. Segretti (who served a brief prison sentence for such "dirty tricks" as sending two hundred copies of a defamatory letter to Democrats) has not in fact been connected to the Watergate conspiracy at all. Almost all his work took place in the primaries *before* any of the Watergate break-ins in June 1972; he was hired by Dwight Chapin in the White House and paid by Herbert Kalmbach, a lawyer for President Nixon, whereas the Watergate group was working for the Committee for the Re-election of the President and received its funds from the finance committee. No evidence has been offered by anyone, including Woodward and Bernstein, that Segretti received any information from the Watergate group, and the putative fifty other Donald Segrettis have never been found, let alone linked to Watergate. In short, neither the prosecutors, the grand jury, nor the Watergate Committee has found any evidence to support the Bernstein-Woodward thesis that Watergate was part of the Segretti operation.

The behavior of the officials who steered Bernstein and Woodward onto this circuitous course makes in itself a revealing case study. Bernstein and Woodward identify their main source only under the titillating code-name of "Deep Throat," and indicate that "Deep Throat" confirmed their suspicion that Segretti—and political spying—were at the root of the Watergate conspiracy. But who was "Deep Throat" and what was his motivation for disclosing information to Woodward and Bernstein? The prosecutors at the Department of Justice now believe that the mysterious source was probably Mark W. Felt, Jr., who was then a deputy associate director of the FBI, because one statement the reporters attribute to "Deep Throat" could only have been made by Felt. (I personally suspect that in the best traditions of the New Journalism, "Deep Throat" is a composite character.) Whether or not the prosecutors are correct, it is clear that the arduous and time-consuming investigation by Woodward and Bernstein of Segretti was heavily based on FBI "302" reports, which must ultimately have been made available by someone in the FBI. The prosecutors suggest that there was a veritable revolt against the directorship of L. Patrick Gray, because he was "too liberal." Specifically, he was allowing agents to wear colored shirts, grow their hair long, and was even recruiting women. More important, he had publicly reprimanded an FBI executive. According to this theory, certain FBI executives released the "302" files, not to expose the Watergate conspiracy or drive President Nixon from office, but simply to demonstrate to the President that Gray could not control the FBI, and therefore would prove a severe embarrassment to his administration. In other words, the intention was to get rid of Gray. . . .

Perhaps the most perplexing mystery in Bernstein and Woodward's book is why they fail to understand the role of the institutions and investigators who were supplying them and other reporters with leaks. This blind spot, endemic to journalists, proceeds from an unwillingness to see the complexity of bureaucratic in-fighting and of politics within the government itself. If the government is considered monolithic, journalists can report its activities, in simply comprehended and coherent terms, as an adversary out of touch with popular sentiments. On the other hand, if governmental activity is viewed as the product of diverse and competing agencies, all with different bases of power and interests, journalism becomes a much more difficult affair.

In any event, the fact remains that it was not the press which exposed Watergate; it was agencies of government itself. So long as journalists maintain their usual professional blind spot toward the inner conflicts and workings of the institutions of government, they will no doubt continue to speak of Watergate in terms of the David and Goliath myth, with Bernstein and Woodward as David and the government as Goliath.

Thinking It Over

1. The author claims that journalists have a "blind spot" when reporting scandals in government. What is this blind spot and why does it affect reporters the way it does?

2. Does it do damage to the role of the press in a democracy if Epstein's case is correct? That is to say, suppose all the press did was to report what the government did in the case at the earliest possible time. Would that be enough?

55.
JOURNALISM, PUBLICITY AND THE LOST ART OF ARGUMENT
by Christopher Lasch

Setting the Scene: Nearly all commentary on the press involves questions of content, accuracy, and bias. In order for a democracy to work, the feeling goes, the public must have all the information it needs to make a decision. This information must be accurate and free of bias. How well does the media meet these standards is the question that dominates. Christopher Lasch steps outside this debate. His concern is not with the degree of accuracy and objectivity of the press. He seeks to question the value of objectivity itself and when he does his conclusion is that less is much better. Here is one of America's leading scholars and essayists taking on an established view on a subject of great importance to the Republic. How could anyone resist?

Let us begin with a simple proposition: What democracy requires is public debate, not information. Of course it needs information, too, but the kind of information it needs can be generated only by vigorous popular debate. We do not know what we need to know until we ask the right questions, and we can identify the right questions only by subjecting our own ideas about the world to the test of public controversy. Information, usually seen as the precondition of debate, is better understood as its by-product. When we get into arguments that focus and fully engage our attention, we become avid seekers of relevant information. Otherwise we take in information passively—if we take it in at all.

From these considerations it follows that the job of the press is to encourage debate, not to supply the public with information. But as things now stand the press generates information in abundance, and nobody pays any attention. It is no secret that the public knows less about public affairs than it used to know. Millions of Americans cannot begin to tell you what is in the Bill of Rights, what Congress does, what the Constitution says about the powers of the presidency, how the party system emerged or how it operates. A sizable majority, according to a recent survey, believe that Israel is an Arab nation. Ignorance of public affairs is commonly attributed to the failure of the public schools, and only secondarily to the failure of the press to inform. But since the public no longer participates in debates on national issues, it has no reason to be better informed. When debate becomes a lost art, information makes no impression.

Though the question at first may seem to have little to do with the issues raised by modern publicity, let us ask why debate has become a lost art. The answer may surprise: Debate began to decline around the turn of the century, when the press became more "responsible," more professional, more conscious of its civic obligations. In the early 19th century the press was fiercely partisan. Until the middle of the century papers were often financed by political parties. Even when they became more independent of parties they did not embrace the ideal of objectivity or neutrality. In 1841 Horace Greeley launched his *New York Tribune* with the announcement that it would be a "journal removed alike from servile partisanship on the one hand and from gagged, mincing neutrality on the other." Strong-minded editors like Greeley, James Gordon Bennett, E. L. Godkin and Samuel Bowles objected to the way in which the demands of party loyalty infringed upon editorial independence, making the editor merely a mouthpiece for a party of faction; but they did not attempt to conceal their own views or to impose a strict separation of news and editorial content. Their papers were journals of opinion in which the reader expected to find a definite point of view, together with unrelenting criticism of opposing points of view.

It is no accident that journalism of this kind flourished during the period from 1830 to 1900, when popular participation in politics was at its height. Eighty percent of the eligible voters typically went to the polls in presidential elections. After 1900 the percentage declined sharply (65 percent in 1904 and 59 percent in 1912), and it has continued to decline more or less steadily throughout the 20th century. Torchlight parades, mass rallies and gladiatorial contests of oratory made 19th-century politics an object of consuming popular interest. Horace Mann's account of the campaign of 1848 conveys something of the vitality of 19th-century politics, all the more impressive when we remember that this particular account came from someone who believed that the attention devoted to politics might better have been devoted to education:

> Agitation pervaded the country. There was no stagnant mind; there was no stagnant atmosphere. . . . Wit, argument, eloquence, were in such demand, that they were sent for at the distance of a thousand miles—from one side of the Union to the other. The excitement reached the humblest walks of life. The mechanic in his shop made his manner chime to the music of political rhymes; and the farmer, as he gathered in his harvest, watched the aspects of the political, more vigilantly than of the natural, sky. Meetings were everywhere held. . . . The press showered its sheets over the land, thick as snow-flakes in a wintry storm. Public and private histories were ransacked, to find proofs of honor or proofs of dishonor; political economy was invoked; the sacred names of patriotism, philanthropy, duty to God, and duty to man, were on every tongue.

Mann's account suggests that 19th-century journalism served as an extension of the town meeting. it created a public forum in which the issues of the day were hotly debated. Newspapers not only reported political controversies but participated in them, drawing in their readers as well. Print culture rested on the remnants of an oral tradition. Print was not yet the exclusive medium of communication, nor had it severed its connection with spoken language. The printed language was still shaped by the rhythms and requirements of the spoken word, in particular by the conventions of verbal argumentation. Print served to create a larger forum for the spoken word, not yet to displace or reshape it.

The "best men," as they liked to think of themselves, were never altogether happy with this state of affairs. Horace Mann, even though he was himself elected to Congress in the 1848 election, regarded party strife as the bane of the republic. . . .

By the 1870s and 1880s, Mann's low opinion of politics had come to be widely shared by the educated classes. The scandals of the Gilded Age gave party politics a bad name. Genteel reformers—"mugwumps," to their enemies—demanded a professionalization of politics, designed to free the civil service from party control and to replace political appointees with trained experts. . . .

The drive to clean up politics gained momentum in the Progressive era. Under the leadership of Roosevelt, Woodrow Wilson, Robert La Follette and William Jennings Bryan, the Progressives preached "efficiency," "good government," "bipartisanship" and the "scientific management" of public affairs, and declared war on "bossism." They attacked the seniority system in Congress, limited the powers of the speaker of the House, replaced mayors with city managers, and delegated important governmental functions to appointive commissions staffed with trained administrators. Recognizing that political machines were welfare agencies of a rudimentary type, which dispensed jobs and other benefits to their constituents and thereby won their loyalty, the Progressives set out to create a welfare state as a way of competing with the machines. They launched comprehensive investigations of crime, vice, poverty and other "social problems." They took the position that government was science, not an art. They forged links between government and the university so as to assure a steady supply of experts and expert knowledge. On the other hand, they had little use for public debate. Most political questions were too complex, in their view, to be submitted to popular judgment. They liked to contrast the scientific expert with the orator—the latter a useless windbag whose rantings only confused the public mind.

Professionalism in politics meant professionalism in journalism. The connection between them was spelled out by Walter Lippmann in a notable series of books: *Liberty and the News* (1920), *Public Opinion* (1922) and *The Phantom Public* (1925). These provided a founding charter for modern journalism—the most elaborate rationale for a journalism guided by the new ideal of professional objectivity. Lippmann held up standards by which the press is still judged—usually with the result that it is found wanting. . . .

The role of the press, as Lippmann saw it, was to circulate information, not to encourage argument. The relationship between information and argument was antagonistic, not complementary. He did not take the position that reliable information was a necessary precondition of argument; on the contrary, his point was that information precluded argument, made argument unnecessary. Arguments were what took place in the absence of reliable information. Lippmann had forgotten what he learned (or should have learned) from William James and John Dewey: that our search for reliable information is itself guided by the questions that arise during arguments about a given course of action. It is only by subjecting our preferences and projects to the test of debate that we come to understand what we know and what we still need to learn. Until we have to defend our opinions in public, they remain opinions in Lippmann's pejorative sense—half-formed convictions based on random impressions and unexamined assumptions. It is the act of articulating and defending our views that lifts them out of the category of "opinions," gives them shape and definition, and makes it possible for others to recognize them as a description of their own experience as well. In short, we come to know our minds only by explaining ourselves to others.

The attempt to bring others around to our own point of view carries the risk, of course, that we may adopt their point of view instead. We have to enter imaginatively into our opponents' arguments, if only for the purpose of refuting them, and we may end up being persuaded by those we sought to persuade. Argument is risky and unpredictable—and therefore educational. Most of us tend to think of it (as Lippmann thought of it) as a clash of rival dogmas, a shouting match in which neither side gives any ground. But arguments are not won by shouting down opponents. They are won by changing opponents' minds—something that can happen only if we give opposing arguments a respectful hearing and still persuade their advocates that there is something wrong with those arguments. In the course of this activity, we may well decide that thee is something wrong with our own.

If we insist on argument as the essence of education, we will defend democracy not as the most efficient but as the most educational form of government—one that extends the circle of debate as widely as possible and thus forces all citizens to articulate their views, to put their views at risk, and to cultivate the virtues of eloquence, clarity of thought and expression, and sound judgment. As Lippmann noted, small communities are the classic locus of democracy—not because they are "self-contained," however, but simply because they allow everyone to take part in public debates. Instead of dismissing direct democracy as irrelevant to modern conditions, we need to recreate it on a large scale. And from this point of view, the press serves as the equivalent of the town meeting.

This is what Dewey argued, in effect—though not, unfortunately, very clearly—in *The Public and Its Problems* (1927), a book written in reply to Lippmann's disparaging studies of public opinion. Lippmann's distinction between truth and information rested on a "spectator theory of knowledge," as James W. Carey explains in his recently published *Communication and Culture.* As Lippmann understood these matters, knowledge is what we get when an observer, preferably a scientifically trained observer, provides us with a copy of reality that we can all recognize. Dewey, on the other hand, knew that even scientists argue among themselves. "Systematic inquiry," he contended, was only the beginning of knowledge, not its final form. The knowledge needed by any community—whether it is a community of scientific inquirers or a political community—emerges only from "dialogue" and "direct give and take."

. . . According to Lippmann, the press was unreliable because it could never give us accurate representations of reality, only "symbolic pictures" and stereotypes. Dewey's analysis implied a more penetrating line of criticism. As Carey puts it, "The press, by seeing its role as that of informing the public, abandons its role as an agency for carrying on the conversation of our culture." Having embraced Lippmann's ideal of objectivity, the press no longer serves to cultivate "certain vital habits" in the community—"the ability to follow an argument, grasp the point of view of another, expand the boundaries of understanding, debate the alternative purposes that might be pursed." . . .

The decline of partisan press and the rise of a new type of journalism professing rigorous standards of objectivity do not assure a steady supply of usable information. Unless information is generated by sustained public debate, most of it will be irrelevant at best, misleading and manipulative at worst. Increasingly information is generated by those who wish to promote something or someone—a product, a cause, a political candidate or officeholder—without arguing their case on its merits or explicitly advertising it as self-interested material either. Much of the press, in its eagerness to inform the public, has become a conduit for the equivalent of junk mail. Like the Post Office—another institution that once served to extend the sphere of face-to-face discussion and to create "committees of correspondence"—it now delivers an abundance of useless, indigestible information that nobody wants, most of which ends up as unread waste. The most important effect of this obsession with information, aside from the destruction of trees for paper and the mounting burden of "waste management," is to undermine the authority of the word. When words are used merely as instruments of publicity or propaganda, they lose their power to persuade. Soon they cease to mean anything at all. People lose the capacity to use language precisely and expressively, or even to distinguish one word from another. The spoken word models itself on the written word instead of the other way around, and ordinary speech beings to sound like the clotted jargon we see in print. Ordinary speech begins to sound like "information"—a disaster from which the English language may never recover.

Thinking It Over

1. What do you think? Do you like "point-counterpoint" presentations on TV or do you like straight news? Take it a step further. Would you like the "point" made on CBS, the "counterpoint" on NBC and the "counter-counterpoint" on ABC? (Today it is unlikely that the city, town, or county in which you live even has competiting newspapers.) Finally, could the American people handle good rugged argumentation today?

2. Where to start? Lasch contends there is a causal sequence among the factors of knowledge, information, and argument. What is the sequence on which his point relies? Do you find it reasonable?

Chapter IX

PARTIES AND ELECTIONS

56.
WILL THE REAL NONVOTER
PLEASE STAND UP?
by Ruy Teixeira

Setting the Scene: Let's face it. If voting is any indicator, Americans don't care much about their democracy. In election after election, minorities of the voting age public turn out to vote. Worse (from the point of view of democratic thinking) voter turnout is decreasing at the very time one could argue it ought to be increasing. Why? More importantly what would happen if this state of affairs changed and large numbers of Americans did begin to vote? This reading suggests a surprising answer.

At times the American left seems like the spurned suitor who, seeing his beloved around town with someone else, insists, "It's really me she loves, she just doesn't know how to express it." One may find such sentiments understandable but still think them ridiculous.

The latest version of such wishful thinking is that nonvoters in America, if allowed and encouraged to come forward, would provide the left with the political support it currently lacks. Before this it was the poor, and before that racial minorities, and before that women, and before that the "new working class" who were going to transform politics. The list is long, but the claim is always the same: "I know these people are for us. They just don't know how to express it." . . .

What, then, are the facts? One need not share Piven and Cloward's [Editor's note: Frances Fox Piven and Richard Cloward are authors of a book (*Why Americans Don't Vote*) that claims that if nonvoters voted, leftist candidates and causes would be the big gainers.]

viewpoint to believe 82 million American nonvoters constitute a problem. It is still worthwhile to try to understand why, in general, Americans don't vote and why, in particular, Americans have voted even less in the recent past (a ten-point drop between 1960 and 1980). In its broadest outlines, the answer to the first question is simple. By and large, the costs of voting are higher in the United States than in other industrialized democracies, while the perceived benefits are lower. This reflects our *individual* system of voting responsibility. In our system the individual must surmount certain bureaucratic obstacles in order to vote. He must make sense out of a relatively narrow range of political alternatives, within which his viewpoint may not be represented. And the individual must, by and large, mobilize himself to go down to the polls and cast a ballot. In short the burden of voting falls on each voter's shoulders.

In contrast, other industrialized democracies typically have a *collective* system of voting responsibility where the state and political parties share the burden of getting voters to the polls. Most other democracies have state-initiated voter registration, for example, where the sate assumes the responsibility for registering its citizens. In addition the political parties in these other democracies play a stronger role in making elections meaningful to voters and in mobilizing voters to cast their ballots.

The benefits of voting—thought of in the sense of expressing ones informed viewpoint and feeling commitment toward party or cause—tend to be lower. (Most voting theorists see these as the key benefits of voting since the probability that a lone vote will actually affect an election outcome is so minuscule.) Because of this relatively unfavorable relationship between benefits and costs, Americans tend to vote at a lower rate than their counterparts in other industrialized democracies. Quite simply, for many Americans voting just doesn't seem worth the bother. Whatever one thinks of such an attitude toward a civic responsibility, it hardly makes nonvoting an indicator of suppressed radicalism or of any political viewpoint.

The Ups and Downs of Nonvoting

This is the basic story behind chronically low voter turnout in the United States. Why, then, did turnout go down ten points in the recent past—that is, what further weakened our already weak system of voter participation? To understand this, it is necessary to understand that, by some very important criteria, turnout should actually have gone *up* in this period.

Registration requirements became somewhat looser between 1960 and 1980, and levels of educational attainment—the single strongest promoter of voter participation—increased sharply. Real income went up, and there was an upgrading of the occupation structure in the direction of white-collar work. . . . [T]his socioeconomic upgrading should have increased voter participation substantially, all other things being equal.[1] But all other things were not equal.

Another series of demographic changes depressed turnout levels. These changes, the

---

[1]Ruy A. Teixeira, *Why Americans Don't Vote: Turnout Decline in the United States, 1960-1984* (Greenwood Press, Westport, Conn.: 1987).

product of the rise of the Baby Boom generation and of a society in economic and cultural flux, produced an electorate that was less rooted in the social fabric. Voters were younger, more likely to be single, and more likely to have moved recently. . . . [T]hese changes pushed turnout downward in a way that roughly counterbalanced the upward push on turnout from socioeconomic upgrading.

The other changes that depressed turnout levels concerned feelings about the political system. Given the weak American party system, such feelings probably play a particularly important role in making elections meaningful. Americans became less partisan, had less faith in their ability to influence the government (less "political efficacy"), and paid less attention to political campaigns. . . . [T]his disconnection from the political system substantially accounts for the rest of the drop in turnout.

This hardly suggests a romantic story of radical nonvoters searching for alternatives; it is instead a pedestrian tale of generalized withdrawal from the political world. It seems more reasonable to assume that most nonvoters lack a basic interest in politics than that they understand the status quo and reject it.

Results from the 1984 election suggest that a basic lack of engagement with politics is still with us. In a situation where observers and statistical models (including my own) predicted a large turnout increase due to favorable social and demographic trends, only a tiny half-point increase occurred. It could be that Americans' disenchantment with politics is only getting deeper as time goes on.

The Changing American Nonvoter

The story told above helps explain why the profile of the American nonvoter has changed so much since 1960. At that time it was justifiable to think of the typical nonvoter as being on the lowest socioeconomic rung of society—a poor high school dropout, for example—and, therefore, among the most deprived members of the social structure. The changes described above in fact *decreased* the concentration of nonvoters in the lowest socioeconomic categories—and more people were moving into the nonvoting camp for nonsocioeconomic reasons. These two trends added up to a substantial shift in the nonvoters' profile . . . .

In 1960, 72 percent of nonvoters had less than a high school education; by 1980 this figure had dropped to 39 percent. Similarly, in 1960, 60 percent of nonvoters were poor (less than $5,000 family income in 1960 dollars), whereas in 1980 only 44 percent were poor (using the same criterion). About 7 percent of nonvoters were under age twenty-five in 1960, while in 1980, 25 percent were under age twenty-five. Thirty-seven percent were mobile, and 26 percent were single in 1960; by 1980 each of these categories captured half of the nonvoting population.

Although in 1960 it might have been quite reasonable to describe the American nonvoter as a poor high school dropout, that definition was no longer so compelling by 1980. These days the pool of nonvoters is much more dispersed among socioeconomic and other categories, so that nonvoters can no longer be easily typecast as the most deprived or oppressed.

If Nonvoters Voted

These, then, are the American nonvoters, for better or worse. What if we could bring them, or a large proportion of them, to the polls? Would it make a difference? If so, how much?

The answer to the first question is, yes, it would make a difference. On this everyone agrees . . . .

These differences would, however, probably not be large. This is because (a) the nonvoting pool, while not a faithful representation of the entire population, is hardly a monolith of the disadvantaged; (b) partisan skews by demographic group, especially compared to other countries, are not overwhelming (skews in political attitudes even less so); and (c) partisan preference itself is a less and less reliable guide to how any individual votes in a given election. These mediating factors mean that massive increases in voting by nonvoters would not necessarily translate into much of an advantage for either party.

Political scientists Raymond Wolfinger and Steven Rosenstone have shown that even the most liberal voter registration laws would produce about a 9-percentage-point increase in the voting rate but only a .3 percent increase for the Democrats.[2] This is based on partisanship, which is becoming a poorer and poorer guide to the actual vote. Some scholarly evidence, in fact, indicates that nonvoters are *less* likely to follow their partisan preference than those who do vote.[3]

In short nonvoters are different from voters, but not so different that their participation in an election is likely to change the outcome dramatically. This is why a poll of newly registered voters in 1984 by Peter Hart Research, Inc. showed a 61 percent majority for Reagan—roughly the same as the rest of the electorate. The average nonvoter is simply too much like the average voter for results to be much different.

This suggests that, from a partisan point of view, the question of mobilizing nonvoters is logically inseparable from the question of mobilizing voters. A party unable to sway the existing pool of voters with its message would be unlikely to change its fortunes by mobilizing more nonvoters to vote. Conversely, if a party is able to reach the current electorate with its message, it could expect an additional increment of support from newly mobilized nonvoters. Hopes of a quick fix from the nonvoting pool are misguided, and the basic problem of winning an election remains the familiar one of getting the American people to support one's policies.

Thinking It Over

1. In his essay Teixeira says the following in a claim that nonvoters were more apt to be high school graduates in 1980 than in 1960: "In 1960, 72 percent of nonvoters had less than a high school education; by 1980 this figure had dropped to 39 percent." Is there anything wrong with using this statement for the purposes intended?

---

[2]Raymond Wolfinger and Steven Rosenstone, *Who Votes?* (Yale University Press, New Haven, Conn." 1980).
[3]John R. Petrocik, "Voter Turnout and Electoral Oscillation." *American Politics Quarterly* 9, 1981: pp. 17-43.

2. Given the fact that political parties and candidates have always believed high turnout would help them, will the knowledge that increased turnout will not change the nature of the electorate serve to dampen voter registration drives and further the decline in turnout?

3. Deal with this comment: "While these data are interesting, the really poor people I know are much less apt to vote than the wealthier people I know. My gut tells me Teixeira is wrong."

57.
IS THE TRUTH NOW IRRELEVANT IN PRESIDENTIAL CAMPAIGNS?
by Kathleen Hall Jamieson

Setting the Scene: In this reading the author not only claims that the 1988 Presidential campaign struck a new low for lies and deceit in televised campaign advertising, she also argues that countervailing forces that have traditionally worked to protect the public no longer do. Written as the 1988 election came to a close, the article ends on a pessimistic note: If we don't discover candidates "self-assured enough to campaign on the facts," there is little that can be done to stem a tide that is washing up some pretty dirty elections on the beaches of American politics.

Never before in a presidential campaign have televised ads sponsored by a major party candidate lied so blatantly as in the campaign of 1988.

Television ads of previous presidential contenders have, to be sure, seized upon votes cast by the opposition candidate and sundered them from context, resurrected political positions from the distant past and interpreted legislative moves as sweeping endorsements of unpopular positions. And, in eras gone by, the penny press, which didn't even feign political neutrality, published scurrilous assaults on would be presidents, albeit to far more limited audiences than those reached by televised broadcasts. But in the era of mass visual communication, major party candidates have, until this year, assumed that outright lying in an ad would create an outcry from the press, a devastating counter-assault from the other side and a discrediting backlash from an incensed electorate.

That assumption no longer governs. Take, for example, this ad from the Bush campaign: The picture shows a pool of sludge and pollutants near a sign reading, "Danger/Radiation Hazard/No Swimming." The text indicts Massachusetts Gov. Michael S. Dukakis for failing to clean up Boston Harbor. But the sign shown has, in fact, nothing to do with Dukakis or his record. Instead, it warns Navy personnel not to swim in waters that had once harbored nuclear submarines under repair.

Here's another from the Bush image mill: A procession of convicts circles through a revolving gate and marches toward the nation's living rooms. The ad invites the inference—false—that 268 first-degree murderers were furloughed by Dukakis to rape and kidnap. In fact only one first-degree murderer, Willie Horton escaped furlough in Massachusetts and committed a violent crime—although others have done so under other furlough programs, including those run by the federal government and by California under the stewardship of then Gov. Ronald Reagan.

There is only one precedent for such visual demagogery in the history of electronic presidential campaigning. In 1968 during the Richard Nixon-Hubert Humphrey contest, the

Republicans aired a wordless sequence of images as "Hot Time in the Old Town" played in the background. The images: Humphrey smiling; carnage in Vietnam. Humphrey smiling; Appalachian poverty. Humphrey smiling; bloodshed outside the Democratic convention. The inference invited was that Humphrey either approved or was responsible for the unsettling images juxtaposed with his own jovial one.

But when the 1968 ad sparked protests, the Republicans quickly withdrew it. No such protests greeted either the Boston Harbor or furlough spots. An electorate numbed by the negative campaigns of 1986—and a press corps preoccupied more with ad strategy than content—simply took the visual demagoguery in stride.

Thus encouraged, the campaigns moved beyond false implications to direct distortion. The Dukakis campaign joined in with an ad claiming that Bush cast "the tie-breaking Senate vote to cut Social Security benefits," when, instead, Bush had voted to eliminate a cost-of-living adjustment in benefits, thus eroding purchasing power but not diminishing the actual level of the checks.

From the Republicans came a portrait of the Democratic candidate looking somewhat silly as he rides in a tank and thus attempts to dramatize his support for a strong defense. "Michael Dukakis has opposed virtually every defense system we have developed," says the ad. Untrue. The Democrat favors the Trident II submarine and the D5 missile and the SSN21 Seawolf attack submarine among others. "He opposed the Stealth bomber . . ." says the ad. Another falsehood. Dukakis supports Stealth.

Has the electorate lost its sense of fair play? Certainly earlier candidates of the electronic era feared that they might forfeit the election if they offended voters' notions of fairness and honesty. Even in 1964, which witnessed the most negative electronic campaign prior to 1988, caution pervaded the politicking. A 1964 Democratic ad highlighting the Ku Klux Klan's endorsement of Barry Goldwater was shelved, unaired, when Goldwater rejected the Klan's embrace. To document Goldwater's position on Social Security, one ad showed five corroborating sources.

Ads dramatizing Goldwater's stands repeated words actually uttered by the candidate. Goldwater had, in fact, said that he wouldn't mind if the "Eastern seaboard were sawed off" and that the nuclear bomb was "merely another weapon." The famous "daisy" commercial certainly played on voters' fears of a Goldwater presidency, but the ad didn't even need to mention his name; the electorate's disposition to believe that the candidate was trigger-happy had been well fanned by his Republican opponents as they vied for the GOP nomination in the spring.

Comforted by such examples from recent decades, I concluded a survey of presidential advertising in a recent book on presidential campaigns with the assurance that the public had little to fear from distortions in TV and other ads. I was wrong.

Just as the Battle of Agincourt demonstrated the vulnerability of French armor to the British longbow, the 1988 campaign showed the deceptive power of visual association and the weaknesses of the protection provided by debates, news broadcasts, counteracting advertising and press coverage.

Part of the fault lies with the Dukakis campaign, which ignored the Bush attacks until they had so pervaded the attitudes of the electorate that Dukakis had plummeted from frontrunner to also-ran.   Part of the fault resides with reporters more disposed to discussing advertising strategy than substance or accuracy.   Part of the fault resides with a public more inclined to gather political information from inadvertent exposure to ads than from news accounts, attention to candidates' speeches or position papers.

Only in the last half of October did Democratic ads attempt to clean up a campaign environment so awash in distortions that Bush's portrayal of Boston Harbor seemed clean by comparison. Without counter-advertising by Dukakis, or clarification in news or debates, the electorate had no reason to doubt the inference invited by the Bush furlough ad.

Only those who had closely followed campaign speeches and position papers, as well as broadcast and print news accounts, would know that the facts provide absolutely no support for the implication that a President Dukakis would usurp the rights of the states and furlough first-degree murderers to mug or murder Reagan Democrats. Among those little-known facts are: Only one first-degree murderer furloughed by the Massachusetts program, Willie Horton, committed a violent crime; that the typical furlough jumper was an unarmed robber, not a murderer; that 72 of the escapees didn't escape at all—they simply returned more than two hours late; that a comparable federal program continues, and that programs comparable to Dukakis' existed in other states (including under the Reagan administration in California) and that both the crime rate and the murder rate in Massachusetts are low for an industrial state

So Dukakis could have knocked the GOP ad for a loop. But by refusing in the debates to rebut the distortions, and by waiting until October to respond in ads, Dukakis squandered two of the three means available to protect the public from deception in political ads.

For its part, the press, the third potential safeguard, spent much of this time focused on revealing the strategy rather than the inaccuracy of the ads. Only when the Bush "tank" ad rumbled into the World Series did its obvious distortion of Dukakis' defense posture prompt ABC, and then the other networks, The Washington Post and the other major papers to set the record straight.

But even if the news outlets had been more vigilant, news alone can't adequately protect the public from deception.   Single news segments cannot erase dozens of exposures to sludge-clotted Boston Harbor or the seemingly endless procession of scot-free murderers. Besides, most viewers in key states will have seen the ads repeatedly, whereas a far smaller number will see the single correction in network news stories. A smaller number still will thumb back from the comics and sports pages to the articles unmasking the distortions.

Nor can the networks be called upon to screen out deceptive political advertising. Were the product a Plymouth and not a president, Bush's claim to leadership on the INF treaty, his assertion that Dukakis opposed the Stealth bomber and the implication that Dukakis freed 268 Willie Hortons would not have aired. Nor would Dukakis' claim that Bush voted to cut Social Security. Whereas the networks protect the consumer from distortions in product ads, the need to protect a candidate's right to free speech means that stations and networks can't reject deceptive presidential ads.

How then can the electorate be protected? The best available defense seems to be the vigilance of the opposing candidate and party. But, as this campaign has shown, a candidate's access to news, counter-advertising and debates protects the public only if the attacked candidate moves quickly and strategically. Moreover, the protections of news and debates presuppose that the attacked candidate is comfortable with personally rebutting untruths and counter attacking. Neither seems to come naturally to Michael Dukakis.

There is also the real risk that a counter-attack may simply legitimize false claims and magnify their impact. It can also reduce the campaign to a shouting match in which each candidate calls the other a liar, leaving the electorate disillusioned and confused. That seems to be where the campaign of 1988 is winding up. It's also where future campaigns are likely to be headed—unless this country can discover among the ranks of its politicians a pair of candidates self-assured enough to campaign on the facts.

Thinking It Over

1. This article was followed (on the same page) in the *Washington Post* by a piece entitled "But Then Truth Has Never Been Important." A comparison of the two articles would form the basis for an interesting essay or term paper.

2. Why is it that the government can prohibit a manufacturer from lying about a competitor's product, but it can't stop political candidates from lying about each other? Are voters less important than consumers?

58.
THE PARTY'S OVER:
THE FAILURE OF POLITICS IN AMERICA
by David S. Broder

Setting the Scene: In the camps of political science, David S. Broder is one of America's most respected journalists. Writing during the massive socio-political disruption of the late 1960s, he recalls his own class work in political science and laments the passing of political parties, which he claims, are the mainsprings of American democracy. We need the parties, he says, as a hedge against extremism. But more than that. We need them for the proper day to day functioning of a democracy that seeks to govern the most complex society on the planet.

The Decline and Fall of Party Government

The reason we have suffered governmental stalemate is that we have not used the one instrument available to us for disciplining government to meet our needs. That instrument is the political party. ~

Political parties in America have a peculiar status and history. They are not part of our written Constitution. The Founding Fathers, in fact, were determined to do all they could to see they did not arise. Washington devoted much of his Farewell Address to warning his countrymen against "the dangers of party in the state." And yet parties arose in the first generation of the nation, and have persisted ever since. Their very durability argues that they fill a need. That need is for some institution that will sort out, weigh, and, to the extent possible, reconcile the myriad conflicting needs and demands of individuals, groups, interests, communities and regions in this diverse continental Republic; organize them for the contest for public office; and then serve as a link between the constituencies and the men chosen to govern. When the parties fill their mission well, they tend to serve both a unifying and a clarifying function for the country. Competitive forces draw them to the center, and force them to seek agreement on issues too intense to be settled satisfactorily by simple majority referendum. On the other hand, as grand coalition, they are capable of taking a need felt strongly by some minority of the population and making it part of a program endorsed by a majority.

When they do not function well, things go badly for America. The coming of the Civil War was marked by a failure of the reconciling function of the existing parties. Long periods of stagnation, too, can be caused by the failure of the parties to bring emerging public questions to the point of electoral decision. When the parties fail, individual citizens feel they have lost control of what is happening in politics and in government. They find themselves powerless to influence the course of events. Voting seems futile and politics pointless charade. These are the emotions millions of Americans express today, after sixteen years of government impasse. By any measure you can take, public opinion is markedly more disenchanted with government and its leaders today than it was in 1955. The Gallup Poll reported in August of 1955 that 79 percent of the adults approved the way President Eisenhower was handling his job. At a comparable point in his term, in August, 1971, President Nixon enjoyed the confidence and approval of 49 percent of the American people. Nor was Nixon alone in public opprobrium. A bit earlier in the year, the Harris Survey reported that Congress got a favorable rating for its work from only 26 percent of the people, the lowest figure it had ever recorded in that category. The credibility of our highest officials is deeply suspect. In February, 1967, 65 percent of the American people told Dr. Gallup they did not believe the Johnson Administration was telling the public all it should know about the Vietnam war. Exactly four years later, with a new President in office, the same survey showed 69 percent did not believe they were getting the facts from Nixon.

"What we are witnessing," said Dr. Warren Miller, director of the Center for Political Studies at the University of Michigan in November, 1971, "is a massive erosion of the trust the American people have in their government." Cynicism about government has increased dramatically. The survey on which Miller was reporting showed that roughly half as many whites and blacks believed in the reality of "government of the people, by the people and for the people" in 1970 as had believed in it in 1958. By 1970 there was virtually a three-fold increase among whites and more than a five-fold increase among blacks who thought government was run by the big interests for their own benefit. The figures show an appalling rise in public distrust and alienation . . .

The governmental system is not working because the political parties are not working. The parties have been weakened by their failure to adapt to some of the social and technological changes taking place in America. But, even more, they are suffering from simple neglect: neglect by Presidents and public officials, but, particularly, neglect by the voters. . . .

Some students of government who share this view of the importance of political parties in American government nonetheless think it futile to exhort readers on their behalf. Such political scientists as James L. Sundquist and Walter Dean Burnham, whose knowledge of American political history is far deeper than my own, believe we are simply in the wrong stage of the political cycle to expect anything but confused signals and weak responses from the parties.

The last major party realignment, it is generally agreed, took place in 1932, and set the stage for the New Deal policies of government intervention in the economy and the development of the welfare state. We are, these scholars argue, perhaps overdue for another realignment, but until an issue emerges which will produce one, an issue as powerful as the Great Depression, it is futile to complain that party lines are muddled and governmental action is all but paralyzed. Their judgment may be correct, but I do not find it comforting. The cyclical theory of party realignment is an easy rationalization for throwing up our hands and doing nothing. But we do not know when the realignment will take place. Some scholars have thought there was a thirty-six-year cycle, with 1896 and 1932 as the last "critical elections." But 1968, the scheduled date, on this theory, for another "critical election," has come and gone, and our drift continues.

The level of frustration in the country is terribly high—dangerously high. I do not think that we can just assume that people will bide their time and wait for relief to arrive from some new party, or some rearrangement of constituents between the Democrats and Republicans. There is clear danger than the frustrations will find expression in a political "solution" that sacrifices democratic freedoms for a degree of relief from the almost unbearable tensions and strains of today's metropolitan centers. Basically, I believe that our guarantee of self-government is no stronger than our exercise of self-government; and today the central instruments of self-government, the political parties, are being neglected or abused. We must somehow rescue them if we are to rescue ourselves.

In 1963, when James MacGregor Burns, the Williams College political scientist and biographer of Roosevelt and Kennedy, published his analysis of the political impasse, calling it *The Deadlock of Democracy*, many of his colleagues in political science dismissed his picture of "drift, delay and devitalization" as overdrawn.

In 1965, when Lyndon Johnson rushed bill after bill through a compliant Congress, some of them argued that Burns's theory had been knocked into a cocked hat. That judgment was, to put it kindly, premature. Today the "Great Society" exists mainly on the pieces of paper collected in the Johnson Library in Austin and in the Souvenir bill-signing pens gathering dust in offices on Capitol Hill. Instead of the "Great Society," what we have is a society in which discontent, disbelief, cynicism and political inertia characterize the public mood; a country whose economy suffers from severe dislocations, whose currency is endangered, where unemployment and inflation coexist, where increasing numbers of people and even giant enterprises live on the public dole; a country whose two races continue to withdraw from each other in growing physical and social isolation; a country whose major public institutions command steadily less allegiance from its citizens; whose education, transportation, law enforcement, health and sanitation systems fall far short of filling their functions; a country whose largest city is close to being ungovernable and uninhabitable; and a country still far from reconciling its international responsibilities with its unmet domestic needs.

We are in trouble. And now, unlike a decade ago, the people know it. The question is, Can we still save ourselves from deadlock without sacrificing our democracy?

. . .

Societies are funny creatures. So long as there is a presumption that disagreements will be settled civilly, that each dispute will not be carried to the ultimate test of strength, the naked force that is at the root of government—the police power—need not be invoked. But when that assumption is no longer made, when every issue has the potential of becoming an "ultimate issue," the police power will become much more evident. Already we have had mass arrests, not by some foolish provincial sheriff, but by the police force of the nation's capital, acting with the approval of the Attorney General of the United States. On the other side, we have had guerrilla raids on draft headquarters and FBI offices, bombings of the Capitol and other government buildings and other acts of terrorism.

To the extent that our dependence on pressure group tactics leaves us open to increasing civil strife and the danger of reflexive repression, it represents yet another limit on how far

had in mind.

They assumed that the House, being directly elected by the people—unlike the Senate, which at first was reelected by the state legislatures—would be the most powerful of the two houses. In The Federalist number 52, "Publius" justified the house two-year term by noting that "the greater the power is, the shorter ought to be its duration."

The fact that House seats are now looking more like life peerages is no accident.

House districts have consistently been gerrymandered following each census to protect incumbents of both parties. Republicans complain that redistricting by the predominantly Democratic state legislatures has cheated them out of 20 to 25 House seats, but one reason their losses were so low this year is the protection that gerrymandering has given their incumbents.

Another reason is that in 1980 the Democrats were rudely surprised by the Republican tide that swamped 27 Democratic House incumbents, including such stalwarts as Al Ullman of Oregon and Richardson Preyer of North Carolina. Themselves duly warned, the Republicans were able to minimize their losses in the recession-ridden 1982 off-year elections, as did the Democrats in President Reagan's 1984 reelection landslide.

This is partly the result of the rise of factors the Founding Fathers couldn't have foreseen—professional campaign consultants armed with opinion polls and computers and the congressional campaign committees of both parties, which provide professional and financial aid that helps reduce surprises and levels out big swings. Both parties made incumbent protection their top priority for 1986.

Early in 1985, for example, the Republicans announced that they had targeted about 35 Democratic House incumbents. Once again duly warned, the Democrats took a close look at strengthening these districts. Their efforts in many cases discouraged GOP candidate recruitment, and these incumbents, several of whom were unopposed, won this year with an average of 62 percent of the vote.

By the same token, about 80 percent of political action committee money goes to incumbents, 10 percent to challengers and 10 percent to open seats. Once again, one reason is that PAC contributions aren't risk capital and PACs contribute only to challengers who have a decent shot.

The low turnout in U.S. elections also is related. One reason for our relatively low turnout is the difficulty in registering in this country, compared to most other democracies. These barriers traditionally have been at least in part the work of elected officials and political bosses who don't want large numbers of new and unfamiliar voters they can't control.

There's not likely to be much change in this stability in the House in the next few years until a generation of members begins to retire or lose because they've gotten complacent and out of touch with their districts.

Right now, however, there's not much complacency on the House side, which is why they had the big reelection numbers.

As Norman Ornstein, a leading student of Congress, points out: "It's healthy for incumbents to get a good scare."

"Publius" could not have agreed more.

Thinking It Over

1. Make a list of items called "advantages of incumbency." Then see if you can construct a list of strategies for challengers; one to counteract each advantage of incumbency. Good luck.

2. Why doesn't Dickenson's article deal with limiting campaign spending so that challengers and incumbents are held to certain levels? Or, what about setting limits on the number of terms? Are there any other structured ways to give challengers a break? What about giving them a handicap (as in golf) of one percent of the vote for every two-year term the incumbent has served?

3. Write an essay entitled: "What's wrong with incumbency?" Take the position that there isn't much wrong with it at all.

65.
HOME STYLE:
HOUSE MEMBERS IN THEIR DISTRICTS
by Richard F. Fenno, Jr.

Setting the Scene: One of the great strengths of Richard Fenno's work is the use of personal interviews in his research. You will hear from Congresspersons themselves as they try to balance their need to maintain a strong presence in their districts with their ambition to become an influential member of the Washington establishment. Fenno masterfully weaves these interviews into his analysis to demonstrate patterns of behavior invisible to the naked eye. You will note that Fenno codes his Congresspersons (Congressman "O," for instance) to protect their anonymity.

When we speak of constituency careers, we speak primarily of the pursuit of the goal of reelection. When we speak of Washington careers, we speak primarily of the pursuit of the goals of influence in the House and the making of good public policy. Thus the intertwining of careers is, at bottom, an intertwining of member goals.

So long as they are in the expansionist stage of their constituency careers, House members will be especially attentive to their home base. They will pursue the goal of reelection with single-minded intensity and will allocate their resources disproportionately to that end. . . . [F]irst-term members go home more frequently, place a larger proportion of their staff in the district, and more often leave their families at home than do their senior colleagues. Building a reelection constituency at home and providing continuous access to as much of that constituency as possible requires time and energy. Inevitably, these are resources that might otherwise be allocated to efforts in Washington. "The trouble is," said one member near the end of his second term,

I haven't been a congressman yet. The first two years, I spent all of my time getting myself reelected. That last two years, I spent getting myself a district so that I could get reelected. So I won't be a congressman until next year.

By being "a congressman" he means pursuing goals above and beyond that of reelection (i.e., power in the House and good public policy).

In a House member's first years, the opportunities for gaining inside power and policy influence are limited. Time and energy and staff can be allocated to home without an acute sense of conflict. At rates that vary from congressman to congressman, however, the chances to have some institutional or legislative effect improve. As members stretch to avail themselves of the opportunity, they may begin to experience some allocative strain. It requires time and energy to develop a successful career in Washington just as it does to develop a successful career in the district. Because it may not be possible to allocate these resources to House and home, each to an optimal degree, members may have to make allocative and goal choices.

A four-term congressman with a person-to-person home style described the dilemma of choice:

> I'm beginning to be a little concerned about my political future. I can feel myself getting into what I guess is a natural and inevitable condition—the gradual erosion of my local orientation. I'm not as enthused about tending my constituency relations as I used to be and I'm not paying them the attention I should be. There's a natural tension between being a good representative and taking an interest in government. I'm getting into some heady things in Washington, and I want to make an input into the government. It's making me a poorer representative than I was. I find myself avoiding the personal collisions that arise in the constituency—turning away from that one last handshake, not bothering to go to that one last meeting. I find myself forgetting people's names. And I find myself caring less about it than I used to. Right now, it's just a feeling I have. In eight years I have still to come home less than forty weekends a year. This is my thirty-sixth trip this year. What was it Arthur Rubinstein said? "If I miss one practice, I notice it. If I miss two practices, my teacher notices it. If I miss a week of practice, my audience notices it." I'm at stage one right now—or maybe stage one and stage two. But I'm beginning to feel that I could be defeated before long. And I'm not going to change. I don't want the status. I want to contribute to government.

The onset of a Washington career is altering his personal goals and his established home style. He is worried about the costs of the change; but he is willing to accept some loss of reelection support in exchange for his increased influence in Congress.

This dilemma faces every member of Congress. It is built into the twin requirements that Congress be a representative and a legislative institution. Some members believe they can achieve reelection at home together with influence or policy in Washington without sacrificing either. During Congressman O's first year as a subcommittee chairman . . . I asked him whether his new position would make it more difficult to tend to district matters. He replied,

> If you mean, am I getting Potomac fever, the answer is, no. If you mean, has the change in my official duties here made me a better congressman, the answer is, yes. If you mean has it taken away from my activity in the constituency, the answer is no.

Congressman O, we recall, has been going home less; but he has been increasing the number and the activity of his district staff. Although he speaks confidently of his allocative solution, he is not unaware of potential problems. "My staff operation runs by itself. They don't need me. Maybe I should worry about that. You aren't going back and say I'm ripe for the plucking are you? I don't think I am."

A three-term member responded very positively when I paraphrased the worries of the congressman friend of his who had quoted Arthur Rubinstein:

> You can do your job in Washington and in your district if you know how. My quarrel with [the people like him] of this world is that they don't learn to be good politicians before they get to Congress. They get there because some people are sitting around the table one day and ask them to do it. They're smart, but they don't learn to organize a district. Once you learn to do that, it's much easier to do your job in Washington.

This member, however, has not yet tasted the inside influence of his friend. Moreover, he does not always talk with such assurance. His district is not so well organized that he has reduced his personal attentiveness to it.

> Ralph Krug [the congressman in the adjacent district] tells me I spoil my constituents. He says, "You've been elected twice; you know your district; once a month is enough to come home." But that's not my philosophy. Maybe it will be someday . . . My lack of confidence is still a pressure which brings me home. This is my political base. Washington is not my political base. I feel I have to come home to get nourished, to see for myself what's going on. It's my security blanket—coming home.

For now, he feels no competing pulls; but he is not unaware of his friend's dilemma.

Members pose the dilemma with varying degrees of immediacy. No matter how confident members may be of their ability to pursue their Washington and their constituency careers simultaneously, however, they all recognize the potentiality of conflict and worry about coping with it. It is our guess that the conflict between the reelection goal on the one hand and the power or policy goals on the other hand becomes most acute for members as they near the peak of influence internally. For, at this stage of their Washington career, the resource requirements of the Washington job make it nearly impossible to meet established expectations of attentiveness at home. Individuals who want nothing from their Washington careers except the status of being a member of Congress will never pursue any other goal except reelection. For these people, the dilemma of which we speak is minimal. Our concern is with those individuals who find, sooner or later, that they wish to pursue a mix of goals in which reelection must be weighted along with power or policy.

One formula for managing a mix of goals that gives heavy weight to a Washington career is to make one's influence in Washington the centerpiece of home style. The member says, in effect, "I can't come home to present myself in person as much as I once did, because I'm so busy tending to the nation's business; but my seniority, my influence, my effectiveness in Washington is of great benefit to you." He asks his supportive constituents to adopt a new set of expectations, one that would put less of a premium on access. Furthermore, he asks these constituents to remain sufficiently intense in their support to discourage challengers—especially those who will promise access. All members do some of this when they explain their Washington activity—especially in connection with "explaining power." And, where possible, they quote from favorable national commentary in their campaign literature. But, though Congressman L . . . comes close, none of the eighteen has made Washington influence the central element of his home style.

One difficulty of completely adopting such a home style is that the powerful Washington legislator can actually get pretty far out of touch with his supportive constituents back home. One of the more senior members of my group, and a leader of his committee, recounted the case when his preoccupation with an internal legislative impasse affecting Israel caused him to neglect the crucial Jewish element of his primary constituency—a group "who contribute two-thirds of my money." A member of the committee staff had devised an amendment to break the deadlock.

> Peter Tompkins looked at it and said to me, "Why don't we sponsor it?" So we put it forward, and it became known as the Crowder-Tompkins Amendment. I did it because I respected the staff man who suggested it and because I wanted to get something through that was reasonable. Well, a member of the committee called people back home and said, "Crowder is selling out." All hell broke loose. I started getting calls at two and three in the morning from my friends asking me what I was doing. So I went back home and discussed the issue with them. When I walked into the room, it made me feel sad and shocked to feel their hostility. They wanted me to know that they would clobber me if they thought I was selling out. Two hours later, we walked out friends again. I dropped the Crowder-Tompkins Amendment. That's the only little flare up I've ever had with the Jewish community. But it reminded me of their sensitivity to anything that smacks of discrimination.

The congressman survived. But he would not have needed so forceful a reminder of his strongest supporters' concerns were he nearer the beginning of his constituency career. But, of course, neither would he have been a committee leader, and neither would the imperatives of a House career bulked so large in his mix of goals.

Another way to manage conflicting reelection and Washington career goals might be to use one's Washington influence to alter support patterns at home. That is, instead of acting—as is the normal case—to reenforce home support, to keep what he had "last time," the congressman might act to displace that old support with compensating new support. He might even accomplish this inadvertently, should his pursuit of power or policy attract, willy-nilly, constituents who welcomed his new mix of goals. The very Washington activity that left him out of touch with previously supportive constituents might put him in touch with newly supportive ones. A newly acquired position of influence in a particular policy area or a new reputation as an effective legislator might produce such a feedback effect. We describe the pattern in conditional terms, because we have not observed such an effect. It would probably take a longer period of observation, with more of a focus on Washington to do so. In theory, however, the Washington and the constituency careers should influence one another reciprocally.

. . . [W]e noted a tendency for successful home styles to harden over time and to place stylistic constraints on the congressman's subsequent behavior. The pursuit of a Washington career helps us explain this constituency phenomenon. That is, to the degree that congressman pursues power or policy goals in the House, he will have that much less time or energy to devote to the consideration of alternative home styles. His predisposition to "do what we did last time" at home will b further strengthened by his growing preoccupation with Washington matters. Indeed, the speed with which a congressman begins to develop a Washington career will affect the speed with which his home style solidifies. We noted . . . that the home styles of Representatives J and K seemed to take permanent shape very quickly. We also noted that their first taste of a Washington career came very quickly. It is our guess, then, that the sooner the Washington career begins, the sooner the home style will harden. . . .

In all of this speculation about career linkages, we have assumed that most members of Congress develop, over time, a mix of personal goals. We particularly assume that most members will trade off some of their personal commitment to reelection in order to satisfy a personal desire for institutional or policy influence. It is our observation, based on only eighteen cases, that House members do, in fact, exhibit varying degrees of commitment to reelection. All want reelection in the abstract, but not all will pay any price to achieve it; nor will all pay the same price. This complex view of House member goals is, we think a realistic view. . . .

One senior member contemplated retirement in the face of an adverse redistricting but, because he had the prospect of a committee chairmanship, he decided to run and hope for the best. He wanted reelection because he wanted continued influence; but he was unwilling to put his present influence in jeopardy by pursuing reelection with the same intensity that marked his earlier constituency career. As he put it,

> Ten years ago, I whipped another redistricting. And I did it by neglecting my congressional duties. . . . Today I don't have the time, and I'm not going to neglect my duties. . . . If I do what is necessary to get reelected and thus become chairman of the committee, I will lose the respect and confidence of my fellow committee members because of being absent from the hearings and, occasionally, the votes.

He did not work hard at reelection, and he won by his narrowest margin ever. But he succeeded in sustaining a mix of personal goals very different from an earlier one.

A Republican member of my group, having finally achieved national prominence, decided to retire nonetheless, because he found it impossible as a member of the minority party in Congress to make "substantive contributions to public policy." If he could not achieve his goal of helping to make good public policy, he did not want reelection. . . . [W]e noted the members' desire to use their home support to secure voting leeway as well as reelection. Many, no doubt, would not seek reelection if it meant the loss of all such leeway. Recall, also, Congressman L . . . who decided to retire rather than undertake a strenuous reelection campaign. Having given greater weight to his Washington career goals, he was unwilling to cycle back to a situation in which reelection was paramount. "What's the use of having high seniority with the opportunity of being influential in Congress if you have to spend all your time in your district?" He did not want reelection at the price of reduced influence in the House.

It is probably fair to say that at some point most members ask themselves how badly they want to be reelected. Doubtless, the question is posed, seriously, at a variety of junctures in their two careers. Like the three members just discussed, however, most members probably ask it when they are in the protectionist stage of their constituency careers and well established in their Washington careers. This, at any rate, is the status of most House members who retire. As for the reasons why members begin to question their devotion to reelection, political scientists cannot say. Doubtless, like any other personal decision, the decision to retire is complicated. But many observers have noted the recent marked increase in retirements from the House of Representatives. . . .

The congressman's home activities are more difficult and taxing than we have previously recognized.   Under the best of circumstances, the tension involved in maintaining constituency contact and achieving legislative competence is considerable. Members cannot be in two places at once, and the growth of a Washington career exacerbates the problem. But, more than that, the demands in both places have grown recently.   The legislative workload and the demand for legislative expertise are steadily increasing. So is the problem of maintaining meaningful contact with their several constituencies.   Years ago, House members returned home for months at a time to live among their supportive constituencies, soak up the home atmosphere, absorb local problems at first hand. Today, they race home for a day, a weekend, a week at a time. Only seven of the eighteen maintain a family home in their district. The other eleven stay with relatives or friends or in barely furnished rooms when they are at home. The citizen demand for access, for communication, and for the establishment of trust is as great as ever. So members go home. But the quality of their contact has suffered. "It's like a one-night stand in a singles bar." It is harder to sustain a genuine two-way communication than it once was. House member worries about the home relationship—great under any circumstances, but greater now—contribute to the strain and frustration of the job. Some cope; but others retire. It may be those members who cannot stand the heat of the home relationship who are getting out of the House kitchen.

Thinking It Over

1. Does Fenno tell us what factor is more important in a Congressperson's decision to retire, the energy he or she must spend in the district in order to secure reelection or other factors in Washington that preclude them from becoming influential policymakers? Comment.

2. Compare this reading with Mayhew's analysis (see below). Is there common ground between them? Do they reinforce each other or do they exhibit contradictions which are impossible to resolve?

3. Does Fenno shed light on the problem of "the untouchable incumbents" discussed in Dickenson's reading (see above)? Might it not be the case that incumbent losses would be greater if Congresspersons who feel threatened didn't chicken out and retire? Try to conceptualize a research project that would test this hypothesis.

66.
CONGRESS:
THE ELECTORAL CONNECTION
by David R. Mayhew

Setting the Scene: In the first part of his classic interpretation of Congress Professor Mayhew reviews the activities that Congresspersons perform to insure their reelection. These are "advertising," "credit claiming," and "position taking." We pick up the analysis as he begins a discussion of how the structural units of Congress (the members' offices and their staff, committees, and political parties) are designed to "meet electoral needs." It is a remarkable discussion that goes a long way to explain why the hugh majority of Congresspersons who seek reelection are successful.

It will be useful to start here with two prefatory points—to be substantiated as the discussion proceeds. The first is that the organization of Congress meets remarkably well the electoral needs of its members. To put it another way, if a group of planners sat down and tried to design a pair of American national assemblies with the goal of serving members' electoral needs year in and year out, they would be hard pressed to improve on what exists. The second point is that satisfaction of electoral needs requires remarkably little zero-sum conflict among members. That is, one member's gain is not another member's loss; to a remarkable degree members can successfully engage in electorally useful activities without denying other members the opportunity successfully to engage in them. In regard to credit claiming, this second point requires elaboration further on. Its application to advertising is perhaps obvious. The members all have different markets, so that what any one member does is not an inconvenience to any other. There are exceptions here—House members are sometimes thrown into districts together, senators have to watch the advertising of ambitious House members within their states, and senators from the same state have to keep up with each other . . . —but the case generally holds. With position taking the point is also reasonably clear. As long as congressmen do not attack each other—and they rarely do . . .—any member can champion the most extraordinary causes without inconveniencing any of his colleagues. The *Congressional Record* is largely a series of disjointed insertions prepared for the eyes of relevant political actors, with each member enjoying final editing rights on his materials . . .

A scrutiny of the basic structural units of Congress will yield evidence to support both these prefatory points. First, there are the 535 Capitol Hill *offices*, the small personal empires of the members. Annual staff salary schedules now run at about $150,000 per office on the House side, with variation upward according to state population on the Senate side. The Hill office is a vitally important political unit, part campaign management firm and part political machine. The availability of its staff members for election work in and out of season gives it some of the properties of the latter. And there is the franking privilege for use on office emanations. The dollar value of this array of resources in an election campaign is difficult to estimate . . . The value has certainly increased over the last decade. It should be said that the availability of these incumbency advantages causes little displeasure among members. In the early 1970s a flurry of court decisions brought the franking privilege under attack. The reaction of the House was to pass a bill outlawing some of the more questionable uses but also rendering the frank less vulnerable to judicial incursion. The spirit of the reform was evident in a statement of the bill's floor manager: "The fact is that 98 or 99 percent of the material going out of the mail room is good, solid information and in the public interest."[1] A final comment on congressional offices is perhaps the most important one: office resources are given to all members regardless of party, seniority, or any other qualification. They come with the job.

Second among the structural units are the *committees*, the twenty-one standing committees in the House and seventeen in the Senate—with a scattering of other special and joint bodies . . . Committee membership can be electorally useful in a number of different ways. Some committees supply good platforms for position taking. The best example over the years is probably the House Un-American Activities Committee (now the Internal Security Committee), whose members have displayed hardly a trace of an interest in legislation . . . Senator Joseph McCarthy used the Senate Government Operations Committee as his investigative base in the Eighty-third Congress; later on in the 1960s Senators Abraham Ribicoff (D., Conn.) and William Proxmire (D., Wis.) used subcommittees of this same unit in catching public attention respectively on auto safety and defense waste.[2] With membership on the Senate Foreign Relations Committee goes a license to make speeches on foreign policy[3] . . .

Some committees traffic in particularized benefits. Just how benefits of this sort are likely to be distributed by governments has been the subject of theoretical speculation. Buchanan and Tullock suggest a kind of round-robin rip-off model, with seriatim majorities coalescing to do in excluded minorities. . . . Specifically, in giving out particularized benefits where the costs are diffuse (falling on taxpayer or consumer) and where in the long run to reward one congressman is not obviously to deprive others . . . the members follow a policy of universalism. . . . That is, every member, regardless of party or seniority, has a right to his share of benefits. There is evidence of universalism in the distribution of projects on House Public Works,[4] projects on House Interior,[5] projects on Senate Interior,[6] project money on House Appropriations,[7] project money on Senate Appropriations,[8] tax benefits on House Ways and Means,[9] tax benefits on Senate Finance,[10] and (by inference from the

[1] *Congressional Record* (daily ed.), April 11, 1973, p. H2601. The floor manager was Morris Udall (D., Ariz.).
[2] On Ribicoff see David Price, *Who Makes the Laws?*, p. 50.
[3] See Fenno, *Congressmen in Committees,* p. 189.
[4] Murphy, "House Public Works Committee," pp. 3, 23, 39.
[5] Fenno, *Congressmen in Committees,* p. 58.
[6] Ibid., pp. 165-66.
[7] Fenno, *Power of the Purse*, pp. 85-87.
[8] Fenno, *Congressmen in Committees,* p. 160; Stephen Horn, *Unused Power: The Work of the Senate Committee on Appropriations* (Washington, D.C.: Brookings, 1970), p. 91.
[9] Manley, *The Politics of Finance*, pp. 78-84; Surrey, "Congress and the Tax Lobbyist."

reported data) urban renewal projects on House Banking and Currency.[11]   The House Interior Committee, in Fenno's account, "takes as its major decision rule a determination to process and pass *all* requests and to do so in such a way as to maximize the chances of passage in the House.   Succinctly, then, Interior's major strategic premise is: *to secure House passage of all constituency-supported, Member-sponsored bills.*"[12]   House Public Works, writes Murphy, has a "norm of mutual advantage"; in the words of one of its members, "[We] have a rule on the Committee, it's not a rule of the Committee, it's not written down or anything, but it's just the way we do things.   Any time any member of the Committee wants something, or wants to get a bill out, we get it out for him . . . Makes no difference—Republican or Democrat.   We are all Americans when it comes to that."[13]   Not surprisingly there is some evidence that members of these distributive committees gain more from them than nonmembers.[14]   But there is also evidence that committee members act as procurers for others in their states or regions.[15]   An interesting aspect of particularistic politics is its special brand of "rules."   There have to be allocation guidelines precise enough to admit judgments on benefit "soundness" (no member can have everything he wants), yet ambiguous enough to allow members to claim personal credit for what they get.   Hence there are unending policy minuets; an example is the one in public works where the partners are the Corps of Army Engineers with its cost-benefit calculations and the congressmen with their ad hoc exceptions.[16]

Particularism also has its position-taking side.   On occasion members capture public attention by denouncing the allocation process itself; thus in 1972 a number of liberals held up some Ways and Means "members' bills" on the House floor.[17]   But such efforts have little or no effect.   Senator Douglas used to offer floor amendments to excise projects from public works appropriations bills, but he had a hard time even getting the Senate to vote on them.[18]

Finally, and very importantly, the committee system aids congressmen simply by allowing a division of labor among members.   The parceling out of legislation among small groups of congressmen by subject area has two effects.   First, it creates small voting bodies in which membership may be valuable.   An attentive interest group will prize more highly

---

[10]Fenno, *Congressmen in Committees,* pp. 156-59; Surrey, "Congress and the Tax Lobbyist" . . .

[11]Charles R. Plott, "Some Organizational Influences on Urban Renewal Decisions," 58 *American Economic Review* 306-11 (May 1968).

[12]Fenno, *Congressmen in Committees,* p. 58.

[13]Murphy, "House Public Works Committee," p. 23.

[14]See, for example, Plott, "Organizational Influences on Urban Renewal Decisions"; and also Carol F. Goss, "Military Committee Membership and Defense-Related Benefits in the House of Representatives," 25 *Western Political Quarterly* 215-33 (1972).

[15]See, for example, Murphy, "House Public Works Committee," p. 8; Fenno, *Power of the Purse,* pp. 87-88; Fenno, *Congressmen in Committees,* pp. 272-73; Barbara Deckard, "State Party Delegations in the United States House of Representatives—An Analysis of Group Action," 5 *Polity* 327-33 (1973).

[16]See Murphy, "House Public Works Committee," pp. 39-47; and also Arthur Maass, *Muddy Waters: The Army Engineers and the Nation's Rivers* (Cambridge: Harvard University Press, 1951), ch. 1 . . .

[17]Eileen Shanahan, "Special Tax Bills Blocked by Reform Drive in House," *New York Times,* March 1, 1972, p. 1.

[18]Douglas, *In the Fullness of Time,* pp. 269-70, 314-18 . . .

the favorable issue positions of members of committees pondering its fortunes than the favorable positions of the general run of congressmen. Second, it creates specialized small-group settings in which individual congressmen can make things happen and be perceived to make things happen. "I put that bill through committee." "That was my amendment." "I talked them around on that." This is the language of credit claiming. It comes easily in the committee setting and also when "expert" committee members handle bills on the floor . . .

A list of the standing committees only begins to show the congressional division of labor. At the beginning of the Ninety-third Congress there were 143 subcommittees in the Senate and 132 in the House.[19] With disaggregation carried to this extreme the number of members covering subject areas becomes small enough to permit relatively easy credit claiming. Thus on the House Agriculture Committee there are no more than about half a dozen members handling each commodity.[20] In small working units formal voting tends to recede in importance as a determinant of outcome, and what individual members do with their time and energy rises in importance. Whatever else it may be, the quest for specialization in Congress is a quest for credit. Every member can aspire to occupy a part of at least one piece of policy turf small enough so that he can claim personal responsibility for some of the things that happen on it. . . . Better yet, he can aspire to rise in seniority and claim ever more responsibility—perhaps even be christened a "czar" or a "baron" by the press.[21] What the congressional seniority system does as a system is to convert turf into property; it assures a congressman that once he initially occupies a piece of turf, no one can ever push him off it. And the property automatically appreciates in value over time. With these advantages for all hands, it is not surprising that congressmen are strongly attached to the seniority system . . .

In recent years there have been efforts to reform seniority in the House, and in fact both parties have changed some of their rules. But the problem here seems to be not that members are against the system but that there is not enough turf to go around. House members are staying on the Hill longer, with the result that there are more members who have lasted several terms and who feel entitled to wield considerable subcommittee influence. The reform drive has produced a devolution (in some committees) of staff and budget resources to the subcommittee level, and a Democratic rule that no member can hold more than one subcommittee chairmanship . . . But the House may have to create more subcommittees to satisfy its members. There is little reform impetus in the Senate, where there are more subcommittees than there are senators.

The other basic structural units in Congress are the *parties*. The case here will be that

---

[19]As listed in *Congressional Quarterly Weekly*, April 28, 1973. There were also sixteen subcommittees of the joint committees.

[20]Charles O. Jones, "The Role of the Congressional Subcommittee," 6 *Midwest Journal of Political Science* 327-44 (1962).

[21]See, for example, Norman C. Miller, "The Farm Baron: Rep. Jamie Whitten [D., Miss.] Works behind Scenes to Shape Big Spending," *Wall Street Journal*, June 7, 1971, p. 1. Whitten is chairman of the Subcommittee on Agriculture of the House Appropriations Committee.

the parties, like the offices and committees, are tailored to suit members' electoral needs. They are more useful for what they are not than for what they are. It is easy to conjure up visions of the sorts of zero-sum politics parties could import into a representative assembly. One possibility—in line with the analysis here—is that a majority party could deprive minority members of a share of particularized benefits, a share of committee influence, and a share of resources to advertise and make their positions known. Congressional majorities obviously do not shut out minorities in this fashion. It would make no sense to do so; the costs of cutting in minority members are very low, whereas the costs of losing majority control in a cutthroat partisan politics of this kind would be very high. . . . A more conventional zero-sum vision is the one in which assembly parties organize in disciplined fashion for the purpose of enacting general party "programs"; the battle is over whose program shall prevail. It should be obvious that if they wanted to, American congressmen could immediately and permanently array themselves in disciplined legions for the purpose of programmatic combat. They do not. Every now and then a member does emit a Wilsonian call for program and cohesion . . . but these exhortations fail to arouse much member interest. The fact is that the enactment of party programs is electorally not very important to members (although some may find it important to take positions on programs).

What is important to each congressman, and vitally so, is that he be free to take positions that serve his advantage. . . . There is no member of either house who would not be politically injured—by being made to toe a party line on all policies (unless of course he could determine the line). There is no congressional bloc whose members have identical position needs across all issues. Thus on the school bussing issue in the Ninety-second Congress, it was vital to Detroit white liberal Democratic House members that they be free to vote one way and to Detroit black liberal Democrats that they be free to vote the other. In regard to these member needs the best service a party can supply to its congressmen is a negative one; it can leave them alone. And this in general is what the congressional parties do. Party leaders are chosen not to be program salesmen or vote mobilizers, but to be brokers, favor-doers, agenda-setters, and protectors of established institutional routines.[22] Party "pressure" to vote one way or another is minimal. . . . Party "whipping" hardly deserves the name. . . . Leaders in both houses have a habit of counseling members to "vote their constituencies." The Senate Democratic whip, Robert C. Byrd (D., W. Va.), studies the voting records of his members, and when they appear on the floor for a roll call, he "tries to steer them in their own direction with a 'this is a no (or yes) for you'"[23] . . .

Of course the congressional parties are still important pieces of Capitol Hill furniture. There remain significant differences between Democrats and Republicans in their roll call voting. . . . Partisan electoral swings, by taking out members sustained by one kind of supporting coalition and bringing in members sustained by another, can change the position-

---

[22] See Nelson W. Polsby, "Two Strategies of Influence: Choosing a Majority Leader, 1962," ch. 3 in Peabody and Polsby, *New Perspectives on the House*; and Robert L. Peabody, "The Selection of a Majority Leader, 1970-71: The Democratic Caucus and Its Aftermath," unpublished manuscript.

[23] Paul R. Wieck, "Keeping Senate Traffic Moving: The Efficiency Byrd," *New Republic*, January 20, 1973, p. 13. See also Clapp, *The Congressman*, p. 288 . . .

taking balance in both houses with detectable legislative effect (as in the Eightieth and Eighty-ninth Congresses). The custom of denying committee and sub-committee chairmanships to minority party members remains one of the two leading forms of invidious discrimination on the Hill (the other being discrimination by seniority). Yet as time goes on, all this adds up to less and less. "Party voting" in the House, however defined, has been declining since the turn of the century and has reached a record low in the last decade.[24] Partisan seat swings in the House have declined considerably in amplitude; one reason is that a fall in the proportion of incumbents holding seats in the marginal range has lowered the casualty rate in times of voter volatility.[25] Alternation in party control has at least temporarily ceased, with the Democrats becoming something of a "party of state" at the congressional level. . . . As for chairmanship discrimination against Republicans, it is made bearable by the fact that minority members on most committees share in the decision making in all its stages . . . some committees look like dual (limited) monarchies, with Democratic chairman and ranking Republican congenially sharing influence. . . . The general picture of the congressional party system is one of a system in slow decline—or, to put it another way, a system whose zero-sum edges have been eroded away by powerful norms of institutional universalism. In a good many ways the interesting division in congressional politics is not between Democrats and Republicans, but between politicians in and out of office. Looked at from one angle the cult of universalism has the appearance of a cross-party conspiracy among incumbents to keep their jobs.

Thinking It Over

1. Is the fact that there is no way to "police" Congress from organizing itself to insure the reelection of its members another argument in favor of limiting the number of terms Congresspersons may serve?

2. It is interesting to speculate on the impact a more disciplined party system would have on many of the points Mayhew makes. Review the article with this question in mind. Would a more disciplined party system solve the problem?

---

[24]Turner, *Party and Constituency*, ch. 2 . . .
[25]See Mayhew, "Congressional Elections" . . .

67.
CONGRESS: KEYSTONE OF THE WASHINGTON ESTABLISHMENT
by Morris P. Fiorina

Setting the Scene: Most us would like to "do something" about the federal bureaucracy. From the citizen's perspective it hovers over us as a vast quagmire of red tape, telephone lines that lead nowhere, and officials that never quite seem to have authority to deal with our particular problem. But believe it or not there is a group of people who *like* the bureaucracy, says Professor Fiorina. Congresspersons. In fact they especially like all the things about it that turn citizens off. That is why they built it the way they did and continue to beef it up with more and more complexity and confusion. How could anyone be that satanic, you ask? Because if the bureaucracy in Washington turns us off, they get to turn us on by helping us deal with it. We become grateful and dependent on them. How better to secure our vote?

Dramatis Personae

I assume that most people most of the time act in their own self-interest. This is not to say that human beings seek only to amass tangible wealth but rather to say that human beings seek to achieve their own ends—tangible and intangible—rather than the ends of their fellow men. I do not condemn such behavior nor do I condone it (although I rather sympathize with Thoreau's comment that "if I knew for a certainty that a man was coming to my house with the conscious design of doing me good, I should run for my life").[1] I only claim that political and economic theories which presume self-interested behavior will prove to be more widely applicable than those which build on more altruistic assumptions.

What does the axiom imply when used in . . . a context peopled by congressmen, bureaucrats, and voters? I assume that the primary goal of the typical congressman is reelection. Over and above the $57,000 salary plus "perks" and outside money, the office of congressman carries with it prestige, excitement, and power. It is a seat in the cockpit of government. But in order to retain the status, excitement, and power (not to mention more tangible things) of office, the congressman must win reelection every two years. Even those congressmen genuinely concerned with good public policy must achieve reelection in order to continue their work. Whether narrowly self-serving or more publicly oriented, the individual congressman finds reelection to be at least a necessary condition for the achievement of his goals. . . .

Moreover, there is a kind of natural selection process at work in the electoral arena. On average, those congressmen who are not primarily interested in reelection will not achieve

---

[1]Henry David Thoreau, *Walden* (London: Walter Scott, n.d.), p. 72.

reelection as often as those who are interested. We, the people, help to weed out congressmen whose primary motivation is not reelection. We admire politicians who courageously adopt the aloof role of the disinterested statesman, but we vote for those politicians who follow our wishes and do us favors.

What about the bureaucrats? A specification of their goals is somewhat more controversial—those who speak of appointed officials as public servants obviously take a more benign view than those who speak of them as bureaucrats. The literature provides ample justification for asserting that most bureaucrats can be expected to seek to expand his agency in terms of personnel, budget, and mission. One's status in Washington (again, not to mention more tangible things) is roughly proportional to the importance of the operation one oversees. And the sheer size of the operation is taken to be a measure of importance. As with congressmen, the specified goals apply even to those bureaucrats who genuinely believe in their agency's mission. If they believe in the efficacy of their programs, they naturally wish to expand them and add new ones. All of this requires more money and more people. The genuinely committed bureaucrat is just as likely to seek to expand his agency as the proverbial empire-builder.[2]

And what of the third element in the equation, us? What do we, the voters who support the Washington system, strive for? Each of us wishes to receive a maximum of benefits from government for the minimum cost. This goal suggests maximum government efficiency, on the one hand, but it also suggests mutual exploitation on the other. Each of us favors an arrangement in which our fellow citizens pay for our benefits.

With these brief descriptions of the cast of characters in hand, let us proceed.

Tammany Hall Goes to Washington

What should we expect from a legislative body composed of individuals whose first priority is their continued tenure in office? We should expect, first, that the normal activities of its members are those calculated to enhance their chances of reelection. And we should expect, second, that the members would devise and maintain institutional arrangements which facilitate their electoral activities. . . .

For most of the twentieth century, congressmen have engaged in a mix of three kinds of activities: lawmaking, pork barreling, and casework. Congress is first and foremost a lawmaking body, at least according to constitutional theory. In every postwar session Congress "considers" thousands of bills and resolutions, many hundreds of which are brought to a record vote (over 500 in each chamber in the 93d Congress). Naturally the critical consideration in taking a position for the record is the maximization of approval in the home district. If the district is unaffected by and unconcerned with the matter at hand, the congressman may then take into account the general welfare of the country. (This sounds cynical, but remember that "profiles in courage" are sufficiently rare that their occurrence

---

[2]For a discussion of the goals of bureaucrats, see william Niskanen, *Bureaucracy and Representative Government* (Chicago: Aldine-Atherton, 1971).

inspires books and articles.) Abetted by political scientists of the pluralist school, politicians have propounded an ideology which maintains that the good of the country on any given issue is simply what is best for a majority of congressional districts. This ideology provides a philosophical justification for what congressmen do while acting in their own self-interest.

A second activity favored by congressmen consists of efforts to bring home the bacon to their districts. Many popular articles have been written about the pork barrel, a term originally applied to rivers and harbors legislation but now generalized to cover all manner of federal largesse.[3] Congressmen consider new dams, federal buildings, sewage treatment plants, urban renewal projects, etc. as sweet plums to be plucked. Federal projects are highly visible, their economic impact is easily detected by constituents, and sometimes they even produce something of value to the district. The average constituent may have some trouble translating his congressman's vote on some civil rights issue into a change in his personal welfare. But the workers hired and supplies purchased in connection with a big federal project provide benefits that are widely appreciated. The historical importance congressmen attach to the pork barrel is reflected in the rules of the House. That body accords certain classes of legislation "privileged" status: they may come directly to the floor without passing through the Rules Committee, a traditional graveyard for legislation. What kinds of legislation are privileged? Taxing and spending bills, for one: the government's power to raise and spend money must be kept relatively unfettered. But in addition, the omnibus rivers and harbors bills of the Public Works Committee and public lands bills from the Interior Committee share privileged status. The House will allow a civil rights or defense procurement or environmental bill to languish in the Rules Committee, but it takes special precautions to insure that nothing slows down the approval of dams and irrigation projects.

A third major activity takes up perhaps as much time as the other two combined. Traditionally, constituents appeal to their Congressman for myriad favors and services. Sometimes only information is needed, but often constituents request that their congressman intervene in the internal workings of federal agencies to affect a decision in a favorable way, to reverse an adverse decision, or simply to speed up the glacial bureaucratic process. On the basis of extensive personal interviews with congressmen, Charles Clapp writes:

> Denied a favorable ruling by the bureaucracy on a matter of direct concern to him, puzzled or irked by delays in obtaining a decision, confused by the administrative maze through which he is directed to proceed, or ignorant of whom to write, a constituent may turn to his congressman for help. These letters offer great potential for political benefit to the congressman since they affect the constituent personally. If the legislator can be of assistance, he may gain a firm ally; if he is indifferent, he may even lose votes.[4]

Actually congressmen are in an almost unique position in our system, a position shared

---

[3]The traditional pork barrel is the subject of an excellent treatment by John Ferejohn. See his *Pork Barrel Politics: Rivers and Harbors Legislation, 1947-1968* (Stanford: Stanford University Press, 1974).

[4]Charles Clapp, *The Congressman: His Job As He Sees It* (Washington, D.C.: Brookings Institution, 1963), p. 84.

only with high-level members of the executive branch. Congressmen possess the power to expedite and influence bureaucratic decisions. This capability flows directly from congressional control over what bureaucrats value most: higher budgets and new program authorizations. In a very real sense each congressman is a monopoly supplier of bureaucratic unsticking services for his district.

Every year the federal budget passes through the appropriations committees of Congress. Generally these committees make perfunctory cuts. But on occasion they vent displeasure on an agency and leave it bleeding all over the Capitol. The most extreme case of which I am aware came when the House committee took away the entire budget of the Division of Labor Standards in 1947 (some of the budget was restored elsewhere in the appropriations process). Deep and serious cuts are made occasionally, and the threat of such cuts keeps most agencies attentive to congressional wishes. Professors Richard Fenno and Aaron Wildavsky have provided extensive documentary and interview evidence of the great respect (and even terror) federal bureaucrats show for the House Appropriations Committee.[5] Moreover, the bureaucracy must keep coming back to Congress to have its old programs reauthorized and new ones added. Again, most such decisions are perfunctory, but exceptions are sufficiently frequent that bureaucrats do not forget the basis of their agencies' existence. For example, the Law Enforcement Assistance Administration (LEAA) and the Food Stamps Program had no easy time of it this last Congress (94th). The bureaucracy needs congressional approval in order to survive, let alone expand. Thus, when a congressman calls about some minor bureaucratic decision or regulation, the bureaucracy considers his accommodation a small price to pay for the goodwill its cooperation will produce, particularly if he has any connection to the substantive committee or the appropriations subcommittee to which it reports.

From the standpoint of capturing voters, the congressman's lawmaking activities differ in two important respects from his pork-barrel and casework activities. First, programmatic actions are inherently controversial. Unless his district is homogeneous, a congressman will find his district divided on many major issues. Thus when he casts a vote, introduces a piece of nontrivial legislation, or makes a speech with policy content he will displease some elements of his district. Some constituents may applaud the congressman's civil rights record, but others believe integration is going too fast. Some support foreign aid, while others believe it's money poured down a rathole. Some advocate economic equality, others stew over welfare cheaters. On such policy matters the congressman can expect to make friends as well as enemies. Presumably he will behave so as to maximize the excess of the former over the latter, but nevertheless a policy stand will generally make some enemies.

In contrast, the pork barrel and casework are relatively less controversial. New federal projects bring jobs, shiny new facilities, and general economic prosperity, or so people believe. Snipping ribbons at the dedication of a new post office or dam is a much more pleasant pursuit than disposing of a constitutional amendment on abortion. Republicans and

---

[5]Richard Fenno, *The Power of the Purse* (Boston: Little, Brown, 1966); Aaron Wildavsky, *The Politics of the Budgetary Process*, 2d ed. (Boston: Little, Brown, 1974).

Democrats, conservatives and liberals, all generally prefer a richer district to a poorer one. Of course, in recent years the river damming and stream-bed straightening activities of the Army Corps of Engineers have aroused some opposition among environmentalists. Congressmen happily reacted by absorbing the opposition and adding environmentalism to the pork barrel: water treatment plants are currently a hot congressional item.

Casework is even less controversial. Some poor, aggrieved constituent becomes enmeshed in the tentacles of an evil bureaucracy and calls upon Congressmen St. George to do battle with the dragon. Again Clapp writes;

> A person who has a reasonable complaint or query is regarded as providing an opportunity rather than as adding an extra burden to an already busy office. The party affiliation of the individual even when known to be different from that of the congressman does not normally act as a deterrent to action. Some legislators have built their reputations and their majorities on a program of service to all constituents irrespective of party. Regularly, voters affiliated with the opposition in other contests lend strong support to the lawmaker whose intervention has helped them in their struggle with the bureaucracy.[6]

Even following the revelation of sexual improprieties, Wayne Hays won his Ohio Democratic primary by a two-to-one margin. According to a *Los Angeles Times* feature story, Hays's constituency base was built on a foundation of personal service to constituents:

> They receive help in speeding up bureaucratic action on various kinds of federal assistance—black lung benefits to disabled miners and their families, Social Security payments, veterans' benefits and passports.
>
> Some constituents still tell with pleasure of how Hays stormed clear to the seventh floor of the State Department and into Secretary of State Dean Rusk's office to demand, successfully, the quick issuance of a passport to an Ohioan.[7]

Practicing politicians will tell you that word of mouth is till the most effective mode of communication. News of favors to constituents gets around and no doubt is embellished in the process.

In sum, when considering the benefits of his programmatic activities, the congressman must tote up gains and losses to arrive at a net profit. Pork barreling and casework, however, are basically pure profit.

A second way in which programmatic activities differ from case work and the pork barrel is the difficulty of assigning responsibility to the former as compared with the latter. No

---

[6]Clapp, *The Congressman: His Job As He Sees It*, p. 84.

[7]"Hays Improves Rapidly from Overdose," *Los Angeles Times*, June 12, 1976, part 1, p. 19. Similarly, Congressman Robert Leggett (D., Calif.) won reelection in 1976 even amid revelations of a thirteen-year bigamous relationship and rumors of other affairs and improprieties . . . [Bryan this footnote has 3 more paragraphs of explanation see p. 148 in the actual book]

congressman can seriously claim that he is responsible for the 1964 Civil Rights Act, the ABM, or the 1972 Revenue Sharing Act. Most constituents do have some vague notion that their congressman is only one of hundreds and their senator one of an even hundred. Even committee chairmen have a difficult time claiming credit for a piece of major legislation, let alone a rank-and-file congressman. Ah, but casework, and the pork barrel. In dealing with the bureaucracy, the congressman is not merely one vote of 435. Rather, he is a nonpartisan power, someone whose phone calls snap an office to attention. He is not kept on hold. The constituent who receives aid believes that his congressman and his congressman alone got results. Similarly, congressmen find it easy to claim credit for federal projects awarded their districts. The congressman may have instigated the proposal for the project in the first place, issued regular progress reports, and ultimately announced the award through his office. Maybe he can't claim credit for the 1965 Voting Rights Act, but he can take credit for Littletown's spanking new sewage treatment plant.

Overall then, programmatic activities are dangerous (controversial), on the one hand, and programmatic accomplishments are difficult to claim credit for, on the other. While less exciting, casework and pork barreling are both safe and profitable. For a reelection-oriented congressman the choice is obvious.

The key to the rise of the Washington establishment (and the vanishing marginals) is the following observation: *the growth of an activist federal government has stimulated a change in the mix of congressional activities.* Specifically, a lesser proportion of congressional effort is now going into programmatic activities and a greater proportion into pork-barrel and casework activities. As a result, today's congressmen make relatively fewer enemies and relatively more friends among the people of their districts.

To elaborate, a basic fact of life in twentieth-century America is the growth of the federal role and its attendant bureaucracy. Bureaucracy is the characteristic mode of delivering public goods and services. Ceteris paribus, the more the government attempts to do for people, the more extensive a bureaucracy it creates. As the scope of government expands, more and more citizens find themselves in direct contact with the federal government. Consider the rise in such contacts upon passage of the Social Security Act, work relief projects and other New Deal programs. Consider the millions of additional citizens touched by the veterans' programs of the postwar period. Consider the untold numbers whom the Great Society and its aftermath brought face to face with the federal government. In 1930 the federal bureaucracy was small and rather distant from the everyday concerns of Americans. By 1975 it was neither small nor distant.

As the years have passed, more and more citizens and groups have found themselves dealing with the federal bureaucracy. They may be seeking positive actions—eligibility for various benefits and awards of government grants. Or they may be seeking relief from the costs imposed by bureaucratic regulations—on working conditions, racial and sexual quotas, market restrictions, and numerous other subjects. While not malevolent, bureaucracies make mistakes, both of commission and omission, and normal attempts at redress often meet with unresponsiveness and inflexibility and sometimes seeming incorrigibility. Whatever the problem, the citizen's congressman is a source of succor. The greater the scope of government activity, the greater the demand for his services.

Private monopolists can regulate the demand for their product by raising or lowering the price. Congressmen have no such (legal) option. When the demand for their services rises, they have no real choice except to meet that demand—to supply more bureaucratic unsticking services—so long as they would rather be elected than unelected. This vulnerability to escalating constituency demands is largely academic, though. I seriously doubt that congressmen resist their gradual transformation from national legislators to errand boy-ombudsmen. As we have noted, casework is all profit. Congressmen have buried proposals to relieve the casework burden by establishing a national ombudsman or Congressman Reuss's proposed Administrative Counsel of the Congress. One of the congressmen interviewed by Clapp stated:

> Before I came to Washington I used to think that it might be nice if the individual states had administrative arms here that would take care of necessary liaison between citizens and the national government. But a congressman running for reelection is interested in building fences by providing personal services. The system is set to reelect incumbents regardless of party, and incumbents wouldn't dream of giving any of this service function away to any subagency. As an elected member I feel the same way.[8]

In fact, it is probable that at least some congressmen deliberately stimulate the demand for their bureaucratic fixit services. . . . Recall that the new Republican in district A travels about his district saying:

> I'm your man in Washington. What are your problems? How can I help you?

And in district B, did the demand for the congressman's services rise so much between 1962 and 1964 that a "regiment" of constituency staff became necessary? Or, having access to the regiment, did the new Democrat stimulate the demand to which he would apply his regiment?

In addition to greatly increased casework, let us not forget that the growth of the federal role has also greatly expanded the federal pork barrel. The creative pork barreler need not limit himself to dams and post offices—rather old-fashioned interests. Today, creative congressmen can cadge LEAA money for the local police, urban renewal and housing money for local politicians, educational program grants for the local education bureaucracy. And there are sewage treatment plants, worker training and retraining programs, health services, and programs for the elderly. The pork barrel is full to overflowing. The conscientious congressman can stimulate applications for federal assistance (the sheer number of programs makes it difficult for local officials to stay current with the possibilities), put in a good word during consideration, and announce favorable decisions amid great fanfare.

In sum, everyday decisions by a large and growing federal bureaucracy bestow significant tangible benefits and impose significant tangible costs. Congressmen can affect these

---

[8]Clapp, *The Congressman: His Job As He Sees It,* p. 94.

decisions. Ergo, the more decisions the bureaucracy has the opportunity to make, the more opportunities there are for the congressman to build up credits.

The nature of the Washington system is now quite clear. Congressmen (typically the major Democrats) earn electoral credits by establishing various federal programs (the minority Republicans typically earn credits by fighting the good fight). The legislation is drafted in very general terms, so some agency, existing or newly established, must translate a vague policy mandate into a functioning program, a process that necessitates the promulgation of numerous rules and regulations and, incidentally, the trampling of numerous toes. At the next stage, aggrieved and/or hopeful constituents petition their congressman to intervene in the complex (or at least obscure) decision processes of the bureaucracy. The cycle closes when the congressman lends a sympathetic ear, piously denounces the evils of bureaucracy, intervenes in the latter's decisions, and rides a grateful electorate to ever more impressive electoral showings. Congressmen take credit coming and going. They are the alpha and the omega.

The popular frustration with the permanent government in Washington is partly justified, but to a considerable degree it is misplaced resentment. *Congress is the linchpin of the Washington establishment.* The bureaucracy serves as a convenient lightning rod for public frustration and a convenient whipping boy for congressmen. But so long as the bureaucracy accommodates congressmen, the latter will oblige with ever larger budgets and grants of authority. Congress does not just react to big government—it creates it. All of Washington prospers. More and more bureaucrats promulgate more and more regulations and dispense more and more money. Fewer and fewer congressmen suffer electoral defeat. Elements of the electorate benefit from government programs, and all of the electorate is eligible for ombudsman services. But the general, long-term welfare of the United States is no more than an incidental by-product of the system.

Thinking It Over

1. Deal with the following as Fiorina would: "Get serious! Even if Congresspersons were that evil, your thesis suggests a conspiracy theory wild beyond imagination."

2. Perhaps what we need in Washington is an "ombudsman's" office. Ombudsmen are people whose specific task is to assist citizens in dealing with the bureaucracy. It could be staffed and financed by transferring one-half of all Congresspersons' personal office resources to it. Good idea? How would you make it accountable? Will Congress approve such a thing in the next thousand years?

68.
LIVE FROM CAPITOL HILL
by Carol Matlack

Setting the Scene: There is near agreement that information will be to the 21st century what financial capital was to the 20th—power. Voters are desperate for information and Congresspersons have large staffs that are only too willing to give it out. In fact they are paid extra to do so. But citizens are naturally skeptical of this kind of information. That is why they turn to the news. But now (are you ready for this?) Congresspersons are making the news. This reading tells you how. I do not mean they make the news by feeding reporters information. They have always done that. I mean they physically take charge of the tape, the interview, the questions. They *become* the network, the reporter, the editor. They even provide the interviewee—themselves.

Glaring into a television camera with the Capitol dome looming behind him, Rep. Larry E. Craig is railing against Speaker Jim Wright of Texas and a proposed congressional pay raise. "The House leadership is ducking," the Idaho Republican says. "I've spoken out against it. I will not take the pay raise."

A few hours later, all three major network affiliates in Boise will air the scene on their local evening newscasts. But viewers won't be told that the man interviewing Craig is his press secretary, that the camera crew works for the National Republican Congressional Committee (NRCC) and that the broadcast is being paid for by Craig's campaign treasury.

Some Members of Congress are giving new meaning to the term "newsmaker." With technical assistance from their political party organizations, they are creating their own "news" reports and beaming them directly to hometown stations—and without ever talking to a reporter. Local stations pay nothing for these broadcasts, and many news directors not only accept them but often also request them.

"If they're offering the service to us, we'd be nuts not to take it," said Mike Desotell, an assignment editor and producer at WBAY-TV in Green Bay, Wis., which frequently uses satellite-fed reports from Rep. Toby Roth, R-Wis., on its newscasts. "You work kind of like a team with some of these stations," said David Fish, Craig's press secretary. "Rural stations depend on that."

This is taking place at a time, ironically, when hometown TV coverage of Congress has grown tremendously, fueled by rapid technological changes that have brought localized coverage within reach of even the smallest station. Only a decade ago, most local stations could only dream of having a reporter in Washington. Today, for $200-$300, a station without any reporters in the capital can have a custom-made story from Washington in a matter of hours.

Membership in the Congressional Radio and Television Galleries has tripled since 1979, with most of the growth in bureaus serving local stations. Hundreds of House Members, long accustomed to toiling in relative obscurity, have suddenly found themselves going "Live at 5" before hometown audiences. . . .

Until recently, a Member of Congress who wanted TV coverage back home

Every Wednesday afternoon when Congress is in session, the NRCC stations a camera crew on the lawn outside the Capitol and invites GOP Members to stop by and make tapes for their local stations. One by one, the Members troop before the camera and answer questions posed by their press secretaries. Later in the day—in plenty of time for evening newscasts—the NRCC beams the tape to local stations that have been alerted to receive the satellite feed . . .

Local news directors defend their use of Members' ready-made broadcasts, saying that they can discard anything that appears slanted or isn't newsworthy. "Just because [a Member] did it doesn't mean we'll use it," John Speciale, news director at WICU-TV in Erie, Pa., said.

But most of the material is carefully crafted to put Members' positions in the best light. For example, Smith's presentations on his oil and gas bill began with his press secretary asking, "Congressman, what are you doing to help the independent oil producers?" Smith replied: "They bear an incredible burden. . . . We need to give them that relief, give them incentives to go out and produce oil and gas." Smith didn't mention the long odds that his proposal faces; even oil and gas lobbyists admit that Congress is unlikely to enact tax relief for their industry this year.

Partisan considerations are evident as well. Craig, for instance, repeatedly blasted the Speaker for trying to block a vote on the pay raise and urged viewers to call or send telegrams to Wright. He didn't mention that his own party's leadership had endorsed Wright's strategy. (The pay raise later was brought to a vote and defeated.)

"It's dangerous to let the press secretaries determine what kind of coverage their politicians are going to get," said Tim Hillard, Washington bureau chief for Fisher Broadcasting Co., which owns stations in the Pacific Northwest. Most congressional offices have quit offering canned video to the Fisher stations because they rarely use it, Hillard said. But sometimes, aides attempt an end run. Once, after Hillard declined to cover a press conference, a Senator's press secretary called a camera crew from one of the political party organizations to cover the event and then sent the tape to the local station, explaining that Hillard had "missed" the story. But the plan backfired when the station news director became suspicious and called Hillard. "I immediately called the Senator's office and said, 'Don't try that again,'" Hillard recalled. "They haven't."

Generally, stations that use Members' prepared videotapes air only the Members' comments, not the press secretaries' questions, and do not disclose the source of the tape to viewers. . . .

As Members of Congress move into the "news" business, they are directly competing with many of the Washington television bureaus whose business boomed in the early 1980s but now appears to have leveled off.

When Bob Petrick, fresh out of graduate school, joined an independent Washington broadcast service in 1979, he was among only a handful of television reporters covering

Washington for local stations. The job was grueling: He and his cameraman hauled around bulky cameras, shooting film and shipping it back to the stations for developing and editing. Same-day coverage was practically impossible unless the film was put on an airplane early in the day.

Barely a year later, Petrick had taken over the bureau, and several forces had converged to transform its future. Relatively inexpensive, lightweight videocameras had come on the market. Videotaped stories could be edited in Washington and transmitted instantly via satellite feeds, which had become widely available and reasonably priced. And, said Petrick, television reporters had learned to catch the interest of local viewers by spicing up Washington stories with visual imagery—cars lining up at gas stations during fuel shortages, and unemployment lines during economic downturns. "By the time the Reagan Administration came in, everybody was really hungry to say, 'What does this new Administration mean for people back home?'"

Most of the major broadcast chains, several small regional chains and even a few individual stations opened Washington bureaus in the early 1980s, and existing bureaus were expanded. Live Washington broadcasts were a hot item; when Hillard arrived in Washington in 1981 to report for Fisher's newly opened bureau, he recalled, "we were so enamored with the technology, for about a year we went live every night." Fisher's stations, in Portland, Ore., and Seattle "were anxious to publicize the fact that they had a Washington bureau," he said. "If one of our delegation sneezed, it was likely to get on the air."

Independent bureaus also flourished, serving local stations under regular contracts or on a pay-as-you-go basis. Petrick's bureau grew, absorbed another bureau and affiliated with Potomac Communications, one of the largest independent. (Petrick's bureau, In Washington/ANB, remains separate from Potomac's own bureau, Potomac News Service.)

Video technology was especially important to the independents because they could make multiple tapes of a single event and market them to several stations by tacking on short customized segments at the end of each tape. "We could leverage our product a lot better," said Bruce Finland, Potomac's chairman.

The independent bureaus, whose bread-and-butter business has traditionally been in smaller markets, are the ones who stand to lose most when Members prepare their own videos for local broadcast. "I met with a group of news directors just last week, and one said, 'Why do we need you? We get that free,'" Finland said. "I said, 'That's pretty dangerous.' And they said, 'Well, we ask the questions.'"

Customized News

Tom Haederle popped the videocassette out of the editing console. "Well, this won't win any awards," he said with wry smile. Haederle, a reporter for In Washington/ANB, had just pieced together a 94-second report on the condition of the U.S. economy—as analyzed by University of Massachusetts chancellor Joseph Duffey at a congressional hearing earlier in the day. less than an hour later, television viewers in Springfield, Mass., would see the report on their evening news, with Haederle signing off, "In Washington, Newswatch 40."

The assignment was a typical one for Petrick's five-person operation, which provides what is known in the business as "custom" Washington coverage for more than 30 local television stations. Petrick and his two reporters—Haederle and Paula Faria, Petrick's wife—spend most of their time covering members of Congress and Washington events involving people from their local television markets. For the independents, national news is usually seen through the lens of local reaction: How does the local Member of Congress respond to the day's headlines? What does the local mayor or university chancellor have to say about the federal budget?

Independent reporters work hard—Petrick says that on a busy day, he and his staff can produce 15 stories—and they seldom have the luxury of working on long-range projects or developing beats. Potomac News Service has four full-time reporters serving nearly 150 stations; Conus Communications, another large independent, has three reporters serving nearly 85 stations.

"We can't really follow Members with any continuity," Petrick said. "Their press people call us and let us know what's going on. We can't keep on top of them as much as the print people do."

The line between journalism and salesmanship often gets blurred in independent bureaus. when business is slow, Petrick and his colleagues often call stations to pitch story ideas. They frequently run errands for client stations, such as picking up credentials for out-of-town reporters covering the presidential inauguration. "It's part of keeping clients happy," Petrick said.

And independents have a subtle disincentive to anger Members and their press secretaries with critical coverage. They depend on the press secretaries to alert them to stories. And, if an irritated Member refuses their interview requests, their client station can shop around for another bureau. . . .

Switchboards at the independent bureaus light up whenever there is an international incident such as the U.S. downing of a Libyan fighter plane in January and local stations are looking for congressional reaction. Events such as the inaugural, governors' and mayors' meetings, and White House awards ceremonies are also favorites.

Independent crews often carry a supply of "mike flags"—plastic cubes emblazoned with local stations' logos. Upon arriving at an event, they shoot some generic footage—a technique called "spraying the room." Then, the reporter tapes a series of virtually identical closings, slipping a new "flag" onto the microphone for each one. . . .

Pressures

Tight news budgets and changing expectations from the home office are putting new pressure on station-owned and chain-owned bureaus as well. "Television stations are flat now in terms of profit," said Stephen Hess, a Brookings Institution scholar who has studied press coverage of Congress. Most stations that maintain their own Washington news bureaus today do so out of "noblesse oblige," Hess said. . . .

For some stations, the mobile satellite truck has replaced "our reporter in Washington" as the latest gimmick. Many stations sent reporters on the road last year to cover the presidential campaign and the political party conventions. . . .

Some stations are calling on their Washington bureaus to deliver more feature material. Consumer and health stories are much in demand, said Louisa Hart, bureau chief for the Newsfeed Washington bureau, which serves 95 domestic and foreign stations.

Many stations try to cover their congressional delegations from the home office via satellite news conferences arranged through the political parties' broadcast facilities or the congressional recording studios. Such sessions rarely produce tough questioning, though. Hometown reporters "basically ask the 'What's your opinion?' kind of question," said Jeffrey Bullock, press secretary to Rep. Thomas R. Carper, D-Del. "They're intelligent people, but they're not people who cover Capitol Hill. They're not familiar with the issues. . . ."

Most Washington bureau reporters predict that they will survive the current shakeout, and that coverage may improve as a result. "We may have to claw to get on the air," Hillard said, "but there is no longer the pressure to have a story on the air every day to justify your existence. What we're doing is better stuff."

But Washington bureau reporters are increasingly disturbed by local stations' willingness to accept Members' packaged television programming. . . .

Members who use the broadcast facilities are enthusiastic about the result. "My ID has gone up dramatically," said Sen. John McCain, R-Ariz., who has a monthly cable television show in which Arizona residents call him on a toll-free telephone number at the Senate Republican Conference studio. Members of Congress aren't the only beneficiaries; the Harriman Center has made videotapes of Democratic governors attending national Governors' Association conferences and beamed them to stations in the governors' home states.

Despite the technology at their disposal, many Members of Congress still appear reluctant to enter the satellite age. Hess of the Brookings Institution recently surveyed a random sampling of House press secretaries and found that on average, they sent video material to their home districts less than once a month. "It's amazing how many of them use no television, considering what's available," he said.

But Finland of Potomac Communications likens ready-made congressional programming to an expansion of the congressional franking privilege. "They're doing this to further their own aims," he said. "Congressmen want to be able to control their over coverage."

Thinking It Over

1. If there is a fault here, isn't it with the local stations? If they edit the tapes correctly, what problems could remain?

2. This is another case of a classic dilemma in controlling Congress: Congress is a *political* institution that makes its own rules. Which is the better tactic: to try to get them to change their rules, or to work outside Congress to establish countervailing mechanisms?

69.
UNELECTED REPRESENTATIVES: CONGRESSIONAL STAFF AND THE FUTURE OF REPRESENTATIVE GOVERNMENT
by Michael J. Malbin

Setting the Scene: One of the most important developments in Congressional politics in the last several decades is the growth of staff—the people that assist Congresspersons. While much of the concern with staff focuses on how they work to keep their boss's image secure *outside* Congress, the impact of staff is equally important in the realm of policy-making *inside* Congress. Knowledge is power. As the public sector expands, Representatives need to know more and more about more and more and more. As society increases in complexity, the job of Representative or Senator becomes more involved and the time one has to learn or even to *think* becomes less and less. In other words as the need for knowledge is increasing at a fantastic rate, the time available to meet this need is decreasing as swiftly. This is where the staff comes in. They are becoming the brains of democracy.

I was nervous. Fresh from academe, on my first assignment as a journalist, I was in the middle of an article about a conference committee that was deadlocked over the use of highway trust fund money for mass transit. I had done all the easy interviews—staffers and lobbyists who filled me in on the issues and players. But sooner or later I knew I would have to interview some elected senators and representatives. The $23 billion authorization bill was the most significant one to come out of the House Public Works Subcommittee on Transportation that year (1973), so it seemed obvious to me that I ought to see the chairman. So there I was, waiting in the office of the late John Kluczynski (D-Ill.) with tape recorder clutched in hand, and, as I said, I was nervous. After all, this interview could be the one to give me the political insights I needed to impress my new editors.

When I first got to Kluczynski's office, the receptionist said the congressman would be glad to see me in a few minutes. Then, while I waited, she telephoned one of the committee staff professionals working on the bill. The chairman wanted him there, she said, in case I raised any technical issues. That seemed a reasonable enough request, until we reached the first "technical" question.

I began the interview with what I thought was a throwaway question. (My experienced colleagues said that was a good way to break the ice.) What makes this issue important, I asked?

"This is a tremendously important bill. It involves millions of dollars," Kluczynski began to answer, and then paused. "No—*billions*, isn't it? he asked, turning to the staff aide.

That did it—the balloon was pricked and my case of nerves was over. The significance of that brief exchange was too clear to be missed, even by a newcomer. I was initially shocked, but quickly began realizing that to understand Congress, I had better start paying attention to the role of its staff.

That realization has only been confirmed by subsequent experience. Rarely do representatives or senators depend as totally on their staffs as Kluczynski did that day, particularly not on a major bill handled by a subcommittee they head. In fact, most members seem broadly to be in control of most of what their own staffs are doing with the authority delegated to them. Nevertheless, it is not unfair to suggest that Congress as a whole has become the institutional embodiment of Kluczynski's spirit. The members cannot begin to control the workload that their staffs collectively help to generate. Yet, Congress could not function in today's world without the staff on which it has come to depend.

This represents a revolutionary change in an institution that, as recently as 1945, saw no need for permanent professional committee staffs. The congressional budget is almost forty-five times as large as it was three decades ago. In that same time committee staffs, the most important element of the congressional bureaucracy in policy terms, have increased almost eightfold, personal staffs have increased fivefold, and support agencies[1] have taken on a new importance. The numbers only begin to tell the story of staff influence, however, More impressive are the kinds of tasks members of Congress have become willing to delegate to their staffs. This has reached the point where some members publicly ask whether they or their staffs are in charge.

In principle, of course, the members hire, fire, and therefore control their staffs. Nevertheless, the staff exercises a great deal of indirect influence over which the members' control is at best tenuous and imperfect. That influence arises from the simple fact the members have more to do than time in which to do it and it extends well beyond the housekeeping functions familiar to most of us. We all know that committee staffs arrange hearings, draft bills, and hold stacks of paper with reams of information for members during debates. But the way these staffs can substantively affect every step in the legislative process may be less familiar. For example, their ability to run committee investigations, the results of which they can skillfully leak to the media, gives them influence over the items members choose to put on the legislative agenda. Once a bill is on the agenda, the staff works to assemble a coalition behind it, arranging detailed amendments with other staff members and with interest group representatives to broaden support for the bill without sacrificing the goals the chairman, often at their urging, has adopted. When conflicts cannot be resolved, the members may then learn enough about the details to weigh the political costs of compromise. But even then, the role of the member is clearly limited. As former Senator Dick Clark (D-Iowa), once said: "There is no question about our enormous dependency and their influence. In all legislation, they're the ones that lay out the options."[2]

The system that leads staffs to have this kind of influence does have a rational basis. The reason for committee staffs, and the source of their influence, is an extension of the

---

[1]The four support agencies are the Library of Congress, General Accounting Office, Office of Technology Assessment, and Congressional Budget Office.

[2]Spencer Rich, "An Invisible Network of Hill Power," *The Washington Post*, 20 March, 1977, A. E5.

reason for having committees: the idea that Congress is best served if members become specialists, with the vast majority accepting the expertise of a few on most issues. Committee staffs grew when it became apparent that even specialized committee members needed help if Congress was to get the information required for making informed decisions. Congress needs staffs, just as it needs specialist members, to help it evaluate the flood of material from the outside and perhaps even come up with ideas of its own. The system clearly provides benefits. It seems no accident that Congress, the most powerful parliamentary body in the world, is also the one with the largest staff. Without its staff, Congress would quickly become the prisoner of its outside sources of information in the executive branch and interest groups.

Yet, the costs have been high. The staffs—individually well educated, hard working, and, in general, devoted to what they perceive to be the public good—collectively create a situation in which many of the elected members fear they are becoming insulated administrators in a bureaucratized organization that leaves them no better able to cope than they were when they did all the work themselves. . . . The seriousness of this situation would be difficult to overemphasize.

We all know from studies of public opinion that the policy messages conveyed by voters to their representatives are at best tenuous and ambiguous. . . . But this tenuous connection becomes stretched to the breaking point when the representatives delegate too much of their control to appointed staff aides. How much delegation is "too much" is open to debate, of course. But there can be no doubt that precisely what staffs do and how they do it are matters that relate to the basic principles underlying representative government—the very principles that give members, and through them their staffs, their reason for being.

The problem has arisen partly from the sheer size of today's congressional staffs and partly from the ways in which members have transformed the role of staff over the past few decades. Congress has been pursuing at least four somewhat conflicting aims as it has increased the size of its staff. Its aims have included: (1) a desire to be less dependent on the executive branch and outside interest groups for information; (2) a desire, especially among Republicans and junior Democrats, to put their own imprint on issues of national importance; (3) a desire on the part of an increasing number of members to devote their time and resources to gaining credit in the media for putting new issues on the legislative agenda instead of working quietly to impress their colleagues through committee specialization; . . . and (4) a desire on the part of almost everyone in Congress to gain some control over their expanding workloads and over the increasingly fragmented nature of their work. Of these different goals, the first suggests an increase in the size of Congress's professional staff but says nothing about the way the staff should be used or how it should be controlled, the second suggests that the staff should not only grow but that staff resources should be dispersed, and the third suggests giving the enlarged staff new kinds of things to do. All three of these objectives have more or less been attained in the years since World War II. However, the first three objectives are incompatible with the fourth—and that is the one that raises the basic question of democratic control.

Congress has failed utterly to cope with its workload. If anything, the growth of staff has made the situation worse. First, on the level of sheer numbers, more staff means more information coming in to each member's office, with more management problems as different staff aides compete for the member's time to present their own nuggets in a timely fashion. The member, under these conditions, is becoming more of a chief executive officer in charge of a medium-sized business than a person who personally deliberates with his colleagues about policy. . . . Second, the problems created by large numbers are exacerbated by the staffs' new roles. Increasingly, the members want aides who will dream up new bills and amendments bearing their bosses' names instead of helping the bosses understand what is already on the agenda. The result is that the new staff bureaucracy and the workload it helps create threaten to bury Congress under its own paperwork, just as surely as if the staff never existed.

. . .

[Editor's Note: The author now turns to a discussion of the impact of staff on policy formation.]

The most direct impact of the role of staff has to do with the reception Congress gives the ideas put forward by groups or individuals that have no identifiable constituency, such as some of the smaller issue groups on the right and left, academicians, and issue specialists in think tanks and consulting firms. Senators and representatives are too busy to see every lobbyist who comes their way and must depend on their staffs to screen them. Organizations and individuals with real political or economic power have little difficulty getting in the door to make their case, but people who have nothing to offer but their ideas have a tougher time. If it were not for the staffs, the latter could easily be frozen out, given the members' limited time for sifting worthwhile ideas from worthless ones. The staffs give these people their chance. But the staffs generally do not go out actively to seek the broadest range of opinion on the subjects within their responsibility. Rather, like members, they tend either to rely on friends and acquaintances or wait passively for people to make themselves known to them. Thus the staffs, like the members, tend to favor people from organizations that have the staff resources to keep up with issues as they develop. However, since the staff people are not themselves elected, and since their future careers in the Washington community often depend on their gaining reputations as innovators, it is to their interest to spend time listening to people whose ideas may help them put something new on the oversight or legislative agenda, even if those people have no political constituencies of their own. The interwoven interests of the participants in the various issue networks lead them to work together to identify problems they can then use their expertise to solve. The future interests of the staff flow directly from the changes in career patterns that we discussed earlier, in which staff jobs are stepping stones for ambitious young lawyers instead of places where mid-level bureaucrats and political cronies end their careers.

The tendency of the staffs' future career interests to enhance the power of experts without constituencies is reinforced by the staffers' backgrounds. The new staffs tend to be young lawyers who came to Washington because they had been political activists and wanted to "make a mark" on "the system." In addition, their undergraduate and law school training has tended to make them more sympathetic to arguments based on general ideological principles (from the left for Democratic aides and from the right for Republicans) than either their classmates with "real jobs" or the elected members. They thus tend to draw members toward precisely what Fenno said members do least well. The technocratic and ideological staffers may be distinct . . . or the same staff person may embrace both attitudes. . . . Moreover, both may work side by side with other staff people whose legal specialization and future ambitions tie them more closely to traditional economic interests . . . or whose past experience and background similarly lead them to act as interest group advocates. . . . But major corporate, trade association, and labor union interests would have little difficulty being heard in a Washington that had no staffs, nor would be issue-based organization that had developed a deliverable political constituency. Where the staffs make a difference, therefore, is in their openness to, career interest in, and institutional need for ideas and slogans whose main political support initially comes only from the fact that staff people and journalists are interested in listening to them.

While the first systematic substantive impact of staff on policy comes out of its entrepreneurial role, the second comes from its role in negotiations. Both have the net effect of increasing the amount of legislation that gets passed and the kinds of interests served by that legislation. The job of a staff negotiator is to help move the process ahead toward a resolution. While a member may pull him back, it almost always is in the interest of the staff negotiator to see a set of negotiations through to a successful conclusion. This is particularly true if the program contains some section the staff member can think of as his own. The program—or the planned hearing, if the person is an investigator—may represent a major investment of time for a staff person whose future may depend on gaining recognition in Washington for having made a difference. As a result, the process of staff negotiation tends to lend practical weight to the view that the purpose of the legislative process is to fashion agreements behind which the greatest number of self-appointed interested parties can unite. . . . The impetus of staff, in other words, is to build coalitions by having programs respond, at least symbolically, to more demands, rather than let them die their natural death. The result is increasingly inclusive, increasingly complex legislation that can only be understood by an expert. Needless to say, this increases the power of permanent Washingtonians with the necessary expertise, such as former staffers.

In the course of building the coalitions just described, programs are considered in isolation from each other. It is not normally in the interest of staff to question how a program affects the budget, the overall structure of government, or the ability of citizens to understand what their government is doing. Of course, members themselves have this same inclination to see programs in isolation from each other. If they did not, they would scarcely tolerate the way staffs negotiate in their name. But a member who serves on several different committees, directly communicates with constituents, and sits down with other members to share the results of their composite experiences, is far more likely than an aide to have a basis for getting beyond the inclinations to think about the relationships between policies in ways that cross lines of issue specialization.

Thinking It Over

1. Construct an essay entitled "Information, Knowledge, and Power: The Roll of Congressional Staff."

2. Let us assume that staff to help Congresspersons make wise decisions is needed, but staff to help them get reelected is not. Is there any way to square that circle?

70.
SHOWDOWN AT GUCCI GULCH
by Jeffrey H. Birnbaum and Alan S. Murray

Setting the Scene: What follows comes from a book that traces how the Congress accomplished the impossible—how the lobbyists were denied the biggest influence-peddling opportunity in modern history. The opportunity was the tax reform bill of 1986. In this case reform means simplifying the tax code by eliminating special interest deductions. It drew lobbyists like honey draws bees because over the years hundreds of deductions had been placed in the tax code to satisfy special interests. When these are threatened, swarms of lobbyists descend on Congress. Here is the situation. Oregon Republican Bob Packwood's tax bill is getting eaten up in the Senate Finance Committee. The special interests are succeeding, one by one, in making sure their favorite deduction survives. Other Senators are also busily protecting their own pet deductions, often in the name of deserving causes. You'll see names here you may not recognize. Moynihan is a Democratic Senator from New York, Armstrong is a Republican Senator from Colorado, Bradley is a Democratic Senator from New Jersey, and Diefenderfer is the top staff worker on the Finance Committee, which Packwood chairs, and which controls the tax reform bill. A "markup" is a closed door committee session in which key decisions are made about a bill's future. The subtitle of the book *Gucci Gulch* comes from the name Congresspersons gave the place in the capitol building where lobbyists used to gather in their expensive suits to wait their turn to influence the tax bill. We join the struggle as the tax reform package faces a disastrous day in the Senate.

As bad as events had been, Friday, April 18, promised to be far worse. The markup schedule dictated that the most costly individual tax items were to be voted on that day. With the downhill slide of the markup thus far, Packwood's chances of winning those votes were shaky at best. Friday was shaping up as the day of reckoning. Huge sums were on the line, and the fate of the entire enterprise hung in the balance. Some $70 billion worth of tax breaks that Packwood wanted to pare were scheduled for a vote in the morning, and it was clear to Diefenderfer that the chairman was likely to lose.

Armstrong had collected enough votes to keep the current deduction for business meals. In addition, Moynihan had teamed with tax-reform opponents to gather enough votes to save the deduction for sales taxes, a big-money item that was vital to preserving revenue neutrality. Dole was on Moynihan's side, and even Bradley was so discouraged that he decided to vote with Moynihan.

Diefenderfer stayed late that Thursday, trying to figure a way out. He frantically contacted senators' offices, trying to find some support, but there was none. It was well past dinner when he called his boss. "It doesn't look good," he told Packwood. "We have problems."

Early the next morning Diefenderfer and his assistants made their way to Packwood's office in the Russell Office Building. Starting at about seven-thirty, they manned the telephones, trying to scare up a vote or two, trying to save the floundering effort, but it was to no avail. The calls only confirmed the fears of the night before. Discipline had broken down. The bill was a goner.

"We'll pull it down," Packwood concluded in his matter-of-fact, businesslike style.

By that time, reporters and staff aides had already gathered in the committee's hearing room and were awaiting Packwood's arrival. They gossiped about the tax-reform carnage the day might produce. Surely there would be plenty. Armstrong's people were crowing about their boss's imminent victory; he had even canceled a trip to see his amendment through. There were whispers as well about Moynihan's potential coup. Two floors below, dozens of lobbyists settled into their seats in the auditorium. Packwood, who was usually punctual, had not arrived and the lobbyists wondered what was delaying him. No one was prepared when he finally entered, took his chair in the center of the horseshoe-shaped hearing table in the front of the room, and delivered his message in rapid-fire fashion.

"I don't want to give any impression that we have any idea of quitting," Packwood said, "but I did not want to run the risk of killing this bill. What I was afraid of today is that if we held votes, it would be the end of the bill." There would be no votes today, he said. There would be no votes for some time to come.

Some lobbyists listening downstairs started to cheer.

To many, Packwood's action signaled the end of reform. The Finance Committee was clearly too wedded to its many tax breaks to accomplish such a massive rewrite of the code. A pessimistic Moynihan declared the effort "in ruins," and said, "it has clearly failed in the Senate." Secretary Baker, the administration's top gun for tax reform, was equally distressed: "We're in the soup."

David Pryor, the folksy Arkansan who was the most junior member of the committee, summed it up best: "We're all riding a lame horse right now. We have to decide whether we want to keep riding it or trade it in. I frankly think this is a horse that's so lame we can't continue to ride it."

The tax bill had reached its lowest ebb.

The Two-Pitcher Lunch

About fifteen minutes after the markup disbanded, Packwood telephoned Diefenderfer from his office. "Lunch?" Packwood asked. "Sure," the aide replied.

Diefenderfer enjoyed his occasional long lunches with the boss, but on this day he knew the conversation would be as gloomy as the overcast skies. They were facing the greatest setback of their many years together on Capitol Hill. Diefenderfer had been Packwood's top aide at the Commerce Committee before moving to the Finance Committee, and the two men had been through many tough battles, but this was the biggest and the hardest to solve. They left the Capitol grounds together, making small talk, trying not to dwell on their failure. They walked the few blocks to their favorite saloon, The Irish Times.

The Irish Times is the kind of place that people go to get drunk. Neon signs on the window flash BUDWEISER and STROH'S, and above the door, a painted sign advertises: GIVE ME YOUR THIRSTY, YOUR FAMISHED, YOUR BEFUDDLED MASSES. Inside, a visitor's first impression is the odor of spilled beer; the second is the lighting—or lack of it. It is not the kind of place that engenders optimism. Even on the sunniest days, its checkerboard tablecloths are shrouded in darkness.

Packwood and Diefenderfer ordered two cheeseburgers, rare, and a pitcher of draft beer. "We're not going any place the way we're going," the senator said. "The bill is getting worse rather than better." Both men knew what vast understatement those words conveyed and solemnly began to review the bidding. It was their task, starting at that moment, to turn around what appeared to be an impossible situation. Tax reform—and Packwood's reputation—hung in the balance.

As they took their first sips of beer, Packwood suggested a new approach. Instead of writing a bill that reached into every corner and crevice of the massive tax code, he asked, why not select just a few, small pieces of the mammoth design and patch together a less far-reaching measure? Maybe it could consist of just a minimum tax and a few repealed deductions. At least it could be called reform.

Diefenderfer disliked that option. The stripped-down approach, he thought, would be considered a humiliating defeat among Washington scorekeepers. If Packwood was unable to persuade his panel to draft a sweeping bill along the lines the president was demanding—and the House already had passed—the press would label the committee a sellout and its fledgling chairman an impotent leader. Packwood would be relegated to the status of legislative loser, one of the worst fates to befall a big-time politician.

Diefenderfer was no tax expert, but he was extremely close to Packwood. His opinions carried tremendous weight. He was more than staff director at the Finance Committee; he was an all-purpose political adviser. It was his job to keep his boss out of trouble, and he usually succeeded. "Diefenderfer is in a category by himself with Packwood," Darman observed several months later. "When Diefenderfer tells Packwood what's on his mind, Packwood listens."

Packwood and Diefenderfer were almost inseparable, and they were a distinctive pair as they walked through the halls of Congress. Diefenderfer was a big, bearded, lumbering man of forty-one years, who was proud of his aggressiveness (he held a brown belt in judo) and his steel-country roots in western Pennsylvania. The shorter Packwood would often walk slightly ahead of Diefenderfer, striding with his high forehead jutting forward, looking oddly like the movie character E.T.

Diefenderfer's analysis of the problems of the stripped-down approach hit home with the ambitious chairman. The two men had often discussed how important it was for Packwood to prove himself a success. The senator's extensive library was stocked with books about great men in history, such as Disraeli and Jefferson, and his office was decorated with biscuit tins bearing likenesses of Winston Churchill. Packwood took the examples of these men seriously. If the Finance Committee failed to approve more than a pale imitation of reform, Diefenderfer argued, it would be three or four years before Packwood could regain his reputation as a leader, before he could recoup his power. This was a possibility that Packwood was loathe to ignore.

There was also Packwood's reelection to consider. On that day, April 18, 1986, Packwood was a month away from what he feared would be a close primary back home in

Oregon, and his political opponents were beginning to make hay out of his committee's many giveaways. Representative James Weaver, the Democratic aspirant, gave a major address that asserted Packwood was "foundering" in his first major test as chairman, and that he was sucking up to "special interests." Oregon newspapers were also chiding him for taking huge campaign contributions from almost every interest group imaginable. He was quickly growing infamous as "Mr. Special Interest."

Another solution was vaguely in the minds of both men. They had discussed the possibility for months and had even done some preliminary research on it, but the notion was so drastic, and its likelihood of success so remote, that almost no one thought it anything but foolhardy.

Packwood and Diefenderfer called it the "radical approach": the paring away of enough deductions, exclusions, and credits in the code to halve the top individual tax rate to 25 percent from 50 percent. With a rate so low, Packwood reasoned, "people would cease to worry about whether or not the particular deduction or exemption they were concerned with stayed or disappeared."

The idea was an extraordinary but simple one. Although many Americans fell into tax brackets as high as 50 percent, few Americans paid more than 25 percent of their income in taxes; there was no reason for the top rate to be any higher than that. The proposal Packwood and Diefenderfer were plotting would be even more audacious than Bill Bradley's landmark proposal in 1982, and in some ways, even more far-reaching than the quickly dismissed Treasury I plan in 1984.

Packwood had dropped hints about his interest in the 25-percent solution before. During Finance Committee hearings, he had asked witnesses: "At what tax rate won't deductions matter anymore?" He had even mentioned a 25-percent plan to the president at a White House meeting with congressional leaders in the summer of 1985, but almost no one took him seriously. Eliminating enough tax breaks to get the rate down to 25 percent was, most everyone in Washington agreed, politically impossible. Packwood himself had originally thought a 25-percent plan would have to be accompanied by a consumption tax to raise additional revenue. Now, however, he was considering something more sweeping. The president had ruled out any new taxes as part of reform; that meant the low rate would have to be paid for by eliminating tax breaks.

During the first pitcher of beer, the two men hashed over the options. They were well into their second pitcher when it became clear there was only one course to take: the radical approach.

These two men—one who had never faced public election, the other who represented a state that had little more than 1 percent of the nation's population—were toying with the most massive redistribution of the tax burden in the nation's history. Hunched over their sandwiches, they were plotting to take hundreds of billions of dollars out of the pockets of those who had made heavy use of tax loopholes and bestow those billions on everyone who had not. It was a plan that would cause fundamental changes in the very structure of American society. It would subtly and deeply affect the lives of every American household and every American business. Packwood, who had spent much of his Senate career poking loopholes in the tax system, was not suggesting the biggest loophole-closing package in history.

To a large extent, the idea that crystallized over beer at The Irish Times was a political ploy. The two men thought it might help quiet the criticism of Packwood at home, and that certainly could not hurt his reelection chances. His political opponents could hardly criticize him for doing what they were demanding.

The plan also had its appeal in Washington. During his seventy hours of meetings with the senators on his panel, Packwood noted that almost every one of them said that they supported "reform—real reform," but of course, they always added, "real" reform was not politically possible. During the two-week deterioration of the markup, the members sometimes justified their piggish votes by claiming the initial Packwood proposal was not real reform anyway, so why should they hold back?

Well, Packwood now thought, if they say they want reform, I'll give them reform. A radical, off-with-their-heads tax-reform plan with a rate as low as 25 percent surely would call the bluff of anyone who was trying to conceal distaste for reform behind a reformer's rhetoric. It would be difficult for the self-righteous members of the Finance Committee to reject out of hand.

In addition, the radical approach had a substantive appeal for Packwood. By this time, he was convinced that 25 percent or thereabouts was a "magic" number for the top individual rate. If rates were that low, he believed, people would stop caring so passionately about their deductions and credits. He had come to believe that Bradley and Kemp were right: the lower the rate, the less political pressure for tax breaks and the more efficient the economy.

Packwood also liked the idea because it was bold, and the combative chairman enjoyed taking bold stands. Like his great-grandfather and father before him, he had a volatile nature. He cherished being unpredictable and independent-minded. If nothing else, the proposal would contribute to that image.

A more prudent lawmaker, steeped in the traditions and policy of tax law, would have concluded that the 25-percent idea would never work, that it probably was suicidal to even attempt it, but Packwood was in a desperate spot, and he chose a desperate strategy. Taking a half-inch-thick slice of onion from Diefenderfer's cheeseburger and placing it atop his own, Packwood looked at Diefenderfer and said, "Why not?" They finished their burgers and a second pitcher of beer and walked back to the Capitol rejuvenated. They had made their decision.

Neither of them knew where their half-crazed plan would lead them. Later, in private, Packwood told several associates that he did not expect the 25-percent plan to succeed and that he was putting it forward mostly for tactical reasons. He and Diefenderfer both doubted the committee would go for it, but at least Packwood would have staked out the high ground on tax reform. Packwood conceded, "It was a long shot."

"I've often described it as sort of like the end of that movie *The Wild Bunch*," Packwood says. In the film, a gang of bandits sells out a young member of their crew to the other side, but later decides to undo the deed. "The next morning they get up and look at each other and strap on their guns and go to get the kid. They know they're going to be killed, but they've got to do this, they've got to try it. Bill and I just felt, OK, this is something we've got to try. If we fail, we fail at a great enterprise. No guts, no glory."

Thinking It Over

1. Is it possible to extract from this case a set of principles that could be used as a model for decision-making? Or is this case simply an interesting exception? Do decisions get made this way often?

2. It'll take a bit of research (including a thorough read of Birnbaum and Murray's excellent book) but I bet you could write a very interesting term paper called "Showdown at Gucci Gulch II" in which you trace the continuing saga of tax reform. Try it.

Chapter XI

THE PRESIDENCY

71.
THE FEDERALIST PAPERS, NO. 70
by Alexander Hamilton

Setting the Scene: Like the other institutions of the national government proposed in the new Constitution, the Presidency needed to be explained and defended. In *Federalist* No. 70, Alexander Hamilton sets about the task. Once again, it is easy to judge that the fear the defenders of the Constitution seek to allay is the fear that too much power will be centered at the federal level. In this case Hamilton attempts the tricky business of convincing his readers that a plural executive would be too weak without raising fears that the single executive he proposed would be too strong. In reading *Federalist* No. 70, remember that when Hamilton wrote it, many states had created councils to check the power of the executive.

There is an idea, which is not without its advocates, that a vigorous executive is inconsistent with the genius of republican government. The enlightened well-wishers to this species of government must at least hope that the supposition is destitute of foundation; since they can never admit its truth, without, at the same time, admitting the condemnation of their own principles. Energy in the executive is a leading character in the definition of good government. It is essential to the protection of the community against foreign attacks; it is not less essential to the steady administration of the laws, to the protection of property against those irregular and high-handed combinations, which sometimes interrupt the ordinary course of justice, to the security of liberty against the enterprises and assaults of ambition, of faction, and of anarchy. Every man, the least conversant in Roman story, knows how often that republic was obliged to take refuge in the absolute power of a single man, under the formidable title of dictator, as well as against the intrigues of ambitious individuals, who aspired to the tyranny, and the seditions of whole classes of the community, whose conduct threatened the existence of all government, as against the invasions of external enemies, who menaced the conquest and destruction of Rome.

There can be no need, however, to multiply arguments or examples on this head. A feeble executive implies a feeble execution of the government. A feeble execution is but another phrase for a bad execution; and a government ill executed, whatever it may be in theory, must be, in practice, a bad government.

Taking it for granted, therefore, that all men of sense will agree in the necessity of an energetic executive, it will only remain to inquire, what are the ingredients which constitute this energy? How far can they be combined with those other ingredients, which constitute safety in the republican sense? And how far does this combination characterize the plan which has been reported by the convention?

The ingredients which constitute energy in the executive are, unity; duration; an adequate provision for its support; competent powers.

The ingredients which constitute safety in the republican sense are, a due dependence on the people; a due responsibility.

Those politicians and statesmen, who have been the most celebrated for the soundness of their principles, and for the justness of their views, have declared in favor of a single executive, and a numerous legislature. They have, with great propriety, considered energy as the most necessary qualification of the former, and have regarded this as most applicable to power in a single hand; while they have, with equal propriety, considered the latter as best adapted to deliberation and wisdom, and best calculated to conciliate the confidence of the people, and to secure their privileges and interests.

That unity is conducive to energy will not be disputed. Decision, activity, secrecy, and dispatch, will generally characterize the proceedings of one man, in a much more eminent degree than the proceedings of any greater number; and in proportion as the number is increased, these qualities will be diminished.

This unity may be destroyed in two ways; either by vesting the power in two or more magistrates, of equal dignity and authority; or by vesting it ostensibly in one man, subject, in whole or in part, to the control and co-operation of others, in the capacity of counsellors to him. . . .

The experience of other nations will afford little instruction on this head. As far, however, as it teaches anything, it teaches us not to be enamoured of plurality in the executive. . . .

Wherever two or more persons are engaged in any common enterprise or pursuit, there is always danger of difference of opinion. If it be a public trust of office, in which they are clothed with equal dignity and authority, there is peculiar danger of personal emulation and even animosity. From either, and especially from all these causes, the most bitter dissentions are apt to spring. Whenever these happen, they lessen the respectability, weaken the authority, and distract the plans and operations of those whom they divide. If they should unfortunately assail the supreme executive magistracy of a country, consisting of a plurality of persons, they might impede or frustrate the most important measures of the government, in the most critical emergencies of the state. And what is still worse, they might split the community into violent and irreconcilable factions, adhering differently to the different individuals who composed the magistracy. . . .

Upon the principles of a free government, inconveniences . . . must necessarily be submitted to in the formation of the legislature; but it is unnecessary, and therefore unwise, to introduce them into the constitution of the executive. It is here, too, that they may be most pernicious. In the legislature, promptitude of decision is oftener an evil than a benefit. The differences of opinion, and the jarrings of parties in that department of the government, though they may sometimes obstruct salutary plans, yet often promote deliberation and circumspection; and serve to check excesses in the majority. When a resolution, too, is once taken, the opposition must be at an end. That resolution is a law, and resistance to it punishable. But no favorable circumstances palliate, or atone for the disadvantages of dissention in the executive department. Here they are pure and unmixed. There is no point at which they cease to operate. They serve to embarrass and weaken the execution of the plan or measure to which they relate, from the first step to the final conclusion of it. They constantly counteract those qualities in the executive, which are the most necessary ingredients in its composition—vigor and expedition; and this without any counterbalancing good. In the conduct of war, in which the energy of the executive is the bulwark of the national security, everything would be to be apprehended from its plurality.

It must be confessed, that these observations apply with principal weight to the first case supposed, that is, to a plurality of magistrates of equal dignity and authority, a scheme, the advocates for which are not likely to form a numerous sect; but they apply, though not with equal, yet with considerable weight, to the project of a council, whose concurrence is made constitutionally necessary to the operations of the ostensible executive. An artful cabal in that council would be able to distract and to enervate the whole system of administration. If no such cabal should exist, the mere diversity of views and opinions would alone be sufficient to tincture the exercise of the executive authority with the spirit of habitual feebleness and dilatoriness.

But one of the weightiest objections to a plurality in the executive, and which lies as much against the last as the first plan, is, that it tends to conceal faults, and destroy responsibility. . . . It often becomes impossible, amidst mutual accusations, to determine on whom the blame or the punishment of a pernicious measure . . . ought really to fall. it is shifted from one to another with so much dexterity, and under such plausible appearances, that the public opinion is left in suspense about the real author. . . .

A little consideration will satisfy us, that the species of security sought for in the multiplication of the executive, is unattainable. Numbers must be so great as to render combination difficult; or they are rather a source of danger than of security. The united credit and influence of several individuals must be more formidable to liberty than the credit and influence of either of them separately. When power, therefore, is placed in the hands of so small a number of men, as to admit of their interests and views being easily combined in a common enterprise, by an artful leader, it becomes more liable to abuse, and more dangerous when abused, than if it be lodged in the hands of one man; who, from the very circumstances of his being alone, will be more narrowly watched and more readily suspected, and who cannot unite so great a mass of influence as when he is associated with other. . . .

I will only add, that prior to the appearance of the constitution, I rarely met with an intelligent man from any of the states, who did not admit as the result of experience, that the unity of the executive of this state was one of the best of the distinguishing features of our constitution.

Thinking It Over

1. Review Hamilton's essay to see if you can discover the points at which the "separation of powers" principle is operative.

2. Construct the conceptual framework for an essay entitled "Hamilton's Presidency in the 1990s: What Remains?"

72.
THE IMPERIAL PRESIDENCY
by Arthur M. Schlesinger, Jr.

Setting the Scene: Arthur Schlesinger, a leading American historian, has also been very close to politics,; working on campaigns, and in the White House. *The Imperial Presidency* is a book about the abuse of political power. Schlesinger, who has written award-wining books about several strong Presidents (Andrew Jackson, Franklin Roosevelt, John Kennedy), knows his subject. The selection you will read is an excellent discussion of the parameters of the President's war making power, the Constitution and the intentions of the framers. Read this well and you will be sufficiently armed to engage 99.99 percent of all Americans on the subject of the President's role in war making—from the War of 1812 to Vietnam and the Persian Gulf.

. . . Congress received other weighty powers related to the conduct of foreign affairs: the power to make appropriations, to raise and maintain the armed forces and make rules for their government and regulation, to control naturalization and immigration, to impose tariffs, to define and punish offenses against the law of nations and, above all, "to declare War, grant Letters of Marque and Reprisal, and make Rules concerning Captures on Land and Water."

This last clause—in Article I, Section 9, of the Constitution—was of prime importance. The Founders were determined to deny the American President what Blackstone had assigned to the British King—"the sole prerogative of making war and peace."[1] Even Hamilton, the most consistent advocate of executive centralization, proposed in the Convention that the Senate "have the sole power of declaring war" with the executive to "have the direction of war when authorized or begun."[2]

In an early draft, the Constitution gave Congress the power to "make" war. Every scholar knows the successful intervention by Madison and Gerry—

Mr. MADISON and Mr. GERRY Moved to insert "*declare*," striking out "*make*" war; leaving to the Executive the power to repel sudden attacks.

—but no one really quite knows what this exchange meant. Among the delegates, Roger Sherman of Connecticut, for example, responded to Madison and Gerry by saying he thought the original language "stood very well" and that it already permitted the executive "to repel and not to commence war." On the other hand, George Mason of Virginia, after announcing that he was "agst. giving the power of war to the Executive, because not safely to be trusted

---

[1] E. S. Corwin, *The President: Office and Powers* (New York, 1940), 154.

[2] C. C. Tansill, ed., *Documents Illustrative of the Formation of the Union of the American States* (Washington, 1927), 224.

with it," then said he preferred "declare" to "make"; obviously he did not think he was thereby giving more power to the untrustworthy executive. Professor Lofgren, a most precise student of the episode, can distinguish at least four different interpretations of the Madison-Gerry amendment.[3]

What does seem clear is that no one wanted either to deny the President the power to respond to surprise attack or to give the President general power to initiate hostilities. The first aspect—the acknowledgment that Presidents must on occasion begin defensive war without recourse to Congress—represented the potential breach in the congressional position and would have the most significance in the future. But the second aspect gained the most attention and brought the most comfort at the time. James Wilson, next to Madison the most penetrating political thinker at the Convention, thus portrayed the constitutional solution: this system "will not hurry us into war; it is calculated to guard against it. It will not be in the power of a single man, or a single body of men, to involve us in such distress."[4]

The Founding Fathers did not have to give unconditional power to declare war to Congress. They might have said, in language they used elsewhere in the Constitution, that war could be declared by the President with the advice and consent of Congress, or by Congress on the recommendation of the President.[5] But they chose not to mention the President at all in connection with the war-making power. Nor was this because they lacked realism about the problems of national security. In a famous passage in the 23rd Federalist, Hamilton said that the powers of national self-defense must "exist without limitation, *because it is impossible to foresee or define the extent and variety of national exigencies. . . .* The circumstances that endanger the safety of nations are infinite, and for this reason no constitutional shackles can wisely be imposed on the power to which the care of it is committed. This power ought to be co-extensive with all the possible combinations of such circumstances." The Founding Fathers were determined that the national government should have all the authority required to defend the nation. But Hamilton was not asserting these unlimited powers for the Presidency, as careless commentators have assumed. He was asserting them for the national government *as a whole*—for, that is, Congress and the Presidency combined.

The resistance to giving a "single man," even if he were President of the United States, the unilateral authority to decide on war pervaded the contemporaneous literature. Hamilton's observations on the treaty-making power applied all the more forcibly to the war-making power: "The history of human conduct does not warrant that exalted opinion of human virtue which would make it wise to commit interests of so delicate and momentous a kind, as those which concern its intercourse with the rest of the world, to the sole disposal of a magistrate created and circumstanced as would be a President of the United States."[6] As Madison put it in a letter to Jefferson in 1798: "The constitution supposes, what the History of all Govts

---

[3]For the Madison-Gerry motion, see Tansill, ed., *Documents*, 562. The indispensable commentary is Charles A. Lofgren, "War-Making Under the Constitution: The Original Understanding," *Yale Law Review*, March 1972 (81 Yale L.J.), 672.

[4]Lofgren, "War-Making Under the Constitution," 685.

[5]Cf. James Grafton Rogers, *World Policing and the Constitution* (Boston, 1945), 21.

[6]75th Federalist.

demonstrates, that the Ex. is the branch of power most interested in war, & most prone to it. It has accordingly with studied care vested the question of war in the Legisl."[7]

At the same time, the Constitution vested the command of the Army and Navy in the President, which meant that, once Congress had authorized war, the President as Commander in Chief has full power to conduct military operations. "Of all the cares or concerns of government," said the Federalist, "the direction of war most peculiarly demands those qualities which distinguish the exercise of power by a single hand."[8] The designation of the President as Commander in Chief also sprang from a concern to assure civilian control of the military establishment. By making the Commander in Chief a civilian who would be subject to recall after four years, the Founders doubtless hoped to spare America tribulations of the sort that the unfettered command and consequent political power of a Duke of Marlborough had brought to England.

There is no evidence that anyone supposed that his office as Commander in Chief endowed the President with an independent source of authority. Even with Washington in prospect, the Founders emphasized their narrow and military definition of this presidential role. As Hamilton carefully explained in the 69th Federalist, the President's power as Commander in Chief

> would be nominally the same with that of the king of Great Britain, but in substance much inferior to it. It would amount to nothing more than the supreme command and direction of the military and naval forces . . . while that of the British king extends to the *declaring* of war and to the *raising* and *regulating* of fleets and armies,—all which, by the Constitution under consideration, would appertain to the legislature.

As Commander in Chief the President had not more authority than the first general of the army or the first admiral of the navy would have had as professional military men. The President's power as Commander in Chief, in short, was simply the power to issue orders to the armed forces within a framework established by Congress. And even Congress was denied the power to make appropriations for the support of the armed forces for a longer term than two years.

In addition to the command of the armed forces, the Constitution gave the President the power to receive foreign envoys and, with the advice and consent of the Senate, to appoint ambassadors as well as to make treaties. Beyond this, it had nothing specific to say about this authority in foreign affairs. However, Article II gave him general executive power; and, as the 64th and 75th Federalist Papers emphasized, the structural characteristics of the Presidency—unity, secrecy, decision, dispatch, superior sources of information—were deemed especially advantageous to the conduct of diplomacy.

The result was, as Madison said, "a partial mixture of powers." Madison indeed argued

---

[7]Madison to Jefferson, April 2, 1798, Madison, *Writings,* Gaillard Hunt, ed. (New York, 1906), VI, 312-13.
[8]73rd Federalist.

that such mingling was indispensable to the system, for unless the branches of government "be so far connected and blended as to give to each a constitutional control over the others, the degree of separation which the maxim requires, as essential to a free government, can never in practice be duly maintained." Particularly in the case of war and peace—the war-making and treaty-making powers—it was really a matter, in Hamilton's phrase, of "joint possession."[9]

In these areas the two branches had interwoven responsibilities and competing opportunities. Moreover, each had an undefined residuum of authority on which to draw—the President through the executive power and the constitutional injunction that "he shall take Care that the Laws be faithfully executed," Congress through the constitutional authorization "to make all Laws which shall be necessary and proper for carrying into Execution . . . all . . . Powers vested by this Constitution in the Government of the United States." In addition, the Constitution itself was silent on certain issues of import to the conduct of foreign affairs: among them, the recognition of foreign governments, the authority to proclaim neutrality, the role of executive agreements, the control of information essential to intelligent decision. The result, as Edward S. Corwin remarked 40 years ago, was to make of the Constitution "an invitation to struggle for the privilege of directing American foreign policy."[10]

One further consideration lingered behind the words of the Constitution and the debates of the Convention. This was the question of emergency. For the Founding Fathers were more influenced by Locke than by any other political philosopher; and, as students of Locke, they were well acquainted with Chapter 14, "Of Prerogative," in the *Second Treatise of Government*. Prerogative was the critical exception in Locke's rendition of the social contract. In general, the contract—the reciprocal obligation of ruler and ruled within the frame of law—was to prevail. In general, the authority of government was to be limited. But in emergency, Locke argued, responsible rulers could resort to exceptional power. Legislatures were too large, unwieldy and slow to cope with crisis; moreover, they were not able "to foresee, and so by laws to provide for, all accidents and necessities." Indeed, on occasion "a strict and rigid observation of the laws may do harm." This meant that there could be times when "the laws themselves should . . . give way to the executive power, or rather to this fundamental law of nature and government, viz., that, as much as may be, all the members of society are to be preserved."

Prerogative therefore was the exercise of the law of self-preservation. It was "the people's permitting their rulers to do several things of their own free choice, where the law was silent, and sometimes, too, against the direct letter of the law, for the public good, and their acquiescing in it when so done." The executive, Locke contended, must have the reserve power "to act according to discretion for the public good, without the prescription of law and sometimes even against it." If emergency prerogative were abused, the people would rebel; but, used for the good of the society, it would be accepted. "If there comes to be a

---

[9]The quotations are from the 47th, 48th and 75th Federalist Papers.
[10]Corwin, *President*, 200.

question between the executive power and the people about a thing claimed as prerogative, the tendency of the exercise of such prerogative to the good or hurt of the people will easily decide that question."[11]

Locke's argument, restated in more democratic terms, was that, when the executive perceived what he deemed an emergency, he could initiate extralegal or even illegal action, but that he would be sustained and vindicated in that action only if his perception of the emergency were shared by the legislature and by the people. Though prerogative enabled the executive to act on his individual finding of emergency, whether or not his finding was right and this was a true emergency was to be determined not by the executive but by the community.

The idea of prerogative was *not* part of presidential power as defined in the Constitution. The Founding Fathers had lived with emergency, but they made no provision in the Constitution, except in relation to *habeas corpus*, for the suspension of law in the case of necessity (and even here they did not specify whether the power of suspension belonged to the executive). The argument of the Federalist Papers, in the words of Clinton Rossiter, was in effect that the Constitution was "equal to any emergency."[12]

Yet there is reason to believe that the doctrine that crisis might require the executive to act outside the Constitution in order to save the Constitution remained in the back of their minds. Even in the Federalist Papers Hamilton wrote of "that original right of self-defence which is paramount to all positive forms of government" and Madison thought it "vain to oppose constitutional barriers to the impulse of self-preservation."[13] The First Congress, which included sixteen members of the Constitutional Convention and many more from state ratifying conventions, has been described as almost an adjourned session of the Convention. It was here that Congressman Alexander White, who himself had led the fight for ratification in western Virginia, argued that it would be better for the President "to extend his power on some extraordinary occasion, even where he is not strictly justified by the constitution, than [that] the Legislature should grant him an improper power to be exercised at all times." In other words, the legal order would be better preserved if departures from it were frankly identified as such than if they were anointed with a factitious legality and thereby enabled to serve as constitutional precedents for future action. The doctrine of emergency prerogative carried with it two corollaries: that the official who thus acted did so at his own peril; and that, having acted, he must report at once to Congress, which would serve as the judge of his action. "That this doctrine was accepted by every single one of our early statesmen," a careful scholar, Lucius Wilmerding, Jr., has written, "can easily be shown."[14]

I am not sure how easy this showing would be. Washington, for example, made clear in his Farewell Address his rejection of "change by usurpation; for though this, in one instance, may be the instrument of good, it is the customary weapon by which free governments are destroyed." But this did not quite meet the Lockean point, for the purpose

---

[11]John Locke, *Second Treatise of Government*, Ch. 14.
[12]Clinton Rossiter, *Constitutional Dictatorship* (Princeton, 1948), 212.
[13]28th and 41st Federalist Papers.
[14]Lucius Wilmerding, Jr., "The President and the Law," *Political Science Quarterly*, September 1952, 324, 338.

of prerogative was precisely not to establish precedents. Yet, however the Founding Fathers lined up on this question, one cannot suppose that Presidents steeped in Locke would have entirely dismissed the idea of action beyond the Constitution if necessary to save the life of the nation.

Thinking It Over

1. As this book goes to print (December, 1990) President Bush is playing chicken with Iraq in the Persian Gulf. I don't know what's going to happen. But you know what has. Write me a letter in which you tell me whether or not this reading helped you to understand what has happened.

2. Write the question for this reading you would have written if you were me and I knew then what you know now.

73.
THE TWILIGHT OF THE PRESIDENCY
by George E. Reedy

Setting the Scene: George Reedy was Press Secretary to President Lyndon Johnson during one of the toughest times there has ever been to hold that job—the Vietnam War. He wrote this book soon after. In the excerpt you will read here, one gets a chance to listen to a very knowledgeable person on how it really is to be President. Reedy is concerned with work load, information, the agony of responsibility and Presidential greatness. How lucky can we be? In effect, we get to ask: "If you could tell me, Mr. Reedy, in about four pages, the most important things I need to know about the day-to-day activities of the President, what would you say?"

One of the American people's most cherished notions about the presidency is that the office somehow ennobles the occupant and renders him fit to meet any crisis. This concept probably achieved its most articulate expression in a book and a movie, *Gabriel Over the White House* (now mercifully forgotten), which was the favorite reading and viewing of millions during the early days of the New Deal.

Those who hold this idea are fond of referring to Harry S. Truman and his unexpected rise (as they see it) from a small-town machine politician to a world statesman possessed of rare qualities of courage and high purpose. They are less fond, of course, of references to Warren G. Harding and Calvin Coolidge who left the presidency looking very little, if any, different than they did when they entered office.

It is a thesis of this book that the office neither elevates nor degrades a man. What it does is to provide a stage upon which all of his personality traits are magnified and accentuated. The aspects of his character which were not noted previously are not really new. They were merely hidden from view in lesser positions, where he was only one of many politicians competing for public attention. It is absurd to contend that Mr. Truman's great courage and patriotism—the most noteworthy of his attributes—came to him when he walked into the Oval Room. The truth—which would be borne out by all of his intimates—is that he always possessed such qualities. But who would notice them in a senator from Missouri—particularly a senator who cared little about the techniques of public relations?

A president is one of the few figures in political life who will not be regarded in terms of stereotypes. A senator who comes to Washington is very quickly put into the class of liberal, conservative, or moderate (the latter usually meaning nondescript). These terms are not truly descriptive of his political ideology but of the symbols which he uses. The stereotypes are useful because without them it would be difficult for the press to analyze events. But they have a tendency to obscure the man. Lyndon Johnson's espousal of civil rights and welfare legislation as president came as a surprise to many people simply because they had spent a number of years looking at a label rather than a person. And Dwight D.

Eisenhower's warning against the military-industrial complex seemed out of character simply because of the popular mythology that had portrayed him as a well-meaning but not overly bright general. Neither of the men actually changed when he entered the White House. Nobody had really looked at him before. . . .

Richard E. Neustadt has observed that expertise in presidential power "seems to be the province not of politicians as a class but of extraordinary politicians." The point is well taken and this writer suggests only a minor modification. The last few words should read "extraordinary *men* who have become politicians." This suggestion is put forward only because it is essential . . . to emphasize the crucial importance of personality to the success of a president.

Before plunging too deeply into the problem of the president and reality, it might be well to explore briefly what a president does—or at least what he should do. . . .

Despite the widespread belief to the contrary, however, there is far less to the presidency, in terms of essential activity, than meets the eye. The psychological burdens are heavy, even crushing, but no president ever died of overwork and it is doubtful whether any ever will. The chief executive can, of course, fill his working hours with as much motion as he desires. . . . He can delegate the "work" to subordinates and reserve for himself only the powers of decision as did Dwight D. Eisenhower or he can insist upon maintaining tight control over every minor detail, like Lyndon B. Johnson.

The concept of the president who works around the clock is deep in American mythology, however, and, with the exception of President Eisenhower, presidents have agreed that it must be maintained. Even in the case of President Eisenhower, his assistants thought they had to keep up appearances regardless of their chief's disdain for dissimulation. Jim Haggerty, his press secretary, was notorious for "saving up" official papers and announcements to release while the president was on vacation—thus preserving the illusion that it was a combination work-and-play holiday. . . .

The concept of the overburdened president represents one of the insidious forces which serve to separate the chief executive from the real universe of living, breathing, troubled human beings. It is the basis for encouraging his most outrageous expressions, for pampering his most childish tantrums, for fostering his most arrogant actions. More than anything else, it serves to create an environment in which no man can live for any considerable length of time and retain his psychological balance.

A president can be rude, insulting, and even downright sadistic to his closest advisers and their only response will be: "How fortunate that he has people around him who understand the tremendous burdens he is carrying." He can display the social manners of a Vandal sacking a Roman villa and his intimates will remark to each other: "We don't care about style. The only thing that is important is his deep feeling for the urban poor. Of course, he is somewhat crude but what does that matter?" He can elevate a mediocre sycophant to high position and members of his entourage will remark to each other: "You know, it is amazing how perceptive and socially conscious that young man is!"

The burdens would be lighter, the urban poor would be better served, and the young men might be more perceptive and socially conscious if presidents had to face the same minor social penalties that the rest of us do. An occasional "go soak your head" or "that's stupid" would clear the murky, turgid atmosphere of the White House and let in some health-giving fresh air.

This, however, is not a likelihood. A president moves through his days surrounded by literally hundreds of people whose relationship to him is that of a doting mother to a spoiled child. Whatever he wants is brought to him immediately—food, drink, helicopters, airplanes, people, in fact, everything but relief from his political problems. And the assistant who is unable to provide a requested service—no matter how unreasonable—automatically blames himself for his shortcomings rather than external circumstances. . . .

The presidential burden, of course, does not lie in the workload. It stems from the crushing responsibility of political decision, with life and death literally hanging in the balance for hundreds of millions of people. A president is haunted every walking hour of his life by the fear that he has taken the wrong turn, selected the wrong course, issued the wrong orders. In the realm of political decision he can turn to no one for *authoritative counsel*. Only *he* is authoritative. The situation was summed up by Harry S. Truman in the sign he kept on his desk, "The Buck Stops Here."

Every reflective human being eventually realizes that the heaviest burdens of his life are not the responsibilities he bears for himself but the responsibilities he bears for others. Where the load becomes too heavy, he can walk out easily if no one else is affected. The escape process becomes more difficult when his family is involved. And as the number of people dependent upon him increases, it becomes virtually impossible. The president's responsibilities literally embrace—either positively or negatively—every living person. There is no escape—no place to hide—not even for a moment.

Those who seek to lighten the burdens of the presidency by easing the workload do no occupant of that office a favor. The "workload"—and especially the ceremonial workload—are the only events of a president's day which make life endurable. They are the only occasions that give him an opportunity to concentrate his mental processes on problems which are amenable to technical solution—and thereby blot out of his consciousness the image of napalm exploding through the houses of an Asian village at his order; of hungry people walking the streets because he might have misused his fiscal authority; of angry opponents sharpening political knives in anticipation of revenge for a slight which he inflicted in a moment of irritation; of jeering cartoons and sneering slogans held aloft on giant placards by college youth alienated because he increased the draft quotas. *Work* is a blessed relief which comes all too rarely. . . .

The real misery of the average presidential day is the haunting sense that decisions have been made on incomplete information and inadequate counsel. Tragically, the information must *always* be incomplete and the counsel *always* inadequate, for the arena of human activity in which a president operates is one in which there are no quantitative answers. He must deal with those problems for which the computer offers no solution; those disputes where rights and wrongs are so inextricably mixed that the righting of every wrong creates a new wrong; those divisions which arise out of differences in human desires rather than differences in the available facts; those crisis moments in which action is so imperative that it cannot wait upon orderly consideration. He has no guideposts other than his own philosophy and his intuition, and if he is devoid of either, no one can substitute. Other people can tell him "what I would do if I were president." But those other people are *not* president. Try as they may, they cannot achieve that sense of personal identification with history which is the hallmark of the chief executive. Presidents are wont to explain those of their decisions which are incomprehensible to their contemporaries on the grounds that they have access to information not available in its entirety to other men. The inference is: "If you knew what I knew, you would understand why I did what I did." That a president has more comprehensive data available to him is true (or at least can be true if a president pays sufficient attention to his sources of information) but is actually irrelevant. On sweeping policy decision, which are, after all, relatively few, a president makes up his mind on the basis of the same *kind* of information that is available to the average citizen. When Franklin D. Roosevelt decided to commit this nation against the Axis powers he had little relevant information on the Nazis, the Fascists, and the Japanese warlords that was qualitatively different from that which could be gleaned from the *New York Times*. When Harry Truman decided to resist Communist aggression in Korea, he knew very little more than that the Forty-ninth Parallel had been crossed by Communist troops, a fact which was already in headlines. When Lyndon Johnson decided to send troops into the Dominican Republic, he had no information advantage over his fellow Americans other than a brief telephone conversation with his ambassador (although later reams of factual data were gathered to justify the action).

Of course, a president usually *knows* more about the situation than other people—not because he has more information but because it is his *business* to know and men usually pay attention to their business. He has the responsibility of making ultimate decisions which will be submitted to the harshest judgment possible—the judgment of history. This is the kind of prospect that tends to concentrate a man's mind wonderfully.

Moreover, the difference in the decision-making process between the president and his fellow Americans is not necessarily that he has taken better advantage of the available facts than they have but that he, and only he, must make the decision. As it is his business to *know*, it is his exclusive business to *decide*. This gives his thought processes a quality which no other person, not even his most trusted adviser, can have. His fellow Americans stand in the position of critics. They can "second guess"; they can be "Monday morning quarterbacks." Quite possibly they will have judgments demonstrably superior to those made by the president. But they do not have to say "yes" or "no" under the pressure of a deadline. They do not have to concern themselves about the prospect that history may damn them eternally. They do not have to take responsibility for action in the sure knowledge that the action will produce consequences which will demonstrate to the whole world that they were right or wrong. Neither do they have to offer leadership to diverse groups of people who are strong-willed and convinced of their own righteousness.

A president is many things. The demands of his office call upon him to be symbol of the nation, to be a teacher, to be a political organizer, to be a moral preceptor, to be an arbiter of taste. But what he must do, in order to earn his keep, can be boiled down to two simple fundamentals. He must resolve the policy questions that will not yield to quantitative, empirical analyses; and he must persuade enough of his countrymen of the rightness of his decisions so that he can carry them out without destroying the fabric of society. . . .

The difference between the great and the mediocre presidents probably centers on the individual ability of each one to grasp this point. The great presidents understood the White House as a focal point of power from which could flow the decisions that shaped the destiny of the nation. They realized that the day-to-day activities of a president were intended to bolster support for policies, to obtain the backing that could translate their intuitive judgment into meaningful action, and to deal with the conflicting forces that lie within our society in such a way that they could be reduced to common denominators and therefore to a degree of coherence. The mediocre presidents, on the other hand, have tended to regard the White House as a stage for the presentation of performances to the public or as a fitting honor to cap a career that was illustrious in some other field.

Thinking It Over

1. When the crisis in the Persian Gulf began and troops were sent, President Bush was heavily criticized for not interrupting his vacation in Maine. Ronald Reagan was often criticized as being "too detached," even lazy. How would Reedy respond to this?

2. To what extent did Reedy's analysis surprise you? Try to outline those notions you had about the Presidency that now need rethinking. Is there any pattern to these disjunctions?

74.
LINE-ITEM LOGIC
by Lawrence J. Haas

Setting the Scene: This is an article that relates to Presidential power, checks and balances and how the President makes decisions. The subject is the line-item veto. Currently the President must sign or veto an entire bill. He or she cannot veto parts of it. Congress, of course, likes it this way, and jealously guards against the President's encroaching on its power. In the debate over the Presidential veto, we have the quintessential case of an issue which can be debated rationally from either side. But any judgment on the question cannot be separated from partisan politics. Which party holds the White House and controls the Congress? So what else is new? We are, after all, studying politics.

"Let's help ensure our future of prosperity by giving the President a tool that—though I will not get to use it—is one I know future Presidents of either party must have," President Reagan told Congress in January 1988, in his last State of the Union message. "Give the President the same authority that 43 governors use in their states, the right to reach into massive appropriations bills, pare away the waste and enforce budget discipline. Let's approve the line-item veto."

To show how powerful this tool could be, Reagan said he would send Congress a list of items that, had he been given the chance, he would have struck from the $600 billion fiscal 1988 continuing resolution that had been enacted a month earlier. He proceeded to ask Congress to strike those items. "What an example we can set," the President said, "that we are serious about getting our financial accounts in order."

When the list arrived on Capitol Hill, however, it seemed almost a parody of Reagan's words. With Washington running annual deficits of about $15 billion, the 17 items that then-Office of Management and Budget (OMB) director James C. Miller III suggested should be struck added up to just $1.15 billion in 1988 outlays.

No, a line-item veto isn't going to solve America's fiscal problems, though some supporters say it could play a significant role. OMB's current deputy director, William M. Diefenderfer III, told the U.S. Chamber of Commerce recently: "Some say, 'Well, yeah, but you can only save three or four or five billion dollars a year by use of the line-item veto' . . . Where I come from and where I know all of you come from, three or four or five billion dollars a year is real money."

But the real issue here is power—that of the President in relation to Congress. Where you stand on the line-item veto or related measures depends a lot on what you think has happened to presidential power over the years. The line-item veto's supporters argue that for one reason or another, the President isn't as powerful in shaping fiscal policy as he once was. Critics of the proposal contend that the President is quite powerful, thank you, and should not be given extra authority that could upset the Constitution's delicate balance between the branches.

The line-item veto is not the only new power President Bush is seeking as a way to control spending. As part of the continuing budget summit between White House aides and congressional leaders, Bush's team is expected to propose altering the budget process to try to prevent any tax hikes he might accept from being diverted from deficit cutting to new spending. . . .

As OMB director Richard G. Darman said . . . on ABC's *This week With David Brinkley,* "If we don't get significant budget process reform, there's no doubt that the money would be spent and it wouldn't reduce the deficit, which is why we shouldn't consider a tax increase independently of major budget process reform."

A Bigger Bully Pulpit

The Bush Administration engaged itself in the debate over presidential power soon after taking office. Darman told the Senate Governmental Affairs Committee in early 1989 why a new President these days needs to avoid important losses in his battles with Congress: "The presidency is a much, much weaker institution than I think most people assume it is, and I think if you start an Administration with a highly visible, highly advertised loss, you permanently weaken that presidency for whatever else it might do."

Many historians scoff at this view. "Increasingly, the question of whether the President is or isn't strong enough has become a polemical issue," said Fred I. Greenstein, a scholar of the presidency at Princeton University. When a Republican occupies the White House, supporters complain about the encumbrances placed upon him, particularly by a Democratic-controlled Congress. It's no coincidence, Greenstein and others say, that the conservative American Enterprise Institute for Public Policy Research (AEI) last year published *The Fettered Presidency*, a set of essays about such constraints.

"There's also an awful lot of 'Whose ox is gored?' in this equation," said Stephen Hess, a senior fellow at the Brookings Institution. "This whole thing is a teeter-totter. When somebody is up, somebody is going to be down. And the system still works that way, although the swings have been long enough that most of us with a short memory forget that there is this fulcrum at work. So the folks who are talking about giving the President extra power are almost the children of those who were worried about the President having too much power. . . .

In the grand sweep of history, the presidency does not seem weakened in the area of fiscal policy. Before 1921, the President did not even propose his own budget; instead, executive agencies sent separate requests to the relevant congressional committees.

Even during the New Deal, the federal budget equaled barely 10 per cent of the gross national product, compared with more than 20 per cent since the late 1970s. In a sense, when it comes to shaping the economy through fiscal policy, the President and Congress are both stronger than they used to be.

Whether in more recent years legal and other types of changes have tied the President's hands a bit is more debatable. Unquestionably, the 1974 Congressional Budget and

Impoundment Control Act was important in establishing Congress as a competing force on fiscal policy. For one thing, it created the Budget Committees and, through them, the process by which Congress adopts a budget resolution. Until that point, Congress had no mechanism for making over-all decisions about fiscal policy. Nor could it offer a single, comprehensive alternative to the President's budget.

For another, the 1974 law institutionalized the concept of a "current services" baseline. Since then, instead of just comparing its tax and spending decisions with presidential proposals, as it had traditionally done, Congress has downgraded the President's budget by comparing legislative decisions with a new measurement that factors in inflation, past budget authority and other variables. . . .

Historically, the push to increase presidential power to control spending is a familiar struggle. President Grant requested a line-item veto in 1873, and lawmakers have proposed it from time to time since. The idea has grown more visible since Reagan began his highly public campaign for it in 1984.

This more recent push seems to derive from two sources: widespread exasperation over the stubborn budget deficit and complaints about an omnipotent Congress.

The deficit, many argue, might be much smaller if the President had enhanced rescission power. "I strongly suspect that were we to pass this legislation, most of the unnecessary pork projects would not even make it to the President's desk," said Coats, whose proposal for enhanced rescission power attracted 40 votes in a test floor vote in November. "It would impose a lot more initial restraint on Members." If the President could force Members to vote on his rescission requests, Coats and others believe, he could publicly embarrass the sponsors of "pork."

That is debatable, given the experience of the 43 states whose governors have line-item power. "The history of item vetoes at the state level reveals that legislatures are willing to appropriate excessive funds to please their constituents and place the onus of deficit reduction on the governor," constitutional scholars Louis Fisher and Neal Devins wrote in the *Georgetown Law Journal* in 1986.

Former OMB chief Miller, who has studied the states' experience with line-item vetoes, suggested that a particularly effective form of the tool is one that allows governors to reduce but not eliminate the amount of money allocated for an account. "We found that these arrangements had a tremendous effect," Miller said, citing recent work by himself and George Mason University economist W. Mark Crane.

But the experiences of states may not be relevant. In the states there has been a stronger tradition of resistance to legislatures than there has been in Washington, according to scholars, and governors have been viewed as the citizens' bulwark against irresponsible state legislators.

How a line-item veto might work at the federal level is anyone's guess. Gradison [Rep. William D. Gradison Jr., R-Ohio] has raised concern that it would prompt Congress to pack appropriations bills with even more pork—and leave it to the President to line-item it out—and that it would encourage creation of more entitlements—spending not subject to annual appropriations—that might be out of the reach of the veto power. Perhaps anticipating that step, Bush's 1991 budget argues that a line-item veto should be applicable to entitlements.

But the most important questions seem to be governmental, not fiscal. One of the Constitutions' hallmarks is the delicate system of checks and balances between the three branches. That a line-item veto would shift power to the executive is disputed by few on either side of the debate. The only question is whether it is a good idea.

Those who favor it tend to complain about congressional practices that, they say, have effectively disenfranchised the executive from fiscal decision making. Their pet peeve is the omnibus spending bill, a package containing as many as 13 appropriations bills that Congress sometimes sends to the President at the end of the session.

Under these circumstances, supporters of a line-item veto have maintained, the President has little choice but to sign the bill. In the AEI's *The Fettered Presidency*, political scientist Judith A. Best wrote: "In presenting the President with last-minute omnibus appropriations bills, Congress is playing the deadly game of chicken; it risks a governmental crisis because it has good reason to believe the President will capitulate. . . . The President is more visible, more conspicuous and thus will appear more culpable when the checks to not go out and the government offices do not open."

True enough. But omnibus spending bills have been around longer than the Republic itself. As Rep. Edwards wrote in "Of Conservatives and Kings," an article for *Policy Review* early last year, "both omnibus appropriations and non-germane riders were common nearly 300 years ago and were well-known to the Founding Fathers." So it is hard to argue that the presidency is somehow weaker today because of them.

Besides, lawmakers and others wonder why the President does not play his own game of chicken. If, for instance, he warned beforehand that he would not accept such an omnibus measure, then his veto of it might shift blame to Congress. "Even though Congress has made it hard for the President, why not [do it]?" asked Rep. Richard K. Armey, R-Texas, who serves on the Budget Committee. . . .

Conservative Split

Reagan's call for the line-item veto highlights a deep-seated split within conservative ranks. On one side are lawmakers, such as retiring Sen. Gordon J. Humphrey, R-N.H., who appear frustrated that a Republican President can't get his way with a Democratic-controlled Congress and say that they must strengthen his tools.

On the other side are those who take a more institutional approach. Edwards, Gradison and others argue that true conservatives should oppose a line-item veto and espouse the prerogatives of a strong legislature against the encroachments of the executive. To do otherwise, they say, is to threaten the uniquely American system that assures individual liberty.

Edwards wrote in *Policy Review*: "We as conservatives, at least in my formative years, opposed the centralization of government. We were diffusionists. We believed our freedoms were best protected if power was not centralized."

Although the line-item veto and enhanced rescission are both aimed at pork, the former is considered more dangerous to the balance of powers than the latter. Congress would need two-thirds of both chambers to overturn a line-item veto; thus, by holding merely a third of one chamber, a President could thwart the will of most Members. An enhanced rescission could be rejected by a majority vote in both chambers.

Where the danger arises, critics of the line-item veto say, is with the President's leverage over individual lawmakers. With the threat of striking funds for Members' pet projects—and making his line-item veto stick—he could entice them into voting for other things he wants, such as foreign aid, in exchange for presidential acquiescence in the pork.

Democrats, of course, might have more to fear from a Republican President; his priorities would be more likely to clash with theirs, and so, he might use the threat of a line-item veto more frequently. It is no surprise, then, that the line-item veto is currently more popular among Republicans than Democrats.

But critics accuse the GOP of myopia. After all, giving the line-item veto to this President would extend it to future ones. Some even might be Democrats. With a Democratic President, Republicans might regret their earlier support for a line-item veto.

"The real head-scratcher in this is that the Republicans must believe that no Democrat will ever be elected President, or that no President will stray from the conservative fold," said John C. Dill, a top aide in the early 1980s to Rep. James R. Jones, D-Okla., when Jones chaired the Budget committee.

Why Bush really wants more fiscal power at a time of high deficits baffles more than a few observers. In a sense, the budget process in its current form is quite convenient for him.

Here's why. After the President sends his budget to Congress, usually in January, attention turns to Capitol Hill. The President has no legislative responsibility over the budget resolution, or over the resulting tax and spending measures, until they reach his desk. As a result, he can blame Congress for the annual fiscal havoc with some justification, simply by pointing out that he had little to do with it. This was one of Reagan's time-honored tactics, and Bush has occasionally adopted it for his own use.

"For the last decade, we seem to have appealed to institutional weaknesses rather than institutional strengths," scholar Fisher, a senior specialist with the Congressional Research Service, told the House Rules Committee in March. "By looking to Congress for comprehensive action, we unwittingly weakened the unity and leadership that must come from the President."

It is no coincidence, Fisher said, that Bush gave Darman so much freedom to negotiate a fiscal 1990 budget agreement with Congress last year; he didn't want to soil his hands. Nor, others have noted, is it coincidental that Bush's message that accompanied his 1991 budget took up just 1 page, whereas Darman's essay in the same document consisted of 15. . . .

If the current arrangement is really so convenient, the White House could be leading itself into an uncomfortable position, particularly if this year's budget summit does not solve the deficit problem. With a victory on any of the budget process changes that he's pushing, Bush could find himself with a bit more power to cut spending—and a lot more public blame for the problem.

Thinking It Over

1. The assumption is that the President's position vis-à-vis Congress would be immensely strengthened had she or he the power to line-item veto. But is that necessarily so? (Hint: Read David Stockman's remarks in this book and ask the question, what if Reagan could have cut the appropriations bill as he saw fit by using the line-item veto? He still would have had a deficit and he no longer could have blamed it on Congress.)

2. What are the odds that the Congress will ever give the President a line-item veto?

75.
THE PLOT THAT FAILED:
NIXON & THE ADMINISTRATIVE PRESIDENCY
by Richard P. Nathan

Setting the Scene: Richard Nathan's book manages to be both insightful and exciting at the same time. What he does is confront a very important question for governance in America: Should the President be given more power to control the bureaucracy? It is vastly ironic to note, for instance, that only two years after Nixon resigned because of the mess (Watergate) he got into trying to control the bureaucracy, Jimmy Carter was elected primarily by telling the American people he was going to make government more accountable. Nathan suggests that what Nixon was trying to do—govern through his own staff officers, ignoring cabinet officers, and the Congress—might have worked and even been applauded had Nixon appointed better people and if Nixon, himself, had stood on higher moral ground. This reading deals with the Presidency as it relates to the Congress on the one hand and to the bureaucracy on the other. President Harry Truman had a sign on his desk that said "The Buck Stops Here." The plot that failed may have failed because the buck got lost and no one even tried to find it.

At the outset of his presidency, Richard Nixon, with little real experience as an executive in government, operated in much the same fashion as his two Democratic predecessors, whose party, it must be remembered, controlled both the Executive Branch and the Congress. Like Kennedy and Johnson, Nixon in 1969 emphasized the development of legislation that would put his unique stamp on domestic policy. White House working groups, very similar to LBJ's perpetual task forces on domestic policy, were set up to develop legislative initiatives in a wide range of field—welfare, revenue sharing, education, health, urban affairs, the environment, and labor-management relations. This was true under Daniel Patrick Moynihan, during the period in which he served as executive director of the Urban Affairs Council, as well as under Dr. Arthur F. Burns, who served in the first year as a Counselor to the President for domestic affairs. It was also true under John Ehrlichman as he increasingly came to the forefront for domestic affairs beginning in the summer of 1969.

On the other hand, the heads of the major domestic agencies in the beginning of the Nixon Administration had been selected in the conventional manner to be representative of a broad range of viewpoints as well as different professions and geographical areas. With the exception of Robert H. Finch at Health, Education, and Welfare and John N. Mitchell at Justice, Nixon's domestic Cabinet choices were not men close to him. George W. Romney, Secretary of Housing and Urban Development and former governor of Michigan, had been his principal primary opponent for the Republican nomination in 1968. Two other domestic Cabinet members were also former governors—John A. Volpe of Massachusetts, Secretary of Transportation, and Walter J. Hickel of Alaska, Secretary of the Interior. In the tradition of American Cabinet-making, all three former governors (Romney, Volpe, and Hickel) were men with independent national reputations. Nixon is reported not even to have met George P. Schultz, his first Secretary of Labor, or Clifford M. Hardin, Secretary of Agriculture, until after the election in 1968.

Only Mitchell in the original domestic Cabinet had strong influence, in the White House policymaking arena during the early period when the Administration's legislative program was being shaped. From the very beginning, he chaired all meetings involving civil rights and other domestic issues coming under the umbrella of the Justice Department and talked personally to the President about legislative recommendations that should be made in these areas. Shultz's influence grew in this period and Finch's diminished. But, with the exception of Mitchell, members of the Cabinet for domestic affairs were called in on an "as-needed" basis and often were not present when critical decisions were made about the legislative proposals they would have to champion in the Congress.

A good illustrative of this standard operating procedure concerned the preparation of the 1971 State of the Union message, which was devoted almost entirely to domestic affairs. It was in this message that the President first revealed his $16 billion revenue-sharing program for fiscal year 1972. The program consisted of what was called "general revenue sharing" (that is, it could be used for basically any purpose and had previously been proposed) and $11 billion for six new "special revenue-sharing" measures. The latter consisted of groups of existing grants pulled together into a single and comprehensive grant for broad functional areas—education, law enforcement, manpower, transportation, and rural and urban development. Taken together, these special revenue-sharing proposals involved many controversial changes in domestic policy. For this reason, it was decided by Ehrlichman (and his predecessors under Kennedy and Johnson undoubtedly would have operated in the same way) to have these bills drafted secretly by the White House staff and the Office of Management and Budget. It was not until the day before the 1971 State of the Union message was to be delivered that the Cabinet officers who would have to carry the freight on special revenue sharing were called in individually and briefed. They were instructed not to tell any of their staff what was being done until after the message had been transmitted. Three of the four Cabinet members involved took the news calmly. After all, it was not out of the ordinary for the White House to control so closely the development of new legislative proposals. The fourth, George Romney, was furious. He took the occasion to lambast White House arrogance in dealings with members of the Cabinet. Citing similar events, his anger was not to be allayed until he had enumerated his grievances and eventually calmed down. When he did, he took his marching orders like the others and was cooperative. In fact, Romney became one of the strongest advocates of special revenue sharing (in his case for urban affairs) because this proposal in so many ways fitted in with his ideas about urban programs.

The Strategy Shifts

Contrasting sharply to the development of new legislation, the relationship between the domestic Cabinet and the White House was the other way around in the management area.

In 1969 and 1970, primarily because of the strong White House emphasis on new legislation, administrative matters were relegated to a quite secondary position. The domestic secretaries essentially were allowed to go their own way in selecting their top program officials, supervising their work, and handling other administrative task.

However, as time passed, this convention approach, which emphasized new legislation with relatively little attention being given to managerial matters was found to have its distinct disadvantages. This was especially true for a Republican president facing a Democratic Congress and presenting the type of an agenda for domestic reform that was then emerging. With the exception of general revenue sharing, few of the President's domestic initiatives succeeded. Some were completely disregarded by the Congress. Gradually the strategy shifted . . . More attention was paid to opportunities to achieve policy aims through administrative action as opposed to legislative change, the former to be accomplished by taking advantage of the wide discretion available to federal officials under many existing laws.

The events involved in this shift from a legislative to a managerial strategy [meant that] . . . by the end of the first term, a completely new view of domestic government had been developed by Nixon and his principal aides. Instead of the traditional legislative strategy, plans were made to adopt a fundamentally different approach for the second term. The legislative agenda was to be sharply pared down. With general revenue sharing enacted, the new order of march, in short, was to *takeover* the bureaucracy and *take on* the Congress, to concentrate on administrative steps and correspondingly to downgrade legislation as the principal route for bringing about domestic policy change. No longer would the Cabinet be composed of men with national standing in their own right who were in a position to go their own way and were disposed by past experience to do so. Unprecedented changes were to be made in the designation (and removal) of appointed officials and in the assignment of their duties. The President's men—trusted lieutenants, tied closely to Richard Nixon and without national reputations of their own—were to be placed in direct charge of the major program bureaucracies of domestic government for the second term. This approach, the "Administrative Presidency" strategy, is new to the modern period. its significance needs to be carefully weighed. Why was it adopted? Is it proper for the president to assume the role of manager of the executive establishment for domestic affairs? And most important, what are the implications for the federal bureaucracy?

The American Federal Bureaucracy

The federal bureaucracy as we know it today, composed of civil servants appointed on the basis of various tests of merit, dates from 1883. The passage of the Pendleton act in that year came within months after President Garfield's assassination by a disappointed office seeker, a violent act that nonetheless gave needed impetus to the 30-year drive for civil service reform, one of the great issues of American government . . .The Pendleton Act . . . marked the transition from the wild, unbridled spoils system of public service to the orderly, unpolitical and infinitely more efficient merit system."[1]

The philosophy of the merit system is grounded in the idea that it is necessary to distinguish between making policy (the job of the politician) and carrying it out (the role of the professional). According to this theory, the president and the Congress decide on the laws and major policies of government, and then professional administrators immune from political pressures and favoritism carry them out. It is this seemingly straightforward distinction between policy and administration on which the civil service reformers based their case. But this distinction between making policies and carrying them out is by no means so simple and clear-cut. No two situations are the same. The line between policy and administration in government is a wavy, constantly shifting boundary that depends on many factors: the newness of the issue involved, its cost, and its relationship to an administration's major purposes for change. different individuals will regard the same conditions differently. What one civil servant views as a policy matter and refers to his presidentially appointed superior, another may define as a ministerial matter and decide himself.

By deploying his appointees as *politician-managers* in line positions, President Nixon, through his Administrative-Presidency strategy for the second term, was trying to move the line between policy and administration in government. Such a change is by no means an easy or small matter. Richard Neustadt has written that the power of the President is the "power to persuade . . . to bargain."[2] Others who have examined the administrative role of the American presidency have similarly called attention to the significant limits on presidential power or what Neustadt, again, describes as the "illusion that administrative agencies comprise a single structure."[3]

. . .

Against this background, the role of the White House and other Executive Office staffs began to change at the end of Nixon's first year in office. Contrary to the original plans, both groups were enlarged and their powers expanded over the next two years. By the end of the third year, the Executive Office staff—instead of contracting—had doubled in cost from the Johnson years. The White House staff itself, along with "borrowed" agency personnel, occupied almost all of the space in the six-floor Executive Office Building next to the White House. The Bureau of the Budget (renamed the Office of Management and Budget in July 1970) was displaced to new quarters across Pennsylvania Avenue. One account in 1972 noted ironically that President Nixon, "distrustful of bureaucracy . . . has built a kind of defense against it—and in doing so he has built his own bureaucracy."[4]

But even more than the increase in numbers, the important changes were in style. Under Ehrlichman as executive director of the Domestic Council, the new technique of the White

---

[1]U. S. Civil Service Commission, *Biography of an Ideal, The Diamond Anniversary History of the Federal Civil Service*, January 13, 1958, p. 3.

[2]Richard E. Neustadt, *Presidential Power*, John Wiley, 1960, Chapter 3.

[3]Ibid., p. 47.

[4]*U.S. News and World Report*, April 24, 1972, p. 72.

House "working group" was adopted. The first working group was assigned to develop the President's welfare-reform program. Headed by one of Ehrlichman's lieutenants, Edward L. Morgan, Jr., it included representation from Labor, HEW, Budget, Moynihan's staff, and that of Counsellor to the President, Dr. Arthur F. Burns, with less regular participation from the Office of Economic Opportunity, the Department of Agriculture, and the Council of Economic Advisors.

The welfare working group met five to six hours a day every day over a period of 10 weeks. Direct relationships were established between White House staff and agency officials well below the level of the Secretary. Only the most astute Cabinet member could keep on top of this policy process. The typical decision pattern was one of consensus-building within the working group, with the lead and arbitrating role assigned to Ehrlichman, or in the case of welfare, to Morgan as his deputy. If a member of a working group could not win his point by effective argument, he had to go back and persuade his secretary to become personally involved. But even then, the Cabinet officer found himself in the difficult position of having to argue on an often detailed and intricate matter of policy where most of the others involved in the decision process were already committed to, and knowledgeable about, a contrary position. It was no wonder that the intervention of Cabinet members in this period became less frequent.

An example of how this process could be frustrating to Cabinet secretaries occurred in the case of welfare. Several times, the welfare working group made a decision to pay cash instead of giving food stamps to needy persons eligible for Family Assistance benefits. Each time this decision surfaced in public, Agriculture Secretary Hardin angrily called the White House demanding to know why he had not been consulted. When it was explained that his representative, an assistant secretary, had been present on the working group, he complained that this was the wrong man and that he should have been told directly . . .

Working groups were relied on increasingly in 1969 and 1970 as the President's domestic program was being formed. Besides welfare, they covered emergency labor disputes, model cities, urban-growth policy, health, revenue sharing, education, social services, and transportation. Many of these groups did good work, and it can be argued that their role in major policy formulation across agency lines was a fully appropriate one. Nevertheless, the position of the Cabinet officers and the structure of White House decision making were changing . . .

John Ehrlichman explained the rationale for the working-group approach in one of his few public statements on the subject in November 1970. He argued that the White House should draw directly on the experts who know best the substance of matters under review.

"Now, some time ago, we sent out a request that we be furnished with the names of the people in the departments and agencies who actually did the work on the documents that come over. We found that everything was signed by the Secretary, and it didn't do much good to call the Secretary, and say: Say, about that paper, you sent over here on so-and-so. As you know very well when somebody has a working knowledge of the document, we want those names because we want to be able to get those people over here to sit down with the President and answer his questions"[5] . . .

Supposedly care was taken in this period to limit the use of the working-group approach to issues that had what Ehrlichman called "a multi-dimensional character," leaving to the individual Cabinet secretary those "strictly within the scope of his authority."[6] But in the field of domestic policy, with its multiplicity of activities and a high degree of overlap among agency and program jurisdictions, opportunities for White House involvement even under this definition are multiple and far-ranging.

Along with the working-group method, as the White House staff grew the natural tendency was for new staff members to become involved at lower levels in the agencies. Increasingly, Domestic Council staff and that of the Office of Management and Budget, with its new policy responsibilities, took on an oversight role for existing programs on routine legislative matters as well as for many purely administrative decisions. White House clearance was required on more and more issues and became harder to obtain. On occasion Cabinet members were completely left out of White Hose deliberations, as with special revenue sharing in 1971, until plans were fully formed. Then, their role in the inner councils of the Administration was cast as that of critics of planned new directions, defenders of the *status-quo*. Access to the President became difficult to obtain and less frequent, with Cabinet members known to briddle hard and complain about the White House running their affairs.

The effects of these changes were predictable. When a junior White House staffer calls a career expert in an agency, the relationship that they develop offers wide latitude for agency personnel to develop their own lines into the White House. This only adds to the problem of isolating the Cabinet secretary. Such relationships reinforce the tendency for the secretary and his close associates to draw up ranks and act on the bases of *we* versus *they*—they being the President's staff. the bigger the White House establishment, the harder it is to avoid the classical adversarial relationship from taking hold and becoming dominant. As the counter-bureaucracy of the executive office grew and prospered, President Nixon's early concept of a strong, independent role for his Cabinet officers increasingly was undermined, *and deliberately so* . . .

. . .

As it happened, the issues raised by the Administrative Presidency were not resolved in terms of democratic theory or the ideas of public-administration experts and political scientists; and they probably would not have been under any conditions. Nevertheless, Watergate adds a dimension that may very well weaken the institution of the presidency permanently . . .

Hence, the question of the Administrative Presidency is in real terms subtly changed. It is not so much, as it might have been, a question or who had the most political, legal, and theoretical support for a particular interpretation of constitutional powers. For we cannot look

---

[5] Federal Executive Institute, U.S. Civil Service Commission, *The Challenges of Leadership for American Federal Executive*, Charlottesville, Va, November 1970.
[6] Ibid.

at the Administrative Presidency without also looking at the more basic question: Do we want to change the presidency because of Mr. Nixon's conduct of office? And here we have a dilemma that cannot be resolved easily. On the one hand, traditional public-administration theory says that the president and his Cabinet should exercise effective managerial control and there should be institutional machinery at the center of government to help him make and clearly explain the hard choices of modern government. On the other, the behavior of Mr. Nixon and the men around him is a cause of concern indicating to many that in our political system too strong a presidency can lead to abuses.

Clearly Richard Nixon erred fatally in the area of political activities by surrounding himself with unprincipled men, lacking a sufficiently strong commitment to public service. The American presidency cannot operate under such conditions; the temptations are too great. One can only speculate what would have happened if other men, for example, Melvin R. Laird or Elliot L. Richardson (both independent men with experience in elective politics), had been at the fateful meetings on Watergate.

The Administrative Presidency—A Riddle

The Administrative Presidency is a riddle. Arthur M. Schlesinger's concept of "the Imperial Presidency" (an idea almost entirely framed in relation to foreign policy) would have us conclude against such a strategy. Yet FDR sought similar goals, and many students of the presidency credit him for doing so. In the present day, there are good arguments to the effect that we need a force to counter entrenched domestic-program bureaucracies and interest groups—organizations adept at protecting and expanding their turf. Theodore J. Lowi in *The End of Liberalism* warned against just such conditions of power flowing to centers of technical expertise, not subject in any real terms to the give-and-take of democratic political processes.[7]

Many scholars on the presidency and in fields of domestic policy will find this riddle easy to solve. For a long time the majority of academics have disliked Nixon. yet there was a time after his trip to China and before Watergate when even this group wavered. The proposition is a serious one: If there had been no Watergate and assuming that Richard Nixon had adhered to higher campaign and personnel standards, are there not serious reasons for concluding that—from his point of view and for his purposes—he was right about the Administrative Presidency?

The essential question comes down to whether we need to have more and stronger checks and balances within the Executive Branch. Nixon's notion that the only way to take on the bureaucracy is to assemble like-minded men and women committed above all to his program raises the same questions regarding political behavior as Watergate. Like-minded men, devoted fully to the president, in the case of Watergate and the White House "plumbers," developed a warped and unbalanced perspective where excesses reinforced and fed on each other. The result was catastrophic for Nixon and for the country. Would this same behavior

---

[7]Theodore J. Lowi, *The End of Liberalism*, W. W. Norton, New York, 1969.

have occurred in the area of domestic policy if the Administrative Presidency had been played out with no Watergate? Would the orientation and views of Mr. Nixon's trusted lieutenant's for domestic affairs, each tied by his reputation and record almost solely to Richard Nixon, have caused men to yield to the same temptations to put ends over means? Or, alternatively, would our traditions of public service have been sufficient in these substantive areas of policy to assure responsible conduct? The decision on these questions can only be a personal one.

This question of whether the Administrative Presidency could have succeeded in the absence of Watergate may never be answered. For Watergate has had a deep impact on political morality in the United States. Post-Watergate, with a new awareness of the need for higher ethical standards in political life, it is possible that a president with a coherent program could organize his administration to navigate a course similar to Nixon's plan for an Administrative Presidency, while also adhering to sufficiently high standards of public service and personal conduct. Yet . . . it is likely that its aftertaste [of Watergate] will discourage an American president from soon again attempting this kind of domestic strategy. . . . Hence, if the Nixon-Ehrlichman diagnosis is correct that many domestic bureaucracies have acquired too much power, the solution in terms of presidential strategy may now be very hard to implement.

Thinking It Over

1. What was the plot? Why did it fail?

2. What was the shift in strategy that Nixon used as his first term drew to a close?

76.
THE PRESIDENTIAL CHARACTER
by James David Barber

Setting the Scene: Judging Presidents is a favorite pastime of scholars. Our purpose here, however, is to consider how one *ought* to judge Presidents. What are the indicators that separate one from the other? James David Barber is the author of the most popular typology used to measure Presidents. The key to understanding Presidents, he says, is understanding a pattern of behavior that reflects their character, world view, and style. Add to these concepts the situation in which they find themselves and the "climate of expectations" that prevails and you can go a long way in predicting their behavior. Follow Barber now as he briefly explains these concepts, develops a four-part typology from them and then shows how it works when matched against a series of Presidents.

I am not about to argue that once you know a President's personality you know everything. But as the cases will demonstrate, the degree and quality of a President's emotional involvement in an issue are powerful influences on how he defines the issue itself, how much attention he pays to it, which facts and persons he sees as relevant to its resolution, and, finally, what principles and purposes he associates with the issue. Every story of Presidential decision-making is really two stories: an outer one in which a rational man calculates and an inner one in which an emotional man feels. The two are forever connected. Any real President is one whole man and his deeds reflect his wholeness.

As for personality, it is a matter of tendencies. It is not that one President "has" some basic characteristics that another President does not "have." That old way of treating a trait as a possession, like a rock in a basket, ignores the universality of aggressiveness, compliancy, detachment, and other human drives. We all have all of them, but in different amounts and in different combinations.

The Pattern of Character, World View, and Style

The most visible part of the pattern is style. *Style is the President's habitual way of performing his three political roles: rhetoric, personal relations, and homework.* Not to be confused with "stylishness," charisma, or appearance, style is how the President goes about doing what the office requires him to do—to speak, directly or through media, to large audiences; to deal face to face with other politicians, individually and in small, relatively private groups; and to read, write, and calculate by himself in order to manage the endless flow of details that stream onto his desk. No President can escape doing at least some of each. But there are marked differences in stylistic emphasis from President to President. The *balance* among the three style elements varies; one President may put most of himself into rhetoric, another may stress close, informal dealing, while still another may devote his energies mainly to study and cogitation. Beyond the balance, we want to see each President's peculiar habits of style, his mode of coping with and adapting to these Presidential demands. For example, I think both Calvin Coolidge and John F. Kennedy were primarily rhetoricians, but they went about it in contrasting ways.

A President's *world view consists of his primary, politically relevant beliefs, particularly his conceptions of social causality, human nature, and the central moral conflicts of the time.* This is how he sees the world and his lasting opinions about what he sees. Style is his way of acting; world view is his way of seeing. Like the rest of us, a President develops over a lifetime certain conceptions of reality—how things work in politics, what people are like, what the main purposes are. These assumptions or conceptions help him make sense of his world, give some semblance or order to the chaos of existence. Perhaps most important: a man's world view affects what he pays attention to, and a great deal of politics is about paying attention. The name of the game for many politicians is not so much "Do this, do that" as it is "Look here!"

"Character comes from the Greek word for engraving; in one sense it is what life has marked into a man's being. As used here, *character is the way the President orients himself toward life*—not for the moment, but enduringly. Character is the person's stance as he confronts experience. And at the core of character, a man confronts himself. The President's fundamental self-esteem is his prime personal resource; to defend and advance that, he will sacrifice much else he values. Down there in the privacy of his heart, does he find himself superb, or ordinary, or debased, or in some intermediate range? No President has been utterly paralyzed by self-doubt and none has been utterly free of midnight self-mockery. In between, the real Presidents move out on life from positions of relative strength or weakness. Equally important are the criteria by which they judge themselves. A President who rates himself by the standard of achievement, for instance, may be little affected by losses of affection.

Character, world view, and style are abstractions from the reality of the whole individual. In every case they form an integrated pattern: the man develops a combination which makes psychological sense for him, a dynamic arrangement of motives, beliefs, and habits in the service of his need for self-esteem.

The Power Situation and "Climate of Expectations"

Presidential character resonates with the political situation the President faces. It adapts him as he tries to adapt it. The support he has from the public and interest groups, the party balance in Congress, the thrust of Supreme Court opinion together set the basic power situation he must deal with. An activist President may run smack into a brick wall of resistance, then pull back and wait for a better moment. On the other hand, a President who sees himself as a quiet caretaker may not try to exploit even the most favorable power situation. So it is the relationship between President and the political configuration that makes the system tick.

Even before public opinion polls, the President's real or supposed popularity was a large factor in his performance. Besides the power mix in Washington, the President has to deal with a national climate of expectations, the predominant needs thrust up to him by the people. There are at least three recurrent themes around which these needs are focused.

People look to the President for *reassurance,* a feeling that things will be all right, that the President will take care of his people. The psychological request is for a surcease of anxiety. Obviously, modern life in America involves considerable doses of fear, tension, anxiety, worry; from time to time, the public mood calls for a rest, a time of peace, a breathing space, a "return to normalcy."

Another theme is the demand for a *sense of progress and action.* The President ought to do something to direct the nation's course—or at least be in there pitching for the people. The President is looked to as a take-charge man, a doer, a turner of the wheels, a producer of progress—even if that means some sacrifice of serenity.

A third type of climate of expectations is the public need for a sense of *legitimacy* from, and in, the Presidency. The President should be a master politician who is above politics. He should have a right to his place and a rightful way of acting in it. The respectability—even religiosity—of the office has to be protected by a man who presents himself as defender of the faith. There is more to this than dignity, more than propriety. The President is expected to personify our betterness in an inspiring way, to express in what he does and is (not just in what he says) a moral idealism which, in much of the public mind, is the very opposite of "politics."

Over time the climate of expectations shifts and changes. Wars, depressions, and other national events contribute to that change, but there also is a rough cycle, from an emphasis on action (which begins to look too "political") to an emphasis on legitimacy (the moral uplift of which creates its own strains) to an emphasis on reassurance and rest (which comes to seem like drift) and back to action again. One need not be astrological about it. The point is that the climate of expectations at any given time is the political air the President has to breathe. Relating to this climate is a large part of his task.

Predicting Presidents

The best way to predict a President's character, world view, and style is to see how he constructed them in the first place. Especially in the early stages, life is experimental; consciously or not, a person tries out various ways of defining and maintaining and raising self-esteem. He looks to his environment for clues as to who he is and how well he is doing. These lessons of life slowly sink in: certain self-images and evaluations, certain ways of looking at the world, certain styles of action get confirmed by his experience and he gradually adopts them as his own. If we can see that process of development, we can understand the product. The features to note are those bearing on Presidential performance.

Experimental development continues all the way to death; we will not blind ourselves to midlife changes, particularly in the full-scale prediction cases. But it is often much easier to see the basic patterns in early life histories. Later on a whole host of distractions—especially the image-making all politicians learn to practice—clouds the picture.

In general, character has its *main* development in childhood, world view in adolescence, style in early adulthood. The stance toward life I call character grows out of the child's experiments in relating to parents, brothers and sisters, and peers at play and in school, as well as to his own body and the objects around it. Slowly the child defines an orientation toward experience; once established, that tends to last despite much subsequent contradiction. By adolescence, the child has been hearing and seeing how people make their worlds meaningful, and now he is moved to relate himself—his own meanings—to those around him. His focus of attention shifts toward the future; he senses that decisions about his fate are coming and he looks into the premises for those decisions. Thoughts about the way the world works and how one might work in it, about what people are like and how one might be like them or not, and about the values people share and how one might share in them too—these are typical concerns for the post-child, pre-adult mind of the adolescent.

These themes come together strongly in early adulthood, when the person moves from contemplation to responsible action and adopts a style. In most biographical accounts this period stands out in stark clarity—the time of emergence, the time the young man found himself. I call it his first independent political success. It was then he moved beyond the detailed guidance of his family; then his self-esteem was dramatically boosted; then he came forth as a person to be reckoned with by other people. The *way* he did that is profoundly important to him. Typically he grasps that style and hangs onto it. Much later, coming into Presidency, something in him remembers this earlier victory and re-emphasizes the style that made it happen.

Character provides the main thrust and broad direction—but it does not *determine,* in any fixed sense, world view and style. The story of development does not end with the end of childhood. Thereafter, the culture one grows in and the ways that culture is translated by parents and peers shapes the meanings one makes of his character. The going world view gets learned and that learning helps channel character forces. Thus it will not necessarily be true that compulsive characters have reactionary beliefs, or that compliant characters believe in compromise. Similarly for style: historical accidents play a large part in furnishing special opportunities for action—and in blocking off alternatives. For example, however much anger a young many may feel, that anger will not be expressed in rhetoric unless and until his life situation provides a platform and an audience. Style thus has a stature and independence of its own. Those who would reduce all explanation to character neglect these highly significant later channelings. For beyond the root is the branch, above the foundation the superstructure, and starts do not prescribe finishes.

Four Types of Presidential Character

The five concepts—character, world view, style, power situation, and climate of expectations—run through the accounts of Presidents in the chapters to follow, which cluster the Presidents since Theodore Roosevelt into four types. This is the fundamental scheme of the study. It offers a way to move past the complexities to the main contrasts and comparisons.

The first baseline in defining Presidential types is *activity-passivity.* How much energy does the man invest in his Presidency? Lyndon Johnson went at his day like a human cyclone, coming to rest long after the sun went down. Calvin Coolidge often slept eleven hours a night and still needed a nap in the middle of the day. In between the Presidents array themselves on the high or low side of the activity line.

The second baseline is *positive-negative affect* toward one's activity—that is, how he feels about what he does. Relatively speaking, does he seem to experience his political life as happy or sad, enjoyable or discouraging, positive or negative in its main effect. The feeling I am after here is not grim satisfaction in a job well done, not some philosophical conclusion. The idea is this: is he someone who, on the surfaces we can see, gives forth the feeling that he has *fun* in political life? Franklin Roosevelt's Secretary of War, Henry L. Stimson wrote that the Roosevelts "not only understood the *use* of power, they knew the *enjoyment* of power, too . . . . Whether a man is burdened by power or enjoys power; whether he is trapped by responsibility or made free by it; whether he is moved by other people and other forces or moves them—that is the essence of leadership."

The positive-negative baseline, then, is a general symptom of the fit between the man and his experience, a kind of register of *felt* satisfaction.

Why might we expect these two simple dimensions to outline the main character types? Because they stand for two central features of anyone's orientation toward life. In nearly every study of personality, some form of the active-passive contrast is critical; the general tendency to act or be acted upon is evident in such concepts as dominance-submission, extraversion-introversion, aggression-timidity, attack-defense, fight-flight, engagement-withdrawal, approach-avoidance. In everyday life we sense quickly the general energy output of the people we deal with.   Similarly we catch on fairly quickly to the affect dimension—whether the person seems to be optimistic or pessimistic, hopeful or skeptical, happy or sad. The two baselines are clear and they are also independent of one another: all of us know people who are very active but seem discouraged, others who are quite passive but seem happy, and so forth. The activity baseline refers to what one does, the affect baseline to how one feels about what he does.

Both are crude clues to character. They are leads into four basic character patterns long familiar in psychological research. In summary form, these are the main configurations:

Active-Positive

There is a congruence, a consistency, between much activity and the enjoyment of it, indicating relatively high self-esteem and relative success in relating to the environment. The man shows an orientation toward productiveness as a value and an ability to use his styles flexibly, adaptively, suiting the dance to the music. He sees himself as developing over time toward relatively well defined personal goals—growing toward his image of himself as he might yet be. There is an emphasis on rational master, on using the brain to move the feet. This may get him into trouble; he may fail to take account of the irrational in politics. Not everyone he deals with sees things his way and he may find it hard to understand why.

Active-Negative

The contradiction here is between relatively intense effort and relatively low emotional reward for that effort. The activity has a compulsive quality, as if the man were trying to make up for something or to escape from anxiety into hard work. He seems ambitious, striving upward, power-seeking. His stance toward the environment is aggressive and he has a persistent problem in managing his aggressive feelings. His self-image is vague and discontinuous. Life is a hard struggle to achieve and hold power, hampered by the condemnations of a perfectionistic conscience. Active-negative types pour energy into the political system, but it is an energy distorted from within.

Passive-Positive

This is the receptive, compliant, other-directed character whose life is a search for affection as a reward for being agreeable and cooperative rather than personally assertive. The contradiction is between low self-esteem (on grounds of being unlovable, unattractive) and a superficial optimism. A hopeful attitude helps dispel doubt and elicits encouragement from others. Passive-positive types help soften the harsh edges of politics. But their dependence and the fragility of their hopes and enjoyments make disappointment in politics likely.

Passive-Negative

The factors are consistent—but how are we to account for the man's *political* role-taking? Why is someone who does little in politics and enjoys it less there at all? The answer lies in the passive-negative's character-rooted orientation toward doing dutiful service; this compensates for low self-esteem based on a sense of uselessness. Passive-negative types are in politics because they think they ought to be. They may be well adapted to certain nonpolitical roles, but they lack the experience and flexibility to perform effectively as political leaders. Their tendency is to withdraw, to escape from the conflict and uncertainty of politics by emphasizing vague principles (especially prohibitions) and procedural arrangements. They become guardians of the right and proper way, above the sordid politicking of lesser men.

Active-positive Presidents want most to achieve results. Active-negatives aim to get and keep power. Passive-positives are after love. Passive-negatives emphasize their civic virtue. The relation of activity to enjoyment in a President thus tends to outline a cluster of characteristics, to set apart the adapted from the compulsive, compliant, and withdrawn types.

The first four Presidents of the United States, conveniently, ran through this gamut of character types. (Remember, we are talking about tendencies, broad directions; no individual man exactly fits a category.) George Washington—clearly the most important President in the pantheon—established the fundamental legitimacy of an American government at a time when this was a matter in considerable question. Washington's dignity, judiciousness, his aloof air of reserve and dedication to duty fit the passive-negative or withdrawing type best. Washington did not seek innovation, he sought stability. He longed to retire to Mount Vernon, but fortunately was persuaded to stay on through a second term, in which, by rising above the political conflict between Hamilton and Jefferson and inspiring confidence in his own integrity, he gave the nation time to develop the organized means for peaceful change.

John Adams followed, a dour New England Puritan, much given to work and worry, an impatient and irascible man—an active-negative President, a compulsive type. Adams was far more partisan than Washington; the survival of the system through his Presidency demonstrated that the nation could tolerate, for a time, domination by one of its nascent political parties. As President, an angry Adams brought the united States to the brink of war with France, and presided over the new nation's first experiment in political repression: the Alien and Sedition Acts, forbidding, among other things, unlawful combinations "with intent to oppose any measure or measures of the government of the United States," or "any false, scandalous, and malicious writing or writings against the United States, or the President of the United States, with intent to defame . . . or to bring them or either of them, into contempt or disrepute."

Then came Jefferson. He too had his troubles and failures—in the design of national defense, for example. As for his Presidential character (only one element in success or failure), Jefferson was clearly active-positive. A child of the Enlightenment, he applied his reason to organizing connections with Congress aimed at strengthening the more popular forces. A man of catholic interests and delightful humor, Jefferson combined a clear and open vision of what the country could be with a profound political sense, expressed in his famous phrase, "Every difference of opinion is not a difference of principle."

The fourth President was James Madison, "Little Jemmy," the constitutional philosopher thrown into the White House at a time of great international turmoil. Madison comes closest to the passive-positive, or compliant, type; he suffered from irresolution, tried to compromise his way out, and gave in too readily to the "war-hawks" urging combat with Britain. The nation drifted into war, and Madison wound up ineptly commanding his collection of amateur generals in the streets of Washington. General Jackson's victory at New Orleans saved the Madison administration's historical reputation; but he left the Presidency with the United States close to bankruptcy and secession.

These four Presidents—like all Presidents—were persons trying to cope with the roles they had won by using the equipment they had built over a lifetime. The President is not some shapeless organism in a flood of novelties, but a man with a memory in a system with a history. Like all of us, he draws on his past to shape his future. The pathetic hope that the White House will turn a Caligula into a Marcus Aurelius is as naive as the fear that ultimate power inevitably corrupts. The problem is to understand—and to state understandably—what in the personal past foreshadows the Presidential future.

Thinking It Over

1. From what you know about President Bush, see if you can place him in Barber's typology.

2. Do you find any face validity in Barber's theory? In other words do you find yourself operating in the kinds of ways he suggests? Do your parents fit? Other people you know?

77.
THE ENIGMA
by Robert J. Samuelson

Setting the Scene: This is another one of those articles that confronts an "accepted wisdom." We all know the popular image of former President Ronald Reagan. "Nice guy but kind of slow," "*Rambo* type," "a cowboy mentally," "a class 'B' actor who looked bad if he strayed from his script." And so on. The following analysis, published in the liberal *New Republic* the month following Reagan's departure from office, argues that Reagan was like TV's popular detective *Columbo*, his greatest advantage was the fact his adversaries tended to underestimate him. Many of you will go into this reading highly skeptical. I don't know how you will come out of it in terms of your view of Reagan but I can guarantee one thing—you'll understand the Presidency much better having read it.

A huge puzzle hangs over Ronald Reagan's presidency. By conventional measures, it's been enormously successful. Double-digit inflation is gone. The economy is in its second-longest expansion since World War II. Reagan championed the most sweeping tax reform in decades. He proposed—and Congress enacted—a program of catastrophic health insurance for the elderly and a major overhaul of welfare. Abroad, he signed the first arms control agreement (the INF treaty) that actually reduces nuclear stockpiles. All these achievements enjoy widespread bipartisan approval. If anyone else (say, Jimmy Carter) had compiled this record, he'd be leaving to loud cheers. Reagan's reputation, however, is more complex.

Everyone concedes his popularity and accomplishments. But he's also treated with casual contempt, as if his success were a fluke. James Reston of the *New York Times* recently ridiculed "Reagan's easy optimism, his amiable incompetence, his tolerance of dubs and sleaze, his cronyism, his preoccupation with stars, his indifference to facts and convenient forgetfulness." This captures the conventional wisdom. Reagan's seen as a public relations president, often ignorant of policy. The picture is more than journalistic invention. The memoirs of White House aides (David Stockman, Donald Regan) show a man aloof from everyday government. So there's the puzzle: How did someone who worked so little at being president do so well at it? The answer is that you don't have to work hard to be a good president.

It's no accident that Reagan is the first two-term president since Eisenhower. Nor is it a coincidence that, despite high personal popularity, both these presidents have been held in low esteem by the journalistic and political elites who dominate presidential commentary. There's an unspoken idea of what a successful president should be like, and neither Eisenhower nor Reagan has conformed. This ideal president should be a forceful leader and activist. He should have a clear national vision and the political savvy to get Congress and the public to follow him. Eisenhower never fit this mold, and Reagan seemed to only at first—when the "Reagan revolution" was a popular political and media myth. Both men reacted to events. Each seemed disengaged. Ike played golf. Ron chopped wood.

The trouble with the idealized president is that it has little to do with the real world. Presidents do not succeed based on how well they advance a personal agenda. These agendas are usually overwhelmed by outside events. Truman is best remembered for the Marshall Plan: a program he didn't design for a problem that barely existed when he replaced Roosevelt. Presidents succeed or fail by how well they make sound judgments on a few issues—where presidential decisions count—that vitally affect the nation's future. Everyday management of government (including most congressional actions) doesn't matter much. Reagan bungled important matters, most obviously the budget deficits. But these lapses were outweighed by his good judgment on inflation, dealing with the Soviets, and tax reform. By contrast, most other recent presidents have failed the good judgment test.

If Presidents Ford and Kennedy aren't counted—because each served only briefly—Reagan is the first president since Eisenhower not to leave the country in a state of acute crisis. For Lyndon Johnson, the crisis was Vietnam. For Nixon, it was Watergate. For Carter, it was mainly spiraling inflation. These presidents had accomplishments: the enactment of Medicare and Medicaid for Johnson; the opening of China for Nixon; the Israeli-Egyptian peace treaty for Carter. But their achievements were overshadowed. The contrast with Reagan and Eisenhower simply confirms that the president's main job is custodial: it is to deal with the central national problems that occur on his watch, whether the problems are inherited or emerge along the way.

Reagan has been given little credit for having done well at this basic task. His glitzy lifestyle, relaxed work habits, and sugary rhetoric all suggested a man who excelled at performing ceremonial functions but disdained doing the actual job of governing. This vindicated the widely held view that Reagan was a mere actor who didn't deserve to be president. The imagery is false. His last feature movie opened in 1957. For a quarter century he's been involved in politics. For 16 of those years he's held two of the nation's highest elective offices. If he's not a professional politician, who is?

To explain Reagan's success, his critics are full of theories. One is "luck." Reagan had little to do with his administration's achievements and everything to do with its failures. Thus: Paul Volcker (former chairman of the Federal Reserve Board and a 1979 appointee of Carter) defeated double-digit inflation; Treasury Secretary james A. Baker III engineered tax reform; Secretary of State George Shultz (and the rise of Mikhail Gorbachev) made arms control possible; other subordinates handled catastrophic health insurance and welfare reform. But Reagan's incompetence led to the fiascos, from budget deficits to Iran-*contra*. Yet how did such a dopey president (tolerant of "cronyism" and "sleaze") manage to have so many competent subordinates? And if the president was merely manipulated by his subordinates, how was it that he repeatedly ignored their advice in many areas—the budget deficits being the best example?

The good-luck theory clearly fails to explain Reagan's greatest accomplishment and the pillar of his popularity: the reduction of double-digit inflation. The idea that Volcker ought to receive all the credit, and Reagan none, is preposterous. It's true that Volcker led the attack. But though nominally "independent" of the White House, the Federal Reserve cannot long oppose presidential wishes without facing intense political pressures that no agency of technocrats can easily withstand. William Greider's *Secrets of the Temple*—a chronicle of Volcker's time at the Fed—shows that his policies had Reagan's encouragement and backing. After one 1981 session between the two men, David Stockman concluded: "Volcker couldn't have come out of that meeting thinking anything but that the White House wanted tightening."

The ensuing 1981-82 recession was more severe than anyone anticipated. Unemployment reached a peak of 10.8 percent in late 1982. But Volcker did not relax the tough, high interest rate policies until inflation was clearly broken—and Reagan didn't force his hand by blasting the Fed in public. That's the important point. It's easy to forget now how much economists agonized in the late 1970s over the difficulty of controlling inflation. Reagan and Volcker showed that government could govern. With nerve and patience, someone could take the unpopular decisions that had huge long-term benefits. Would Carter have done the same? The answer surely is no.

Carter had trouble sticking with any anti-inflation policy. He tinkered with price and credit controls. As unemployment passed nine percent, he probably would have panicked and forced Volcker to relent. The risk would have been continued stagflation. With inflation at six to eight percent (down from 1979's 13.3 percent), fear of going back into double digits would have inhibited the recovery. Carter partisans say he's unfairly maligned. They blame his inflation on oil prices and credit him for naming Volcker. The first argument is wrong. By 1978—before the second oil shock—inflation had reached nine percent, up from 4.8 percent in 1976, and was rising. As for Volcker, he was an afterthought. Carter was firing Treasury Secretary W. Michael Blumenthal and replacing him with Fed Chairman G. William Miller. Someone had to run the Fed, and Volcker wasn't even the first choice . . .

It's true, as charged, that the United States has lived beyond its means. Part of Reagan's prosperity was borrowed from the future. Our excess spending was covered by imports. Now that the trade deficit is dropping, choices can't be postponed indefinitely. There are two ways to restrain our excess national spending: we can do so explicitly by reducing the budget deficits; or we can let the market do the job through higher interest rates, exchange rate changes, more inflation, or some other mechanism that will restrain private spending. The danger of leaving the job to the market is that the ultimate social costs may be higher. For example, higher interest rates could depress private investment, which might harm future productivity growth and living standards.

These economic consequences are serious, but not calamitous. The economy's main problem is actually the poor growth of productivity—the ability to raise our national wealth. This is the basic cause of the budget deficits. When productivity rose rapidly in the 1950s and '60s, people felt they could afford more government and more private spending. Now the conflict is acute. Economists don't fully understand the productivity slowdown. Nor can government easily cure it. But the Reagan years coincided with an improvement. Since 1979 business productivity has grown 1.4 percent annually. That's twice the 0.6 percent rate between 1973 and 1979, but below the 1947-73 average of three percent. Despite budget deficits and other problems—stubborn poverty and the savings and loan crisis, to mention two—the economy is far healthier today than a decade ago. . . .

No, they misjudged Reagan. His Presidency has been more cautious than conservative. In the end, it's been a triumph of competence, not ideology.

Thinking It Over

1. I like oxymorons. "Jumbo shrimp." "Military intelligence." ("Political Science"?) Is there such a thing as "goofy competence"? Does Samuelson mean you have to be simple to be President?

2. Compare Samuelson's piece to James David Barber's and then formulate the Reagan character as you think Barber would.

Chapter XII

THE BUREAUCRACY

78.
THE AMERICAN BUREAUCRAT:
A HISTORY OF A SHEEP
IN WOLVES' CLOTHING
by Barry D. Karl

Setting the Scene: Barry D. Karl is a leading American historian and essayist. He is deeply concerned with the role of politics in history and within that framework the position of administration in politics. In early 1987 the American Society for Public Administration published a "Symposium in Observance of the Bicentennial of the Constitution of the United States and the Centennial of the American Administrative State." Included in that symposium was Karl's essay. His position is quite clear. We have dressed up our bureaucrats in wolves' clothing. Fear of "administrative tyranny" has been with us since the beginning. While the growth of the bureaucratic state that we are familiar with today was both an unexpected and unintended consequence of the framers' design, our hostility toward it was clearly consistent with their intentions.

For most of American history the terms "bureaucrat" and "bureaucracy" have been used in popular discourse as epithets, when they have been used at all. Although both terms have achieved a certain amount of academic credibility in American social science over the last 30 or 40 years, it is an acceptance which is grudging. That is true, in many respects, even in the worlds of political science and public administration where the influence of European theory since the end of World War II has brought about a broader understanding of comparative administrative practices. Nonetheless, in the sophisticated professions that now constitute the complex fields of journalism and political commentary the terms are part of a political language that has evolved in American political life. They evoke negative images. Even when they appear in debates that are ostensibly about deregulation and the role of the state in the life of the citizen, they are in fact expressions of an American suspicion of government that goes back to our national origins. Americans believed that power was essentially corrupting long before Lord Acton articulated the idea for them; and "bureaucracy" is a term that can easily be used to describe the inherent corruption of power. . . .

In the decades that followed the New Deal both its defenders and its critics distorted the picture by claiming either that it was an era of effective reform to which one could return by finding an attractive and compassionate leader or that it was a threatening period of dictatorial centralization or national management in Washington. It was, in fact, neither one. Both of the pictures have at their center conceptions of bureaucracy which, for better or for worse, bear little relation to the actual role of bureaucracies in American history.

Americans have coped with the introduction of the bureaucratic state by castigating it all the while and attempting to place upon it every limitation of which they could think.

The good New Deal bureaucrat is a trained and benevolent public servant dutifully carrying out the programs of a popularly elected American philanthropist. The bad New Deal bureaucrat is a tyrannical ideologue attempting to impose a narrow intellectual elite's standard of well-being on a complex, pluralist society. The real New Deal bureaucrat was, by and large, something quite different. "He," and the surprising number of "shes" among them, were administering politically designed programs with the expressed intention of maintaining intact the political system that had designed them.[1] While their distaste for partisan politics matched that of their Progressive forebears, their commitment to the two-party political debate was profound. While they were aware of the academic distinction between politics and administration, they were never fooled by it. The civil servant called for by their civil service reforms was a servant of political interests backed by the voters, not an administrative neuter fulfilling scientific objectives rationally defined. The protection of civil service was a protection from the mindless victimization produced by partisan politics, not a protection from the responsibility of serving the political aims signified by such changes. It was certainly never intended to certify scientifically defined policies believed by adherents to be above political judgment and control.

Bureaucratic agencies established by the New Deal took it from both sides. They were, on the one hand, evidence of the radical takeover of authority by a suspect elite. They were, on the other hand, partisan boondoggles writ large. Critics and supporters alike would, for half a century after the New Deal, continue to enjoy the parks, roadways, waterways, and public buildings built by the New Deal without ever associating them with the work of a federal bureaucracy.

---

[1]The presence of women is traceable not to any premonitions of the liberation movement that followed the era but to the fact that women were represented in such overwhelming numbers among the managers and providers of social services at the state and local levels, services now being transferred to the federal government.

Both labels stuck. Bureaucracy was radical and wasteful, revolutionary, tyrannical, and dishonest. Abolishing it would remain the most attractive and popular remedy, while making it more efficient and effective would gradually drift toward a private professional preserve where political scientists, teachers of public administration, and, by the 1950s a new group of sociologically oriented social scientists interested in bureaucratic theory would debate a curious historical reality only they seemed able to understand.

Modern technology, post-industrialism, and the ideas of Max Weber and Talcott Parsons were now ways of describing the consciousness that had emerged. When by 1962 the *New International Encyclopedia of the Social Sciences* appeared, its article on bureaucracy marked the essential transformation. Reinhard Bendix quickly swept past the pejoratives of the Anglo-American tradition and presented his readers with a brilliant panoramic view of the new Euro-American social thought. The American bureaucrat had come of age, or so it seemed.

The fact that by 1976 the Democratic Party could support a winning candidate whose campaign could be directed against the bureaucracy in Washington was certainly not envisaged by the proud academicians of the *Encyclopedia*. Nor was the fact that the argument would be sustained successfully by the Republicans as well, to become by the 1980s a major movement that could be defined not only as bipartisan but as a return to democracy, the recapture of a lost heritage. Sweeping aside a century of regulatory idealism built on the dream of a federal government that would protect its citizens from predatory interests, leaders in both parties extolled a new freedom, the freedom from bureaucratic dictation. Even the Supreme Court in its recent attack on Gramm-Rudman could call on the tradition by criticizing the power of an appointed bureaucrat, the Comptroller General, rather than raising the issue of separation of powers.

Bureaucracy, the Threat to Democracy: The Real Battle

Americans make no distinction, in political terms, between public needs and popular desires. Their refusal to accept such a distinction and to agree to an objective standard of public need defined by rationally determined considerations may distinguish Americans from members of societies where the state defines needs and debates only the degree and the timing of their fulfillment. Americans charge their government with the responsibility of meeting their individual needs in accordance with the shifting moods and perceptions that determine exactly what those needs are. The public will accept decisions that seem plausible if they are defended as expansions of democratic opportunity. But as the consequences of those decisions unfold, the American public will assume no responsibility for its own role in the process. The mood swings are precipitous and the penalties severe. Americans who elect leaders who reflect a current consensus on their attitudes toward political issues of the day will turn against those same leaders if and when that consensus changes.

Men who are elected for their administrative skills rather than their presence as popular public figures may find themselves sorely taxed by an unexpected public need for drama and charismatic leadership. The public wanted what Herbert Hoover represented in 1928. By 1931 it was clear that they sensed a need for something else, qualities which Hoover himself considered objectionable. He was never forgiven for his inability, in fact his refusal, to transform himself into the new, needed, public image.

In an important sense the problem is not a new one. The debates that began in the Progressive Era used the terms "politics" and "administration" as the way of defining what has variously been viewed as a Manichaean opposition, a pair of correlative terms, or a necessary, if not altogether happy, partnership in the management of the democratic state. What seems clear, however, is that the dynamics of the relationship are and have continued to be historically volatile, more so, perhaps, than in any of the familiar cultures of western society where the growth of the administrative state and its relation to the social order are traced by students of administrative history. It might be useful to try to suggest some reasons for that volatility.

First, as Tocqueville suggested, Americans may be more committed believers in the essential politics of self-government than any other people on earth. As he pointed out, the belief that the passage of a law will solve every problem tends to be at the root of the American reform impulse. Even the most popular presidents have been forced to subject their administrative judgment to Congress and the courts. The Supreme Court has been pressed to respond to political judgments, at times to forestall legislative punishment.

Secondly, Americans have tended to look on government, and the federal government in particular, as the distributor of resources and the opportunities for advancement which such resources represent. Such distribution has always been subjected to the rule that benefits must be available to all, not just to the needy, and that there be as little administrative intervention as possible in what is essentially a process of democratic redistribution. That was as true of public lands in the nineteenth century as it is of educational opportunities, social security, medical benefits, and jobs today. Americans do not want to think of themselves as dependent upon state managers whose jobs they cannot threaten by the casting of a ballot or the rewriting of a law. The attractiveness of the short ballot and the growth of appointed rather than elected officialdom in American government has always been limited by the public's sense that it could find substitute controls and the legislature's sense that its threatened rebellions would elicit appropriate responses. Control over jobs and resources remains the basis of the cry of corruption, whether the target be a lowly ward heeler whose living depends on the voters he drags to the polls on election day or the management of a high level technology industry supplying the armed services with absurdly expensive screwdrivers.

Thirdly, Americans hold their elected administrators responsible for serving them and accept patronage as part of the process. The justice meted out to political and administrative decision makers has no equivalent of the legal distinction between involuntary manslaughter and premeditated murder. This ruthlessness of public judgment leads politicians and administrators alike to at least two recourses. They can try to please every one a little, thereby lessening the impact of criticism even though the end result may be the equivalent of doing nothing at all; or they can set up an opponent, one enemy who is preventing the action they really want to take, thereby directing attention away from themselves.

Nothing has done more to strengthen the role of administrative courts and the battles over the use of the legislative veto than the confusion of the political and administrative processes and the resulting conflicts among administrators charged with managing the programs. Frustrated presidents resort to the invention of new methods, the questionable use of old ones, and the inevitable force of public exhortation, which in itself may become a highly questionable theater in the world of public affairs. Presidential candidates running against incumbents, presidents seeking reelection, second-term presidents fighting unresponsive congresses, and vice-presidents hoping to succeed to candidacy, if not to office, all face the problem of attempting to turn administrative problems into political theater. The situation is an open invitation to irresponsibility, if not, under certain circumstances, a guarantee of it. Suggestions that there be a single term for presidents are all built on the belief that such a restriction would separate the office from the politics of reelection; but that, in a way, is too close to the logic that dictated the mischievous twenty-second amendment in the first place. A president without political clout ceases to be a political leader. From a historical point of view, the only real answer to the problem of maintaining administrative power in the presidency would be to remove the limitation on reelection entirely, thereby giving the political public the only kind of leader it feels it can control.

The unwillingness of Americans to believe that administration might be an elite function . . . governed the way public administration developed and complicated beyond belief, almost, its relation to politics as a career.

The dream of removing partisanship from American politics is essentially an elite dream that has no place in the American public's most profound conception of its own political power. Part of the hostility to bureaucracy stems from the fact that Americans see it as an inhibiting force, blocking their access to political power. Part of the inherent inefficiency of bureaucracy in the American administrative tradition is a result of that hostility, a consciousness on the part of even the most committed administrator that meeting the public's perception of need is the bottom line.

John Kennedy's *Profiles in Courage* may be the clearest expression of the paradox. Each of his courageous figures sacrifices a political career in the interest of some principle. They do not stay in Congress, or win the presidency, or succeed in gaining whatever career prize they set out to win. Most of them are martyrs; and while martyrs may be useful models for developing certain kinds of character, losing, as our Kennedys were raised to understand, is not the name of the game.

The threat of some kind of administrative tyranny is the oldest threat to democracy in our 200 years of independent history. It is the menace in twentieth century communism, just as it was in nineteenth century monarchy. The inefficiency, irrationality, and corruption we are willing to sustain in order to protect ourselves from it have succeeded, perhaps, in creating bureaucratic forms that are uniquely ours. We demand a bureaucracy we can control, by our votes, our bribes, our capacity for public wrath, and, if necessary, by the price we are willing to pay for inefficiency.

This is not to argue the impossibility of administratively efficient democracy, only its fragility. For our commitment to individual autonomy, to self-interest, and to material well-being as the touchstones of American democracy places limits on the definitions of efficiency that are acceptable to us, particularly in times of economic stringency. Politics remains our method of requiring the state to serve us.

The growth of the bureaucratic state may be the single most unintended consequence of the Constitution of 1787, in a sense, perhaps, the heart of the partisanship the framers thought they could avoid. What may be the most consistent with their intention, however, is the hostility to bureaucracy we inherited from them, and that we have continued to preserve. It is a reality with which we have learned to live, albeit somewhat uncomfortably; but it is a reality that should give pause to those who believe that there is in the intentions of the framers of the Constitution of 1787 a world to which we can return. All of the current interest in deregulation cannot obliterate the existence of the bureaucratic state or relieve us of the responsibility of adjusting our democracy to it. The battle between bureaucracy and democracy is written into our history. So is the fact that democracy must win. All we have left to debate is the cost.

Thinking It Over

1. While Karl believes "the battle between bureaucracy and democracy is written into our history," does he also believe that the conflict is inevitable?

2. You are in a cafe in Zurich talking with a new acquaintance. You tell him you are an American studying political science and are asked "Do you plan to work for the government when you graduate?"
    "Not in this lifetime!"
    He is surprised by your response. "What is it with you Americans and your bureaucracy?"
    You thank your lucky stars you've read Barry Karl's article and prepare to blow him away with the profundity of your answer. Run it through your mind once now.

79.
BUREAUCRATIC GOVERNMENT USA
by David Nachmias and David H. Rosenbloom

Setting the Scene: There are few political scientists who would debate the proposition that in the ever changing distribution of power in our national government, the bureaucracy has been the big winner in the last half century. What follows is a clearly reasoned explanation of why this is so. Professors Nachmias and Rosenbloom start at the beginning by defining power itself. They then craft a relationship between this definition and the bureaucratic state. Finally they place their analysis in the context of leading scholarship in the field. Readers of this selection will never want for an explanation of why the bureaucracy is deservedly called the "fourth branch of government."

For many years American politics could have been studied with little or no attention to bureaucracy. A long intellectual tradition in political science separated politics from bureaucracy (administration). Politicians were supposed to make public policies and decisions about the structure of government and the allocation of scarce resources; administrators were supposed to implement those policies and decisions. Although this tradition had its roots in the efforts of reformers in the 1870s and 1880s to depoliticize the federal bureaucracy, it may also have described public administration in an earlier age. However, as the roles of government increased and expanded and public policies grew more complex, politics and administration became thoroughly intertwined.

Today the federal bureaucracy is at the core of American government and a dominant force in the political system. The executive, legislative, and judicial branches of government are also becoming bureaucratic institutions in their organization and behavior, partly as a response to the growing power of the federal bureaucracy. Thus the political power of elected and politically appointed . . . authorities is diminishing relative to that of the administrators and staffs of governmental organizations. Not only do administrators implement public policies; they also play a major role in policymaking.

Political parties and interest groups, the traditional links between government and citizens, are also in a period of transition and change. Party activists are being replaced by campaign managers, organization specialists, and media experts. Candidates for office rely more and more on their personal organizations rather than on their parties. And after the campaign is over, elected candidates tend to carry their personal staffs into office with them. As for interest groups, they are increasingly organized bureaucratically, with power becoming concentrated among the professional executives and the operating administrators.

No longer can we understand American government without a careful examination of bureaucracy and its dominant position in the political system. But first we need to know something about the nature of power, its shifting bases, and its concentration.

Power and Authority

One of the most important characteristics of a society is the way it organizes power. For power, the medium of exchange in politics, is a key to the public life and government of any nation. Indeed, this proposition has been central to Western political thought since the days of Plato and Aristotle.

What is power? Robert Dahl defines it as follows: "A has power over B to the extent that he can get B to do something B would not otherwise do."[1] Thus power has to do with the relationships between two or more actors (individuals, groups, organizations, or nations) when one of them can affect the behavior of another . . .

Max Weber (1864-1920) drew an important distinction between power and authority. Power may involve force or coercion. Authority, on the other hand, is a form of power that does not imply coercion; it involves a "suspension of judgment" on the part of its recipients. People follow the orders given by someone in authority because they believe that they should. Their compliance is voluntary. To comply, however, they must have a common value system. When the members of a society do not accept the same values, other forms of power, such as coercion, become dominant. A society's value system legitimizes authority as a means of exercising power.

Weber further distinguished between three "ideal types" of authority: charismatic, traditional, and rational-legal. He describes the evolution of polities in terms of the type of authority relations within them. The earliest of the three is the *charismatic* authority that "rests on the affectual devotion of the follower to the lord and his gifts of grace (charisma). They comprise especially magical abilities, revelations of heroism, power of the mind and speech . . . The purest types are the rule of the prophet, the warrior hero, the great demagogue."[2] The positions of the followers who depend upon their leader's charisma are most threatened at times of leadership succession. To secure their positions and prerogatives, they may institutionalize and routinize the process of selecting successors. This creates the *traditional* type of authority. Traditional authority, in Weber's words, "rests on the belief in the sacredness of social order and its prerogatives as existing yore . . . The body politic is based on communal relationships, the man in command is the 'lord' ruling over obedient 'subjects.' People obey the lord personally since his dignity is hallowed by tradition; obedience rests on piety."[3]

Bureaucratic Power

Modern society, according to Weber, is based upon *rational-legal* authority. This type of authority

---

[1]Robert A. Dahl, *Modern Political Analysis* (Englewood Cliffs, N.J.: Prentice-Hall, 1963), p. 40.

[2]Max Weber, "The Three Types of Legitimate Rule," in Amitai Etzioni, ed., *A Sociological Reader on Complex Organizations*, 2nd ed. (New York: Holt, 1969), p. 12.

[3]Ibid., p. 9.

rests on enactment; its pure type is best presented by bureaucracy. The basic idea is that laws can be enacted and changed at pleasure by formally correct procedure. The governing body is either elected or appointed and constitutes as a whole and in all its sections rational organizations . . . obedience is not owed by anybody personally but to enacted rules and regulations which specify to whom and to what rule people owe obedience.[4]

Yet even in modern society, Weber said, charismatic leaders may emerge in times of crisis and emergency, and charismatic authority may become institutionalized. Charismatic patterns of authority may coexist with rational-legal authority, as is the case with the American presidency and in some modern organizations.[5] Similarly, traditional authority can be found in modern rational-legal organizations. We are all familiar with voluntary compliance that is evoked by statements like "The Old Man wants it that way." But on the whole, rational-legal authority is the preponderant type of authority around which political life is organized in the United States.

Since Weber's time there have been several attempts to classify the concept of power in greater detail. One typology, developed by John French and Bertram Raven, is based on the nature of the relationship between the power holder and the power recipient.[6]

- *Reward* power, or "power whose basis is in the ability to reward," can appear in situations where the reward is meaningful for the power recipient.

- *Coercive* power is based on the recipient's perception of the ability of the power holder to distribute punishments.

- *Legitimate* power operates when the recipient acknowledges that the power holder has the right to influence him and that he has an obligation to comply.

- *Referent* power is observed when a power recipient identifies with a power holder and tries to behave in the same way. (In these situations, power holders may not even be aware that they have power.)

- *Expert* power is based on the special knowledge attributed to the power holder by the recipients. They believe that the holder possesses knowledge which they need but do not have. The obvious example is a professional-nonprofessional relationship, such as that of doctor and patient.

All these forms of power are found in modern society. All are also part of the legitimate

---

[4]Ibid., p. 7.

[5]See, for example, Victor Thompson, *Modern Organizations* (New York: Knopf, 1961), p. 439.

[6]John R. P. French and Bertram Raven, "The Bases of Social Power," in Dorwin Cartwright and Alvin Zander, eds., *Group Dynamics*, 3rd ed. (New York: Harper & Row, 1968), pp. 259-269.

authority system. But recent research has demonstrated that legitimate and expert power are more prevalent in American society than referent, reward, and coercive power.[7] This fact is important in accounting for the concentration of power among our nonelected authorities.

Concentration of Bureaucratic Power

Power relationships are found in most aspects of life. At a very early age children learn what positions have authority over other positions and when and where different authority relations are binding. A major reason for the prevalence of power relations is that they reduce the individual's sense of complexity by increasing the predictability of the patterns of people's behavior.

Ours is often called a complex society, and much of our behavior consists of attempts to organize and manage this complexity. If "there is a unique quality to the modern era, it is that the conditions of existence have changed to such a degree that something explicitly recognized as 'complexity' now continually forces itself into our awareness."[8] The changes that have created complexity were brought on by the growth of modern science, the emergence of a large-scale technological environment, and the proliferation of immense social and political organizations that include more and more individuals. We are currently experiencing an unprecedented rate of change, and one accelerating so rapidly that it has become exponential. (An example of exponential growth is a town whose population trebles every ten years—3,000 in 1960, 9,000 in 1970, 27,000 in 1980, and so on.[9]) Many scientific, technological, and social processes are exponential in their patterns of growth. A good example is computer technology. Moreover, the actual number of scientific and technological developments impinging on society each year continues to grow so much that the developments become metaphors of human activity.

These changes take place in a highly differentiated, fragmented, and specialized environment. Indeed, knowledge itself has become fragmented and specialized:

> Modern science is characterized by its ever-increasing specialization, necessitated by the enormous amount of data, the complexity of techniques and of theoretical structure within every field. Thus science is split into innumerable disciplines continually generating new subdisciplines. In consequence, the physicist, the biologist and the social scientist are, so to speak, encapsulated in their private universes, and it is difficult to get from one cocoon to the other.[10]

---

[7]See, for example, Curt Tausky, *Work Organizations*, 2nd ed. (Itasca, Ill.: Peacock, 1978), p. 138, and Guy Benveniste, *The Politics of Expertise* (San Francisco: Glendessary, 1972).

[8]Landgon Winner, "Complexity and the Limits of Human Understanding," in Todd R. La Porte, ed., *Organized Social Complexity: Challenge to Politics and Policy* (Princeton, N.J.: Princeton University Press, 1975), p. 41.

[9]In general, exponential models are formed by a series of points in fixed intervals, each of which represents the same base raised to a higher power each time, e.g., $3, 3^2, 3^3 \ldots 3^n$.

[10]Ludwig von Bertalanffy, *General Systems Theory* (New York: Braziller, 1968), p. 30.

Closely related to differentiation and fragmentation is the problem of interdependence. Before collective action can be taken, all the fragments of knowledge about that action must be brought together. But the process of integrating the fragments is often so difficult that it can result in "decreased efficiency of operation, neglect of creative combinations, erratic behavior in a climate of uncertainty, unpredictable breakdowns in the system, and at the extreme, disintegration of the organization itself."[11]

Today it is more and more difficult for individuals (including political decision makers) to comprehend any system as a whole. Whereas the knowledge required to understand both the separate components and their interdependence is rapidly increasing, the knowledge that is actually available grows relatively slowly. While he was in the Senate, Walter Mondale introduced the Full Opportunity and Social Accounting Act of 1967 in a speech that reviewed a variety of social programs. He concluded: "Our intentions are good, but we lack a systematic and integrated approach to social problems. When they miss their mark, we may not even realize it. If they are damaging, it may be years before we know it. Our successes are difficult to document; they suffer the attacks of the ignorant while we in our ignorance have no way to defend them."[12]

Power reduces the problem posed by the gap between the required and the available knowledge. In the economic arena, John Kenneth Galbraith points out, many large firms have given up trying to comprehend the uncertainties of the markets of supply and demand. Instead, they set out to influence the behavior of the markets: "This consists of reducing or eliminating the independence of action of those to whom the planning unit sells or from whom it buys. Their behavior being subject to control, uncertainty as to that behavior is reduced."[13] The basic motivation of the large corporation is no longer simply to maximize profits per se but to minimize uncertainties: "The firm is required . . . to control or to seek to control the social environment in which it functions—or any part which impinges upon it."[14] The result is that fewer and fewer corporations control a greater share of the market, and more and more individuals are employed in these fewer corporations. In the mid 1970s the 500 largest industrial corporations in the United States had a newt worth of over $600 billion, employed over 14 million people, and held total assets of $44 billion (Exxon) to $1.5 billion (Lockheed Aircraft).[15] Some observers estimate that about 5 percent of all private and public organizations account for over 60 percent of employment.[16]

Ability to control the environment does help to overcome the uncertainties inherent in complexity. But it does not always guarantee success, and it creates additional problems. Differentiation is further accelerated, bringing increased needs for interdependence, which in turn raises the level of complexity. In such situations, power rests with those who can reduce

---

[11]Winner, "Complexity and the Limits of Human Understanding," p. 63.

[12]U.S. Senate, 90th Congress, Hearings before the Subcommittee on Government Research of the Committee on Government Operations, *Full Opportunity and Social Accounting Act Seminar* (Washington, D.D.: Government Printing Office, 1967), p. 34.

[13]John Kenneth Galbraith, *The New Industrial State* (New York: Signet, 1968), p. 39.

[14]John Kenneth Galbraith, *Economics and the Public Purpose* (Boston: Houghton Mifflin, 1973), p. 39.

[15]*Fortune* (May 1976), p. 318.

[16]Tausky, *Work Organizations*, pp. 2-3.

the decision makers' *sense* of complexity.

It is often said that specialized bureaucratic skills are needed in government in order to manage the complexity of our environment. Complexity poses a serious problem for public policy. The demands made on government are increasing rapidly; problems that used to be handled in other ways now come under governmental jurisdiction. Consequently the number of areas that public policy is supposed to affect has been expanding. In the economic realm, for instance, the variety of national and multinational corporations that governments regulate in order to effect coherent policy has markedly grown. The interdependence among various corporations and their motives, markets, resources, and so on, creates a highly uncertain environment that government can only manage through further organization, regulation, and coordination. These activities have produced a new locus of power—bureaucratic power.

In the early 1920s Thorstein Veblen predicted that there would be a revolution in which power would become concentrated in the hands of scientists and engineers.[17] In the 1930s Harold Laski believed that power would shift to experts.[18] In the early 1940s James Burnham declared, "Managers . . . will be the ruling class society . . . their preferential treatment in distribution will be allotted to them in terms of status in the political-economic structure."[19] In the 1950s Lasswell, Lerner, and Rothwell said that the revolution of our time is a shift in influence from "specialists in bargaining" to intellectuals ("symbol specialists" or "masters of persuasion"), to "specialists in violence," or to those with "administrative and police skills."[20] These strategic elites were expected to cope with uncertainty and to reduce the decision makers' sense of complexity. Just as traditional societies developed the roles of warriors to control their environments, modern society has created specialized roles to manage complexity. Individuals occupying these roles have become irreplaceable and central to the functioning of modern economic, social, and political organizations. In the process, their power has increased relative to other groups.

The new locus of power lies in bureaucracies, and the power of bureaucrats as a group has expanded: "Often possessing little technical knowledge beyond a somewhat intangible ability to organize others, administrators now control the allocation of the organization's resources."[21] Harold Wilensky, studying problems of knowledge and policy in government and industry, concluded:

> The managerial revolution has taken place but its form is less dramatic than that envisioned by Max Weber and Thorstein Veblen and popularized by James Burnham. Instead of scientists, engineers and other technical staff coming to power by virtue of their indispensability, there is a shift of power to administrative leaders.[22]

---

[17]Thorstein Veblen, *The Engineers and the Price System* (New York: Viking, 1921).

[18]Harold J. Laski, *The Limitations of the Expert* (London: Fabian Society, 1931).

[19]James Burnham, *The Managerial Revolution* (Bloomington, Ind.: Indiana University Press, 1960), pp. 70, 72, 80.

[20]Harold D. Lasswell, Daniel Lerner, and E. C. Rothwell, *The Comparative Study of Elites* (Stanford, Calif.: Stanford University Press, 1952), esp. pp. 16-18.

[21]Robert Presthus, *The Organizational Society*, rev. ed. (New York: St. Martin's, 1978), p. 16.

[22]Harold L. Wilensky, *Organizational Intelligence* (New York: Basic Books, 1967), p. 173.

In political institutions, forms of dual authority frequently emerge. Public officials run for election and fulfill expressive functions, such as voicing the public's needs, preferences, and moods. In contrast, bureaucratic staffs concentrate on dealing with complexity by managing information, organizing and coordinating productive efforts, setting agenda, controlling resources, and formulating and implementing public policies. The authority of elected officials and that of bureaucrats interact and my overlap, but they are nevertheless distinct. Furthermore, as the elected and politically appointed officials become more dependent on administrators, the latter's power expands. Power, as Robert Michels argued, has a self-perpetuating aspect.[23] Those who have power tend to remain in power, since they have the resources to do so. The very fact that legitimacy is such an important consideration in democratic regimes means that existing power distributions can be perpetuated . . .

Power relationships are prevalent in many aspects of life, and the way in which power is distributed and legitimized affect the nature of public policy and the public's well-being. In the United States, large-scale bureaucracies increasingly take over functions previously carried out by individuals, families, and neighborhoods. Within these bureaucracies, the locus of power has shifted from expressive authorities who speak to popular aspirations into the hands of administrators. The American polity, like American business, places power in organizations that are becoming increasingly bureaucratic in terms of structure, process, and behavior. Power is bureaucratized, and bureaucrats emerge as major power holders.

Thinking It Over

1. Given the nature of modern society and assuming the authors' assessment is correct, what does the future hold for our elected institutions such as Congress?

2. Deal with the following hypothesis: "The authors are correct and that makes it necessary to reinstate a balance between the Congress and the President on the one hand and the bureaucracy on the other." *Is* it necessary? Are the Congress and the President together on the same side of the fulcrum?

---

[23]Robert Michels, *Political Parties* (Glencoe, Ill.: Free Press, 1949). See also Charles P. Snow, *Science and Government* (Cambridge, Mass.: Harvard University Press, 1960), and Suzanne Keller, *Beyond the Ruling Class* (New York: Random House, 1963).

80.
THE CASE FOR BUREAUCRACY
by Charles T. Goodsell

Setting the Scene: This is an unabashed defense of bureaucracy. The author is convinced that a close look at how Americans actually feel reveals their judgments of bureaucracy are benign indeed. Point by point he takes us through an analysis that suggests Barry Karl was right (see above): for some strange reason opinion leaders have dressed up a lot of nice folks to look like wolves. But he may have been wrong about rank and file Americans who are not hostile toward bureaucracy at all. Goodsell deals with each kind of evidence brought by the critics of bureaucracy and explains how it fits an overall pattern. It is an essay that will give you plenty of ammunition to make the "case for bureaucracy" youself.

Let us begin by elaborating common depictions of public bureaucracy so that we can appreciate what making the case for it confronts. As for portrayals in mass media, we encounter a relatively simple picture, confidently expressed. The employee of bureaucracy, that "lowly bureaucrat," is seen as lazy or snarling, or both. The office occupied by this pariah is viewed as bungling or inhumane, or both. The overall edifice of bureaucracy is pictured as over-staffed, inflexible, unresponsive, and power-hungry, all at once. These images are agreed upon by writers and groups of every shade of opinion. One is hard pressed think of a concept more deeply ingrained and widely expressed in American cultural life.

To exemplify popular culture's image of bureaucracy, a newspaper feature on the subject describes it as "a brontosaurus of unimaginable size, appetite, ubiquity and complexity." At the federal level alone, the feature notes, this dinosaur owns 413,000 buildings, leases 228 million square feet of space, operates 450,000 automobiles, and owes a trillion dollars in debt.[1] In another illustration, a columnist likens American bureaucracy to "several hundred lidless baskets of snakes placed in a single room," with confusion rampant within and between baskets.[2] A Sunday supplement article solemnly proclaims that despite the tradition of individualism in America, bureaucracy is reducing us to "a nation of paper-shuffling petitioners, forever waiting for permission from some government office for our next step, continually putting aside the work of the world in order to fill out forms."[3] An article in a monthly magazine declares that "the performance of the bureaucracy constitutes the biggest crisis facing our country today," comparable to Watergate or Vietnam.[4]   In short, the

---

[1]Saul Pett, "The Bureaucracy," AP article published 14 June 1981.

[2]Russell Baker, as quoted in John D. Weaver, *The Great Experiment* (Boston: Little, Brown, 1965), p. 15.

[3]Jack Anderson, "How to Outsmart the Bureaucrats," *Parade*, 27 July 1980, p. 18.

[4]Michael Nelson, "Bureaucracy: The Biggest Crisis of All," originally published in the *Washington Monthly* and reprinted in *The Culture of Bureaucracy*, ed. Charles Peters and Michael Nelson (New York: Holt, Rinehart and Winston, 1979), p. 43.

phenomenon of bureaucracy is seen as so terrible that metaphors of snakes and jurassic monsters are needed to describe it, and disasters like military defeat and presidential perfidy are required as standards of comparison to indicate the magnitude of crisis involved.

What evidence do the popular writers have for their attacks on bureaucracy? If we asked them, they would rephrase the question by wondering where evidence to the contrary could be found. One source the popular critics always draw upon is that item found in almost every edition of every daily newspaper, the bureaucratic horror story. This is the graphic and sympathetic account of how some poor citizen has been mistreated by incompetent bureaucrats or how in some other way a great bureaucratic error has been committed. Here are summaries of a few such stories:

- A Chicago woman undergoing chemotherapy for cancer of the breast applied for Medicare. She received a computer-produced letter indicating she was ineligible since she had died the previous April.
- A chronic alcoholic was arrested and mistaken for another man. When he protested, his claims of misidentification were diagnosed as paranoia and schizophrenia, and he was committed to a mental hospital.
- The Department of Energy set out to declassify millions of documents inherited from the Atomic Energy Commission. Eight of the released documents contained the basic design principles for the hydrogen bomb.
- A woman on welfare ran up astronomical medical bills because of terminal illness. She was denied Medicaid on ground that her welfare payments created a personal monthly income $10.80 above the eligibility maximum.
- A unit of what is now the Department of Health and Human Services sent fifteen chimpanzees to a Texas laboratory for the purpose of launching a chimp-breeding program. All were males.

All right, you will say, these stories were newsworthy precisely *because* such horrible and ridiculous things happened. And "bureaucracy" let them happen! Is this not *proof* that bureaucrats are heartless, asinine, and plain stupid?

Notice, however, that the bureaucratic horror story is usually short. Often not many details of the case are included, and those that are given stress the citizen's anguish or the incident's adverse effects. Certainly any extenuating circumstances or the government's side of the story are not covered. Journalists are perfectly aware that what arouses reader interest is the maligned citizen and the horrific outcome, not restrictions faced by bureaucrats in terms of rules with which they must live and workloads with which they must cope. With respect the Chicago breast cancer case, for example, who would care that a new computer-based information system was at the time being installed and many bugs had yet to be worked out? As for the misidentified alcoholic, how many readers are interested in the fact that another man with the name, similar physique, and almost identical birth date was entered on police records? On the Medicaid case, how newsworthy is the fact that personal income maximums are not set by local welfare departments and, if exceeded by them in any amount, result in an adverse state audit and charge-back?

Another point on bureaucratic horror stories has to do with what social scientists would call a sampling problem. The cases appearing in print are selected for attention and not because they are representative. This is so despite the implication often given that repeated occurrence is precisely why these stories are published so often. (One story begins, "Brace yourself. It's more bureaucratic madness."[5]) Actually, a random selection of cases would yield routine and thereby uninteresting subject matter; nothing could be less newsworthy than the smoothly processed eligibility claim or by-the-book police arrest. Moreover, a selection of instances of unusual government efficiency would violate the media's desire to appear independent by being skeptical.

What *is* of interest, to journalists and readers alike, is the bizarre case. In a country as large as the United States, and in a society as efficient in transmitting news as the American, plenty of bizarre cases can be singled out each day. But by definition they are atypical. Especially of interest is the atypical case that reinforces stereotypes of bureaucracy and thereby strikes a responsive chord. All citizens old enough to have conscious memory have experienced incidents from time to time in which officials have acted toward them in baffling and frustrating ways. Hence, everyone can relate personally to the bureaucratic horror story. That is why it is printed. Nevertheless, such stories are not a good research source for finding out how bureaucracy actually operates.

Another kind of evidence frequently cited by popular critics is poll results that reflect the negative overall image of bureaucracy propagated in the media and ingrained in our culture. This is a highly abstract, depersonalized image that I later analyze as central to a grand bureaucratic myth. The polls quoted by critics tap this abstract level almost exclusively, which merely reinforces the conventional wisdom. Gallup, for instance, asked a national sample whether federal employees "work harder or not so hard as they would in nongovernmental jobs." He also questioned whether the federal government "employs too many or too few people to do the work that must be done."[6] In both instances he was surveying abstract images of the federal government and not personal, concrete experience with its agencies or personnel. We are not surprised that about two-thirds of the sample said bureaucrats work "not so hard," and a similar proportion replied that government "employs too many." The conclusion then drawn is that Americans are alienated over poor government services. Yet the questions asked are nicely set up with dichotomous phrasing, and there is little doubt as to the "right" answer in terms of accepted norms. Also, the questions reflect national frustrations that go beyond bureaucratic performance; pollsters have found an erosion of confidence in almost all national institutions in recent years. When we move, in the next chapter, to survey questions where citizens are asked specifically about past personal experiences with government agencies, a radically different picture emerges. This more meaningful set of survey results is ignored by the high priests of popular culture—it is too damaging to their preconceptions and intentions.

---

[5] Mike Royko column published 16 September 1980.

[6] Both questions were asked in 1977. The results of the first are from George H. Gallup, *The Gallup Poll: Public Opinion, 1972-1977* (Wilmington, Del.: Scholarly Resources, 1978), 2:1112. Information on the second question is from the *Washington Post*, 1 October 1978, p. A16.

To frame this discussion in terms of "evidence" actually elevates popular discussion of bureaucracy above its usual level.   Most of the antibureaucratic commentary assumes everyone hates bureaucracy and does not bother substantiating its negative attributes.   The impression is given that consensus is so complete on this issue that the time and trouble needed for verification are unnecessary.   Bureaucracy is portrayed as so wicked that its sins could hardly be subject to exaggeration.

It is easy, then, for individuals and enterprises to exploit this fixation against public bureaucracy without fear of being called to account.   Their interest is not in describing American government but in using antibureaucratic sentiment to their own ends.   Countless politicians run for office (including the highest posts in the land) on platforms that blame society's problems on "the bureaucrats" and their burdensome rules, wasteful extravagance, social experimentation, and whatever else nettles.   Candidates promise that when they are elected, they will deal fiercely and conclusively with these enemies; when, after the election, neither the bureaucrats nor the perceived problems disappear, voters conclude that the survival of the former has caused the perpetuation of the latter.

The exploitation of antibureaucracy sentiment is not restricted to politics.   Comfortable livings are made from the phenomenon.   Numerous amusing books are written that ridicule government servants and agencies, and they sell well.   Public lectures are given on the subject at substantial fees.   Parlor games on evil bureaucracy are manufactured and marketed.   Literary reputations are made by fictional depictions of bureaucracy that use the imagination of the novelist to satisfy the keenest cravings for cynicism and despair.   Futurists make best-seller lists by contending that the rejection and replacement of bureaucracy is the inevitable wave of the future—and indeed is already upon us.

It could all be considered harmless.   After all, politicking by scapegoat and buck-chasing by entrepreneurship are the American way.   Yet, as a result we are treated to the spectacle of the opinion molders of a national culture bent on reinforcing dismal perceptions of a government that is unusual by world standards.   It is a government subject to periodic review in relatively honest elections.   It is a government massively constrained by law and constitution.   It is a government widely admired by foreigners for organizational innovation and technological prowess.   Is American bureaucracy really that bad?

. . .

Our starting point for making the case for bureaucracy is the proposition that its true nature is not outlined in Sunday supplement diatribes, nor even in the reasoned argument found in most scholarly writings on the subject.   Rather, understanding the quality of American bureaucracy begins with exploring the meaning of actual government agencies for the millions of citizens that experience them every day.   The question for these citizens is simply whether the administrative entities encountered do or do not deliver.   These "students" of public administration do not approach the subject as a literary or academic plaything but as a set of concrete institutions upon which they depend for obtaining crucial information, providing vital services, alleviating personal problems, and maintaining a safe community.   In such "study" the stakes are immediate and the impressions direct and fresh.

Direct reports from citizens on their experiences with bureaucracy—as distinct from generalized conventional wisdom on the subject—indicate that they perceive far more good than bad in their daily interactions with it.   Client polls, public opinion surveys, exit interviews, and mailed questionnaires all repeat the basic finding that the majority of encounters are perceived as satisfactory.   Bureaucracy is reported as usually providing the services sought and expected.   Most of the time it lives up to acceptable standards of efficiency, courtesy, and fairness.   Sometimes government agencies perform poorly, of course; innumerable acts of injustice, sloth, and plain rudeness are committed daily in government offices around the country.   No one is claiming perfection for bureaucracy.   At the same time, the basic conclusion of satisfactory citizen treatment as the *norm* rather than the *exception* flies radically in the face of most literature on the subject.   Citizens have an understanding of bureaucracy that those of us who "know" about it professionally seldom seem to attain . . .

Our insights into American bureaucracy are sharpened further when it is studied comparatively rather than as a whole or in isolation.   We use the single noun "bureaucracy" but in so doing refer to a vast multitude of enormously varying institutions.   The extreme heterogeneity of government agencies is underscored when formally identical or similar pairs of organizations are found, beneath the surface, to differ radically.   The bankruptcy of stereotyped thinking about bureaucracy is made even clearer when we discover contrast in aspects of bureaucracy that by reputation are particularly locked into gray uniformity.   We noted, for example, that welfare application forms and welfare waiting rooms vary enormously.

Then, too, we find that certain disparaging differentials thought to exist in relation to public bureaucracy disappear under close scrutiny.   One of these is the long-standing allegation, made by urban liberals, that municipal bureaucracies deliberately discriminate against the poor and racial minorities.   The evidence is overwhelming against this proposition.   An even older denunciation of bureaucracy, advanced by probusiness conservatives, is that public bureaucracy performs poorly compared to the private sector. Comparison between public and private administration is difficult; but when it is possible to compare, business performance is by no means always shown to be superior to governmental. In fact, government is sometimes favored in measures of efficiency, productivity, and innovation.

Finally, a comparison of American bureaucracy to that of other countries underscores the fact that we in this country have much to be grateful for.   Americans usually entertain more favorable perceptions of bureaucratic performance than do citizens of other countries.   In the functional area in which every government in the world invests substantial resources—postal service—program statistics rank the United States as a world leader.   Doubtless the most caustic critics of American bureaucracy sigh with relief when, after traveling abroad, they return to the relatively efficient public services found in the United States.

A major cause for chronic underestimations of American bureaucratic performance is our tendency to hold unrealistic expectations concerning it.   Belonging to a culture used to optimism and problem solving, Americans tend to assume that if announced objectives are not met, something is "wrong."   The initial feasibility of the goals tends to remain unconsidered.   Belonging also to a business civilization, Americans are used to tangible indicators of achievement, that, a "bottom line."   But in bureaucracy goals tend to be idealistic, diffuse, and vague. They often conflict or even contradict. As a result, observers are easily led to conclude that "failure" has occurred because one or more objectives have not been met. Hence, in a way, public bureaucracy does not "fit" American culture too well, which is one reason why its cultural images are so negative. Although individual citizens have mostly satisfactory concrete experiences with bureaucracy, they too encounter divergence from time to time between personal goals and bureaucratic behavior. Regardless of whether this divergence is justified or not, it is transformed into an objectified symbol of contempt: "red tape" . . .

Bureaucracy is further handicapped by the tendency of Americans to expect more from it than just a good job. Bureaucracy is supposed to manipulate successfully conditions in society so as to remove "problems," that is, things identified by someone as painful or unfortunate. But defining a problem does not make it removable. Moreover, because of intervening variables, bureaucracy may do everything possible to correct an external condition without removing it. A manufacturing firm can control the product it produces and is thus in a position to influence the terms on which its work is evaluated. A public bureaucracy, evaluated on the resultant effects of its output, must largely hope for the best.

Bureaucracy is often portrayed as incapable of fostering social change. This is in part also an inflated expectation in that bureaucracies must be recognized as dependent on power and authority external to themselves (even though also possessing both in ample amounts); they cannot be expected to overturn power structures that establish them in the first place. Beyond this limitation, public agencies constantly stimulate and implement changes, although the changes wrought may not always be the particular ones the critics themselves want. Even so, the kinds of substantive change encountered by different public bureaucracies are so manifold in character that somewhere in the society administrative "change agents" operate to please just about everybody, regardless of their position on the political spectrum.

Our misleading stereotypes of bureaucracy extend to the men and woman who staff them, the bureaucrats. Yet a sixth of the working population are bureaucrats, broadly speaking. One needs a creative imagination indeed to classify all of these millions as dullards, lazy bums, incompetents, and malicious oppressors. Actually, apart from race and gender considerations, this sector of the population is very similar to the population at large in terms of demographics. Yet, despite the bureaucrats' "ordinariness," the academic model builders have for some forty years entertained the notion of an ominous "bureaucratic mentality." Under empirical examination such an attitudinal syndrome evaporates into thin air. Bureaucrats are no more authoritarian than any citizen, and their attitudes toward clients are a far cry from patronizing or oppressive . . .

Several misconceptions also prevail about bureaucracy's tendencies with respect to organizational size, growth, and aging. Loose talk of giantism—often centering on the huge size of federal budgets and the largest federal agencies—misrepresents the range of bigness versus smallness found in administrative institutions within the public sector. The daily experiences of people with bureaucracy have little to do with gross expenditure totals or the aggregated vastness of the Department of Defense or Postal Service. What counts is the actual offices and institutions where citizens work and obtain services. Most of these entities are surprisingly small, even tiny, in terms of numbers of employees. According to our admittedly imperfect data, the vast majority of federal installations and local governments employ less than twenty-five people.

Moreover, bureaucracies by no means continually or inevitably grown in size. Some get bigger, some remain stable, others actually decline in numbers of employees. Much of the growth that occurs is due to population or work-load expansion rather than Parkinson's Law or similar imperatives, whether jocular or not. Regardless of changes in size, no evidence is available to support contentions that bigness creates "badnesses" of inefficiency and rigidity. In fact, some empirical studies come to the opposite conclusion. Still another misconception is that bureaucracies never die and become ossified and captured with age. All of these venerable notions collapse when confronted by evidence.

Bureaucracy is often regarded as possessing uncontrollable political power and hence engaging in subversion of democracy. Certainly public agencies possess political power, as they must to perform at all. But this power is not unrestrained. Multiple controls exist, and bureaucrats have incentives to follow as well as lead. Bureaucracies check each other, and in the United States external sources of restriction operate in unusual number and with a particularly strong net effect. American bureaucracy may well be the most inhibited on earth.

Bureaucracy is accused of contributing to socioeconomic inequities in society and a sense of policy drift within the polity. The underlying notion here is that administration corrupts politics, a reversal of the causal direction propounded at an earlier time in the field of public administration. Such a view gives far too much credit to bureaucracy's influence. Public administrators may not mount revolutionary barricades or initiate moral crusades, but at the same time they are hardly to blame for the existence of either capitalism or pluralism. In fact, public bureaucracies help considerably to ameliorate the adverse consequences of each.

Thinking It Over

1. Go to today's paper. See if you can find an example of what Goodsell calls "the bureaucratic horror story."

2. In thinking about the kinds of charges discussed by Goodsell, is it your view that the same charges are made against private bureaucracies as well? Or is there something about public bureaucracies that draw special attention?

81.
THE BUREAUCRATIC EXPERIENCE
by Ralph P. Hummel

Setting the Scene: It is not the bureaucrats who are at fault for the incapacity of bureaucracies to meet human needs, says the author. The evil is found in the nature of the beast. Bureaucracies are *designed* to work inhumanely. Efficiency and humanity are set at odds with one another on purpose in large organizations that process public services. Hummel's piece is thus a fundamental frontal attack on bureaucracy. He argues effectively that bureaucracies, with their lines of authority, rules of procedure, impersonality and routine change human personalities into bureaucratic personalities. Ironically and tragically, these structures end up helping those populations that need help the most—the least.

People have difficulties with bureaucracy. This is true for the administrator who suddenly finds himself or herself in charge of and held responsible for an instrument of purported power and control that eternally squirms and wriggles to escape the grasp. It is true for newly hired workers in a bureaucracy who have to learn a new set of behaviors, norms, and speech patterns to get along and keep their jobs. And it is true for the outsider who wants to do business with a bureaucracy—get a tax refund, register a birth or death, secure a passport, license an enterprise, obtain police protection, or enter a child in school. Quite similar problems exist for the manager trying to control a corporation's sales force; the employee learning to talk, act, and think the way employees typically talk, act, and think at IBM and GM, or ITT; and the customer attempting to get Macy's credit department to correct a mistake the computer made.

If we have experienced bureaucracy in any of these roles, and none of us can long avoid such contact, we have to admit to ourselves that we have great difficulty with bureaucracy—attuning to it, communicating our needs to it, and obtaining satisfactions from it. No matter how astute we are, these difficulties exist, and we may feel that if only we could explain the reasons for such tensions we might be able to do better for ourselves in future contacts.

Bureaucratic Society

The fundamental reasons for our difficulties were spelled out by Max Weber in warnings to which we seem not to have paid much attention. Perhaps to do so would result in too painful a recognition of the vastness of the chasm between social life and bureaucratic existence. Bureaucracy in its modern form, Weber concluded, constitutes the creation of a new world of human interaction. A transformation of normal human life began specifically with the development of modern organization.

In this new world of organized human interaction, it is entirely possible that a baby entrusted to welfare agencies may die of neglect even though in the words of a welfare administrator "everyone concerned did his or her job conscientiously."[1]

In normal human life, Weber points out, people relate to one another through the meaning each attaches to his or her actions—a meaning to which the other responds.[2] Responsibility means acting in keeping with mutually defined meanings. The bureaucrat, on the other hand, is restricted to those actions permitted by the job rules and program requirements. These are defined systemically and from the top down. As a welfare administrator said in the case of the baby cited above—an eight-month-old who died weighing only seven (7) pounds: "There was never a complaint filed with the state's Central Registry charging neglect or abuse."[3]

In the organized system, the bureaucrat is not officially allowed to tune in to the subjective meanings and needs that a client may be trying to convey. The bureaucrat must tune in only to those meanings and needs that have official standing. The result: it is possible for a baby to die even though advocates for the homeless may charge that the baby "spent repeated nights without shelter sleeping on the floor" of a welfare office and that "he was constantly seen dying by Human Resource Administration workers, but none intervened to protect him."[4]

When social interaction becomes organized, those actions become rational that are logically in line with the goals of the organization. This is what Weber meant when he said, "Bureaucracy is *the* means of transforming social action into rationally organized action."[5] Personal responsibility becomes systemic accountability. The system may have faults, but this does not mean we can assign blame to persons operating the system according to rules defined by those faults.

Thus the press may roast the Pentagon bureaucracy for being unable to find an officer who would shoulder responsibility for a crash that, in 1985, killed 248 soldiers aboard a chartered plane at Gander, Newfoundland, but such criticism is simply inappropriate.[6] Accountability, like the military's transport system as a whole, is systemic: the system might be maldesigned but, at best, the dutiful officer is accountable to that system and not responsible to outsiders with their separate social values.

That generals act like bureaucrats rather than warriors may be frustrating, but it is surprising only to the uninitiated.

In the case of the dying baby, the government charged with his care could honestly report that while the system had weaknesses—which could be corrected after the fact by introducing nurses and physicians to welfare offices—all the system's workers did their jobs properly.[7]

The goals of the bureaucratic social system may in themselves be human or humane. It

---

[1] Barbara Basler, "A Blind and Deaf Infant's Short Life on the Rolls of New York's Homeless," *New York Times*, Dec. 20, 1985, pp. B1 and B5; citation from p. B1.

[2] Weber, *Economy and Society*, p. 4.

[3] Basler, p. B5.

[4] Ibid., p. B1.

[5] Weber, *Economy and Society*, p. 987.

[6] "The Broken Chain of Command," editorial, *New York Times*, Dec. 21, 1985, p. 26.

[7] Basler, p. B5.

is just that other human and humane goals not encompassed in the system's objectives cannot be considered by those functionaries who carry out its objectives—at least not in their official capacity. Such goals or needs stand logically outside the goals and needs of the bureaucratic system. They are, in the system's terms, "illogical" and therefore "irrational." It is one of the great ironies of bureaucratic interference in social life that those most in need of whatever help bureaucracy might be able to offer also feel least effective in dealing with it. A study for the U.S. Congress showed that only 46 percent of people with an income below $5,000 felt themselves to be highly effective when dealing with bureaucracy; the figure was 69 percent for those with an income over $15,000.[8]

Great care must therefore be taken, it would seem, in the design of the objects of bureaucratic systems so as to give a chance to human interaction at the functionary/client level. But this may not be enough. Bureaucracy's need for control may impose a form of social interaction incompatible with situations in which people need to care for each other. It may be true, as defenders of public bureaucracy have argued, that "Governments get the messy jobs, and government agencies have many goals imposed on them,"[9] goals that private bureaucracy—business—can't handle. But the problem may be that *any* type of organization that insists on rationally organizing social interaction may be systemically unfit to take *care* of goals and policies that require caring human interaction.

In summary, bureaucracy changes the way human beings relate to one another as social beings:

1. Bureaucracy replaces ordinary *social interaction*, in which individuals act by mutually orienting themselves to each other, by *rationally organized action*, in which individuals orient themselves to goals and meanings defined from the top down.

2. Bureaucracy replaces mutually defined *meaning* of social action by orientation toward systems *functions*.

The extent to which the bureaucratic world is not the normal human world can also be understood psychologically. Weber himself pointed out that bureaucratization favors the development of "the [new] personality type of the professional expert."[10] Because Weber did not develop this theme further in psychological terms, we may have missed that he was speaking about the creation of a new, truncated type of human being.

The Bureaucratic Personality

---

[8]U.S. Congress, Committee on Government Operations, Subcommittee on Intergovernmental Relations *Confidence and Concern: Citizens View American Government* (Washington, D.C., U.S. Government Printing Office, 1973), part 2, pp. 275-76.

[9]H. Brinton Milward, and Hal G. Rainey, "Don't Blame the Bureaucracy!" *Journal of Public Policy*, vol. 3, Pt. 2 (May 1983), pp. 149-168; citation from pp. 154-55.

[10]Weber, *Economy and Society*, p. 998.

Clients find bureaucrats cold and impersonal. But clients have an escape. They can sacrifice what bureaucracy has to offer. They can cut down on dealing with bureaucratic personalities. Most clients, except the most dependent, can turn to other aspects of life—like economic enterprise, social life, and politics. Their own personality is shaped by other than bureaucratic demands.

Bureaucrats are not so lucky. Their job contract with bureaucracy soon becomes a psychological contract. This they cannot escape. Pulled on a daily basis between the human demands of social life and the organizational demands of work life, they live in the tension between two personalities. One is integrated and in charge of itself. The other is fragmented by division of labor and hierarchy and under the control of others. . . .

Two forces originating in organizations' structure shape the bureaucratic personality. First, there is always someone else who is in charge of what you do (hierarchy): deciding whether what you do is socially right or wrong. Hierarchy relieves you of personal conscience and guilt. In psychological terms, hierarchy acts as the individual's superego. Second, what you do is predefined by job description, rules, and the division of labor. This relieves you of having to decide for yourself what work activity is most appropriate for the task at hand. In psychological terms, job definition replaces ego function, the function of mastering the world out of one's own sense of what works.[11]

Individuals respond quite differently to modern organization's demand that, when push comes to shove, members must check their conscience and sense of mastery at the plant gate or office door. One consultant reports this response from bureaucrats to whom the institution's demand for ego and superego control was pointed out.[12]:

> Now, clearly, they would make this argument: Yeah, there are those people who work there whose ego may be questioned in terms of the fact that they are conformist or that they are terribly compliant civil servants, and therefore will do whatever their superiors tell them to do.

But this total collapse in front of bureaucracy's demands is not the experience of most:

> Their experience was more often that political appointees in leadership positions, for example, would make things difficult for them, but that they could make things difficult for those political appointees, given their position in bureaucracy over time and the history they have in their organization, and so forth. So in that sense what they were describing was this tension: given the constraints how can they maintain ego integrity or self integrity?

Psychologically, then, the bureaucrat lives a daily life suspended in the tension between

---

[11]The technical terms "superego" and "ego" used here are Sigmund Freud's. But any modern psychology focuses on the conscience and mastery functions.

[12]Personal communication with Prof. Michael A. Diamond of the university of Missouri, who has served as consultant for federal and state governments.

organization structure and self. Psychology itself, however, cannot tell us anything about the ultimate degree to which bureaucracy is the enemy of self. Human beings, it could be argued, have always had to adapt themselves to their environment. Yet, in the bureaucratic environment, which human beings themselves constructed, they may have overemphasized essentials of human nature that so finally challenge other essentials as to nearly destroy human nature. There is something fundamentally wrong with bureaucracy and not with the individual bureaucrat. The individual always retains his or her human potential. This becomes apparent only when the psycho-logic of bureaucracy is pushed to its logical conclusions. The result becomes clear in two ways: when bureaucracy pushes a human being to the ultimate extreme by "terminating" him or her, and when bureaucracy's basic values themselves are changed as has happened in recent attempts to humanize bureaucracy.

Douglas LaBier, a Washington psychoanalyst dealing with government employees, describes the pain of a perfectly well-adapted federal bureaucrat when the environment became less bureaucratic:

A federal bureaucrat went along for years perfectly happy in his role of giving pain to other bureaucrats on behalf of his boss. This individual's sado-masochistic personality fitted his official role of "hatchet man." The hatchet man's boss upheld a strictly top-down chain of command by a reign of terror. Finally the boss was replaced by a new boss who believed in letting employees help in deciding policy as part of a participative management style.

No longer afforded a legitimate channel for expression the hatchet man's previously "well adjusted pathology" now "erupted as the work environment changed to become healthier."

The hatchet man now began to actively interfere in the work of the division, badmouthing people behind their backs, sabotaging projects that were being worked on, trying to disrupt communications by impeding the flow of memos, and the like. Finally, in pain, he went to see the psychoanalyst, who asked not the usual questions about childhood, but: "Has anything changed in your work lately?"[13]

The symptoms and the pathology are specific to the hatchet man and his situation, but the pain is universal. An entire new movement of psychoanalytically oriented organization analysis beginning in the 1970s has found that bureaucracy produces pain. . . . The efforts of psychoanalysts focusing on work is to alleviate such pain. But there is something that psychoanalysts are specifically prevented from doing by their own competence in dealing with the psyche. This is to undertake the social and cultural analysis that shows *why* bureaucracy is an ultimate challenge to all human beings.

---

[13]Case paraphrased from personal communication with Douglas LaBier, Jan. 2, 1986. The case is discussed in Douglas LaBier, *Modern Madness: The Emotional Fallout of Success* (Reading, Mass.: Addison-Wesley, 1986).

The origin of emotional tension at work, of pain, of an ultimate challenge to the humanity of people lies in the structure of modern organizations itself. It is not to be sought in the individual weaknesses of inmates. This becomes most clear when the bureaucracy "terminates" a bureaucrat. A former contract administrator for a private bureaucracy—the office of mining company[14]:

I didn't really mind getting fired. The company had been in trouble for a long time. What I did mind was passing my boss every day in the hallway and his being unable to look me in the eye, say hello, much less smile. I still had two weeks to go before I'd actually have to leave. He'd see me coming down the hall and he'd turn away.

How did that feel?

Why, it makes you feel like you're nobody—a *nonentity*!

The challenge of bureaucracy to all humankind is not essentially a psychological one. Bureaucracy is not satisfied with disordering the psyche by breaking away large chunks of it and reordering the psyche by distributing it over in organizational structures. Bureaucracy also challenges an individual's entire being. The Greeks had a work for it: being = *ontos*. The fundamental challenge of bureaucracy is not merely a psychological one, it is an ontological challenge. The individual submits to it in agreeing to the initial work contract. Once major functions of the self are placed outside the self—conscience in hierarchy and mastery in job definition—the individual has surrendered his or her being to the organization. This also explains how the organization retains its hold over the individual. An individual trained in letting the organization make decisions of conscience and mastery for her or him over many years loses the ability to refer to her or his own standards for what is right or wrong and whether work is done well. Without the functions originally surrendered to the organization and now lodged there, she or he is—nobody. Not accidentally do we speak of "incorporation." The driving force for all social relations, political power, and administrative control in bureaucracy therefore is the experience of a nameless fear that without one's job one will cease to exist. The driving force of bureaucracy, its hold over humankind, is existential anxiety. . . .

In summary, bureaucracy radically alters the psyche of human beings:

1. Bureaucracy replaces autonomous *personality* with organizational *identity*.

2. Bureaucracy takes the functions of *conscience* (superego) and *mastery* (ego) out of the individual's psyche and distributes them across organizational structures: *hierarchy* and the *division of labor*.

---

[14]Personal communication with Cynthia Confer, Jan. 13, 1986.

3. Bureaucracy, in creating *dependency* of the individual self on structures of the organization (in effect, mingling self and organization), controls its functionaries by manipulating the *existential anxiety* over loss of being that a separation from the job threatens.

Thinking It Over

1. Is it the design of bureaucracy that is at fault or its size? Put another way, is large size part of the definition of bureaucracy? Should it be?

2. If you compare the readings by Hummel and Goodsell, they seem to pass in the night. Why? Can you bring them together?

82.
THE INSTITUTIONAL IMPERATIVE: HOW TO UNDERSTAND THE UNITED STATES GOVERNMENT AND OTHER BULKY OBJECTS
by Robert Kharasch

Setting the Scene: While Professor Hummel deals with bureaucracy from the point of view of the impact of its structure on human behavior (see above), Robert Kharasch approaches bureaucracy from the perspective of the goals institutions seek and the definition of the work they do. While Kharasch's work is intended to be funny (and it is), one finds in its exaggerations and its simplicity many insights into the workings of the administrative state. And it goes down easy.

Nothing seems to work right. The chief products of our society are public bafflement, frustration and rage. The great agencies of government appear to be purposeless, ineffective and yet curiously incapable of improvement.

Our government institutions bear titles promising alleviation of all the ills of our society. Yet the recipients of the regular mercies of welfare agencies insist that they are not faring well. The multiple foreign policy machineries of the United States government have for a decade yielded to an uncontrollable urge to drop bombs on Asian grass huts.

The malaise extends to a profound distrust of the workings of the world's corporations. Even *Business Week*, a journal not noted as the voice of the underground, reports that big companies are viewed with "a great deal" of confidence by only 27 percent of the scientifically sampled public.[1]

Profit-making institutions are not alone to blame; Russian industries have polluted the Caspian Sea as diligently as American industries have destroyed Lake Erie. The convergence of Communists and Capitalists is a popular theme, and is nowhere better illustrated than by the parallel malfunctioning of the instruments of production and government. From the right, the left, and the center there is uneasy agreement that the machinery requires major repairs, and maybe even a factory recall.[2]

The frustration of organized society appears to be widespread, structural and inevitable. It appears to be so, and it *is* so. . . .

---

[1]*Business Week*, June 17, 1972, p. 98.

[2]Mr. Clark Clifford, lately Secretary of Defense and a practiced intoner of high credentials, intones: "The history of the rise and fall of great nations discloses that their decline was not due to lack of power or influence abroad, but to the loss of the confidence of their own people at home—confidence in their Government and confidence in their economy." *The New York Times*, July 2, 1972.

The Devil Didn't Do It

At times, the blame for the malfunctioning of our institutions has been assigned to those individual devils who find themselves temporarily at the helm. Foreign policy will be denounced as the evil product of an Acheson, a Dulles, a Rusk or a Kissinger. Economic policy is attributed to the baleful workings of the Wall Street bankers, the Socialists, or the professorial chairholders of the eastern universities. In their least sophisticated form these theories of government amount to fundamentalist theologies calling for the casting out of devils. Joe McCarthy screamed for the expulsion of Commies and their sympathizers. Other plain Joes regularly interpret the morning news from Washington as the gnawing of termites at the timbers of the Republic.

The trouble with the devil theories of government and institutional action is twofold. *First*, government agencies go through the same notions whether a Democrat, a Republican, or a claimed party-liner occupies the Cabinet seat. The Pinkos and the tools of the Wall Street bankers so often and so noisily exposed in the past have somehow been unable to further their secret causes. Asmodeus is just not the Assistant Secretary for Policy and Plans in any branch of the American government. No way. *Second*, the devil theories are unable to explain why Chinese or Russian foreign policy or economic policy bears such strong family resemblances to American or French policies. If the faults of our institutions were attributable to the evil motives of the bad men running the establishment, then somewhere, sometime, good men ought to do better—but they don't. . . .

What is necessary, then, if the functioning of our institutions is to be understood, is a short statement of the laws which institutions follow. . . .

The institutions that are the subject matter of this work are human creations, and the first definition is as follows:[3]

DEFINITION OF INSTITUTION

An institution is a continuing recognizable group of individuals working together where the group's existence is not measured by a human life.

By this definition the United States Government in all its awful majesty and bureaucratic proliferation is an institution. So is every other High Contracting Party to any international treaty. So is General Motors, and so is the General Staff of the Army, which is itself a sub-

---

[3]Stating our first principles is a matter of some delicacy. Parkinsonian pith is surely to be desired, but overcompression has the undesirable consequence of losing any meaning except to the author. That "love is all" is true, no doubt, but hardly an all-purpose guide to daily action. At the same time, properly complex and qualified statements lack conviction. history does not report that Galileo said, "under carefully controlled laboratory conditions and all other things remaining unchanged, the Earth may be regarded as moving." He said (or we are told he said): "and still it moves." That kind of effect is worth some effort.

institution of a bigger institution. The Upper Suburban Garden Club is exclusive in its membership, but a perfectly acceptable institution by the definition. The moral beauty of an institution concerns us not a bit: the Gestapo, the Red Cross, the Weathermen and the Hospital for the Destitute and Infirm are all alike subject to the institutional laws.

Within every institution, there is a prescribed pattern of activity for those who are members of the institution. This may be filing a form, writing a memorandum or, in the higher reaches of human achievement, arranging for national rehabilitation by aerial bombardment.

In a very general way we can include the pattern of all these scurryings in the anthills by the following:

DEFINITION OF INTERNAL
MACHINERY (WORK)

**The internal machinery of an institution is
the patterns of work established for the
individuals who are a part
of the institution.**

Note, please, that the definition says the patterns of work are "established," but not by whom or for what purpose. In most institutions the reasons for the patterns of work are lost in the mists of time. In some, the reason for the work pattern is sensible and immediately apparent. In all institutions there is a pattern, and whether the pattern first appeared on tablets of stone or an organizational memorandum concerns us not.

Note also, please, the distinction between "the pattern of work" and the purpose of work. The pattern of the work set the Head Torturer is to torture by the accepted means of rack and thumbscrew. The *purpose* of the torture may be declared to be Protection of the Faith during the Inquisition, protection of the Reich in Hitler's Germany, or Protection of Perversion in a motorcycle gang. Whatever the ostensible purpose, the pattern of work set for all Head Torturers is the same.

Equipped with two definitions, we can now state our axioms. Appropriately, they appear in triplicate:

THREE AXIOMS OF
INSTITUTIONAL ACTION

**First Axiom: Any institutional action is
merely the working of the institution's
internal machinery.**

**Second Axiom: Institutional existence depends
upon the continual working of the internal
machinery.**

Third Axiom: Whatever the internal machinery does is perceived within the institution as the real purpose of the institution (i.e., function is seen as purpose).

As any geometry student knows, there is no arguing about axioms. They are given to be accepted. Nevertheless, a little discussion at this point is appropriately directed to those who find the axioms either (a) so obvious as to be meaningless or (b) so meaningful as to be offensive.

The Axioms are meant to be taken quite literally. The First Axiom says: "Any institutional action is merely the working of the institution's internal machinery." Is it not plainly so that an institution cannot act unless its internal machinery (as defined) runs? Pick an institution—any institution. The Outer Exurbs Tennis and Garden Club cannot name Creeping Gadwort the weed of the month without the functioning of the internal machinery for proposing, considering and promulgating such weighty decisions. The institution of the Inner City Police Department cannot arrest a suspect unless the internal machinery functions. If a policemen grabs a suspect but does not go through the machinery of "arresting," the suspect has been conked with a billy club, but he is not "arrested" because the institution did not act.

Put another way, institutional action is recognizable only because the institutional machinery has functioned. If you hire a plane and drop a bomb, you are a nut, properly loathed by all. If you drop a bomb as part of the 923d Wing, duly following Air Force procedures, you may be a hero (to some).

An institution may be insanely complex, as the Department of Defense is, so that the machinery is broken into thousands of subdivisions—those who report and those who plan alternatively, and those who weigh alternatives and those who decide, and those who write decisions and so on, and on. The action of the machinery may be so minor as to be ludicrous: perhaps a directive as to the permissible length of sideburns in the Army. . . . But, there can be no action, no memorandum re: sideburns, unless there are internal procedures—machinery—to consider and act upon sideburneal matters.

The working of this machinery *is* the agency's action. There is just nothing else there but the machinery. To say "The White House tonight sent troops" or "The President sent troops" misses the institutional point. Neither the building nor the man did any such thing. The building couldn't, and the man used (or was used by) the established institutional machinery.

The Second Axiom ("Institutional existence depends upon the continual working of the internal machinery") says no more than that if the machinery stops, so does the institution. A little reflection makes this self-evident. If the machinery for issuing license plates for automobiles stops working—for whatever reason—the existence of the institution called the Automobile License Division of the Bureau of Motor Vehicles also stops. While an institution can wait for work (say, the Fire Department, or the Office of Civil Defense), if there is no work ever in sight, in due course there will be no institution. . . . Stop to note that the absence of *useful* work is no threat to institutional health. Lots of institutions do nothing at all worth doing, but they are in the pink of condition—busy filing, writing memos and seeking more staff. A mild anecdote about auto licensing makes this clear.

The Naïve Commissioner

Upon his appointment to high office, the Commissioner of Motor Vehicles of a midwestern state surveyed his domain. The walls of one large room were lined with rank upon rank of gleaming metal file cabinets. Inquiry revealed that each cabinet held records of all the leases of all the motor vehicles in the state. The files were beautifully kept by a staff dedicated to alphabetization.

The new Commissioner was impressed by the competence of this branch, and turned to go. But an idle thought struck him. "What do we do with these records?" he asked. The answer, solemnly supplied as a full explanation, was: "Why, we file them."

Further inquiry disclosed that never had a record left the file room after it arrived; the filing of vehicle leases had precisely no purpose whatsoever.

The point of the story is not that bureaucracies do nothing with purpose (which is false), but that the institution requires only work, not purposeful work, to survive. This brings us to the Third Axiom.

The Third Axiom declares that Function is seen as Purpose: "Whatever the internal machinery does is perceived within the institution as the real purpose of the institution." Here is a distinction of high significance, offering the clue to much otherwise mysterious institutional behavior. This all-important distinction is between *what is said to be the purpose* of the institution and *what is perceived within the institution as its real purpose.* What is usually said to be the purpose of our institutions is always something noble. Assertions of noble purpose make excellent oratory, but the significant operative purpose is what the worker within the institution thinks is the purpose. The Third Axiom states that the worker thinks the purpose of the institution is *whatever the internal machinery does.* . . .

Those readers who are logicians, systems analysts, or attentive will have noticed a circular aspect of the Three Axioms of Institutional Action.

If whatever the institution's machinery does is perceived by the workers as the real purpose (Third Axiom) and the working of the machinery *is* the action of the institution (First Axiom), and existence depends on continued operation of the machinery (Second Axiom)—well, then the whole business is circular, self-perpetuating and without higher purpose. If you saw this, you saw clearly. It is this axiomatic circularity that leads us at once to the prime directive controlling all institutional action, the Institutional Imperative. . . . Bold-faced type is again indicated, as we are in the presence of truth.

THE INSTITUTIONAL IMPERATIVE

Every action or decision of an institution must be intended to keep the institutional machinery working.

And, as a natural corollary to the Imperative:

COROLLARY TO THE I.I.

To speak of any goal or purpose of an institution other than keeping the institutional machinery running is no more meaningful than to speak of the goal of an automobile exhaust or the purpose of the hum of a sewing machine.

The Institutional Imperative is an absolute law of action, never broken in practice. It is felt in the bone and gut by every person working in every institution. Yet language has such strange powers to overcome both instinct and reason that the workings of the Imperative are never revealed to outsiders. Inside the walls, there is a terrible and irresistible compulsion; the outsider is told the institution acts only from the highest motives.

Again, we pause to consider a few examples.

The Story of the Blank Tariff (A Tale of Simple Virtue)

A tariff, be it known, is a schedule of rates and conditions charged by some public utility.

The ostensible purposes of tariff-filing are high ones. They are: to inform the public of a utility's charges, and to assure that the charges are equally applicable to all. These are, let us concede, most useful and admirable goals, to be accepted with satisfaction. We accept with less satisfaction the operations of the institutional machinery established to carry out such high purposes.

Each regulatory agency has a Tariff Office, or Section, or Bureau. The excellent public servants in the Tariff Office devote themselves to assuring that the tariffs filed by the regulated utilities meet the standards laid down for tariffs by the agency's Tariff Circular. The Tariff Circular contains all the rules and regulations about where, when and how to file tariffs, on what paper and in what form. In general the Tariff Circular deals with matters of form, not substance; it tells how to express a rate, but not how high or low the rate should be.

Many tariffs nowadays appear in loose-leaf form, for easy and cheap revision. As revisions are made, an earlier page is canceled and a new page substituted. A system is prescribed, by Tariff Circular, for recording these changes. The upper-right-hand corner of the seventeenth revision of a tariff page will look like this:

United Carriage Company
Tariff No. 6
17th Revised Page No. 10
Cancels 16th Revised Page No. 10
Issued: April 1, 1984
Effective: May 1, 1984

The system is simple and effective, and hardly seems worth the labor of description. But, we learn as much from an ant as from an elephant. We cannot understand matters of state until we know in the smallest detail how the machinery of the state operates.

A generation ago, an agency which could be nameless but will not be—it was the Civil Aeronautics Board (or "CAB" to its many friends)—required all international airlines to file tariffs. These airline tariffs could be altered only on thirty days' notice. A certain airline—call it Air Anterior—had, on March 1, filed a tariff page as the ninth revision of page 21 of its tariff, to be effective April 1. This ninth revised page named rates which, the page stated, would become effective April 1 and *expire* on April 30. Since future rates had not been decided on, a tenth revised page 21 was filed which was perfectly blank, except for the legend stating it was effective May 1. A few days later Air Anterior filed an eleventh revision of page 21, now naming rates effective May 1, and subsequently filed a twelfth revised page 21, duly canceling eleventh revised page 21, and naming rates effective May 10.

Disaster struck! Air Anterior received a curt notice from the CAB stating that twelfth revised page 21 and eleventh revised page 21 had been rejected for noncompliance with the CAB's tariff circular. A call followed to the airline's regular Washington law firm, and the youngest and hence lowest lawyer on the totem pole was dispatched to the CAB to investigate.

Upon inquiry, the head of the CAB's tariff office revealed that twelfth revised page 21 had been rejected because eleventh revised page 21 had been rejected. And why had eleventh revised page 21 been rejected? Why, because it failed to say "eleventh revised page 21 cancels tenth revised page 21," which meant that tenth *and* eleventh revised page 21 were both still effective, which violated the tariff circular's plain commandment. So also, twelfth revised page 21 had to be rejected because it canceled only eleventh revised page 21 and not tenth revised page 21. All quite correct; thine tariff circular is a just tariff circular, but thine tariff circular is a jealous tariff circular.

But, the eager young lawyer was quick to point out, everything on tenth revised page 21 was perfectly blank. No harm could come by failing to say the magic words "cancels tenth revised page 21" because the tenth revised page was a mere blank—a smile without the Cheshire cat.

This argument was rejected: a violation of the tariff circular was a violation. A blank page is a page, and a page must be canceled. So, the lawyer tried an appeal to grace. Pray grant "special permission" to publish on short notice a new eleventh revised page 21 bearing the proper incantation canceling tenth revised page 21. The chief of the Tariff Bureau, who has such discretionary powers, refused. Making a mistake was not a justifiable reason for asking special permission.

Next, the lawyer tried an argument on a higher plane. The purpose of tariffs is to notify the public, and if the tariff pages were rejected and could not be immediately refiled, either (a) the airline could not operate for the first two weeks in May, having no valid tariff on file, which would leave the public with no air service, or (b) the airline would operate without a tariff, leaving the public open to all the dangers of tariffless transportation. In fact, the lawyer said to the Tariff Bureau Chief, "If you report my client I'll tell the world and the judge just what happened, and they'll laugh you out of court."

The Tariff Bureau Chief's response to this impassioned logic is the point of the parable. Looking with some astonishment at a lawyer so young and unsophisticated, the Bureau chief said kindly: "It's not my job to enforce the tariffs, it's my job to see that they're filed right."

Thinking It Over

1. Try the "institutional imperative" out on the process of registering for your next semester's courses. Does it work?

2. How does Kharasch's analysis fit Hummel's more serious essay? Is Hummel an extension of Kharasch, or vice versa?

83.
BUREAUCRACY
by James Q. Wilson

Setting the Scene: James Q. Wilson is one of the nation's leading political scientists. His main interest is in the field of bureaucracy and public policy. No reader in American government would be complete without a word from him. In the selection reprinted below, Wilson offers a solution to the malfunctions that seem endemic to organizational society. He builds his argument through case studies, one of which you will consider here. In it he suggests something quite remarkable, indeed: the success of the German army early in World War II is to be found, not in its discipline, but in the fact that by most contemporary bureaucratic standards it was highly *undisciplined.* It is in the seeds of this finding that Wilson builds his formula for a workable administrative state.

On May 10, 1940, Army Group A of General Gerd von Rundstedt left its positions in Germany, moved through Luxembourg unopposed and through the southern part of Belgium with only slight opposition, and attacked France. By May 13, the 7th Panzer Division led by General Erwin Rommel had crossed the Meuse River near Dinant and elements of General Heinz Guderian's 19th Panzer Corps had crossed the Meuse near Sedan. On May 14, Guderian sent two armored divisions racing west; by May 19 they had crossed the Somme and later that day had reached Abbeville, a short distance from the English Channel. By the end of the month, the British had been evacuated from Dunkirk. On June 22, France capitulated. In six weeks, the German army had defeated the combined forces of Britain, France, and Belgium. It was, in the opinion of many, the greatest military victory of modern times.

The German success was an example of *blitzkrieg* (literally, lightning war). The word has become so familiar that we mistake it for an explanation. Military officers and historians know differently, but the public at large probably thinks that the key to the German victory can be found in some of the connotations *blitzkrieg* suggests to our minds: A fully mobilized German nation, striking suddenly and without warning, uses its numerical superiority and large supply of advanced tanks and aircraft to overpower a French army hiding in the forts and pillboxes of the Maginot line. The Germans, in this view, were superior to the French in strategy, in resources, and in the fanatical will to fight that had been achieved by ideological indoctrination and centralized command.

Virtually every element in this explanation is either wrong or seriously misleading. The Germans gave the French and British plenty of notice that war was imminent: In September 1939, Germany invaded Poland; France and Britain mobilized; and Allied troops moved into forward positions to defend against an expected German thrust. To be sure, the French and British armies were largely idle and increasingly demoralized during the eight-month-long

"Phony War," but after the fall of Poland (and later of Norway) there was ample warning of German intentions. By March the French intelligence service had acquired a quite accurate understanding of the German military build-up opposite Sedan; the French military attaché in Switzerland had reported that the Germans had built eight military bridges across the Rhine and even predicted, quite correctly, that the Germans would attack toward Sedan between May 8 and 10.[1] Unfortunately, French aerial reconnaissance was almost entirely lacking; no one believed the report of a French bomber pilot that there was a sixty-mile long column of German vehicles, all with their headlights on, moving toward the Ardennes. But the clues were there.

The German army was smaller than the French army[2] and did not have as many tanks as did the French. In 1939, the French army had over 2,342 tanks (compared to the German's 2,171), and the best French tanks were larger and more powerful than the best German ones.[3] (But French tanks, unlike German ones, lacked radios, and so it was hard to maneuver them in concert.) French aircraft were marginally inferior to those of the Germans, but if one adds to the French resources the air forces of Britain and Belgium, the strength of the Luftwaffe was probably no greater than—and may have been less than—that of its adversaries.[4] While the Panzer Corps that made the initial attack were heavily motorized, the German Army as a whole was not. In our vague recollections of lightning thrusts by tank formations, we forget that most of the Germany army in 1940 walked and most of its supplies were pulled along in horse-drawn wagons. (As late as 1943, the typical German infantry division had 942 motor vehicles and 1,133 horse-drawn vehicles and for its supply required twice as many tons of hay and oats as it did of oil and gasoline.[5])

Moreover, the key breakthroughs along the Meuse River front were not accomplished by tanks or aircraft. They were accomplished by foot soldiers who paddled rubber rafts across the water, after which they had to climb up steep banks or dodge across open fields under enemy fire. Supporting fire from artillery, aircraft, and tanks helped the crossing, but these crucial engagements were decided by the infantry.

Unlike the First World War, in the Second the French soldiers did not respond to their mobilization orders in a burst of patriotic enthusiasm. There was no crush outside the recruiting offices. "The memories of the Great War were still too recent," historian Alistair Horne was later to write. "The slogan of the moment . . . became 'Let's get it over with.'"[6] But there is little reason to believe that Germans flocked to their recruiting offices, either; after all, both sides had suffered horribly in 1914-18. The German political leadership attempted to instill Nazi ideology in their rebuilt armies and may have succeeded with the officer corps; they certainly succeeded in the case of the SS divisions. At one time scholars

---

[1] Alistair Horne, *To Lose a Battle: France 1940* (New York: Penguin Books, 1979), 233.

[2] Martin van Creveld, *Fighting Power: German and U.S. Army Performance, 1939-1945* (Westport, Conn.: Greenwood Press, 1982), 5; Barry R. Posen, *The Sources of military Doctrine: France, Britain, and Germany Between the World Wars* (Ithaca, N.Y.: Cornell University Press, 1984), 82-83, and sources cited therein.

[3] Len Deighton, *Blitzkrieg: From the Rise of hitler to the Fall of Dunkirk* (New York: Alfred A. Knopf, 1980), 172-73.

[4] Ibid., 164-65; Posen, *Sources*, 84.

[5] Deighton, *Blitzkrieg*, 175.

[6] Horne, *To Lose*, 126.

were unanimous in their view that ideology played no role in German combat cohesion; now, newer studies are challenging that view. But however successful the Nazis were in motivating German soldiers, it is still not clear that this motivation took the form of Nazi zealotry among the rank and file. . . . The Germans fought hard in 1940 (and just as hard in 1944, when they were retreating in the face of vastly superior Allied forces), but there is no reason to think that political fanaticism had much to do with their combat cohesion. In Germany as in any nation, then as now, soldiers fight out of some mixture of fear and a desire not to let down (or appear to let down) one's buddies in the squad or platoon.

One might suppose that Germany's brilliant strategy was sufficient to overcome all these limitations in men and matériel. Because it worked, the German strategy was, indeed, brilliant, but it was also an extremely risky strategy that could well have failed. Moreover, it is not clear that the strategy itself was decisive.

Originally, Hitler had wanted to attack France by sending the German army through Holland and Belgium to the Channel coast. In October 1939, General Erich von Manstein acquired a copy of the plan and concluded that it would not work: It lacked any clear strategic objective and would not lead to an opportunity to destroy the French army, the bulk of which would presumably be stationed south of the German attack. Moreover, a German officer carrying top-secret documents fell into Belgian hands when his plane crashed; the papers pointed clearly to a German attack on Belgium, and accordingly elements of the French army moved north.

But if not through Belgium, then where? Manstein suggested the Ardennes Forest in the southernmost tip of Belgium and Luxembourg. This route had the advantage of putting the German army on a direct course toward Paris over a route that was flat and open—once it got through the Ardennes and across the Meuse River. But how could one get tanks, trucks, and tens of thousands of troops through that forest and over that river?

Consider the risks: To transport a single Panzer division by railway required no fewer than eighty trains of fifty-five cars each. And once the armored column left the train and started off down a decent road, it would stretch out in a line seventy miles long and move at a pace not much faster than that at which a man could walk.[7] One French reconnaissance airplane could spot this movement and know immediately the direction of the German attack days before it was launched. Now put that armored column on a narrow road that twisted and turned through rocky gorges and over hilly, forested terrain. If the lead tank breaks down, hundreds of tanks and trucks behind it are stalled and the invasion stops.

But suppose that there are no air attacks, no unmanageable breakdowns. The converging tank columns must avoid becoming entangled with one another as they emerge from the forest and then cross a river that is one or two hundred yards wide with a steep bank on the other side—a bank that is hard for attackers to climb but easy for defenders to hold. And then suppose that somehow these barriers are surmounted. At last you are in open country, rolling toward Paris and the English Channel. But by turning from south to west, you expose the entire southern flank of your column to the French army. German Field Marshall Fedor

---

[7]Deighton, *Blitzkrieg*, 154.

von Bock argued that it was "transcending the frontiers of reason" to suppose that such a plan could succeed. "You will be creeping by ten miles from the Maginot line with the flank of your breakthrough and hope the French will watch inertly! . . . And you then hope to be able to lead an operation as far as the coast with an open southern flank 200 miles along, where stands the mass of the French Army!"[8]

The French Maginot line, much derided by contemporary opinion, weighed heavily on the German planning. This system of fortifications, running from the southwest corner of Luxembourg south and southeast to the Swiss border, was thought to be impregnable, and so far as history will ever tell us, we must assume it was. Except for one small fort, it held out against the Germans until France surrendered.[9] The Germans were not inclined to attack it in force and they worried that counterattacks from it against the German flank would create a serious threat.

Bock's arguments were unavailing. Just three months before the offensive began, Hitler endorsed the Manstein plan. It worked.

. . .

The German army . . . did a better job than [its] rivals because [it was a] better organization. . . .

The key difference between the German army in 1940 and its French opponents was not in grand strategy, but in tactics and organizational arrangements well-suited to implementing those tactics. Both sides drew lessons from the disastrous trench warfare of World War I. The Germans drew the right ones.

By the end of that war, it was evident to all that large frontal assaults by infantry against well-entrenched soldiers manning machine guns and supported by artillery would not be successful. A rifleman who must cross three hundred yards of No Man's Land, slipping and staggering through the countless shell holes made by his own side's artillery bombardment and desperately trying to get over or around barbed-wire barricades, had no chance against the murderous fire of dug-in machine guns. The French decided that under these circumstances the advantage belonged to the defense, and so organized their armies around a squad (or *groupe de combat*) of twelve men whose task it was to fire, serve, and support a machine gun. The rifle was regarded as a subsidiary weapon; only three riflemen were assigned to a *groupe* and their level of training was low. These soldiers, dedicated to the support of the machine gunners, were ideally suited to defend a trench but hopelessly ill-suited to a war of maneuver.[10]

The Germans drew a different lesson. Trench warfare led to stalemate, and Germany, surrounded on all sides by potential enemies with larger, manpower reserves, could not afford a stalemate. Therefore, the defensive advantage of entrenched machine gunners had to be overcome. But how? There were only two ways—to make the attacking soldiers bulletproof by putting them in armored vehicles, or to make them hard to shoot by deploying them as infiltrators who could slip through weak points in the enemy's line and attack the machine

---

[8]Quoted in Horne, *To Lose*, 197.

[9]Vivian Rowe, *The Great Wall of France* (London: Putnam, 1959).

[10]John E. English, *A Perspective on Infantry* (New York: Praeger, 1981), 67-70.

guns from the rear.[11] When we recall the Panzer divisions with their hundreds of tanks, we may suppose that the Germans chose the first way. They did not. The Panzers were chiefly designed to exploit a breakthrough, not to create one. To create it, the Germans emphasized infiltration warfare.

Their first experiment with this method occurred in 1916 at the battle of Verdun. Abandoning the conventional massed infantry attack preceded by a prolonged artillery barrage (that eliminated surprise and chewed up ground that had to be crossed), the Germans used a brief barrage followed by small groups of infantrymen who probed for weak spots.[12] Gains were made but they were not exploited. A year later a German army used these tactics systematically to attack Riga; the city fell in two days.[13] Further successes along these lines followed at Caporetto.

The Germans sought to use infiltration tactics to produce a *kesselschlacht* (literally, cauldron battle): a grand envelopment of the opponent's position by turning his flank and spreading out in his rear, exploiting the gains with deep thrusts toward headquarters units (*blitzkrieg*). Under the leadership of General Hans von Seeckt, chief of the army in the early 1920s, this doctrine of maneuver was refined and expounded. It not only fit the lessons of World War I, it fit the realities of Germany's geopolitical position. Under the Treaty of Versailles, Germany was limited to a small professional army that would have to contend with enemies on both the east and the west. It could not match the combined manpower of all of these rivals and it could not afford a war of attrition. Thus, a quick and decisive offensive waged by numerically inferior forces was essential to success.[14]

Such tactics required a certain kind of organization, and the Germans set about creating it. An army that could probe enemy defenses, infiltrate weak points, and rapidly exploit breakthroughs with deep encircling moves could not be an army that was centrally directed or dependent on detailed plans worked out in advance. It had to be an army equipped and organized in such a way as to permit independent action by its smallest units—squads, platoons, and companies. The squad (*gruppe*) should not be tied down to the task of carrying or serving a heavy, water-cooled machine gun. Instead, it should be organized into two sections. The largest (the *stoss trupp*) would consist of seven men armed with rifles and, as resources permitted, with light, rapid-firing machine pistols and submachine guns. The other, smaller section of four men would service a new, light machine gun weighing only twenty-five pounds.[15]

Designing and equipping such a unit were the easiest tasks. The difficult—and crucial—job was to staff and lead it in such a way that it was capable of intelligent, aggressive, and independent action. This meant that the best soldiers would have to be placed in the squads, especially the *stoss* (or assault) *truppen*, not assigned to headquarters or other rear elements. The officers and noncommissioned officers commanding these small

---

[11]B. H. Liddell Hart, *The Future of Infantry* (London: Faber and Faber, 1933), 27.

[12]Alistair Horne, *The Price of Glory* (New York: Penguin, 1964), 337, 342-44; English, *Perspective*, 24.

[13]English. *Perspective*, 26.

[14]Barry R. Posen, *The Sources of Military Doctrine* (Ithaca, N.Y.: Cornell University Press, 1984), 182-88.

[15]English, *Perspective*, 24, 64; Len Deighton, *Blitzkrieg* (New York: Alfred A. Knopf, 1980), 143.

units would have to be given substantial freedom of action. Officers and men alike would have to be given incentives that rewarded fighting prowess, especially that which required them to run risks. Following each battle there would be a rigorous evaluation of the efforts and results. For two decades, the German army devoted itself to solving these organizational problems.

What resulted was a system wholly at odds with the stereotypical view of the German army as composed of fanatical soldiers blindly obeying the dictates of a Prussian general staff. Discipline was severe but it was discipline in service of a commitment to independent action on behalf of combat objectives. In this regard, the post-1920 plans represented a continuation of a military tradition stretching back well into the nineteenth century. The central concept was *auftragstatik*, translated by martin van Creveld in his brilliant analysis of German fighting power as a "mission-oriented command system."[16] Commanders were to tell their subordinates precisely what was to be accomplished but not necessarily how to accomplish it. The mission must "express the will of the commander in an unmistakable way," but the methods of execution should be limited "only where essential for coordination with other commands."[17] The German army, compared to its rivals (or even to the contemporary American army), had remarkably little paperwork. Orders were clear but brief.

The best German soldiers were expected to be the storm troopers, the best German officers were those that distinguished themselves by leading men in battle. Selecting personnel for specific military specialties (infantry, motor transport, supply, and so on) was not the responsibility of a personnel organization located in the rear but of combat (usually regimental) commanders.[18] In choosing officers, character, especially willpower and a readiness to accept responsibility, counted more than education.[19] Officers at first were chosen by the regimental commanders to whom the candidates had applied; when later this was replaced by a central screening office, the testing focused on physical, pedagogical, and leadership abilities. Even then, the final choice was left in the hands of the regimental commanders.

Soldiers and officers were indoctrinated with the primacy of combat and the central importance of initiative. The 1936 command manual put it this way: "The emptiness of the battlefield demands independently thinking and acting fighters who exploit each situation in a considered, determined, and bold way. They must be thoroughly conscious of the fact that only results matter . . . *Thus decisive action remains the first prerequisite for success in war.*"[20] Though there were efforts at Nazi indoctrination, they were not centrally managed by Nazi leaders and probably had little effect. The real indoctrination was called "spiritual strengthening" (*geistige betreuung*) and was the responsibility of the commanding officers.

Medals were awarded chiefly for taking successful independent action in combat (Creveld estimates that medals were given much more commonly for this reason in the German army

---

[16]Martin van Creveld, *Fighting Power* (Westport, Conn.: Greenwood Press, 1982), 36.

[17]General von Lossow, quoted in Creveld, *Fighting Power*, 36.

[18]Creveld, *Fighting Power*, 62.

[19]Ibid., 132, 137.

[20]Quoted in ibid., 28-29 (emphasis in the original).

than in other armies). Punishment was often harsh (it is estimated that over eleven thousand German soldiers and officers were executed during the Second World War, many for "undermining the war effort,"[21] but discipline did not fall disproportionately on hapless soldiers. There were almost as many officers and NCOs punished for mishandling subordinates as there were soldiers punished for attacking their superiors.[22] Perhaps because of this, perhaps because German officers (unlike French and American ones) were allowed to fraternize with soldiers when off duty, German soldiers, when interviewed, had a high opinion of the NCOs and officers, describing them as brave and considerate.[23]

To maintain fighting spirit among the squads, platoons, and companies on which combat success so heavily depended, the German army was built up on a local basis. Military units up to the size of a division were formed out of men with the same regional backgrounds—Prussians, Saxons, Bavarians, and so on.[24] When replacements were necessary, they were drawn, so long as wartime exigencies permitted, from the same regions and organized into groups that were then given their final training by a division's field-replacement battalion so as to insure that the new troops would be organized and trained by the men alongside whom they would fight.[25]

The result was an organization well adapted to the task of getting men to fight against heavy odds in a confused, fluid setting far from army headquarters and without precisely detailed instructions. As Creveld summarizes it, the German soldier "fought for the reasons men have always fought: because he felt himself a member of a well-integrated, well-led team whose structure, administration, and functioning were perceived to be . . . equitable and just."[26]

Of course, strategic and technological factors helped. The Manstein plan, despite its risky features, had the advantage of leading to a decisive engagement, not to an inevitable stalemate. The *Stuka* dive bomber was an effective psychological weapon against French troops that had never seen it nor heard its screaming descent. German tanks had radios, French tanks did not. The French advanced too many of their best troops north into Belgium, where the main attack did not come, and too few toward Sedan, where it did. But in war, good tactics can often save a flawed strategy, whereas bad tactics can rarely make even an excellent strategy succeed. The French prepared, tactically as well as strategically, to refight World War I, a war of fixed positions and massed firepower. For such a war they made reasonably good preparations—drawing up detailed mobilization plans, building heavy fortifications, acquiring large quantities of tanks and artillery, organizing their squads around heavy machine guns, and maintaining tightly centralized control over operations. Had they adopted different tactics embedded in a more flexible organization, their strategic errors might

---

[21]Ibid., 114.

[22]Ibid., 115.

[23]Edward A. Shils and Morris Janowitz, "Cohesion and Disintegration in the Wehrmacht in World War II," *Public Opinion Quarterly* 12 (1948): 280-315.

[24]Creveld, *Fighting Power*, 45.

[25]Ibid., 75-76,

[26]Ibid., 163-64.

not have counted so heavily against them.

. . .

The German army beat the French army in 1940; the Texas prisons for many years did a better job than did the Michigan prisons; Carver High School in Atlanta became a better school under Norris Hogans. [Here Wilson is referring to other examples used in his book.] These successes were the result of skilled executives who correctly identified the critical tasks of their organizations, distributed authority in a way appropriate to those tasks, infused their subordinates with a sense of mission, and acquired sufficient autonomy to permit them to get on with the job. The critical tasks were different in each case, and so the organizations differed in culture and patterns of authority, but all three were alike in one sense: incentives, culture, and authority were combined in a way that suited the task at hand.

By now . . . the reader may find [these points] painfully obvious. If . . . obvious to the reader, then surely they are obvious to government officials. Intellectually perhaps they are. But whatever lip service may be given to the lessons I have drawn from the agencies discussed in this book, the daily incentives operating in the political world encourage a very different course of action.

Thinking It Over

1. Take an organizational structure with which you are familiar and apply Wilson's logic to it. Does it make sense? Is it organized in a way that would please Wilson? If you are having trouble thinking of an example of an organization, use the one in which the class for which this reading is assigned is located.

2. Read (if you haven't) either or both of the two critiques of administration included in this chapter. Would Wilson's thesis survive based on the arguments used in one or both of these other perspectives?

Chapter XIII

THE COURTS

84.
THE FEDERALIST PAPERS, NO. 78
by Alexander Hamilton

Setting the Scene: Here Alexander Hamilton defends several principles that the framers of the Constitution built into the Supreme Court. As in other readings from *The Federalist Papers*, the important thing to bear in mind is the linkage between the theory (the principles) and structure (the architecture) of the Court. Pay attention, too, to the *language* Hamilton uses. It may seem strange at first—it always does when you read *The Federalist*—but on reflection one must agree that what needs to be said gets said and in a way that has a resonance, even a majesty, that seems fitting.

We proceed now to an examination of the judiciary department of the proposed government.

In unfolding the defects of the existing confederation, the utility and necessity of a federal judicature have been clearly pointed out. It is the less necessary to recapitulate the considerations there urged; as the propriety of the institution in the abstract is not disputed; the only questions which have been raised being relative to the manner of constituting it, and to its extent. To these points, therefore, our observations shall be confined.

The manner of constituting it seems to embrace these several objects: 1st. The mode of appointing the judges; 2nd. The tenure by which they are to hold their places; 3rd. The partition of the judiciary authority between different courts, and their relations to each other.

First. As to the mode of appointing the judges: This is the same with that of appointing the officers of the union in general, and has been so fully discussed . . . that nothing can be said here which would not be useless repetition.

Second. As to the tenure by which the judges are to hold their places: This chiefly concerns their duration in office; the provisions for their support; the precautions for their responsibility.

According to the plan of the convention, all the judges who may be appointed by the United States are to hold their offices *during good behavior*; which is conformable to the most approved of the state constitutions. . . . The standard of good behavior for the continuance in office of the judicial magistracy is certainly one of the most valuable of the modern improvements in the practice of government. In a monarchy, it is an excellent barrier to the despotism of the prince; in a republic, it is a no less excellent barrier to the encroachments and oppressions of the representative body. And it is the best expedient which can be devised in any government, to secure a steady, upright, and impartial administration of the laws.

Whoever attentively considers the different departments of power must perceive, that, in a government in which they are separated from each other, the judiciary, from the nature of its functions, will always be the least dangerous to the political rights of the constitution; because it will be least in a capacity to annoy or injure them. The executive not only dispenses the honors, but holds the sword of the community. The legislature not only commands the purse, but prescribes the rules by which the duties and rights of every citizen are to be regulated. The judiciary, on the contrary, has no influence over either the sword or the purse; no direction either of the strength or of the wealth of the society; and can take no active resolution whatever. It may truly be said to have neither FORCE NOR WILL, but merely judgment; and must ultimately depend upon the aid of the executive arm for the efficacious exercise even of this faculty.

This simple view of the matter suggests several important consequences: It proves incontestably, that the judiciary is beyond comparison, the weakest of the three departments of power, that it can never attack with success either of the other two; and that all possible care is requisite to enable it to defend itself against their attacks. It equally proves, that, though individual oppression may now and then proceed from the courts of justice, the general liberty of the people can never be endangered from that quarter; I mean so long as the judiciary remains truly distinct from both the legislature and executive. For I agree, that "there is no liberty, if the power of judging be not separated from the legislative and executive powers." It proves, in the last place, that as liberty can have nothing to fear from the judiciary alone, but would have everything to fear from its union with either of the other departments; that, as all the effects of such an union must ensue from a dependence of the former on the latter, notwithstanding a nominal and apparent separation; that as, from the natural feebleness of the judiciary, it is in continual jeopardy of being overpowered, awed or influenced by its co-ordinate branches; that, as nothing can contribute so much to its firmness and independence as PERMANENCY IN OFFICE, this quality may therefore be justly regarded as an indispensable ingredient in its constitution; and, in a great measure, as the CITADEL of the public justice and the public security.

The complete independence of the courts of justice is peculiarly essential in a limited constitution. By a limited constitution, I understand one which contains certain specified exceptions to the legislative no *ex post facto* laws, and the like. Limitations of this kind can be preserved in practice no other way than through the medium of the courts of justice, whose duty it must be to declare all acts contrary to the manifest tenor of the constitution void. Without this, all the reservations of particular rights or privileges would amount to nothing.

Some perplexity respecting the right of the courts to pronounce legislative acts void, because contrary to the constitution, has arisen from an imagination that the doctrine would imply a superiority of the judiciary to the legislative power. It is urged that the authority which can declare the acts of another void, must necessarily be superior to the one whose acts may be declared void. As this doctrine is of great importance in all the American constitutions, a brief discussion of the grounds on which it rests cannot be unacceptable.

There is no position which depends on clearer principles than that every act of a delegated authority, contrary to the tenor of the commission under which it is exercised, is void. No legislative act, therefore, contrary to the constitution, can be valid. To deny this would be to affirm, that the deputy is greater than his principal; that the servant is above his master; that the representatives of the people are superior to the people themselves; that men, acting by virtue of powers, may do not only what their powers do not authorize, but what they forbid.

If it be said that the legislative body are themselves the constitutional judges of their own powers, and that the construction they put upon them is conclusive upon the other departments, it may be answered, that this cannot be the natural presumption, where it is not to be collected from any particular provisions in the constitution. It is not otherwise to be supposed that the constitution could intend to enable the representatives of the people to substitute their *will* to that of their constituents. It is far more rational to suppose that the courts were designed to be an intermediate body between the people and the legislature, in order, among other things, to keep the latter within the limits assigned to their authority. The interpretation of the laws is the proper and peculiar province of the courts. A constitution is, in fact, and must be, regarded by the judges as a fundament law. It must therefore belong to them to ascertain its meaning, as well as the meaning of any particular act proceeding from the legislative body. If there should happen to be an irreconcilable variance between the two, that which has the superior obligation and validity ought, of course, to be preferred; in other words, the constitution ought to be preferred to the statute, the intention of the people to the intention of their agents.

Nor does his conclusion by any means suppose a superiority of the judicial to the legislative power. It only supposes that the power of the people is superior to both; and that where the will of the legislature declared in its statutes, stands in opposition to that of the people declared in the constitution, the judges ought to be governed by the latter, rather than the former. They ought to regulate their decisions by the fundamental laws, rather than by those which are not fundamental. . . .

It can be of no weight to say, that the courts, on the pretense of a repugnancy, may substitute their own pleasure to the constitutional intentions of the legislature. This might as well happen in the case of two contradictory statutes; or it might as well happen in every adjudication upon any single statute. The courts must declare the sense of the law; and if they should be disposed to exercise WILL instead of JUDGMENT, the consequence would equally be the substitution of their pleasure to that of the legislative body. The observation, if it proved anything, would prove that there ought to be no judges distinct from the body.

If then the courts of justice are to be considered as the bulwarks of a limited constitution, against legislative encroachments, this consideration will afford a strong argument for the permanent tenure of judicial officers, since nothing will contribute so much as this to that independence spirit in the judges, which must be essential to the faithful performance of so arduous a duty.

This independence of the judges is equally requisite to guard the constitution and the rights of individuals, from the effect of those ill-humors which the arts of designing men, or the influence of particular conjunctures, sometimes disseminate among the people themselves, and which, though they speedily give place to better information, and more deliberate reflection, have a tendency, in the meantime to occasion dangerous innovations in the government, and serious oppressions of the minor party in the community. . . . Until the people have, by some solemn and authoritative act, annulled or changed the established form, it is binding upon themselves collectively, as well as individually; and no presumption, or even knowledge of their sentiments, can warrant their representatives in a departure from it, prior to such an act. But it is easy to see, that it would require an uncommon portion of fortitude in the judges to do their duty as faithful guardians of the constitution, where legislative invasions of it had been instigated by the major voice of the community.

But it is not with a view to infractions of the constitution only, that the independence of the judges may be an essential safeguard against the effects of occasional ill-humors in the society. These sometimes extend no farther than to the injury of the private rights of particular classes of citizens, by unjust and partial laws. Here also the firmness of the judicial magistracy is of vast importance in mitigating the severity, and confining the operation of such laws. It not only serves to moderate the immediate mischiefs of those which may have been passed, but it operates as a check upon the legislative body in passing them; who, perceiving that obstacles to the success of an iniquitous intention are to be expected from the scruples of the courts, are in a manner compelled by the very motives of the injustice they meditate, to qualify their attempts. . . .

That inflexible and uniform adherence to the rights of the constitution, and of individuals, which we perceive to be indispensable in the courts of justice, can certainly not be expected from judges who hold their offices by a temporary commission. Periodical appointments, however regulated, or by whomsoever made, would, in some way or other, be fatal to their necessary independence. If the power of making them was committed either to the Executive or legislature, there would be danger of an improper complaisance to the branch which possessed it; if to both, there would be an unwillingness to hazard the displeasure of either; if to the people, or to persons chosen by them for the special purpose, there would be too great a disposition to consult popularity, to justify a reliance that nothing would be consulted but the Constitution and the laws.

There is yet a further and a weightier reason for the permanency of the judicial offices, which is deducible from the nature of the qualifications they require. It has been frequently remarked, with great propriety, that a voluminous code of laws is one of the inconveniences

89.
DAVID SOUTER:
TESTIMONY BEFORE THE SENATE
JUDICIARY COMMITTEE

Setting the Scene: There is no doubt that politics has been clearly involved in the process of selecting Justices to the Supreme Court in recent years. Interest groups mobilize. Polls are taken. Demonstrations are held. Politicians posture and pronounce. Serious thinkers do not agree if this is a good thing or not. But one thing is clear. It is not surprising. If the Court is going to make the final decisions in major areas of public policy in a democracy, one would surely expect the people to be involved. What follows is a series of questions and answers from the Senate confirmation hearings of Justice David Souter. These questions focused on the abortion issue because everyone knew that Souter might be the swing vote that changed America's fundamental law in this area. The Senate wanted to know. We *all* wanted to know. Souter didn't want to say. What you will be reading here is *critical* stuff, history in the making. In terms of the high drama of politics it doesn't get any better than this. We begin as Senator Biden tries to tease out Souter's views on the "right to privacy" (found in the Griswold case) that stands behind the *Roe v. Wade* decision.

September 13, 1990

SENATOR BIDEN. Do you agree with Justice Harlan's opinion in *Griswold* [*v. Connecticut*] that the due process clause of the 14th Amendment protects the right of a married couple to use birth control, to decide whether or not to have a child?

JUDGE SOUTER. I believe that the due process clause of the 14th Amendment does recognize and does protect an unenumerated right of privacy. . . . The only reservation I have is a purely formal reservation in response to your question, and that simply is no two judges, I am sure, will ever write an opinion the same way, even if they share the same principles. . . .

QUESTION: Now, you've just told us that the right to use birth control and decide whether or not to become pregnant is one of those fundamental rights, the value placed on it is fundamental. Now, let's say that a woman and/or her mate uses such birth control device and it fails. Does she still have a constitutional right to choose not to become pregnant?

ANSWER: Senator, that's the point at which I will have to exercise the prerogative which you were good to speak of explicitly. I think for me to start answering that question, in effect, is for me to start discussing the concept of *Roe v. Wade.* And I would be glad—I don't think I have to do so for you—but I would be glad to explain in some details my reasons for believing that I cannot do so, but of course they focus on the fact that ultimately the question which you are posing is a question which is implicated by any possibility of the examination of *Roe v. Wade*. And that, as we all know, is not only a possibility, but a likelihood that the Court will be asked to do it. . . .

SENATOR HOWARD METZENBAUM. I want to start—talk with you on a personal level, not as a constitutional scholar nor as a lawyer. This year, I held hearings on legislation that would codify the principles of *Roe v. Wade*. I heard stories from two women who had had illegal abortions prior to 1973. They were women about your age. They told horrifying stories. One woman was the victim of a brutal rape, and she could not bear raising a child from that rape alongside her own two children. Another woman who was poor and alone self-aborted. It's a horrible story, just a horrible story, with knitting needles and a bucket. I heard from a man whose mother died from an illegal abortion when he was 2 years old after doctors told her that she was not physically strong enough to survive the pregnancy.

I will tell you, Judge Souter, that the emotion that those people still feel after more than 20 years is very real. It's sufficiently strong to have conveyed it to those of use who heard their testimony. Each woman risked her life to do what she felt she had to do. One of those women paid the price.

My real question to you isn't how you will rule on *Roe v. Wade* or any other particular case coming before the Court. But what does a woman face when she has an unwanted pregnancy, a pregnancy that may be the result of rape or incest or failed contraceptives or ignorance of basic health information? And I would just like to get your own view and your thoughts of that woman's position under those circumstances.

ANSWER: Senator, your question comes as a surprise to me. I wasn't expecting that kind of a question. And you have made me think of something that I have not thought of for—24 years.

When I was in law school, I was on the board of freshman advisers at Harvard College. I was a proctor in a dormitory at Harvard College. One afternoon, one of the freshman who was assigned to me—I was his adviser—came to me, and he was in pretty rough emotional shape, and we shut the door and sat down. And he told me that his girlfriend was pregnant. And he said, "She's about to try to have a self-abortion, and she doesn't know how to do it." And he said, "She's afraid to tell her parents what has happened, and she's afraid to go the health services." And he said, "Will you talk to her?" And I did.

I know you will respect the privacy of the people involved, and I will not try to say what I told her. But I spent two hours in a small dormitory bedroom that afternoon in that room, because that was the most private place we could get so that no one in the next suite of rooms could hear, listening to her and trying to counsel her to approach her problem in a way different from what she was doing. And your question has brought that back to me. And I think the only thing I can add to that is I know what you are trying to tell me, because I remember that afternoon.

QUESTION: Well, I appreciate your response. I think it indicates that you have empathy for the problem. . . .

September 14, 1990

SENATOR CHARLES E. GRASSLEY. Under our system of government, of course, our face-to-face meeting these few days is likely to be the last time any of use will be able to ask you questions. And so I hope that we can continue our dialogue not to seek commitment from you on specific cases, but rather to more fully understand your approach to deciding these cases. . . .

Judge Souter, a recent nominee to the Supreme Court once said . . . "in a constitutional democracy, the moral content of law must be that of a framer or a legislator, never that of the morality of the judge." Do you share that philosophy of judging?

JUDGE SOUTER. Yes, I share the demand that we look outside ourselves, the demand that we guard against simply imposing our views of morality or public policy, however passionately we may hold them and however profound our principle may be. We have not been placed upon courts in effect to impose our will. We have been placed upon courts to impose the will that lies behind the meaning of those who framed and, by their adoption, intended to impose the law and the constitutional law of this country upon us all.

QUESTION: So, when it comes to the judge's own values and beliefs, there is little or no room for those in his constitutional interpretation.

ANSWER: He has got to guard constantly against substituting his values for the values which he has sworn to uphold. . . .

SENATOR GORDON J. HUMPHREY. Judge, you were a member of the board of trustees at the Concord Hospital from 1971 to 1985. In 1973, the trustees voted to begin performing abortions in that hospital. Have you said for the record how you voted on that issue?

ANSWER: I think I have, but the—I voted for the resolution. . . .

QUESTION: So you voted in support of the policy change, the result of which the hospital began to perform abortions, consistent with the law, of course.

ANSWER: That abortions could be performed within the hospital and my, also, my recollection also is that the resolution was explicit in saying that this did not obligate a given hospital employee or medical staff member to do anything against conscience.

QUESTION: Right. Good, good. Well, I'm not asking you, in this next question, to comment on *Roe v. Wade*, that is, its correctness, but I would ask you to explain your vote as a trustee of the Concord Hospital. Clearly the hospital was under no obligation to begin performing abortions. Why did you choose to support a change in policy such that the hospital began to perform abortions?

ANSWER: Well, the change in policy was to allow doctors who choose to perform abortions as a medical procedure in that hospital to do so consistently with *Roe v. Wade*. . . . The reason the hospital took that position, and the reason I voted for it, was that the Concord Hospital was a community hospital; it was not tied to any sectarian affiliation; it served people of all religious and moral beliefs; its medical staff represented all religious and moral beliefs, and so did the patients who went through the hospital. We did not believe that it was appropriate for us, whatever might be the moral views of a given trustee, to impose those views upon the hospital when in fact it was the law of the United States that a given procedure was lawful.

There was, of course, a further justification. . . . One of the functions which the hospital was giving to the community was the function of the greatest degree of safety in medical care. And if abortions are going to be performed, as by law they could be performed, it was appropriate in a non-sectarian hospital to allow the full range of backup services for the safety of the mother. . . .

QUESTION: So you did not feel in that case that it was appropriate to bring to bear any moral judgment. Is that what you're saying?

ANSWER: I did not.

QUESTION: Does your vote in any way indicate, back then, any way indicate that you feel that unborn human beings are not persons?

ANSWER: My vote has no such implication. My judgment with respect to the appropriateness of the procedure in a hospital of which I was a trustee is no more a reflection of a personal moral view of mine, pro or con, than would be any judgment that I was required to make as a judge of a court. . . .

SENATOR HERB KOHL. Just a couple of questions on *Roe v. Wade*. In 1973 when it was promulgated . . . do you recall your feelings about *Roe v. Wade* back when it was promulgated?

JUDGE SOUTER. I frankly don't remember the early discussions on it. I mean, everybody was arguing it. . . .

QUESTION: You had no—you had no opinion about it other than just to say, "Wow"?

ANSWER: Oh, I doubtless—I doubtless had an opinion. No, I didn't just way wow.

QUESTION: What was your opinion in 1973 on *Roe v. Wade*?

ANSWER: Well, with respect, Senator, I'm going to ask you to let me draw the line there. . . .

QUESTION: O.K. With respect to *Roe v. Wade* just once more, is it fair to state even though you're not prepared to discuss it, understandably, that you do have an opinion on *Roe v. Wade*?

ANSWER: It—I think it would be misleading to say that. I have not got any agenda on what should be done with *Roe v. Wade* if that case were brought before me.

I will listen to both sides of that case. I have not made up my mind. And I do not go on the Court saying I must go one way or I must go another way. The—as you know, the issue that arises when an established and existing precedent is attacked is a very complex issue. It involves not only the correctness or the incorrectness, by whatever lights we judge it, of a given decision. It can also involve extremely significant issues of precedent. And I do not sit here before you under oath having any commitment in my mind as to what I would do if I were on that Court and that case were brought before me. . . .

SENATOR EDWARD M. KENNEDY. Judge, just a few moments ago, in response to the questions of Senator Thurmond, you talked about the moral dilemma that some judges might face who are against the death penalty and yet must impose it, and I thought you demonstrated some legitimate concern for those particular judges. And then you talked about the whole question of the morality of sentencing in terms of white collar criminals, and I thought was—you were very eloquent when you talked about the fact that some of those who are involved in white collar crime might expect that they should at least in the first offense not do time, and you expressed your own kind of moral concern that that was not correct.

Well, picking up on that question, let me ask you this, whether—as a matter of your own individual and personal moral beliefs, do you believe that abortion is moral or immoral?

JUDGE SOUTER. Senator, I'm going respectfully to ask to decline to answer that question for this reason: that whether I do or do not find it moral or immoral will play absolutely no role in any decision which I make, if I am asked to make it, on the question of what *Wade* should or legitimately may be given to the interest which is represented by the abortion decision. And I think to answer that question and to get into a matter of personal morality of mine, when it would not affect my judgment, would go far to—to dispel the promise of impartiality in approaching this issue if it comes before me.

Thinking It Over

1. A friend of mine said the following to me during the Souter hearings. "The abortion issue matters—a lot to the people of America. Souter's vote will be critical. Why shouldn't we know what it will be? And while we're at it, does anyone doubt he's lying? How could he *not* have thought through how he would have voted on *Roe*. Hell, everyone in America has and he's a judge!" What should my response to my friend have been?

2. What about it? Can you gather from Souter's testimony what his view on abortion is?

90.
THE SUPREME COURT: HOW IT WAS, HOW IT IS
by William H. Rehnquist

Setting the Scene: Often we live in awe of persons who rise to high ranks like justices on the Supreme Court. It's important to understand, however, that many of them are just like you. What follows is Chief Justice Rehnquist's own account of his first trip to Washington to work for the Court—as a clerk to Justice Robert H. Jackson. Driving across the heartland, racing a snowstorm in a car without a heater, a solitary young person on the threshold of life heading for Washington and . . .   It could be you. Rehnquist's account also takes us through his first day at work and his first case. In doing so, he gives us a lesson in how important staff work can be, how the Court goes about its work, and also how judges learn to make decisions in a world of complexity and incomplete information.   In a word, how does one fight off the insecurities that plague the human condition even (and especially) for those among us who are called upon to make the biggest decisions of all.

It was the morning of January 30, 1952, in Wooster, Ohio. I had spent the night in a tourist home, where, despite the inflation resulting form the Korean War, one could still get a room for four dollars. I was en route from my parents' home in Milwaukee, Wisconsin, to Washington, D.C. I was due there two days later to report for duty as a law clerk to Robert H. Jackson, one of the eight associate justices of the Supreme Court of the United States. It was a highly prized position; I was surprised to have been chosen for it, and I did not want to be late for the start of my work. . . .

Concern with the weather for the remaining part of my trip to Washington became more acute as I read the weather report. It had apparently been snowing farther south in Ohio yesterday and that storm was expected to move eastward across the Appalachians today. The morning in Wooster was overcast, and there was snow on the ground, although none was falling at present. Since my transportation for this trip consisted of a 1941 Studebaker Champion, a good little car but eleven years old, I decided that I had best be on my way as soon as possible. Driving through the Great Lakes states in the middle of winter I had become acutely aware of a seasonal shortcoming of my car. It had no heater. Looking back from the present time, it is hard for me to believe that even as long ago as 1941 a heater would have been optional equipment on a car sold in Milwaukee, Wisconsin. But I know from occasionally bitter memory that the car did not have a heater, and therefore I certainly did not want to be on the road after sundown if I could avoid it . . .

I was a twenty-seven-year-old bachelor, somewhat late in completing my education because of three years' service in the military during World War II. By going through two summer sessions, I had managed to finish Stanford Law School in December 1951. The clerkship with Justice Jackson would be my first job as an honest-to-goodness graduate lawyer.

A large element of luck seemed to me to have entered into my selection as Justice Jackson's law clerk. Through studying about constitutional law in law school, and picking up bits of information here and there, I of course knew that justices of the Supreme Court had law clerks. Indeed, two recent Stanford graduates, Warren Christopher in the class of '49 and Marshall Small in the class of '51, had been clerks to Justice William O. Douglas. But Justice Douglas himself had western roots, and had arranged for the committee that chose his clerks to interview applicants on the West Coast. The chance of getting a clerkship with one of the other justices seemed remote indeed to a Stanford student such as I was, in a day when one did not fly across the country except in the event of a major emergency, and when one did not spend one's small savings on transcontinental train trips for interviews that seemed to have little prospect of success.

But, as fate would have it, Justice Jackson came to dedicate the new Stanford Law School building in the summer of 1951, when I was attending my second summer session. Phil Neal, my administrative-law professor, had himself clerked for Justice Jackson several years before. Shortly before Justice Jackson was due to arrive for the dedication ceremonies, Professor Neal asked me if I would be interested in clerking for the justice; the suggestion came to me out of a clear blue sky, but I naturally said that I would be. Neal then arranged for Justice Jackson to interview me for the position while he was at Stanford.

It cannot be difficult to imagine the fear and trembling with which I approached the interview. My academic record at Stanford Law School was excellent, but Stanford at that time did not enjoy as much national prestige as it now does. I first tried to bone up for my meeting with the justice by reading some of his opinions, and by trying to steep myself in constitutional law. After a few hours, however, I decided that it was utterly futile; if I had not learned enough constitutional law in my course on the subject to quality for the position, I would probably not learn it in a few additional hours of cramming.

I met with Justice Jackson in one of the faculty offices, and his pleasant and easygoing demeanor at once put me at ease. After a few general questions about my background and legal education, he asked me whether my last name was Swedish. When I told him that it was, he began to reminisce about some of the Swedish clients he had had while practicing law in upstate New York before he had moved to Washington. I genuinely enjoyed listening to the anecdotes, but somehow I felt I should be doing more to make a favorable impression on him. He, however, seemed quite willing to end the interview with a courteous thanks for my having come by, and I walked out of the room sure that in the first minutes of our visit he had written me off as a total loss.

I was naturally surprised, therefore, to receive a litter from him in November 1951, telling me that his efforts to get by with only one law clerk that term were not working out well, and that both he and the clerk felt that some added assistance was in order. I had told him that because of my going through the summers I would graduate from Stanford in December, and he requested that I come to Washington on February 1, 1952, and plan to serve as his clerk from then until June 1953. I was surprised and delighted to receive this offer, and accepted it immediately.

As I noted the steady lowering of the southeastern sky, I thought to myself that a Swedish surname might have helped in the interview last summer but it wasn't going to help me perform the presumably demanding tasks associated with my new job. I crossed the Ohio River at Wheeling, West Virginia, and by the time I was in Pennsylvania, it had started to snow. An hour or so later, when I angled south across the Pennsylvania line into western Maryland, it was snowing hard. I was following United States highway number 40, the old "national road," which would take me to within forty miles of Washington . . .

. . . I came over the Appalachians, went through Hagerstown, and climbed back over the Blue Ridge without much more improvement in visibility. But when I finally turned south toward Frederick the skies began to brighten some, and the snow first let up and then stopped. During the last forty miles from Frederick to Washington the sun emerged from behind the clouds, and I had the feeling that it was personally welcoming me to the Nation's Capital.

. . . I had been in Washington only once before in my life, when I came with my cousins from Iowa between my junior and senior year in high school. But I had absolutely no recollection of ever having seen the Supreme Court building; as I looked at it now, I felt sure that I would have remembered it if I had seen it before.

Behind me and across the Capitol plaza was the United States Capitol building, with its familiar dome thrusting up into the chilly gray February sky. In front of me was the main portico that provided entrance to the Supreme Court building, flanked on either side by two large, seated, marble figures. The portico itself is supported by sixteen massive Corinthian marble columns. Above these on the architrave is inscribed in large letters the familiar phrase "Equal Justice Under Law." Capping the entrance is a pediment with a sculptured group in bas-relief. The whole impression is of a magnificent Greek temple of white marble, flanked by two low wings extending outward on each side.

. . . I climbed the seemingly endless steps leading up to the front entrance of the building, opened the large door, and walked through a vestibule. Beyond the vestibule I entered the Great Hall, and here again paused to feast my eyes on the sight. The ceiling looked to be at least twenty feet high, and on each side were double rows of marble columns. Arrayed along each side of the hall in niches designed for that purpose were busts of each of the eleven former Chief Justices of the Court, from John Jay to Harlan F. Stone.

But the fact that impressed me as much as the architecture was how quiet the Great Hall was. With the exception of the guard on duty, I was the only person in the hall. I explained to the guard my mission—to report for work to Justice Jackson—and he directed me to the Marshal's Office. From there I was taken by messenger down a corridor, just as deserted as the Great Hall, through some brass gates and down another corridor to a door where a bronze plaque contained the black letters MR. JUSTICE JACKSON. . . .

Robert H. Jackson had been born sixty years earlier in a hamlet in northwest Pennsylvania, but at the age of five his family moved north across the New York state line to the village of Frewsburg.

Because he adhered to the political faith of his fathers, he was one of the few Democrats in otherwise staunchly Republican upstate New York. Combining service to his party, to his state, and to his profession with his practice, he was known throughout the state when at the age of forty-two President Franklin Roosevelt appointed him general counsel for the Bureau of Internal Revenue in Washington. Jackson rose rapidly in the legal hierarchy of the New Deal; that rise culminated in his appointment as an associate justice of the Supreme Court in June 1941. As I stood before him on this February morning in 1952 he was in the midst of his eleventh year on the Court.

He was a friendly-looking man, a little on the stout side, with thinning a dark hair that came to a widow's peak. His face was broad, his complexion somewhat florid, and his eye had an incipient twinkle. He was, I would judge, five feet nine inches or ten inches in height.

He greeted me warmly, and after an exchange of pleasantries, I told him that I supposed I ought to go to work. He allowed as how this was so, but said that we first had to do an even more important thing—have me put on the federal payroll. After signing the appropriate form, I became a GS-9 at a salary of $6,400 per year. While this doesn't seem like a lot of money today, it was far and away the most I had ever earned in my life. Justice Jackson then remarked rather casually that he supposed I had a general idea of how the Supreme Court operated. Actually, I had only the foggiest notions of how the Supreme Court operated, but I was naturally loath to volunteer this fact. . . .

I had taken a course in constitutional law in my second year of law school, but had done no work at all in the field called "federal jurisdiction," which dealt with the niceties of when a case might be brought in federal court, as opposed to state court. I decided that I would have to work hard, keep my eyes and ears open, and hope to benefit from what was obviously going to be on-the-job training. Back in the law clerks' office, I confided some of my self-doubt to George Niebank [Jackson's other clerk] while he was explaining to me what Justice Jackson expected of his law clerks. George assured me that his law-school education at the University of Buffalo Law School had not included any course in federal jurisdiction either, and although it might have been nice if it had, he had since been able to pick up whatever knowledge was necessary in that field. He went on to explain that the principal tasks of the law clerks were to write short memoranda on each petition for certiorari, and to help edit or make suggestions on Court opinions or dissents that Justice Jackson had written.

I was glad that, after I received the letter from Justice Jackson in November, I had done a little outside reading on the way the Supreme Court does its business. I did know the difference between petitions for certiorari and Court opinions. Petitions for certiorari was a term applicable almost exclusively to practice in the Supreme Court of the United States, and had its origin in the way the docket of the Supreme Court had grown from the time that our nation first began. . . .

Since the Supreme Court was primarily an appellate court, it started out with very little to do because the principal source of its appeals—the lower federal courts—had not been in existence long enough to decide any cases that could be appealed to the Supreme Court. There was obviously no docket congestion in the Supreme Court of the Unite States for the first few years of its existence. But all of this change in the next sixty years, as the United States expanded its territory. First the Louisiana Purchase in 1803 and then the Mexican Cession in 1848 established a nation whose boundaries extended from the Atlantic Ocean to the Pacific Ocean. In 1789, the population of the United States had been 3 million; by 1850, that population had increased to more than 23 million.

As might be expected, the increase in population meant new courts in the new territories and states, and thus more business for the Supreme Court. By 1850, the Supreme Court, which had always been very much up-to-date with its docket, was gradually falling behind. The situation worsened until 1891, when Congress stepped in an created the federal circuit courts of appeals, which were placed between the federal district courts and the Supreme Court of the United States to siphon off many of the appeals that had previously gone directly to the Supreme Court. This measure alleviated the docket congestion until after World War I, but in 1925 Congress stepped in again and passed what is commonly called the Certiorari Act. This act provided that in most cases there would be no right to appeal from a lower court to the Supreme Court of the United States; instead, review of a lower-court decision would take place only upon the agreement of the Supreme Court to hear the case. An application for such review was called a petition for certiorari. . . .

During the term of court in which I came to work for Justice Jackson, about thirteen hundred petitions for certiorari were file. Sitting there and talking to George Niebank, I suddenly realized that about thirty or forty of these petitions were currently stacked on my desk. George explained that he thought we should divide up the petitions equally between us as soon as I got the hang of the work, but that the would be glad to take the lion's share until I felt I had gotten my sea legs. This generous arrangement suited me fine . . .

With some trepidation I picked up the certiorari papers on the top of the stack on my desk, and began reading through them. I was relieved to find that when I came to grips with an actual real-life petition, many of the abstract problems as to how a memorandum should be written faded away. The set of papers on which I was now working consisted of a petition for certiorari, printed and bound in the traditional form of a legal brief, and a memorandum in opposition from the prevailing party in the lower court. The petitioner in my case—that is, the party who had lost in the court of appeals wanted the Supreme Court to review his case—had been indicted in the federal district court in Philadelphia on a narcotics charge, and after trial a jury had found him guilty. He had then appealed to the Court of Appeals for the Third Circuit, which sat in Philadelphia, and that court had handed down a written opinion upholding his conviction. I dutifully noted the numerous contentions raised by the petitioner: The government had not produced sufficient evidence at his trial to support the verdict of guilty, several of the trial judge's rulings on the admissibility of evidence had been wrong, and the trial judge's charge to the jury, in which he advised the jury of the governing law which they should apply to their deliberations, had incorrectly stated that law. Each of these three points was covered in a petition containing sixteen pages, and after reading only the petition I thought that perhaps there was some merit to the claim that the trial judge hadn't properly stated the law in his instructions to the jury.

But reading the memorandum in opposition filed by the United States, I got a totally different picture of what had been going on in the lower courts. The government pointed out that in all probability the trial judge's charge to the jury did correctly state the law, but that even if it didn't, the defendant's lawyer had made no objection to it at the time the trial judge informed the parties that he would charge to that effect. The government also made the point that even if there had been an isolated misstatement of the law in the judge's instructions, it was very likely "harmless error": That is, the evidence of guilt presented to the jury was so overwhelming in this case that an isolated misstatement of the law could not possibly have affected the conclusion reached by the jury. Finally, the government pointed out, in the best tradition of the advocate, that *even* if the instruction to the jury had been wrong, and *even* if it did not constitute merely harmless error, this was simply not the kind of case that the Supreme Court typically decided to review. In the government's view, the case was of no general importance, no new principles of law were involved, and if the wrong result had been reached in the lower courts, they had at least gone through the right motions in reaching it.

This last argument by the government troubled me considerably as I sat there pondering it, and I more or less put it to one side to think about for a while. I then turned to the opinion that had been written by one of the judges of the Court of Appeals for the Third Circuit in Philadelphia. I realized as I read the opinion that much of the government's memorandum in opposition to the petition for certiorari was based on this opinion, and it seemed to be a thoughtful, workmanlike job. As I made this observation, I mentally asked myself the question, "Who are you, two months out of law school, to give such a patronizing evaluation of an opinion written by a judge of a United States courts of appeals who was appointed to his office by the president of the United States and confirmed by the United States Senate?" While the question may have been a good one, I rapidly realized that I must cast aside such modesty if I was to get through my share of the hundreds of certiorari petitions that had to be processed between February 1 and the time that the Court adjourned in June.

The petitioner who had been convicted of the narcotics offense in Philadelphia relied on two Supreme Court decisions which he claimed had not been followed by the lower courts in his case; the government in opposition said that these two cases weren't applicable, and that a third decision, which had not even been cited by the petitioner, was controlling. I dutifully read the opinions in each of the three cases and concluded that the government was probably right. I now tentatively decided that my recommendation to Justice Jackson should be that he vote to deny this petition for certiorari. The rule followed by the Supreme Court ever since the Certiorari Act of 1925 was that the votes of four of the nine justices were required in order to grant certiorari in a case; if Justice Jackson and at least five other members of the Court voted to deny certiorari in the case I was working on, the effect would be to leave standing the opinion of the Court of Appeals for the Third Circuit in Philadelphia, leaving the petitioner to serve his time in prison.

I decided I would write all but the last paragraph, which gave the reasons for the recommended action, now, and think about the recommendation a little more. . . .

I composed as I went along, summarizing what had happened in the trial court, what the court of appeals had said in its written opinion, the defendant's contentions, and the government's response to them. I then sat at the typewriter for a few minutes, wondering if I should compose the final paragraph now or wait until later. . . .

. . . George Niebank tapped me on the shoulder and suggested that it was time to go to lunch. As we stood waiting for our trays, George explained to me that all the law clerks who were eating in the building on a given day usually ate together in a dining room set aside for them just across the hall from the cafeteria proper. When we had paid the cashier, he led the way to the clerks' dining room where the rest of the law clerks, ahead of us in the lunch line, had already made their way.

I was naturally an object of some curiosity, since all the rest of the clerks had come to work sometime during the preceding summer and had gotten to know one another pretty well by this time. I was fortunate in knowing Justice Douglas's single clerk, Marshall Small, because he had graduated from Stanford Law School a year ahead of me. . . . Unfortunately, Marshall was not there that day. . . .

. . . There were probably ten or twelve of us seated around the clerks' dining table that noon, and I made an effort to size up the others. The majority came from a very few law schools—Harvard, Yale, Columbia, Pennsylvania, Chicago, and Northwestern. We all seemed to be roughly of an age, since it was almost impossible to have finished law school in 1951 or 1952 without having spent some time in the service during the Second World War or immediately afterward. I was not surprised by the fact that of all the clerks that term only Marshall Small and I came from law schools west of the Mississippi River, but sitting there at the lunch table I began to feel a little bit defensive about it.

The conversation turned to a proposed opinion for the Court which Justice Jackson had authored and, unbeknownst to me, circulated to the other justices the preceding day. Opinions for the Court were issued after the Court had heard arguments in a case in which certiorari had been granted, and the opinion was supposed to be based on the discussion among the justices at their conference on the case in question. The justices sat on the bench in the courtroom from noon until 2:00 P.M. and from 2:30 until 4:30 P.M., Monday through Friday during each week of oral argument. They then met in conference on Saturday morning to discuss and vote on the cases they had heard argued during the week. The Court's schedule generally called for two one-week sessions of oral argument, and then two weeks of recess in which opinions could be prepared and considered by the justices. At the end of each two-week session of oral argument, the Chief Justice would assign the writing of the draft opinion in a particular case to one of the members of the Court who had voted with the majority, and it then became the task of that justice to draft an opinion that would explain the reasons why the Court was deciding the way it did.

The case about which the law clerks were not talking was entitled *Sacher v. United States*, 343 U.S. 1, and it had been orally argued to the Court during the second week of January. I was vaguely aware that the case involved the actions of Judge Medina, who had presided at the trial of the communist party members in New York a few years earlier, in citing several of the defense lawyers for contempt of court. Judging from the discussion among the clerks, the Court had been sharply divided in voting on the case at conference, and Justice Jackson's opinion upholding the contempt citations was not very popular at this particular lunch table.

George, who knew about the case and had apparently helped Justice Jackson with it, stoutly defended the result, but he seemed to have few supporters. There were dark predictions of stirring dissents from justices who disagreed with the majority of the Court, and I became quite uneasy about what would happen to Justice Jackson's opinion. Only later did I come to realize that it would be all but impossible to assemble a more hypercritical, not to say arrogant, audience than a group of law clerks criticizing an opinion circulated by one of their employers. Their scorn—and in due time it became my scorn too—was not reserved for Justice Jackson, but was lavished with considerable impartiality upon the products of all nine chambers of the Court.

When I returned to my office, I debated whether I should go ahead and type the last paragraph of the memorandum I had been working on before lunch, or whether I should read through some other petitions to get more of a feel for how the merits of the various claims stacked up against one another. I began thumbing through another petition in a rather desultory manner, but found my mind wandering back to the earlier memo. I finally decided to take the bit in my teeth and go back and finish it up. I thereby began to teach myself a lesson that most law clerks and most judges have to teach themselves somewhere along the line. Ideally speaking, one never knows as much as one ought to know about the particular matter being judged, whether it be a law clerk trying to make up his mind what recommendation to make with respect to a petition for certiorari, or an appellate judge making up his mind whether to vote to affirm or reverse the decision of a lower court. After immersing oneself in the materials at hand in order to reach a conclusion, albeit a tentative one, the crucial question is "When will I know more than I do now?" Perhaps it is just my own way of working, but I have always preferred where possible to go through one thing from beginning to end, do what I had to do with it, and move on to the next thing . . .

The first day on the job, of course, is a time for feeling out as deftly as possible some of the contours of one's employment. . . .

I was, of course, fully determined to do the job assigned to me, but I was also curious as to the normal daily schedule which Justice Jackson kept, because I assumed I was expected to be in my office during the time that he was in his chambers or on the bench. Conversely, I guess, I assumed that I was free to absent myself if I was current with my work before Justice Jackson arrived in the morning and after he left in the evening. I didn't actually want to ask even George Niebank about what hours I should keep, because it somehow seemed to indicate less than complete devotion to the job.

I solved part of the problem that first evening by simply staying until everyone else had left. Mrs. Douglas left shortly before 6:00 o'clock, Justice Jackson left around 6:00 o'clock, and George Niebank left around 6:15. I departed at about 6:20, and felt that I could probably set my minimum hours around Justice Jackson's schedule. I proved correct; morning rush-hour traffic in Washington was bad even in 1952, and it seemed to me that most of my clerk colleagues tried to get into the office about 9:30 A.M. Justice Jackson almost invariably arrived around 10:00 A.M. and left about 6:00 P.M.

As I turned out the lights and locked the door of my office, I had a feeling of almost complete satisfaction with my first day on the job. The work interested me greatly, I enjoyed the people I had met, and I felt very enthusiastic about the immediate future.

Thinking It Over

1.   What is a petition of certiorari? How does the Certiorari Act of 1925 square with *Marbury v. Madison?*

2.   What is Rehnquist's rule for making decisions? Do you think it's a good one? Would you use it yourself?

91.
THE BRETHREN
by Bob Woodward and Scott Armstrong

Setting the Scene: The book from which the reading below is taken is perhaps the most controversial popular book ever written on the Court. It didn't hurt that one of its authors (Bob Woodward) was played by Robert Redford in the Watergate movie *All the President's Men.* The value of the book for students of government is its insider accounts of how decisions really get made on the Court. Much of it would make Machiavelli blush. While the authors may be fairly accused of a little sensationalism here and there, the book as a whole rings true. One suspects that those who find the behavior of the judges surprising have been blinded by the image of the Court in our popular culture—that they are intellectual gods, high priests of rationality, and free from the temptations of the human condition.

The four main death penalty cases had not resolved a fifth one *(Moore v. Illinois).* Lyman A. "Slick" Moore had been sentenced to death for a shotgun murder, but his appeal raised issues other than the "cruel and unusual" nature of the death penalty. With the death penalty now struck down, the Court had to decide these other issues—or Moore was doomed to life in prison.

Moore argued that he had been unfairly convicted. The prosecution had withheld from the defense the fact that the three principal witnesses who claimed to have heard a "Slick" brag of the murder had all told police that they didn't think this Moore was the same "Slick." A judge had also permitted prosecutors to wave a sawed-off shotgun in front of the jury, though the prosecution admitted at trial that it was not the murder weapon.

At conference, the vote was 7 to 2 to uphold Moore's conviction, with Marshall and Douglas the only dissenters. Moore would not get a new trial, but the death penalty decision in the other four cases would keep him from being executed.

The Chief assigned the case to Blackmun. As usual, Blackmun was late with his circulation. Douglas expressed his exasperation over the delay at conference. "Circulations from Harry are like returns in an election from rural counties—late," Stewart once said.

When the opinion finally came around, it said the information, if withheld, did not prove Moore's innocence, but only tended to show that he was not the same man who had bragged about the murder. Waving the shotgun before the jury, Blackmun stated, was not a sufficiently significant error to justify a new trial.

Marshall was upset. During his days of criminal-law practice, he had seen many men convicted by distorted presentations of the facts. He had a clerk prepare a detailed analysis of the evidence, challenging Blackmun's reading.

The identification by eyewitnesses had been crucial to obtaining the conviction and Blackmun was ignoring many of the facts damaging to their testimony. This was a miscarriage of justice. Marshall's analysis was circulated as a dissent. Blackmun responded in a set of footnotes arguing his own version of the facts.

Powell and Stewart quickly switched their votes, and Marshall needed only one more to take away Blackmun's majority. His friend Brennan would surely provide the fifth vote. Brennan, after all, was the author of a landmark 1963 decision *(Brady v. Maryland)* that required prosecutors to turn over all exculpatory evidence to the defense.

One of Brennan's clerks thought that if Brennan had seen the facts as Marshall presented them, he would not have voted the other way. he went to talk to Brennan and, thirty minutes later, returned shaken. Brennan understood that Marshall's position was correct, but he was not going to switch sides now, the clerk said. This was not just a run-of-the-mill case for Blackmun. Blackmun had spent a lot of time on it, giving the trial record a close reading. he prided himself on his objectivity. If Brennan switched, Blackmun would be personally offended. That would be unfortunate, because Blackmun had lately seemed more assertive, more independent of the Chief. Brennan felt that if he voted against Blackmun now, it might make it more difficult to reach him in the abortion cases or even the obscenity cases.

Sure, "Slick" Moore deserved a new trial. But more likely than not, it would result in his being convicted again. After all, Moore had a long record. He was not exactly an angel. Anyway, the Court could not concern itself with correcting every injustice. They should never have taken such a case, Brennan said. He felt he had to consider the big picture.

"He won't leave Harry on this," Brennan's clerk reported to Marshall's clerk.

The clerks were shocked that such considerations would keep a man in prison. They wondered whether Brennan still would have refused to switch if the death penalty had not been struck.

Marshall's clerk asked his boss to talk to Brennan.

Marshall refused. It was not his style. He resented pressure from the Chief and he was not about to imitate his methods.

Marshall's clerk made a final appeal through Brennan's clerks.

Brennan had his priorities. His priority in this case was Harry Blackmun. There would be no new trial for "Slick" Moore.

. . .

Brennan was at his desk one afternoon when Blackmun called with a question about a sticky legal technicality. Did Brennan have any ideas?

"Harry, I'll be right over," Brennan said. Dropping his own work, he hurried down the hall to Blackmun's chambers.

A clerk passing by Blackmun's office observed the two Justices a short time later. Blackmun was at his desk and Brennan stood behind him, one arm on Blackmun's shoulder, the other extended to some memo or law book. It was part of Brennan's "cultivation of Harry project," as one clerk called it.

Brennan thought that Blackmun was continuing to drift away, not only from the Chief's influence but from his own conservatism, and he was determined to encourage it. He had no hope that Blackmun would ever be a regular liberal vote. But Blackmun at least took each case as it came, with a minimum of prejudice. Keenly aware that Blackmun was always fearful that his language in opinions might someday come back to haunt him or the Court, Brennan showed him how narrow decisions were possible in several cases.

The clerks in the Chief's chambers joked that after Blackmun circulated certain opinions, Brennan would take him to lunch out of gratitude. Once, the Chief's clerks were sure that Brennan had joined a Blackmun draft even before he had read it. Even on the tax cases, which Brennan hated, he gave extra consideration to them because they were Blackmun's area of expertise. "This is a tax case. Deny." That was Brennan's normal reaction to a cert request in a tax case. But when Blackmun circulated a tax opinion, Brennan responded with a florid note, praising the work and scholarship. On a major securities case *(Blue Chip Stamps v. Manor Drug Stores)* Blackmun had charged that the majority opinion "graves into stone" with "three blunt chisels" certain arbitrary principles, exhibiting "a preternatural solicitousness for corporate well-being." Brennan readily joined the over-written dissent.

In another case, the question was whether the city of Chattanooga, Tennessee, could prohibit the production of the controversial rock musical *Hair* in its civic auditorium *(Southeastern Promotions, Ltd. v. Conrad).* Onstage nudity, simulated sex, four-letter words, pro-drug and anti-war themes marked it as a distinctively 1960s protest. Religious and historical figures were mocked, and interracial love was hailed.

One of the street people in the play was called Burger. The insult was not intentional, since the Chief had not been on the Court when the script was written in 1967. Nonetheless, no play could have been more designed to offend the Chief.

Burger wanted to uphold a decision not to allow the play in a city-owned auditorium. He assumed that his five-man majority in the 1973 obscenity cases, including Blackmun, would stand firm. But Brennan felt that, because the city had banned the play before seeing it or even its script, the question was really one of prior restraint. He bombarded Blackmun with memos and other material and spoke with him at length about the application of prior-restraint law to the case. The issue was not the right of the local community to define or ban obscenity, but the banning of something *before* it appeared. This was a denial of the very sort of hearing that in the 1973 obscenity cases Blackmun had insisted each pornographer be given before anything could be declared obscene.

Blackmun finally voted with Brennan at conference, making Brennan the senior member of the majority present. Brennan assigned the case to Blackmun, and Blackmun agreed to undertake the opinion on the condition that he would not be breaking new ground. He wrote an odd opinion, saying that such a play could be banned only if there was a "clear and present danger." Brennan was so anxious to nail down Blackmun's vote that he joined before talking with his clerks. What was the possible "clear and present danger"? they asked. Nudity? Rape? Brennan got Blackmun to drop the phrase.

Burger was aghast. He remarked several times to his clerks that he didn't understand what Blackmun was doing. It had to be the influence of Stewart and Brennan, The Chief gave no credit to Blackmun.

Burger was also having more and more trouble with Powell, who seemed to constantly flirt with the Court's left wing. At times Burger found Powell unreachable, willing to listen but seemingly unable to understand his points. When the conference considered a

Jacksonville, Florida, law banning the showing of films with any nudity at drive-in movie theaters, Powell voted to uphold the ban *(Erznoznik v. City of Jacksonville)*. Despite some nudity the movie, *Class of '74*, rated R, was not obscene in Powell's view, but the local law regulating its showing was a reasonable and permissible exercise of police power. Not only could the movie screen be seen from nearby highways, but also from a church parking lot.

The conference was deadlocked 4 to 4, with Douglas back in the hospital. After the conference, Powell's clerks besieged him. Even his most conservative clerk argued that since the movie was not obscene, its showing at the drive-in was protected by the First Amendment. Ordinarily his vote ended the chambers debate, but this time he seemed to encourage it, even though he had already voted. His clerks knew which arguments to push. It was really a matter of balancing the privacy interests of those offended by the drive-in with the First Amendment rights of the theater owner and customers. Could not the passersby readily avert their eyes?

Powell disagreed. Moreover, the case just wasn't that important.

But the principle was, the clerks insisted. Clearly the government could not regulate expression simply because it was offensive to the majority. Could a billboard erected by an unpopular political candidate be banned because it was offensive to a majority and could be seen from the street, or a church parking lot?

The clerks also raised the matter of economic consequences. They had come to realize, as they got to know Powell, that his business bias was even greater than it appeared to be in is final written opinions. The clerks called it "Lew's corporate dignity doctrine." He seemed convinced that business did little or no wrong. They joked that cert petitions in business cases might well be addressed, "Dear Lew."

Now in this case, they pointed out that a theater owner in a similar instance had had to spend nearly $250,000 to construct a barrier to block the view. The result was an unfair burden, almost a tax, on theater owners who wanted to show R-rated movies that were, after all, protected by the Constitution. It wasn't exactly the corporate dignity argument they were making, but a corporate survival argument.

The clerks finally turned to the sort of hairsplitting, literal-minded argument that appealed to the lawyer in Powell, to his legal fastidiousness. The jacksonville regulation prohibited the showing of "the human male or female bare buttocks." As Blackmun had said earlier at oral argument, that meant a ban on all backsides, even those of a newborn baby. It was absurd.

By now, even Sally Smith, Powell's jovial, fiercely loyal secretary, had joined the discussion. Powell often found Smith a kind of good-sense barometer. They asked for her opinion. There was nothing wrong with a baby's backside on an outdoor movie screen, she said.

After further reflection, Powell decided to change his vote. The ban should be struck down on First Amendment grounds. He actually felt good about the switch. it had been the right kind of family conference. Everyone had had his say, and he—the pater familias, the senior partner, the corporate president, the school board head—had made the final decision.

Burger was surprised at Powell's vote switch, but he was alarmed when he saw Powell's first draft. It was a powerful opinion reasserting the prohibition of government regulation of aesthetic, political and moral expression. And before Burger knew it, Blackmun, and Douglas of course, had joined it, making it a 6-to-3 decision.

"What the hell is going on in Powell's chambers?" the Chief grumbled.

Thinking It Over

1. Did Brennan do the right thing on the "Slick" Moore case? Explain.

2. Remembering that the Court is playing a more and more important role in the policy-making process in our democracy and also remembering that politics and the human condition are inseparable, write an essay for which one of the following two titles works: "The Brethren: It's Time for Reforms," or "The Brethren: What's the Big Deal?"

Credits (continued from copyright page)

Chapter II (9.) From "The Constitution as an Elitist Document," by Michael Parenti in *How Democratic is the Constitution?* by Robert A. Goldwin (Washington: American Enterprise Institute for Public Policy Research, 1980). Reprinted with the permission of the American Enterprise Institute for Public Policy Research, Washington, D.C. (10.) From "The Founding Fathers: A Reform Caucus in Action," by John Roche, *American Political Science Review*, December, 1961. Reprinted by permission of the American Political Science Association and the author. (11.) From "The American Constitution as Ideology," by Everett Carll Ladd, *The Christian Science Monitor*, February 2, 1987. Reprinted by permission of the author. (13.) From "A Man for 1987, James Madison: Unsung Hero of the Constitution," by Fred Barbash, *Washington Post*, March 15, 1987. Copyright © 1987 *The Washington Post*, reprinted by permission. (14.) From *Pluralist Democracy in the United States: Conflict and Consent*, (Chicago: Rand McNally, 1967). Reprinted by permission of the author. (15.) From *Why We Lost the ERA*, by Jane J. Mansbrige. Copyright © 1986 by University of Chicago Press. Reprinted by permission.

Chapter III (17.) From *The Declining Significance of Race*, by William J. Wilson. Copyright © 1980 by University of Chicago Press. Reprinted by permission. (18.) From *The Myth of Black Progress* by Alphonso Pinkney. Copyright © Cambridge University Press 1984. Reprinted with the permission of Cambridge University Press. (22.) From "Hate Goes to College," by Steve France, *American Bar Association Journal*, July, 1990. Reprinted by permission of the author.

Chapter IV (25.) From *The Maligned States*, by Ira Sharkansky. Copyright © 1978 by McGraw-Hill, Inc. All rights reserved. (26.) From "21 or Else Mandate Angers States," by Elaine S. Knapp, *State Government News*, August, 1984. Copyright © 1984 The Council of State Governments. Reprinted with permission from *State Government News*. (27.) From *New Federalism: Inter Governmental Reform from Nixon to Reagan* by Timothy J. Conlan. Copyright © 1988 Reprinted with permission of Brookings Institute. (28.) From "Crazy-Quilt Federalism," by W. John Moore, *National Journal*, November 26, 1988. Copyright © 1988 by *National Journal* Inc. All rights reserved. Reprinted by permission. (29.) From *Kennedy Justice* by Victor S. Navasky. Reprinted by permission of International Creative Management, Inc. Copyright © 1970/71 by Victor S. Navasky.

Chapter V (32.) From *The Power Game: How Washington Works* by Hedrick Smith. Copyright © 1988 by Hedrick Smith. Reprinted by permission of Random House, Inc. (33.) Excerpt from *The Triumph of Politics* by David A. Stockman. Copyright © 1986 by David A. Stockman. Reprinted by permission of HarperCollins Publisher. (34.) From *The Deadlock of Democracy* by James MacGregor Burns. Copyright © 1963 Reprinted by permission of the publisher, Prentice-Hall, Inc., Englewood Cliffs, New Jersey 07632. (35.) From "The Decline of the American National Government," by Robert J. Pranger. Reprinted with permission from *Publius: The Journal of Federalism* 3 (Fall 1973).

Chapter VI (36.) From the book, *The Political Life of Children* copyright © 1986 by Robert Coles. Used by permission of Atlantic Monthly Press. (37.) From *Chilren in the Political System*, by David Easton and Jack Dennis. Copyright © by University of Chicago Press. (38.) Reprinted with permission of Macmillan Publishing Company from *The Phanton Public* by Walter Lippmann. Copyright © 1925, renewed 1953 by Walter Lippmann. (39.) From "Teflon Politics," by Michael Jay Robinson and Maura Clancey, *Public Opinion* April/May 1984. Reprinted with the permission of the